Demography Principles and Methods

Second Edition

T. LYNN SMITH

Graduate Research Professor of Sociology
University of Florida

PAUL E. ZOPF, Jr.
Dana Professor of Sociology
Guilford College

Alfred
PUBLISHERS

ALFRED PUBLISHING CO., INC., 75 Channel Drive, Port Washington, N.Y. 11050

Demography: Principles and Methods

Published by Alfred Publishing Co., Inc.,
75 Channel Drive, Port Washington, N.Y. 11050

Copyright © 1976 by Alfred Publishing Co., Inc.

Printed in the United States of America

Library of Congress Cataloging in Publication Data

Smith, Thomas Lynn, 1903–
    Demography: principles and methods.

    Includes bibliographies and indexes.
      1. Demography. I. Zopf, Paul E., joint author.
II. Title.
HB881.S599 1976   301.32   75-23243
ISBN 0-88284-033-9

To the Memory of John Graunt, J. D. B. DeBow, and Walter F. Willcox
Who Firmly Established Some of the Basic Landmarks in the
Development of Population Study

PREFACE
to the Second Edition

The basic purpose of the second edition of this book is the same as that of the first; that is, to provide a volume which will enable teachers in colleges and universities to introduce undergraduates to the fundamentals of population study. Moreover, the frame of reference remains basically the same and the format is essentially unchanged. However, much of the content of the book has been revised substantially, especially by the updating of maps, graphs, tables, and other statistical data, but also by the revision of the discussions of trends and various other topics in line with the most recent data available. In addition to a comprehensive general frame of reference, the book is intended to present detailed expositions of demographic realities, a wide range of comparisons between and within societies, and a considerable variety of demographic techniques and methods. It involves consideration of all the principal aspects of demography, including the number and geographic distribution of the inhabitants, the composition or characteristics of the population, the vital processes, migration, and the growth of population. The last occupies a particularly important place with emphasis placed on the press of humanity upon available resources. In addition, at appropriate places throughout the text, the writers treat some of the social and cultural factors that produce population conditions as well as those that result from demographic conditions. This is because the complex structure, functions, forces, and processes of social life are assumed to act in concert with basic values, attitudes, and other subjective orientations to produce population components with certain geographic distributions, arrangements of characteristics, and particular patterns of growth or, occasionally, decline.

Sections dealing with genetics, the demographic aspects of economic development, techniques of controlling population growth, and the like, deliberately have been omitted in the preparation of this text. This is not because the writers depreciate the value of such fields, nor because they would not have population materials closely integrated with other aspects of sociological and economic analysis. On the contrary they believe that such subjects deserve places in the curriculum as separate courses, and they are convinced that demographic matters, considered both as independent variables and as dependent variables, must constitute an important part of any comprehensive and well-integrated system of sociological or economic analysis. Primarily, however, the limitations were imposed because of the belief, which these authors share with a large number of others who have population courses as part of their teaching loads, that a three-hour course for one semester is not too much time for the undergraduate major in sociology, economics, biology, and so forth, to devote exclusively to the principles and methods of population study. Certainly even the most able of the students must concentrate at least to this extent upon demographic essentials if they are to master a few of the most fundamental population facts, to gain a knowledge of a basic frame of reference, to become familiar with the sources from which the materials are drawn, to acquaint themselves with even the most elementary techniques of population analysis, and to learn about the best-known relationships between demographic phenomena.

The teaching aids which accompany each of the chapters are those the authors have used throughout the years, along with others suggested by friends and associates who have also had much experience with the population course. In the lists of suggested readings a variety of important works has been included to assist the teachers in acquainting the students with alternative approaches to the various subjects, to supply the facts of publication about works that readily might be assigned for book reports, and to help the students locate the more basic sources that should be consulted in the preparation of term papers.

The junior author wishes to express his profound appreciation to T. Lynn Smith for the privilege of working closely with him in the preparation of both editions of this text. The former feels particular pleasure over the fact that the writings of many of T. Lynn Smith's students and colleagues show considerable consistency and continuity. This has made the senior author of this book responsible for a great deal of agreement among many demographers on basic concepts, terminology, rationale, and methods. Both authors wish to thank their colleagues and students at the University of Florida and at Guilford College for the encouragement and insight which they have helped to provide. Finally, they wish to express profound gratitude to Louvina J. Smith and to Evelyn Zopf and Eric Zopf for their patience and understanding during the time that this volume has been in preparation. Without them its completion would have been impossible.

T. Lynn Smith
Paul E. Zopf, Jr.

CONTENTS

5 MIGRATION

6 GROWTH OF POPULATION

LIST OF FIGURES

LIST OF FIGURES (Cont'd)

LIST OF TABLES

LIST OF TABLES (Cont'd)

LIST OF TABLES (Cont'd)

PART ONE

The Nature and Development of Population Study

1
THE SCOPE AND METHOD
OF POPULATION STUDY

People are the most important thing in the world. As people, you and we and billions of our kind spread over the face of the earth are at once the means and the end of all of society's endeavors. Everything done in the fields of economics or industry, government or politics, education, religion, recreation — and all the rest — is done by people and for people. Furthermore, the number of people involved, the manner in which they are distributed over a territory, the rate at which they are increasing or decreasing, and the extent to which they are young or old, male or female, married or single, rural or urban, in or out of the labor force, of one racial or ethnic group or another, literate or illiterate, native or foreign born, and so on are of basic importance in nearly all of mankind's undertakings. For example, those responsible for the military activities of a country are avid for certain facts about the people of their country and of a potential enemy. Those in charge of educational programs want other information about the population just as badly. Dozens of other comparable needs for population facts might be listed, for virtually all questions of public policy have their population aspects. This is true at the local, state, national, and even international levels.

At the national level, information about the number of inhabitants and their characteristics and recent trends affecting each are basic to the formulation of policies relating to agriculture and industry, immigration, education, social security, health and medical insurance, taxation, and military service. At the state level, population facts and principles are of fundamental importance in connection with plans and policies relative to old-age benefits and other welfare measures, equalization of educational opportunities, construction of highways, apportionment of seats in the legislature, and hospitalization. Even at the local level, knowledge of basic facts about the people involved is essential for the

3

intelligent shaping of public policies. Questions such as those related to the location of schools, school construction and consolidation, locating and building of hospitals and other health facilities, and planning and improvement of roads and highways must all be studied in close relationship to population facts and trends. Thus, with much reason, one might contend that comprehensive, tested facts about people, their numbers and their characteristics, are among the materials most useful to modern society. Certainly, these matters deserve careful, objective, scientific study.

The prime objective of this volume is to introduce college and university students to the important and rapidly developing field of population study. An attempt has been made to treat in a systematic manner all the major divisions of the modern field of demography. In preparing this introduction the authors have felt it necessary to present in considerable detail relevant materials on each of the following aspects of the general topic: the systematized set of concepts, classifications, and principles, or the frame of reference, used by those who are most experienced in the field of population; the more important primary and secondary sources of information used in the study and analysis of each of the general topics included in demography; and various analytical devices and techniques which may be employed to extract meaningful results from vast masses of raw materials pertaining to the numbers, geographic distribution, characteristics, vital processes, migrations, and changes in human populations.

SCOPE AND CONTENT

The scope and content of population study or demography as developed in the United States and other parts of the modern world are fairly well agreed upon by those teaching the subject in colleges and universities and by most of those doing comprehensive research in the field. They may be set forth rather explicitly by means of a brief consideration of each of the principal divisions of the subject.

Number and Geographic Distribution of the Inhabitants

The number of its inhabitants is the most important demographic fact about any area, large or small. Therefore, the first task of the student of population is to determine as accurately as possible and to maintain as current and up-to-date as feasible the actual numbers of people in the various areas with which he is concerned (continents, nations, regions, congressional districts, counties, cities, boroughs, towns, villages, townships, wards, precincts, census tracts, and so forth). The taking of periodic censuses is the basic way of securing such information, but frequent postcensus estimates also are a prime necessity. If the counts are properly tabulated and if the figures are given separately for each of the smaller units into which a given area is subdivided, the basis has been laid for significant study and analysis of the geographic distribution of the population. Thus, for a state such as Michigan or Mississippi, the tabulation of the data gathered in each census of the population, such as the ones made each ten years by the United States Bureau of the Census, should indicate clearly and exactly the number of persons in: (1) the state as a whole; (2) each of the counties of which it is composed; (3) each of the townships or other minor civil divisions into which the counties are subdivided; (4) every center of population (city, town, village, or hamlet), incorporated or unincorporated, in all of the counties; (5) every political subdivision (ward, precinct, and so forth) within each city, town, or village; and (6) for the cities in which the necessary preparatory work has been done, each census tract into which the urban or urbanized area has been sub-divided. Given such tabulations the experienced student of population is enabled — by careful study and especially by means of various mapping devices — to extract and present facts and relationships of the utmost theoretical and practical importance.

Composition or Characteristics of the Population

A second fundamental division of demography relates to the composition or characteristics of the population. These two expressions are commonly employed by census technicians and population analysts to designate the common and rather obvious, but highly significant, features which distinguish one person from another and, therefore, are used as the basis for classifying human populations into the most fundamental categories. Each of these characteristics is mentioned briefly in turn. The first to be listed, however, are four (age, sex, rural or urban residence, and race or color) which are of greatest importance for purposes of demographic analysis. They are most basic in that data about them should enter into the cross-tabulations with the materials on all the other characteristics. In a very real way they are the four principal threads in the "warp and woof" of modern census tabulations. For example, a meaningful table of data on the marital condition of a population should show the materials properly subdivided by age, sex, race, and residence so that a given column of figures will give the information for the white (or Negro), urban (or rural), male (or female) population in each age group.

Age, a little reflection will convince almost anyone, is the person's most important characteristic, the most fundamental determinant of one's behavior. For this reason, the data on the age distribution of the population are of the utmost significance in the field of demography. The extent to which adequate age classifications (those by five-year age groups are by far the most useful) are employed in combination with all the other subclassifications of population materials determine to a high degree the ultimate value of the costly materials gathered by a nation's census and by its registration system. The student of population must exercise the utmost care in the study of this factor in order to insure that the other relationships and differentials he is seeking to test or to establish are not merely reflections of differences or similarities in the age compositions of the populations he is comparing.

Sex is the person's second most important personal characteristic, and the ratio of males to females in a given population rivals in demographic significance its age composition. As indicated above, proper classification of population facts according to the sexes of the persons involved is one of the principal threads in the warp and woof of modern census tabulations. The population analyst can make little headway until he is able to control through subsorting, or in other ways, the variations in the sex composition of the population he is studying.

Rural or urban residence is the third characteristic of a population that the student must have in mind constantly. After long experience, the technicians in charge of United States census tabulations use the rural-urban division of the population as the first of the highly elaborate sets of classifications employed in our decennial census reports. Some of the tables which appear on the opening pages of the national and state reports subdivide the population into the urban, rural-nonfarm, and rural-farm categories, and these categories wisely are retained throughout a large part of the tables that follow. This is because the demographic characteristics and processes of persons who live in the country are radically different from those of people who reside in cities. As will be abundantly clear throughout this volume, the classification of the population into rural and urban segments, or into various categories along a rural-urban continuum, is one of the primary concerns of the census that is conducted by a competent and professional staff and one of the features most urgently needed by the population analyst.

Race or color is the fourth of the strands or threads that should run through all census tabulations and figure prominently in endeavors to understand and interpret demographic materials. From time immemorial human groups have attached significance to the differences in pigmentation, hair texture, and other distinguishing characteristics of *Homo sapiens.* From the most remote times, these criteria have been used to establish great categories of mankind, such as the white, the black, and the yellow races. It matters little that contemporary scientific findings and theories (in biology, psychology, anthropology, and sociology) give scant support to the belief that these physical characteristics are in any way related to native intelligence, innate capacities, or moral capabilities. As long as any considerable portion of a society *thinks* that such physical features are significant, they will continue to be the basis for fundamental divisions of the population. In the United States Census of Population the classification of the inhabitants as white and nonwhite, with the latter subdivided into Negro and other races, is carried through a substantial part of the tabulations. Together, the materials on the four characteristics just discussed occupy the bulk of the space in the voluminous reports of the decennial censuses of population.

National origin is another characteristic of considerable significance in countries, such as the United States, Canada, Australia, Argentina, and Brazil, which have received considerable numbers of immigrants. In our own country the classification of the population into native born and foreign born, with each of these categories further subdivided, gives valuable information on another important population characteristic. In the reports of many of our censuses, because of the high proportion of immigrants in the population of the United States and because of the pressures exerted by the organizations representing the various nationality groups, materials on this subject loom very large. They are useful not merely in connection with the subject of national and ethnic origins, but also in endeavors to check upon conclusions relative to immigration and emigration that have been based upon studies of the records of the agencies responsible for administering our immigration laws.

The *marital condition* of the population is of tremendous sociological significance. The modern census of population includes queries relating to this characteristic and generally the replies to these questions are properly tabulated in relation to the characteristics already discussed and those to be considered below. Most censuses, including that of the United States, give elaborate data on this highly significant demographic feature.

Occupation, industry, labor force, and *employment* loom large in the modern population census. Of course, only the first of these, occupation, actually may be considered as a characteristic of the population, but its adequate study involves the other concepts as well. For this reason the occupations of those employed or seeking work fills a considerable part of most modern census reports. However, the student of population has less of a monopoly on the study of occupational characteristics than he has on many other features of the composition of the population. This subject quickly leads into various other aspects of sociology and economics that go considerably beyond the proper range of demography.

Educational status of the population is a feature about which the modern census secures mountains of data. Until recently, however, this material has been studied very little, and such analysis as has been done was made, for the most part, by those who were working on other aspects of the composition of the population. Probably this is because the demographer, through his greater familiarity with the reports on the census of population, has most frequently been challenged by the comprehensive materials that have been collected on the subjects of literacy and illiteracy and the number of years of schooling completed by the various groups in the general population. The facts, relationships, and trends in this respect belong, of course, fully as much in the sociologist's study of educational institutions and the professional educator's analyses of the results of his efforts, as they do in demography.

Religious affiliations and preferences is another population characteristic of no slight importance. Very frequently in historical times whether one was Christian or Jew, Catholic or Protestant, Moslem or unbeliever has been by far his most important characteristic. No census of population in the United States has included queries on religious affiliations or preferences, but such questions are integral parts of many modern censuses, such as those made in Brazil, Canada, and Pakistan.

The Vital Processes

A third broad area encompassed within the field of demography is the study of the natural increase in population, that is, of births and deaths and the resulting surplus or deficit that results when one is weighed against the other. Birth, death, and migration are the only factors that can influence directly the size of a population or its geographic distribution. Hence, when one has a knowledge of birth rates and death rates, only materials regarding migrations are needed in order to account completely for all increases or decreases in the number of inhabitants and for all changes in the geographic distribution of population. This is the basic reason for postponing any discussion of the growth of population until after the rate of reproduction, the mortality rate, and migration have been studied.

Ordinarily the *fertility* of the population is the major element in the changing number and distribution of a given area. The study of this factor usually involves the keeping and systematic organization of detailed records of births in the population or populations being analyzed. Thus the basic data are not secured by means of a census but by entirely different procedures from those by which we obtain our fundamental information relative to the number, geographic distribution, and characteristics of the population. Registration, instead of enumeration, is the basic technique employed for the collection of data about births and also for the collection of information on the other of the vital processes, that is, mortality or death.

Mortality, as indicated, is the second of society's two vital processes. At most times and in most places, the death rate is considerably lower than the birth rate, thus producing a natural increase of population. As in the case of births an elaborate registration system is required to secure the detailed records of deaths, along with the characteristics of deceased persons, with which the student of population works. Since comprehensive morbidity or health statistics are rarely assembled, most of our knowledge of the health of various populations consists of inferences based on mortality data. Thus it is sometimes difficult to determine exactly where the study of population terminates and that of health begins.

The number of births minus the number of deaths in a given population during a specified length of time (usually one year) gives the *natural increase* of population. This, in turn, is the primary element in the study of population growth and population redistribution. Ordinarily, however, attention is not focused upon natural increase *per se*, but the birth rate and the death rate are considered separately, along with migration, as the factors directly involved in the increase, decrease, and changing geographic distribution of a population.

Migration

The migration of persons from one country to another, or from place to place within a given country, is the fourth large area of study in the field of demography. As indicated above, this movement of persons from one area to another is the third factor (along with births and deaths) that must be considered before one can account for the growth or decrease of population or for changes in the geographic distribution of the inhabitants. As yet, however, the ways and means of securing the necessary data on migrations, especially those that involve movement from one part of a nation to another, have not been perfected; and much of what is known on the subject is inference based upon successive counts of the population and a knowledge of the other two factors involved.

Immigration and *emigration* are of concern to the student of population because they denote the international movement of persons from one society to another. The records kept by the national agencies concerned with the control of such movements and the naturalization of immigrants are the basic sources of data for studies in this aspect of demography. They are supplemented, however, by the census enumerations and classifications of the population as native and foreign born and the various subclassifications of the latter category.

Internal or *intranational migration* remains the greatest unknown in contemporary population study, although for many areas the exodus or the influx of population is a major factor in the decrease or the growth of population. Few countries have anything remotely resembling an accurate system for accounting for the movement of population from one place to another, although many attempt rigid controls of such movements. In the United States the census of population has tried in various ways to secure partial information on this subject, but the problems involved are among the most serious with which the contemporary student of population is faced. Even such common and badly needed materials as current estimates of state populations made regularly by the Bureau of the Census and various state and private agencies are subject to tremendous error for want of reasonably accurate data on the annual interstate migrations of the population.

The Growth and Geographic Redistribution of Population

The material relating to the changing number and geographic distribution of the population is the fifth and final set of data with which the demographer is concerned. Studies of these subjects naturally lead to making estimates of future populations or population "projections," a commodity for which modern society seems to have an insatiable appetite. Of course, successive census counts supply the substantial information needed for the determination and description of past changes, and the knowledge of recent trends and of the three factors involved in population growth or decline offers some basis for predicting the immediate future.

Population Problems and Policies

In addition to the scientific study, analysis, and interpretation of the data in the five general areas outlined above, the student of population may well carry his thinking to the point of indicating certain problems inherent in demographic situations and trends; and logically, too, he may try to formulate statements as to what national, state, or local population policies should be. In fact, matters such as these command the principal attentions of a substantial number of demographers and of those who are responsible for formulating public policies and planning for human welfare.

SOURCES OF DATA

Most of the data utilized by demographers are secured, mainly for other purposes, in the periodic censuses of population which most nations conduct and from the registries of births, deaths, and immigration which they maintain. These are supplemented at critical points by materials the demographers themselves collect by surveys organized specifically for the purpose of filling some of the gaps in the essential statistical information. For this reason the student of population must be expert in the collection, testing, tabulation, manipulation, analysis, description, and interpretation of statistical materials. If he is working in the United States, he soon comes to know that the information gathered, tabulated, and published in the decennial censuses of population since 1790, plus the data on deaths registered since 1900 and on births registered since 1915, constitute one of the world's greatest repositories of social and economic facts.

Brief mention may be made of the specific sources in which the student will find a large share of the demographic information which he may need. Nowadays it is relatively easy to secure the basic population facts about any nation as a whole, if they are to be had at all. These are readily available in the several editions of the *Demographic Yearbook* which the United Nations has published annually since 1948 - 49. The various issues of this indispensable compendium vary considerably, since each volume is devoted to a considerable extent to the presentation of detailed figures on just one of the major divisions of demography, such as mortality, fertility, or the growth of population. Since the Population Commission established by the United Nations secures directly from the nations involved, tabulates, and publishes these materials, the student, by consulting the various issues of the *Demographic Yearbook,* may easily secure the more important demographic data for any or all of the world's nations, territories, dependencies, colonies, and so one, if such information is to be had at all. This is a remarkable improvement over the situation existing prior to 1948. If, however, one needs demographic information for the various national subdivisions, such as the states, provinces, or departments, he must consult the census reports, statistical yearbooks, and other sources published by the respective nations.

For the United States, there are two primary sources of demographic data. The first of these is the comprehensive reports of the censuses of population, which give the definitive tabulations of the data assembled each ten years since 1790. The latest of these enumerations, the nineteenth, was made in 1970, and most of the published results were available by the end of 1973. The second fundamental source is the annual publications issued by the National Center for Health Statistics which give summary tabulations of the data on births and deaths. Departments of public health in most of the states also publish vital statistics data for their respective states, some of them slightly earlier and in somewhat greater detail than those given in the reports issued by the National Center for Health Statistics.

It requires a considerable amount of time and effort for the student of population to inform himself adequately concerning the contents of the various reports of the Bureau of the Census and the National Center for Health Statistics. For the serious student, however, the hours spent in this endeavor will prove highly rewarding.

The National Center for Health Statistics also issues each year a series of *Vital Statistics — Special Reports* in which current and historical materials on births, deaths, marriages, and divorces are published in a convenient form that makes this set of great value for reference purposes.

If only the more general demographic materials are needed, the *Statistical Abstract of the United States,* issued annually by the Government Printing Office, is a convenient and thoroughly reliable source of information.

Population Index, a periodical issued quarterly by Princeton University and the Population Association of America, is devoted almost exclusively to annotated bibliographies of population literature appearing throughout the world. By consulting this periodical regularly the student may keep abreast of the more important surveys conducted in this and other countries and keep himself informed with respect to the most important current books and articles in the demographic field.

METHOD

The population student or demographer employs the scientific method in his endeavor to expand the frontiers of knowledge through intensive study of the materials in the areas mentioned above. In fact, demography may be defined as the systematized body of knowledge that has been derived through the application of the scientific method to the study of population materials. This study includes the gathering, organization, manipulation, analysis, description, and interpretation of the data relating to the number, geographic distribution, characteristics, vital processes, and changing numbers and distribution of human beings.

Science itself should be thought of as one of the species of human knowledge, of which philosophy, history, and theology are other well-known varieties. From the standpoint of subject matter there is the utmost variety in scientific phenomena, ranging all the way from those studied by the astronomer to those in the province of the social psychologist. The technical aids or devices employed by scientists working in the various subject matter fields also are of the utmost variety. Each branch of science develops and perfects its own, such as the telescopes of the astronomers, the microscopes of the biologists and the chemists, the scales and vacuums of the physicists, and the schedules, tests, and interviewing techniques of the psychologists and sociologists. In these technical methods of science there is no unity.

But there is unity in the logical methods employed by those working in all parts of the realm of science, and this unity makes it possible to think of science as a whole and not merely of the specific parts or disciplines of which it is composed.

Two types of mental activity are involved in the scientific method: (1) *observation* and (2) *inference*. Skill in securing unbiased, pertinent, and accurate observations and facility in making significant, logical inferences from these observations constitute the essence of the scientific method. Observation is "the act of apprehending things and events, their attributes and their concrete relationships," including the direct awareness of one's own mental experiences, whereas inference is the formulation of propositions (judgments, beliefs, opinions) based on these observations or as a consequence of other judgments already formed.[1]

Observation is of two types: (1) *bare observation* of phenomena subject to no control and (2) *experiment*. The importance of bare observation is generally overlooked, since it is so commonplace, whereas the role of experiment is lauded by almost all who write on the scientific method. Indeed it is not unusual to encounter on the college campus the proposition that "science is experimentally verified knowledge," and it was upon this ground that many authorities for many years sought to exclude the social sciences from the general realm of science. The untenability of such a position is amply demonstrated by astronomy, universally recognized as the most highly perfected branch of science, which by its very nature must depend almost exclusively upon bare observation. Experimentation, or the control of all factors except the one purposely being varied, is a great aid to observation, and as mentioned above the various fields of science all have devices to facilitate the process of observation. In the field of population study the individual's powers of observation are greatly aided by the schedules of questions prepared for use by census enumerators, the highly perfected forms employed by registrars of vital statistics, the tried and tested systems of tabulation, and the ingenious tables and charts designed for analytical purposes.

There are two principal types of inference: *induction* and *deduction.* Induction, or reasoning from the particular to the general, is the process of formulating propositions that describe or assert some general regularity or uniformity among the phenomena that have been observed. Deduction, or reasoning from the general to the particular, is the process of postulating attributes of the specific from a knowledge of the general. As will be indicated below, both induction and deduction are indispensable parts of the scientific method. Induction supplies the generalizations that may be true, and deduction sets forth what should follow if such propositions are valid. Providing the proposition, or hypothesis, itself is of significance, the hypothesis is a good one if some of the consequences that one deduces should follow may be tested empirically.

In the use of the logical scientific method, scientists in all disciplines are guided, consciously or unconsciously, by three fundamental characteristics of science: (1) critical discrimination, (2) generality and system, and (3) empirical verification. *Critical discrimination* is the ability to be cognizant of the significant facts. The skilled individual is not misled by mere appearances, preoccupied with the trivial, or bewildered by the multiplicity of insignificant details in which the fact of scientific consequence may be enmeshed. For example, critical discrimination of a high order was necessary before the whale was classified as a mammal instead of a fish. It alone can prevent much purportedly scientific investigation from being merely an elaboration of the obvious. It is sadly lacking in the social scientist who spends years of his time manipulating masses of statistical data, expending enough time and energy to make himself the best informed man in the world on the topic, and then presents the reader with an elaborate set of statistical tables and a few statements to the effect that "the facts speak for themselves." Since the phenomena with which any segment of science must deal are infinite in number and variety, critical discrimination is the first requisite of all scientific endeavor; and this is especially true in demography, where the masses of raw materials that have accumulated over the years almost defy description.

Generality and system is a second requisite of all science, irrespective of the particular subject matter with which a given branch is concerned. Man would be unable to survive in a universe that was lacking in order and regularity. Therefore, to discover, to describe, and to understand the order or regularity prevailing in nature is a chief task of man's intellectual endeavors, including those known as science. For this reason, since even the smallest part of nature is infinitely complex, the scientist must not be concerned with a phenomenon or a fact as such, but instead with the object or thing as a representative of many, as a specimen of an entire class of similar objects or things. For him the important facts are those that occur repeatedly in time and space; and the unique is of little value. He seeks instead individual objects and particular events merely as specimens of the types and classes his search for general uniformities and principles leads him to establish.

Finally, all science rests in a very special way upon *empirical verification*. In astronomy, physics, chemistry, zoology, geology, psychology, anthropology, sociology every proposition sustained for more than temporary consideration must be based solidly upon facts gained through sensory impressions. Every generalization must arise through induction from stimuli received through one or more of the senses. If it is anything more than a mere hunch or working hypothesis, the more critical deductions as to what should follow, providing they are valid, already must have been made and tested empirically. Such empirical tests involve the "look and see" procedures to determine if the things that should follow, providing the proposition is valid, actually do.

Since systematized bodies of knowledge other than science, such as history and philosophy, also make use of observation and inference, and since they too require critical discrimination, generality and system, and empirical verification, it is well to consider the distinction between science and one of the others, let us say philosophy. The essential feature distinguishing the two lies not in the nature of the cognitive processes employed but rather in the varying orders in which observation and inference appear in scientific endeavor and in philosophic inquiry. Philosophical endeavors may, and probably usually do, start with observation, just as do scientific activities. In both realms of thought, also, since the human mind has a tendency to leap forward from the observation of a few examples or cases to the formulation of some general rule or principle, induction generally follows immediately after a limited number of observations have been made. At this point the two mental disciplines may part company. The philosopher has the privilege of making his observations, inductions, and deductions in any order that suits his purpose, providing only that no internal conflicts are permitted in his line of reasoning. Thus he may proceed with observation — induction — deduction — deduction — observation — deduction, and so forth, or the three in any other sequence he may choose to utilize.

The scientist has no such freedom. For him, after observation comes induction, or the formulation of some general proposition that may be true. At this point he must resort to deduction, to intensive reflection on the query, "If this generalization is true or valid, what consequences should follow?" Naturally, as he reflects upon the things that should follow, previous facts of observation in large numbers are brought to bear on the hunch or working hypothesis he is entertaining; and unless all these are in accord with the proposition, it is quickly discarded. The active scientific mind conceives and discards hundreds of such tentative propositions for every one that merits more formal testing. In this stage, too, even for the generalization which is supported by the scientist's previously acquired knowledge, not all of the possible deductions as to what should follow are entertained for further empirical testing. In most instances the possibilities are far too numerous to allow for that. Rather the ingenious researcher asks himself, "If this proposition is not valid, under what circumstances is it most likely to prove defective?" In other words he attempts to resort immediately to the critical case. He seeks ways and means of making additional observations, under experimental conditions if at all possible, at the points of greatest significance. But under no circumstances, no matter how important the proposition he is seeking to test, may he proceed to further inferences until additional empirical tests have demonstrated that the results to be expected, providing the proposition is valid, actually do follow. Thus, in the scientific method, in contrast with the philosophical method, the sequence is always as follows: observation – induction – deduction – observation – induction – deduction – observation and so on.

ORDER OF PRESENTATION

The order followed above in outlining the field of population study, or demography, is followed closely throughout this volume. Before commencing with the discussion of the number and geographic distribution of the inhabitants, which constitutes Part Two of this book, however, a second introductory chapter is included to help familiarize students with various events that the present writers consider the principal landmarks in the development of population study. In selecting the items included, the writers have been influenced heavily by the course of events in the United States and the needs of college and university students in this country. No separate chapters are devoted to problems of tabulation, map making, the construction of charts, the making and testing of indexes, and other methodological considerations. Instead, such explanations as appear to be necessary are given in connection with the application of a given measure, index, or technique.

NOTES

1. A. Wolf, *Essentials of the Scientific Method* (New York: The Macmillan Company, 1930), pp. 17 - 18. Cf. Carlo L. Lastrucci, *The Scientific Approach* (Cambridge: Schenkman Publishing Company, Inc., 1963), pp. 3 - 26; and Thelma F. Batten, *Reasoning and Research* (Boston: Little, Brown and Company, 1971), Part I.

SUGGESTED SUPPLEMENTARY READINGS

BENJAMIN, BERNARD. *Demographic Analysis*, Chaps. 1 - 4. New York: Frederick A. Praeger, 1969.

BERTRAND, ALVIN L. *Basic Sociology*, 2nd ed., Chap. 19. New York: Appleton-Century-Crofts, 1973.

BOGUE, DONALD J. *Principles of Demography*, Chaps. 1, 4, and 5. New York: John Wiley & Sons, Inc., 1969.

COX, PETER R. *Demography*, 4th ed., Chaps. 1 - 4. London: Cambridge University Press, 1970.

DAVIS, KINGSLEY. "The Sociology of Demographic Behavior," in *Sociology Today: Problems and Prospects*, edited by Robert K. Merton, Leonard Broom, and Leonard S. Cottrell, Jr., Chap. 14. New York: Basic Books, Inc., 1959.

HAUSER, PHILIP M., and OTIS DUDLEY DUNCAN. *The Study of Population: An Inventory and Appraisal*, Chaps. 3 - 5. Chicago: University of Chicago Press, 1969.

HOLLINGSWORTH, T. H. *Historical Demography*, Chap. 1. Ithaca: Cornell University Press, 1969.

PETERSEN, WILLIAM. *Population*, 2nd ed., Chap. 1. New York: The Macmillan Company, 1969.

SHRYOCK, HENRY S., JACOB S. SIEGEL, and associates. *The Methods and Materials of Demography*, Vol. 1, Chaps. 1 - 3 and 22. Washington: Government Printing Office, 1971.

SPENGLER, JOSEPH J., and OTIS DUDLEY DUNCAN, eds. *Demographic Analysis*. New York: The Free Press, 1956.

THOMPSON, WARREN S., and DAVID T. LEWIS. *Population Problems*, 5th ed., Chap. 1. New York: McGraw-Hill Book Company, 1965.

UNITED NATIONS. *Demographic Yearbook, 1971*, Chap 1. New York: United Nations, 1972.

UNITED NATIONS. *Principles and Recommendations for the 1970 Population Censuses*, pp. 3 - 9. New York: United Nations, 1967.

WILLCOX, WALTER F. *Studies in American Demography*, Appendix 1. Ithaca: Cornell University Press, 1940.

WRONG, DENNIS H. *Population and Society*, 3rd ed., Chap. 1. New York: Random House, Inc., 1967.

2
IMPORTANT LANDMARKS IN THE DEVELOPMENT OF POPULATION STUDY

Interest in the number of inhabitants and inventories of those with special characteristics arose very early in the history of civilization, but disinterested, objective attempts to determine relationships, trends, and principles seem to date from comparatively recent historical times. At least a search through contemporary compendia of demographic knowledge reveals very few items in which contemporary scholars indicate that ancient and medieval intellectuals had any significant theoretical interest in demographic matters.

The Romans, of course, early used ingenious census procedures to determine for military and other practical administrative purposes the number, geographic distribution, and a few of the most significant characteristics of the population. Servius Tullius (578 - 534 B.C.), sixth legendary king of Rome, is credited with the institution of the census. According to the ancient chronicler,[1] this monarch ordered his people to erect altars to the gods who were the guardians of the district and directed them to assemble once a year to honor these gods with public sacrifices. These occasions he made into solemn festivals, the Paganalia, and he laid down laws to govern the sacrifices. To cover the expenses of the sacrifices and festivities he ordered that all persons in a given district should each contribute a certain piece of money, the men paying with one kind, the women with another, and children with a third. Accordingly when these coins were counted, the number of the inhabitants, the sex distribution, and certain features of the age distribution of the population were known. Furthermore, in order to keep account of the number of inhabitants in the various cities, of births, of deaths, and of those arriving at manhood, he prescribed the type of coin that the relatives should pay into the treasury at Juno Lucina on the occasion of a birth, that which should be paid into the treasury of Venus of the Grove when a person died, and that to be paid into the treasury of Juvenatas for one who arrived at manhood. "By means of these pieces of money he would know every year both the number of all the inhabitants and which of them were of military age." Certainly for administrative purposes these data were much more complete, current, and accurate than those available to the heads of many modern states, but there is little or no information available as yet that would indicate that they served any particular purpose for the kinds of abstraction and inference of which the science of demography is composed. If the Romans did secure and systematize such knowledge, modern scholars still must do the work of integrating it with contemporary systems. As yet the interesting activities of the Romans can hardly be cited as one of the principal landmarks in the development of population study.

The same is true of censuses and other concerns about population matters among the ancient Hebrews and other peoples of antiquity. As we see in the writings assembled in the *Old Testament* the peoples in much of the ancient world long harbored a fear of any attempts to "number the people." The association in time between the census ordered by David and the pestilence which swept away seventy thousand men (II. Samuel, 24) gave rise to this fear. Modern demography was affected seriously because the pestilence was attributed directly to God's anger over the taking of the census. This Hebrew tradition long made many Christian peoples fearful that similar results would follow any other attempts at census taking.[2] Even now this fear lingers among some segments of the populations of a number of countries. However, aside from this, the census and other demographic efforts of the ancient Hebrews have affected modern population study little if at all.

In the pages that follow, the effort is made to indicate and describe briefly the works of greatest importance in the perfection of scientific methodology in the demographic field, developing the necessary frame of reference and providing for the collection and systematic tabulation of essential data on the number of the inhabitants, their principal characteristics, and the three factors (births, deaths, and migrations) involved directly in population change. The development of population study in the United States was the primary consideration in the selection of items to be included.

JOHN GRAUNT: OBSERVATIONS ON THE BILLS OF MORTALITY (1662)

The publication, in 1662, of *Natural and Political Observations Mentioned in the following Index and made upon the Bills of Mortality*, by John Graunt, Citizen of London,[3] is one of the great landmarks in the development of the science of population study. It is believed to be the first one sufficiently important to deserve listing in a summary account such as this. Others credit Graunt with being not only the founder of demography but of statistics as well.[4]

Graunt's method was truly scientific. From the records of burial permits issued in the city of London after the plague of 1592 gave rise to the practice of requiring such authorizations for interments of the deceased, Graunt carefully assembled the data for the years 1604 to 1661, inclusive. Wisely, he included the materials for the surrounding districts, or "out-parishes," as well as the urban districts. These he supplemented with data on births taken from parish registers of christenings. For the years 1629 to 1659 he was able to get detailed information on causes of death, and for the period 1629 - 1660 he secured the data on all burial permits and christenings classified according to the sex of the persons involved. These materials he

> reduced into Tables (the Copies whereof are here inserted) so as to have a view of the whole together, in order to the more ready comparing of one *Year, Season, Parish,* or other *Division* of the City, with another, in respect of all the *Burials,* and *Christenings,* and of all the *Diseases,* and *Casualties* happening in each of them respectively; I did then begin, not only to examine the Conceits, Opinions, and Conjectures, which upon view of a few scattered *Bills* I had taken up; but did also admit new ones, as I found reason, and occasion from my *Tables.* [5]

The observations, stated concisely in the "Index" and elaborated upon in the text are 106 in number. The great majority of these propositions are genuine inductions, suggested as Graunt indicated by a study of various specific "bills" and tested by means of the comprehensive tables. Many of the demographic generalizations he formulated and stated on the basis of these studies are supported by the results of most inquiries made since he wrote and by the work of contemporary students of population. A few noteworthy examples are as follows:

1. There is a heavy migration of persons from the country to the city (observations 37, 46, 47, 58, 66, 89).

2. This migration is selective of "breeders," that is, of persons in the reproductive ages (observations 46, 50).

3. The natural increase of population is higher in the country than in the city (observations 43, 44).

4. The rate of reproduction is higher in rural districts than in urban (observations 49, 50, 51).

Graunt also observed that the urban death rate was higher than the rural, a differential that has prevailed generally since he wrote and probably is still true in many parts of the world.

THE FIRST CENSUS OF POPULATION OF THE UNITED STATES: 1790

The United States Census of population, probably entitled to be called the first modern census, has been called a political accident because of the manner in which the conflict between the large and the small states was resolved by the framers of the Constitution of the United States. In the early days of the new republic, as the work on the constitution progressed, the small states held out for equal representation in the Congress, whereas the larger states insisted that they were entitled to greater representation in the legislative bodies. In the end a compromise was effected giving each state the right to send two members to the Senate and providing in paragraph 3, section 2, of Article I that members of the House of Representatives should be apportioned among the several states "according to their respective Numbers. . . ." This paragraph further stipulated that "the actual Enumeration shall be made within three Years after the first Meeting of the Congress of the United States, and within every subsequent Term of ten Years, in such Manner as they shall by Law direct."

In accordance with this constitutional provision, the first census of the population of the United States was taken in 1790 and subsequent enumerations have been made each ten years from then to the present time. So began the work of assembling the vast store of concrete facts which today is fully entitled to be designated as the world's greatest repository of social and economic data. Even though decades were to pass before any considerable scientific study would be made of the rapidly accumulating mass of material, the beginning of the United States Census of Population in 1790 is a prominent landmark in the development of population study. With the improvements made in 1800 it got well underway the procedures that supplied the all-important data on the number and distribution of the inhabitants.

MALTHUS: ESSAY ON POPULATION (1798)

The closing decades of the eighteenth century were marked by considerable interest in population matters, particularly in the rapidity with which human populations were increasing and in the economic effects of population increase. Both Benjamin Franklin and Thomas Jefferson devoted considerable time and thought to such subjects. The demographic event of greatest consequence in this period, however, was the appearance in 1798 of the first edition of the *Essay on Population*, published anonymously in England by a young Episcopalian clergyman named Thomas R. Malthus. A second edition of the work, tempered down and expanded considerably, appeared in 1803. The basic thesis of this volume, that the growth of population tends consistently to outstrip the increase in the means of subsistence, for decades was a chief bone of contention among those writing and debating upon social and economic questions. The pessimistic conclusions inherent in Malthus' propositions had much to do with economics coming to be known as "the dismal science." Even today it is not difficult to stir up an argument among sociologists, economists, biologists, and public-health personnel by raising a query relating to the validity of Malthusian theory.

Malthus wrote, of course, before modern censuses had yielded any considerable amounts of reliable demographic data and before much in the way of analytical techniques had been perfected. Even so, to many he appears still to be the ultimate authority on all demographic questions. There are those, of course, with whom the present writers are inclined to side, who maintain that the Malthusian principles and especially the debates over them which have preempted the time and energy of those interested in population matters may have hindered rather than helped the progress of demographic study and investigation. For example, as recently as 1959, Davis held that the doctrinal encumbrances of the Malthusian heritage still pervaded what was thought of as population theory to such a great extent that a large number of those working in this area did "not contribute to, or even have much understanding of, formal demography."[6] Since then, however, demographers have critically refined theory that is basically demographic and have made increasing use of theory developed in the broader realm of social science. An example of the former is the "Demographic Transition",[7] a case of the latter is the application of systems theory to demographic matters.[8] Nevertheless, even today the demographer must have more than a passing acquaintance with Malthus' ideas, eloquent testimony that the publication of the *Essay on Population* constitutes an important landmark in the course of the development of population study.

COMPREHENSIVE DATA ON THE CHARACTERISTICS OF POPULATION: 1854

Most of the insight and organization needed to give value to census statistics on the characteristics of the population dates from the years 1853 - 1854 when J. D. B. DeBow served as superintendent of the United States Census. A native of South Carolina, DeBow moved to New Orleans, Louisiana, where he founded and developed to greatness a periodical called *DeBow's Review*. This journal soon became the outlet for essays by its editor and others on numerous social and economic topics, including many of the first demographic treatises to be published in the United States. His vision, energy, and general leadership resulted in his appointment in 1848 to organize and direct a state bureau of statistics, the first to be established in this country. The same year he also was appointed professor of political economy and commerce at Tulane University. In these capacities he developed an outline for use in the study of Louisiana parishes (counties) and communities, which he then employed to stimulate leaders in various parts of the state to assemble, organize, and present in written form the more significant social and economic facts about their respective localities. Of the fourteen general topics included in his outline, the following dealt specifically with demographic matters:

I. Time of *settlement* of your parish or town; dates of oldest land grants; number and condition of first settlers; whence emigrating; other facts relating to settlements and history.

VI. Instances of *longevity* and *fecundity*; observations on diseases in your section; localities, healthful or otherwise; statistics of diseases; deaths; summer seats, &c.

VII. *Population* of your parish; increase and progress, distinguishing white and black; Spanish, French, American or German origin; foreigners, classes of population; number in towns; growth of towns and villages, &c.; condition, employment, ages; comparative value of free and slave labor; comparative tables of increase; marriages, births, &c.; . . .[9]

Reports for about one-half of Louisiana's parishes were published in *DeBow's Review*.

In 1853 President Franklin Pierce appointed DeBow as superintendent of the United States Census. At that time the work of enumeration and tabulation of the 1850 census had already been completed. Fortunately, the schedules had been greatly improved, due mostly to the efforts of Mr. Lemuel Shattuck of Boston. The new schedules made provision for the first time for recording the name and characteristics of each person enumerated. With the data thus subject to manipulation, DeBow — familiar with the work of Quételet and other European scholars, acquainted with the accomplishments of various European censuses, and driven by his own inquiring genius — proceeded to revolutionize the handling of the census materials and particularly those on the characteristics of the population. He also made detailed specific recommendations for the improvement of forms and tabulations in subsequent censuses. As a result many of the series of characteristics with which contemporary demographers deal in the United States go back to the census of 1850. In addition, the comprehensive *Statistical View of the United States*, cited above, which DeBow prepared as a compendium of the results of the seventh and earlier censuses, both theoretically and practically must be regarded as one of the principal landmarks in the entire history of demographic studies. While he headed the Census Office, DeBow also was responsible for the first official attempts to assemble data on mortality and fertility of the population of the United States.

These accomplishments, to be properly evaluated, need to be reflected against those of the superintendents of the preceding six censuses, those from 1790 to 1840, inclusive. The first census set forth and secured information on only five particulars relating to the population: white males under sixteen, white males over sixteen, white females, slaves, and all other free persons "except Indians, not taxed." The second census, in 1800, improved this schema only by classifying white males and white females, separately, into the following age groups: under ten, ten to sixteen, sixteen to twenty-six, twenty-six to forty-five, and forty-five and over. Exactly the same procedure was followed in the third census. In the fourth census, the following innovations appeared: white males between sixteen and eighteen were classified separately, the number of unnaturalized foreign-born persons was indicated, and the free colored and slave populations were classified by sex into the following age categories: under fourteen, fourteen to twenty-six, twenty-six to forty-five, and over forty-five. In the fifth census (1830) white males and females were classified into five-year age groups up to the age of twenty, and into ten-year age groups from twenty to a hundred; the free colored and the slaves, of each sex, were classified by age into those under ten, those ten to twenty-four, those twenty-four to thirty-six, those thirty-six to fifty-five, those fifty-five to 100, and those of 100 and over; and the numbers of those born in another country who had not been naturalized were indicated. On population matters, the 1840 census followed exactly the preceding one. "These enumerations were published, within one, two, or three years, severally, from the time when they were made, but in such a manner as unfitted them for general use, understanding, or reference, and with very little tabular system and accuracy. A complete set of them does not exist in the public departments at Washington, and one or two are nearly, if not entirely, out of print."[10]

Unfortunately, DeBow's connection with the Census of the United States ended on December 31, 1854, when the work of the Seventh Census terminated, and, as was the practice in the censuses from 1790 to 1890, the Census Office was closed. When preparations for the Census of 1860 got underway, the same man DeBow had replaced in 1853 was again in charge of the Census Office established for the purpose of making the new enumeration.

INTERNATIONAL RESUME OF POPULATION STATISTICS: 1866

The publication of *Statistique Internationale (Population)*, by Adolph Quételet and Xavier Heuschling, presented to those interested in population study a comprehensive summary of population materials for most of the countries that had engaged seriously in the collection of demographic data. It is true that the compilation had comparatively little influence in the United States, but it deserves mention here because it did break the ground in this highly important part of population study and because even now the volume is of great value to those who desire to study demographic changes over a considerable period of time. Quételet was president and Heuschling secretary of Belgium's Commission Centrale de Statistique; and the book was published as Tome X of the *Bulletin de la Commission Centrale de Statistique*, Brussels, 1866. In its preparation they had the cooperation of the official statisticians of Austria, Bavaria, Denmark, England, France, Greece, Hanover, Italy, the Netherlands, Prussia, the two Saxonies, Spain, Sweden, Switzerland, the United States and Württemberg.

The proposal for this compilation of primary international data developed in connection with various meetings of the International Statistical Association and crystallized at the fourth gathering of that body held in London in 1860. Here the Association acted favorably upon Quételet's proposal "for a conference of the official delegates to agree upon a common set of forms for use in their respective countries." Following this, Quételet and Heuschling drew up plans for the compilation, which then were circulated among the others for criticism and advice. It was the consensus that the initial venture should concentrate principally upon "the number of inhabitants in each country, their distribution by sexes and by ages, and, wherever possible, upon mortality tables." In compiling and publishing the tabulations the authors wisely included information from as many census enumerations as possible, and the vital statistics for a series of years. Subsequently, important international compilations of population data were made by the French Ministère du Travail et de la Prévoyance Social,[11] and the International Institute of Statistics at The Hague.[12]

Following the organization of the League of Nations, the *Statistical Yearbook of the League of Nations*, beginning in 1927 and terminating with the 1942 - 1944 issue, presented current data on the number of inhabitants in various nations and territories. After the establishment of the United Nations, this body's Population Commission began issuing annually a *Demographic Yearbook*, but this represented such an important new step that it deserves mention below as another important landmark in the development of population studies.

COMPREHENSIVE OFFICIAL MORTALITY STATISTICS: 1902

The struggle for comprehensive, reliable, official mortality statistics for the United States was a long one. It is somewhat difficult to establish precisely the time when the struggle was won, a victory surely entitled to a place in the list of outstanding landmarks in the development of population study in the United States, but 1902 is probably the most appropriate year. That is when the Census Office was established on a permanent basis, renamed the Bureau of the Census, and specifically charged with responsibility for making annual compilations and reports on mortality and birth statistics in the United States. From an official report, a few of the more salient facts relative to the problem and the struggle may be seen:

> The United States until 1900 was the only civilized country of the occidental world in great areas of which deaths and births were not registered. This gap in American statistics was due mainly to the fact that registration was, and still is, exclusively under State control. The Federal Government has no authority to legislate about it and, before 1900, few of the States maintained good registration laws and good administration of them. During the second half of the last century the Federal Government asked of each family at the time of a decennial census whether during the preceding 12 months a death had occurred therein or a child been born and died before the enumeration. But less than three-fourths of the deaths were thus reported . . . the half century of experiment accomplished little more than to set up a "no thoroughfare" sign against further effort to make a census alone yield the information needed for vital statistics.[13]

ESSENTIAL DATA ON POPULATION FERTILITY

Those interested in population study in the United States found the procurement of adequate data on the fertility of the population even more difficult and more delayed than getting the necessary material on mortality. The attempts between 1850 and 1900 to determine the birth rate of the population by use of the numbers of children under one year of age reported in the decennial censuses yielded little of value for the nation as a whole and nothing significant for its various subdivisions. Nor did the establishment in 1902 on a permanent basis of the Bureau of the Census, charged with the responsibility of preparing annual reports of the numbers of births registered throughout the country, quickly overcome the difficulties. The birth registration area was not established until 1915, and it did not cover the entire nation until 1933. Even then tremendous difficulties, far greater than those encountered in getting full coverage in the registration of deaths, had to be solved. Not the least of these was the length of time that had to pass before those using the birth statistics became aware that the data were not to be taken at their face value. The failure to register large proportions of the births, especially those occurring in rural areas and those to Negro parents, and the practice of registering births according to place of occurrence instead of according to the mother's place of residence long made the birth statistics of little or no value to any except the most skilled demographers. In fact, it was not until after 1950 that the official birth statistics for various parts of the United States were more or less adequate for use in comparative studies of the rate of reproduction of the population.

By the early 1930's, however, the ingenuity of American demographers had developed a substitute for the birth rate for use in the study of the rate of reproduction. As a result, since the publication of the results of the 1930 census, population study in the United States has been greatly facilitated by the demographer's ability to take that important factor into account. The ratio of young children to women of child-bearing age, commonly known as the *fertility ratio*, is the measure which has been substituted for the birth rate. It is computed variously as the number of children under five per thousand or hundred women aged fifteen to forty-four, twenty to forty-four, fifteen to forty-nine, and so on.

Walter F. Willcox seems to have been the first to devise and employ this measure of population fertility. Following the census of 1900, he "attacked the problem from a different angle, abandoning the effort to obtain a true birth rate from census figures and studying instead the proportion of children enumerated under 5 years of age to women of child-bearing age."[14] As early as 1911 he presented a paper to the American Statistical Association describing his method and comparing fertility trends in the United States with those in France.[15] Others were slow to follow, however, and most of those writing on population matters in the United States used the birth statistics that soon thereafter became available, apparently blissfully unaware of their primary defects.

In 1931, the Bureau of the Census published a monograph entitled *Ratio of Children to Women: 1920*[16] prepared by Warren S. Thompson. For some reason, Thompson made no mention of the earlier work by Willcox, but the publication of his study made the fertility ratio almost immediately known and used by other students of population throughout the nation. This, in turn, represented a significant landmark in the development of population study in the United States.

DATA FOR THE FARM POPULATION: 1930

From 1874 to the present time, rural-urban classifications and analyses have figured prominently in population study throughout the United States. However, separate data for the rural-farm part of the rural population have played such an important role in the development of demographic studies in this country that the date on which they became generally available for use by men and women engaged in research work at the state agricultural experiment stations and other research centers deserves special mention. This is because detailed materials concerning the farm population in the various counties and other subdivisions of the states were a necessity, both practically and legally, before rural sociologists at such centers could devote any considerable amount of time to population study. Such data became available just at the time Franklin Delano Roosevelt became president of the United States and just as the men working in this field were called upon for exceptional demographic activity in order to secure and analyze the materials needed to guide the federal relief and federal works programs.[17] As a result, population studies were the principal activity of the men working in the field as rural sociology came to maturity in the years following 1930, and they continue to receive considerable attention. In turn, the contributions of those who are employed as rural sociologists at the agricultural experiment stations, or who once were so employed, loom large in the whole field of demography. It must be stressed, therefore, that the provision of detailed materials on the numbers, distribution, and characteristics of the farm population deserves a place of prominence as one traces the development of population studies in the United States.

Charles J. Galpin, well-known for his pioneering work in rural sociology, is chiefly entitled to the credit for this important innovation. In 1919, Galpin left the University of Wisconsin, where he pioneered the work in the study of the rural community, to become head of the Division of Farm Population and Rural Life in the newly established Bureau of Agricultural Economics of the U. S. Department of Agriculture. In his new position he received eventually the multitude of requests for data on the farm population which annually reached Washington from persons and agencies all over the United States. He quickly found that the materials for the rural population fell far short of meeting the needs of his clients in the forty-eight states. However, those in charge of the U. S. Bureau of the Census gave scant heed to his suggestions and requests that the materials about the rural population, then coming in from the 1920 census, be presented separately for the farm and nonfarm (then largely village) segments of which it consisted. He did receive permission, however, to have one of his assistants sort by hand the pertinent information for eight selected counties distributed throughout the United States.[18] The reception accorded this fragmentary material was such that Dr. Leon E. Truesdell of the Bureau of the Census quickly had the necessary information tabulated for the entire United States and prepared a Census Monograph to make it available.[19] In the preparation of plans for the 1930 census, the sub-classification of the data for the farm and nonfarm portions of the rural population became a basic consideration. As a result, in the reports of the 1930 and subsequent censuses, in the county tables, and to a certain extent in those for minor civil divisions as well, the materials of age, sex, race and nativity, educational status, occupations, and so forth, are given in most of the detail needed for administrative purposes. In addition, they constitute the basic facts that may be manipulated by demographers and other sociologists and economists in order to test empirically a large share of the working hypotheses they are able to develop. The present writers are of the opinion that the introduction of the rural-farm and rural-nonfarm categories as integral portions of the 1930 census tabulations constituted the most important innovation relative to the characteristics of the population since DeBow gave form to this all-important aspect of demography in the years immediately following the 1850 census.

COMPREHENSIVE CURRENT INTERNATIONAL DEMOGRAPHIC DATA: "THE DEMOGRAPHIC YEARBOOK, 1948"

The Economic and Social Council of the United Nations at its fourth session, in 1947, recommended that the international organization publish a demographic yearbook "containing regular series of basic demographic statistics, comparable within and among themselves, and relevant calculations of comparable rates. . . ." The Statistical Commission and the Population Commission, to which the planning of the compilation was assigned, recommended forty-eight general topics for inclusion. These are as follows, with those selected for use in the first (1948) issue indicated with asterisks:

   I.   Area and population

       1. Area*
       2. Total population*
       3. Population density*
       4. Annual percentage rate of population change

    5. Population of major cities
    6. Population by age and sex — absolute numbers and proportions*
    7. Population by age, sex, and marital condition — absolute numbers and proportions*
    8. Population by urban and rural divisions*
    9. Population by race and nationality (or citizenship)
   10. Population by age, sex, and literacy*
   11. Households — number and distribution by size*
   12. Women by number of children ever born and by number of children living*

II.   Economically active population

   13. Active population (labor force) by age and sex*
   14. Active population by industry*
   15. Active population by industrial status (class of worker)*

III. International migration

   16. Emigrants by country of destination*
   17. Immigrants by country of origin and nationality*
   18. Emigrants and immigrants by age, sex, and occupation

IV.   Natality

   19. Total number of births*
   20. Crude birth rates*
   21. Births by month of occurrence
   22. Births by age of mother and father*
   23. Fertility rates by age of mother*
   24. Births by parity*
   25. Births by legitimacy
   26. Births by duration of marriage*
   27. Stillbirths*
   28. Gross and net reproduction rates*
   29. Ratio of children under five years of age to women aged fifteen to forty-nine years

V.   Mortality

   30. Total deaths
   31. Crude death rates*
   32. Deaths by month of occurrence
   33. Deaths by age and sex*
   34. Death rates by age and sex*
   35. Infant mortality rates*

    36.   Deaths by cause
    37.   Maternal (puerperal) mortality rates
    38.   Life table death rates (q_x)*
    39.   Life table survivors (l_x)*
    40.   Mean expectation of life*

VI. Morbidity

    41.   General morbidity

VII. Marriage and divorce

    42.   Total marriages*
    43.   Crude marriage rates*
    44.   Marriages by age of partners*
    45.   Marriage rates by age and sex*
    46.   Total divorces
    47.   Crude divorce rates
    48.   Divorces by duration of marriage and number of children

The first issue of the *Demographic Yearbook*, corresponding to the year 1948, appeared in 1949. As was to be expected, it contained a wealth of data never before available to the student of population. Another edition in 1951 gave materials through 1949 and 1950. Since then the volumes have been issued annually. All contain many of the more general data with the series brought up to date, but gradually the various issues have extended the time series into the past as far as possible. Furthermore, each number specializes to a considerable extent in a particular topic. Thus, for example, the 1949 - 50 issue featured marriage and fertility; the 1951, 1957, 1961, 1966, and 1967 numbers mortality; the 1954, 1959, and 1969 compilations of natality; the 1955 volume the statistics from censuses taken in the decade 1945 - 1954; the 1956 edition ethnic and economic characteristics; the 1958 and 1968 publications marriage and divorce; the 1960 and 1970 numbers population trends; the 1962, 1963, and 1964 issues the materials from census enumerations made in the ten-year period 1955 to 1964; and the 1971 and 1972 volumes the results of censuses taken between 1962 and 1972.

AT LAST –
MINIMUM ESSENTIAL MIGRATION DATA: 19??

As yet no event connected with the development of data on the important factor of migration nor its analysis deserves mention in this brief sketch of the major landmarks in the development of population study. The present stage of the science and its immediate needs, however, make it unlikely that this state can continue as it now exists in most countries for much longer. Perhaps the 1980 Census of the United States will innovate another fundamental "breakthrough" in population study. Or possibly vigorous leadership in some of the other countries may entitle one of them to take credit for the next important landmark in the development of demography.

It is true, of course, that for the first time in 1940 the United States Bureau of the Census collected a relatively large amount of data on internal migration. It continued the effort, using modified procedures, in the 1950 and the 1960 enumerations and tabulated the results in several of its *Special Reports* and *Subject Reports*, respectively. In 1970, that agency also collected some data on the subject and has published them in five *Subject Reports* and in some sections of the general summary reports. The Census Bureau also has accumulated other materials on the subject during intercensal periods, largely as part of its *Current Population Survey*. These materials make it possible to learn some things about interregional, interstate, and intercounty migration as well as about persons who move from house to house within counties. But the data are based upon samples and estimates and their accuracy depends upon the person's recollection at the time of the enumeration of his place of residence at another period of time, either five years earlier or one year earlier. In fact, the magnitude of the errors remains largely unknown.[20] Moreover, the data reveal little about such highly important movements as those from rural areas to urban centers, from urban fringes to city centers, from cities to suburbs, from one city to another, and so on.[21]

While the need for adequate migration data is as patent today as in centuries past, most of what is known on the subject in virtually all parts of the world is based on inference from the data yielded by successive population counts and a knowledge of births and deaths, the other two factors involved directly in the changing number and distribution of the population. Only when an attempt is made to measure all three of the factors involved (births, deaths, *and* migrations), so that the student may then compare the net change indicated by the factors with the net change indicated by the successive counts, for a state, a city, a county, or other division, will there be any substantial improvement in the situation.

The absolute minimum of information needed could be secured if, in the course of the decennial count, each person aged ten years or more were asked whether at the time of the previous census he was residing in the county in which he is being enumerated or in some other county, and if each person of less than ten years were classified as being born in the county of residence or in another county. To be sure, this procedure would force the individual to recall his place of residence ten rather than five years earlier, but it also would provide him with a stable reference point; that is, the occasion on which he was contacted by the census enumerator. These data should then be tabulated to indicate for each county the number of persons who had moved to it from another county during the intercensal period. Of course, other details, such as the age, sex, and other characteristics of the migrants, would add immensely to the value of the tabulations.

Once such an innovation is introduced, the attempt will have been made to account for all the factors in population change. Then if the difference between two successive census counts of the population of a county does not equal the net change indicated by subtracting the number of deaths during the interim from the number of births, plus or minus the number of migrants, it will follow that one or more of the figures (one or both of the census counts, the registry of births, the registry of deaths, or the reported migrations) is wrong. The demonstration of such errors would be the first step in their correction. As indicated above, when they get these data on migration, students of population will be able to attempt to balance the equation. All of the other materials are now being assembled as a matter of course. The census that places the lacking data on migration in the hands of demographers will represent another fundamental contribution to the developing study of population.[22]

1. Earnest Cary, *The Roman Antiquities of the Dionysius of Halicarnassus* (Cambridge: Harvard University Press, 1939), II, pp. 317 - 319.

2. Cf. Clarence G. Dittmer, *Introduction to Social Statistics* (Chicago and New York: A. W. Shaw Company, 1926), p. 5.

3. Conveniently available in *Natural and Political Observations made upon the Bills of Mortality by John Graunt,* edited by Walter F. Willcox (Baltimore: The Johns Hopkins University Press, 1939).

4. See the "Introduction" by Willcox, *ibid.,* pp. iii - xiii, and the literature cited therein. Willcox himself concludes that Graunt, "more than any other man, was the founder of statistics," p. xiii.

5. *Ibid.,* pp. 17 - 18.

6. Kingsley Davis, "The Sociology of Demographic Behavior," in *Sociology Today: Problems and Prospects,* edited by Robert K. Merton, Leonard Broom, and Leonard S. Cottrell, Jr. (New York: Basic Books, Inc., 1959), p. 311.

7. Cf. Dennis H. Wrong, *Population and Society* (3rd ed.) (New York: Random House, 1969), pp. 17 - 23, and David M. Heer, *Society and Population* (Englewood Cliffs, N. J.: Prentice-Hall, 1968), pp. 10 - 12.

8. One of the most extensive efforts is Thomas R. Ford and Gordon F. DeJong (eds.), *Social Demography* (Englewood Cliffs, N.J.: Prentice-Hall, 1970). See especially Chapters 1 and 12.

9. J. D. B. DeBow, *Statistical View of the United States. . .Being a Compendium of the Seventh Census. . .* (Washington: Beverley Tucker, Senate Printer, 1854), p. 19.

10. *Ibid.,* p. 11.

11. *Statistique internationale du mouvement de la population* Paris: Imprimerie Nationale, 1913), 2 Vols.

12. *Aperçu de la demographie des divers pays du monde:* 1922, 1925, 1927, 1929, 1931, 1929 - 1936 (La Haye, 1923 - 1939).

13. Walter F. Willcox, *Introduction to the Vital Statistics of the United States: 1900 - 1930* (Washington: Government Printing Office, 1933), p. 13.

14. *Ibid.,* p. 56.

15. *Ibid.,* p. 57.

16. Washington: Government Printing Office.

17. For details on this development, see T. Lynn Smith, "The Development of Rural Sociology in the United States, with a Few Annotations on Its Development in the South," *Revue Internationale de Sociologie*, VIII, 1 (April, 1972), pp. 76 - 78.

18. Charles J. Galpin and Veda B. Larson, *Farm Population of Selected Counties: Composition, Characteristics, and Occupations in Detail for Eight Counties, Comprising Otsego County, N. Y., Dane County, Wis., New Madrid and Scott Counties, Mo., Cass County, N. Dak., Wake County, N. C., Ellis County, Tex., and King County, Wash.* (Washington: Government Printing Office, 1924).

19. Leon E. Truesdell, *Farm Population of the United States: An Analysis of the 1920 Farm Population Figures.* . . . Census Monograph VI (Washington: Government Printing Office, 1926).

20. For a report on the quality of these data, see Henry S. Shryock, Jr., *Population Mobility Within the United States* (Chicago: Community and Family Study Center, University of Chicago, 1964), Chap. 4.

21. In 1973, the United States Department of Agriculture, the University of Georgia, and the Office of Economic Opportunity cooperated in producing *Poverty Dimensions of Rural-to-Urban Migration: A Statistical Report* (Washington: Government Printing Office, 1973). This is intended to be the first of an important series on migration in the United States, but it too is limited by being the result of survey data, in this case those for 1967. It does, however, refer to cumulative migration rather than to a single move in a specified time period.

22. The importance of this step was indicated at the 1954 meetings of the Population Association of America, *Population Index*, 20, 3 (July, 1954), p. 148; and in a report to the Rural Sociological Society. See T. Lynn Smith, "Levels and Trends in Rural Migration," *Rural Sociology*, 19, 1 (March, 1954), pp. 80 - 81.

SUGGESTED SUPPLEMENTARY READINGS

CARR-SAUNDERS, ALEXANDER M. *The Population Problem: A Study in Human Evolution.* Oxford: The Clarendon Press, 1922.

COX, PETER R. *Demography*, 4th ed., Chap. 18. London: Cambridge University Press, 1970.

DeBOW, J. D. B. *Statistical View of the United States . . . Being a Compendium of the Seventh Census . . .* Washington: Beverley Tucker, Senate Printer, 1854.

HAUSER, PHILIP M., and OTIS DUDLEY DUNCAN. *The Study of Population: An Inventory and Appraisal,* Part II. Chicago: University of Chicago Press, 1958.

HOLLINGSWORTH, T. H. *Historical Demography*, Chaps. 2 - 8. Ithaca: Cornell University Press, 1969.

KISER, CLYDE V., ed. *Forty Years of Research in Human Fertility*, Part I. *Milbank Memorial Fund Quarterly*, Vol. XLIX, No. 4 (October, 1971).

MALTHUS, THOMAS R. *An Essay on the Principle of Population or a View of Its Past and Present Effects on Human Happiness. . . .* Various editions and publishers.

ROBINSON, WARREN C. "The Development of Modern Population Theory," in *Population and Society*, edited by Charles B. Nam, pp. 97 - 108. Boston: Houghton Mifflin Company, 1968.

SAUVY, ALFRED. *General Theory of Population.* New York: Basic Books, Inc., 1969.

THOMLINSON, RALPH. *Population Dynamics: Causes and Consequences of World Demographic Change*, Chap. 3. New York: Random House, Inc., 1965.

THOMPSON, WARREN S., and DAVID T. LEWIS. *Population Problems*, 5th ed., Chaps. 2 and 3. New York: McGraw-Hill Book Company, 1965.

UNITED NATIONS. "History of Population Theories," in *Population and Society*, edited by Charles B. Nam, pp. 63 - 97. Boston: Houghton Mifflin Company, 1968.

WILLCOX, WALTER F., ed. *Natural and Political Observations Made upon the Bills of Mortality by John Graunt.* Baltimore: Johns Hopkins University Press, 1939.

WILLCOX, WALTER F. *Studies in American Demography*, Chaps. 4, 13, 17, and 24. Ithaca: Cornell University Press, 1940.

PART TWO

Number and Distribution of the Inhabitants

3
THE NUMBER AND GEOGRAPHIC DISTRIBUTION OF THE POPULATION

The number of persons in the populations of various geographical units and their distribution with respect to area are among the most important facts of demography. The number of its inhabitants is the first population fact called for with respect to a given nation, state, city, county, or any other political subdivision, and the number of persons per given unit of area is the second. In fact, as a general rule, first judgments with respect to the size and importance of a nation or other political unit are based on these two indicators. Fortunately, both are thoroughly objective items and are subject to accurate quantitative measurement. Moreover, where abundant demographic information is available for study and use, the facts relating to the number and geographic distribution of the population generally will be among the most reliable.

The essential facts about the number and geographic distribution of the inhabitants are not only of intrinsic value, but in contemporary society they also are the population facts most commonly needed for various research and administrative purposes. Thus, sociologists must have the facts relative to the numbers of inhabitants in various areas before they can compute indexes of criminality, juvenile delinquency, marriage, and so on; administrators must have them in order to determine how state and federal funds for education, agriculture, road construction, and so on, are to be apportioned among the counties, states, or other political divisions with which they are concerned; and economists must have exact information on the numbers of persons involved before they can determine the ratios that constitute the units employed in so many of their analyses. Even demographers find that reliable facts about the number and geographic distribution of the population are among the basic elements needed for almost all the other facets of their discipline, such as the study of the characteristics of the population, the analysis of fertility, and the investigation of mortality or the expectation of life. For these reasons it is well to begin the systematic study of demographic phenomena with a consideration of fundamental matters relative to the number of inhabitants and their geographic distribution.

BASIC CONCEPTS AND INDEXES

A concise understanding of the meaning and significance of several specific concepts and indexes is essential in the study of the number and geographic distribution of the population. In the first place, perhaps, it is advisable to explain why the modifier "geographic" is used instead of merely saying "the distribution of population." The simpler construction would be preferable in many ways. However, in recent years some demographers have been including under the heading of "distribution of population" such matters as "age distribution," "distribution by sex," and so on. These are matters which probably should be treated under the general topic of the composition of characteristics; nevertheless, in order to avoid any possible ambiguity the expression "geographic distribution" is used consistently throughout this volume.

Our principal sources of information about the number and geographic distribution of the population are derived from the periodic enumerations, or *censuses* of population, made officially by governments throughout the world. The term *census* comes from the Roman word that designated the practice of registering adult males and their property, a procedure that has little in common with the modern census. Its object was to provide the basis for administering programs of military service and taxation. In modern demography, however, a census is a count of the population effected through direct querying of all the households in the political unit involved. Strictly speaking, the United States Census could satisfy constitutional requirements merely by enumerating the population of the various states every ten years. Actually, the modern census invariably includes a long list of items on the characteristics of the population, housing, income, and various other social, cultural, and economic matters.

The United Nations, in the *Demographic Yearbook, 1962*,[1] presents as its definition of a population census and the one currently in use, "the total process of collecting, compiling and publishing demographic, economic and social data pertaining, at a particular time, to all persons in a defined territory." Its five most essential characteristics are: (1) universality — it should include every person in the area, without omission or duplication; (2) simultaneity — all census facts should refer to one specific point of time; (3) individual units — the data are recorded separately for each individual; (4) defined territory — the coverage should be of a precisely defined territory; and (5) compilation — "the compilation and publication of data by geographic areas and by basic demographic variables is an integral part of a census."

Despite the length and complexity of the schedules of questions used in the modern census, its primary task is still that of ascertaining the number of the inhabitants or the population of the unit under consideration. Since this is the most elemental demographic fact, it is necessary to ask what is a *population*? The applicable definition of population given in the second unabridged edition of *Webster's New International Dictionary* is "the whole number of people or inhabitants in a country, section, or area." But this omits one basic consideration. In modern times there is a vast difference between the persons who actually are in a state such as New York or Florida on April 1 of a census year and the persons who for legal or social reasons may be said to belong there. Likewise at the time of the census in Brazil, Canada, or France, to mention only three nations, many nationals of these countries are abroad, whereas tourists, businessmen, diplomatic and consular personnel, and mere transients are present in each in goodly numbers. This raises the question as to whether the population of a given town, city, county, state, or nation includes the persons *found* there at the time of the census or whether it includes all those who *belong* there. In attempts to resolve this issue, those in charge of modern censuses usually decide upon one or the other of the two following alternatives. In Great Britain, for example, the *de facto* approach is employed, that is, all persons found in a given area the day the census is taken are included in the population. In the United States, on the other hand, the *de jure* approach is used, that is, the attempt is made to assign to their usual place of residence all persons enumerated in areas other than the one in which they customarily reside. In still other countries, of which Brazil is a good example, the attempt is made to prepare certain of the tabulations on both the *de facto* and the *de jure* bases.

The assumption that each person has one and only one usual place of abode, heretofore implicit in the procedures of the U. S. Census of population is becoming increasingly invalid with the passage of each decade. Millions of men and women are in the armed forces, large numbers of them stationed abroad; and not only they themselves but the members of their immediate families are shifted from one place to another with considerable frequency. Hundreds of thousands of persons maintain legal residences in states or counties other than the ones in which they actually reside, a phenomenon that is particularly acute with those who live and work in the District of Columbia. Additional hundreds of thousands actually have two residences and spend approximately one half of the year in states such as Florida, Arizona, or California and the other half elsewhere. Finally, the mobility of the population in general is increasing by leaps and bounds, and the elements in the population that have no fixed residence are becoming more numerous year by year. Under these circumstances the definition of population on the *de jure* basis is becoming more and more unsatisfactory.

Census procedures also vary with respect to the time allowed for the making of the enumeration. In the United States the census of population is taken as of April 1 of the census year. The enumerators begin the task of counting on April 1 and continue for four or five months until all households have been contacted; and on the schedules the information for the members of each family is entered as though all the questions had been asked on April 1. In many other countries, only one day is allowed for the enumeration. In these cases large numbers of workers are employed and everyone else is required to stay indoors throughout the day until all the visits have been completed and the all clear signal has been given.

Several concepts used in connection with the geographic distribution of the population also require brief specific mention. As indicated above, any population figure has reference to the number of persons found in or classified as belonging to a given portion of the earth's surface, such as town, city, county, state, or nation. If the ratio between the number of the inhabitants and the area of the unit is calculated, so as to determine the average number of persons per square mile, per square kilometer, and so forth, one has an index of *density of population.*

The *center of population* is a second concept of importance in the study of the geographic distribution of the population. For the nineteenth census of the United States, "the Bureau of the Census defines the 'center of population' as the point at which an imaginary flat, weightless, and rigid map of the United States would balance if weights of identical value were placed on it so that each weight represented the location of one person on April 1, 1970."[2]

Tabulations of census data for the various divisions and subdivisions of nations, states, cities, counties, minor civil divisions, and census county divisions are the raw materials for the study of the geographic distribution of the population. For many years, the tables prepared and published by the U. S. Bureau of the Census have been fairly adequate on this score insofar as the rural population is concerned. Only recently, however, with the development and use of the concept of the *census tract,* has it been possible to do very much analysis of the geographic distribution of population within the limits of a city or in the suburban fringe which surrounds it. Analysis of the rural materials has been facilitated because established legal subdivisions of a state include not only the counties but also *minor civil divisions* (designated variously as townships, commissioners' districts, wards, beats, precincts, and so forth in the several states). In addition, the designation *census county divisions* was used in twenty-one states in the 1970 census. These units represent "community areas" which have relatively stable boundaries that either follow physical features, coincide with incorporation lines, or approximate the limits of trade and service areas of principal settlements. Census county divisions have replaced some minor civil divisions for statistical purposes, especially where the boundaries of the latter were subject to frequent changes, had little correspondence to the limits of real social communities, or were poorly known by the inhabitants. The census county divisions represent yet another attempt to report population data as much as possible for genuine social groupings. Therefore, when the Bureau of the Census has prepared and published the population data showing for each state the number of inhabitants in each county and (with the materials further subdivided) the number of persons in each population center (village, town, or city) within the county, and each minor civil division or census county division, the demographer has the materials he needs for the study of the geographic distribution of the rural population.

Similar procedures, however, are far from adequate for supplying the information needed for study and analysis of the geographic distribution of the population in a city and the built-up area surrounding it. The wards or other political subdivisions of a city may be small in area, but they invariably are large in terms of the numbers of inhabitants. The city has no minor civil divisions corresponding in size (as measured by population) to those which the division of the counties into townships, precincts, and so forth automatically supplies for the rural portions of the nation. For this reason sociologists in many of the nation's larger cities have cooperated with the Bureau of the Census in dividing the urban area into small and fairly homogeneous units.

> Census tracts are small areas into which large cities and adjacent areas have been divided for statistical purposes. In each standard metropolitan statistical area, tracts were established by the Bureau of the Census in cooperation with a local committee. Tracts were generally designed to be relatively uniform with respect to population characteristics, economic status, and living conditions. The average tract has about 4,000 residents. Tract boundaries are established with the intention of being maintained over a long time so that comparisons may be made from census to census.[3]

Tables and maps of various kinds are indispensable in the study of the geographic distribution of the population in any area, but these will be introduced and described in the following pages as the occasion arises.

THE NUMBER AND GEOGRAPHIC DISTRIBUTION OF THE WORLD'S INHABITANTS

The number of people on the earth has never been known with any degree of exactitude. In some of the more densely populated parts of the world there has never been anything deserving the name of population census. Furthermore, there is little uniformity in the years selected for census taking, so the counts made in some populous nations are out of date before those in others get underway. Finally, there is a considerable margin of error in all enumerations. For these reasons any total figure arrived at is at best an approximation of what actually is the number of the earth's inhabitants.

During the last century, however, there has been a notable increase in census activities throughout the world, so that our present knowledge of the number and geographic distribution of the earth's population is far superior to what it has been. Thus, according to the information assembled in the 1962 *Demographic Yearbook*,[4] in the 1855 - 1864 decade only around 200 million persons were covered by census enumerations made during that period. This figure rose to approximately 839 million in the decade ending in 1904. The 1964 issue[5] indicates that the population of the world enumerated in the 1955 - 1964 period had increased to almost 2.2 billion. However, since the same source estimated the total population of the world in 1964 at about 3.2 billion,, it is evident that only a little over two-thirds of the earth's inhabitants were included in the territory in which censuses were taken during the decade 1955 - 1964. In the period 1855 - 1864, censuses were conducted by only twenty-four sovereign countries, of which seventeen were in Europe, four in North America, two in South America, and one in Asia and Oceania. This figure rose to forty-four for the decade 1895 - 1904, twenty-three countries in Europe, seven in North America, seven in Asia and Oceania, five in South America, and two in Africa. For the period 1945 - 1954, the total was sixty-five including twenty-eight countries in Europe, fifteen in Asia and Oceania, twelve in North America, eight in South America, and two in Africa. These compilations include a reported census of China for 1953. In the period 1955 - 1964, 119 sovereign nations enumerated their populations. This group included thirty-six in Africa, thirty-one in Asia and Oceania, thirty-one in Europe, twelve in North America, eight in South America, and the U.S.S.R. The censuses of the 1970's are, of course, not yet complete. The *Demographic Yearbook* for 1971, the first of the reports on these enumerations, is to be continued in two or three subsequent issues. Between January 1, 1965, and December 31, 1971, however, 181 censuses were taken. Twenty-eight of the countries and possessions involved are in Africa, thirty-three in North America, six in South America, thirty-five in Asia, forty-two in Europe, thirty-six in Oceania, and the U.S.S.R.[6] Yet the total population enumerated during this period was about 2.3 billion, which compares with an estimate of the world's population in 1971 of approximately 3.7 billion.[7]

Table 1 has been prepared in an attempt to give as concisely as possible the most essential facts pertaining to the number and geographic distribution of the world's inhabitants. For each country, territory, or dependency having as many as 10,000 inhabitants, it gives the date of the latest census, the population enumerated, the area in square kilometers, estimates of the population in 1971, and the density of population. For all countries or territories with 1971 populations of 10 million or more, the percentage each country or territory contains of the total world population also is presented. The materials in this table are by far the most complete and accurate ever available to students of population relative to the number of inhabitants of the earth and their geographic distribution. They include the totals as given for the various continents or major regions.

TABLE 1

Population, area, and density of population for each country and territory of the world: latest census and midyear estimates for 1971

Region and country or territory	Latest census		Population 1971 (Mid-year estimates in thousands)	Percentage of world population	Area (Square kilometers)	Density 1971 (Persons per sq. kilometer)
	Year	Population				
World	....	....	3,706,000	100.0	135,783,000	27
Africa			354,000	9.6	30,320,000	12
Algeria	1966	11,821,679	14,769	0.4	2,381,741	6
Botswana	1964	543,105	668	....	600,372	1
Burundi	1970-71	3,250,000*	3,615	....	27,834	130
Cameroon	1960-65	5,017,000	5,470a	....	475,442	11b
Central African Republic	1959-60	1,202,910	1,637	....	622,984	3
Chad	1963-64	3,254,000	3,800	....	1,284,000	3
Congo	1960-61	581,600	958	....	342,000	3
Dahomey	1961	2,106,000	2,760	....	112,622	25
Egypt	1966	30,075,858	34,130	0.9	1,001,449	34
Equatorial Guinea	1960	245,989	289	....	28,051	10
Ethiopia	....	....	25,248	0.7	1,221,900	21
Gabon	1960-61	448,564	473a	....	267,667	2b
Gambia	1963	315,486	375*	....	11,295	33
Ghana	1970	8,545,561*	8,858	....	238,537	37
Guinea	1955	2,570,219	4,010	....	245,857	16
Ivory Coast	1957-58	3,100,000	4,420	....	322,463	14
Kenya	1969	10,942,705	11,694	0.3	582,645	20
Lesotho	1966	852,361	935	....	30,355	31
Liberia	1962	1,016,443	1,571	....	111,369	14
Libyan Arab Republic	1964	1,564,369	2,010	....	1,759,540	1
Madagascar	1966	6,200,000	6,350a	....	587,041	11b
Malawi	1966	4,039,583	4,549	....	118,484	38

TABLE 1 (Cont'd)

Population, area, and density of population for each country and territory of the world: latest census and midyear estimates for 1971

Region and country or territory	Latest census		Population 1971 (Mid-year estimates in thousands)	Percentage of world population	Area (Square kilometers)	Density 1971 (Persons per sq. kilometer)
	Year	Population				
Mali	1960-61	3,484,500	5,143	...	1,240,000	4
Mauritania	1964-65	1,050,000*	1,200	...	1,030,700	1
Mauritius	1962	701,016	774[a]	...	2,045	343[b]
Morocco	1971	15,379,259*	15,234	0.4	445,050	34
Namibia	1960	526,004	650	...	824,292	1
Niger	1959-60	2,501,800	4,126	...	1,267,000	3
Nigeria	1963	55,670,055	56,510	1.5	923,768	61
Rwanda	1970	3,724,000*	3,827	...	26,338	145
Senegal	1960-61	3,109,840	4,022	...	196,192	21
Sierra Leone	1963	2,180,355	2,600	...	71,740	36
Somalia	....	....	2,864	...	637,657	4
South Africa	1970	21,448,169*	22,092	0.6	1,221,037	18
Southern Rhodesia	1969	4,846,930[c]	5,500	...	390,580	14
Sudan	1956	10,262,536	16,087	0.4	2,505,813	6
Swaziland	1966	374,697	421[c]	...	17,363	24
Togo	1970	1,955,916	2,022	...	56,000	36
Tunisia	1966	4,533,351	4,560[a]	...	163,610	28[b]
Uganda	1969	9,548,847	10,127	0.3	236,036	43
United Republic of Tanzania	1967	12,313,469	13,637	0.4	945,087	14
Tanganyika	1967	11,958,654	13,244	0.4	942,626	14
Zanzibar	1967	354,815	386	...	2,461	157
Upper Volta	1960-61	4,300,000	5,491	...	274,200	20
Zaire	1955-58	12,768,706	22,477	0.6	2,345,409	10

Zambia	1969	4,056,995*	4,275	...	752,614	6
Non-Sovereign Countries						
Angola (Portugal)	1970	5,673,000*	....	...	1,246,700	5[b]
Cape Verde Islands (Portugal)	1970	272,071*	264	...	4,033	65
Comoro Islands (France)	1966	243,948	250[a]	...	2,171	112[b]
French Territory of Afars and Issas	1960-61	81,200	97	...	22,000	4
Mozambique (Portugal)	1970	8,233,000*	15,234	...	783,030	11[b]
Portuguese Guinea	1970	487,448*	563	...	36,125	16
Reunion (France)	1967	416,525	455	...	2,510	181
São Tomé & Príncipe (Portugal)	1970	73,811*	66	...	964	68
Seychelles (U.K.)	1960	41,425	53	...	376	141
Spanish Sahara	1970	76,425*	50	...	266,000	d
America, North	....		326,000	8.8	24,249,000	13
Barbados	1970	238,141*	239	...	431	555
Canada	1971	21,569,000*	21,786	0.6	9,976,139	2
Costa Rica	1963	1,336,274	1,786	...	50,700	35
Cuba	1970	8,553,395*	8,657	...	114,524	76
Dominican Republic	1970	4,006,405	4,188	...	48,734	86
El Salvador	1971	3,541,010*	....	...	21,393	166[b]
Guatemala	1964	4,287,997	5,348	...	108,889	49
Haiti	1971	4,243,926*	4,969	...	27,750	179
Honduras	1961	1,884,765	2,445[a]	...	112,088	22[a]

TABLE 1 (Cont'd)

Population, area, and density of population for each country and territory of the world: latest census and midyear estimates for 1971

Region and country or territory	Latest census		Population 1971 (Mid-year estimates in thousands)	Percentage of world population	Area (Square kilometers)	Density 1971 (Persons per sq. kilometer)
	Year	Population				
Jamaica	1970	1,865,400*	1,897	:.:	10,962	173
Mexico	1970	48,381,547	50,830	1.4	1,972,547	26
Nicaragua	1971	1,911,543*	....	:.::	130,000	15^b
Panama	1970	1,428,082	1,478	:.::	75,650	20
Trinidad and Tobago	1970	945,210*	1,030	:.::	5,128	201
United States	1970	203,210,158	207,006	5.6	9,363,123	22
Non-Sovereign Countries						
Antigua (U.K.)	1970	70,000*	...	:.::	442	158^b
Bahamas (U.K.)	1970	175,192*	185	:.::	13,935	13
Bermuda (U.K.)	1970	52,330	54	:.::	53	1,019
British Honduras	1970	119,645*	124	:.::	22,965	5
British Virgin Islands	1970	10,484*	11	:.::	153	72
Cayman Islands (U.K.)	1970	10,652*	10	:.::	259	39
Dominica (U.K.)	1970	70,300*	72	:.::	751	96
Greenland (Denmark)	1965	39,600	50	:.::	2,175,600	d
Grenada (U.K.)	1970	94,500*	96	:.::	344	279
Guadeloupe (France)	1967	312,724	332	:.::	1,779	186
Martinique (France)	1967	320,030	341	:.::	1,102	309
Montserrat (U.K.)	1970	12,300*	12	:.::	98	122
Netherlands Antilles	1960	188,914	225	:.::	961	234
Panama Canal Zone (U.S.)	1970	44,198	45	:.::	1,432	31
Puerto Rico (U.S.)	1970	2,712,033	2,757	:.::	8,897	310
St. Kitts-Nevis-Anguilla (U.K.)	1970	64,000*	62	:.::	357	174

St. Lucia (U.K.)	1970	101,000*	103	...	616	167
St. Vincent (U.K.)	1970	89,100*	90	...	388	232
U.S. Virgin Islands	1970	62,468	65	...	344	189
America, South	...	...	195,000	5.3	17,834,000	11
Argentina	1970	23,362,204*	23,552	0.6	2,776,889	8
Bolivia	1950	2,704,165	5,063	...	1,098,581	5
Brazil	1970	93,215,301*	95,408	2.6	8,511,965	11
Chile	1970	8,834,820*	8,992	...	756,945	12
Colombia	1964	17,484,508*	21,772	0.6	1,138,914	19
Ecuador	1962	4,649,648	6,297	...	283,561	22
Guyana	1970	714,000*	736	...	214,969	3
Paraguay	1962	1,819,103	2,161[a]	...	406,752	5[a]
Peru	1972	13,567,939*	14,015	0.4	1,285,216	11
Uruguay	1963	2,595,510	2,921	...	177,508	16
Venezuela	1971	10,721,522*	9,352[a]	...	912,050	10[a]
Non-Sovereign Countries						
French Guiana	1967	44,392	...	...	91,000	d
Surinam (Netherlands)	1964	324,211	406	...	163,265	2
Asia	...	...	2,104,000	56.8	27,532,000	76
Afghanistan	...	...	17,480	0.5	647,497	27
Bahrain	1971	216,078	220	...	622	354
Bhutan	...	...	854	...	47,000	18

TABLE 1 (Cont'd)

Population, area, and density of population for each country and territory of the world: latest census and midyear estimates for 1971

Region and country or territory	Latest census		Population 1971 (Mid-year estimates in thousands)	Percentage of world population	Area (Square kilometers)	Density 1971 (Persons per sq. kilometer)
	Year	Population				
Burma	1941	16,823,798	25,811[a]	0.7	678,033	38[a]
Ceylon	1971	12,747,755*	12,669	0.3	65,610	193
China	1953	582,603,417	787,176	21.2	9,596,961	82
Cyprus	1960	577,615	639	....	9,251	69
India	1971	547,367,926*	550,374*	14.9	3,280,483	168
Indonesia	1971	118,309,059*	124,894	3.4	1,491,564	84
West Irian	1971	923,440*	....	...	412,781	2[b]
Iran	1966	25,785,210	29,783*	0.8	1,648,000	18
Iraq	1965	8,047,415	9,750	...	434,924	22
Israel	1972	3,124,000*	3,013	...	20,700	146
Japan	1970	103,720,060	104,661	2.8	370,073	283
Jordan	1961	1,706,226	2,383	...	97,740	24
Khmer Republic	1962	5,728,771	6,415[a]	...	181,035	35[a]
Korea						
Democratic Peoples Republic	....	....	14,281	0.4	120,538	118
Republic	1970	31,469,132*	31,917	0.9	98,477	324
Kuwait	1970	737,909	831	...	17,818	47
Laos	....	....	3,033	...	236,800	13
Lebanon	1970	2,126,325	2,873	...	10,400	276
Malaysia						
East Malaysia	1970	1,632,635*	1,673	...	198,161	8
Sabah	1970	655,622*	674	...	73,711	9
Sarawak	1970	977,013*	999	...	124,450	8

West Malaysia	1970	8,801,399*	8,978	...	131,588	68
Maldives	1967	103,801	110	...	298	369
Mongolia	1969	1,197,600	1,283	...	1,565,000	1
Nepal	1971	11,290,000*	11,290	0.3	140,797	80
Oman	...	....	678	...	212,457	3
Pakistan	1961	93,831,982	116,598*	3.1	946,719	123
Philippines	1970	36,684,486	37,959	1.0	300,000	127
Qatar	...	....	81	...	22,014	4
Saudia Arabia	1962-63	e	7,965	...	2,149,690	4
Sikkim	1971	204,760*	198*	...	7,107	28
Singapore	1970	2,074,507	2,110	...	581	3,632
Syrian Arab Republic	1970	6,292,000*	6,451*	...	185,180	35
Thailand	1970	34,152,000*	35,335	1.0	514,000	69
Turkey	1970	35,666,549*	36,162	1.0	780,576	46
United Arab Emirates	1968	179,126	197	...	83,600	2
Viet-Nam						
Democratic Republic	1960	15,916,955	21,595	0.6	158,750	136
Republic	...	....	16,973[a]	0.5	170,906	99[a]
Yemen	...	....	5,900	...	195,000	30
Yemen, Peoples Democratic Republic	...	....	1,475	...	287,683	5
Non-Sovereign Countries						
Brunei (U.K.)	1971	136,256	135	...	5,765	23

TABLE 1 (Cont'd)

Population, area, and density of population for each country and territory of the world: latest census and midyear estimates for 1971

Region and country or territory	Latest census		Population 1971 (Mid-year estimates in thousands)	Percentage of world population	Area (Square kilometers)	Density 1971 (Persons per sq. kilometer)
	Year	Population				
Gaza Strip (Israel)	1967	356,261	....	....	378	942[a]
Hong Kong (U.K.)	1971	3,948,179	4,045	....	1,034	3,912
Macao (Portugal)	1970	248,636	321	....	16	20,063
Portuguese Timor	1970	610,500*	614	....	14,925	41
Ryuku Islands (U.S.)	1970	945,111	950	....	2,196	433
Europe	....	....	466,000	12.6	4,936,000	94
Albania	1960	1,626,315	2,226	....	28,748	77
Austria	1971	7,456,400	7,456	....	83,849	89
Belgium	1970	9,650,944*	9,726	....	30,513	319
Bulgaria	1965	8,227,866	8,540*	....	110,912	77
Czechoslovakia	1970	14,362,000*	14,500*	0.4	127,869	113
Denmark	1970	4,937,784*	4,966*	....	43,069	115
Finland	1970	4,622,299*	4,684*	....	337,009	14
France	1968	49,778,540*	551,260*	1.4	547,026	94
Germany						
Federal Republic	1970	59,378,500*	59,175	1.6	247,973	239
German Democratic Republic	1971	15,956,060*	15,954	0.4	107,771	148
East Berlin	1971	1,084,866*	1,086	....	403	2,695
West Berlin	1970	2,129,900*	2,105	....	481	4,377
Greece	1971	8,768,648*	8,957	....	131,944	68
Hungary	1970	10,315,600*	10,364*	0.3	93,030	111
Iceland	1970	204,930	214	....	103,000	2
Ireland	1971	2,971,230*	2,971*	....	70,283	42

	Year					
Italy	1971	53,770,331*	54,078	1.5	301,225	180
Liechtenstein	1970	21,350	21	...	157	134
Luxembourg	1970	332,434*	341	...	2,586	132
Malta	1967	315,765*	325	...	316	1,030
Monaco	1968	23,035	24	...	1	16,107
Netherlands	1960	11,461,964	13,194	0.4	40,844	323
Norway	1970	3,888,305*	3,905*	...	324,219	12
Poland	1970	32,589,209	32,749*	0.9	312,677	105
Portugal	1970	8,668,267	9,440[a]	...	92,082	94[b]
Romania	1966	19,103,163	20,470	0.6	237,500	86
San Marino	1947	12,100	18	...	61	293
Spain	1970	33,956,376*	34,134	0.9	504,782	68
Sweden	1970	8,076,903	8,105*	...	449,750	18
Switzerland	1970	6,269,783	6,345	...	41,288	154
United Kingdom	1971	55,348,957*	55,566*	1.5	244,044	228
England and Wales	1971	48,593,658*	48,815*	1.3	151,126	323
Northern Ireland	1971	1,527,593*	1,534*	...	14,146	108
Scotland	1971	5,227,706*	5,217*	...	78,772	66
Yugoslavia	1971	20,504,216*	20,550	0.6	255,804	80
Non-Sovereign Countries						
Channel Islands (U.K.)	1971	123,063	121	...	195	621
Guernsey	1971	53,734	50	...	78	641
Jersey	1971	69,329	71	...	116	612

TABLE 1 (Cont'd)

Population, area, and density of population for each country and territory of the world: latest census and midyear estimates for 1971

Region and country or territory	Latest census		Population 1971 (Mid-year estimates in thousands)	Percentage of world population	Area (Square kilometers)	Density 1971 (Persons per sq. kilometer)
	Year	Population				
Faroe Islands (Denmark)	1966	37,122	41	....	1,399	29
Gibralter (U.K.)	1970	26,833*	27*	....	6	4,475
Isle of Man (U.K.)	1971	56,289	56	....	588	96
Oceania	....	.....	19,800	0.5	8,510,000	2
Australia	1971	12,728,461*	12,728	0.3	7,686,848	2
Fiji	1966	476,727	531	....	18,272	29
New Zealand	1971	2,862,631	2,853	....	268,676	11
Tonga	1966	77,429	90	....	699	129
Western Samoa	1971	143,547*	143	....	2,842	50
Non-Sovereign Countries						
American Samoa (U.S.)	1970	27,159	29	....	197	147
British Solomon Islands	1970	160,998	166	....	28,446	6
Cook Islands (New Zealand)	1971	21,317*	25	....	234	107
French Polynesia	1971	119,168	121	....	4,000	30
Gilbert & Ellice Islands (U.K.)	1968	53,517*	57	....	886	64
Guam (U.S.)	1970	84,996	90	....	549	164
New Caledonia (France)	1969	100,579*	107	....	19,058	6
New Guinea (Australia)	1966	1,578,650*	1,790	....	238,693	7
New Hebrides (U.K. & France)	1967	76,582	84	....	14,763	6
Pacific Islands (U.K.)	1970	90,940	107	....	1,779	60
Papua (Australia)	1966	606,336*	691	....	222,998	3

U.S.S.R.	1970	241,720,134	245,066*	6.6	22,402,200	11
Byelorussian S.S.R.	1970	9,002,338	9,110	....	207,600	44
Ukrainian S.S.R.	1970	47,126,517	47,680	1.3	603,700	79

Source: Compiled and computed from data in United Nations, *Demographic Yearbook, 1971* (New York: Statistical Office of the United Nations, 1972), p. 111, Table 1; pp. 112-124, Table 2. States or territories having less than 10,000 inhabitants are omitted.

*Provisional.

[a]1967.

[b]At date of latest census.

[c]African population only.

[d]Less than 1.

[e]Results officially repudiated.

Observation and study of the substantial data given in Table 1 enable one to draw many important conclusions concerning the geographic distribution of the world's inhabitants. Note that the inhabitants of Asia make up well over one-half of the human race, even with those living in the Asiatic part of the U.S.S.R. not included. Europe, also without the corresponding portion of Russian territory, is second with about 13 per cent of the earth's population, Africa third with almost 10 per cent, and North America fourth with approximately 9 per cent.

Communist-controlled China alone has over one-fifth of the world's total population, followed by India with about one-seventh. Nearly 7 per cent of the inhabitants of our planet live within the 1971 limits of Soviet Russia and slightly under 6 per cent in the United States. The seven other most populous nations are Indonesia, Pakistan, Japan, Brazil, the Federal Republic of Germany, Nigeria, and the United Kingdom.

The number of inhabitants per square kilometer of land surface ranges from a low of two in Oceania, due largely to the inclusion of huge and sparsely populated Australia in this world division, to ninety-four in Europe. Asia's teeming millions result in an index of seventy-six for the continent. These figures for Europe and Asia do not include the appropriate portions of Soviet Russia, for which the density of population is computed at eleven per square kilometer. The index for North America is thirteen, for Africa twelve, and for South America eleven.

Because of the large numbers involved, the indexes of density of population in Japan, India, Pakistan, Indonesia, and China command special attention. They are 283, 168, 123, 84, and 82 persons per square kilometer of territory, respectively; the corresponding figure for the United States is only 22. However, it should not be overlooked that there was in 1971 an average of 323 persons per square kilometer in the Netherlands and England and Wales, 319 in Belgium, and 239 in the Federal Republic of Germany. Barbados, with 555 persons per square kilometer of territory, Puerto Rico with 310, Trinidad and Tobago with 201, Haiti with 179, Jamaica with 173, and El Salvador with 166, claim particular attention in the Americas.

THE NUMBER AND GEOGRAPHIC DISTRIBUTION OF THE INHABITANTS OF THE UNITED STATES

In the United States significant study of the geographic distribution of the population may be made with a minimum of trouble and wasted effort, because all of the essential data and materials are readily available to the student. Fairly current and highly reliable data are supplied in detail by censuses taken only ten years apart. The indispensable maps showing boundaries of all major and minor civil divisions are kept up to date and are obtainable at a nominal charge. In addition, for most of the nation's major cities the data are tabulated for units (the census tracts) which are much smaller than any administrative entities, and maps are published showing the location and boundaries of all these small areas in each city. In many other parts of the world, however, it is difficult or impossible to secure population counts for small areas, and even if these are available, very frequently maps showing the boundaries of the corresponding units are long out of date, if indeed they are available at all. The comparative stability of the boundaries of counties and minor civil divisions is another advantage enjoyed by demographers using data for the United States over those who work with materials for many countries throughout the world.

Tabulations concerned with the number and distribution of the inhabitants are given a primary place in the publications of the United States Census of Population. Counts of the number of persons are presented not only for each of the fifty states and for the District of Columbia, but for each county, minor civil division (township, ward, beat, etc.), incorporated center, and unincorporated place of a thousand inhabitants or more in each of the states. In addition special tabulations for "urbanized areas," "standard metropolitan statistical areas," "state economic areas and economic subregions," and, for most of the larger cities, the census tracts, greatly facilitate the study of many aspects of the geographic distribution of the inhabitants.

The nineteenth decennial census, taken as of April 1, 1970, enumerated 203,210,158 persons in the United States.[8] As may be noted from Table 1, this figure is equal to approximately one-eighteenth of the population of the globe. There will not be another rather exact determination of the number of inhabitants in this country until the first results from the 1980 census are published late that year or early in 1981. Even then only the data on number and distribution will be available, and several years more will pass before the comprehensive materials on the characteristics of the population will have been tabulated and published. In the interim, the Bureau of the Census publishes annual estimates, and for the nation as a whole the calculations probably are quite accurate, especially because of the significant improvements in the accuracy of population estimation after 1950. For example, estimates made in the years prior to the 1970 census were only slightly lower than the number eventually enumerated. Even so, it would be unwise to put too much trust in the estimates for the later years of the intercensal period, particularly those for any state. Even the national estimate of 210,404,000 for July 1, 1973, will need revision after the definitive counts are made in 1980, and those for the years near the end of the decade are likely to contain even larger margins of error.

A broad idea of the general geographic distribution of the inhabitants of the United States is given by a consideration of the numbers and proportions of the population residing in the four major regions in the nation, as these regions are delineated by the Bureau of the Census. As indicated by the 1970 census, the bulk of the population lives in the North, with 49,040,703 (24.1 per cent)

TABLE 2
Number, geographic distribution, and density of population in
the United States, 1970

Division and state	Population 1970	Per cent of national population	Rank in population	Population per square mile
United States	203,210,158	100.0	....	57.5
New England	11,841,663	5.8	....	188.1
Maine	992,048	0.5	38	32.1
New Hampshire	737,681	0.4	42	81.7
Vermont	444,330	0.2	49	47.9
Massachusetts	5,689,170	2.8	10	727.0
Rhode Island	946,725	0.5	39	902.5
Connecticut	3,031,709	1.5	24	623.6
Middle Atlantic	37,199,040	18.3	....	370.8
New York	18,236,967	9.0	2	381.3
New Jersey	7,168,164	3.5	8	953.1
Pennsylvania	11,793,909	5.8	3	262.3
East North Central	40,252,476	19.8	....	164.9
Ohio	10,652,017	5.2	6	260.0
Indiana	5,193,669	2.6	11	143.9
Illinois	11,113,976	5.5	5	199.4
Michigan	8,875,083	4.4	7	156.2
Wisconsin	4,417,731	2.2	16	81.1
West North Central	16,319,187	8.0	....	32.1
Minnesota	3,804,971	1.9	19	48.0
Iowa	2,824,376	1.4	25	50.5
Missouri	4,676,501	2.3	13	67.8
North Dakota	617,761	0.3	46	8.9
South Dakota	665,507	0.3	45	8.8
Nebraska	1,483,493	0.7	35	19.4
Kansas	2,246,578	1.1	28	27.5
South Atlantic	30,671,337	15.1	....	114.9
Delaware	548,104	0.3	47	276.5
Maryland	3,922,399	1.9	18	396.6
District of Columbia	756,510	0.4	41	12,401.8
Virginia	4,648,494	2.3	14	116.9
West Virginia	1,744,237	0.9	34	72.5
North Carolina	5,082,059	2.5	12	104.1

TABLE 2 (Cont'd)

Number, geographic distribution, and density of population in the United States, 1970

Division and state	Population 1970	Per cent of national population	Rank in popu- lation	Population per square mile
South Carolina	2,590,516	1.3	26	85.7
Georgia	4,589,575	2.3	15	79.0
Florida	6,789,443	3.3	9	125.5
East South Central	12,803,470	6.3	....	71.5
Kentucky	3,218,706	1.6	23	81.2
Tennessee	3,923,687	1.9	17	94.9
Alabama	3,444,165	1.7	21	67.9
Mississippi	2,216,912	1.1	29	46.9
West South Central	19,320,560	9.5	....	45.2
Arkansas	1,923,295	0.9	32	37.0
Louisiana	3,641,306	1.8	20	81.0
Oklahoma	2,559,229	1.3	27	37.2
Texas	11,196,730	5.5	4	42.7
Mountain	8,281,562	4.1	....	9.7
Montana	694,409	0.3	44	4.8
Idaho	712,567	0.4	43	8.6
Wyoming	332,416	0.2	50	3.4
Colorado	2,207,259	1.1	30	21.3
New Mexico	1,016,000	0.5	37	8.4
Arizona	1,770,900	0.9	33	15.6
Utah	1,059,273	0.5	36	12.9
Nevada	488,738	0.2	48	4.4
Pacific	26,522,631	13.1	....	29.7
Washington	3,409,169	1.7	22	51.2
Oregon	2,091,385	1.0	31	21.7
California	19,953,134	9.8	1	127.6
Alaska	300,382	0.1	51	0.5
Hawaii	768,561	0.4	40	119.6

Source: Compiled from data in U.S. Bureau of the Census, *U.S. Census of Population 1970, Number of Inhabitants,* Final Report PC(1)-A1, *United States Summary* (1971), p. 21, Figure 21; pp. 48-49, Table 8; p. 51, Table 10; p. 52, Table 11.

residing in the Northeastern states and 56,571,663 persons (27.8 per cent) in the North Central states. The South, with a total of 62,795,367 inhabitants, accounted for 30.9 per cent of the total; and the West, with 34,804,193 residents, for 17.1 per cent. The indexes showing the average number of persons per square mile line up with these differences in the populations of the respective regions. In comparison with the figure of 57.5 persons per square mile in the United States as a whole, the indexes of density of population in the various regions are as follows: Northeast, 300; North Central, 75; South, 72, and West, 20. These differences in the density of population are reflected in popular thinking with respect to the congestion in the Northeast and the "wide open spaces" of the West. On the other hand, in the middle sections of the country both in the North and in the South, the number of persons per square mile most nearly approaches the mean for the nation.

Further understanding of the distribution of population in the United States may be obtained through careful study of the data given in Table 2 and the map which is Figure 1. That California, New York, and Pennsylvania ranked in that order in 1970 as the three most populous states in the Union is fairly well known, even though California was only in fifth place as recently as 1940. Less well known is the fact that Texas, Illinois, and Ohio ranked fourth, fifth, and sixth, respectively; and not many people are aware that Michigan, New Jersey, Florida, and Massachusetts, in the order named, completed the list of the ten most populous states. It is well known that Alaska has not only the lowest density but also the smallest population of any state of the Union, and that it is most closely rivaled in this latter respect by Wyoming, Vermont, Nevada, and Delaware. At the time of the 1970 enumeration, the other five of the ten least populous states, in ascending order of the number of inhabitants, were as follows: North Dakota, South Dakota, Montana, Idaho, and New Hampshire.

More useful for many purposes than the tabular materials just referred to is the map showing the geographic distribution of population throughout the United States. The dots and volumetric spheres represent the distribution in 1970 and emphasize urban places of various sizes. A study of Figure 1 will prove highly rewarding to one who wishes to know the essentials of the geographic distribution of population in the United States, and the construction and study of comparable maps for the various regions and states will prove highly informative for those who wish more detailed information on one or more important divisions of the nation.

In 1970, the center of population in the United States was located in St. Clair County, Illinois, about five miles east-southeast of the city of Mascoutah. (See Figure 2.) Ten years earlier it was 26.9 miles to the east and 9.4 miles to the north, still in Illinois; in 1790 it was 700 miles east and 60 miles north, near Baltimore, Maryland. At every census from the first to the nineteenth, the center of population in the United States moved steadily westward, with the progress

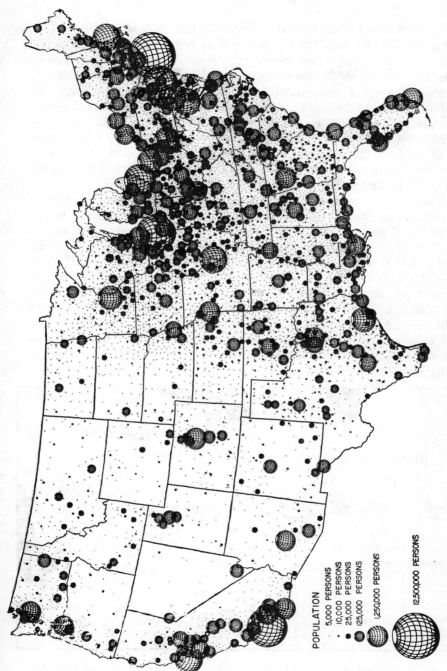

POPULATION

5,000 PERSONS

10,000 PERSONS

25,000 PERSONS

125,000 PERSONS

1,250,000 PERSONS

12,500,000 PERSONS

Figure 1. Distribution of population in the United States, 1970.

between 1830 and 1840, 1850 and 1860, 1870 and 1880, and 1940 and 1950 being especially marked. The distance spanned in the latest intercensal period was considerably greater than in most decades since 1880, although only about half that which occurred between 1950 and 1960. Because of tremendous gains in population in California and other western states and those in Florida, Texas, and other states to the south and the southwest, by 1980 the center of population may be expected to be still farther west and somewhat to the south of its 1970 location. Although the concept of the center of population is of some use in the study of the geographic distribution of the population, it does not have sufficient utility to make its determination of primary concern to those largely interested in the demographic study of a given state or region.

The density of population, or the ratio of people to land, serves many useful purposes in the study of the geographic distribution of the population. As indicated above, there was in 1970 an average of 57.5 persons per square mile of territory in the United States. With the areas of Alaska and Hawaii included, this index stood at 50.6 in 1960, 42.6 in 1950, 37.2 in 1940, and 34.7 in 1930. As may be seen from Table 2, the District of Columbia, with over 12,000 persons for each square mile of territory, was by far the most densely populated unit in the nation, followed most closely by New Jersey (953 persons), Rhode Island (902 persons), Massachusetts (727 persons), and Connecticut (624 persons). At the other extreme was Alaska, averaging one-half person per square mile, followed by Wyoming (three persons), Nevada (four persons), Montana (five persons), and New Mexico (eight persons).

Figure 2. The westward march of the center of population in the United States, 1790 to 1970. Illustration from the Bureau of the Census.

SOME OF THE USES OF DATA ON THE
GEOGRAPHIC DISTRIBUTION OF THE INHABITANTS

The materials relating to the geographic distribution of the population make up the portion of demographic information that is most directly applicable for a host of social and economic purposes with the least expenditure of effort and the minimum of analytical skill and experience. Indeed, from the time the population counts made in the census of 1790 were used to apportion the seats in the House of Representatives among the thirteen original states to the present, the tabulations showing the numbers of inhabitants in the various states, counties, towns and cities, and minor civil divisions have been used increasingly in myriads of useful ways. During the second and third quarters of the twentieth century, for example, rarely has the Congress of the United States made an appropriation of funds to be distributed among the several states in which the number of inhabitants was not a primary factor in the formula by which the share going to each state was determined. Indeed, since the 1930's this fact alone has made accurate estimates of the populations of the various states for postcensal years of critical importance, especially for the combined federal-state programs in the most rapidly growing states. Today, the self-protection and interest of every state in the Union demands that it make every effort to see that full counts of the population are made in every census and that the postcensal population estimates are as accurate as possible.

Similar uses of the materials on the geographic distribution of the population, in the form in which the data are organized and published in the census reports, are made on a large scale in each of the fifty states. In this case, however, it is the material relating to the distribution in the counties of a segment of the population, namely the children of school age, which figures most largely in the apportionment of state tax funds. Nevertheless, the number of inhabitants in any political subdivision and the proportion this constitutes of the state's total population are primary considerations in its contemporary fiscal policies.

For many modern uses the data on the geographic distribution of the population must be processed to a considerable extent before they can be used in making policy decisions and for other matters. For example, the maps prepared by the demographer showing the distribution of the population within a city, county, or district, along with those showing recent changes, are widely employed by those who must determine the locations and attendance areas of new schools. One such illustration is Figure 3, which shows the distribution of population in an eleven-county planning region in North Carolina. When, as in Figure 4, a map of the geographic distribution of the population is correlated with one showing another feature, such as the zones surrounding hospitals, some basic relationships easily may be shown.

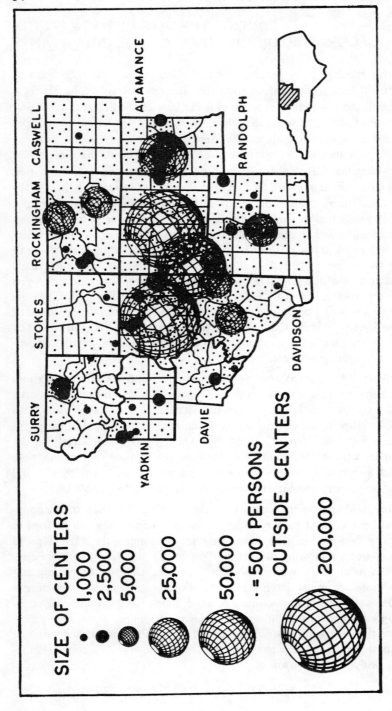

64

Figure 3. Distribution of population in North Carolina State Planning Region G. Reproduced from Paul E. Zopf, Jr., *A Demographic and Occupational Profile of State Planning Region G*, Report to the Regional Committee on Environmental Affairs, Piedmont Triad Council of Governments, 1972.

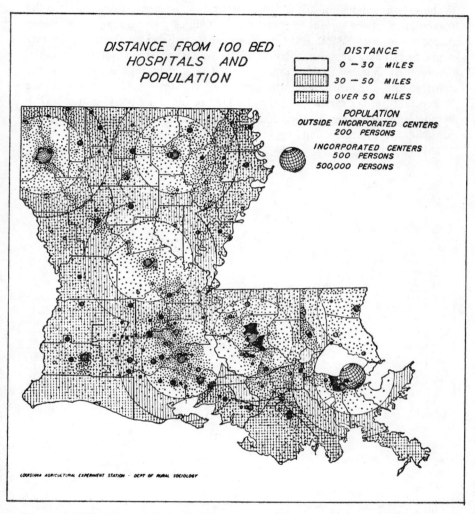

Figure 4. Distribution of population in Louisiana, 1940, in relation to the location of hospitals having a hundred or more beds, 1945. Reproduced from Homer L. Hitt and Alvin L. Bertrand. "The Social Aspects of Hospital Planning in Louisiana." Baton Rouge: Louisiana Agricultural Experiment Station and the Office of the Governor, 1947.

By far the most important use of the data showing the number of inhabitants in the various subdivisions of a nation, state, city, or county, however, is in the computation of the various rates and ratios which play such an important role in demographic, sociological, economic, and other study and analysis. An accurate count or estimate of the population of the area involved is absolutely essential before such indexes as the crime rate, the rate of juvenile delinquency, the marriage rate, the divorce rate, the death rate, the birth rate, per capita income or expenditure, per capita wealth, and a host of other important indicators can be computed. One hardly need mention that indexes of these types are indispensable for the understanding of and conduct of modern economic social affairs.

NOTES

1. (New York: Statistical Office of the United Nations, 1963), p. 1.

2. U.S. Bureau of the Census, *U.S. Census of Population: 1970, Number of Inhabitants,* Final Report PC(1)-A1, *United States Summary* (Washington: Government Printing Office, 1971), p. vi.

3. *Ibid.,* p. xv.

4. *Op. cit.,* p. 1.

5. (New York: Statistical Office of the United Nations, 1965), p. 2.

6. (New York: Statistical Office of the United Nations, 1972), p. 3.

7. *Ibid.,* p. 111, Table 1.

8. The total of 203,210,158 persons is from *General Social and Economic Characteristics,* Final Report PC(1)-C1, *United States Summary* (1972), p. 361, Table 68. It differs slightly from totals supplied by the Bureau of the Census in other reports of the 1970 enumeration but because it is the most recent revision, the present writers use it consistently throughout this volume.

SUGGESTED SUPPLEMENTARY READINGS

BOGUE, DONALD J. *The Population of the United States,* Chaps 4 and 5. Glencoe, Ill.: The Free Press, 1959.

BOGUE, DONALD J., and CALVIN L. BEALE. *Economic Areas of the United States.* New York: The Free Press, 1961.

CHANDRASEKHAR, S. "India's Population: Fact, Problem and Policy," in *Asia's Population Problems,* edited by S. Chandrasekhar, Chap. 3. New York: Frederick A. Praeger, 1967.

CLÁRKE, JOHN I. *Population Geography,* 2nd ed., Chaps. III and IV. New York: Pergamon Press, 1972.

DAVIS, KINGSLEY. *The Population of India and Pakistan,* Part I. Princeton: Princeton University Press, 1951.

HO, PING-TI, *Studies on the Population of China, 1368 - 1953,* Chap. V. Cambridge: Harvard University Press, 1959.

ORLEANS, LEO A. "The 1953 Chinese Census in Perspective." *Journal of Asian Studies,* Vol. XVI, No. 4 (1957), pp. 565 - 573.

PETERSON, WILLIAM. *Population,* 2nd ed., Chap. 2. New York: The Macmillan Company, 1969.

SHRYOCK, HENRY S., JACOB S. SIEGEL, and associates. *The Methods and Materials of Demography,* Vol. 1., Chaps. 4 and 5. Washington: Government Printing Office, 1971.

SMITH, T. LYNN. *Brazil: People and Institutions,* 4th ed., Chap. III. Baton Rouge: Louisiana State University Press, 1972.

SMITH, T. LYNN, and HOMER L. HITT. *The People of Louisiana,* Chap. II. Baton Rouge: Louisiana State University Press, 1952.

TAEUBER, CONRAD, and IRENE B. TAEUBER. *The Changing Population of the United States,* Chap. 1. New York: John Wiley & Sons, Inc., 1958.

THOMLINSON, RALPH. *Population Dynamics,* Chaps. 21 and 22. New York: Random House, Inc., 1965.

U.S. BUREAU OF THE CENSUS. *U.S. Census of Population: 1970. Number of Inhabitants.* Final Report PC(1)-A1, *United States Summary.* Washington: Government Printing Office, 1971.

WRONG, DENNIS H. *Population and Society,* 3rd ed., Chap. 2. New York: Random House, Inc., 1967.

ZOPF, PAUL E., JR. *North Carolina: A Demographic Profile,* Chap. II. Chapel Hill: University of North Carolina Population Center, 1967.

PART THREE

The Characteristics of the Population

RURAL OR URBAN RESIDENCE

Logically, any one of four chapters might be the first in this section on the composition or characteristics of the population. As indicated in Chapter 1, the factors of rural or urban residence, race and nativity, age, and sex constitute the warp and woof of modern census tabulations. Through sorting and subsorting of the data, it must be possible for the population student to control all four of these before he can go very far in the analysis of any other demographic phenomenon. Therefore, the treatment of any one of them would constitute a suitable point of departure. Since the U. S. Bureau of the Census regularly makes its first classification of materials on the basis of residence, this subject is placed first in this part. The other three are treated in the chapters that follow immediately.

As is stressed in the study of the sociology of both urban and rural life, a person's residence is among his most distinguishing characteristics. Whether one lives in the city or in the country, or in the indistinct area between the two made into a reality of considerable magnitude by the transportation facilities of the twentieth century, determines in a general way what he does and the conditions of life under which he lives. Thus, rural society presents a sharp contrast to urban society, and this is true to a certain extent even in the United States during the early decades of the space age. Outstanding in rural society is the preponderance of agricultural occupations, low population density, small population aggregates or communities, and a high degree of ethnic and cultural homogeneity. The farmer still lives in an environment that is vastly different from the one surrounding the typical urban resident. In general, nature in all its benevolent as well as its malevolent aspects impinges directly upon the people who live in the country, whereas the inhabitants of the city have placed a thick shield of man-made environment or culture between themselves and the natural environment. The farmer has relatively few social contacts with others, and those he does have are restricted to more limited geographical and social spheres and generally are more personal and informal.

The sum of all these and other dissimilarities determines that the country person and the urban man are surrounded and conditioned by radically different natural, cultural, and social environments. The urban environments form and shape urban personalities and behavior patterns in ways considerably different from the ones the rural environment gives to those conditioned by it. Consequently, the resident of an urban center is distinguished from one who lives in the country by a long list of important social, cultural, and economic differentials. Fortunately, this is fairly clear to most of those who have continued responsibility in planning and administering broad state and national policies in connection with health, welfare, education, and other services. From the demographic point of view, sizable differences between the rural and urban segments of the population with respect to age distribution, sex composition, income and economic resources, morbidity, mortality, and rate of reproduction are facts with which the successful administrator must be acquainted.

This has been particularly true since the federal treasury became the source of significant proportions of the funds used to maintain health programs, agricultural activities, educational services, welfare measures, hospital development and construction, and so on. Apparently the time has passed when Congress would appropriate for a given program equal amounts of money to each of the states, regardless of the size and composition of its population. This was done, however, in the first federal grants for highway construction and agricultural research. The funds are being apportioned increasingly on a per capita basis, and frequently the formulas used specify that certain definite segments of the population, such as the rural or the rural-farm categories, shall be the ones to figure in the computations. Nowadays, before they can vote intelligently on many bills awaiting action, members of the Congress must know well the distinctions between the urban, rural-nonfarm, and rural-farm populations. In these and many other ways, knowledge of the basic facts concerning the rural or urban residence of a given population now has considerable application.

DEFINITIONS AND CLASSIFICATIONS

Sociologists have difficulty in making a satisfactory distinction between rural and urban society, because the whole of society is not sharply divided into two clearly differentiated parts. Instead, society in general resembles a spectrum in which the elements most clearly identifiable as rural are concentrated at one extreme, and those most indisputably urban at the other, with the two gradually changing in relative importance as one moves from either end to the center. From the standpoint of the size of the community, the relative importance of agriculture and stockraising activities, the degree of social differentiation, or any other criterion that may be employed to distinguish between rural and urban, the rural features become less important and the urban features more so as one passes from the single farmstead to the homes and other buildings clustered at a cross-roads, to a rural hamlet, to an agricultural village, to a village trade center, to the town, to a small city, to a large city, and to a great metropolitan center and its satellites. In addition, somehow one must fit into this continuum situations representing the various degrees of urbanization or its opposite that are represented by the more remote sections of the metropolitan area, the heterogeneous situations that constitute what is known as the rural-urban fringe, and many other combinations of the rural and urban patterns of living. The vast majority of communities are neither purely urban nor purely rural, but they are localities in which the rural and urban features are combined in varying proportions. In spite of all this, sociologists generally agree that for census and other statistical purposes it may be necessary to take one, and only one, criterion, such as the size of the community as measured by the number of its inhabitants, as the basis for classifying the population into rural and urban categories. Such is the position of the present writers. As sociologists they set forth nine basic differences between the rural and urban worlds that should be understood by one who would differentiate the rural from the urban.[1] They also identify at least nine basic changes which generally occur as urban-oriented society grows out of rural-dominated society in many parts of the globe.[2] But as demographers they are well content when the census of a given country classifies as urban all of its inhabitants living in communities having more than a stated number of inhabitants and as rural the remainder of the population.

Even though allowance is made for a necessary difference between definitions that are best for logical purposes and those that are practicable in census classifications, there is no international agreement as to where to draw the line between urban and rural populations or even upon the criteria that should be employed in separating the two categories. The procedure of making the division arbitrarily at a given place on the population scale is used in many countries, including Mexico, France, and the United States. (See Table 3.) But some nations categorize as urban population centers which for some reason have been "elevated" to a certain rank, received distinctions which authorize them to designate themselves as towns or cities, or have come to enjoy other social, political, or administrative distinctions over other places of equal size and importance. Perhaps the situation today, as evidenced by the material in Table 3, is even more confused than it once was. After France selected (in 1846) the numerical criterion of 2,000 inhabitants as the point for separating the rural from the urban portions of the population, the practice spread rapidly throughout Central Europe. This type of criterion was recommended by the International Institute of Statistics in 1887.[3] Nevertheless, today there still remains almost complete lack of comparability between the residential classifications employed in the census publications of various countries throughout the world. Indeed, so much individuality is expressed in this respect that much effort and ingenuity must be employed before any accu-

TABLE 3

The absolute and relative importance of the urban population in each country and territory having 1 million or more inhabitants for which data are available

Country or territory	Year	Total population	Urban population	Per cent urban	Definition of urban[a]
Africa					
Algeria	1966	11,821,679	4,613,259	39.0	Fifty-five most important communes having local self-government.
Angola	1960	4,830,449	512,543	10.6	Agglomerations of 2,000 or more inhabitants.
Burundi	1965	3,210,090	71,390	2.2	Commune of Bujumbura.
Central African Republic	1965-66	1,473,000	392,000	26.6	Twenty principal centers with populations of over 3,000 inhabitants.
Chad	1963-64	2,524,370[b]	173,210[b]	6.9	Ten urban centers.
Dahomey	1961	2,082,511	194,130	9.3	Towns of Cotonou, Fort-Novo, Ouidah, Parakou, and Djougou.
Egypt	1966	30,075,858	12,384,502	41.2	Governorates of Cairo, Alexandria, Port Said, Suez, frontier governorates and capitals of other governorates as well as district capitals (Markaz).
Ghana	1960	6,726,815	1,551,360	23.1	Urban centers.
Guinea	1955	2,570,219[b]	212,989[b]	8.3	Urban centers.
Kenya	1969	10,942,705	1,079,908	9.9	Town of 2,000 or more inhabitants.
Liberia	1970	1,523,050	399,670	26.2	Localities having more than 2,000 inhabitants.
Libyan Arab Republic	1964	1,564,369	385,239	24.6	Total population of Tripoli and Benghazi plus the urban parts of Beida and Derna.
Malawi	1966	4,039,583	203,303	5.0	All townships, town planning areas, district centers.
Mali	1960-61	3,680,000	411,100	11.2	Not available.
Mauritania	1964-65*	1,050,000	70,000	6.7	Urban centers.
Morocco	1971*	15,379,259	5,409,725	35.2	117 urban centers.
Nigeria	1963	55,670,055	8,971,464	16.1	Not available.

Country	Year	Population	Urban	%	Description
Rwanda					Not available.
South Africa	1970*	3,724,000	130,340	3.5	Areas of 500 or more inhabitants, and adjoining suburban areas; well-established towns of fewer than 500 but at least 100 white inhabitants and with specified urban characteristics; certain "rural" portions of districts containing metropolitan areas.
	1970*	21,448,169	10,280,202	47.9	
Southern Rhodesia	1969	5,099,344	856,911	16.8	Main towns including suburbs.
Sudan	1956	10,262,536	853,873	8.3	Sixty-eight towns.
Togo	1970	1,955,916	254,709	13.0	Localities having been given the status of communes.
Tunisia	1966	4,533,351	1,819,719	40.1	Population living in communes.
Uganda	1969	9,548,847	732,854	7.7	Not available.
United Republic of Tanzania					
Tanganyika	1967	12,313,469	679,291	5.5	Sixteen gazetted townships.
	1967	11,958,654	610,801	5.1	Fifteen gazetted townships.
Zanzibar	1967	354,815	68,490	19.3	Gazetted township of Zanzibar.
Zaire	1955-58	12,733,590	2,795,249	22.0	Agglomerations of 2,000 or more inhabitants where the predominant economic activity is non-agricultural; mixed agglomerations which are urban because of type of economic activity but rural in size.
Zambia	1969	4,056,995	1,232,669	30.4	Main towns and as many small townships as could be separately identified.

TABLE 3 (Cont'd)

The absolute and relative importance of the urban population in each country and territory having 1 million or more inhabitants for which data are available

Country or territory	Year	Total population	Urban population	Per cent	Definition of urban[a]
America, North					
Canada	1966	20,014,880	14,726,759	73.6	Centers of 1,000 or more, including urbanized fringes of metropolitan areas, other major urban areas, and those having 10,000 or more inhabitants in the city and its urban fringe.
Costa Rica	1963	1,336,274	460,543	34.5	"Metropolitan area" of San Jose, Cartago, and administrative centers of all cantons except San Pablo, Nandayure, and Buenos Aires.
Cuba	1971	8,657,160	5,234,846	60.5	Population living in a nucleus of 2,000 or more inhabitants.
Dominican Republic	1970	4,006,405	1,593,235	39.8	Administrative centers of *municipios* and municipal districts.
El Salvador	1971*	3,541,010	1,396,059	39.4	Administrative centers of *municipios*.
Guatemala	1964	4,209,820	1,443,020	34.0	*Municipio* of Guatemala Department and officially recognized centers of other departments and municipalities.
Haiti	1950	3,097,220	377,355	12.0	Administrative centers of commune.
Honduras	1961	1,884,765	437,818	23.2	Localities of 1,000 or more having essentially urban characteristics.
Jamaica	1970*	1,861,300	690,200	37.1	Kingston metropolitan area and selected main towns.
Mexico	1970	48,381,547	28,377,932	58.7	Localities of 2,500 or more inhabitants.
Nicaragua	1963	1,535,588	627,292	40.9	Administrative centers of departments and *municipios*.
Panama	1970	1,428,082	679,418	47.6	Localities of 1,500 or more inhabitants having essentially urban characteristics.
Puerto Rico	1970	2,712,033	1,575,491	58.1	Places of 2,500 or more inhabitants and densely settled urban fringes of urbanized areas.

United States	1970	203,210,158	149,332,119	73.5	Places of 2,500 or more inhabitants and densely settled urban fringes of urbanized areas.
America, South					
Argentina	1964	22,186,800	13,622,695	61.4	Communities of 2,000 or more inhabitants.
Bolivia	1950	3,019,031	1,013,350	33.5	Administrative centers of departments, provinces, and cantons.
Brazil	1970	93,204,379	52,098,495	55.9	Urban and suburban zones of administrative centers of *municípios* and districts.
Chile	1970	8,853,140	6,725,820	76.0	Populated centers which have definite urban characteristics contributed by certain public and municipal services.
Colombia	1964	17,484,508	9,239,626	52.8	Not available.
Ecuador	1962	4,476,007	1,616,584	36.1	Cities, capitals of provinces and cantons.
Paraguay	1962	1,819,103	651,869	35.8	Towns.
Peru	1961	9,906,746	4,698,178	47.4	Capitals of districts and populated centers with specified urban characteristics.
Uruguay	1963	2,592,600	2,132,000	82.2	Cities.
Venezuela	1961	7,523,999	5,073,845	67.4	Centers with a population of 1,000 or more inhabitants.
Asia					
Ceylon	1963	10,590,060	1,997,930	18.9	Municipalities, urban councils, local board areas and towns proclaimed under the Births and Deaths Registration Ordinance.

TABLE 3 (Cont'd)

The absolute and relative importance of the urban population in each country and territory having 1 million or more inhabitants for which data are available

Country or territory	Year	Total population	Urban population	Per cent	Definition of urban[a]
Hong Kong	1961	3,133,131	2,292,621	73.2	Districts in which high density building is permitted and adjoining districts in which an intermediate scale of density is permitted.
India	1961	438,774,729	78,929,755	18.0	Towns; also, all places having 5,000 or more inhabitants, a density of not less than 1,000 persons per square mile, and certain other features.
Indonesia	1971*	118,309,059	20,614,486	17.4	Municipalities, regency capitals and other places with urban characteristics.
Iran	1966	25,143,700	9,840,400	39.1	Cities, towns and villages of 5,000 or more inhabitants.
Iraq	1965	8,047,415	4,112,291	51.1	The area within the boundaries of Municipality Councils (Al-Majlis Al-Baldei).
Israel	1970	3,001,407	2,465,147	82.1	All settlements of more than 2,000 inhabitants, except where at least one-third of the heads of households earn their living from agriculture.
Japan	1970	103,720,060	74,853,337	72.2	City (shi) having 30,000 or more inhabitants with 60 per cent or more of the houses located in the main built-up areas and 60 per cent or more of the population (including their dependents) engaged in manufacturing, trade or other urban type of business.
Khmer Republic	1962	5,728,771	590,011	10.3	Towns.
Korea, Republic of	1970	31,469,132	12,955,265	41.2	Seoul city and municipalities of 50,000 or more inhabitants (shi).
Malaysia, West	1970*	8,801,399	2,527,988	28.7	Gazetted areas with population of 10,000 or more.

Mongolia	1969	1,197,600	527,400	44.0	Capital and district centers.
Nepal	1961	9,412,996	336,222	3.6	Cities of 10,000 or more inhabitants in identifiable agglomerations with essentially urban characteristics.
Pakistan	1961	90,282,674	12,254,730	13.6	Municipalities, civil lines, cantonments not included within municipal limits, any other continuous collection of houses inhabited by not less than 5,000 persons and having urban characteristics and also a few areas having urban characteristics but fewer than 5,000 inhabitants.
Philippines	1970	36,684,486	11,645,459	31.7	Cities and municipalities having a population density of 1,000 or more persons per square kilometer. Central districts of municipalities and cities having a population density of 500 or more persons per square kilometer. Central districts regardless of population density having certain specified services.
Singapore	1970	2,074,507	2,074,507	100.0	City of Singapore.
Syrian Arab Republic	1970*	6,292,000	2,740,000	43.5	Cities, *Mohafaza* centers and *Mantika* centers.
Thailand	1960	26,257,916	4,778,648	18.2	Municipal areas.
Turkey	1970*	35,666,549	13,817,717	38.7	Population of the localities within the municipality limits of administrative centers of provinces and districts.
Viet-Nam, Democratic Republic of	1960	15,916,955	1,518,754	9.5	Cities.

TABLE 3 (Cont'd)

The absolute and relative importance of the urban population in each country and territory having 1 million or more inhabitants for which data are available

Country or territory	Year	Total population	Urban population	Per cent	Definition of urban[a]
Europe					
Albania	1969*	2,079,800	696,000	33.5	Towns, and other industrial centers of more than 400 inhabitants.
Austria	1971	7,456,400	3,866,600	51.9	Communes (Gemeinden) of more than 5,000 inhabitants.
Belgium	1968	9,618,756	8,346,525	86.8	Cities, urban agglomerations and urban communes.
Bulgaria	1971*	8,540,000	4,565,000	53.5	Towns, i.e. localities legally established as urban.
Czechoslovakia	1961	13,745,577	6,539,012	47.6	Large towns, usually of 5,000 or more inhabitants, having a density of more than 100 persons per hectare of built-up area, and specific urban characteristics; small towns, usually of 2,500 or more inhabitants, having a density of more than seventy-five persons per square hectare of built-up area, and specific urban characteristics.
Denmark	1969	4,890,687	2,216,801	45.3	Provincial capitals plus capital city.
Finland	1970*	4,691,679	2,384,939	50.8	Urban communes.
France	1968	48,654,556	34,751,364	70.0	Communes of more than 2,000 inhabitants.
Germany					
Federal Republic	1969*	60,842,100	23,379,800	38.4	Not available.
Democratic Republic	1970	17,058,229	12,552,816	73.6	Communities with 2,000 and more inhabitants.
Greece	1961	8,388,553	3,628,105	43.3	Municipalities and communes with 10,000 or more inhabitants.
Hungary	1970	10,315,600	4,648,300	45.1	Budapest and all legally designated towns.
Ireland	1966	2,884,002	1,419,064	49.2	Cities and towns, including suburbs, of 1,500 or more inhabitants.

Italy	1961	50,623,569	24,168,720	47.7	Communes with less than 50 per cent of the economically active population engaged in agriculture (1936).
Netherlands	1970	13,028,681	10,158,892	78.0	Municipalities with a population of 2,000 and more inhabitants.
Norway	1970*	3,879,104	1,649,254	42.5	Town municipalities.
Poland	1970	32,589,209	17,007,423	52.2	Towns and settlements of urban type.
Portugal	1960	8,889,392	2,016,878	22.7	Aggolmerations of 2,000 or more inhabitants (1940).
Romania	1970	20,252,541	8,258,138	40.8	Cities, towns and 183 other localities having urban socio-economic characteristics.
Sweden	1970	8,076,903	6,574,933	81.4	Built-up areas with at least 200 inhabitants and usually not more than 200 meters between houses.
Switzerland	1970	6,269,783	3,422,862	54.6	Communes of 10,000 or more inhabitants including suburbs.
United Kingdom England and Wales	1971*	48,593,658	38,025,355	78.3	Areas classified as urban for local government purposes.
Northern Ireland	1971*	1,527,593	841,923	55.1	Administrative county boroughs, municipal boroughs, and urban districts.
Scotland	1971*	5,227,706	3,703,733	70.8	Cities and all burghs.
Yugoslavia	1961	18,549,291	5,264,735	28.4	Localities of 15,000 or more inhabitants; others with specified proportions of workers not engaged in agriculture.

TABLE 3 (Cont'd)

The absolute and relative importance of the urban population in each country and territory having 1 million or more inhabitants for which data are available

Country or territory	Year	Total population	Urban population	Per cent	Definition of urban[a]
Oceania					
Australia	1971	12,728,461	10,888,635	85.5	For the larger urban centers: Population clusters of 1,000 or more persons having a minimum density of 500 persons per square mile and some areas of lower population and/or density classified on other grounds. For other urban centers: Built-up areas as determined from aerial photographs.
New Guinea	1966*	1,578,650	74,067	4.7	Centers with population of 500 or more but excluding a variety of rural clusters regardless of size.
New Zealand	1969	2,780,839	1,765,200	63.5	Cities, boroughs and all town districts.
U.S.S.R.	1970	241,720,134	135,991,514	56.3	Cities and urban-type localities, officially designated as such by each of the constituent Republics.
Byelorussian S.S.R.	1970	9,002,338	3,907,783	43.4	
Ukrainian, S.S.R.	1970	47,126,517	25,688,560	54.5	

Source: Compiled from data in United Nations, *Demographic Yearbook, 1962*, pp. 304-315, Table 10; *1963*, pp. 162-230, Table 5; *1964*, pp. 648-664, Table 27; *1967*, pp. 132-205, Table 5; *1968*, pp. 315-322, Table 11; *1969*, pp. 144-150, Table 5; *1970*, pp. 136-165, Table 5; *1971*, pp. 139-158, Table 5.

*Provisional

[a]For fully detailed definitions of urban areas, see various editions of the *Demographic Yearbook*.

[b]African population only.

rate comparisons may be made of the degree of urbanization in two or more countries. Even more labor is needed if one would attempt a comparison of trends.

The definitions of urban and rural currently in use for census purposes fall into several fairly clear categories. The first of these is employed in the countries which follow the French pattern and classify as urban persons living in population centers which have more than a specified number of inhabitants. Indeed the actual criterion applied by the French — to consider as urban the persons residing in communes having 2,000 or more inhabitants — is rather widely used in Europe. The slight modification of this procedure that long has been standard in the United States, which sets the basic division between rural and urban at 2,500 inhabitants, is used by several other American countries. Other nations employ variations of essentially the same criterion, and use such criteria as 250, 1,000, 1,500, 5,000, 20,000 and 40,000 as the number of inhabitants required before a given population center is classified as urban.

A second category of rural-urban classification consists of those in which various towns and cities have been given charters or other privileges and distinctions which entitle them to status as urban centers whereas all places lacking such honorific titles are classed as rural. Such bases for the rural or urban classification of the population prevail for the United Kingdom, Romania, and elsewhere in Europe.

Somewhat related to this procedure is that rather widely used throughout Latin America, which designates as urban those population centers which serve as seats of local, state or departmental, and national government, and as rural all other localities, irrespective of their size. Various American countries, too, are experimenting with the use of other urban characteristics, such as the provision of municipal water systems (Chile) or the existence of municipal lighting, water, and sewage-disposal systems (Peru).

A new and promising approach to the problem of rural-urban classification was employed in Brazil's 1940, 1950, 1960, and 1970 censuses. Since this procedure may point the way to considerable improvements elsewhere, it deserves detailed description. During the preparatory work for the 1940 census a decree was issued making the prefect of each *município* (or county-like unit) responsible for having drawn and deposited with the Regional Geographic Office a map of his *município*, prepared in accordance with instructions supplied by the National Geographic Council. Among the instructions was one requiring each map to contain inserts showing the plan of the seat of the *município* and of the seats of all the *distritos* of which it was composed. The instructions also stipulated that "the urban and suburban areas of each *vila* (district seat) together shall include at least thirty dwellings; the urban area of the *cidade* (seat of the *município* shall include a minimum of two hundred dwellings." It was provided, however, that all existing *cidades* and *vilas* should be mapped even though they did not meet the minimum requirements. Additional instructions were as follows:

Article 8: The determination of the urban part of the seat, whether of *municipio* or *distrito*, shall consist in the clear and simple description of a line, easily identifiable on the ground, surrounding the center of the greatest concentration of houses, in which, as a general rule, are located the principal public edifices and where the commercial, financial, and social life of the seat is manifested most intensely, and where, in many cases, there is the imposition of special taxes, as for example the urban tenth.

Single Paragraph — The said line of delineation of the urban area shall describe preferably, a polygon, made of straight lines, which follows closely the periphery of the above-mentioned center of concentration of the houses in the seat.

Article 9: The delineation of the suburban portion of the seats (of *municipios* or *distritos*) shall consist in the clear and simple description of a line, also easily recognized on the ground, embracing an area that surrounds, at a variable distance, the urban section, an area into which the expansion of the urban zone is already proceeding or to which, due to its favorable topographic conditions, this expansion is naturally destined. The boundary line of the suburban zone should circumscribe as rigorously as possible, the area that really corresponds to the present or future expansion of the urban center, it being prohibited to delimit under any pretext whatsoever that may be invoked, even that of regularizing the form, a suburban perimeter which is removed in distance and confrontation, from the area of expansion mentioned above.[4]

Thus it is evident that the territory of each *municipio* is divided into three residential categories, namely, one or more urban areas, one or more suburban zones, and the remaining rural territory. This division was used in the 1940, 1950, 1960, and 1970 censuses for classifying the population into the urban, suburban, and rural categories. As will be indicated below, somewhat analogous procedures were used in the 1950, 1960, and 1970 censuses of population in the United States for determining zones about cities of 50,000 or more inhabitants that were to be placed in the urban category and in delineating the boundaries of unincorporated centers of a thousand or more population.

United States Census Definitions and Classifications

More than fourscore years elapsed between the taking of the first census of population in the United States and the official inclusion of a classification of population according to rural or urban residence. However, the importance of the deficiency was recognized by J. D. B. DeBow, who during the short interim in 1853 and 1854, when he served as Superintendent of the Census, salvaged the results of the seventh census and did so much to plot the course of development of the modern census. Consider the understanding and vision expressed in some of his comments on the subject:

The Census does not furnish material for separating the urban and rural population of the United States, so as to admit of a statement showing the extent of either. Such a table to each of the States would be very valuable and it is much to be regretted that it can be deduced from none of the census publications.

So imperfect is the Census of 1850 in this respect that hundreds of important towns and cities in all parts of the country, and especially in the South and West, are not even distinguished on the returns from the body of the counties in which they are situated, and therefore their population cannot be ascertained at all. Again, slaves are often included in the towns, simply because their owners reside there. But what is of more importance and the greatest cause of embarrassment is the fact that in New England and the Northern States, what are returned as cities, and towns, often include whole rural districts. If the information in regard to town and city population is ever to be correctly ascertained, there must be explicit instructions to separate upon the returns, distinctly, all places having an aggregation of over fifty or a hundred persons, with a store, tavern, blacksmith shop or school house and post office, or some or all of those, and to include within such village, town, or city, no person not resident within its limits proper. It would not be difficult to frame suitable instructions upon this point.[5]

It is readily evident that if DeBow had participated in planning the 1860 census, the necessary improvements would have been made at an early date.

As it was, however, the first appearance of the rural-urban classification of the population came in 1874 with the publication of the *Statistical Atlas of the United States*, prepared under the supervision of Francis A. Walker.[6] At this time the division between rural and urban was placed at 8,000; persons living in cities having that many or more inhabitants were placed in the urban category, and all others in the rural. In this volume the data for all the previous censuses were reclassified, and the numbers of urban people so defined were tabulated for all the decennial censuses through 1870. There is no way of knowing to what extent or in what manner the basic difficulties pointed out by DeBow were overcome. With primary interest still focused upon the urban group, the census of 1880 employed the criterion of 4,000 inhabitants as the dividing line between the rural and urban segments of the population.

Attention was shifted somewhat from the rural segment of the population in the 1890 census, when all persons living in aggregates of 1,000 or more inhabitants were classified as urban. Ten years later the 4,000 criterion again was employed to define the lower limit of the urban category, with the remainder of the inhabitants being divided into two subclasses: the semi-urban, those residing in incorporated centers of less than 4,000 population, and the rural, those residing in unincorporated territory.

In 1910, the line of demarcation between rural and urban was set at 2,500, and this continues to be the basic element in the classification of the population into the rural and urban categories. However, those who use the results of the 1950, 1960, and 1970 censuses of population should be familiar with the "current" definition first employed in connection with the 1950 enumeration. As revised for use in the most recent count, it is as follows:

> According to the definition adopted for use in the 1970 census, the urban population comprises all persons living in urbanized areas and in places of 2,500 inhabitants or more outside urbanized areas. More specifically, the urban population consists of all persons living in (a) places of 2,500 inhabitants or more incorporated as cities, villages, boroughs (except Alaska), and towns (except in the New England States, New York, and Wisconsin), but excluding those persons living in the rural portions of extended cities; (b) unincorporated places of 2,500 inhabitants or more; and (c) other territory, incorporated or unincorporated, included in urbanized areas. . . . The population not classified as urban constitutes the rural population.[7]

For many purposes, the student must also be acquainted with the "previous" definition of urban employed for comparative purposes in the 1950, 1960, and 1970 censuses and the only one used in the still highly important 1940 and 1930 enumerations.

According to the previous definition, "the urban population had been limited to all persons living in incorporated places of 2,500 inhabitants or more and in areas (usually minor civil divisions) classified as urban under special rules relating to population size and density."[8]

As indicated above, for many purposes the simple rural-urban dichotomy is inadequate, and the concept of the continuum is much more satisfactory. Therefore, it is fortunate that the Bureau of the Census employs subdivisions of both the urban and the rural categories in the majority of its basic tabulations, and that special compilations of data enable the student to determine many of the demographic variations that occur as one passes from the most highly rural to the most highly urban portions of the population.

The *urban category* is the one for which, from the standpoint of the population analyst, the data are tabulated and published in the most satisfactory manner. The category as a whole is employed, or the facts for it may be obtained by subtraction, in nearly all the state and county tables; and in addition fairly complete information is given separately for every city of 100,000 or more inhabitants, rather plentiful materials for each place having between 10,000 and 100,000 residents, and considerable data for each smaller center. Furthermore, in the 1970 census tabulations a wealth of demographic detail was published for each of the 248 *urbanized areas* that had been delineated, as well as for each of 243 *standard metropolitan statistical areas* scattered throughout the nation. The materials were supplemented for the first time in 1970 by some for *extended cities*.

The principal goal in delineating *urbanized areas* is to distinguish the urban and rural populations in and around the nation's major cities and to emphasize the significance of urban influence beyond political boundaries. As defined for census purposes, an urbanized area contains the following:

1a. A central city of 50,000 inhabitants or more in 1960, in a special census conducted by the Census Bureau since 1960, or in the 1970 census; or

b. Twin cities, i.e., cities with contiguous boundaries and constituting for general social and economic purposes, a single community with a combined population of at least 50,000, and with the smaller of the twin cities having a population of at least 15,000.[9]

The portion of the urbanized area lying outside its central city or cities is designated as the *urban fringe*. It is closely settled territory that excludes the rural parts of the extended cities and includes the following:

a. Incorporated places of 2,500 inhabitants or more.

b. Incorporated places with fewer than 2,500 inhabitants, provided that each has a closely settled area of 100 housing units or more.

c. Small parcels of land normally less than one square mile in area having a population density of 1,000 inhabitants or more per square mile. The areas of large nonresidential tracts devoted to such urban land uses as railroad yards, airports, factories, parks, golf courses, and cemeteries are excluded in computing the population density.

d. Other similar small areas in unincorporated territory with lower population density provided that they serve
   — to eliminate enclaves, or
   — to close indentations in the urbanized areas of one mile or less across the open end, or
   — to link outlying enumeration districts of qualifying density that are not more than 1½ miles from the main body of the urbanized area.[10]

In any case, the urbanized area is characterized as the physical city as distinguished from both the legal city and the metropolitan community. Urbanized areas are smaller than the standard metropolitan statistical areas and usually are embraced within the limits of the latter.

The concept of the *extended city* represents yet another effort to describe the relationships between urban centers and their outlying territory, particularly the manner in which the two merge. Those who prepared the reports of the 1970 census observe that

> Over the 1960 - 1970 decade there has been an increasing trend toward the extension of city boundaries to include territory essentially rural in character. . . . The classification of all the inhabitants of such cities as urban would include in the urban population persons whose environment is primarily rural in character. In order to separate these people from those residing in the closely settled portions of such cities, the Bureau of the Census examined patterns of population density and classified a portion or portions of each such city as rural. These cities — designated as extended cities — thus consist of an urban part and a rural part. An extended city contains one or more areas, each of at least 5 square miles in extent and with a population density of less than 100 persons per square mile according to the 1970 census. The area or areas constitute at least 25 per cent of the land area of the legal city or total 25 square miles or more. The delineation of extended cities was limited to cities in urbanized areas.[11]

The *standard metropolitan statistical area* (SMSA), as the concept was employed in the 1970 census for the purpose of giving detailed tabulations of information for the 243 most highly urbanized segments of the United States, is a county or a group of contiguous counties containing at least one city of 50,000 inhabitants or more or "twin cities" with a combined population of at least

50,000.[12] Other counties may be included if they meet certain criteria of metropolitan character and social and economic integration with the central city or cities. The criteria of metropolitan character of a county or counties relate to such things as: (1) the number and proportion of the labor force engaged in nonagricultural jobs; (2) the percentage of population living in contiguous minor civil divisions with densities of at least 150 persons per square mile; and (3) the ratio between the number of nonagricultural workers in counties whose metropolitan character is being tested and the number in the county containing the largest city. The criteria of integration relate primarily to the extent of social and economic communication between the outlying counties and the central county.[13] They include consideration of two principal factors: (1) the proportion of workers in the county in question who work at jobs in the county containing the central city or cities; and (2) the percentages of those who work in the outlying county but who live in the county or counties containing the central city or cities. Other criteria, such as telephone communication between an outlying county and the central one, newspaper circulation, official traffic counts, and so on may be used for further clarification of the integration of counties into standard metropolitan statistical areas.

In 1970, for the second time, the Bureau of the Census employed the term *standard consolidated area* to identify the huge urban complexes around New York and Chicago. Each of these units contains several contiguous standard metropolitan statistical areas as well as other counties which do not meet the criteria of integration set forth above but which do have close social and economic relationships with these great urban agglomerations. The two were named the New York-Northeastern New Jersey and the Chicago-Northwestern Indiana Standard Consolidated Areas, respectively.[14]

The *rural population* as given by the 1970 census, as is evident from the above, relative to the definition of urban, consists of all persons who resided neither within the limits of an urbanized area (including its "urban fringe") nor in any other center of 2,500 or more inhabitants. It is divided into two principal subcategories, and the data for each of these figure in most of the state and county tables. In order to appreciate the fundamental distinction between these two segments, it is necessary to know that the 1970 *rural-farm population* includes all persons considered to reside on tracts of land that were classified as farms, irrespective of their occupations. In turn, farms were classified as

> . . . places of 10 or more acres from which sales of farm products amounted to $50 or more in the preceding calendar year, or on places of less than 10 acres from which sales of farm products amounted to $250 or more in the preceding year.[15]

The basic element in the definition is that the land in question be used for or connected with agricultural operations. Therefore, those living on what might appear to be farm land who paid cash rent merely for the use of a house and yard were not included in the farm population. Furthermore, in 1970 as in 1960, the only persons classified as "farm" resided in rural territory. In earlier censuses, some farm persons were classified as "urban."

The *rural-nonfarm population* is the residual group. It includes all persons who were classified neither as urban nor as rural-farm. Therefore, it is a hodge-podge embracing some of the most widely divergent segments of the entire population. The village population, that is, those living in centers of less than 2,500 inhabitants, and the people living just outside urbanized areas and the corporate limits of towns and cities of less than 50,000 population make up two of the most important groups in this category. But the category also embraces a wide variety of nonagriculturists (miners; trappers; woodsmen; fishermen; filling station operators and attendants; personnel engaged in the operation of motels, tourist courts and resorts; the keepers of stores, bars, beer parlors, and fish camps; and so forth) dispersed throughout the countryside.

In addition to the rural-farm and the rural-nonfarm categories, for which the data are presented with all detail that reasonably may be expected, the census reports for the states also give the more important data for each center having from 1,000 to 2,499 inhabitants. In addition, in 1970, the Bureau consolidated and published several data for all such rural population centers taken collectively in each state.

Indexes and Scales of Urbanization and Rurality

Very frequently there is need for an index showing the points on the rural-urban continuum at which the various counties and minor civil divisions of a given state are located. Such need arises principally where it is desired to include this variable in the analysis of demographic interrelationships or trends and particularly where correlation analysis is essential. Many demographers, sociologists, economists, and political scientists, when confronted with the problem, have found it difficult to devise a satisfactory index. The proportion of the total population that is classified as urban frequently is suggested and employed. However, in practice this is highly unsatisfactory because so many of the counties in a given state, and an even larger percentage of the minor civil divisions, contain no urban populations whatsoever. For example, the student attempting to correlate the degree of urbanization with one or more other factors in the state of Kentucky with the percentage of urban population in the total population as an index would discover that in 1970, 52 of the 120 counties in the state contained no urban centers. If Colorado were the state for which the analysis were to be made, he would find that urban populations were lacking in 33 of the 63 counties in the state. Since the logic of correlation analysis breaks down completely when any considerable number of the items have a value of zero, the measure that at first glance appears to be the most appropriate is entirely unsuited for use in these cases. The situation is similar in many other states, and the defects are even more pronounced if minor civil divisions are the units employed in the analysis. Also frequently encountered is a very sparsely populated county, far removed from metropolitan centers and slightly exposed to direct influences from the city, but which contains a town of more than 2,500 inhabitants. Indeed, counties of this type may contain extremely high proportions of persons classified as urban. This is another reason why the proportion of urbanites in the population in a county is a very poor indicator of the degree to which such a county is urbanized. What are the alternatives? After considerable exploratory study, it would appear that the best readily available index for use in the type of problem under discussion is the proportion of the population in the county, or in the minor civil division, that is resident in places (incorporated centers of all sizes and unincorporated places having 1,000 or more inhabitants) for which separate tabulations are prepared by the Bureau of the Census. In 1970, materials were published giving the total populations of all minor civil divisions no matter what their size, but if in the 1980 and subsequent censuses, the data are published separately for unincorporated centers of less than 1,000 inhabitants, this index will be even more satisfactory as a measure of the degree of urbanization of the various counties and minor civil divisions in a given state.

Frequently, the population student needs more than a simple division of the population into rural and urban categories, and this is the case especially when he desires to relate to other factors of populations according to the size of their communities of residence. The need in this case is for a series of categories that will reflect the various grades or degrees encountered as one moves from the most rural to the most urban situations or populations. Usage in this respect is not standardized, and the terminology employed frequently is confusing. Substantial progress was made, however, in connection with the 1950, 1960, and 1970 censuses when the population living in the urban fringes of cities of 50,000 or more was included in the urban category and the data published for each such urbanized area as a unit. The value of the information assembled in 1970 was enhanced by the publication of data on selected items for the whole nation, based on 15 and 20 per cent samples of the population separately, for the total area, central cities, and fringes of urbanized areas. In addition, materials were supplied for other urban places of 10,000 or more inhabitants, those of 2,500 to 9,999 persons, and, of course, for standard metropolitan statistical areas. The rural class was further subdivided into the farm and nonfarm categories. Yet the materials on the smallest places were so limited that they did not permit sufficiently refined classifications of the populations of the various states, a feature that would be even more useful than the national data that are available. Under these circumstances, the present writers have found the following arrangement of considerable use.

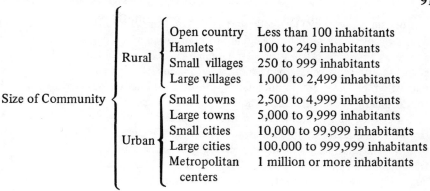

SOME INTERNATIONAL COMPARISONS

Prior to 1949 it was almost impossible for the student of population to secure any comprehensive and reliable information about the absolute and relative importance of the rural and urban populations in most parts of the world. Anyone vitally interested in the matter could easily spend weeks or months in the endeavor, only to discover eventually that all his efforts were fruitless.[16] Fortunately, this was one of the first items to which the Population Commission established by the United Nations turned its attention, and comprehensive tabulations of such data as could be secured appeared in the first issue of the *Demographic Yearbook*.[17] Much more inclusive tabulations were included in the 1962, 1963, 1964, 1967, 1969, 1970, and 1971 editions of this magnificent source of information. The materials presented in Table 3 have been taken from these compilations.

The lack of uniformity in the definitions of rural and urban makes it impossible to make fair comparisons between most countries; and even if the definitions were uniform, one could never be sure that a place of a given size in one country was equally urban, or equally rural, with one of the same size in another. For example, both the United States and Mexico employ 2,500 inhabitants as the point at which the line is drawn between the rural and urban portions of the population. But in Mexico the agriculturists commonly reside in villages and towns from which they commute daily to work on their lands in the surrounding territory; whereas, in the United States farmers more generally live on their lands. For this reason a Mexican population center of three or four thousand inhabitants is likely to be largely agricultural, while in the United States a village of no more than one thousand inhabitants generally is highly commercial and may be industrial as well. Again, a population aggregate of three thousand people in England or Belgium is almost certain to represent a much higher concentration of urban traits and practices than is one of comparable size in Spain or Bulgaria, not to mention towns of this size in India, China, and many other parts of the world.

For these reasons it is likely that many of the variations in the extent to which various nations in the world are rural or urban are even greater than might appear at first glance from the data which have been assembled in Table 3. Nevertheless, the most outstanding fact to be obtained from this material is the extent to which the world's inhabitants still reside in highly rural territory and are conditioned by rural influences and ways of life. Note that more than four-fifths of India's teeming millions are in the rural category, undoubtedly highly rural from the qualitative standpoint as well. Were data available for China, the degree of urbanization hardly could be much higher. As a matter of fact, in all of Asia, Iraq, Israel, and Japan are the only nations in which the urban population is larger than the rural (except, of course, for Hong Kong and Singapore). In the Americas, where the data are most complete, the urban population is more numerous than the rural in eleven of twenty-four countries. These are Argentina, Brazil, Canada, Chile, Colombia, Cuba, Mexico, Puerto Rico, Uruguay, the United States, and Venezuela. In Africa, the largest proportion of urban inhabitants is found in South Africa, and there the percentage is only forty-eight. Even in Europe, twelve of the twenty-five countries for which data are available are more rural than urban, even though England and Wales, Northern Ireland, and Scotland are all counted as separate countries.

It is obvious that the wide range of definitions of "urban" used by the various countries and the fact that rural and urban distinctions are available for only about half of all existing nations and territories make it necessary to seek other data which enable better comparisons on the basis of residence. For about 90 per cent of all nations and territories, the United Nations publishes annually the numbers of people living in capital cities of all sizes, in other centers of 100,000 or more, and, when they exist, in densely settled "urban agglomerations" which consist of large cities and their densely settled peripheries. At present, these data are the only ones which make it possible to distinguish populations on any residence basis whatsoever in virtually all of the world's sovereign countries and in a great majority of the territories and possessions of other nations. Also, there is greater uniformity in these data than can be found in the materials separating rural and urban, simply because in the former case the United Nations applies certain uniform definitions and makes its own estimates when other figures are unavailable. By including capitals, these materials on cities have the advantage of being available for at least the principal urban center in almost every society. In practice, the data apply to some urban centers possessing as few as 6,000 inhabitants and to others containing as many as ten million persons.[18]

By employing the materials described above, Figure 5 has been prepared to show for nearly all nations and most territories the percentages of people living in the capital cities, in other centers of 100,000 or more, and in urban agglomerations. Three groups of countries may be distinguished. First, those whose total populations contain relatively high proportions (30 or more per cent) of city dwellers number less than thirty and are concentrated in North America above the Rio Grande, the northern and southern parts of South America, North-western Europe, and Oceania (largely Australia and New Zealand). They also include Israel and Japan. In general these are societies in which industrial growth is far advanced and in which urbanization is a long-term phenomenon. To be sure, there are large numbers of rural people in these places, but their proportions are not so great that an agrarian way of life can be said to dominate any of the countries in this group.

Second, the nations and territories which contain moderate proportions (15 to 29.9 per cent) of persons living in the kinds of cities under consideration cover relatively broad areas and include Mexico and parts of the Caribbean, the central portion of South America, North and South Africa, Eastern Europe both north and south, sections of the Near East and the Middle East, and the vast Soviet Union. These countries total nearly 100. Some of them have become important industrially in fairly recent years, and many are just now witnessing significant reductions in the relative importance of agriculture and an agrarian way of life. This is certainly the case in Mexico, Brazil, and a few other countries of

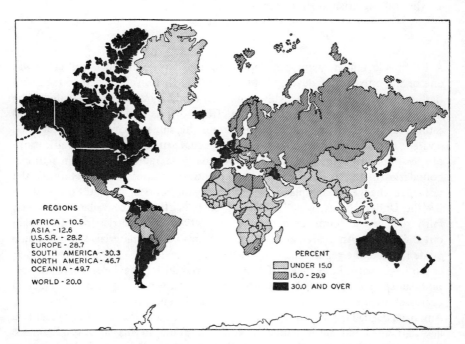

REGIONS

AFRICA - 10.5
ASIA - 12.6
U.S.S.R. - 28.2
EUROPE - 28.7
SOUTH AMERICA - 30.3
NORTH AMERICA - 46.7
OCEANIA - 49.7

WORLD - 20.0

PERCENT

UNDER 15.0
15.0 - 29.9
30.0 AND OVER

FIGURE 5. Percentages of people living in capital cities, other urban centers with 100,000 or more inhabitants, and urban agglomerations, each nation and territory.

Latin America. Much the same might be said of South Africa, the Soviet Union, parts of Eastern Europe, and the Scandinavian countries. Still other societies in this intermediate group are those whose balance between rural and urban people has changed comparatively little but which became rather highly urbanized early in their histories. Several countries in the Middle East and a few in North Africa may be placed in this category.

Third, the nations and territories which have small relative shares (less than 15 per cent) of their people living in the kind of cities in question also number almost 100. However, despite the fact that their distribution is fairly wide, they represent a smaller share of the world's countries than was the case only a decade or two ago. In the Western Hemisphere, only Bolivia in South America, three of the countries of Central America, and sparsely inhabited Greenland fall into this category. In the eastern half of the world, India and mainland China, of course, are the most conspicuous of these slightly urbanized countries. In addition, nearly all of the rest of Asia and practically all of Africa south of the Sahara must be placed in this group. These societies, many of which have become independent or have endured disruptive political revolutions in the years since World War II, are the truly agrarian portions of the globe.

TRENDS

A worldwide tendency for populations to concentrate in towns and cities was one of the outstanding developments during the first seventy years of the twentieth century, and the same highly significant tendency continues unabated. The importance of the economic and social effects of this trend can hardly be overestimated. The demographic data concerning this subject leave a great deal to be desired: not only do some countries lack adequate rural and urban classifications of the population, but so many have undergone radical changes in national boundaries in recent decades that it is practically impossible to determine the residence changes taking place during intercensal periods. In addition to those for the United States, which will be given later, there are available, however, fairly reliable and comparable materials for sixty-seven countries spread throughout the world. An analysis of the trends seen in these materials should be adequate to make the general tendency sufficiently clear.

To begin with, in eighteen of these countries during the latest intercensal period, substantial increases in the urban population were accompanied by actual decreases in the rural population. Interestingly enough, five countries in the Americas (Canada, Jamaica, Puerto Rico, the United States, and Chile) and two in Asia (Japan and the Republic of Korea) are found in this category. Eight are European countries, namely Bulgaria, France, Greece, Hungary, Ireland, Romania, Sweden, and Northern Ireland. Australia, New Zealand, and the Soviet Union also fall into this category.

Only slightly less striking is a second category of countries in which substantial increases in the urban population were accompanied by relatively minor (10 per cent or less) increases in the rural population. Eleven of the sixty-seven belong in this group: Algeria, Egypt, Zambia, Brazil, Venezuela, Iraq, Turkey, Austria, Finland, Poland, and Switzerland.

Those countries in which the number in both the urban and rural populations rose substantially, but in which the rate of increase in the former was at least twice that in the latter, may be placed in a third group. The twenty-two countries included are: Kenya, Morocco, Nigeria, Togo, Tunisia, Uganda, the Dominican Republic, Guatemala, Mexico, Nicaragua, Panama, Colombia, Ecuador, Ceylon, Indonesia, Iran, Jordan, Mongolia, Nepal, Pakistan, the Syrian Arab Republic, and Albania.

In eight countries, the rate of growth of the urban population was higher than that of the rural, but not as much as twice as high. These are South Africa, Tanganyika in the United Republic of Tanzania, Costa Rica, El Salvador, Paraguay, India, Sabah in East Malaysia, and the Philippines. In four, the rate of growth of the rural population exceeded that of the urban. They are Southern Rhodesia, Czechoslovakia, Denmark, and England and Wales. Three countries experienced absolute and relative growth in their rural populations but numerical and proportional decreases in their urban populations. These are West Malaysia, Portugal, and Scotland. Finally, in the Federal Republic of Germany, the total, urban, and rural populations all decreased between the two most recent censuses.

Were data available for China, many of the countries recently achieving national status, and various "underdeveloped" sections of the world, the tendency for the population to concentrate in towns and cities would probably be seen to be as strong as it is in virtually all parts of the earth mentioned above. Indeed, the urbanization of the world and the contemporary dominant position of urban values and philosophies must be considered among the most potent forces shaping civilization during the last decades of the twentieth century.

THE RURAL AND URBAN POPULATIONS OF THE UNITED STATES

Of the 203,210,158 inhabitants of the United States shown by the census of April 1, 1970, a total of 149,332,119[19] (73.5 per cent) were classified as urban and 53,878,039 (26.5 per cent) as rural on the basis of the new definition of urban employed for the first time in 1950. In 1960, under the new definition of urban, 69.9 per cent of the national population was classed as urban and 30.1 per cent as rural. Thus, in the interval between 1960 and 1970 enumerations, the urban population increased significantly, whereas the rural decreased on the absolute basis as well as the relative, just as was true in the preceding decade. The number of urban centers in 1970 totaled 7,062. In 1960, the corresponding number was only 6,041; in 1950, it was 4,077; and in 1940, it was 3,485. The change during the 1960's represents the net influence of adding centers that passed the 2,500 mark in population between 1960 and 1970, subtracting a few that dropped below that figure during the decade, and adding all unincorporated places and nearly all newly incorporated centers having more than 2,500 inhabitants in 1970.

The rural population of the United States in 1970 was subdivided into 45,586,707 persons (22.4 per cent of the national total) classified as rural-non-farm, and 8,292,150 (4.1 per cent) classified as rural-farm. In the former category, the number of persons increased over 1960 but the percentage decreased; in the latter group, both the number and the proportion declined.

POPULATION BY SIZE OF PLACE

Apart from the standard consolidated area, of which there are only two, the largest urban unit for census purposes is the standard metropolitan statistical area. The principal metropolitan areas as identified in 1970 are shown in Figure 6, in which the volume of each sphere represents the total population, the core represents the population of the central city or cities, and the outer ring represents the population residing outside the central city. In 1970, all of the 243 SMSA's together contained 139,418,811 persons or 68.6 per cent of the nation's total population. Of this group, 63,796,943 persons or 45.8 per cent of the metropolitan population lived in central cities, 59,210,328 persons or 42.5 per cent resided in urban areas outside the central cities, and 16,411,154 or 11.7 per cent dwelt in the rural portions of the standard metropolitan statistical areas. The SMSA's range in size from New York, with 11,571,899 persons, to Meriden, Connecticut, with 55,959. Thirty-three of them have 1 million or more inhabitants and are given in Table 4, along with a few of their more important features; 33 have between 500,000 and 999,999; 61 have from 250,000 to 499,999; and 218 have from 50,000 to 249,999.

The numbers and proportions of the population residing in places of stated sizes as shown by the 1970 census, with comparable data for 1920, are shown in Table 5. The year 1920 was chosen for comparison because it was about 1918 that the United States became more urban than rural. In 1970, 58.3 per cent of the people of the United States resided in urbanized areas, including central cities and urban fringes. When all of these urban inhabitants are allocated to the places of various sizes listed in Table 5, in 1970, 56,463,833 persons or 27.7 per cent of all of those in the United States are found to have been residing in large cities, that is, places having populations of 100,000 or more, whether they were central cities of urbanized areas or part of the urban fringe within those areas. In addition, 46,797,033 persons (23.1 per cent of the national total) were living in other population centers of various sizes that were included within urbanized

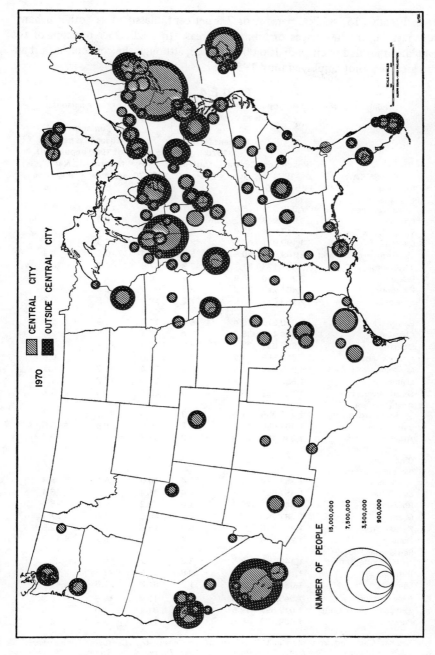

Figure 6. Populations of the principal standard metropolitan statistical areas of the United States, 1970.

areas. Finally, 15,185,700 persons or 7.5 per cent, classified as "other urban," were residing in the fringes of urbanized areas. In 1920, 25.9 per cent of the population resided in cities of 100,000 or more, although the concept of "urbanized area" was not employed until 1950.

TABLE 4

Populations of standard metropolitan statistical areas of 1 million or more persons, ranked by size, 1970

SMSA	Population 1970	Per cent Negro 1970 Central cities	Outlying areas	Per cent change, 1960-70	Components of change (as per cent of 1960 population) Natural increase	Net migration
New York	11,571,899	21.2	5.9	8.2	8.6	−0.8
Los Angeles-Long Beach	7,032,075	16.5	6.2	16.4	12.3	4.2
Chicago	6,978,947	32.7	3.6	12.2	12.0	0.2
Philadelphia	4,817,914	33.6	6.6	10.9	9.9	1.0
Detroit	4,199,931	43.7	3.6	11.6	12.9	−1.3
San Francisco-Oakland	3,109,519	20.5	5.4	17.4	10.5	6.9
Washington, D.C.	2,861,123	71.1	7.9	37.8	18.4	20.2
Boston	2.753,700	16.3	1.1	6.1	−	−
Pittsburgh	2,401,245	20.2	3.5	−0.2	6.8	−7.0
St. Louis	2,363,017	40.9	7.2	12.3	11.5	0.8
Baltimore	2,070,670	46.4	6.0	14.8	11.9	2.9
Cleveland	2,064,194	38.3	3.4	8.1	10.5	−2.4
Houston	1,985,031	25.7	8.9	40.0	18.1	21.9
Newark, N.J.	1,856,556	54.2	9.6	9.9	9.3	0.6
Minneapolis-St. Paul	1,813,647	4.0	0.2	22.4	15.7	6.7
Dallas	1,555,950	24.9	5.2	39.0	17.3	21.7
Seattle-Everett	1,421,869	6.5	0.4	28.4	11.8	16.7
Anaheim-Santa Ana-Garden Grove	1,420,386	1.6	0.3	101.8	23.5	78.3
Milwaukee	1,403,688	14.7	0.2	9.8	12.8	−3.0
Atlanta	1,390,164	51.3	6.2	36.7	17.0	19.7
Cincinnati	1,384,851	27.6	2.9	9.2	12.0	−2.9
Paterson-Clifton-Passaic	1,358,794	17.4	2.4	14.5	9.1	5.4
San Diego	1,357,854	7.6	1.4	31.4	15.1	16.4
Buffalo	1,349,211	20.4	1.6	3.2	9.6	−6.4
Miami	1,267,792	22.7	12.2	35.6	8.4	27.2
Kansas City	1,253,916	22.1	5.2	14.8	12.3	2.5
Denver	1,227,529	9.1	0.4	32.1	15.2	14.9
San Bernardino-Riverside-Ontario	1,143,146	7.4	3.3	41.2	14.3	26.9
Indianapolis	1,109,882	18.0	0.8	17.5	13.7	3.8
San Jose	1,064,714	2.5	1.2	65.8	21.6	44.1
New Orleans	1,045,809	45.0	12.5	15.3	14.5	0.8
Tampa-St. Petersburg	1,012,594	17.5	4.4	31.1	3.6	27.5
Portland, Ore.	1,009,129	5.6	0.3	22.8	8.4	14.4

Source: Compiled from data in U.S. Bureau of the Census, *U.S. Census of Population: 1970, Number of Inhabitants,* Final Report PC(1)-A1, *United States Summary* (1971), pp. 171-178, Table 32; *General Demographic Trends for Metropolitan Areas, 1960 to 1970,* Final Report PHC(2)-1, *United States* (1971), pp. 34-46, Table 10; pp. 47-60, Table 11.

TABLE 5

Numbers and percentages of the population of the United States residing in places of stated size, 1970 and 1920

Size of place	Number of places		Number of inhabitants		Percentage of inhabitants	
	1970[a]	1920	1970[a]	1920	1970[a]	1920
Total	20,768	15,597	203,210,158	106,021,537	100.0	100.0
Urban	7,062	2,725	149,332,119	54,253,282	73.5	51.1
1,000,000 or more	6	3	18,769,365	10,145,532	9.2	9.6
100,000-999,999	150	65	37,694,468	17,283,794	18.5	16.3
10,000-99,999	2,145	686	55,986,720	17,467,368	27.5	16.4
2,500-9,999	4,134	1,971	20,961,994	9,356,588	10.4	8.8
Under 2,500	627	–	726,683	–	0.4	–
Other urban territory	–	–	15,185,700	–	7.5	–
Rural	13,706	12,872	53,878,039	51,768,255	26.5	48.9
1,000-2,499	4,191	3,034	6,656,007	4,718,651	3.3	4.5
Under 1,000	9,515	9,838	3,851,873	4,262,255	1.9	4.0
Other rural territory.[b]	–	–	43,379,116	42,787,349	21.3	40.4

Source: Compiled from data in U.S. Bureau of the Census, U.S. Census of Population: 1970, Number of Inhabitants, Final Report PC(1)-A1, United States Summary (1971), pp. 46-47, Table 7.

[a]The "new" urban definition is used.

[b]Unincorporated places of less than 1,000 inhabitants and the open country.

The second big mass of the nation's citizens is composed of those who live either on farms, in other portions of the open country, or in unincorporated villages and hamlets of less than 1,000 inhabitants. In 1970, 26.5 per cent of the population was in this category. Such a distribution makes it clear that the resident of the large city or its area of influence is the typical American and that the person living in one of the types of rural territory described above has the second best claim to such a distinction. Those who live in the nation's "Littletowns" and "Middletowns," on the other hand, definitely are in third place. This point is further emphasized by an examination of the data for the urban places lying outside of the urbanized areas. Collectively the 3,840 places in this category contained only 30,878,364 inhabitants or 15.2 per cent of the nation's population. Of this total the proportions corresponding to these smaller urban centers of various sizes are as follows: places of 25,000 or more, 3.4 per cent; places of 10,000 to 24,999, 4.8 per cent; places of 5,000 to 9,999, 3.8 per cent; and places of 2,500 to 4,999, 3.2 per cent.

REGIONAL AND STATE DIFFERENCES

As is well known, within the United States the relative importance of the urban, rural-nonfarm, and rural-farm portions of the population varies tremendously. (See Table 6 and Figure 7.) Whereas in California 90.9 per cent, in New Jersey 88.9 per cent, in Rhode Island 87.1 per cent, and in New York 85.6 per cent of the population in 1970 was classified as urban, in Vermont, West Virginia, North Dakota, and Mississippi well under half of the inhabitants were placed in the urban category, the exact percentages being 32.2, 39.0, 44.3, and 44.5, respectively. Massachusetts (84.6 per cent) ranked fifth from the top in percentage of urban population and South Dakota (44.6 per cent) fifth from the bottom in this respect. With the exception of Indiana, all of the states extending eastward from Illinois to Massachusetts were more than seven-tenths urban, as were Hawaii, Nevada, Florida, Utah, Texas, Arizona, Colorado, Maryland, Ohio, Michigan, Washington, and Missouri. In general the southeastern states, with the exception of Florida, and the northern plains and mountain states, along with Iowa, make up the most highly rural parts of the nation, whereas the northeastern area, except for the northernmost part of New England, part of the region around the Great Lakes, California, the Southwest, and peninsular Florida, constitute the most urbanized sections. (See Figure 1 in Chapter 3 for geographic distribution of the population.) In 1970, the seven states having the largest urban populations together contained 50 per cent of the nation's urban total. These states and the urban populations of each are as follows: California, 18,136,045; New York, 15,602,486; Illinois, 9,229,821; Texas, 8,920,946; Pennsylvania, 8,430,410; Ohio, 8,025,775; and Michigan, 6,553,773.

In 1970, the rural-nonfarm population was more than five times as large as the rural-farm group and totaled 45,586,707 or 22.4 per cent of the nation's population. The number and relative importance of these people in the various states are shown in Table 6. In Vermont, 61.9 per cent of the 1970 population fell into the rural-nonfarm class, and it was most closely rivaled in this respect by West Virginia (57.7 per cent) and Alaska (50.8 per cent). In none of these states were cities of 50,000 or more inhabitants sufficiently numerous for large numbers of persons to be residing in the urban fringes. However, at the other end of the scale the situation was quite different. The states with the smallest proportions of their populations in the rural-nonfarm category are those with populations most highly concentrated in large cities and the areas adjacent to them. Thus, in 1970, the states with the lowest percentages of the population classified as rural-nonfarm were as follows: California, 8.2; New Jersey, 10.6; Rhode Island, 12.8; Illinois, 13.1; New York, 13.4; Massachusetts, 15.1; Hawaii, 16.2; and Texas, 16.8. Yet many of these same states have relatively large numbers of rural-nonfarm people. Twelve of them taken together accounted for 51 per cent of the rural-nonfarm population of the United States in 1970. These are as follows: Pennsylvania, 3,141,289; New York, 2,441,877; North Carolina, 2,421,846; Ohio, 2,257,727; Michigan, 2,042,377; Texas, 1,880,724; Georgia, 1,651,447; California, 1,635,124; Virginia, 1,524,556; Illinois, 1,458,822; Indiana, 1,448,069; and Tennessee, 1,300,163. A perusal of the list will suggest the extremely heterogeneous nature of the rural-nonfarm category. In Virginia, for example, the total group is made up of some persons who reside in suburbs not far from the nation's capital but outside of its urban fringe, others who inhabit small towns and villages scattered throughout the state, and still others who reside on small patches of land that are too small or unproductive to be classified officially as farms but who may have relatively little in common socially and economically with those residing in the "bedroom towns" of Washington, D.C.

In 1970, the rural-farm population of the United States totaled a mere 8,292,150 and made up only 4.1 per cent of the nation's inhabitants. The manner in which they were distributed among the states is shown in Table 6. Especially noteworthy are the high concentrations in certain parts of the South (particularly the Mississippi Delta, the tidewater areas of the Carolinas and Virginia, and Appalachia), the rather heavy and regular distribution throughout the Midwest, and the sparsity of farm residents in the western Great Plains, the Rocky Mountain area, northern New England and New York, and in Florida. Nevertheless, only in North Dakota, South Dakota, Iowa, Nebraska, Idaho, Kentucky, Minnesota, Montana, and Kansas did the rural-farm population make up more than one-tenth of the inhabitants and in no case were they as much as one-quarter of the total. Eleven states taken together contained 53 per cent of the 1970 rural-farm population of the nation. They are as follows: Iowa, 512,371; Minnesota, 454,516; Illinois, 428,726; Wisconsin, 415,206; Texas, 386,174; Kentucky,

TABLE 6

Population of the various states by type of residence, 1970

State	Urbanized areas				Other urban		Rural-nonfarm[a]		Rural-farm[a]	
	Central cities		Urban fringe							
	Number	Per cent	Number	Per cent	Number	Per cent	Number	Per cent	Number	Per cent
United States	63,921,684	31.5	54,524,882	26.8	30,878,364	15.2	45,586,707	22.4	8,292,150	4.1
Alabama	881,825	25.6	398,500	11.6	731,616	21.2	1,271,951	36.9	159,641	4.6
Alaska	....	....	....	....	145,512	48.4	152,740	50.8	1,113	0.4
Arizona	844,495	47.7	313,046	17.7	251,323	14.2	339,546	19.2	23,273	1.3
Arkansas	334,396	17.4	44,228	2.3	582,241	30.3	787,162	40.9	173,677	9.0
California	7,267,139	36.4	8,880,631	44.5	1,988,275	10.0	1,635,124	8.2	184,875	0.9
Colorado	814,061	36.9	609,950	27.6	309,300	14.0	385,188	17.5	85,989	3.9
Connecticut	993,878	32.8	1,107,780	36.5	243,394	8.0	673,183	22.2	14,948	0.5
Delaware	80,386	14.7	269,288	49.1	45,895	8.4	141,583	25.8	11,360	2.1
District of Columbia	756,510	100.0	....	....	....	....	....	....	....	....
Florida	1,945,662	28.7	2,188,121	32.2	1,334,354	19.7	1,250,111	18.4	72,261	1.1
Georgia	1,024,400	22.3	855,760	18.6	887,914	19.3	1,651,447	36.0	171,544	3.7
Hawaii	324,871	42.3	117,526	15.3	196,286	25.5	124,878	16.2	5,933	0.8
Idaho	74,990	10.5	10,197	1.4	300,247	42.1	231,759	32.5	93,708	13.2
Illinois	4,285,814	38.6	3,587,968	32.3	1,356,039	12.2	1,458,822	13.1	428,726	3.9
Indiana	1,789,622	34.5	605,511	11.7	976,927	18.8	1,448,069	27.9	374,590	7.2
Iowa	631,666	22.4	210,488	7.5	774,251	27.4	695,180	24.6	512,371	18.1
Kansas	401,565	17.9	384,368	17.1	698,937	31.1	524,400	23.3	237,944	10.6
Kentucky	549,183	17.1	571,690	17.8	563,180	17.5	1,151,565	35.8	381,696	11.9
Louisiana	1,142,809	31.4	560,317	15.4	703,024	19.3	1,118,627	30.7	113,757	3.1
Maine	129,266	13.0	42,545	4.3	332,346	33.5	464,716	46.8	22,840	2.3

Maryland	905,759	23.1	1,683,160	42.9	415,016	10.6	855,116	21.8	62,385	1.6
Massachusetts	1,726,298	30.3	2,607,898	45.8	476,253	8.4	860,043	15.1	18,831	0.3
Michigan	2,468,063	27.8	3,190,780	36.0	894,930	10.1	2,042,377	23.0	277,529	3.1
Minnesota	928,411	24.4	973,423	25.6	625,474	16.4	823,895	21.7	454,516	11.9
Mississippi	243,245	11.0	77,347	3.5	666,050	30.0	1,019,277	46.0	210,323	9.5
Missouri	1,375,686	29.4	1,200,872	25.7	701,104	15.0	1,040,366	22.2	359,319	7.7
Montana	121,672	17.5	20,430	2.9	228,574	32.9	239,936	34.6	82,129	11.8
Nebraska	496,846	33.5	91,446	6.2	324,306	21.9	331,457	22.3	237,978	16.0
Nevada	198,650	40.6	137,718	28.2	58,968	12.1	85,801	17.6	7,716	1.6
New Hampshire	143,574	19.5	30,369	4.1	242,097	32.8	311,917	42.3	9,073	1.2
New Jersey	1,146,346	16.0	4,932,026	68.8	295,033	4.1	762,468	10.6	32,432	0.5
New Mexico	243,751	24.0	53,700	5.3	411,324	40.5	267,808	26.4	37,487	3.7
New York	9,311,018	51.1	4,956,786	27.2	1,334,682	7.3	2,441,877	13.4	190,659	1.0
North Carolina	955,746	18.8	256,686	5.1	1,072,736	21.1	2,421,846	47.7	374,692	7.4
North Dakota	53,365	8.6	55	b	220,022	35.6	191,858	31.1	152,261	24.5
Ohio	3,380,238	31.7	3,262,136	30.6	1,383,401	13.0	2,257,727	21.2	370,946	3.5
Oklahoma	761,540	29.8	287,532	11.2	691,065	27.0	642,862	25.1	175,349	6.9
Oregon	527,261	25.2	456,791	21.8	418,652	20.0	586,689	28.1	102,185	4.9
Pennsylvania	3,341,951	28.3	3,580,028	30.4	1,508,431	12.8	3,141,289	26.6	225,238	1.9
Rhode Island	339,891	35.9	405,347	42.8	79,692	8.4	121,206	12.8	2,359	0.2
South Carolina	241,695	9.3	407,741	15.7	582,759	22.5	1,247,095	48.1	111,528	4.3
South Dakota	72,488	10.9	3,518	0.5	220,622	33.2	206,147	31.0	162,730	24.5
Tennessee	1,353,336	34.5	135,288	3.4	816,683	20.8	1,300,163	33.1	316,817	8.1

TABLE 6 (Cont'd)

Population of the various states by type of residence, 1970

State	Urbanized areas				Other urban		Rural-nonfarm[a]		Rural-farm[a]	
	Central cities		Urban fringe							
	Number	Per cent	Number	Per cent	Number	Per cent	Number	Per cent	Number	Per cent
Texas	5,386,628	48.1	1,530,717	13.7	2,003,601	17.9	1,880,724	16.8	386,174	3.4
Utah	324,223	30.6	408,956	38.6	118,293	11.2	179,662	17.0	26,297	2.5
Vermont	....	....	....	....	142,889	32.2	275,031	61.9	26,427	5.9
Virginia	1,124,889	24.2	1,272,117	27.4	537,835	11.6	1,524,556	32.8	192,784	4.1
Washington	909,550	26.7	963,868	28.3	603,050	17.7	820,846	24.1	111,826	3.3
West Virginia	221,139	12.7	119,475	6.8	338,877	19.4	1,007,267	57.7	57,445	3.3
Wisconsin	1,345,887	30.5	720,758	16.3	843,773	19.1	1,093,074	24.7	415,206	9.4
Wyoming	....	....	....	....	201,111	60.5	100,276	30.2	31,263	9.4

Source: Compiled and computed from data in U.S. Bureau of the Census, *U.S. Census of Population: 1970, Number of Inhabitants,* Final Report PC(1)-A1, *United States Summary* (1971), p. 43, Table 4; Final Reports PC(1)-A2-A52, Reports for States, Table 2; *General Social and Economic Characteristics,* Final Report PC(1)-C1, *United States Summary* (1972), p. 359.

aThe rural population reflects corrected totals. In the total rural populations of the nation and the states the corrections are negligible but for the rural-nonfarm and rural-farm subdivisions they often are substantial. Therefore, it was deemed advisable to employ the corrected figures even though this produces a discrepancy of 0.02 per cent in the total rural population of the nation as reported at various places in this chapter.

bLess than 0.1 per cent.

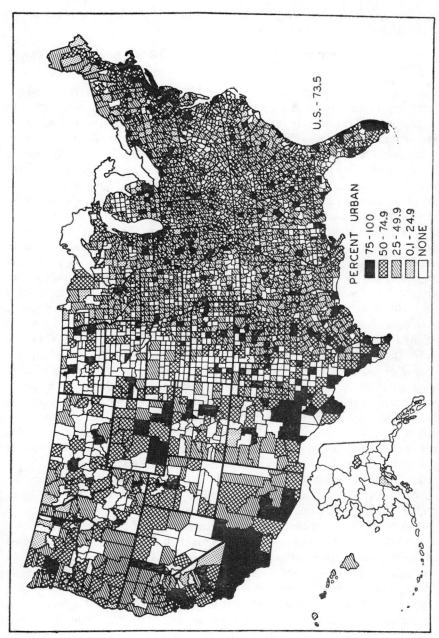

Figure 7. Relative importance of the urban population in the general population, by counties, 1970.

381,696; North Carolina, 374,692; Indiana, 374,590; Ohio, 370,946; Missouri, 359,319; and Tennessee, 316,817. In no state in 1970 did the rural-farm population exceed the urban or the rural-nonfarm populations.

TRENDS

From the time the first census was taken in 1790 there has been a strong and uninterrupted tendency for the population of the United States to concentrate in urban districts. (See Figure 8.) In the period after 1840 this tendency was most pronounced in the decade ending in 1920, during which the rate of population increase in the urban centers was 9.06 times as high as that in the rural portions of the nation. It was least pronounced in the ten-year period that opened with the great economic depression, 1930 to 1940, when the urban population grew at a rate of only 1.23 times that of the rural. The years 1920 to 1930, when the rate of urban population increase was 6.2 times as high as that of the rural, most closely rivaled the preceding intercensal period in the extent to which urban population gains outstripped the rural; whereas the period ending in 1950, in which the urban population increased only 2.47 times as fast as the rural is the second lowest in this respect. Between 1950 and 1960, the urban population increased 3.10 times as fast as the rural. Changes in the other decades from 1840 to 1960 are as follows: 1840 - 1850, rate of increase of the urban population 3.16 times as high as that of the rural; 1850 - 1860, 2.65; 1860 - 1870, the period of the Civil War, 4.36; 1880 - 1890, 4.22; 1890 - 1900, 2.98; and 1900 - 1910, 4.37. These comparisons are on the basis of the "old" definition of urban, employed exclusively through the census of 1940 and for comparative purposes in those of 1950 and 1960. In presenting the results of the 1970 census, however, the Bureau of the Census used only the "new" definition of urban. Changes in the relative importance of the urban and rural populations based upon that definition are as follows: between 1950 and 1960, the urban population grew 29.3 per cent but the rural declined 0.8 per cent; between 1960 and 1970, the urban population increased 19.2 per cent and the rural decreased 0.3 per cent. In the latter decade, the urban group expanded by 24,056,180 persons and the rural declined by 167,429, making it the smallest rural population since 1920. The urban population was, of course, the largest in the nation's history.

Obviously, there are tremendous differences among the regions and the states with respect to the comparative rates of growth in the urban and rural segments of the population. In order to explore this aspect of the subject, a detailed study was made of the trends over the forty years between 1930 and 1970. The basic situation in each of the states is shown in Figure 9, in which the circle to the left represents the population in 1930, that to the right the increase (or decrease) in population between 1930 and 1970. The shading in each circle represents the relative importance of the rural and urban segments in the total population. In

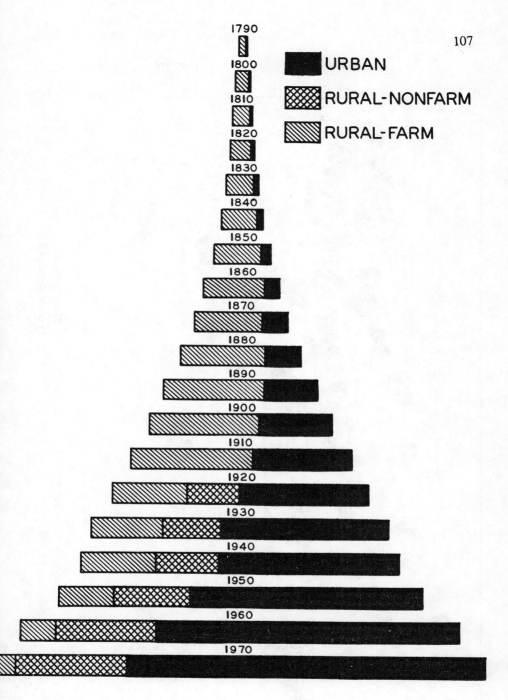

Figure 8. The growth of population in the United States, by residence, 1790 to 1970. The "old" definition of urban applies in years prior to 1950, the "new" definition in 1950 and thereafter.

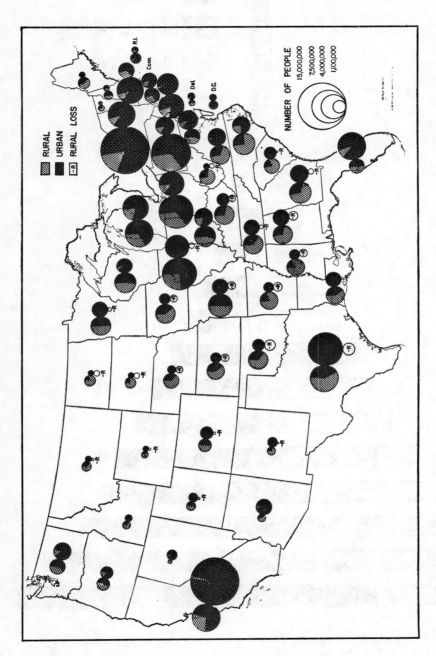

Figure 9. Changes in the rural and urban populations of the United States, by states, 1930 to 1970. The circle on the left represents the population in 1930, that on the right the increase (or decrease) in population between 1930 and 1970.

these four decades, the urban population of the nation increased 116 per cent and the rural decreased 0.3 per cent. The rate of increase of the urban population in the West was the greatest (301 per cent), followed by those in the South (214 per cent), the North Central (81 per cent), and the Northeast (48 per cent). The rural population, however, increased in the Northeast (24 per cent) and the West (16 per cent) and decreased in the South (11 per cent) and the North Central (1 per cent). No state had a smaller urban population in 1970 than it had in 1930, and percentage increases range from lows of 20 in Vermont, 26 in Massachusetts, 29 in Pennsylvania, 30 in Rhode Island, and 38 in West Virginia, to highs of 1,756 in Alaska,[20] 1,047 in Nevada, 840 in Arizona, 620 in Florida, and 564 in New Mexico. Most of these states had comparatively small urban populations in 1930, but this should not discount the significance of the rates at which they are urbanizing. On the other hand, twenty-five states had smaller rural populations in 1970 than in 1930. These decreases ranged from 48 per cent in Oklahoma to 1 per cent in South Carolina.

There are substantial differences in the rates of change of the urban population by size of place. In general, however, the major cities located in the Northeast and the North Central regions have grown more slowly than those in the West and certain parts of the South. (See Figure 10.) Notable among the last are Atlanta, a few cities in Virginia, and several in Florida and Texas. Furthermore, the cities that have grown the fastest are neither the largest nor the smallest. Between 1930 and 1970, the population of cities with 1 million or more inhabitants increased only 25 per cent, that in places with 100,000 to 999,999 inhabitants increased 76 per cent, that in centers of 10,000 to 99,999 grew 154 per cent, and that in places of 2,500 to 9,999 expanded 97 per cent. Many of the smaller cities, of course, are tributary to larger ones, but no matter what their placement, they are experiencing the greater rates of increase. The comparatively slow growth of the largest urban centers is further illustrated by comparing rates of increase of the central cities and the urban fringes of urbanized areas. This is only possible for the period from 1950 to 1970, but during that time the total population residing in urbanized areas increased 71 per cent, that in the central cities grew only 32 per cent, and that in the urban fringes expanded 161 per cent.

Because the rural population as of 1970 used in some of the above comparisons includes such large numbers of those classified as urban under the new definition, it would be well to consider the recent trends in the rural-farm population. However, this category too was influenced significantly by the changes in definition of a farm introduced in the 1959 census of agriculture and used in the 1960 and 1970 censuses of population. For that reason, it is well to examine the trends which existed prior to 1950 as well as those from 1950 to 1970.

In 1940, the rural-farm population of the United States numbered 30,216,188 men, women, and children, a total corresponding almost exactly to that enumerated in 1930, 30,157,513. By 1950, however, the number of persons in this

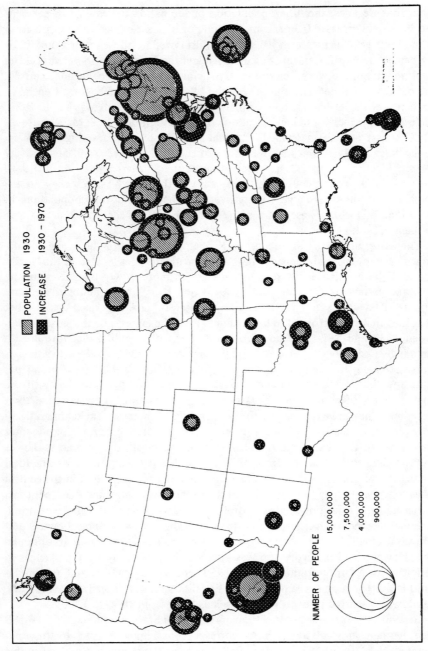

Figure 10. Growth of the major cities in the United States, 1930 to 1970.

category had fallen to 23,076,539, a decrease of 7,139,649 or 23.6 per cent from the figure for 1940. On a relative basis, the rural-farm population fell from 24.6 per cent of the total in 1930 to 23.3 per cent in 1940 and to 15.3 per cent in 1950. Furthermore, in every one of the forty-eight states there were fewer persons in the rural-farm category in 1950 than in 1940. Between 1950 and 1960, under the new definition of a farm, the rural-farm population fell from 23,076,539 to 13,444,898 persons, a decrease of 9,631,641 or 41.7 per cent. In the 1960's, it declined to 8,292,150 persons, the decrease amounting to 5,152,748 persons or 38.3 per cent. Some of the reduction after 1950 was due to changes in the definition of a farm, but even so one could hardly ask for more convincing data relative to the extent to which the nation is urbanizing. Moreover, these trends are so pervasive that the four major regions and the fifty states all lost rural-farm population during the 1960 - 1970 decade. The proportional loss was greatest in the South (50 per cent), followed by the Northeast (41 per cent), the West (35 per cent), and the North Central (26 per cent). In the states, the greatest rate of loss was in South Carolina (68 per cent), followed by Mississippi (61 per cent), Alabama (60 per cent), Georgia (58 per cent), and North Carolina (54 per cent). The lowest rate was in South Dakota (21 per cent), followed by Montana (22 per cent), and Minnesota, Iowa, and Indiana (23 per cent each).

In evaluating the changes in the rural-farm population, it should be stressed that increasingly large proportions of those residing on tracts of land that are classified as farms do not receive the bulk of their income from agricultural activities. This general impression is supported by the data showing the occupational classification of the employed male members of the labor force in 1940 and 1970. According to these, of the male labor force resident on farms in 1940, 56.1 per cent was employed as farmers or farm managers and 26.7 per cent as farm laborers or foremen. By 1970 the comparable proportions were down to 39.3 per cent and 9.5 per cent, respectively. Both sets of data make it evident that the farm population is by no means synonymous with that engaged in agriculture. These materials also support the fact that many persons who have moved to farms in recent decades have done so for residential rather than business purposes. This is part of the larger process of homogenization of society in the United States, in which such factors as migrations, transplantation, borrowing, and others bring about an intermingling of populations, societal patterns, and cultural traits and thereby create a greater heterogeneity in the composition of society in each given locality while at the same time they are reducing the differences between any two segments of the general society. In other words, it is the bringing about of a situation in which all of the sociocultural components are more evenly distributed throughout the entire social body.

Before closing this chapter, reference should be made to the rate of population growth in the areas that were classified as rural-nonfarm territory. Between 1950 and 1960, this segment of the population increased by 30.2 per cent, doing so much more rapidly than the total and the urban populations. Between 1960 and 1970, however, the rate decreased and the rural-nonfarm group expanded by only 10.9 per cent as compared with 13.3 per cent for the total and 19.2 for the urban populations, although the reduction in the rate of increase of the rural-nonfarm segment is partly due to the fact that many persons residing in the fringes of large cities were redefined as urban in the 1970 census. The four major regions all gained rural-nonfarm inhabitants during the decade, with the Northeast and the South increasing by 12 per cent, the North Central by 11 per cent, and the West by only 2 per cent. Forty-two states had larger rural-nonfarm populations in 1970 than in 1960, the greatest percentage increases occurring in Vermont (44), New Hampshire (33), Connecticut (28), Mississippi (25), and Wisconsin (25). Eight of the states lost rural-nonfarm population during the 1960's. Their names and percentage decreases are California (9.7), Hawaii (9.4), North Dakota (6.6), West Virginia (2.1), Nebraska (1.5), Kansas (0.9), South Dakota (0.7), and Utah (0.2). In the 1950's, the growth of this segment of the population was by far the most important of the several residence changes that were going on, but in the 1960's it yielded in significance to urbanization, especially in the middle-sized cities. The suburbs surrounding urban centers of all sizes continue to mushroom, but as we move toward the last two decades of the century, the growth of cities and their spheres of influence is probably the most fundamental residence factor conditioning American society and culture.

1. Cf. T. Lynn Smith and Paul E. Zopf, Jr., *Principles of Inductive Rural Sociology* (Philadelphia: F. A. Davis Company, 1970), Chap. 2; T. Lynn Smith and C. A. McMahan, *The Sociology of Urban Life* (New York: The Dreyden Press, 1951), pp. 42 - 58; and T. Lynn Smith, "Rural Sociology: A Trend Report and Bibliography," *Current Sociology*, VI, 1 (1957), pp. 5 - 7.

2. See Paul E. Zopf, Jr., *North Carolina: A Demographic Profile* (Chapel Hill: University of North Carolina Population Center, 1967), pp. 118 - 119.

3. Cf. Adna Ferrin Weber, *The Growth of Cities in the Nineteenth Century* (New York: Columbia University Press, 1899), p. 14.

4. Conselho Nacional de Geografia, *Resolucao N. 3, de 29 de Marco de 1938* (Rio de Janeiro: Directoria de Estatistica de Producao, 1938), pp. 7 - 8.

5. J. D. B. DeBow, *Statistical View of the United States . . . Being a Compendium of the Seventh Census. . . .* (Washington: Beverley Tucker, Senate Printer, 1854), p. 192.

6. (Washington: Government Printing Office, 1874).

7. U. S. Bureau of the Census, *U. S. Census of Population: 1970, Number of Inhabitants*, Final Report PC(1)-A1, *United States Summary* (Washington: Government Printing Office, 1971), p. IX.

8. U. S. Bureau of the Census, *U. S. Census of Population: 1950*, Vol. I, *Number of Inhabitants* (Washington: Government Printing Office, 1952), p. XIV.

9. *U. S. Census of Population: 1970, op. cit.*, p. XII.

10. *Ibid.*

11. *Ibid.*, p. IX.

12. *Ibid.*, p. XIII.

13. See U. S. Bureau of the Budget, *Standard Metropolitan Statistical Areas: 1967* (Washington: Government Printing Office, 1968).

14. *U. S. Census of Population: 1970, op. cit.*, p. XIV.

15. U. S. Bureau of the Census, *U. S. Census of Population: 1970, General Social Economic Characteristics*, Final Report PC(1)-C1, *United States Summary* (Washington: Government Printing Office, 1972), p. App-2.

16. Cf. T. Lynn Smith, *Population Analysis* (New York: McGraw-Hill Book Company, 1948), p. 28.

17. *Demographic Yearbook, 1948* (Lake Success, New York: United Nations, 1949), pp. 18 and 213 - 229.

18. See Statistical Office of the United Nations, *Demographic Yearbook, 1967* (New York: United Nations, 1968), pp. 206 - 230, Table 6.

19. Includes 100,651 persons classified as rural within extended cities.

20. 1929 to 1970.

BEALE, CALVIN L. "Rural Depopulation in the United States: Some Demographic Consequences of Agricultural Adjustments," in *Population and Society*, edited by Charles B. Nam, pp. 415 - 423. Boston: Houghton Mifflin Company, 1968.

BOGUE, DONALD J. *Principles of Demography*, Chap. 15. New York: John Wiley & Sons, Inc., 1969.

DAVIS, KINGSLEY. "The Origin and Growth of Urbanization in the World," in *Population and Society*, edited by Charles B. Nam, pp. 407 - 415. Boston: Houghton Mifflin Company, 1968.

DAVIS, KINGSLEY. *World Urbanization, 1950 - 1970*, Vol. I. Berkeley: Institute of International Studies, 1969.

HATHAWAY, DALE E., J. ALLAN BEEGLE, and W. KEITH BRYANT. *People of Rural America* (A 1960 Census Monograph), Chaps. I and II. Washington: Government Printing Office, 1968.

HAWLEY, AMOS H. "World Urbanization: Trends and Prospects," in *Population: The Vital Revolution*, edited by Ronald Freedman, Chap. 5. New York: Doubleday & Co., Inc. (Anchor Books), 1964.

PETERSEN, WILLIAM. *Population*, 2nd ed., Chap. 8. New York: The Macmillan Company, 1969.

SHRYOCK, HENRY S., JACOB S. SIEGEL, and associates. *The Methods and Materials of Demography*, Vol. 1, Chap. 6. Washington: Government Printing Office, 1971.

SMITH, T. LYNN. *Brazil: People and Institutions*, 4th ed., Chap. XXV. Baton Rouge: Louisiana State University Press, 1972.

SMITH, T. LYNN. "The Emergence of Cities," in *The Urban South*, edited by Rupert B. Vance and Nicholas J. Demerath, Chap. 2. Chapel Hill: University of North Carolina Press, 1954.

SMITH, T. LYNN. *Studies of the Great Rural Tap Roots of Urban Poverty in the United States*. New York: Carlton Press, 1974.

SMITH, T. LYNN, and HOMER L. HITT. *The People of Louisiana*, Chap. III. Baton Rouge: Louisiana State University Press, 1952.

SMITH, T. LYNN, and PAUL E. ZOPF, JR. *Principles of Inductive Rural Sociology*, Chap. 3. Philadelphia: F. A. Davis Company, 1970.

TAEUBER, CONRAD, and IRENE B. TAEUBER. *People of the United States in the 20th Century* (A 1960 Census Monograph), Chaps. II and XV. Washington: Government Printing Office, 1971.

UNITED NATIONS. *Demographic Yearbook, 1967,* Chap. I. New York: United Nations, 1968.

UNITED NATIONS. *Growth of the World's Urban and Rural Population, 1920 - 2000.* New York: United Nations, 1969.

ZOPF, PAUL E., JR. *North Carolina: A Demographic Profile*, Chap. V. Chapel Hill: University of North Carolina Population Center, 1967.

5

RACE, COLOR, ETHNIC STOCK,

AND NATIVITY

Of all the features that distinguish one population from another, or different segments of a given population from one another, the characteristics variously known as race, color, ethnic stock or affiliation, and nativity are among the most obvious. At most times and places throughout the historical period, they also have been the attributes to which people in general have attached the most significance. Perhaps at some future date the reservations which most of those working in the fields of anthropology, psychology, and sociology have with respect to the validity of reputed innate differences in the intelligence and capabilities of the various racial and ethnic subgroups of mankind may gain popular acceptance. If so, possibly many of the causes of tension and turmoil during the twentieth century will be removed; but as these lines are written, as we move well along into the space age and men land on the moon, the prospects of any such development in the decades immediately ahead do not appear bright.

Many modern censuses, including that of the United States, use a classification of the population by race (or color) and nativity as one of the primary subdivisions in their tabulations of the data. In the United States, as indicated in the previous chapter, only the rural-urban differentiation takes precedence over this fundamental breakdown. This is sound procedure, for so great are the differences between the cultural backgrounds and the economic status of the native-born and the foreign-born and of the white and nonwhite races that considerable differentials in their birth rates, mortality rates, mobility, levels of education, and other social indexes are generated. Usually it is a waste of time to attempt comparisons of any demographic phenomenon in one region with that in another, in rural and urban areas, or of the same population at two different points of time, unless the data are first subdivided according to race (or color) and nativity. This is especially true in countries such as Brazil, Colombia, Peru, and the United States, where the various racial groups are unevenly distributed among the regions, where the rural populations contain different proportions of the colored races than the urban, and where the racial composition of the population is undergoing considerable change. For example, in the United States, there is very little value in the comparison of a southern state, such as South Carolina, with a northern one, such as Wisconsin, unless the comparisons are made separately for the white and Negro populations with each further subdivided according to rural or urban residence. To do otherwise is likely to demonstrate nothing more than that the former is the home of large numbers of rural Negroes, a fact that is well known and which may be demonstrated very simply.

CONCEPTS AND CLASSIFICATIONS

The 1970 census of the United States employed a three-way classification as the basis for all further subdivisions having to do with race, color, ethnic stock, and nativity. The fundamental categories are *white, Negro and other races,* and *Negro.* This represents a substantial improvement over the 1960 enumeration, in which the dichotomy of *white* and *nonwhite* was the essential classification, with relatively few data reported separately for the Negro population. Some materials collected in 1970 also include cross-classifications for *native* and *foreign-born* persons, and in a few cases for *Indians, Japanese, Chinese, Filipinos,* and *all others.* In addition, for the first time in 1970, several subjects were reported separately for *persons of Spanish heritage,* although a more rudimentary form of this distinction was used previously. In the cross-tabulations of such data with those for residence, age, employment status, and other characteristics, however, the division is almost invariably according to white, Negro and other races, and Negro. Similarly, in the reports for the various states, this racial classification is most generally employed in furnishing the detailed statistics for counties and other units, although some separate tables give information for Indians, Japanese, Chinese, and Filipinos and for persons of Spanish heritage in selected counties and cities.

As with the definition of rural and urban, it is essential to emphasize that the racial classifications employed by the modern census do not correspond with those developed by the scientists most concerned with the subject. For example, many of the persons classified as Negro for census purposes possess few of the physiological features that would be used by the zoologist or the anthropologist to distinguish Negroids from the other principal racial divisions of mankind. Strictly speaking, social and cultural criteria are the ones employed. In the words employed in the census reports themselves:

The concept of race as used by the Census Bureau does not denote clear-cut scientific definitions of biological stock. Rather, it reflects self-identification by respondents. Since the 1970 census obtained the information on race principally through self-enumeration, the data represent essentially self-classification by people according to the race with which they identify themselves.

For persons of mixed parentage who were in doubt as to their classification, the race of the person's father was used. In 1960, persons who reported mixed parentage of white and any other race were classified according to the other race; mixtures of races other than white were classified according to the race of the father. [1]

Expanding upon the racial identifications, the report states:

The category "Negro" includes persons who indicated their race as Negro or Black, as well as some persons who did not classify themselves in one of the specific race categories on the questionnaire but who had such entries as Jamaican, Trinidadian, West Indian, and Ethiopian.

The category "Indian" includes persons who indicated their race as American Indian or who reported for this item only the name of an Indian tribe. [2]

It should be stressed, however, that the more precise definitions of race, those based upon three or more physical characteristics such as color, height, and the cephalic index, hardly would be practicable for census purposes.

The division of the white population according to nativity into the native-born and the foreign-born categories is another of the threads that runs through a considerable part of the tabulations prepared in connection with the census of population in the United States. These concepts, though, are too self-evident to require definition. Similar classifications are employed in the census reports in many other countries. In several U. S. censuses, and particularly those for 1930 and earlier, the division of the native white population into persons of native parentage and those of foreign or mixed parentage occupied a prominent place, but as the foreign-born stocks have decreased in importance this feature has been relegated to a position of minor importance.

Ethnic stocks or affiliations are terms applied to groups of mankind discriminated on the basis of common customs and characteristics. When one refers to an ethnic group, all connotations of physiological uniformities are not necessarily ruled out, but certainly they occupy a position of secondary importance to those such zoological features have when the concept of race is employed. As will be indicated below, in some countries considerable use is made of ethnic classifications of the population. Yugoslavia is a case in point, with the population classified into categories such as Serbs, Croats, and Slovenes, in addition to those, such as Hungarians, Czechs, Poles, and so forth, which indicate cultural and nationality affiliations with other large groups not mainly resident within Yugoslavia itself. In the United States, comparatively little has been done, in connection with the census, to secure demographic data separately for such important ethnic groups as the Pennsylvania Dutch, the Louisiana French, or the Mexican-American people of the Southwest. In 1940, 1950, and 1960, however, special or subject reports did supply information about the languages spoken in the home and mother tongue, which is of some value for one interested in ethnic stocks, and for 1960 a subject report was published giving considerable detail about persons of Spanish surname. In addition, seven *Subject Reports* from the 1970 census deal in great detail with national origin, language, and race. Various minority races and Spanish-speaking groups are accorded a particularly important place in these compilations.[3]

INTERNATIONAL COMPARISONS

Anything resembling a definitive classification of the world's population, country by country, according to race or ethnic affiliation, is still to be done. In a general way it is known that the bulk of the population in China, Japan, and some of the neighboring countries belongs to the Mongoloid or yellow varieties of mankind, that Europe is peopled mainly by those of the Caucasoid or white races, that the population of India is the result of a blending over a long period of various white and nonwhite races, that Africa and Australia originally were the homes of Negroid or black peoples, and that the Americas were occupied at the time of Columbus' discovery by various copper-colored stocks whom he designated as Indians and who are commonly referred to as redmen. Known also is the fact that persons of European stocks supplanted the natives in many parts of the New World, including Canada, the United States, Costa Rica, Argentina, and Uruguay, and that they came to dominate politically and economically, if not numerically, most other sections of the Americas. Known, finally, is something of the extent to which the Europeans, in the dominant roles they occupied in world affairs from the sixteenth to the twentieth centuries, forcibly transplanted the Negroes from Africa to various parts of the New World, persons from India to South Africa and Trinidad, and workers of various colors and hues from many sections of the world to plantation areas in the West Indies, Hawaii, and elsewhere. But anything resembling a summary statement of the racial or ethnic composition of the world's population is still to be developed.

Not until the eighth issue of the *Demographic Yearbook*[4] did those responsible for the collection and collation of international demographic statistics turn their attention to racial and ethnic classifications employed in the various countries of the world; and the results they were able to assemble reveal how much is still lacking in this respect, particularly uniformity. These subjects were emphasized again in the 1963 issue and supplemented in that for 1964, and they appeared once more in the 1971 edition. A brief summary of the types of data secured and published in these four invaluable compendia should serve to establish the present status of attempts in this field.

Not surprising, perhaps, is the extent to which censuses in various parts of Africa have supplied information relating to the racial and ethnic composition of the population. Many of the countries provide listings of tribal populations, generally under the heading "African population." Among those notable for the detail of their efforts are Gabon, Gambia, Ghana, Guinea, Kenya, Niger, Senegal, Sudan, Togo, Uganda, the United Republic of Tanzania, and Upper Volta. Several others have attempted less detailed racial and ethnic classifications, generally involving the following groups: white or European; African, Bantu, or Negro; colored; Asiatic; and mixed. They are Botswana, Lesotho, Malawi, Namibia, Nigeria, South Africa, Southern Rhodesia, Swaziland, and Zambia. In some cases, the classifications are greatly affected by official policies concerning the races and some designations may carry considerable stigma. The few African countries which continue to be the possessions or territories of European nations tend to have less detailed classifications of their populations on the basis of race and ethnicity. Often the only distinction made is between Africans and non-Africans, although variations of "mixed" occasionally appear.

For America, too, on the basis of censuses taken between 1945 and 1971, those preparing the *Yearbook* were able to secure some kind of ethnic or racial classification on the population for a number of countries. In addition to the materials for the United States, already discussed, others were secured for Barbados, Canada, Costa Rica, Cuba, the Dominican Republic, Guatemala, Honduras, Jamaica, Trinidad and Tobago, Bolivia, Brazil, Guyana, and Surinam. In Canada, the basic division is into thirty-six ethnic groups identified by the language spoken by the paternal ancestor on first arrival on the North American continent. In most of the Latin American countries, some designations for white, black, Indian, and the mixed groups usually appear, with the last sometimes provided in considerable detail. In addition, some of the countries provide classifications by national origin.

For all of Asia, the four pertinent issues of the *Demographic Yearbook* include racial and ethnic classifications for only eleven major political entities. They are Bahrain, Brunei, Burma, Ceylon, Cyprus, Sabah and Sarawak in East Malaysia, Mongolia, the Philippines, Singapore, Thailand, and the Democratic Republic of Viet-Nam. The classifications of most of these countries are extremely detailed compendia usually based on ethnicity, but sometimes involving major races and subraces as well.

Most European countries are inhabited almost exclusively by those of the Caucasoid races, so it is not strange that few of their censuses include racial or ethnic classifications in the tabulations. Only Albania, Bulgaria, Romania, the Vatican, and Yugoslavia figure in the compilations under discussion in these paragraphs. Virtually all of the classifications are based upon national origin, frequently in considerable detail.

In Oceania, apart from several island countries with fewer than 10,000 inhabitants, Australia, the British Solomon Islands, Fiji, French Polynesia, the Gilbert and Ellice Islands (United Kingdom), New Caledonia (France), the New Hebrides

(France and the United Kingdom), New Zealand, Tonga, and Western Samoa figure in the list of countries included in the United Nations compilations of data on race and national origin. In most cases, both racial and ethnic categories are prominent, although the latter tend to be the most comprehensive. In a number of cases, materials for mixtures of various groups are accorded an important place in the tabulations.

The vast Soviet Union, as reported in its 1970 census, consists of almost 100 separate groups designated according to "ethnic nationality." Each of twenty-two of them contained at least one million persons.

For all of the countries and groups or categories mentioned above, some fairly recent statistical information is available. However, for many of the more thickly populated parts of the world the data are completely lacking; and there is little comparability in the approach, criteria, or classifications for the countries and territories that it was possible to include. Distinctions comparable to those made by some of the countries would be legion if they were attempted for such nations as China or India; and even within small countries such as Belgium, Switzerland, or Czechoslovakia, several fairly distinct ethnic groups are to be found. It is to be hoped that those in charge of making the compilations for the *Demographic Yearbook* will continue their efforts to assemble and present comprehensive international statistics on race, nativity, and ethnic affiliations, although relatively little was done after 1964.

COLOR, RACE, AND NATIVITY OF THE POPULATION OF THE UNITED STATES

From the tabulations of the United States Census it is possible to determine in great detail the color or racial composition and the nativity of the population. The most recent count, that for 1970, showed a white population of 177,748,975 and a nonwhite population of 25,462,951; or 87.5 per cent of the inhabitants was classified as white and 12.5 per cent as Negro and other races (nonwhite). In 1960, the corresponding percentages were 88.6 and 11.4, respectively; in 1950, they were 89.5 and 10.5. Of the whites in 1970, a total of 169,015,205 fell in the native-white category and 8,733,770 in the foreign-born group; and of the nonwhites, 22,580,289 were classified as Negroes and 2,882,662 as belonging to other races. The latter were subdivided as follows: Indian, 792,730; Japanese, 591,290; Chinese, 435,062; Filipino, 343,060; and all other, 720,520. On the relative basis, 83.2 per cent of the total population was classified as native white, 4.3 per cent as foreign-born white, 11.1 per cent as Negro, and 1.4 per cent as belonging to other races.

Data showing the country of birth of the foreign-born white population are available and have been assembled in Table 7. Materials are included for the most recent census and for that of 1930, when the foreign-born white population of

TABLE 7

Country of birth of the foreign-born white population of
the United States, 1930 and 1970

Country of birth	1970		1930	
	Number	Per cent	Number	Per cent
All countries	8,773,770	100.0	13,983,405	100.0
Italy	1,005,687	11.5	1,790,424	12.8
Germany	830,498	9.5	1,608,814	11.5
Canada	798,782	9.1	1,278,512	9.2
Mexico	746,327	8.5	639,017	4.6
United Kingdom	681,140	7.8	1,402,044	10.0
Poland	547,010	6.3	1,268,583	9.1
U.S.S.R.	461,444	5.3	1,153,624	8.2
Cuba	425,974	4.9	31,600	0.2
Ireland	250,492	2.9	744,810	5.3
Austria	213,501	2.4	370,914	2.7
Hungary	182,681	2.1	274,450	2.0
Greece	176,025	2.0	174,526	1.2
Czechoslovakia	160,672	1.8	491,638	3.5
Yugoslavia	153,020	1.8	211,416	1.5
Sweden	126,843	1.5	595,250	4.3
Netherlands	109,709	1.3	133,133	1.0
France	104,491	1.2	135,265	1.0
Norway	96,938	1.1	347,852	2.5
Lithuania	75,806	0.9	193,606	1.4
Denmark	61,307	0.7	179,474	1.3
Switzerland	49,547	0.6	113,010	0.8
Other Europe	401,342	4.6	554,847	4.0
Other America	389,407	4.5	62,095	0.4
Asia	273,598	3.1	94,218	0.6
All other and not reported	411,529	4.7	134,283	1.0

Source: Compiled and computed from data in U.S. Bureau of the Census, *Sixteenth Census of the United States: 1940, Characteristics of the Population, United States Summary* (1943), p. 36, Table 14; *U.S. Census of Population: 1970, General Social and Economic Characteristics,* Final Report (PC(1)-C1, *United States Summary* (1972), pp. 382–383, Table 86.

the United States was at its largest. Foreign-born Negroes and members of other races are omitted because in 1970, they were less than one-tenth of the total foreign-born population. Notable is the large number of countries that have sent sizable contingents of white immigrants to the United States, even though in 1970 those born in Italy made up almost one-eighth of the foreign-born population. The 1970 census indicates that slightly over one-half of those born outside the United States came from six countries: Italy, Germany, Canada, Mexico, the United Kingdom, and Poland. Even greater were the numbers, proportions, and heterogeneity of the foreign-born population in 1930, the basic materials for which appear in Table 7 and which are analyzed more intensively below.

Rural-Urban Differences

It has long been known that the "foreign" elements in a given population tend to concentrate in the cities, whereas the "native" elements constitute relatively high proportions of the people of the rural areas.[5] The validity of this principle is illustrated excellently with data from the most recent census of population in the United States, although the materials from each of the earlier enumerations also might be used for this purpose. In 1970, in the country as a whole, only 1.3 per cent of the rural-farm and 1.8 per cent of the rural-nonfarm population were foreign-born, whereas 5.8 per cent of the urban population had been born in another country. If each residential category had contained precisely the same proportion of the foreign born as it did of the general population, it might be said to have had exactly its pro rata share of those born outside the United States. As it was, however, the percentages just given indicate that in 1970 the rural-farm population contained only 29 per cent, the rural-nonfarm population 36 per cent, and the urban population 123 per cent of their pro rata shares of the nation's foreign-born inhabitants. On the other hand, the same year the native-white population made up 81.2 per cent of the urban, 89.0 per cent of the rural-nonfarm, and 91.5 per cent of the rural-farm population, and the indexes of the extent to which each of these residential categories contained more or less than its pro rata share of this nativity group are 97, 107, and 110, respectively. The differences between the urban and the two rural populations in this respect reflect the degree to which the other large group of the native-born, the Negroes, are concentrated in the cities and are scarce in the suburbs and on the farms.

The data for the Negro portion of the native-born population are especially interesting. To a far greater extent than is true of the native-white population, the Negroes are the descendants of persons who have been in the United States for two centuries or more. Prior to the outbreak of the first World War they were largely concentrated in the rural sections of the nation's most rural region – the South. The labor shortage accompanying that war resulted in a mass transfer of Negro workers to northern cities, and the one produced by the second World War and its aftermath brought about their exodus in large numbers from the South to the cities of the Pacific Coast. For these reasons there is considerable validity in thinking of the Negro as a native element in the South and as a recent arrival in other sections of the country.[6] So great has been the migration of Negroes to the nation's cities that in 1970, their proportions in the urban, rural-nonfarm, and rural-farm populations were 12.3 per cent, 8.2 per cent, and 6.5 per cent, respectively. Since exactly 11.1 per cent of the nation's population in 1970 was classified as Negro, this indicates that the urban population contained 111 per cent, the rural-nonfarm population 79 per cent, and the rural-farm population only 59 per cent of their pro rata shares of the members of this racial group. Ten years earlier the comparable indexes were 106, 80, and 105. Even in the South, as defined by the Bureau of the Census, Negroes in 1970 were over-represented in the urban population, although to a lesser extent than was true in the other major regions. In the South, 64.6 per cent of the total population but 67.3 per cent of the Negro group were classified as urban. For the remainder of the United States, 97.7 per cent of the Negro population fell into the urban category. In the South, 27.3 per cent of the Negroes fell in the rural-nonfarm and 5.4 per cent in the rural-farm category in comparison with corresponding percentages of 2.6 and 0.3, respectively, in the rest of the nation. Expressed as the extent to which each of these residential groups contained more or less than its share of the area's Negro population, the indexes for the southern region are as follows: urban, 104; rural-nonfarm, 94; and rural-farm, 84. For all other sections of the country taken together, the comparable indexes are: urban, 132; rural-nonfarm, 12; and rural-farm, 6. All of this points up the rapid rate at which the nation's Negro population, including that of the South, has been urbanizing in the last few decades and the great speed at which the Negro farm population is diminishing.

The Geographic Distribution of the Race and Nativity Groups

The materials already presented make the vast differences in the manner in which the various race and nativity groups are distributed throughout the United States evident, but the subject deserves a much more complete treatment. Data showing the proportions that whites, Negroes, and members of other races constitute of the population of the fifty states and the District of Columbia have been assembled in Table 8. A few other of the most pertinent facts, especially those concerning the foreign-born, are presented as called for in the discussion that follows.

Because the foreign-born are highly concentrated in urban areas, a few of the states containing the nation's major cities also contain the majority of the foreign-born population. In fact, in 1970 ten states accounted for four-fifths of the total. To be specific, New York State alone contained 2,109,776, or 21.9 per cent of the total foreign-born population of the United States. This aggregate was at least three times as large as that for any other state except California, which counted 1,757,990 of the foreign-born among its inhabitants. Taken together, New York, California, New Jersey (634,818), and Illinois (628,898) contained 53 per cent of the nation's foreign-born population, and if the total (540,284) for the fifth-ranking state, Florida, is included, the proportion is swelled to 58.9 per cent. If, however, the relative importance of the foreign-born in the population is considered, then the five ranking states in the order named are New York, Hawaii, New Jersey, California, and Massachusetts. They have 247, 209, 189, 187, and 185 per cent, respectively, of their pro rata shares of the nation's foreign-born population. Comparable indexes for the ten largest cities are as follows: New York, 387; Chicago, 236; Los Angeles, 311; Philadelphia, 138; Detroit, 168; Houston, 64; Baltimore, 68; Dallas, 45; Washington, 94; and Indianapolis, 32.

It is interesting to note some of the other significant variations in the distribution of the foreign-born population among the nation's major cities. As suggested by the low indexes for Indianapolis, Dallas, Houston, Baltimore, and Washington, the sources from which the various cities have recruited their populations differ radically from one part of the country to another. In general, except in parts of Florida, the cities in the South have grown by attracting migrants from the rural areas surrounding them, whereas the industrial centers and great ports in the Northeast and the urban centers on the Pacific Coast have received many immigrants from other countries. On this point the tabulations showing the proportions of the foreign-born in the 156 cities of 100,000 or more inhabitants deserve careful study. The general rule is for cities located in the census South to have lower proportions, and those outside the region to have higher proportions of the foreign-born than is true for the nation as a whole. In the entire South only El Paso, Fort Lauderdale, Hialeah, Hollywood, Miami, St. Petersburg, San Antonio, and Tampa contain proportions of the foreign-born that are above the national average of 4.7 per cent. Six of them are Florida cities whose populations were swelled in the 1960's by large numbers of persons from Cuba. Outside the South, thirty-five cities had proportions below the national mean and sixteen of them had percentages that were less than half the national figure. They are Albuquerque, Cedar Rapids, Columbus, Dayton, Des Moines, Evansville, Fort Wayne, Independence, Indianapolis, Kansas City (Kansas), Kansas City (Missouri), Oklahoma City, Springfield (Missouri), Topeka, Tulsa, and Wichita. It is significant, however, that in 1960 only twenty-three non-Southern cities had less than their pro rata share of the nation's foreign-born. The change between 1960 and 1970 indicates both the decreasing statistical importance of the foreign-born and their tendency to concentrate in fewer large cities. In 1970, the highest percentage of foreign-born was in Miami (41.8),

TABLE 8

Changes in the racial composition of the population of the United States, by states, 1960 to 1970

Region and state	White		Negro		Other races		Per cent change, 1960 to 1970		
	Number	Per cent	Number	Per cent	Number	Per cent	White	Negro	Other
United States	177,748,975	87.5	22,580,289	11.1	2,882,662	1.4	11.9	19.7	78.0
New England	11,388,774	96.2	388,398	3.3	64,491	0.5	11.2	59.6	173.1
Maine	985,276	99.3	2,800	0.3	3,972	0.4	2.3	-15.6	49.5
New Hampshire	733,106	99.4	2,505	0.3	2,070	0.3	21.3	31.6	202.6
Vermont	442,553	99.6	761	0.2	1,016	0.2	13.7	46.6	276.3
Massachusetts	5,477,624	96.3	175,817	3.1	35,729	0.6	9.0	57.2	162.9
Rhode Island	914,757	96.6	25,338	2.7	6,630	0.7	9.1	38.2	171.3
Connecticut	2,835,458	93.5	181,177	6.0	15,074	0.5	17.0	68.6	279.8
Middle Atlantic	32,921,730	88.5	3,955,755	10.6	321,555	0.9	5.2	42.0	211.5
New York	15,834,090	86.8	2,168,949	11.9	233,928	1.3	3.6	53.0	201.0
New Jersey	6,349,908	88.6	770,292	10.7	47,964	0.7	14.6	49.6	271.7
Pennsylvania	10,737,732	91.0	1,016,514	8.6	39,663	0.3	2.7	19.2	214.5
East North Central	36,160,135	89.8	3,872,905	9.6	219,436	0.5	8.7	34.2	152.9
Ohio	9,646,997	90.6	970,477	9.1	34,543	0.3	8.3	23.4	225.8
Indiana	4,820,324	92.8	357,464	6.9	15,881	0.3	9.8	32.8	240.1
Illinois	9,600,381	86.4	1,425,674	12.8	87,921	0.8	6.5	37.4	163.0
Michigan	7,833,474	88.3	991,066	11.2	50,543	0.6	10.6	38.1	155.9
Wisconsin	4,258,959	96.4	128,224	2.9	30,548	0.7	10.4	72.0	66.7
West North Central	15,481,048	94.9	698,645	4.3	139,494	0.9	5.0	24.5	66.7
Minnesota	3,736,038	98.2	34,868	0.9	34,065	0.9	10.8	56.6	70.3
Iowa	2,782,762	98.5	32,596	1.2	9,018	0.3	2.0	28.6	159.6
Missouri	4,177,495	89.3	480,172	10.3	18,834	0.4	6.5	22.9	214.3
North Dakota	599,485	97.0	2,494	0.4	15,782	2.6	-3.2	221.0	30.1

TABLE 8 (Cont'd)

Changes in the racial composition of the population of the United States, by states, 1960 to 1970

Region and state	Population in 1970						Per cent change, 1960 to 1970		
	White		Negro		Other races		White	Negro	Other
	Number	Per cent	Number	Per cent	Number	Per cent			
South Dakota	630,333	94.7	1,627	0.2	33,547	5.0	-3.5	46.1	27.5
Nebraska	1,432,867	96.6	39,911	2.7	10,715	0.7	4.2	36.4	46.7
Kansas	2,122,068	94.5	106,977	4.8	17,533	0.8	2.1	17.0	106.3
South Atlantic	24,112,395	78.6	6,388,496	20.8	170,446	0.6	20.3	9.3	113.9
Delaware	466,459	85.1	78,276	14.3	3,369	0.6	21.4	29.0	163.8
Maryland	3,194,888	81.5	699,479	17.8	28,032	0.7	24.1	34.9	235.3
District of Columbia	209,272	27.7	537,712	71.1	9,526	1.3	-39.4	30.6	36.9
Virginia	3,761,514	80.9	861,368	18.5	25,612	0.6	19.7	5.5	210.5
West Virginia	1,673,480	95.9	67,342	3.9	3,415	0.2	-5.5	-24.7	275.3
North Carolina	3,901,767	76.8	1,126,478	22.2	53,814	1.1	14.8	0.9	31.7
South Carolina	1,794,430	69.3	789,041	30.5	7,045	0.3	15.7	-4.9	208.9
Georgia	3,391,242	73.9	1,187,149	25.9	11,184	0.2	20.4	5.8	239.2
Florida	5,719,343	84.2	1,041,651	15.3	28,449	0.4	40.7	18.3	279.7
East South Central	10,202,810	79.7	2,571,291	20.1	29,369	0.2	9.2	-4.7	138.8
Kentucky	2,981,766	92.6	230,793	7.2	6,147	0.2	5.7	6.9	189.4
Tennessee	3,293,930	83.9	621,261	15.8	8,496	0.2	10.6	5.9	245.4
Alabama	2,533,831	73.6	903,467	26.2	6,867	0.2	11.0	-7.8	140.1
Mississippi	1,393,283	62.8	815,770	36.8	7,859	0.4	11.0	-10.9	62.0
West South Central	16,104,903	83.4	3,010,174	15.6	205,483	1.1	14.3	8.7	121.2
Arkansas	1,565,915	81.4	352,445	18.3	4,935	0.3	12.2	9.3	176.9
Louisiana	2,541,498	69.8	1,086,832	29.8	12,976	0.4	14.9	4.6	112.7
Oklahoma	2,280,362	89.1	171,892	6.7	106,975	4.2	8.2	12.3	59.0
Texas	9,717,128	86.8	1,399,005	12.5	80,597	0.7	16.0	17.8	354.8

Mountain	7,798,087	94.2	180,382	2.2	303,093	3.7	19.7	46.4	39.3
Montana	663,043	95.5	1,995	0.3	29,371	4.2	1.9	36.0	30.2
Idaho	698,802	98.1	2,130	0.3	11,635	1.6	6.3	41.8	40.1
Wyoming	323,024	97.2	2,568	0.8	6,824	2.1	a	17.6	37.6
Colorado	2,112,352	95.7	66,411	3.0	28,496	1.3	24.2	66.1	115.0
New Mexico	915,815	90.1	19,555	1.9	80,630	7.9	4.6	14.6	38.5
Arizona	1,604,948	90.6	53,344	3.0	112,608	6.4	37.2	22.9	26.2
Utah	1,031,926	97.4	6,617	0.6	20,730	2.0	18.1	59.5	63.9
Nevada	448,177	91.7	27,762	5.7	12,799	2.6	70.1	105.9	53.3
Pacific	23,579,093	88.9	1,514,243	5.7	1,429,295	5.4	22.1	57.3	55.4
Washington	3,251,055	95.4	71,308	2.1	86,806	2.5	18.1	46.3	64.4
Oregon	2,032,079	97.2	26,308	1.3	32,998	1.6	17.3	45.1	78.2
California	17,761,032	89.0	1,400,143	7.0	791,959	4.0	22.9	58.4	109.4
Alaska	236,767	78.0	8,911	3.0	54,704	18.2	35.6	31.6	22.0
Hawaii	298,160	38.8	7,573	1.0	462,828	60.2	47.4	53.2	8.7

Source: Compiled and computed from data in U.S. Bureau of the Census, *U.S. Census of Population: 1960, General Population Characteristics,* Final Report PC(1)-1B, *United States Summary* (1961), p. 164, Table 56; *U.S. Census of Population: 1970, General Population Characteristics,* Final Report PC(1)-B1, *United States Summary* (1972), p. 293, Table 60.

aLess than 0.1 per cent.

followed by Hialeah (36.0), San Francisco (21.6), Elizabeth (20.6), and Passaic (18.9). The lowest proportion of all is that of 0.4 per cent in Jackson, Mississippi, and Macon, followed by 0.5 per cent in Chattanooga and Evansville, and 0.6 per cent in Shreveport.

An examination of Table 8 also makes apparent the tremendous variations found throughout the United States in the relative importance of Negroes in the population. In the District of Columbia, over 71 per cent of the inhabitants are Negroes, in Mississippi 37 per cent, in South Carolina 31 per cent, and in Louisiana 30 per cent. In Alabama, Georgia, and North Carolina, at least one out of every five persons is a Negro. On the other hand, in Vermont and South Dakota only 0.2 per cent of the population at the time of the 1970 census was classified as Negro, and in Maine, New Hampshire, Montana, and Idaho the proportion was 0.3 per cent. In absolute numbers, nine states had 1 million or more Negroes. New York, with 2,168,949 persons so classified had the largest group, followed by Illinois (1,425,674), California (1,400,143), Texas (1,399,005), Georgia (1,187,149), North Carolina (1,126,478), Louisiana (1,086,832), Florida (1,041,651), and Pennsylvania (1,016,514). Together these nine states had, in 1970, 52 per cent of the Negroes in the United States.

Within the states, too, the proportions of Negroes in the population vary tremendously from one county or minor civil division to another, and within a city the tendency is for the Negro population to be concentrated largely in a few well-defined areas. Both in rural and urban areas the practice is rather general of designating as a "black belt" the districts in which Negroes constitute the large majority of the population. Most noted of the urban sections inhabited almost exclusively by Negroes are a large portion of southside Chicago, Los Angeles' Watts district, and Harlem, a part of Manhattan borough in New York City. The great rural "black belts" are those portions of the "old South" in which early in the nineteenth century the most fertile lands were monopolized by large proprietors and the plantation system of agriculture was established to produce cotton, sugar cane, and rice. Slave labor was utilized almost exclusively in the monoculture of these large, highly commercialized estates, so that Negroes greatly outnumbered whites in the counties where the southern gentry established their dominions. As evidenced by the distribution of slaves in 1860 (see Figure 11), on the eve of the Civil War, the three principal "black belts" in the United States were (1) that extending along both sides of the Mississippi River, in the rich deltas of the Mississippi and Yazoo valleys, from Tennessee to the "sugar bowl" in Louisiana; (2) a large crescent-shaped area extending from northeastern Mississippi, through the central portions of Alabama and Georgia, and overspreading most of South Carolina; and (3) tidewater Virginia and the adjacent parts of North Carolina. In 1970, as delineated on the basis of the counties in which 50 per cent or more of the inhabitants were Negroes, the major "black belts" were the first two of the three just mentioned. (See Figure 12.) These are

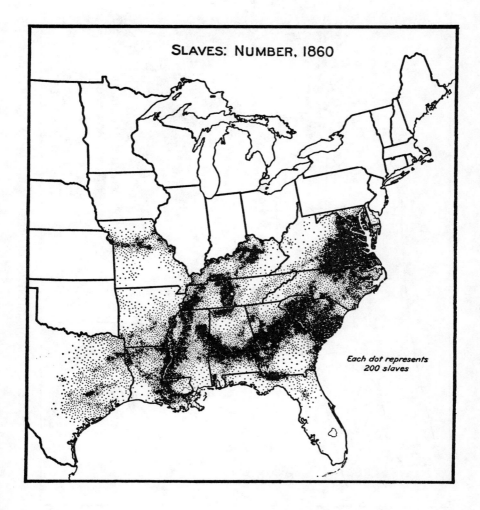

Figure 11. Distribution of slaves in the United States, 1860. Illustration from the U.S. Bureau of Agricultural Economics.

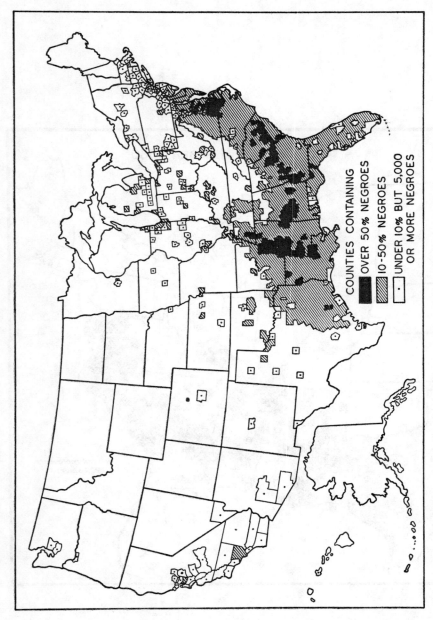

COUNTIES CONTAINING

OVER 50% NEGROES

10-50% NEGROES

UNDER 10% BUT 5,000
OR MORE NEGROES

Figure 12. Relative importance of Negroes in the population, by counties, 1970.

areas in which the close association between the best land, the plantation system, and a high proportion of Negroes in the population has persisted for more than 150 years. In sharp contrast, in 1970, as in 1860, the poorest rocky and mountainous sections of the same states were practically devoid of Negro inhabitants.[7]

Almost 52 per cent of those classified in the other races category resided, at the time of the 1970 census, in the states of California, Hawaii, and New York, and another 19 per cent in Arizona, Oklahoma, Illinois, Washington, New Mexico, and Texas. Of this heterogeneous group, the largest contingents of American Indians lived in the states of Oklahoma (98,468), Arizona (95,812), California (91,018), New Mexico (72,788), and North Carolina (44,406). These numbers amounted to 51 per cent of all the Indians in the United States. Most of the Japanese were in two states, Hawaii (217,307 or 37 per cent) and California (213,280 or 36 per cent). California had the largest number of Chinese (170,131), with New York second (81,378), and Hawaii third (52,039). Together these three states contained seven-tenths of all persons so classified in the United States. Finally, the great bulk of persons designated as Filipino resided in two states, California with 138,859 or 40 per cent, and Hawaii with 93,915 or 27 per cent.

States in which the native-white population made up more than 90 per cent of the population are nineteen in number, and include Maine, New Hampshire, and Vermont in New England; West Virginia from the South Atlantic group; Kentucky from the East South Central Division; Indiana and Wisconsin in the East North Central States; all of the West North Central States except Missouri and North Dakota; all of the Mountain States except New Mexico, Arizona, and Nevada; and Washington and Oregon in the Pacific group. This subject is better explored, however, when the materials for the native-white population are divided into those for the native whites of native parentage and those for native whites of foreign or mixed parentage. Figure 13 was prepared to facilitate their study in relation to the geographical distribution of the various race and nativity groupings. This illustration emphasizes the extent to which the native whites of native parentage predominated in most of the states just enumerated.

In order to show more clearly the portions of the United States in which the immigrants from the various countries and their descendants have made their greatest contributions to our civilization, a series of detailed maps showing the geographic distribution of the principal groups was constructed. The materials used in the preparation of this series are those from the 1930 census, since that was the census year in which the foreign-born population was at its maximum (13,983,405) and the relevant tabulations were prepared in the greatest detail. Comments on each of these maps are limited to the barest essentials. Moreover, the distribution is shown only for nine large contingents, which are the Italian, German, Polish, Russian, Swedish, Norwegian, Danish, Irish, and French groups.[8]

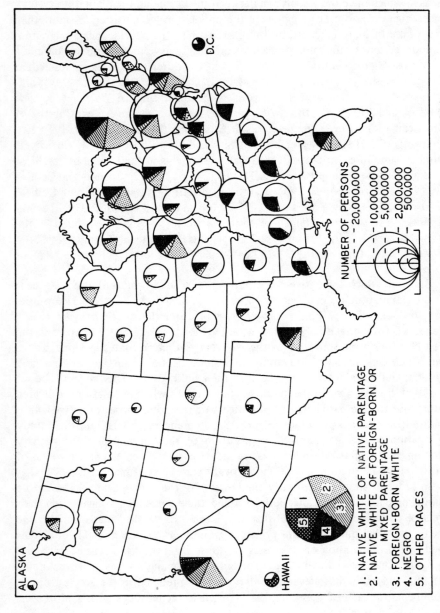

NUMBER OF PERSONS

20,000,000
10,000,000
5,000,000
2,000,000
500,000

ALASKA

HAWAII

D.C.

1. NATIVE WHITE OF NATIVE PARENTAGE
2. NATIVE WHITE OF FOREIGN-BORN OR MIXED PARENTAGE
3. FOREIGN-BORN WHITE
4. NEGRO
5. OTHER RACES

Figure 13. Distribution of the population of the United States, by race and nativity, 1970.

The 1,790,429 persons born in Italy and enumerated in the 1930 census of the United States were highly concentrated in a few great urban industrial centers. (See Figure 14.) More than any of the other nationality groups, they had settled in New York City and closely adjacent parts of the Northeast.

The 1,608,814 immigrants from Germany, on the other hand, ranked with those from England in the extent to which they were disseminated throughout the length and breadth of the land. (See Figure 15.) There was, to be sure, one very large aggregation in New York City and another in Chicago, but other major cities also had large contingents. In addition, those born in Germany were widespread throughout the rural sections of the northern, midwestern, and northwestern states.

In 1930, the number of persons born in Poland totaled 1,268,583. (See Figure 16.) They were highly concentrated east of the Mississippi and north of the Ohio, and especially in New York City, Chicago, and Detroit.

New York City alone contained almost 40 per cent of the 1,153,628 persons born in Russia who figured in the 1930 census. (See Figure 17.) Undoubtedly, large numbers of those of the Jewish faith are included in this total.

As shown by the 1930 inventory, the three Scandinavian countries had supplied 1,122,576 of the immigrants who were counted in the census of that year. Of these, 595,250 were reported as born in Sweden, 347,852 in Norway, and 179,474 in Denmark. (See Figures 18, 19, and 20.) The concentration of these groups in Minnesota and other states of the North Central region is proverbial, and this is largely borne out by the facts, especially with reference to the Swedes and the Norwegians. Persons born in these countries early found their way in considerable numbers to the states on the Pacific Coast.

The survivors of the tremendous immigration of persons from Ireland that got underway about the middle of the nineteenth century totaled 923,642 at the time of the 1930 census, of whom 744,810 were from Eire and the remainder from Northern Ireland. (See Figure 21.) The extent to which they remained in a few of the large cities is remarkable.

Finally, in 1930, 135,492 persons were counted who had migrated from France. (See Figure 22.) The largest groups were located in New York City, San Francisco, Chicago, Detroit, Los Angeles, and New Orleans.

TRENDS

Since the United States began its life as an independent nation, two major trends have been dominant among all the changes in the color or racial composition and the nativity of the population. These are, first, the long-continued decrease in the relative importance of Negroes in the population, which was only reversed between 1930 and 1940; and, second, the sharp decline in the absolute numbers, as well as in the relative importance, of the foreign-born population taking place since Congress passed the Immigration Act of 1924.

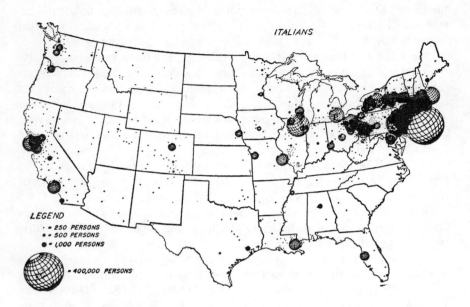

Figure 14. Distribution of immigrants from Italy, 1930.

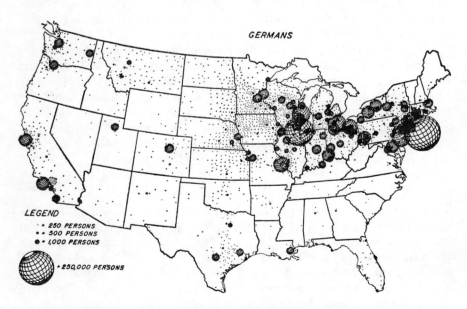

Figure 15. Distribution of immigrants from Germany, 1930.

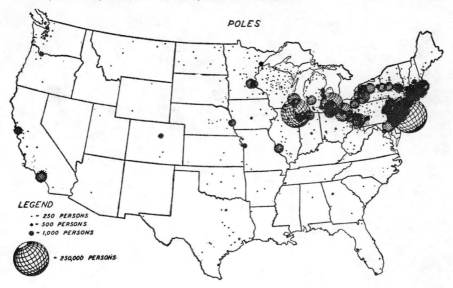

Figure 16. Distribution of immigrants from Poland, 1930.

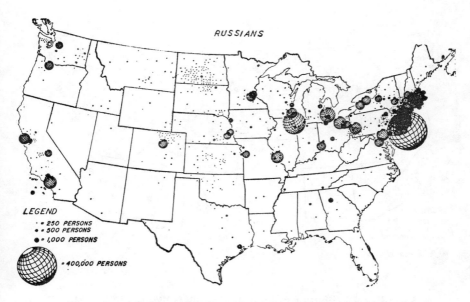

Figure 17. Distribution of immigrants from Russia, 1930.

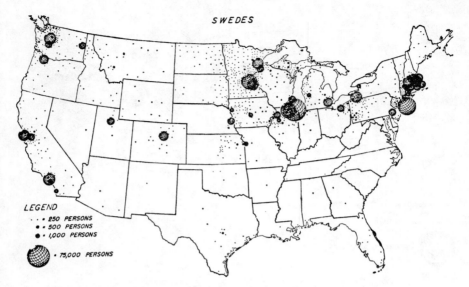

Figure 18. Distribution of immigrants from Sweden, 1930.

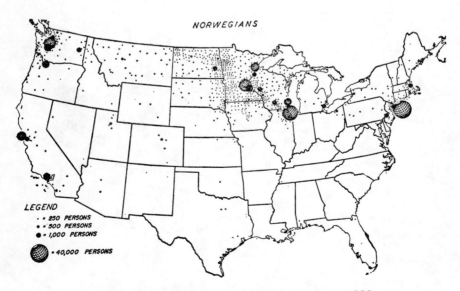

Figure 19. Distribution of immigrants from Norway, 1930.

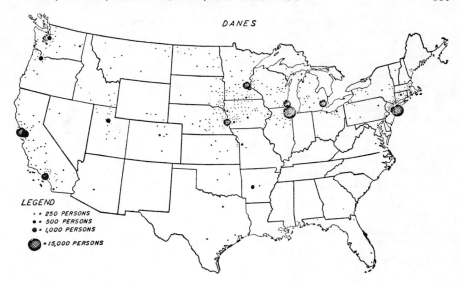

Figure 20. Distribution of immigrants from Denmark, 1930.

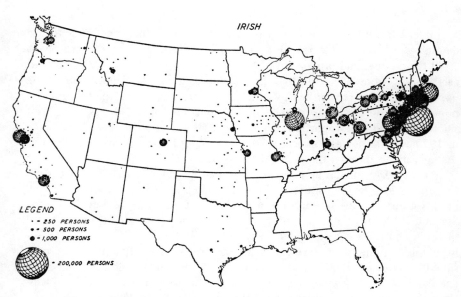

Figure 21. Distribution of immigrants from Eire, 1930.

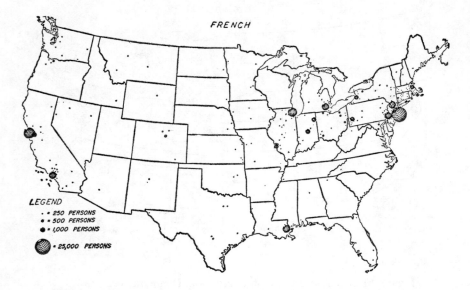

Figure 22. Distribution of immigrants from France, 1930.

Table 9 has been prepared to make readily available the principal statistical data on which these statements are based. It gives for each census from 1790 to 1970 the number and proportion of Negroes in the national population, and for each census from 1850 to 1970 comparable data for the foreign-born white population. Unless replenished by other immigrants, of course, the foreign-born population soon disappears. The number enumerated in 1970 was the lowest since 1880; and the proportion of those born abroad of the nation's inhabitants in 1970 was the lowest on record, the percentage being less than one-third of that prevailing through the period 1860 to 1920. The number of Negroes rose from about 0.75 million in 1790 to more than 22 million in 1970. Since 1930 the proportion they consitute of the total population also has risen. Nearly all of this growth is due to the natural increase of those who were in the United States in 1800, for the importation of slaves was prohibited and almost stopped in 1808, and there has been practically no immigration of Negroes. The "breeding farms" of the older slave states, particularly Virginia, were largely responsible for the increase of Negroes under slavery. From them, following the Louisiana Purchase, slaves were carried to the new plantations being opened in Mississippi, Arkansas, and Louisiana, and later on to the Black Waxy and other sections of Texas.

TABLE 9

Numbers and proportions of Negroes and foreign-born whites
in the population of the United States, 1790 to 1970

Year	Number of Negroes	Percentage of Negroes in total population	Number of foreign-born whites	Percentage of foreign-born whites in total population
1790	757,208	19.3	....	....
1800	1,002,037	18.9	....	....
1810	1,337,808	19.0	....	....
1820	1,771,656	18.4	....	....
1830	2,328,642	18.1	....	....
1840	2,873,648	16.8	....	....
1850	3,638,808	15.7	2,240,535	9.7
1860	4,441,830	14.1	4,096,753	13.0
1870	4,880,009	12.7	5,493,712	14.2
1880	6,580,793	13.1	6,559,679	13.1
1890	7,488,676	11.9	9,121,867	14.5
1900	8,883,994	11.6	10,213,817	13.4
1910	9,827,763	10.7	13,345,545	14.5
1920	10,463,131	9.9	13,712,754	13.0
1930	11,891,143	9.7	13,983,405	11.4
1940	12,865,518	9.8	11,419,138	8.7
1950	15,042,286	10.0	10,161,168	6.7
1960	18,871,831	10.5	9,294,033	5.2
1970	22,580,289	11.1	8,733,770	4.3

Source: Compiled from U.S. Bureau of the Census, *Negroes in the United States, 1920-1932* (1935), p. 1; U.S. Bureau of the Census, *U.S. Census of Population: 1950,* Vol. II, *Characteristics of the Population* (1952), p. 88, Table 36; *U.S. Census of Population: 1960,* Vol. 1, *Characteristics of the Population,* Part 1 (1964), p. 165, Table 57, p. 251, Table 108; and *U.S. Census of Population: 1970, General Social and Economic Characteristics,* Final Report PC(1)-C1, *United States Summary* (1972), p. 361, Table 68.

By 1860, as indicated above, the distribution of slaves in the United States, which is almost the same as saying the distribution of Negroes, was that depicted in Figure 11. This pattern remained almost unchanged until the outbreak of the First World War and the development of the severe labor shortage in northern industrial centers which accompanied it. For over half a century, while the white population was pushing to the west, making farms on the land that was to be had for the taking (from the Indians), the Negro population remained rooted in the same sections of the South in which it was located at the time slavery was abolished. (See Figures 23, 24, and 25, which were constructed to be as comparable as possible with Figure 12.) Over the years the "black belt" has tended to become gray, but the expansion of its limits has been very slow. Indeed, during the last few decades its area has tended to contract. (Compare Figures 12 and 24.)

The first big change came when World War I generated a large exodus of Negroes from the rural South to Chicago and other northern industrial centers. For example, between 1910 and 1930 the Negro population of Chicago increased from 44,103 to 233,903, that of Cleveland from 8,448 to 71,899, that of Detroit from 5,741 to 120,066, that of New York from 91,709 to 327,706, and that of Philadelphia from 84,459 to 219,599.

Next, with the great economic depression in 1929, much of the migration of Negroes to the North was halted, but by this time the increased awareness of the southern rural Negroes that there were alternatives to their customary mode of existence caused them to flock into southern towns and cities in unprecedented

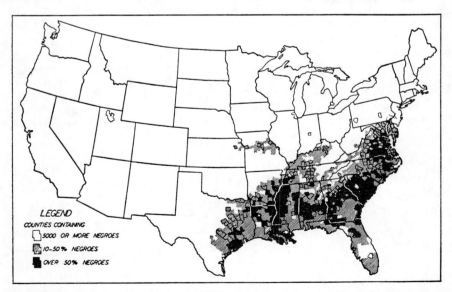

LEGEND
COUNTIES CONTAINING
☐ 5000 OR MORE NEGROES
▨ 10–50% NEGROES
■ OVER 50% NEGROES

Figure 23. Relative importance of Negroes in the population, by counties, 1880.

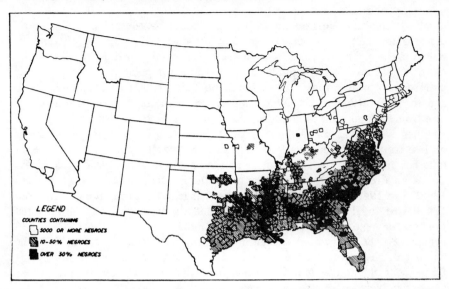

Figure 24. Relative importance of Negroes in the population, by counties, 1920.

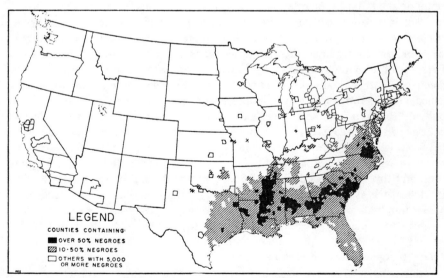

Figure 25. Relative importance of Negroes in the population, by counties, 1950.

numbers. This trend was accentuated to a considerable degree by the federal relief program and the advantages enjoyed by those who were near the distribution points in the major cities and in county seats in general over those residing in the more remote areas.[9] As a result the Negro urban population of the South, as defined for census purposes, rose from 2,966,325 in 1930 to 3,616,218 in 1940, and the proportions of the Negro population of the region classified as urban rose from 31.6 per cent to 36.5 per cent during the same decade.

When World War II and the necessities connected with fighting a global war on two fronts produced a vast shortage of labor for all purposes, the Negroes at long last made their way in considerable numbers to the cities on the Pacific Coast. As a result the Negro population of the Pacific census division rose from 134,295 in 1940 to 504,392 in 1950, the change in California alone being from 124,306 to 462,172. In the succeeding decade, the growth of the Negro population in this region continued unabated, the number rising by 1960 to 962,446 persons, 883,861 of whom resided in California. Between 1960 and 1970, the number of Negroes in the region increased to 1,514,243 persons, 1,400,143 or 92 per cent of whom were in California, giving that state a larger contingent than any except New York (2,168,949) and Illinois (1,425,674).

During the two decades 1950 - 1970 the Negro exodus from southern farms reached climactic proportions. The pressure of two almost inexorable forces made it practically impossible for any able, intelligent, and fairly young Negro to continue on the farms in the role that had been played by his father and grandfather or even in a considerably modified version of that role. On the one hand were the pressures from groups of Negroes and whites which made it treason to the race for him to continue the traditional ways; and on the other hand was the fierce resolution on the part of the planters and other farmers, now able to mechanize cotton production, that the Negro worker must continue in the established inferior order-and-obey relationship or leave the premises entirely. The bulk of sharecroppers and wage hands chose the second alternative, strongly believing in many cases that their greatest advantages lay in the cities. Actually, between 1960 and 1970 the number of Negroes living on the farms of the southern region (as defined by the Bureau of the Census) fell off by 55.3 per cent, and this followed a decline of 53.2 per cent during the preceding decade. In states such as Mississippi, North Carolina, South Carolina, Georgia, and Alabama, hundreds of thousands of persons are represented by the percentage decreases taking place between 1960 and 1970, which were 63.2, 49.6, 61.4, 61.2, and 63.8, respectively. All of these proportional decreases are larger than those which took place in the preceding decade.

These trends are continuing at an undiminished rate. Negroes from the South are finding their way in large numbers to the cities of the Northeast and the Pacific Coast, and Negroes from the farms of the region continue migrating into the towns and cities which extend from Richmond, Savannah, and Jacksonville to those of which Texas is so proud. There is little reason to expect, however, that the movement can continue much longer, for the supply of potential Negro migrants remaining on the farms has grown extremely small.

NOTES

1. U.S. Bureau of the Census, *U.S. Census of Population: 1970, General Population Characteristics,* Final Report PC(1)-B1, *United States Summary* (Washington: Government Printing Office, 1972), p. App-7.

2. *Ibid,* p. App-8.

3. The reports are the following: *National Origin and Language; Negro Population; Persons of Spanish Origin; Persons of Spanish Surname; Puerto Ricans in the United States; American Indians; Japanese, Chinese, and Filipinos in the United States.*

4. (New York: Statistical Office of the United Nations, 1957.)

5. Cf. Pitirim A. Sorokin and Carle C. Zimmerman, *Principles of Rural-Urban Sociology* (New York: Henry Holt & Company, Inc., 1929), pp. 23, 108 - 109; and T. Lynn Smith and Paul E. Zopf, Jr., *Principles of Inductive Rural Sociology* (Philadelphia: F. A. Davis Company, 1970), pp. 56 - 58.

6. See T. Lynn Smith, "The Redistribution of the Negro Population of the United States, 1910 - 1960," *Journal of Negro History,* LI, 3 (July, 1966), pp. 155 - 173.

7. One interested in more of the details about the association between good land, the plantation system, and the Negro, will find them in T. Lynn Smith, *The Population of Louisiana: Its Composition and Changes,* Bulletin No. 293 (Baton Rouge: Louisiana Agricultural Experiment Station, 1937), pp. 8 - 14; T. Lynn Smith and Homer L. Hitt, *The People of Louisiana* (Baton Rouge. Louisiana State University Press, 1952), pp. 38 - 46; and Smith and Zopf, *op cit.,* chapter 18.

8. The distribution of fifteen other groups may be found in T. Lynn Smith, *Population Analysis* (New York: McGraw-Hill, 1948).

9. On this point consult Smith, "Redistribution of the Negro Population," *op. cit.*

SUGGESTED SUPPLEMENTARY READINGS

BARNES, HARRY E. *Society in Transition,* 2nd ed., Chap VI. New York: Greenwood Press, Publishers, 1968.

BOGUE, DONALD J. "Color-Nativity-Race," in *Population and Society,* edited by Charles B. Nam, pp. 378 - 394. Boston: Houghton Mifflin Company, 1968.

KISER, CLYDE V., ed., "Demographic Aspects of the Black Community." *Milbank Memorial Fund Quarterly,* Vol. XLVIII (April, 1970).

PRICE, DANIEL O. *Changing Characteristics of the Negro Population* (A 1960 Census Monograph), Washington: Government Printing Office, 1969.

SHRYOCK, HENRY S., JACOB S. SIEGEL, and associates. *The Methods and Materials of Demography,* Vol. 1, Chap. 9. Washington: Government Printing Office, 1971.

SMITH, T. LYNN. *Brazil: People and Institutions,* 4th ed., Chap. IV. Baton Rouge: Louisiana State University Press, 1972.

SMITH, T. LYNN. "The Redistribution of the Negro Population of the United States, 1910 - 1960." *Journal of Negro History,* Vol. LI, No. 3 (July, 1966), pp. 155 - 173.

SMITH, T. LYNN. *Studies of Latin American Societies,* Selection 5. New York: Doubleday & Co., Inc., 1970.

SMITH, T. LYNN, and HOMER L. HITT. *The People of Louisiana,* Chap. IV. Baton Rouge: Louisiana State University Press, 1952.

TAEUBER, CONRAD, and IRENE B. TAEUBER. *The Changing Population of the United States,* Chap. 4. New York: John Wiley & Sons, Inc., 1958.

TAEUBER, IRENE B. "Migration, Mobility, and the Assimilation of the Negro." *Population Bulletin,* Vol. 14, No. 7 (1958), pp. 127 - 151.

TAEUBER, KARL E., and ALMA F. TAEUBER. *Negroes in Cities.* Chicago: Aldine Publishing Company, 1965.

THOMLINSON, RALPH. *Population Dynamics,* pp. 439 - 452. New York: Random House, Inc., 1965.

UNITED NATIONS. *Demographic Yearbook, 1971,* pp. 26 - 32. New York: United Nations, 1972.

U.S. BUREAU OF THE CENSUS. *U.S. Census of Population: 1970. Subject Reports. National Origin and Language.* Washington: Government Printing Office, 1973.

U.S. BUREAU OF THE CENSUS. *U.S. Census of Population: 1970. Subject Reports. Negro Population.* Washington: Government Printing Office, 1973.

6
AGE COMPOSITION

For three reasons a knowledge of the age distribution is basic in nearly all population analyses. First, age is one of the most fundamental of one's own personal characteristics; what one is, thinks, does, and needs is closely related to the number of years since he was born. Second, as indicated more fully below, the absolute and relative importance of the various age groups are determinants of primary social and economic importance in any society. Third, the qualified student of population must possess the technical skills needed to bring out the significant features of the age composition of a population with which he is concerned, and also those required to make the proper allowances or corrections for the age factor in all the comparisons he may attempt. Because the age factor is so closely related to the birth rate, the mortality rate, marital status, the incidence of migration, and so on, if it is not controlled adequately, analyses and comparisons involving these phenomena are likely to be worse than useless.

Some of the most obvious of the uses of age data are those connected with the planning of military activities, educational facilities, and social welfare programs. Large employers, the entire life insurance business, and a host of other private and governmental organizations and agencies also rely in great measure upon comprehensive, current, and reliable information about the age distribution of the population. For the social scientist the age structure of the population is paramount in importance, because in a multitude of ways, some of them extremely subtle, age conditions practically all social phenomena. This is especially true for the demographer, since, as indicated above, until the effects that should be attributed merely to differences in the age composition of two or more populations have been eliminated or corrected for, little significance may legitimately be attached to any seeming differences with respect to their mortality rates, birth rates, marriage rates, and so on.

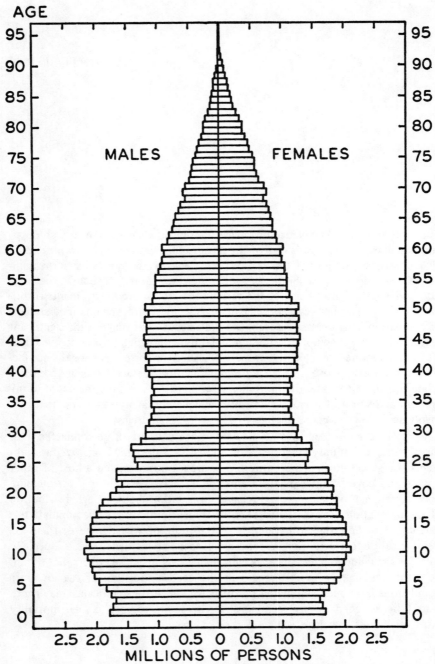

Figure 26. The population of the United States, by single years of age and sex, 1970.

GAUGING THE RELIABILITY OF AGE DATA

There are certain errors in the age data gathered in any census enumeration, and frequently these errors are of considerable magnitude. Most obvious of these is the tendency for many persons to report their ages as the numbers ending with zero. (See Figure 26.) This is particularly true after the attainment of middle age. and usually produces a considerable concentration of persons in the ages forty, fifty, sixty, and so forth. Only slightly less pronounced is the tendency for the reported ages to concentrate on the numbers ending with five, and especially on forty-five, fifty-five, sixty-five, and seventy-five. In addition, even numbers such as thirty-six and thirty-eight or forty-six and forty-eight tend to be considerably more popular in various distributions showing the population by single years of age than are the uneven numbers such as thirty-seven or forty-seven. The older the age group, the greater is the percentage of error introduced by this practice of rounding off the numbers reported. For some strange reason there also is a tendency for the newest member of the family, the baby of less than one year of age, to be omitted when the mother or the father is supplying information to the census enumerator; or it may be that the census enumerators miss inordinately large proportions of families in which there is only one child, and it less than one year old. As a nation gains experience in the taking of censuses and as the educational status of the population improves, all of these types of errors decrease in frequency but they do not entirely disappear. For this reason indexes of the extent to which ages are reported correctly have considerable diagnostic value to the investigator who is concerned with the reliability of census materials in general.

Some years ago, while he was engaged in a series of population studies in the state of Louisiana, the senior author devised a method for rating, grading, or scoring any given population with respect to the accuracy of age reporting in connection with census enumerations. Briefly the procedure is as follows. Take the distribution of ages by single years, from under one to ninety-nine, which most modern censuses publish, and ignore the very few who have passed their hundredth birthdays or whose ages are unreported. If all of the ages were known and reported correctly, almost exactly 10 per cent of the total should be in the first year of age and the others ending with 0, another 10 per cent in the other ages exactly divisible by five, 40 per cent in other even-number ages, and the remaining 40 per cent in the odd-numbers not divisible exactly by five. Thus, all of the tendencies to concentrate mentioned above should reduce the percentages in the last of these four categories. Consequently, by comparing the total number of persons reported in the age groups one, three, seven, nine, eleven, thirteen, . . . ninety-three, ninety-seven, and ninety-nine, with the figure corresponding to 40 per cent of the total, one may secure an indicator of the reliability with which the ages have been reported. Perfect reporting would produce a score of 100, whereas any concentration of the ages ending in zero, five, or the other even numbers would produce an index of less than 100. The greater the error, the smaller the score.

In the studies referred to above, these scores were computed for a considerable number of populations. For example, the score for the total population of the United States in 1940 was 95.5, indicating a considerable amount of error in the data. The scores for the urban, rural-nonfarm, and rural-farm populations for the same year were 95.5, 96.2, and 95.0, respectively, and that for the white population was 96.1 as compared with 90.1 for the nonwhite population. Males scored slightly higher than females, or 96.0 in comparison with 95.5. Rural-farm nonwhites scored lowest of all, 88.5, although the index for urban nonwhites was only 91.3. Rural-farm whites, on the other hand, scored 96.3, slightly higher than the index, 95.9, for urban whites.[1] However, despite the persistence of the distortions mentioned above, by 1970, considerable improvement had been made in the accuracy of age reporting, essentially because of two changes effected by the Bureau of the Census in the method of collecting the statistics. These were the use of self-enumeration with the respondent consulting birth records; and re-phrasing of the appropriate question to ascertain date of birth rather than age in number of years.[2] Therefore, in 1970, the score for the nation's total population was 99.1, indicating a substantial reduction in the amount of error in the data. In the same year, the scores for the urban and rural populations were 99.2 and 98.6, respectively. Unfortunately, however, the materials on single years of age, used in computing these scores, were not compiled separately for the rural-farm and rural-nonfarm groups. The score for the total white population was 99.3 compared with 98.3 for the nonwhite. The differential between males and females was reversed, with the former scoring 98.9 and the latter 99.2. The lowest score, 97.6, was that for rural nonwhites. These results all indicate a significant improvement over 1940 in the accuracy of age reporting, although they also represent somewhat greater inaccuracy than was obtained in 1960. Nevertheless, the most recent data allow for substantial confidence in the use of the materials on age.

The appearance of the 1955 edition of the *Demographic Yearbook* first made it possible to extend this type of analysis to many populations throughout the world, and the publication of the 1962, 1963, and 1971 issues permitted the analysis to be updated and to include a larger number of countries.[3] Unfortunately, several of the countries listed in 1955 did not figure in the later compilations. See Table 10 for the scores computed from the latest census data, along with information, for those cases for which it is available, showing the percentage of illiteracy among the population aged fifteen and over. A study of these materials makes it evident that there is a close association between accuracy in reporting ages and the general educational level of the population,[4] and it also suggests that long experience in census taking probably helps reduce the margin of error in this and other items included in the inventory of the population.

TABLE 10

Scores indicative of the extent of error in reporting ages along with the percentages of illiteracy in various countries with 1 million or more inhabitants, most recent censuses

Country	Year	Score on age reporting	Percentage of illiteracy among those aged 15 and over
Africa			
Algeria	1966	86.9	81.0
Ghana	1960	76.1	79.5[a]
Kenya	1969	84.1	....
Liberia	1962	72.9	91.1
Morocco	1960	55.2	86.2
Nigeria	1963	76.6	....
Senegal	1960-61	91.9	94.4
Southern Rhodesia	1969	112.2[b]	....
Togo	1958-60	80.0	....
Tunisia	1966	90.3	75.6
Uganda	1969	81.9	....
United Republic of Tanzania			
Tanganyika	1967	79.7	72.1
Zanzibar	1967	63.2	64.3
Zambia	1969	101.7	51.3
America, North			
Canada	1966	97.1	....
Costa Rica	1963	91.4	15.6
Dominican Republic	1950	81.0	57.1
El Salvador	1950	76.3	59.0
Guatemala	1964	84.1	62.0
Haiti	1950	70.1	89.3
Jamaica	1960	91.9	18.1
Mexico	1970	87.3	25.9
Nicaragua	1963	79.8	50.2
Panama	1960	91.7	26.7
Puerto Rico	1970	96.7	10.8[c]
United States	1970	99.1	1.4[a,d]
America, South			
Argentina	1947	98.5	13.3[d]
Bolivia	1950	72.3	67.9
Brazil	1950	88.4	50.5

TABLE 10 (Cont'd)
Scores indicative of the extent of error in reporting ages
along with the percentages of illiteracy in various countries with 1 million or more inhabitants, most recent
censuses

Country	Year	Score on age reporting	Percentage of illiteracy among those aged 15 and over
Chile	1952	91.0	19.6
Colombia	1964	86.3	27.1
Ecuador	1962	79.1	32.5
Paraguay	1962	90.6	25.4
Uruguay	1963	97.6	9.5
Venezuela	1950	80.9	49.0
Asia			
Ceylon	1963	81.7	24.5
Cyprus	1960	88.7	24.1
Hong Kong	1961	96.9	28.6
Iran	1966	75.5	77.0
Iraq	1965	79.0	73.7
Israel	1948	92.3	6.2
Japan	1965	98.4	0.7[a]
Khmer Republic	1962	91.6	59.0
Korea, Republic of	1966	98.3	31.9
Philippines	1960	87.1	28.1
Singapore	1957	96.5	50.2
Thailand	1960	95.6	32.3
Turkey	1955	72.0	61.4
Europe			
Austria	1951	101.6	....
Belgium	1947	99.1	3.3
Bulgaria	1965	100.6	9.8
Czechoslovakia	1961	100.3	0.7[a]
Denmark	1960	98.2	....
Finland	1960	99.3	....
France	1968	99.1	....
Germany			
Federal Republic	1961	99.3	....
Democratic Republic	1964	98.3	....
West Berlin	1961	101.1	....
Greece	1951	87.3	25.7

TABLE 10 (Cont'd)

Scores indicative of the extent of error in reporting ages along with the percentages of illiteracy in various countries with 1 million or more inhabitants, most recent censuses

Country	Year	Score on age reporting	Percentage of illiteracy among those aged 15 and over
Hungary	1963	100.4	2.6
Ireland	1966	100.1	....
Netherlands	1960	99.1	....
Norway	1970	98.7	....
Poland	1970	99.0	....
Portugal	1960	95.3	37.2
Romania	1966	99.0	....
Sweden	1970	98.8	....
Switzerland	1970	98.9	....
United Kingdom			
England and Wales	1966	99.4	....
Northern Ireland	1966	97.9	....
Scotland	1966	99.2	....
Yugoslavia	1953	97.3	27.3
Oceania			
Australia	1966	98.1	0.8[a]
New Zealand	1966	97.7	....

Source: Scores computed from data in United Nations, *Demographic Yearbook, 1955,* Table 11; *1962,* Table 6; *1963,* Table 30; *1971,* Table 7. Percentages of illiteracy compiled and computed from data in *ibid., 1955,* Table 13; *1963,* Tables 13 and 14; *1970,* Table 11; *1971,* Tables 18 and 19.

[a]Percentage having less than a first-grade education.

[b]African population only.

[c]10 years and over.

[d]14 years and over.

The score for Morocco is by far the lowest for any of the seventy-four countries included, with those for Zanzibar, Haiti, Turkey, and Bolivia coming next in order. Fourteen countries have scores that are within 1.0 point of 100, indicating a high degree of accuracy in the age data collected by their respective censuses. Thirteen of them are European nations and the other is the United States. In all other European countries except Greece, and in Zambia, Canada, Puerto Rico, Argentina, Uruguay, Hong Kong, Japan, the Republic of Korea, Singapore, Thailand, Australia, and New Zealand the indexes also are within 5.0 points of 100. In much of Latin America, however, the scores are comparatively low, and the same is true for nearly all of the African countries listed and several in Asia. In the case of Southern Rhodesia, Zambia, Austria, Bulgaria, Czechoslovakia, West Berlin, Hungary, and Ireland the indexes are above 100. Inspection of the data upon which the scores are based, however, generally indicates relatively high concentrations of persons in the ages nineteen and twenty, twenty-nine and thirty, thirty-nine and forty, and so on. Therefore, any index that is markedly above 100, such as that for Southern Rhodesia, also indicates substantial inaccuracy in age reporting.

THE AGE-SEX PYRAMID

In their raw state the millions or even hundreds of millions of observations relative to ages gathered by a modern nation in its periodic census of population would be absolutely useless. No mind could begin to grasp their significance or use them for any meaningful purposes. They must all be classified and organized in various ways before they can contribute to understanding. The tabular organization is, quite naturally, the principal device used for such purposes, but a number of graphic forms also are employed to a considerable extent. Of these, the most widely used is the one known as the age and sex pyramid. Various examples of such pyramids are presented in this chapter.

Construction of an age and sex pyramid is fairly simple. Age groupings are placed in order on the vertical scale, with the youngest age group located at the bottom and the oldest age group at the top of the diagram. Thus, for the age classes conventionally used, the group aged zero to four, inclusive, is placed at the base; immediately above it, the group five to nine; and so on, with the age group seventy-five and over at the top of the scale. On the horizontal axis are plotted the percentages that each specified age group constitutes of the total, with the portion corresponding to the male segment placed to the left of the central dividing line and that representing the female part placed to the right of it. Building from bottom to top with bars representing the percentages of the total population constituted by males and females of the respective age groups gives rise to the age and sex pyramid. The pyramid itself represents the entire group or 100 per cent. If the diagram is not to be used for purposes of comparison, absolute numbers rather than percentages, as in Figure 27, may be used in its construction.

The age and sex distribution of a given population is a record of nearly a century of societal experience. Just as the geologist may read much of the earth's history by examining the exposed strata near its surface, one familiar with the subject may see reflected in the profile of a given society's age and sex distribution many important events which have occurred over the century prior to the census involved. Wars, epidemics, migrations to or from the area concerned, precipitous declines or sharp increases in the birth rate — all of these leave distinctive marks or scars upon the age-sex pyramid.

FACTORS AFFECTING THE AGE DISTRIBUTION

The primary factors with which one must reckon in explaining the general configuration of any age-sex distribution, any specific features it may exhibit, and any changes it may undergo, are, of course, the same three that may be involved in any population change: births, deaths, and migrations. However, for some purposes it is well to include some of the secondary factors, such as war and epidemics, mentioned above, which by exerting special influences upon mortality, fertility, or migration, leave very distinctive marks upon the age-sex pyramid.

The General Levels of the Birth Rate and the Mortality Rate

As is indicated in the following section, the proportions of those under five, between five and fifteen, between fifteen and sixty-five, and those aged sixty-five and over, differ drastically from one country to another. In Mexico (see Figure 27), for example, which is fairly representative of most of the Latin American countries, in 1970, 16.9 per cent of the population was less than five years of age, 29.4 per cent between five and fifteen, 50.1 per cent in the ages fifteen to sixty-four, inclusive, and only 3.6 per cent in the more advanced ages of sixty-five and over. The same year in the United States the corresponding percentages were 8.4, 20.0, 61.8, and 9.8. (See Table 11 for comparable data for other countries throughout the world.) Leaving aside for the moment the details with respect to the peculiarities of each of the pyramids, which are discussed to some extent below, it is well to concentrate first upon why the proportions of the young, those in the productive ages, and those at or near the retirement ages differ so greatly from one nation to another. Why do some age-sex pyramids such as those for Canada, the United Kingdom, and the United States, have the elongated form, whereas others, such as those prevailing rather generally in Latin America, the Near East, and parts of the Far East, have such broad bases? Why are the latter so squat in form?

TABLE 11

Proportions of the population in four broad age groups in countries of 1 million or more inhabitants for which data are available

Country	Year of census	Per cent of the population aged			
		Under 5	5-14	15-64	65 and over
Africa					
Algeria	1966	19.4	27.8	48.3	4.4
Angola	1960	17.1	24.5	55.7	2.7
Egypt	1960	15.9	26.9	53.8	3.5
Ghana	1960	19.3	25.3	52.3	3.2
Kenya	1969	19.2	29.1	48.1	3.6
Liberia	1962	16.3	20.9	58.9	4.0
Libyan Arab Republic	1964	18.2	25.5	51.2	5.1
Malawi	1966	18.5	25.4	52.1	4.0
Morocco	1960	18.9	25.5	51.8	3.8
Nigeria	1963	17.2	25.8	55.0	2.1
Sierra Leone	1963	17.3	19.4	58.2	5.1
South Africa	1960	15.0	25.1	56.0	3.9
Southern Rhodesia	1969	16.5	30.7	50.6	2.2
Togo	1958-60	21.5	25.4	48.9	4.1
Tunisia	1966	18.5	27.8	50.1	3.6
Uganda	1969	19.3	26.9	50.0	3.8
America, North					
Canada	1966	11.0	22.0	59.4	7.7
Costa Rica	1963	19.8	28.7	48.4	3.2
Dominican Republic	1960	18.4	28.9	49.7	3.0
El Salvador	1961	17.2	27.6	52.0	3.2
Guatemala	1964	17.6	28.4	51.2	2.8
Honduras	1961	19.0	28.8	49.7	2.4
Jamaica	1960	16.6	24.5	54.5	4.3
Mexico	1970	16.9	29.4	50.1	3.6
Nicaragua	1963	18.2	30.1	48.8	2.9
Panama	1960	16.9	26.5	53.0	3.5
Puerto Rico	1970	11.7	24.9	56.8	6.6
Trinidad and Tobago	1960	15.9	26.5	53.5	4.1
United States	1970	8.4	20.0	61.8	9.8
America, South					
Argentina	1960	10.6	20.2	63.6	5.6
Brazil	1960	16.0	26.8	54.5	2.7
Chile	1960	15.0	24.7	56.1	4.3

TABLE 11 (Cont'd)

Proportions of the population in four broad age groups in countries of 1 million or more inhabitants for which data are available

Country	Year of census	Per cent of the population aged			
		Under 5	5-14	15-64	65 and over
Colombia	1964	17.6	29.0	50.4	3.0
Ecuador	1962	17.0	28.0	51.6	3.3
Paraguay	1962	17.1	28.6	50.4	3.9
Peru	1961	16.9	26.4	52.9	3.8
Uruguay	1963	9.9	18.3	64.2	7.6
Venezuela	1961	18.3	27.4	51.7	2.6
Asia					
Ceylon	1963	15.3	26.4	54.6	3.6
Hong Kong	1961	16.0	24.8	56.4	2.8
India	1961	15.1	26.0	55.8	3.1
Indonesia	1961	17.7	24.4	55.4	2.5
Iran	1966	17.7	28.4	49.9	3.8
Iraq	1965	19.8	28.2	46.8	5.1
Israel	1961	12.2	23.9	58.7	5.2
Japan	1970	8.5	15.4	69.0	7.1
Jordan	1961	17.9	27.5	50.1	4.4
Khmer Republic	1962	14.9	28.9	53.4	2.8
Korea, Republic of	1966	15.4	28.1	53.2	3.3
Nepal	1961	14.3	25.7	57.2	2.8
Pakistan	1961	17.4	27.1	51.4	4.1
Philippines	1960	16.9	28.8	51.6	2.7
Singapore	1970	11.3	27.4	57.9	3.3
Syrian Arab Republic	1960	19.5	26.8	49.0	4.8
Taiwan	1966	15.1	28.2	54.1	2.6
Thailand	1960	16.2	27.0	54.0	2.8
Turkey	1965	14.7	27.2	54.1	4.0
Europe					
Austria	1961	8.3	14.1	65.3	12.3
Belgium	1961	8.3	15.5	63.9	12.2
Bulgaria	1965	7.6	16.2	67.6	8.6
Czechoslovakia	1961	8.3	18.9	64.0	8.8
Denmark	1965	8.3	15.5	64.8	11.4
Finland	1960	9.2	20.9	62.5	7.4
France	1968	7.0	16.8	62.8	13.4

TABLE 11 (Cont'd)

Proporations of the population in four broad age groups in countries of 1 million or more inhabitants for which data are
available

Country	Year of census	Per cent of the populátion aged			
		Under 5	5-14	15-64	65 and over
Germany					
Federal Republic	1961	8.1	13.9	67.1	10.8
Democratic Republic	1964	10.1	13.9	61.6	14.4
East Berlin	1964	9.3	10.1	64.0	16.5
West Berlin	1961	4.4	8.7	68.9	18.0
Greece	1961	9.4	17.3	65.1	8.2
Hungary	1963	6.9	17.7	65.8	9.6
Ireland	1966	11.0	20.3	57.6	11.2
Italy	1961	8.3	16.2	66.0	9.5
Netherlands	1960	10.9	19.8	60.7	8.7
Norway	1970	8.5	16.0	62.6	12.9
Poland	1970	7.7	18.7	65.1	8.5
Portugal	1960	10.1	19.0	62.9	7.9
Romania	1966	7.3	18.7	66.1	7.8
Spain	1960	9.7	17.7	64.4	8.2
Sweden	1970	7.2	13.7	65.4	13.7
Switzerland	1970	7.8	15.6	65.2	11.4
United Kingdom					
England and Wales	1961	7.8	15.2	65.1	11.9
Northern Ireland	1966	10.8	18.7	59.9	10.5
Scotland	1961	9.1	16.8	63.5	10.6
Yugoslavia	1961	10.4	20.7	62.7	6.2
Oceania					
Australia	1966	9.9	19.5	62.1	8.5
New Zealand	1966	11.5	21.1	59.1	8.3
World[a]	....	13.8	20.5	59.4	6.3

Source: Compiled and computed from data in United Nations, *Demographic Yearbook,
1970* (New York: United Nations, 1971), pp. 166-407, Table 6; and *ibid., 1971,* pp. 160-
328, Table 7.

[a]Authors' estimate based upon data in *ibid.*

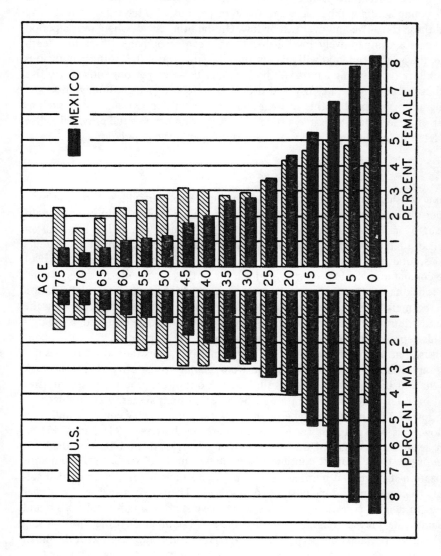

Figure 27. A comparison of the age-sex pyramids for Mexico and the United States, 1970.

In any country in which both the birth rate and the death rate are very high, the age-sex pyramid will be a very squat one, that is, the proportions of children and young adults will be high, and those of persons who have passed forty-five and those sixty-five and over will be low. On the other hand, where over a period of years a comparatively low birth rate has been accompanied by a low death rate, the age-sex pyramid will take on the elongated form, that is the proportions of children and young adults will be low, and those of persons above forty-five and especially those sixty-five and over will be relatively high. Immigration and emigration will modify this to some extent, but only in extreme cases, such as that of Israel since it became a state, does migration become the principal factor in determining the proportions of the various ages in the population.

War

Next, consider briefly the ways in which the age-sex pyramids get some of their other distinctive features. Highly important among these is sculpturing brought about by a major war in which the nation has been involved. The principal effects of such a struggle are two: first, that produced by the deaths of combatants and second, that brought about by the sharp decline in the birth rate. Most of the combatants who lose their lives in war are in the ages twenty to thirty. Therefore, deaths among members of this age group produce a huge scar or indentation on the male side of the pyramid (see, for example, Figure 28 representing the age distribution for Germany in 1934), and this scar is to be observed in the pyramids representing the age-sex distributions of the population for subsequent censuses, at progressively older ages, for some sixty years thereafter. It does not entirely disappear until all those who were coming to maturity at the outbreak of the war have passed up the age ladder and out of the group aged seventy-five and over. Of even greater duration is the other substantial scar, that produced by the lowered birth rate that goes with war. Other things being equal (as indicated below, this was not the case in the United States between 1941 and 1945), in any serious and sustained war, within a year after general mobilization the birth rate begins to fall, and it continues to go down until the war is over and demobilization has enabled married men to return to their wives and unmarried soldiers to consummate long-postponed marriages. Then it rises sharply for a year or so to heights considerably above prewar levels, after which it falls again and resumes the prewar trend. As a result, the small number of babies born during the war years stands out sharply as an age group, in comparison with the much larger numbers born in the years just before and just after the war. Thus, in Germany in 1934 the smallness of the age group fifteen to nineteen was due to the low birth rate during the First World War. The most striking examples for the United States were produced by the small number of babies born during the Civil War, especially in the South, where the struggle's ravages were felt most deeply. This was reflected at successive censuses in every age group through which those born between 1860 and 1865 passed, until in 1930 it was directly responsible for the relatively small numbers of persons aged sixty-five to sixty-nine.[5] An interesting study of the effects of the First World War upon the birth rates in the countries most seriously affected has been published in the *Statistical Bulletin* of the Metropolitan Life Insurance Company.[6] In this publication, the minimum birth rate during the war for each of the countries was expressed as a percentage of the rate prevailing 1911 to 1913. These are as follows: Bulgaria, 41.7; Hungary, 47.5 Germany, 49.5; Belgium, 49.8; France, 50.5; Italy, 56.7; Austria, 57.1; and England and Wales, 73.1.

Sharp Changes in the Birth Rate

Precipitous declines in the birth rate and rapid upsurges in the rate of reproduction quickly produce some of the more pronounced changes in the configuration of the age and sex pyramid for a given country. Such rapid and pronounced changes have characterized the age distribution of the United States since 1920.

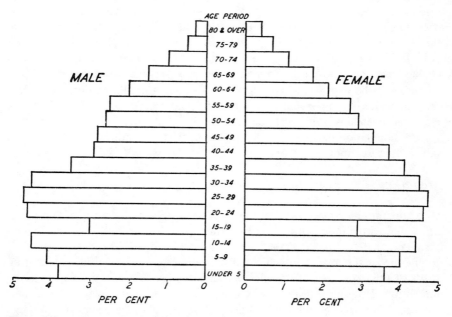

Figure 28. Age-sex pyramid for Germany, 1934.

Thus, the decline in the birth rate of the United States, which had been going on for more than a century, became precipitous between 1920 and 1935. As a result, in the fifteenth census, children aged zero to four were fewer in number than those aged five to nine, and in the sixteenth census there was a marked scarcity in the population of all persons less than fifteen years of age. Therefore, the age-sex pyramids for the United States in 1930 and 1940 were characterized by truncated bases, making them very different from those representing the age distributions for 1920 and earlier years. Even so, the long-continued downward trend of the birth rate was largely responsible for the steady decrease in the proportion of those of less than five years of age in the population, which was 15.4 per cent in 1860, 12.1 per cent in 1900, 10.9 per cent in 1920, and only 9.3 per cent in 1930. In the years between the two world wars, rapidly declining birth rates in many of the European countries were producing similar changes at the bases of the age-sex pyramids representing their populations. Observe again in this connection Figure 28 for Germany in 1934.

Although checked to some extent by the Second World War (see Chapter 14), the sharp rise in the birth rate following 1936, and especially after 1945, produced each year from 1945 to 1949 almost 4 million babies to add to the base of the age distribution, in comparison with less than 2.5 million per year from 1932 to 1939, so that by 1970 the age-sex pyramid for the United States took the form portrayed in Figure 27. As a result of these changes in the birth rate, since 1920 tremendous gyrations have taken place in the configuration of our own age-sex pyramid. Rarely in historical times has the age distribution of any nation experienced transformations equal to these. Because the birth rate remained at its 1950 level until about 1957, at the time of the 1960 census the pyramid was characterized by a broad base, formed by the three bars representing the ages up to fifteen, and the severe pinched effect, corresponding in 1950 to the age groups ten to twenty-five appeared in the bars for those aged twenty to thirty-five. However, decreases in the birth rate in the 1960's are reflected in the age profile for the population in 1970 in the form of a new truncation in the ages zero to ten, adding yet another fluctuation to the already highly varied pyramid of ages.

Migration

Great migrations constitute other significant forces which have a direct influence upon the configuration of age-sex pyramids, both in the areas in which the migrants originate and to which they move. As will be indicated below (Chapter 20), the nature of the migration and the distance spanned are the principal determinants of the extent to which males and females of various ages participate in the migrations. Thus, most of those who emigrate from one country to establish new homes in another are young adults and predominantly of the male sex; whereas those who flock into the nation's cities from the rural districts immediately sur-

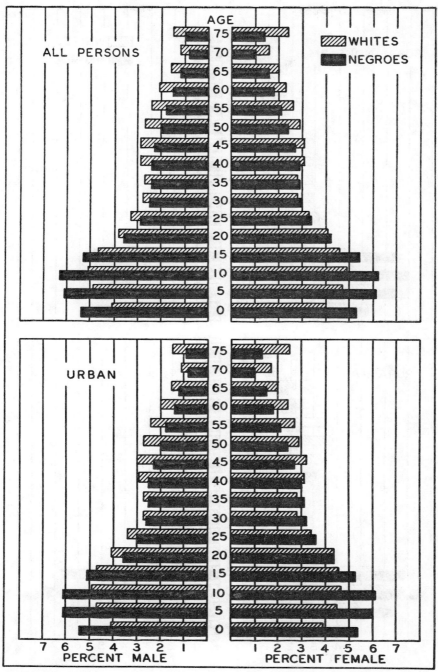

Figure 29. Age-sex pyramids for the total and urban populations of the United States, by race, 1970.

166

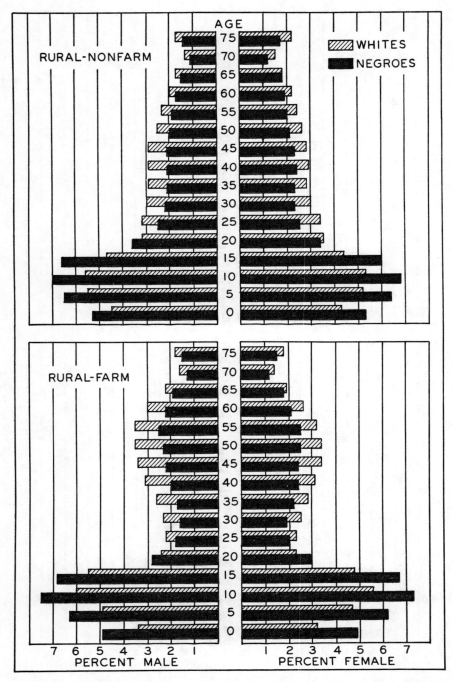

Figure 30. Age-sex pyramids for the rural-nonfarm and rural-farm populations of the United States, by race, 1970.

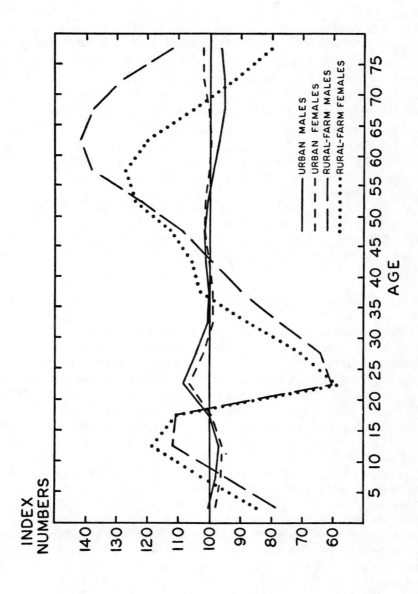

Figure 31. Index numbers showing the relative importance of each age group in the urban and rural-farm populations of the United States, by sex, 1970.

rounding them, although mostly in the ages from seventeen to twenty-five, include many more females than males. Consequently, the country that is sending out large numbers of emigrants will have, other things being equal, an age-sex pyramid that is decidedly indented at the ages near the middle of the scale, and this will be much more so on the side representing the males than on the one representing females; and the pyramid for a rural district from which large numbers of persons are moving to nearby cities will exhibit the same general features, except that the scarcity of those from about twenty-five to forty-five years of age will be more pronounced for females than males. On the other hand, the pyramid for the country receiving the immigrants or for the city to which the farm-born migrants have moved will have considerable bulges in the portions of their pyramids representing the ages involved. For example, the pyramid for the United States in 1930 showed decidedly the influences of almost 15 million immigrants who were in the country at that time, whereas the age distribution of an urban population (see Figures 29, 30, and 31) generally reflects clearly the fact that high proportions of young adults, preponderantly females, have moved from the rural districts to towns and cities. The other selective features of migration, discussed in Chapter 20, each leaves its specific impress both upon the age-sex pyramid for the section in which the migrants originate and upon that for the one in which they settle.

Abrupt Changes in the Mortality Rate

A long-continued downward trend in the mortality rate has been an important factor in producing the elongated age-sex pyramids now characteristic of such countries as Australia, the Netherlands, and the United States. But one may be curious about the effects of recent precipitous declines of death rates throughout much of the world, including the Latin American countries and most of Africa and Asia. These abrupt changes in the death rates have not produced transformations in the age-sex pyramids comparable to those brought about by the rapid drop in the birth rate in the United States, Germany, and other countries, discussed above. This is mainly because the reduction of deaths was spread over many age groups and not largely confined to a few of them. In addition, since in a given population the number of births usually exceeds the number of deaths, often by a considerable margin, mortality generally is of less importance than fertility in explaining population changes of any kind. It appears, however, that a substantial share of the increase in the United States after 1940 in the number of persons aged sixty-five and over was due to lowered mortality rates of those above the age of fifty-five. The so-called "wonder drugs" and other important medical advances no doubt were responsible for this abrupt change in the expectation of life of those at or near the retirement ages.[7]

SOME INTERNATIONAL COMPARISONS

Thanks to the work of statistical bureaus in various countries and to the efforts of the Population Commission of the United Nations, it is now possible for the student of population to obtain fairly recent and comparable data relative to the age distributions in many countries. For present purposes, the materials indicating the proportions of the population falling into four large age groups (under five, five to fourteen, fifteen to sixty-four, and sixty-five and over) are most important; and, accordingly, the necessary computations were made and Table 11 was prepared. The decision to employ these particular categories was influenced by the following: (1) certainly children should be separated from adults, and age fifteen is the most practicable point at which to draw the line between the two; (2) some important changes in birth rates are now occurring in various parts of the world and are having considerable impact on numbers and proportions of young children, so that it is well to subdivide the category of children into those less than five and those five to fourteen, although for part of the analysis that follows they are better grouped together; (3) in many countries, including the United States, sixty-five is the age rather generally employed as the lower limit of eligibility for social welfare services, such as "old age assistance," that established for the beginning of voluntary or compulsory retirement, and that generally used for statistical purposes to separate the "aged" portion of the population from the others; and (4) if the two criteria designating children and the aged are employed, the persons in between the stated limits automatically constitute another category. Included in Table 11 are the results of the authors' attempts to estimate the proportions of the inhabitants of the earth as a whole which fall in each of the four specified broad age categories. The computations carried out for this purpose indicate that approaching the last quarter of the twentieth century approximately 14 per cent of mankind were children of less than five, 20 per cent were aged five to fourteen, 59 per cent were in the ages fifteen to sixty-four, and 6 per cent were in the ages sixty-five and over. For purposes of grouping and analyzing the countries, however, those less than five years of age and those aged five to fourteen may be placed in a single category.

Most of the eighty-six countries included in Table 11 fall into a few rather sharply distinguished categories, if several criteria are employed as the basis for making such groupings. Guided by the percentages for the whole world, indicated above, the present writers used the following specifications to determine whether the population of each country was characterized by a *high, medium,* or *low* percentage of persons in each of the three broad age groups. If less than 30 per cent of the population were in the ages under fifteen, the proportion was considered as low, 30 to 37.9 per cent as medium, and 38 per cent or more as high. Similarly, if less than 57 per cent of the population were aged fifteen to sixty-four, the proportion was evaluated as low, 57 to 61.9 per cent as medium, and 62 per cent or more as high. Finally, less than 5 per cent in the ages sixty-five and over was designated as low, 5 to 7.9 per cent as medium, and 8 per cent or more as high. On the basis of these criteria, the largest group of nations consists of those in which a high proportion of children is the dominating feature in the age distribution, so that the proportions of both those in the productive ages and those of sixty-five and over are low. This group includes Algeria, Angola, Egypt, Ghana, Kenya, Malawi, Morocco, Nigeria, South Africa, Southern Rhodesia, Togo, Tunisia, Uganda, Costa Rica, the Dominican Republic, El Salvador, Guatemala, Honduras, Jamaica, Mexico, Nicaragua, Panama, Trinidad and Tobago, Brazil, Chile, Colombia, Ecuador, Paraguay, Peru, Venezuela, Ceylon, Hong Kong, India, Indonesia, Iran, Jordan, the Khmer Republic, the Republic of Korea, Pakistan, the Philippines, Syria, Taiwan, Thailand, and Turkey. Iraq, Nepal, and Singapore come very close to inclusion in this group. The other large category consists of those countries in which a high expectation of life is the factor of prime importance in determining the general configuration of the age distribution. In this group the proportion of children is low, and the percentages of both those in the productive ages and the most advanced ages are high. Austria, Belgium, Bulgaria, Czechoslovakia, Denmark, France, the Federal Republic of Germany, East and West Berlin, Greece, Hungary, Italy, Norway, Poland, Spain, Sweden, Switzerland, the United Kingdom, and Australia make up this group, although the United States, Uruguay, the Democratic Republic of Germany, Portugal, and Romania closely approximate its limits. Four of the nations, namely Sierra Leone, Canada, Puerto Rico, and Israel, rank medium in all three of the age categories. Three countries (Argentina, Finland, and Yugoslavia) rank as medium with respect to the proportions of children and the elderly and high in their pro rata shares of productive adults. Three other countries (Ireland, the Netherlands, and New Zealand) are medium in the percentages of children and productive adults and high in that of the aged. Liberia's rankings for the three age ranges in question are medium, medium, and low, respectively. Those for Libya are high, low, and medium, respectively; and those for Japan are low, high, and medium, respectively.

Several of the specific percentages given in Table 11 also call for mention, and this is especially true of the extremely low percentages of children and exceedingly high proportions of the aged in both East and West Berlin. Likewise it is evident from the table that the aging of the population has progressed greatly in East Germany, Sweden, France, Norway, Austria, Belgium, Denmark, Switzerland, Ireland, West Germany, and the United Kingdom; and that children make up very low proportions of the populations of most of those same countries along with that of Japan. Finally, Australia is the country in which the distribution of the population as gauged by the proportions in the three age groups under consideration is most similar to that of the United States.

THE AGE DISTRIBUTION IN THE UNITED STATES

Largely because of the extreme gyrations in the birth rate since 1920, the age distribution of the United States for 1970 exhibits some very distinctive features. Its form differs markedly from those of 1930, 1940, 1950, and 1960, as these did from one another. Likewise it is radically different from the more conventional age-sex pyramids representing the data gathered in the 1920 and earlier censuses. Moreover, in 1980 and 1990 the age distributions of population in the United States are sure to take on additional rather unique or distinctive shapes. The cause of much of this is, of course, the small numbers of babies born in this country between 1925 and 1945. On the age-sex pyramid for 1970 these small baby crops are reflected in the shortness of the bars representing the age groups twenty-five to twenty-nine, thirty to thirty-four, and thirty-five to thirty-nine, that is to say, in the "pinched" effect in the portion of the pyramid corresponding to these ages. This relative scarcity will pass on up the age scale, at successive censuses, and give a series of other distinctive shapes to the distribution corresponding to the years 1980, 1990, and 2000. Along with this, the relatively high annual birth rates of several years after 1950 added new broad bars to the pyramid for 1970 in the ages thirteen to twenty. (See Figure 26.) However, the lower rates of the late 1950's and of the 1960's were reflected in 1970 in significant abbreviations of the bars representing the single years of age from zero through twelve.

The proportion of 9.8 per cent in the ages sixty-five and over also deserves comment. This is very high in comparison with anything hitherto prevailing in the United States, although smaller than the corresponding proportions in fifteen of the countries of western Europe.

The age distribution of the population varies widely from one state to another, from one city to another, between rural and urban areas, among the various racial and nativity groups, and so on. Some attention is given in turn to each of these.

State-to-State Variations

As is well known, there is considerable variation from state to state in the proportions of the young, those in the productive ages, and the old. In 1970, the relative importance of those less than fifteen years of age in the population, for example, ranged from highs of 34.3 per cent in Alaska, 33.3 per cent in New Mexico and Utah, and 31.8 per cent in Louisiana, to lows of 24.9 per cent in the District of Columbia, 25.8 per cent in Florida, and 26.4 per cent in Rhode Island. (See Table 12.) Much less pronounced were the state-to-state variations in the proportions of the population aged fifteen to sixty-four, but even so the extremes were 65.7 per cent in the District of Columbia, 64.3 per cent in Hawaii,

TABLE 12

Proportions of the population in four broad age groups and median
age by color for the United States, by states, 1970

State	Under 5	5-14	15-64	65 and over	White	Nonwhite
		Per cent			Median age	
United States	8.4	20.0	61.8	9.8	28.9	22.7
Alabama	8.7	20.9	60.9	9.5	28.8	21.5
Alaska	10.7	23.6	63.4	2.3	22.9	18.7
Arizona	9.0	21.4	60.5	9.1	27.3	18.9
Arkansas	8.2	19.9	59.5	12.4	30.7	21.2
California	8.2	19.5	63.3	9.0	28.6	24.1
Colorado	8.4	20.7	62.3	8.5	26.4	22.6
Connecticut	8.4	19.8	62.3	9.5	29.7	21.9
Delaware	8.8	21.3	61.8	8.0	27.7	21.9
District of Columbia	7.9	17.0	65.7	9.4	41.0	25.1
Florida	7.4	18.4	59.7	14.6	34.8	21.7
Georgia	9.2	20.7	62.1	8.0	27.5	21.6
Hawaii	9.2	20.8	64.3	5.7	23.8	26.8
Idaho	9.0	21.4	60.1	9.5	26.6	20.6
Illinois	8.4	20.1	61.6	9.8	29.6	22.5
Indiana	8.9	20.7	61.0	9.5	27.6	22.1
Iowa	8.3	20.3	59.0	12.4	29.0	21.6
Kansas	7.8	19.6	60.8	11.8	29.2	22.6
Kentucky	8.4	20.2	60.9	10.5	27.8	23.8
Louisiana	9.6	22.2	59.8	8.4	26.8	20.7
Maine	8.5	20.3	59.6	11.6	28.6	22.8
Maryland	8.8	20.8	62.8	7.6	28.1	22.8
Massachusetts	8.3	19.3	61.3	11.2	29.3	22.8
Michigan	9.1	21.4	61.0	8.5	26.9	22.8
Minnesota	8.7	21.5	59.0	10.7	26.9	20.9
Mississippi	9.5	22.1	58.4	10.0	28.8	19.4
Missouri	7.9	19.7	60.4	12.0	30.3	23.0
Montana	8.2	21.7	60.2	9.9	27.7	18.2
Nebraska	8.1	20.2	59.3	12.4	28.9	20.8
Nevada	9.0	20.5	64.2	6.3	28.4	21.5
New Hampshire	8.9	20.2	60.3	10.6	28.0	23.0

TABLE 12 (Cont'd)

Proportions of the population in four broad age groups and median
age by color for the United States, by states, 1970

State	Under 5	5-14	Per cent 15-64	65 and over	Median age White	Nonwhite
New Jersey	8.2	19.6	62.5	9.7	31.4	23.0
New Mexico	9.5	23.8	59.7	6.9	24.6	18.3
New York	8.2	18.6	62.5	10.8	31.6	24.9
North Carolina	8.6	20.0	63.3	8.1	28.2	21.4
North Dakota	8.3	21.8	59.2	10.7	26.8	17.2
Ohio	8.7	20.5	61.5	9.4	28.1	23.7
Oklahoma	7.7	19.2	61.4	11.7	30.2	22.4
Oregon	7.8	19.4	61.9	10.8	29.2	22.7
Pennsylvania	7.9	19.1	62.3	10.8	31.4	24.8
Rhode Island	8.0	18.4	62.6	11.0	29.5	23.0
South Carolina	9.1	21.3	62.2	7.4	27.1	19.9
South Dakota	8.2	21.5	58.2	12.1	28.2	17.4
Tennessee	8.3	19.7	62.3	9.8	29.2	22.5
Texas	8.9	20.8	61.4	8.9	27.1	22.6
Utah	10.6	22.7	59.4	7.3	23.2	19.8
Vermont	8.9	20.6	59.8	10.7	26.8	25.3
Virginia	8.4	20.0	63.7	7.9	27.6	23.2
Washington	8.2	19.9	62.5	9.4	27.8	22.9
West Virginia	7.9	19.2	61.7	11.1	30.0	27.6
Wisconsin	8.7	21.2	59.5	10.7	27.6	19.6
Wyoming	8.5	21.2	61.2	9.1	27.4	20.5

Source: compiled and computed from data in U.S. Bureau of the Census, *U.S. Census of Population: 1970, General Population Characteristics,* Final Report PC(1)-B1, *United States Summary* (1972), pp. 269-275, Table 52; pp. 297-309, Table 62.

64.2 per cent in Nevada, and 63.7 per cent in Virginia, at one end of the scale, and 58.4 per cent in Mississippi, 58.2 per cent in South Dakota, and 59.0 per cent in Iowa and Minnesota, at the other. Most striking of all are the variations in the proportions of those aged sixty-five and over. The relative importance in the population of this group, the one considered as aged for statistical purposes, ranged from 14.6 per cent in Florida and 12.4 per cent in Arkansas, Iowa, and Nebraska, to 2.3 per cent in Alaska, 5.7 per cent in Hawaii, 6.3 per cent in Nevada, and 6.9 per cent in New Mexico.

The factors immediately responsible for variations in the relative importance of the different age groups are the same as those involved in all population changes, namely, births, deaths, and migrations. The high proportion of the young in New Mexico, for example, probably is largely due to the high birth rate in the state combined with a heavy influx of young married couples and their children. It may be that a relatively high death rate among parts of the Mexican-American and Indian populations is also partly responsible. On the other hand, the low proportions of the young in the District of Columbia undoubtedly are due mainly to the low birth rate of a highly urban population along with the recent movement to the nation's capital of hundreds of thousands of young men and women seeking jobs in government service. Migrations, including those of persons from abroad, probably are primarily responsible for the varying percentages of those in the productive ages. Thus, on the one hand, the high proportions of persons fifteen to sixty-four in California, the District of Columbia, and Hawaii undoubtedly reflect for the most part the very large numbers of migrants from other parts of the nation and from abroad who are numbered in their populations. The reverse of this, the low proportions of men and women in these ages in Mississippi, Utah, and the Dakotas, on the other hand, is due largely to the heavy migration to other more urbanized and industrialized sections of the country of those born and reared in these states. In all cases, though, the patterns of causation involved are highly complex, and the situation prevailing in any state at a given time represents a balancing of many forces.

This proposition is illustrated best, perhaps, in connection with the very large variation from state to state in the relative importance of the aged portion of the population. If one merely considers the factor of migration, one state, for example, may have had a high proportion of those sixty-five and over in 1970 because a boom at the beginning of the century attracted to it tens of thousands of young men and women who have gradually aged; whereas another may now have a high percentage of aged in its population largely because of immigrants who settled there immediately prior to the First World War. Or, as in the case of Alaska, a boom may be in progress, drawing large proportions of young adults but very few old people, causing the percentage of the latter to be extremely low. A state such as Montana may now be experiencing a rapid aging of its population primarily because the men and women who pioneered its development are now reaching the advanced ages, whereas another, such as Iowa, should attribute the increasing proportions of the aged in its population largely to the fact that so many of its young men and women are migrating to other states. In Oklahoma, both of these factors figured in producing the present rather high proportion of old people in the state. Finally, Florida must attribute its high proportions of the aged to the fact that so many of those at or near the retirement ages have moved to it from other parts of the nation. Were it not for the fact that many hundreds of thousands of those in the younger ages also were migrating to that state, by 1970 the aged parts of its population would have reached startling proportions. In fact, in California between 1960 and 1970, it was precisely this heavy migration of young adults along with the movement of the elderly which caused the latter to increase from 8.8 per cent to only 9.0 per cent of the state's total population while their number grew by almost 31 per cent. These are only a few of the ways in which migration has entered into the causal pattern, and equally complex are the influences exerted by variations in the birth rate and the death rate.[8]

Observation of the materials in Table 12, though, suggests strongly that the degree to which a state is rural or urban may be the primary force in determining exactly how the factors of births, deaths, and migrations have combined to produce the variations in the proportions of the young, those in the productive ages, and those sixty-five and over currently prevailing. Accordingly, it is well to turn next to the analysis of ways in which the age distributions of the urban, the rural-farm, and the rural-nonfarm parts of the population differ from one another.

Rural-Urban Differences

The differences between the age distributions of rural and urban populations are best shown by means of charts, such as those in Figures 31, 32, and 33. The last two are designed to show for the United States the extent to which the urban and rural-farm groups each contained more or less than its pro rata share of those in each age group, zero to four to seventy-five and over.

The differences are striking and most of them have persisted census after census. In general, the urban population contains relatively few children and high proportions of those in the productive ages. This was true at every census from 1920 to 1970, although both conditions have grown less pronounced in those fifty years as the urban population has become a larger percentage of the total. In 1920, the urban population included far less than its pro rata share of the nation's old people. Such ceased to be the case by 1940, however, and in 1960 and 1970 the towns and cities of the United States had almost exactly their fair share of those aged sixty-five and over. In 1970, due to the fact that in the years 1940 to 1970 the urban birth rate either rose more rapidly or declined more slowly than the rural, the scarcity of children under fifteen in urban districts was

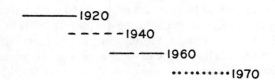

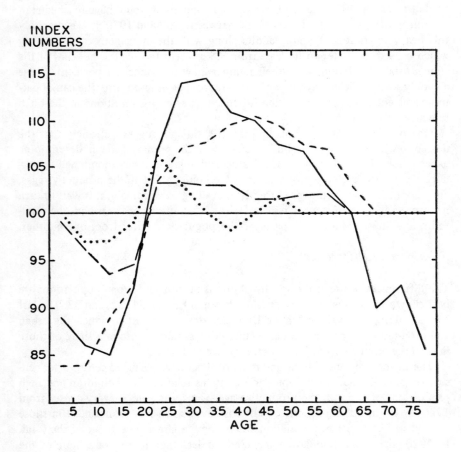

Figure 32. Index numbers showing the relative importance of each age group in the urban population of the United States, 1920, 1940, 1960, and 1970.

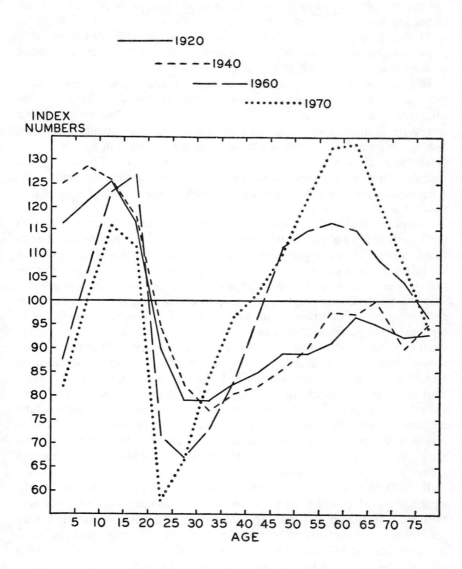

Figure 33. Index numbers showing the relative importance of each age group in the rural-farm population of the United States, 1920, 1940, 1960, and 1970.

less pronounced than in earlier years, but even so the urban population still contained less than its pro rata share of the youngest age groups. Interestingly, in 1970, the age group thirty-five to thirty-nine was underrepresented in the urban population, largely because high proportions of these people have established themselves in suburbs rather than in cities.

High proportions of those aged five to nineteen and very low proportions of those in the productive ages below forty are the distinguishing features of the rural-farm population. In addition, this category consistently has less than its pro rata share of those over seventy-five. By 1970, due to the trends mentioned above, the proportion of children under five in the rural-farm population had fallen far below the national level, but that of persons aged fifty to sixty-nine had risen far above the national average. In part, the latter was the result of the aging of the farm population that was enhanced by the continued migration of younger adults from the farms.

The catch-all category designated as rural-nonfarm long has had more than its pro rata share of children. In 1970, for example, the index for those aged zero to fourteen was 109 as compared with 100 in the rural-farm population and 98 in the urban. In large part this stems from the fact that a substantial portion of the rural-nonfarm population consists of adults and their children residing in suburbs. In 1920, when the category was made up largely of villagers, it also contained excessively large proportions of the aged. This was in an epoch in which the village truly was America's "old folks' home"[9] and before the rise of retirement cities had progressed to any considerable extent.[10] By 1940, however, the relative importance of the elderly in the rural-nonfarm population had fallen off greatly, and in 1970, those sixty-five and over were overrepresented in this residential group only slightly (index 102). This situation, too, results partly from the relative deficiency of the elderly in the suburban part of the rural-nonfarm category. Finally, the age groups from fifteen to twenty-nine are underrepresented in the rural-nonfarm population, largely because many persons in these ranges have not yet married and migrated to the suburbs. Most of these same age groups, of course, are overrepresented in the nation's cities.

In 1970, the most striking features of the age distribution in each of the principal residential groups were as follows: (1) the concentration of those aged twenty to thirty-four and forty to seventy-five in the urban districts; (2) the scarcity of those aged fifteen to twenty-nine and forty to fifty-nine in the rural-nonfarm areas; and (3) the high proportions of those from ten to nineteen and forty-five to sixty-nine and the very low proportions of those twenty to thirty-four in the rural-farm districts.

In considerable part the distinctive features of the 1970 age distribution are the direct result of the operation of the following factors during the decade 1960 to 1970: a substantial decrease in the birth rates of all residence groups; a decline in the birth rate of the rural-farm population that was greater than the

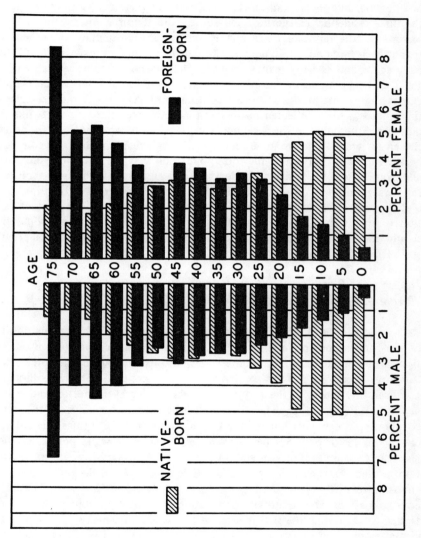

Figure 34. Age-sex pyramid for the native white and foreign-born white populations of the United States, 1970.

corresponding changes for the urban and the rural-nonfarm populations; an extremely heavy movement of young adults from the farms, principally to the cities; and the mushrooming of the suburban parts of rural-nonfarm territory brought about by the location there of thousands of young couples who were just commencing their families. However, most of the distinguishing features of the three residential categories listed above, with the probable exception of the scarcity on the farms of those in the younger portion of the most productive span of years are unlikely to persist. Those living in the suburbs in 1970 are gradually aging, and as a result they are having fewer babies than was the case in the 1950's. Their presence in the rural-nonfarm population offsets to a considerable extent the effects produced by the continuing movement of young couples to the suburbs. This is reflected in the fact that those aged thirty to thirty-nine are now overrepresented in the rural-nonfarm population, whereas those in the ages fifteen to twenty-nine are underrepresented. The urban population is coming to be such a major portion of the total population that the influx of young men and women from the farms, which leaves such a great void in the age structure of the rural-farm population, has relatively little effect upon that of the urban population. As a result of this and the increasing importance of the retirement function of many towns and cities, the age distribution of the urban population should gradually come to be more and more similar to that of the total population. That fact is especially apparent in Figure 32.

Differences Between the Age Distributions of the Foreign-Born and the Native-Born

Relatively little need be said concerning the ways in which the age distribution of the foreign-born population differs from that of the native-born. By definition, babies and other young children are almost excluded from the foreign-born category. Therefore, the age-sex pyramid for this population looks as though it had been inverted, with the very narrow bars coming at the bottom rather than at the top. Figure 34, showing the age distributions of the native white and foreign-born white populations of the United States in 1970, brings this out very clearly. In 1970, only 5.9 per cent of the foreign-born white population were less than fifteen years of age, and 34.1 per cent were sixty-five or over. In addition, of the 60.0 per cent in what are here considered as the productive ages, almost three-fifths were in the ages forty to sixty-four, inclusive. This is, of course, the inevitable result of the flocking of millions of young adults to the United States during the first quarter of the twentieth century, followed by the virtual elimination of immigration during the First World War, the drastic curtailment of it by legislation passed in 1922 and 1924, and the effects of the great economic depression beginning about 1929, which for several years produced a net migration of persons from the United States. As a result, in 1970 the median age of the foreign-born white population was 54.6 compared with 28.1 for the population as a whole, 27.7 for native whites, and 22.5 for Negroes.

Racial Differences

There are still important differences between the age distributions of whites and Negroes, as the data just given indicate, even though the great differentials prevailing in 1900 between the birth rates and the death rates of the two have been reduced substantially. (See Figure 29.) In 1970, in the national population, the proportions of native whites and Negroes, respectively, in each of the three large age groups being used in this discussion were as follows: under fifteen, 28.8 and 35.4 per cent; fifteen to sixty-four, 62.2 and 57.5 per cent; and sixty-five and over, 9.0 and 7.0 per cent. Although the racial differentials in all three age groups were somewhat greater in 1970 than in 1960, continuing the trend that appeared between 1950 and 1960, this is likely to be a temporary condition. Perhaps by 1980, but certainly not long beyond that year, because of the continued heavy migration of Negroes to urban districts and the extent to which this reduces the birth rate of those involved and because of the continued rapid rise in the expectation of life of the Negro population, the differences between the age distributions of the white and Negro populations are likely to grow smaller. That this process is already underway is suggested by an important change that took place in the two years prior to the 1970 census. Although the racial differentials increased between 1960 and 1970 in all of the broad age categories, they decreased among children in the single years of age from zero to one and from one to two, which is to say that the percentages of children in the first two years of life became more similar for the races. Therefore, the overall increase in the category aged zero to fourteen, inclusive, was the net result of lingering divergence in the upper portion of the range and convergence at the two youngest ages. If the pattern continues, by 1980 the growing similarity between the races in age distribution will have begun to move up the age-sex pyramid until at some future point little difference will remain at any age.

Trends

In addition to the current tendencies just mentioned, two long-time trends deserve special attention. The first of these is the steady decline for almost a century in the proportions of children in the population, a trend that was only arrested and reversed to a slight extent by the rise in the birth rate since 1936 but which began again after 1957, when the birth rate started a new downward swing. The second is the current "aging of the population" that has been so widely publicized during recent years. Each of these is discussed in turn.

In the middle of the nineteenth century, the proportions of children in the population of the United States were comparable to those currently found in most Latin American countries and other "underdeveloped" portions of the world. At that time, in our own country, a high birth rate combined with a high death rate made for an extremely squat age-sex pyramid. As a result, in 1850, 41.6 per cent of the population were less than fifteen years of age; and in 1860, on the eve of the Civil War, the corresponding percentage was 40.5. Even after the very short baby crop of the war years had exerted its influence, in 1870, the proportion of those in this age group in the total population was still 39.2 per cent. Thereafter the proportion continued to fall slowly and steadily, to 34.4 per cent in 1900, 32.1 per cent in 1910, 31.8 per cent in 1920, 29.4 per cent in 1930, and 25.0 per cent in 1940. Only between 1940 and 1950 were the effects of the upturn in the birth rate sufficient to halt the decline and to reverse the trend. By 1950, the proportion of those less than fifteen years old had risen to 26.9 per cent and by 1960 it had increased to 31.1 per cent. The proportion decreased to 28.4 per cent in 1970, however, since the annual number of births declined after 1957, dropping below 4 million in 1965. In 1970, fewer than 3.5 million persons were less than one year of age.

The aging of the population − that is, the increase in the number and proportion of those sixty-five years old and over − is the second highly important trend in the age structure of the population of the United States now under way. General awareness of the importance of this trend began shortly after the 1940 census revealed a total of 9,019,314 persons (6.8 per cent of the population) in these older ages. This awareness received great impetus and led to considerable concern when the 1950 census revealed that the number of those in this age group had risen to 12,269,637 and the proportion to 8.1 per cent of the population and when the 1960 enumeration showed that their number had increased to 16,173,492 and their relative importance to 9.2 per cent of the nation's total population. Furthermore, the pattern has not changed, for the 1970 counts indicated that the elderly had increased to 20,065,502 or 9.8 per cent of the total. Merely by projecting this trend for a few decades, it was possible for some to create a widespread belief that very shortly the United States would become a nation of elderly people. Such predictions are extremely unreliable, as will be readily apparent to anyone who will make proper allowance for the effects of the rise in the birth rate since 1936.

In 1900, in the United States, persons aged sixty-five and over totaled 3,080,498 and they made up 4.1 per cent of the population. For the next thirty years the increase of those considered as aged for statistical purposes slightly more than kept pace with the growth of population in general; but, even so, in 1930 only 5.4 per cent of the population were aged sixty-five and over. Had it not been for the small numbers of births during the years of the Civil War, a factor which sharply reduced the number of those aged sixty-five to sixty-nine in the 1930 enumeration, this proportion would have been significantly higher.

However, it was not until after 1930 that the rise in the numbers and proportions of the aged became spectacular. Then, just before the outbreak of the Second World War, the combined effects of the post-Civil War rise in the birth rate, the precipitous fall in the birth rate between 1900 and 1934, the gradual aging of the millions of immigrants who had flocked to the United States from Europe during the early years of the twentieth century, and a significant rise in the expectation of life at age sixty-five, led to the situation presently prevailing. These conditions were augmented by the decrease in the birth rate after 1957. The magnitude of the recent changes may be illustrated as follows. Between 1900 and 1970 the number of persons aged sixty-five and over increased by 551 per cent, whereas the population as a whole grew by only 167 per cent. At the opening of the century only one person out of every twenty-four was in the aged category, whereas in 1970 the corresponding ratio had risen to nearly one in ten.

In a study cited above, the senior author attempted to determine the relative influence for the three factors involved in the recent aging of the population.[11] For the changes taking place between 1940 and 1950, the decade in which a spectacular rise in the numbers and proportions of the aged occurred just as it did in the period 1950 to 1970, this study showed the factors and their relative importance to be as follows: the increased size of the generation caused by the larger number of births in the decade 1875 - 1884 than in the decade 1865 - 1875 — 57 per cent; immigration (during the early years of the twentieth century, of course) — 23 per cent; and lower mortality rates after 1940 of those aged fifty-five and over that year — 20 per cent.

An analysis of the three factors involved gives every reason to expect a continued sharp rise in the number and proportion of aged persons in the immediate future. Specifically, the upward trend of the birth rate until 1957 was neither great enough nor sustained enough to offset fully the long period during the nineteenth century and the first one-third of the twentieth century in which the birth rate was falling rapidly. If the world experiences no tremendous catastrophe, such as would result from a war with nuclear weapons, there should be in the United States in 1980 about 24 million persons aged sixty-five and over, and in 1990 about 29 million. If in the meanwhile there are other spectacular medical discoveries, such as the perfection of "wonder drugs" or successful large-scale organ transplants that aid greatly in controlling the causes of death among those who have passed their sixty-fifth birthdays, the numbers may be slightly larger than these. Unless there are such discoveries, however, the number of the aged should continue to increase until about 1990, after which the low birth rates of the years 1925 to 1934 should be reflected in an abrupt drop in the figure representing those aged sixty-five and over in the year 2000. Thereafter another rapid increase in the number of people sixty-five and over should begin until the low birth rates of the 1960's are reflected in yet another decrease at the end of the first third of the twenty-first century. The most probable estimates seem to be that the proportion of those aged sixty-five and over will be about 10.4 per cent in 1980 and 11.5 in 1990. If the birth rate continues to drop before these dates, the proportions may be slightly higher; and if the birth rate begins to climb or if large reductions in infant mortality rates occur, the proportions may be a little lower.

NOTES

1. See T. Lynn Smith, *Population Analysis* (New York: McGraw-Hill Book Company, 1948), pp. 90 - 91; and T. Lynn Smith and Homer L. Hitt, *The People of Louisiana* (Baton Rouge: Louisiana State University Press, 1952), pp. 50 - 51. For application of the technique to North Carolina in 1960, see Paul E. Zopf, Jr., *North Carolina: A Demographic Profile* (Chapel Hill: University of North Carolina Population Center, 1967), pp. 31 - 33.

2. See U. S. Bureau of the Census, *U. S. Census of Population: 1970, General Population Characteristics*, Final Report PC(1)-B1, *United States Summary* (Washington: Government Printing Office, 1972), p. App-8.

3. (New York: United Nations, 1956), Table 11; *1962*, Table 6; *1963*, Table 30; *1971*, Table 7. Those in charge of the preparation use another device, called "Whipple's Index" for grading the reliability of the age data. See the 1971 edition, pp. 8 - 9.

4. For an early suggestion of this fact, see Ellsworth Huntington, "Society and Its Physical Environment," *An Introduction to Sociology*, edited by Jerome Davis and Harry E. Barnes (rev. ed.) (Boston: D. C. Heath and Company, 1931), pp. 272 - 276.

5. See T. Lynn Smith, "The Demographic Basis of Old Age Assistance in the South," *Social Forces*, 17, 3 (March, 1939), pp. 356 - 361.

6. Vol. 21 (March, 1940), pp. 3 - 6.

7. See T. Lynn Smith, "The Changing Number and Distribution of the Aged Population," *Journal of the American Geriatrics Society*, III, 1 (January, 1955), pp. 2 - 4.

8. For a study of several of the variations in patterns of aging, see T. Lynn Smith and Douglas G. Marshall, *Our Aging Population – The United States and Wisconsin*, Wisconsin's Population Series No. 5 (Madison: University of Wisconsin, 1963).

9. See Edmund deS. Brunner and John H. Kolb, *Rural Social Trends* (New York: McGraw-Hill Book Company, 1933), p. 23; T. Lynn Smith, "Some Aspects of Village Demography," *Social Forces*, 20, 1 (October, 1941), pp. 15 - 25; and T. Lynn Smith, "The Role of the Village in American Rural Society," *Rural Sociology*, 7, 1 (March, 1941), pp. 18 - 19.

10. See T. Lynn Smith, "The Aging of the Population and the Rise of Retirement Towns and Cities in the United States," in *Proceedings of the World Population Conference, 1954* (New York: United Nations, 1955), III, pp. 753 - 764; and Smith and Marshall, *op. cit.*, pp. 2 - 6.

11. See Smith, "The Changing Number and Distribution of the Aged Population," *loc. cit.*

SUGGESTED SUPPLEMENTARY READINGS

BOGUE, DONALD J. *The Population of the United States*, Chap. 6. Glencoe, Ill.: The Free Press, 1959.

BOGUE, DONALD J. *Principles of Demography*, pp. 147 - 165. New York: John Wiley & Sons., Inc., 1969.

COALE, ANSLEY J. "The Effects of Changes in Mortality and Fertility on Age Composition." *Milbank Memorial Fund Quarterly*, Vol. 34 (1956), pp. 79 - 114.

HATHAWAY, DALE E., J. ALLAN BEEGLE, and W. KEITH BRYANT. *People of Rural America* (A 1960 Census Monograph), Chap. 3. Washington: Government Printing Office, 1968.

SCHMID, CALVIN F. "Age and Sex Composition of Urban Subareas," in *Population and Society*, edited by Charles B. Nam, pp. 423 - 426. Boston: Houghton Mifflin Company, 1968.

SHRYOCK, HENRY S., JACOB S. SIEGEL, and associates. *The Methods and Materials of Demography*, Vol. 1, Chap. 8. Washington: Government Printing Office, 1971.

SMITH, T. LYNN. *Brazil: People and Institutions*, 4th ed., pp. 83 - 86. Baton Rouge: Louisiana State University Press, 1972.

SMITH, T. LYNN. *Latin American Population Studies*, pp. 12 - 20. Gainesville: University of Florida Press, 1960.

SMITH, T. LYNN, and DOUGLAS G. MARSHALL. *Our Aging Population—The United States and Wisconsin* (Wisconsin's Population Series No. 5), Madison: University of Wisconsin, 1963.

TAEUBER, CONRAD, and IRENE B. TAEUBER. *The People of the United States in the 20th Century* (A 1960 Census Monograph), Chap. IV. Washington: Government Printing Office, 1971.

THOMLINSON, RALPH. *Population Dynamics*, pp. 427 - 439. New York: Random House, Inc., 1965.

UNITED NATIONS. "Accuracy Tests for Census Age Distributions Tabulated in Five-Year and Ten-Year Groups." *Population Bulletin*, No. 2 (October, 1952), pp. 59 - 79.

UNITED NATIONS. *The Aging of Populations and its Economic and Social Implications*. New York: United Nations, 1956.

VAN DE WALLE, ETIENNE. "Some Characteristic Features of Census Age Distributions in Illiterate Populations." *American Journal of Sociology*, Vol. 71, No. 5 (March, 1966), pp. 549 - 557.

ZOPF, PAUL E., JR. "Variations in Support Burdens as Measured by the Dependency Ratio." *Social Science Review*, No. 17 (Spring, 1974).

7
SEX COMPOSITION

The sex composition of the population is the fourth of the demographic characteristics to receive attention in this volume. But no particular significance should be attached to this order, since, as indicated in earlier chapters, the classification of the census data according to sex constitutes (along with age, rural or urban residence, and race and nativity) one of the principal threads in the pattern of modern census tabulations. Logically, this discussion of the proportions of the sexes in the population might just as well have come before as after the three immediately preceding chapters.

The sex characteristic in population study has much the same reasons for importance as those given in the preceding chapter for the age factor. This is to say that: (1) whether one is male or female is a primary determinant of the person's needs, attitudes, activities, and social and economic roles throughout life; (2) the proportions of males and females in its population do much to shape the form and set the tempo of a given society; and (3) the population analyst must be able to control or correct for the influences arising from the sex composition of the population before he is in position to isolate and measure other demographic attributes or variables. There is no point, for example, to comparisons of the birth rates of two areas, such as that of Alaska or some other pioneer zone (where males greatly predominate) and that of the District of Columbia (where women greatly outnumber men), unless the necessary adjustments are made for the differences in the sex composition of the respective populations.

A little study and reflection will make it evident that the proportion of the sexes in a nation, state, county, or community has a direct bearing upon the marriage rate and the death rate, as well as upon the birth rate. Furthermore, many of the more important social and economic relationships are largely dependent upon a balance between the sexes or the lack of it. Thus, the comparative scarcity of women is probably mainly responsible for the reckless abandon that is so characteristic of life on the frontier, and the same demographic factor contributes to a high degree in shaping the distinguishing features of life in mining camps, in centers of heavy industry, in cities that are primarily seaports, and in many agricultural districts. The social activities in the Yukon and in the Amazon Basin, in Gary and Youngstown, in Butte and Kimberley, in Marseilles and Hong Kong, or in the farming districts of Alberta and Iowa would be far different if there were not so many more males than females in their populations. On the other hand, the relative shortage of males (and especially of those eligible for marriage) is keenly felt in most textile centers and other towns and cities in which light industry prevails; in residential cities such as Washington, D. C.; in cities such as Atlanta, Georgia, and Recife, Brazil, which constitute the metropolises of large districts from which heavy currents of migration have been flowing to distant parts of their respective nations; and in tens of thousands of villages and small towns, spread throughout the agricultural sections of the world, where women, especially widows and elderly spinsters who have moved in from the surrounding farms, are principal elements in the population. In brief, to a high degree the tempo of life in any community is a function of the ratio of males to females in its population.

DATA AND INDEXES

Every modern census ascertains the numbers and proportions of males and females in the population. In the United States, even the first census taken in 1790 determined the sex composition of the white population, and beginning with 1820 the numbers of males and females in the other segments of the population also have figured prominently in tabulations of the data gathered in each census. Since the inquiry respecting sex is the simplest question on the census schedule, census officials probably were correct in concluding as early as 1930 that the sex classification of the total population is the most reliable of all those included in the tabulations.[1] There is no ambiguity about the terms and rarely any motive for misrepresentation. In the United States imperfections do arise in connection with the tabulations of the data for the various racial, nativity, and residential groups, since there is a large floating male population, including many foreign-born. Of special significance in this connection are the substantial numbers of Mexican "wetbacks" and others who have entered the country illegally, for whom it is difficult or impossible to secure complete and accurate returns. No doubt a part of these, and more males than females, is incorrectly enumerated as native-born, thus giving rise to errors in the reported sex distributions.

It is unlikely, though, that such discrepancies exert any considerable influence upon the reported numbers of males and females in the country.

In censuses prior to that of 1970, however, there was one striking and consistent error in the sex classifications. For decades there was reported a larger number of females than of males among Negro children of less than one year of age. In 1960, for example, the numbers of nonwhite males and females of less than one year of age were reported as 305,825 and 306,154, respectively. Yet in that same year the number of reported births in the nonwhite population, adjusted for members of each sex dying in the first year of life, placed females in the minority. Nor was the reported balance consistent with the ratio between the sexes among all those of less than five years of age, in the ages five to nine, and so on. In 1970, however, the number of Negro males of less than one year of age was reported as 244,504, that of females as 242,694, and while there was probably still a considerable error, it did not produce as much distortion as it had in previous censuses. As a result of a study of the situation as it existed prior to the 1970 census, the senior author has suggested that the data for many young Negroes may have been collected from overseers on plantations and other persons who were not the parents of the children involved and who could report only in a general way. If so, it is not unlikely that the error was introduced in this way.[2] Be this as it may, the fact remains that the incorrect reporting of the sex of young Negro children must be reckoned with by those who use the materials for the 1960 census and earlier enumerations.

The indexes commonly employed in the study of the sex composition of the population are few, simple, and easily understood. Logically, any one of the four following relative numbers might very well serve the purpose: the percentage of males in the population; the percentage of females in the population; the ratio of males to females multiplied by a constant; and the ratio of females to males multiplied by a constant. One need not look far in the literature on population subjects to encounter examples of all four of these usages. However, the one most commonly employed by demographers is known as the sex ratio. It is computed by dividing the number of males in the population by the number of females and then multiplying by 100. Therefore, as used in this volume, sex ratio and number of males per hundred females are exactly synonymous. This is the index long relied upon by the U. S. Bureau of the Census. It also conforms to the most standard usage around the world during the last century by those most experienced in population study, and much confusion would be avoided if all those writing on population matters would employ this conventional device when discussing the proportions of the sexes.

The sex ratio would be more useful by itself and in correlations with other factors if it were possible to get reliable data showing how the proportions of males and females vary with age. However, the popular supposition that women are prone to understate their ages is amply substantiated by an analysis of the

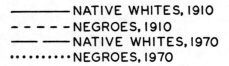

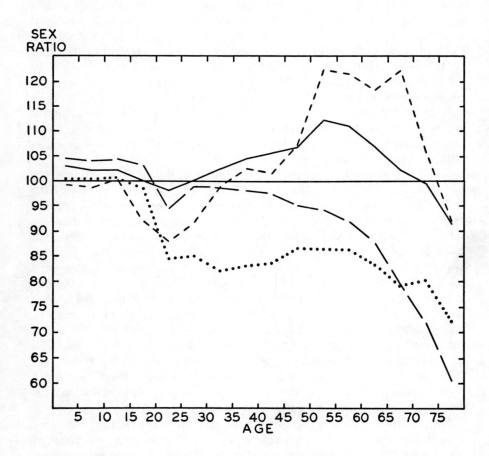

Figure 35. Sex ratios for the native white and Negro populations
of the United States, by age, 1910 and 1970.

materials they furnish to census enumerators.[3] (See Figure 35 and Table 13.) The diagram is based on data from the 1910 and 1970 censuses, the table on materials from the two most recent enumerations. The data are limited to those for native whites and Negroes because these groups are practically unaffected by either emigration or immigration. It is important to observe that for 1910 the curve representing the sex ratios by age among native whites takes the form of a long, drawn-out S. It begins, as should be expected, well above 100 and declines steadily for the first twenty years. This is what the known sex ratio at birth and the higher mortality rates of males in comparison with females lead one to expect. After age twenty has been passed, however, the curve rises sharply to a high between the ages of fifty and fifty-four. Thereafter another decline sets in which carries it down to the relatively low levels among the group of those seventy-five and over. The variations are even more pronounced in the curve representing the Negro population than they are in that for whites, although the general situation is the same. The curves for 1970 conform more closely to the pattern that would be expected, given the different rates of death of males and females, but they too exhibit the sharp decreases between the ages of twenty and twenty-four and increases thereafter. There is, however, no rise in the curve for whites after age twenty-five and only a modest one in that for Negroes after age forty.

Theoretically, the failure of all of these curves to decrease steadily as each successive age group is passed and their tendency to assume some form of the S-shape might arise in either of two ways: (1) if there were a tendency for males in the ages of from fifteen to twenty-four to overstate their ages, the result would be the dip in the curve followed by a sharp rise such as appears in Figure 35; or (2) a similar result would occur if there were a tendency among women in the early portion of adulthood to report themselves as somewhat younger than their chronological ages. Both alternatives seem to be responsible to some degree, although the latter to a considerably greater extent than the former. The statistics presented in Table 13 indicate the degree to which both possibilities were involved in the 1970 enumerations by age and sex. Among the native white and Negro populations, the age groups five to nine, ten to fourteen, and fifteen to nineteen of one census should include the same persons as those fifteen to nineteen, twenty to twenty-four, and twenty-five to twenty-nine at the succeeding census, except for the reductions brought about by the death of some of the persons in the interim between the two decennial censuses. Among males, both native white and Negro, it will be observed that the decreases taking place as the last two of the three age groups involved figured in the 1960 and the 1970 censuses were strictly in line with expectations. This was not the situation, however, among males who were aged five to nine in 1960 and fifteen to nineteen in 1970. In fact, increases were reported during the decade for both whites and Negroes in this group! This clearly implies a discrepancy in reporting on age and

TABLE 13
The reported numbers of males and females in selected age
groups in 1960 and 1970

	1960		1970	Difference	
Age	Population	Age	Population	Number	Per cent
		Native white males			
5-9	8,114,197	15-19	8,238,958	+124,761	+1.5
10-14	7,376,422	20-24	6,647,675	−728,747	−9.9
15-19	5,801,340	25-29	5,612,749	−188,591	−3.3
		Native white females			
5-9	7,800,966	15-19	7,984,897	+183,931	+2.4
10-14	7,078,705	20-24	7,050,949	−27,756	−0.4
15-19	5,673,801	25-29	5,675,672	+1,871	a
		Negro males			
5-9	1,194,593	15-19	1,205,273	+10,680	+0.9
10-14	989,150	20-24	803,355	−185,795	−18.8
15-19	740,196	25-29	647,145	−93,051	−12.6
		Negro females			
5-9	1,195,013	15-19	1,222,355	+27,342	+2.3
10-14	983,302	20-24	949,606	−33,696	−3.4
15-19	755,837	25-29	763,522	+7,685	+1.0

Source: Compiled and computed from data in U.S. Bureau of the Census, *U.S. Census of Population: 1960,* Vol. I, *Characteristics of the Population,* Part 1 (1964), pp. 359-360, Table 158; *U.S. Census of Population: 1970, Detailed Characteristics,* Final Report PC(1)-D1, *United States Summary* (1973), pp. 591-592, Table 189; pp. 593-595, Table 190.
[a]Less than 0.1 per cent.

sex. In the case of females of both races, the numbers recorded in 1960 in the age groups five to nine, ten to fourteen, and fifteen to nineteen either failed to decrease appreciably or increased during the ten years required for them to figure as the age groups fifteen to nineteen, twenty to twenty-four, and twenty-five to twenty-nine in 1970. Such a buoying effect required the inclusion at the later date in the groups aged fifteen to nineteen, twenty to twenty-four, and twenty-five to twenty-nine of considerable numbers of women who actually belonged in higher age groupings.

It hardly needs to be said that these discrepancies limit the usefulness of the data on the sex composition of the population, even though they were not as serious in the most recent census as they were in many earlier enumerations. For those interested in the study of migration particularly, it is extremely unfortunate that the defective nature of the data on the proportions of the sexes by age precludes the employment of these materials in many of the analyses that otherwise would be simple.

FACTORS DIRECTLY AFFECTING THE SEX RATIO

Most of the ways in which births, deaths, and migrations affect the proportions of the sexes in the population are simple and easily understood. One must merely keep in mind the following facts, which are set forth more fully elsewhere in the appropriate places in this volume: (1) the sex ratio at birth is comparatively high, averaging probably about 105 in the United States and having comparable magnitude in most other parts of the world; (2) in general the death rate of males, at all ages, is higher than that for females; (3) in migrations in which long distances are spanned, such as the overseas movements of population and most other types of immigration and emigration, males greatly outnumber females among the migrants; and (4) in migrations in which only short distances are covered, such as the exodus from the rural districts to nearby cities, females constitute disproportionately large numbers of those making the move.

In a population influenced by migration to a minor degree, the sex ratio among the general population depends almost entirely upon the magnitude of the birth rates and death rates. If both of these are high, so as to produce a heavy concentration of population in the younger years of life, the overall sex ratio will be comparatively high, perhaps about 100; if, on the other hand, both are very low, so as to make for relatively high proportions of persons aged forty or more, the sex ratio will be low, perhaps less than ninety-five. Other than this, the extent to which a country is losing by emigration or gaining by immigration is the major force determining the proportions of males and females in its population, with emigration tending to lower the sex ratio materially, or conversely, immigration exerting a buoying influence upon it.

As will be noted in Chapter 16, there may be some countries, such as India, in which the death rates of females exceed those of males. In such cases, this differential mortality will cause the proportions of males, already high at birth, to rise steadily as age increases.

SOME INTERNATIONAL COMPARISONS

As indicated above, the division of the population according to sex is probably the classification of census materials most generally employed throughout the world. Therefore, by using the data assembled in the *Demographic Yearbook* of the United Nations it is fairly easy to prepare and to keep up to date a table such as Table 14. Furthermore, observation of such material serves to bring out the more important variations in the proportions of the sexes throughout the world, and it also serves to illustrate the manner in which the factors mentioned above have combined to produce the differences recorded. In making comparisons it may be well to keep in mind as a norm the sex ratio of about ninety-seven or ninety-eight which the present writers estimate as the probable current index for mankind as a whole.

Colonial areas, to which large numbers of workers for highly commercialized plantations are attracted or carried, are, of course, among the sections of the world in which males most greatly outnumber females in the population. Note the high sex ratio in Malaysia. Even greater is the scarcity of women in frontier districts, such as Alaska (sex ratio 119), to which people have been attracted mainly by the hope of quick and rich rewards from prospecting and mining, and the territory of Guaporé (sex ratio 131) in northern Brazil where new colonization and settlement are taking place. Also some nations have attracted immigrants in sufficient numbers, within a period corresponding to man's life span, to increase materially the sex ratios among their populations. Hong Kong, Israel, Singapore, Taiwan, Cuba, Panama, Venezuela, and Australia owe the considerable preponderance of males in their populations largely to immigration. In addition, in South Africa, Canada, the United States, Brazil, and New Zealand, the sex ratios indicated by the latest censuses would have been considerably lower than those recorded had large contingents of immigrants not been included in their populations.

Migration, however, definitely is not the explanation of the very high sex ratios noted in Pakistan, Ceylon, and India, and probably it is not responsible for the high proportion of males in Libya. To a minor degree a tendency on the part of Moslems to be reticent about their women, to the extent that some of the females may have been omitted from the census enumerations, may be a factor in all of these countries except India. That it is not a major factor, however, seems to have been definitely demonstrated by those responsible for the 1951 census of Pakistan, so that some other explanation must be sought.[4] The most likely possibility is that females in these parts of the world have higher mortality rates than males. Certainly, this is a likely explanation for the relatively high sex ratios in the ages fifteen through sixty-four.

TABLE 14

Population classified according to sex and sex ratios for all countries and territories of 1 million or more inhabitants for which recent data are available

Country	Year	Number of males	Number of females	Sex ratios by age			
				Total	Under 15	15-64	65 and over
Africa							
Algeria	1966	6,079,900	6,022,100	101	105	98	92
Angola	1960	2,459,015	2,371,434	104	106	101	120
Egypt	1960	13,068,012	12,916,089	101	107	98	86
Ghana	1960	3,400,270	3,326,545	102	102	101	113
Kenya	1969	5,482,381	5,460,324	100	103	97	111
Liberia	1962	503,588	512,855	98	105	93	119
Libyan Arab Republic	1964	813,386	750,983	108	107	107	122
Malawi	1966	1,913,262	2,126,321	90	98	83	103
Morocco	1960	5,809,172	5,817,060	100	106	94	147
Nigeria	1963	28,111,852	27,558,203	102	106	98	142
Sierra Leone	1963	1,081,123	1,099,232	98	104	93	115
South Africa	1960	8,039,240	7,954,941	101	100	103	80
Southern Rhodesia	1969	2,562,251	2,518,113	101	99	103	112
Togo	1958-60	689,557	750,243	92	107	78	111
Tunisia	1966	2,314,419	2,218,932	104	107	101	116
Uganda	1969	4,818,449	4,730,398	102	101	100	129
United Republic of Tanzania							
Tanganyika	1967	5,838,076	6,113,857	95	102	89	113
Zanzibar	1967	177,936	176,216	101	102	98	130
Zambia	1969	1,987,011	2,069,984	96	100	92	123
America, North							
Canada	1966	10,054,344	9,960,536	101	103	101	87
Costa Rica	1963	691,969	686,736	101	103	98	97
Cuba	1953	2,985,155	2,843,874	105	104	105	112

TABLE 14 (Cont'd)

Population classified according to sex and sex ratios for all countries and territories of 1 million or more inhabitants for which recent data are available

Country	Year	Number of males	Number of females	Total	Sex ratios by age Under 15	15-64	65 and over
Dominican Republic	1960	1,535,820	1,511,250	102	104	100	103
El Salvador	1961	1,236,728	1,274,256	97	103	93	88
Guatemala	1964	2,105,780	2,104,040	100	104	97	103
Haiti	1950	1,504,736	1,592,484	94	101	92	80
Honduras	1961	939,029	945,736	99	104	95	93
Jamaica	1960	773,439	836,375	92	101	89	69
Mexico	1970	24,140,315	24,237,048	100	104	96	92
Nicaragua	1963	757,922	777,666	97	104	93	81
Panama	1960	545,774	529,767	103	103	103	102
Puerto Rico	1970	1,329,949	1,382,084	96	103	93	94
United States	1970	98,912,192	104,299,734	95	104	95	72
America, South							
Argentina	1960	10,005,897	10,004,642	100	102	100	91
Bolivia	1950	1,326,099	1,378,066	96	106	90	91
Brazil	1960	35,010,717	35,108,354	100	103	98	95
Chile	1960	3,612,807	3,761,303	96	101	94	80
Colombia	1964	8,614,652	8,869,856	97	103	93	85
Ecuador	1962	2,236,476	2,239,531	100	104	97	89
Paraguay	1962	894,164	924,939	97	105	91	79
Peru	1961	4,925,518	4,981,228	99	103	97	78
Uruguay	1963	1,290,386	1,305,124	99	103	99	82
Venezuela	1961	3,821,720	3,702,279	103	103	105	73
Asia							
Burma	1954	1,311,740	1,367,979	96	100	93[a]	98[b]

196

	Year						
Ceylon	1963	5,498,674	5,083,390	108	103	111	121
Hong Kong	1961	1,610,650	1,522,481	106	108	109	42
India	1961	226,060,908	212,713,821	106	106	107	97
Indonesia	1961	47,493,854	48,824,975	97	102	94	95
Iran	1966	12,981,665	12,097,258	107	109	105	113
Iraq	1965	4,102,514	3,944,901	104	108	101	89
Israel	1961	1,106,069	1,073,422	103	107	102	95
Japan	1970	50,778,300	52,577,600	97	104	96	79
Jordan	1961	867,597	838,629	103	112	96	105
Khmer Republic	1962	2,862,939	2,865,832	100	102	98	92
Korea, Republic	1966	14,684,147	14,475,493	101	107	100	65
Malaysia							
East Malaysia							
Sabah	1960	236,616	217,805	109	105	112	103
Sarawak	1960	375,846	368,683	102	105	99	104
West Malaysia	1957	3,237,579	3,041,179	106	104	108	104
Nepal	1961	4,636,033	4,776,963	97	104	94	86
Pakistan	1961	47,516,890	42,765,784	111	109	112[a]	128[b]
Philippines	1960	13,662,869	13,424,816	102	106	98	100
Singapore	1970	1,062,127	1,012,380	105	106	106	79
Syrian Arab Republic	1960	2,344,224	2,220,897	106	111	100	106
Taiwan	1966	6,587,770	6,222,778	106	106	108	77
Thailand	1960	13,154,149	13,103,767	100	102	100	80
Turkey	1965	15,996,964	15,394,457	104	108	103	74

TABLE 14 (Cont'd)

Population classified according to sex and sex ratios for all countries and territories of 1 million or more inhabitants for which recent data are available

Country	Year	Number of males	Number of females	Sex ratios by age			
				Total	Under 15	15-64	65 and over
Europe							
Albania	1955	713,316	678,183	105	110	106	77
Austria	1961	3,296,400	3,777,407	87	104	87	63
Belgium	1961	4,496,860	4,692,881	96	104	98	73
Bulgaria	1965	4,114,167	4,113,699	100	105	101	81
Czechoslovakia	1961	6,704,674	7,040,903	95	104	96	67
Denmark	1965	2,362,496	2,405,101	98	105	99	82
Finland	1960	2,142,263	2,303,959	93	104	93	59
France	1968	24,196,528	25,458,028	95	104	100	62
Germany							
Federal Republic	1961	25,484,357	28,493,061	89	105	89	68
Democratic Republic	1964	7,748,134	9,255,497	84	105	82	62
East Berlin	1964	468,727	602,735	78	105	79	51
West Berlin	1961	929,005	1,268,403	73	105	75	51
Greece	1961	4,091,894	4,296,659	95	106	94	76
Hungary	1963	4,863,350	5,208,350	93	105	93	71
Ireland	1966	1,449,032	1,434,970	101	104	102	87
Italy	1961	24,783,859	25,839,710	96	105	97	73
Netherlands	1960	5,706,874	5,755,090	99	105	98	88
Norway	1970	1,933,700	1,954,605	99	105	102	77
Poland	1970	15,834,525	16,754,684	95	104	95	65
Portugal	1960	4,254,416	4,634,976	92	104	90	66
Romania	1966	9,351,075	9,752,088	96	105	96	71
Spain	1960	14,726,222	15,649,542	94	104	94	70
Sweden	1970	4,033,937	4,042,966	100	106	103	80

Switzerland	1970	3,089,326	3,180,457	97	105	101	68
United Kingdom							
England and Wales	1961	22,303,833	23,800,715	94	105	97	62
Northern Ireland	1966	723,884	760,891	95	106	95	71
Scotland	1961	2,482,734	2,969,610	92	105	93	64
Yugoslavia	1961	9,043,424	9,505,867	95	104	94	70
Oceania							
Australia	1966	5,816,359	5,734,103	101	105	105	72
New Zealand	1966	1,343,743	1,333,176	101	105	103	75
U.S.S.R.	1970	111,399,000	130,321,000	85	104	86[a]	48[b]

Source: Compiled and computed from data in United Nations, *Demographic Yearbook*, various editions.

[a]15-59

[b]60 and over.

The lowest sex ratios in the world are found in those countries which long have been sending out considerable numbers of emigrants and in which World War II resulted in a decimation of the male population. Germany, Austria, Finland, Hungary, and the Soviet Union are the most striking examples, but the group includes as well most other countries in southern and eastern Europe. In some of these, birth rates and mortality rates are comparatively high, so that their sex ratios are significantly above what would have been the case had young children constituted smaller proportions of their total populations.

In comparison with the situation in other parts of the world, most Latin American countries have fairly well-balanced proportions of the sexes in their populations. On the whole the sex ratio for the countries taken collectively does not differ greatly from the figure of ninety-seven or ninety-eight, which, as stated above, probably is a fair approximation of the index for all mankind in the last quarter of the twentieth century. This means, of course, that few of the Latin American countries have experienced any large influx of persons from abroad such as those which are responsible for the high sex ratios in Hawaii, Malaysia, Israel, Australia, and South Africa. Nevertheless, Argentina, to a considerable extent, and Brazil, Cuba, Panama, Uruguay, and Venezuela, to a lesser degree, have had the proportions of males in their populations significantly increased by immigration. In the second place, this also means that none of the Latin American countries has had the sex ratio of its population considerably reduced by a heavy emigration, as has been the case in countries such as Scotland, England and Wales, Portugal, Spain, Romania, Poland, and Italy; nor in spite of frequent so-called "revolutions" have any large proportions of their male populations been killed off in recent wars. However, the proportions of males in Haiti, El Salvador, Mexico, and Paraguay doubtless are considerably lower than would have been the case had not considerable numbers of their nationals migrated to Cuba (prior to 1960), Honduras, the United States, and Argentina, respectively. Finally, there is little indication in the data that any of the Latin American countries have had the sex ratios of their populations inflated by lower death rates among males than among females.

Additional comments may be made about the sex ratios in Jamaica and the Republic of Ireland. The former has contributed heavily from its young male population to the labor forces in Cuba, Panama, and other Caribbean countries; and the latter, with a sex ratio of 101, may appear to be somewhat of an enigma for a country that has lost so heavily by emigration. Probably a large movement of young Irish women to Liverpool, London, and other large cities on the neighboring island, where they obtain positions as domestic servants, is the major factor in producing and maintaining the relative shortage of women in Ireland.

THE SEX COMPOSITION OF POPULATION
IN THE UNITED STATES

The sex composition of the United States varies greatly from place to place, group to group, and time to time. It is well to examine all of these in considerable detail, for the ratio of 94.8 males per hundred females in the population as a whole, as shown by the census of 1970, represents merely the balancing of many varying and often contradictory influences.

Variations Among the Race and Nativity Groups

There are some very striking differences in the proportions of the sexes found among the various race and nativity groups which make up the population. (See Table 15.) Several of these call for comment, although it suffices to point out that the sex ratio among the principal component of the population, the native white category (95.9), is very little higher than that among the total population; and that the high ratios among the Chinese, Filipinos, and miscellaneous group of non-whites are to be expected among those who have migrated in large part from other countries. The ratio for the Japanese is relatively low, of course, because in recent decades the bulk of Japanese immigrants has been the wives of servicemen. The same is true for the Koreans.

The comparatively low ratio among the foreign-born whites (83.8) may appear strange in view of what was said above about the preponderance of males among the immigrants. In this connection, however, it should be mentioned that the foreign-born population of the United States consists for the most part of persons who came to this country prior to the First World War. They now are heavily concentrated in the ages in which the greater longevity of the females has had time to reduce greatly the disproportions between the sexes that once existed. In addition, the immigration of European wives of servicemen in the years following World War II has helped to reduce the sex ratio among the foreign-born white population of the United States. In 1910, it was 129.2; in 1920, 121.7; in 1940, 111.1; and as late as 1950 it stood at 103.8. By 1960 it had fallen to 94.2.

The sex ratio of 96.5 among the American Indians demands attention, even though the population involved is relatively small. In 1900, the corresponding index was 101.5, and in 1930, 1940, 1950, and 1960 it was 105.1, 105.5, 108.7, and 101.2, respectively. The fact that conditions among the Indians favor the survival of the male in comparison with the female seems to be the only possible explanation of the high ratios in the years prior to 1970. Improvements in these conditions, especially ones related to childbearing, so as to reduce the death rate among females seems to be the factor which has depressed the ratio close to that of the total population.

TABLE 15

Sex ratios of various racial and nativity groups in the population
of the United States, 1970

Race and nativity	Number of males	Number of females	Sex ratio
White	86,892,828	91,226,393	95.2
Native	82,910,031	86,475,420	95.9
Foreign-born	3,982,797	4,750,973	83.8
Nonwhite	11,988,882	13,102,055	91.5
Negro	10,721,885	11,817,477	90.7
Other races	1,266,997	1,284,578	98.6
Indian	373,514	387,058	96.5
Japanese	270,926	315,749	85.8
Chinese	227,163	206,306	110.1
Filipino	183,010	153,813	119.0
Korean	28,491	42,107	67.7
Hawaiian	48,710	50,126	97.2
All other	135,183	129,419	104.5

Source: Compiled and computed from data in U.S. Bureau of the Census, *U.S. Census of Population; 1970, Detailed Characteristics,* Final
Report PC(1)-D1, *United States Summary* (1973), pp. 591–592, Table 189,; pp. 593–595, Table 190.

The very low sex ratio among Negroes (90.7), the second largest component of the population, also deserves special comment. Since 1920, when there were 99.2 males per hundred females among the Negro population, the index has fallen steadily, being 97.0 in 1930, 95.0 in 1940, 94.3 in 1950, and 93.4 in 1960. In a large measure the low proportion of males in the Negro population stems from the low sex ratio at birth (approximately 102 as compared with 105 among the whites).[5]

Immigration and emigration are of practically no consequence in determining the number of Negroes in the United States, since in 1970 there were only 253,438 foreign-born Negroes in the population, of whom 115,406 were male and 138,032 female, and since there is practically no emigration of Negroes from this country. Therefore, migration has very little influence in determining the sex ratio among the American Negro population. The other significant factor that may have a bearing upon the sex ratio, namely the extent to which the population is concentrated in the younger ages of life (determined in turn by the levels of the birth rate and the death rate) makes for slightly higher sex ratios among Negroes than otherwise would be the case. This was demonstrated some years ago by the senior author by the use of the materials from the life tables for 1939 - 1941. At that time if there had been sex ratios at birth of 100 for both whites and Negroes, if the population of each race had been stationary, and if no factors other than the differences in expectation of life had influenced the sex ratios, there would have been only 93.7 males per hundred females among the whites as compared with 94.2 among the Negroes.[6] Therefore, the prevailing low sex ratios among Negroes in the United States would be even lower were it not for the fact that the average duration of their lives is still somewhat less than that of the whites. Because neither migration nor the average length of the life span helps account for the low sex ratio among the Negro population, the low sex ratio at birth, and the lower death rates among females than among males are the only factors to which the phenomenon may be attributed. Nevertheless, the recent marked increases in expectation of life at birth among Negroes, at a rate that is faster than the one for whites, helps explain why the sex ratio among Negroes has fallen significantly during the last several decades.

Rural-Urban Differences

There are also sharp differences between the sex ratios of the populations in rural and urban areas. With few exceptions urban populations are characterized by very low sex ratios and farming populations by very high ones. (See Table 16, which gives the most recent data for the United States.) Much of the same disproportions prevail among the various residential groups census after census. It also should be recalled that among persons who report themselves as married and among children the proportions of the sexes are approximately equal. Therefore,

TABLE 16

Sex ratios among the urban, rural-nonfarm, and rural-farm populations of the United States, by race and nativity, 1970

Race and nativity	All categories	Urban	Rural-nonfarm	Rural-farm
Total population	94.8	93.0	99.0	105.7
Native white	95.9	94.2	99.3	106.0
Foreign-born white	83.8	83.2	87.7	111.4
Negro	90.7	89.1	98.4	98.1

Source: Compiled and computed from data in U.S. Bureau of the Census, *U.S. Census of Population: 1970, General Social and Economic Characteristics,* Final Report PC(1)-C1, *United States Summary* (1972), pp. 380-381, Table 85; *Detailed Characteristics,* Final Report PC(1)-D1, *United States Summary* (1973), pp. 591-592, Table 189.

such a high sex ratio in the farming districts means that the farmer seeking a mate has the odds strongly against him, whereas the low sex ratio in urban areas determines that hundreds of thousands of young women in the cities are similarly disadvantaged. Undoubtedly both the marriage rate and the birth rate are below what they would be if the sexes were more equitably distributed in rural and urban areas. It is significant, however, that the exodus of Negro males from the farms has been so great that the sex ratio for this racial group in the rural-farm population dropped from 101.7 in 1960 to 98.1 in 1970.

State-to-State Variations

Most of the differences in the sex ratios of the various states are due to the differing proportions of the white and Negro, native-born and foreign-born, and rural and urban categories in their respective populations. Nevertheless, there are still other important variations from one state to another, such as that brought about by the rush of males to frontier and mining areas. Today the disproportions produced by such phenomena are much less than once was the case, but even so they are not to be entirely overlooked by one who would understand the reasons for observed differences in the sex ratios throughout the United States. In order to note the state-to-state variations in the proportions of the sexes in the two principal race and nativity groups, further subdivided into the three residential categories, and also in the population as a whole, the materials presented in Table 17 have been selected from the mass of information that is available. By such subsorting it is possible for one to study the manner in which the sex ratios differ from one part of the nation to another without running the risk of proving no more than that there are great differences from state to state in the extent to which the population resides in towns and cities, in the proportions of Negroes in the population, and in the relative importance of the foreign-born white population.

TABLE 17

Sex ratios in the various states, by race and residence, 1970

State	Total population	White population			Negro population		
		Urban	Rural-nonfarm	Rural-farm	Urban	Rural-nonfarm	Rural-farm
United States	94.8	93.5	99.1	104.7	89.1	98.4	98.1
New England							
Maine	95.0	91.1	98.3	105.9	...	...	...
New Hampshire	95.7	93.3	98.5	99.7	...	...	...
Vermont	95.6	87.4	98.6	107.6	...	...	...
Massachusetts	91.5	90.4	97.8	101.2	87.2	132.3	...
Rhode Island	96.1	92.7	122.4	92.7	93.1	...	...
Connecticut	94.2	93.0	99.3	99.2	88.8	130.6	...
Middle Atlantic							
New York	91.5	90.8	99.1	104.0	85.2	137.1	...
New Jersey	93.6	93.7	97.8	100.6	88.8	105.9	...
Pennsylvania	92.4	90.5	97.8	102.6	86.9	127.9	...
East North Central							
Ohio	94.0	92.6	98.9	103.0	89.7	120.4	...
Indiana	95.0	93.0	98.5	100.6	90.7	264.6	...
Illinois	94.2	93.8	98.2	103.7	88.6	171.3	...
Michigan	96.0	94.7	99.7	105.1	92.5	132.6	...
Wisconsin	96.3	92.8	100.2	110.0	93.3	...	...
West North Central							
Minnesota	96.0	92.0	99.8	112.0	101.0	...	...

TABLE 17 (Cont'd)

Sex ratios in the various states, by race and residence, 1970

State	Total population	White population			Negro population		
		Urban	Rural-nonfarm	Rural-farm	Urban	Rural-nonfarm	Rural-farm
Iowa	94.6	90.9	94.2	106.7	95.3	...	...
Missouri	93.2	91.3	96.4	104.8	88.4	102.6	...
North Dakota	101.7	97.0	98.8	114.7	...	...	...
South Dakota	98.4	93.2	96.5	110.9	...	...	...
Nebraska	95.5	92.3	95.1	108.2	93.0	...	...
Kansas	96.1	94.3	95.9	106.4	95.9	150.9	...
South Atlantic							
Delaware	95.2	94.9	96.7	103.7	91.9	92.6	...
Maryland	95.5	94.3	101.4	102.7	90.7	104.6	106.0
District of Columbia	86.8	81.9	...	...	88.7	...	...
West Virginia	93.7	88.1	97.5	102.9	84.8	88.3	...
Virginia	97.6	97.6	99.2	101.4	91.2	100.2	98.4
North Carolina	95.9	96.7	96.8	98.4	88.9	94.7	98.3
South Carolina	96.4	99.1	98.2	98.7	88.9	92.5	96.5
Georgia	94.4	94.5	98.8	102.0	85.3	95.5	94.9
Florida	93.2	92.0	99.6	100.3	90.2	99.8	97.0
East South Central							
Kentucky	96.2	93.6	97.8	103.5	90.1	106.9	106.6
Tennessee	93.6	91.8	97.4	100.5	86.5	94.5	101.1

Alabama	93.2	92.5	98.3	100.8	85.0	92.6	96.0
Mississippi	94.0	93.7	97.5	102.9	85.0	92.7	97.6
West South Central							
Arkansas	94.1	90.8	97.5	104.7	85.9	95.5	96.0
Louisiana	94.7	95.2	99.1	102.8	87.3	95.7	98.2
Oklahoma	94.9	93.6	96.9	105.6	88.1	97.5	97.2
Texas	95.8	95.3	99.2	103.7	91.1	100.2	100.4
Mountain							
Montana	99.8	95.7	101.8	113.7	...	...	...
Idaho	99.7	95.4	102.7	109.2	...	...	...
Wyoming	100.6	98.1	102.0	110.3	...	...	...
Colorado	97.4	95.7	100.9	107.8	104.7	...	...
New Mexico	97.2	96.3	101.0	102.2	102.3	...	...
Arizona	96.7	95.2	104.0	101.8	95.9	...	...
Utah	97.6	95.9	102.3	107.4	148.2	...	...
Nevada	102.8	101.5	108.2	124.2	98.8	...	...

TABLE 17 (Cont'd)

Sex ratios in the various states, by race and residence, 1970

State	White population				Negro population		
	Total population	Urban	Rural-nonfarm	Rural-farm	Urban	Rural-nonfarm	Rural-farm
Pacific							
Washington	98.7	96.7	102.3	107.3	110.1	....	....
Oregon	95.9	92.6	102.0	106.1	100.2	....	....
California	96.8	95.6	107.4	108.2	93.7	179.5	....
Alaska	118.9	119.8	123.5	.....	134.4	....	....
Hawaii	108.1	115.7	123.3	.....	191.4	....	....

Source: Compiled and computed from data in U.S. Bureau of the Census, *U.S. Census of Population: 1970, General Social and Economic Characteristics,* Final Report PC(1)-C2-52, state reports (1971), Table 48.

Because of the low sex ratios in urban areas and among Negroes, it is not surprising that the District of Columbia, entirely urban and with Negroes comprising 71 per cent of its inhabitants, has a sex ratio considerably below that for any of the states. It is most closely rivaled in this respect by two of the most highly urbanized states, Massachusetts and New York, with Pennsylvania, Missouri, Alabama, and Florida following in the order named. At the other extreme, the highest sex ratios in the nation prevail in those portions of the country in which the frontier epoch is not long past, in which there are very few Negroes, and in which agricultural and mining activities either predominate now or have done so until recently. Alaska, with almost 119 males for each hundred females is the extreme in this respect, followed by Hawaii, Nevada, North Dakota, and Wyoming in the order named. In 1970, these were the only states with sex ratios above 100.

In addition to the relatively high proportions of males in the Mountain and Pacific geographic divisions, all of the states which border on any of the Mountain states, from Texas to North Dakota, are ones in which the relative importance of males is above that in the national population. Only in North Dakota, however, do males actually outnumber females. From the Dakotas this area of greater male representation extends eastward along the northern tier of states to include Minnesota, Wisconsin, and Michigan.

Southern New England, the highly urbanized Middle Atlantic states, and parts of the South, with its high proportions of Negroes, are the sections in which the females most greatly outnumber males in the population.

Because more than 63 per cent of the people in the United States are whites residing in urban areas, it is well to give special attention to the data for them. These are given separately in Table 17. Among this highly important segment of the population, only in the urban populations of Nevada, Alaska, and Hawaii do males outnumber females. In addition to the sex ratio of only 81.9 for whites in the District of Columbia, which reveals the extent to which women from all over the nation have flocked to Washington to work in government jobs, indexes of less than 92 are characteristic of the towns and cities of such widely distributed states as Maine, Vermont, Massachusetts, Pennsylvania, Iowa, Missouri, West Virginia, Tennessee, and Arkansas. Among the urban white population, sex ratios below the national average are found in one or more of the states in every census division except the Mountain, and even there the sex ratio for Arizona is only 95.2.

Other than in the South, Negroes are almost entirely an urban population; even so, eight of the states have less than 5,000 urban Negroes each. In a few of the others, to which the bulk of the Negroes residing in their towns and cities had migrated during the interim between the 1940 and 1970 censuses, males outnumber females among this group of recent arrivals from distant parts. Minnesota, Colorado, New Mexico, Utah, Washington, Oregon, Alaska, and

Hawaii are the states in this category. In the South, from whose rural districts the exodus of Negroes has been especially marked during recent decades, sex ratios of less than 90 among urban Negroes are the rule rather than the exception. Note especially the ratios of 84.8, 85.0, 85.0, and 85.3 in West Virginia, Alabama, Mississippi, and Georgia, respectively. The last three of these are the states in which the proportions of Negroes traditionally have been the highest in the nation, the ones which contain the bulk of the counties wherein the number of Negroes exceeds that of whites. In the flight of Negroes from the farms of these states, large numbers of the males have gone to the cities of the North and the West in search of jobs, whereas the females in very large numbers have moved to nearby cities such as Atlanta, Jackson, and Birmingham. As a result, in 1960 and 1970, the sex ratios among the Negroes in these cities, respectively, were as follows: Atlanta, 86.1 and 85.7; Jackson, 85.8 and 85.8; and Birmingham, 87.9 and 84.6. In addition, sufficient Negro women moved to Charleston, West Virginia, to produce a sex ratio in 1970 of 81.8 for the Negro population of that city. Such northern states as New York, Pennsylvania, and Illinois, whose principal cities attracted hundreds of thousands of Negroes early in the present century, also now have comparatively low sex ratios among the black residents of their cities and towns, with the number of males per hundred females in New York being especially low.

The rural-farm population is, of course, the residential group in which the excess of males is most pronounced. Among the whites, who constitute the major share of this residential category, males exceed females in number in every state but five (New Hampshire, Rhode Island, Connecticut, North Carolina, and South Carolina), with the sex ratio of 92.7 in Rhode Island being the lowest on the list. In general, however, male preponderance in the white rural-farm population is least pronounced of all throughout the Middle Atlantic region and the South. Thus, every state in the Middle Atlantic region and every one in the South except Oklahoma has a sex ratio for this group that is at or below the national average of 104.7. On the other hand, outside these two regions, in no states except New Hampshire, Massachusetts, Rhode Island, Connecticut, Ohio, Indiana, Illinois, New Mexico, and Arizona are the sex ratios for this group below the national norm. The highest ratios of all, among the whites residing on the nation's farms, are those for Nevada, North Dakota, Montana, Minnesota, and South Dakota, in the order named. Among Negroes, too, the sex ratios in the rural-farm parts of the various states are considerably higher than those for the other residential groups, with the highest (106.6) being in Kentucky.

For the most part, the sex ratios of the rural-farm population, white and Negro, are intermediate between the very low ones of the urban population and the relatively high ones of the rural-farm population. However, in states such as Iowa and Nebraska, in which the village population, with its high proportions of widows and spinsters, makes up the bulk of the category, the sex ratio is comparatively low; whereas, in the states such as those in the Mountain division, in which considerable groups of persons engaged in mining, lumbering, and other extractive industries are included in the rural-nonfarm population, the corresponding sex ratios are higher. In this connection, it should be repeated that the high sex ratios in this region, in all residential categories, are due in large measure to the large numbers of males who followed the frontier into these states in the opening years of the twentieth century. In other states such as Massachusetts and New Jersey, in which much of the rural-nonfarm population consists of suburbanites, the sex ratios tend to be close to 100.

Other Significant Variations

The economic base or bases upon which a city or other area rests also is a powerful force in determining the proportions of the sexes. This has already been demonstrated by the data showing the relatively high proportions of males prevailing in the rural-farm areas and the sections of the country in which mining, lumbering, and other extractive industries are of considerable importance. But it seems well to note some of the extremes in the degree to which the sex ratio varies from city to city throughout the United States. In general, if other factors are equal, cities which function chiefly as naval bases or great seaports, centers of heavy industry, and mining centers tend to have comparatively high proportions of males, whereas those devoted largely to light industrial activities (such as textile manufacturing), residential cities, and those based largely on distribution services run heavily to females. With these points in mind it is interesting to note that in 1970 the cities of 100,000 or more inhabitants having the highest sex ratios were: Columbia, South Carolina, 127.5; Norfolk, 117.6; Virginia Beach, 110.3; Newport News, 107.3; San Diego, 106.3; Hampton, 100.7; Las Vegas, 100.4; and Honolulu, 100.3. All of these were more than seven points above the ratio of 93.0 prevailing among the urban population as a whole, but they also were the only ones with ratios of 100 or more among the 153 cities that were studied. At the other extreme was St. Petersburg, with only 82.1 males per hundred females, followed by thirteen other cities which had sex ratios more than seven points below that of the nation's urban population as a whole. Their names and ratios are: Chattanooga, 83.1; St. Louis, 83.7; Albany, New York, 83.9; Glendale, 84.2; Minneapolis, 84.4; Richmond, 84.8; Birmingham, 84.9; Pasadena, 85.2; Boston, 85.4; Little Rock, 85.4; Montgomery, 85.4; Macon, 85.7; and Scranton, 85.9. In all, 110 of the large cities had sex ratios that were below the nation's urban average, for despite the few that contain more males than females, the latter predominate in the overwhelming majority of cases. Even in places such as Gary, San Francisco, and Detroit, in which males outnumbered females as recently as 1950, females now are in a substantial majority.

Sex Ratio: 1900 to 1970

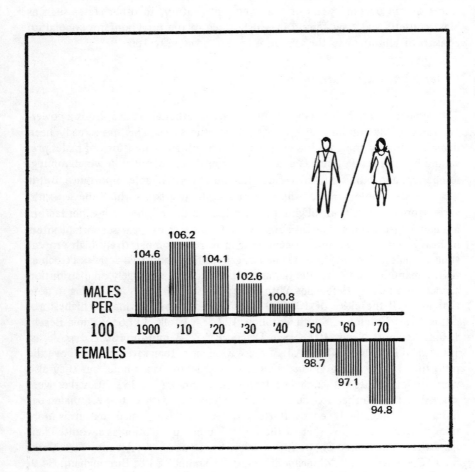

Figure 36. Changes in the sex ratio in the United States, 1900 to 1970. Illustration from the Bureau of the Census.

TRENDS IN THE SEX RATIO

Changes in the sex ratio in the United States result largely from the flow and ebb of the immigrant tide. As indicated above, more males than females migrate long distances. Therefore, the relative numbers of males and females in a nation are strongly influenced by the numbers and proportions of the foreign-born in its population. Prior to 1910, when the sex ratio in the United States was at an all-time high of 106.0, the highest proportions of males in this country occurred in 1890 (105.0), and 1860 (104.7). These indexes are considerably above the ratios of 103.1 registered in 1830 and 102.2 in 1870. The latter, coming at a time shortly after hundreds of thousands of males had been slain in battle and war had practically halted immigration to this country, is the lowest on record except for 1940, when the sex ratio was 100.7; 1950, when it was 98.6; 1960, when it had fallen to 97.0; and 1970, when it was 94.8. (See Figure 36.) Due mostly to the practical cessation of immigration brought about by the First World War, which was maintained by the imposition of restrictions and the quota system (1922 and 1924) and shut off almost entirely by the great economic depression, the number of males per hundred females in this country fell from the all-time high registered in 1910 to 104.0 in 1920, 102.5 in 1930, 100.7 in 1940, and then, for the first time in history, to less than 100 by 1950. The large loss of men during the Second World War and in Korea and Viet-Nam contributed materially, along with the high mortality rates of the rapidly aging foreign-born population, in bringing the sex ratio to the low of 94.8 at the time of the latest census.

The sex ratio for native whites was reported as 103.1 in 1850 and as 103.7 in 1860, on the eve of the great Civil War. After the termination of this conflict, the next census, that of 1870, reported only 100.6 males per hundred females in the native white population, a strong reflection of the carnage that took place during the four years of conflict. Thereafter, the sex ratio for this group rose to 102.1 in 1880 and to 102.9 in 1890. Then it began to fall steadily, reaching 101.1 in 1930, 100.1 in 1940, and affected perceptibly by the years of conflict during the ensuing decade, to 98.6 in 1950. By 1960, it had dropped to 97.5 and ten years later it had fallen to 95.9.

Only during the early years of the Republic, when the heavy importation of male slaves was a factor, has the Negro population included more males than females. In 1820, the first census to make available the necessary data, the sex ratio among Negroes in the United States was 103.4, but by 1830 it had fallen to 100.0. Ever since this time the index has been less than 100, with the lows coming at the end of the Civil War (96.2), in 1940 (95.0), 1950 (94.3), 1960 (93.4), and 1970 (90.7). Undoubtedly there is a considerable margin of error in these indexes, but even so the sex ratio among Negroes is low and getting lower. In addition to the effects of the wars, which reduce the sex ratios through the deaths of combatants, the factors treated in the preceding chapter which are producing the rapid aging of the population, white and Negro, are the principal causes of the falling sex ratios in the United States during the twentieth century. By increasing the numbers and proportions of the population in the ages above forty, in which the lower death rates of females than of males have brought the sex ratio to very low levels, such a trend has contributed greatly to the gradual fall of the sex ratios of both the native white and the Negro populations. Moreover, the annual decreases in birth rates and in the numbers of babies born in the late 1950's and all of the 1960's have decreased the relative importance of males in the population.

Between 1920 and 1960 there was a tendency for the differences in the sex ratios of the rural and urban populations to become more pronounced. The two had drawn considerably apart by 1920, when there were only 100.4 males per hundred females in the urban population of the United States in comparison with indexes of 106.5 for the rural-nonfarm and 109.1 in the rural-farm portions of the nation. At that time the sex ratio of the native white, urban population was only 96.9, whereas in rural-nonfarm territory the corresponding figure was 102.7, and in rural-farm areas it was 109.5. Similarly among Negroes the sex ratios were 95.4, 103.7, and 100.3, in the urban, rural-nonfarm, and rural-farm residential groups, respectively. By 1960, however, the sex ratio for the urban population had fallen to 94.0, a decrease of 6.4 points, whereas that of the rural-nonfarm population was down only to 103.3, a decrease of 3.2 points, and that of the rural-farm category was 107.2, a decrease of 1.9 points. The sex ratio of the rural-farm portion of the native white population in 1960 was 107.9, which is a decrease of 1.6 points over the level at which it stood in 1920, whereas for rural-farm Negroes the 1960 index of 101.7 is 1.4 points above the one prevailing forty years earlier. In sharp contrast, between 1920 and 1960 in the urban districts the sex ratio for native whites fell to 94.5, a decrease of 2.4 points, and that for Negroes fell to 90.3, a decline of 5.1 points. Thus, the concentration of males on the nation's farms and of females in its cities became much greater during these forty years. Between 1960 and 1970, however, the pattern changed, for the decreases in the urban population, both native white and Negro, were smaller than those in the two rural populations. For the urban population the sex ratio decreased to 93.0 in 1970 (1.0 point), whereas that for the rural-nonfarm group declined to 99.0 (4.0 points) and that for the rural-farm population fell to 105.7 (1.5 points). For the native white population, the decreases for the urban, rural-nonfarm, and the rural-farm populations were 0.3 point, 3.8 points, and 1.9 points, respectively; for the Negro population the comparable decreases in the three residence categories were 1.2 points, 3.4 points, and 3.6 points. Thus, between 1960 and 1970, the patterns of distribution by sex grew more alike for the various residence groups, especially the urban and the rural-nonfarm. This is simply another reflection of the process of homogenization in American society by which its various components tend to become more evenly distributed and many of the differences between its parts to diminish.

As has been suggested above, the pushing forward of the frontier from the Atlantic to the Pacific brought about severe imbalances between the proportions of the sexes in the various geographic divisions of the United States. Westward to the frontier went the males, making the sex ratios in many western states extremely high, whereas in the East and the South, the migrations left disproportionately large numbers of females in their wake. With the passing of the frontier, however, each succeeding census has revealed a strong tendency for these state and regional differences in the proportions of males and females in the population to become smaller or for the sex ratios in the various parts of the nation to cluster more closely around the national mean. For example, in the Mountain states, as late as 1920 there were 115.7 males for every hundred females in the population. By 1930, however, this ratio had fallen to 111.3, by 1940 to 107.4, by 1950 to 104.4, by 1960 to 101.2, and by 1970 to only 98.1. Whereas at the close of the First World War the sex ratio in this geographic division was 11.7 points above the national average, at the time of the latest census it was only 3.3 points above. The tendency was even more pronounced in the Pacific states (excluding Alaska and Hawaii). In 1920, there were on the West Coast 113.9 males for every hundred females, but by 1970 the corresponding index was only 97.0. As a result, at the time of the 1970 census the three coterminous states in the Pacific geographic division together had a sex ratio only 2.2 points above that for the nation as a whole, whereas fifty years earlier the index was 9.9 points above. Likewise, in the East North Central, the West North Central, the South Atlantic, and the West South Central geographic divisions, where the sex ratios are above the national average, as one census after another is consulted one may observe the tendency for the sex ratios in the areas to approach the national average. Thus, in the East North Central states the sex ratio declined from 1.7 points above that of the United States in 1920 to only 0.1 point above in 1970. In the West North Central states, the corresponding change was from 2.1 points above to 0.4, and in the West South Central states it was from 1.8 points above to 0.6. In the South Atlantic division the ratio went from 0.4 point below the national average in 1920 to 0.2 point above in 1970.

In sharp contrast with these reductions in the sex ratio were the changes in the geographic divisions in which the ratios consistently have been lower than that for the nation. In two of these, during the interim between 1920 and 1970, the difference between the sex ratio of the division and that of the United States became less pronounced by the end of the period than it had been at the beginning. However, the Middle Atlantic division, the section of the country having the lowest sex ratio, had an index in 1970 that was 2.6 points below the national average, the same as it was in 1920. This was entirely due to the fact that the sex ratio of the nation fell at the same rate as that of the region, and not because of any increase in the proportions of males in that part of the country. In 1970, New England had a sex ratio 1.5 points below that for the United States and the East South Central states a ratio 0.5 point under the national average. However, fifty years earlier the sex ratios in both of these geographic divisions were less than the one for the entire country by 2.9 points. The narrowing of the difference was due in each case to the lowering of the national index, and not because the number of males per hundred females rose in either of these sections of the country. By 1970, the sex ratios in all of the nine divisions were within 3.3 points or less of the national average and the spread between the highest ratio (the Mountain division) and the lowest (the Middle Atlantic division) was only 5.9 points. The net effect of these various regional trends is readily apparent: now that all portions of the United States are well settled, with the passing of each decade the regional differentials are being reduced and the ratios between the sexes in all parts of the nation are approaching the national average.[7]

The nature of the current trends is indicated by an examination of the changes in the sex ratios of the various states in the decade 1960 to 1970. During this period, the fall in the sex ratio in the nation as a whole was accompanied by decreases in the indexes for all of the states and the District of Columbia. Nineteen of them and the nation's capital had indexes in 1960 lower than the national average. During the decade under consideration, the indexes for ten of them (Alabama, Connecticut, Georgia, Louisiana, Massachusetts, Missouri, New Hampshire, Rhode Island, Tennessee, and Vermont) and the District of Columbia fell less rapidly than that for the nation, so that in 1970, the relative importance of males and females in their populations was nearer the national mean than had been the case ten years earlier. However, in eight of the states (Arkansas, Florida, Illinois, New Jersey, New York, Ohio, Pennsylvania, and West Virginia), the sex ratio fell off more rapidly between 1960 and 1970 than it did in the United States as a whole so that the "femininity" of their populations, compared to the nation, became even greater during the ten years. Finally, in Mississippi, the amount of reduction in the sex ratio was the same as that in the nation as a whole.

In thirty-one of the states, the sex ratios in 1960 were above the national average. In twenty-five of them (Alaska, Arizona, California, Delaware, Hawaii, Idaho, Iowa, Kansas, Kentucky, Maine, Maryland, Michigan, Minnesota, Montana, Nebraska, Nevada, New Mexico, North Dakota, Oklahoma, Oregon, South Dakota, Texas, Washington, Wisconsin, and Wyoming), the fall in the index during the period was more rapid than that in the nation, bringing the proportions of males and females in their populations closer to the national average. The most pronounced changes in this respect were the reductions of the sex ratios by 12.9, 6.2, 4.4, and 4.4 points in the states of Alaska, Hawaii, New Mexico, and Wyoming, respectively. In Indiana, the drop in the index (2.2 points) was the same as that in the nation as a whole. In the remaining five states (Colorado, North Carolina, South Carolina, Utah, and Virginia), the fall in the index for the state was less rapid than that in the one for the United States. Therefore, the five are the exceptions to the rule. Nevertheless, in the country as a whole, the tendency is clear: between 1960 and 1970 the changes generally reduced the extent to which the sex ratios in the various regions and states differed from that in the United States as a whole.

NOTES

1. Cf. U.S. Bureau of the Census, *Fifteenth Census of the United States, 1930, Population,* Vol. II, *General Report, Statistics by Subjects* (Washington: Government Printing Office, 1933), p. 93.

2. See T. Lynn Smith, "Errors in the Sex Classification of Negro Children in the United States Census," *Congrés international de la population* (Paris: Herman & Cie, 1938), V, pp. 97 - 106. See also Rupert B. Vance and Nadia Danilevsky, *All These People* (Chapel Hill: University of North Carolina Press, 1945), pp. 44 - 47; and Paul E. Zopf, Jr., *North Carolina: A Demographic Profile* (Chapel Hill: University of North Carolina Population Center, 1967), p. 79.

3. A detailed study of this phenomenon will be found in T. Lynn Smith and Homer L. Hitt, "The Misstatement of Women's Ages and the Vital Indexes," *Metron,* XIII, 4 (Dec., 1939), pp. 95 - 108.

4. E. H. Slade, *Census of Pakistan, 1951* (Karachi: Manager of Publications, Government of Pakistan, 1955), I, pp. 54 - 56.

5. In turn this low sex ratio at birth probably is due to a considerable extent to the high proportion of stillbirths among births of Negro women. See T. Lynn Smith, "A Demographic Study of the American Negro," *Social Forces,* 23, 3 (March, 1945), pp. 382 - 383. This is because, for some unknown reason stillbirths run heavily to the masculine sex, the sex ratio probably being about 110 among all pregnancies and between 120 and 170 among stillbirths. See Sanford Winston, "The Influence of Social Factors upon the Sex Ratio at Birth," *American Journal of Sociology,* 37, 1 (July, 1931), pp. 8 - 12.

6. T. Lynn Smith, *Population Analysis* (New York: McGraw-Hill Book Company, 1948), p. 125.

7. For discussions of this factor as one element in the homogenization of American society, see T. Lynn Smith, "The Homogenization of Society in the United States," *Memoire du XIX Congress International de Sociologie,* 2 (1960), pp. 245 - 275, and T. Lynn Smith and Paul E. Zopf, Jr., *Principles of Inductive Rural Sociology* (Philadelphia: F. A. Davis Company, 1970), Chapter 18.

BOGUE, DONALD J. *The Population of the United States,* Chap. 8. Glencoe, Ill.: The Free Press, 1959.

BOGUE, DONALD J. *Principles of Demography,* pp. 165 - 172. New York: John Wiley & Sons, Inc., 1969.

HUNT, CHESTER L. "Female Occupational Roles and Urban Sex Ratios in the United States, Japan, and the Philippines." *Social Forces,* Vol. 43, No. 3 (March, 1965), pp. 407 - 417.

SCHMID, CALVIN F. "Age and Sex Composition of Urban Subareas," in *Population and Society,* edited by Charles B. Nam, pp. 423 - 426. Boston: Houghton Mifflin Company, 1968.

SHRYOCK, HENRY S., JACOB S. SIEGEL, and associates. *The Methods and Materials of Demography,* Vol. 1, Chap. 7. Washington: Government Printing Office, 1971.

SMITH, T. LYNN. *Brazil: People and Institutions,* 4th ed., pp. 87 - 88. Baton Rouge: Louisiana State University Press, 1972.

SMITH, T. LYNN. *Latin American Population Studies,* pp. 20 - 34. Gainesville: University of Florida Press, 1960.

SMITH, T. LYNN, and HOMER L. HITT. *The People of Louisiana,* Chap. VI. Baton Rouge: Louisiana State University Press, 1952.

TARVER, JAMES D., and LEE CHE-FU. "The Sex Ratio of Registered Live Births in the United States, 1942 - 1963." *Demography,* Vol. 5, No. 1 (February, 1968), pp. 374 - 381.

THOMPSON, WARREN S. *Growth and Changes in California's Population,* Chap. V. Los Angeles: The Haynes Foundation, 1955.

ZOPF, PAUL E., JR. *North Carolina: A Demographic Profile,* Chap. IV. Chapel Hill: University of North Carolina Population Center, 1967.

8
MARITAL CONDITION

An individual's personal happiness is probably more closely dependent upon his marital condition or status than on any other factor. Likewise, the well-being of any society is influenced highly by the proportions of its population that are single, married and living with their mates, separated, widowed, and divorced. For both of these reasons the subject is of concern to students of population. In addition, such important demographic processes as the birth rate and the death rate seem to be correlated to some significant degree with the marital condition of the population.

DATA AND CLASSIFICATIONS

Every modern census includes items on the marital condition of the population, and the tables presenting the information secured from these questions figure prominently in the published tabulations. Indeed, in many of the census reports, including those of the United States, the amount of space given to such materials looms large in the total. In the United States a query on marital status was used for the first time in 1880, but the data for that year were never published. Beginning with the reports of the 1890 census, however, and continuing through those for 1970, information on this important characteristic fills many pages in the census volumes.

During the eighty years in which information on marital condition has been supplied for the population of the United States, much has been learned about the most effective and efficient manner of tabulating such material. For example, the 1970 tables refer only to the population fourteen years of age and over, a practice that is widely used in reports issued in other countries. Excluding children of less than fourteen is good procedure under the conditions prevailing in most countries at the present time, since very few persons nowadays either contract matrimony or are given in marriage before they have passed through adolescence. Thus, in the United States in 1970 only 20,768 of the 2,136,818 boys aged fourteen were reported as married, and the corresponding figure for girls was only 22,010 in a total of 2,049,056. In countries in which child marriage still prevails to any considerable extent, there might be more reason for including the very young in the tabulations, but throughout most of the modern world inclusion of the children in the tables merely introduces unnecessary complications in the organization, manipulation, analysis, and interpretation of the data. It also is expensive and highly wasteful of space that might be much better used for other valuable tabulations.

There are four standard categories used for classifying the population according to marital status: single, married, widowed, and divorced. Naturally, since the legal, religious, and moral sanctions governing unions between men and women vary so widely from time to time, from one society to another, and even within a given society at a stated time, those responsible for a census may experience considerable difficulty in deciding precisely whom to place in the married group. Much of the perplexity is related to the proper handling of common-law or other fairly stable unions entered into without benefit of clergy or commissioned representatives of the state. Even the courts sometimes have trouble in determining whether or not one of these unions should be considered a marriage. Therefore, it is not likely that the census taker will be able to classify all cases perfectly. Nevertheless, many countries do attempt to distinguish in their census tabulations between the persons who are legally married and those who are united only by some common-law contract.

In the United States the attempt is made to include in the married category those living under common-law arrangements and those reported as separated. Those whose marriages have been annulled, on the other hand, are classified as single. The fact that in the United States the ordained representatives (priests, ministers, rabbis) of various religious bodies are authorized to act for the state in the performance of legal marriage ceremonies spares our census officials some of the difficulties encountered in some countries. In Brazil, for example, the couple wishing to marry legally and also according to the rites of the church must have two separate and distinct ceremonies performed, one by the commissioned officer of the state and the other by the priest, minister, or rabbi.[1] Otherwise, the union will lack either legal validity or religious sanction. Under these circumstances, census takers must determine what distinction, if any, shall be made between those who are legally married only, those united in a church union only, and those married both in accordance with the law and in accordance with the rules of the church.

There also are important differences among those who are married at any given time with respect to previous marriages of part of the married population and the ways in which any earlier marriage contracts were terminated. The married category includes, of course, many persons who remarried after one or more earlier unions had ended. Thus, those classified as married at the time of the census include those for whom the current union is the only one, widows and widowers

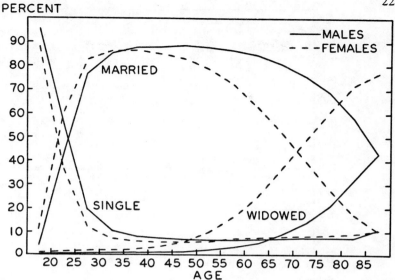

Figure 37. The relationship of age to marital status among the population of the United States, by sex, 1970.

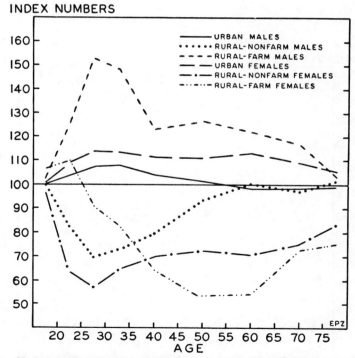

Figure 38. Index numbers showing the extent to which the white urban, rural-nonfarm, and rural-farm populations of the United States had more or less than their pro rata shares of single persons of each age group, by sex, 1970.

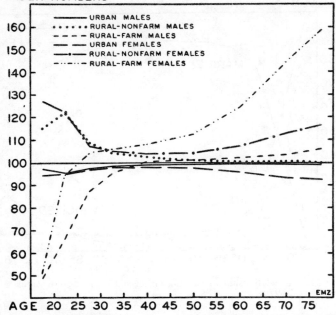

Figure 39. Index numbers showing the extent to which the white urban, rural-nonfarm, and rural-farm populations of the United States had more or less than their pro rata shares of married persons of each age group, by sex, 1970.

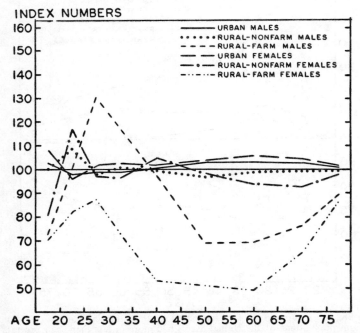

Figure 40. Index numbers showing the extent to which the white urban, rural-nonfarm, and rural-farm populations of the United States had more or less than their pro rata shares of widowed persons of each age group, by sex, 1970.

who have remarried, divorcees who have remarried, and those who have had two or more previous wives or husbands. As yet, however, it has not proved practicable for a census to attempt detailed classifications of the married which would set forth precisely the facts about previous marital conditions of the persons involved.

In 1940, 1950, 1960, and 1970, the United States Census classified the population of fourteen years of age and over into the four broadly recognized groups (single, married, widowed, and divorced), with the married category subdivided into the cases in which the spouses were living together in the home and those in which they resided in different households. In 1960 and 1970, an attempt was made to distinguish those who had been married more than once.

AGE AND MARITAL STATUS

The average person's marital condition depends largely upon his age; and the proportions of the single, married, and widowed in a population are determined to a large extent by its age distribution. Therefore, the first step in all well-conceived attempts to analyze and compare the marital status of various populations must be the adoption or development of adequate methods for controlling the age factor. Some of the ways of doing this were employed in constructing Figures 37 through 40. These are relied upon heavily in the comparisons attempted in this chapter. First, it is well to examine in some detail the manner in which marital condition varies with age.

In most modern societies child marriages are almost nonexistent. Therefore, in a population such as that of Japan, France, Turkey, or the United States, the beginning of adolescence finds 100 per cent of the population in the single category. (See Figure 37, which compares the marital status of the male and female populations of the United States in 1970 and which is fairly representative of the contemporary situation in many western societies.) A very small number of marriages involves those of about twelve years of age, but it is not until age fifteen has been reached that significant proportions enter into the marriage contract. Thereafter the curve showing the percentage single falls as age advances, precipitously at first, very slowly later on, until about the age of fifty-five. After this age has been attained, very few persons marry for the first time. As is evident from Figure 37, in the United States in 1970 about one out of eleven persons in the age group of eighty-five and over had never married at all, the exact proportions being 10.8 per cent for males and 10.7 per cent for females. In 1960, the corresponding proportions were 7.1 per cent and 9.6 per cent.

As indicated above, by the time age fifteen has been reached, significant numbers of people transfer from the category of single to that of married. Accordingly, the curve showing the proportion married rises rapidly, to accompany the fall in the one representing the single. Females marry at somewhat younger ages than males, so that the curve for the former rises somewhat earlier than for the latter. The data in Figure 37 indicate that before women had completed their twentieth year of life, wives already outnumbered their unmarried sisters; but it was only while men were in their twenty-third year that the number of the married came to exceed that of the single. The curves for both sexes continue to rise with increasing age, since the number of new marriages is more than sufficient to offset the ones disrupted by death or divorce. That for females reaches its maximum height (86.6 per cent married) in the age group thirty-five to thirty-nine; and that for males, which rises more slowly, arrives at its zenith (88.3 per cent married) in the age group forty-five to forty-nine.

After these maximum proportions have been attained, the percentage married begins to fall off, rather rapidly among women and not so fast among men. As a result, by the time the ages above eighty-five had been reached, only 10.7 per cent of the women remained in the married category, in comparison with 43.4 per cent of the men. This differential is explained, of course, by the facts that women outlive men, widowers are more likely than widows to remarry, and women tend to marry slightly older men.

The proportions of the widowed in the population are insignificant during the years of late adolescence and early adulthood, but they rise steadily with increasing age. The curve representing the females rises more rapidly than that for the males, and the former also ascends to heights considerably above those attained by the latter. At about the age of forty-five the number of widows comes to exceed the number of single females in the population, whereas among males the curve for the widowers does not rise above that for the single until age sixty-five has been reached. At age seventy, one out of every seven males is a widower and one out of every two females a widow.

Since the expectation of life at birth in the United States in 1970 was about seventy, it is interesting to note the marital condition of the population at that age. For the man who had attained his seventieth birthday, the chances were about one in thirteen that he would have remained a bachelor, seven out of ten that he would be living with his first wife or a subsequent one, and only about one out of seven that he would be a widower. For the woman, however, the probabilities are very different. the chances that she would have lived to age seventy without marrying at all also were one in thirteen, but that she would be living in the married condition only two out of five and that she would be a widow, one in two.

SOME INTERNATIONAL COMPARISONS

Although it is obvious that marriage patterns and the marital condition of the population vary widely from country to country, it is not easy to make valid international comparisons of marital status. This is largely because of the relationship between age and marital status just discussed, coupled with the fact that the age distributions of various populations are so different from one another. Unless the age factor is carefully controlled, it is nonsense to attempt comparisons of the marital condition of the population in such a country as Mexico or India, in which high proportions of the adult population are concentrated in the ages at which large percentages are married, and one, such as the United Kingdom or the United States, in which large proportions of the adult population are beyond the age of fifty when many are widowed.

In an attempt to make readily available to the student some of the more significant features of the marital condition of people throughout the world, Table 18 was prepared. In it is presented, for a large share of the countries for which the data permit such comparisons, current information pertaining to the following "indicators" of marital status: (1) the age group in which the curve showing the proportion of that population that is married reaches its maximum height; (2) the percentage of the persons in this age group who are classified as married; and (3) the proportion of those who have passed their seventy-fifth birthdays who are still single, and who therefore in all probability will never marry. Each of these three indicators is given separately for both the male and the female portions of the population.

From the materials in Table 18 a number of significant generalizations may be made relative to the marital condition of various populations throughout the world.

1. Without exception, the curve showing the percentage married reaches its maximum at an earlier age for females than for males.

2. In more than 66 per cent of the countries, the figure showing the maximum height of the curve representing the proportion of married in the various age groups in the population is higher for males than the one for females.

3. India, the Khmer Republic (Cambodia), and Pakistan are the countries in which the tendency to marry at the earliest ages is most pronounced, and Paraguay, Ireland, Sweden, England and Wales, and the Soviet Union are the ones in which the tendency to postpone marriage until later in life is the strongest. In the last two cases, however, women marry fairly young, whereas the curves showing the proportions of the married among the male population continue to rise until the age group fifty to fifty-four is reached.

4. The curves showing the marital status of the population in Belgium, Canada, Ceylon, England and Wales, and the United States are very similar.

5. The countries in which persons are most likely to marry during the course of their lifetimes are Senegal, Tunisia, Japan, the Republic of Korea, and Bulgaria.

6. Those in which they are least likely to contract formal marriage arrangements are the Latin American countries, including El Salvador, Honduras, Panama, Colombia, and Paraguay,[2] although the tendency to remain single is also relatively great in Ireland, Portugal, Sweden, Switzerland, and Northern Ireland.

TABLE 18

Some indicators of marital condition of the population in selected
countries, latest census

Country	Year	Males Age group	Males Per cent married	Females Age group	Females Per cent married	Percentage of those 75 & over who are single Males	Percentage of those 75 & over who are single Females
Africa							
Angola	1960	45-49	88.9	30-34	90.7	7.4	12.7
Egypt	1960	45-49	94.9	30-34	89.7	0.9	0.5
Liberia	1962	45-49	81.7	30-34	90.7	3.7	2.2
Morocco	1960	45-49	94.1	25-29	91.0	1.6	2.3
Senegal[a]	1960-61	45-49	92.2	30-34	93.9	0.4	0.2
South Africa[a]	1960	45-49	89.0	35-39	84.2	4.5	4.5
Tunisia	1966	45-49	93.4	30-34	92.4	2.0	1.7
Zambia	1969	45-49	90.0	30-34	86.7	4.6	7.1
America, North							
Canada	1966	45-49	88.2	35-39	89.5	10.2	10.1
Costa Rica[a]	1963	45-49	83.6	35-39	76.8	12.2	20.3
Dominican Republic[a]	1960	45-49	82.4	30-34	81.1	20.1	27.0
El Salvador[a]	1961	45-49	81.2	35-39	74.3	17.5	35.0
Guatemala[a]	1964	40-44	85.6	30-34	83.3	11.5	20.5
Honduras[a]	1961	45-49	83.4	30-34	77.2	19.1	36.1
Mexico[a]	1960	45-49	86.7	35-39	80.9	4.9	9.6
Panama[a]	1960	40-44	77.1	35-39	78.4	27.6	33.2
Pureto Rico[a]	1960	45-49	84.9	35-39	81.5	5.7	6.2
United States	1970	45-49	88.3	35-39	86.6	8.0	9.0
America, South							
Argentina[a]	1960	45-49	83.3	35-39	82.0	13.5	15.1
Chile[a]	1970	40-44	83.4	35-39	77.4	7.5	14.9
Colombia[a]	1964	45-49	81.7	35-39	74.2	12.6	21.5
Ecuador[a]	1962	45-49	85.8	35-39	81.0	7.4	15.7
Paraguay[a]	1962	50-54	85.1	35-39	74.7	14.9	38.4
Peru[a]	1961	45-49	85.6	35-39	81.6	8.0	13.9
Uruguay[a]	1963	45-49	81.4	35-39	80.4	14.1	19.9
Asia							
Ceylon[a]	1963	45-49	88.6	35-39	89.8	7.8	6.2
Hong Kong	1961	45-49	91.4	30-34	91.4	2.3	3.4
India	1961	35-39	90.9	25-29	94.2	2.8[b]	0.4[b]
Iraq	1965	45-49	90.3	30-34	88.3	4.0	2.9
Israel	1961	45-49	93.4	35-39	92.0	2.8	3.2
Japan	1970	45-49	95.5	30-34	89.8	1.0	1.0
Khmer Republic	1962	35-39	94.5	30-34	90.1	3.0	2.4
Korea, Republic	1966	40-44	97.5	30-34	93.9	0.1	0.1
Pakistan	1961	35-39	91.0	25-29	93.7	1.6[c]	0.6[c]
Syrian Arab Republic	1960	45-49	92.2	35-39	91.8	1.3	1.9
Thailand	1960	40-44	91.6	35-39	86.3	1.7[b]	1.7[b]

TABLE 18 (Cont'd)

Some indicators of marital condition of the population in selected countries, latest census

Country	Year	Age group in which the proportion married is maximum				Percentage of those 75 & over who are single	
		Males		Females			
		Age group	Per cent married	Age group	Per cent married	Males	Females
Europe							
Belgium	1961	40-44	88.6	30-34	87.9	7.6	12.1
Bulgaria	1965	45-49	96.3	30-34	93.0	1.0	0.9
Czechoslovakia	1961	45-49	90.7	30-34	88.9	3.6	7.6
Denmark	1965	45-49	84.4	30-34	86.4	7.2	15.1
Finland	1960	40-44	85.6	35-39	79.6	9.0	16.4
France	1968	45-49	86.1	30-34	86.8	6.2	10.9
Germany, Democratic Rebublic[d]	1964	40-44	95.6	30-34	85.5	2.1	8.3
Hungary	1970	45-49	91.7	30-34	89.6	3.8	5.7
Ireland	1966	50-54	69.0	40-44	77.4	25.6	23.9
Netherlands	1960	40-44	90.6	35-39	86.9	7.8	13.5
Norway	1960	45-49	83.3	35-39	85.7	11.9	21.0
Poland	1960	40-44	93.9	30-34	85.7	3.0[b]	7.8[b]
Portugal	1960	45-49	85.8	35-39	78.7	7.9	14.9
Romania	1966	40-44	95.1	30-34	89.9	1.7	2.6
Spain	1960	45-49	91.1	35-39	82.3	7.5	12.0
Sweden	1970	50-54	80.4	35-39	85.0	12.2	20.4
Switzerland	1960	45-49	84.7	35-39	80.0	10.2	17.5
United Kingdom							
England and Wales	1966	50-54	88.3	30-34	89.2	6.4	15.4
Northern Ireland	1966	45-49	80.6	35-39	82.7	17.9	24.0
Scotland	1966	40-44	86.2	30-34	87.4	10.5	22.5
Oceania							
Australia	1966	45-49	84.6	30-34	88.8	9.2	12.8
New Zealand	1966	45-49	86.7	30-34	90.3	8.4	12.6
U.S.S.R.	1970	50-54	95.2	30-34	85.3	—	—

Source: Compiled and computed from data in United Nations, *Demographic Yearbook, 1968,* pp. 190-277, Table 7; *1971,* pp. 412-472, Table 12.

[a] Includes those classified separately as consensually married.
[b] 70 and over.
[c] 60 and over.
[d] Includes East Berlin.

DIFFERENTIALS IN MARITAL STATUS

In addition to the relationship between age and marital condition discussed above. it is possible to demonstrate the manner in which several other factors influence the marital condition of a population. These include sex, residence in rural or urban areas, and race or color. It is likely that there also are regional differences in marital condition, quite over and above those that may appear because the age, sex, racial, and residential composition of the population varies widely from one region to another, but much meticulous work, with all of the factors just enumerated carefully controlled, would be necessary in order to discover exactly what they are and to measure their magnitude. Unless this were done, any comparisons attempted would merely demonstrate that one region is more rural or urban, has higher proportions of whites or nonwhites, or has a different sex ratio than another. These facts are well known and susceptible of demonstration in much less cumbersome ways. As yet, however, there has been little effort to discover the extent to which such regional differences are present in the United States or any other country. Likewise, any substantial efforts to determine the nature of the relationship, if any, between marital condition and such factors as religious affiliations, occupational status, educational status, and social status are still to be made.

In the discussions that follow, the data for the United States are used for purposes of illustration. All are for persons aged fifteen and over.

Sex and Marital Condition

The nature and extent of the differences between the marital status of males and females are readily apparent through an examination of Figure 37. During the early years of life women are much more likely to be married, or less likely to be single, than men. After the age of thirty-five or forty has been passed, however, men are more likely than women to be married, although the difference between the sexes with respect to the percentage single tends to disappear. This is explained, of course, by the fact that at any time widows greatly outnumber widowers in the population. After the age of sixty-nine has been passed, widowhood becomes the lot of the average woman, whereas only after the age of eighty-five has been passed do widowers come to outnumber married men.

Race or Color and Marital Status

The associations between race and marital status and residence and marital status are so interdependent that the two must be analyzed simultaneously. To handle these two relationships at the same time that the essential age and sex classifications also are included is an involved procedure. This has been done by the senior author, however, for 1940 and 1950,[3] and by both writers for 1960 and 1970. The results for 1970 may be presented in summary form.

The Negro male population of the United States marries at an earlier age than the white and is less likely than the white to reach the most advanced ages without marrying at all. The peak ages of marriage are thirty-five to thirty-nine for Negroes (80.9 per cent married) and forty-five to forty-nine for whites (89.1 per cent married). However, in 1970, the percentage of Negro males who were married was higher than that of white males only between the ages of fifteen and nineteen and eighty-five and over. At all other ages the proportion was lower among Negroes than whites, with the result that 56.9 per cent of the entire Negro male population but 66.8 per cent of the white male group was classified as married. Conversely, the percentage of Negro men who were single was higher than that of whites at all ages except fifteen to nineteen and eighty to eight-four, resulting in the classification as single of 35.5 per cent of the Negro males and 27.7 per cent of the white males. Negro males also are more likely than the whites to be in the widowed category at all ages except eighty-five and over and are more apt than the whites to be identified as divorced at all ages above twenty-four. Consequently, for all ages taken together, 4.3 per cent of the Negro males and 2.8 per cent of the whites were classified as widowed; 3.3 per cent of the Negroes and 2.6 per cent of the whites were categorized as divorced. The data on divorce should be treated with caution, however, for they reflect a person's status at the time of the census and indicate little about rates of divorce and remarriage, both of which are much higher than the data on the status of the divorced might seem to imply. The proportions of the widowed among the Negro male population are considerable, of course, because of the relatively high mortality rates of the Negro female population, although as is suggested below, the rates for Negro males are even higher.

As identified in 1970, the Negro and white female populations reached the highest proportions married in the same age group (thirty-five to thirty-nine) when 77.2 per cent of the Negro women and 87.8 per cent of the whites were in the married category. The percentage married, however, was lower for Negroes than for whites at every age except eighty-five and over. As a result, 53.0 per cent of all Negro females and 63.1 per cent of all whites were classed as married. Higher percentages of Negro than white females were identified as single in all age groups through fifty-four, after which the situation was reversed. As a result, 28.7 per cent of all black females and 21.8 per cent of all white females were in that category. Negro women at virtually all ages are substantially more likely than white women to be widowed, essentially because of the very high mortality rates of Negro males and the comparatively low sex ratios that make remarriage statistically impossible for many black women in every age group. Even in the ages fifteen to nineteen, the sex ratio is only 98.7 (as compared with 103.1 for whites) and it diminishes thereafter. It is especially low among those persons who are eligible for marriage. At the ages thirty to thirty-four, for example, for each 100 Negro women who are single, widowed, and divorced, and presumably eligible for marriage, there are only 74 men in the same categories. This contrasts with a ratio of 105 for whites. Assuming marriage between persons of approximately the same age, from a purely statistical standpoint, more than a quarter of the Negro women in these ages cannot marry. This intensifies to half in the ages fifty to fifty-four and to three-fifths in the groups sixty-five and over, although the situation is little different for whites in the ages beyond fifty. Finally, the proportions classified as divorced are higher for Negro than for white females at all ages above twenty-four, so that 5.1 per cent of all black females and 3.7 per cent of all the whites fall into this category.[4]

The data for the Negro population, classified by residence, are not sufficiently accurate to make it worthwhile to carry the analysis much beyond these points; and for this reason, in the following section, the comparisons are based exclusively on the materials for the white portion of the population.

Residence and Marital Status

The association between residence and marital condition is a very close one. The central portions of a city, the suburbs, the town, the village, and the open country differ greatly in their power to attract and hold single, married, widowed, and divorced persons. Furthermore, the nature of the social and cultural environments in each of the residential categories has much to do with whether or not a person will marry and, for those who do, with whether or not the marriage will be terminated by death or divorce.

In order to bring out the more essential differences between the marital condition of the urban, rural-nonfarm, and rural-farm populations of the United States in 1970, Figures 38, 39, and 40 were prepared. These show the extent to which the white population in each of these three residential categories had more or less than its pro rata share of the nation's single, married, and widowed persons in each age group from fifteen to nineteen to seventy-five and over. Naturally, the indexes were computed separately for each of the sexes. A study of these charts brings out clearly the nature of the principal associations between residence and marital status.

Thus, they indicate that the most pronounced feature of the urban districts in this respect is the extent to which they attract single persons of both sexes, although single women are overrepresented in the cities at all ages, single men only between the ages of twenty and fifty-four. The urban population also has more than its fair share of widows of practically all ages. On the other hand, the urban areas have less than their pro rata share of married persons of both sexes in all age categories, although the deficiency of married women is somewhat greater than that of married men. Finally, widowers are underrepresented in the cities, but only in the ages from twenty to thirty-four. Older widowers are found with somewhat greater frequency in the urban districts than they are in the total population, although their overrepresentation is not spectacular. In short, the city is more the haven for the single and for widows than it is for persons in other marital categories.

The rural-nonfarm areas, which it is well to remember are now largely suburban, stand out because of their high proportions of married women of all ages, but especially the young and the old. They are only somewhat less notable for their percentages of married men, particularly in the ages below thirty. This is to be expected, of course, because these areas are heavily populated by couples and families, many of them in their early years. The rural-nonfarm population also contains more than its fair share of widowers aged twenty to twenty-four and roughly its equitable proportion of those in the older ages. Young widows, too, are overrepresented, but those in most of the ages past twenty-four are underrepresented. Most noteworthy, perhaps, is the great deficiency of single persons of both sexes in the rural-nonfarm areas. This is the case for women of all ages and for men between the ages of twenty and fifty-five. Older bachelors are about as well represented as they are in the total population, although they are more likely to be living in places that still have close associations with agriculture than in suburban areas.

The rural-farm population contains a great overabundance of single men of virtually all ages, but a substantial deficiency of single women above the age of twenty-five, principally because of their migration to urban centers. The farm group also contains far more than its pro rata share of the nation's married women in all ages above twenty-four, a fact that is closely associated with the extreme scarcity of marriageable women, be they single, divorced, or widowed, in the farming districts. Married men below the age of thirty-five are significantly underrepresented because of this scarcity. Yet in spite of the difficulties they encounter in finding a mate because of the exceedingly high sex ratios among the marriageable population of the farming areas, the rural-farm males who have passed the age of fifty-four are actually more likely to be married than are their fellows in the urban and rural-nonfarm districts. The proportion of very young widowers is high in the rural-farm population, although the numbers involved are not large; but for the ages above thirty-four the indexes indicate that this residential group has considerably less than its pro rata share of this category. Widows of all ages, however, are inordinately scarce on the farms.

TRENDS

In the United States, the proportion of married persons in the population increased substantially during the first seventy years of the twentieth century, although it decreased in the last ten years of the period. (See Table 19.) In 1970, the percent-

TABLE 19

Changes in the marital status of the population of the United States, by age and sex, 1900 to 1970

Age	Per cent married			
	Male		Female	
	1900	1970	1900	1970
14 years	0.1	1.0	0.5	1.1
15–19	1.0	3.9	10.9	11.3
20–24	21.6	42.9	46.5	60.5
25–29	52.6	77.1	68.9	82.5
30–34	69.8	85.7	78.0	86.1
35–44	78.8	87.9	79.5	85.9
45–54	82.2	88.1	73.9	81.1
55–64	79.7	85.6	60.5	68.0
65 and over	67.1	72.4	34.2	36.5
Total	52.8	65.7	55.2	61.2

Source: Compiled and computed from data in U.S. Bureau of the Census, *U.S. Census of Population: 1960*, Vol. I, *Characteristics of the Population*, Part 1 (1964), pp. 436–438, Table 177; *U.S. Census of Population: 1970, Detailed Characteristics*, Final Report PC (1)-D1, *United States Summary* (1973), pp. 640–648, Table 203.

age of married persons in each age group was above the corresponding figure for 1900 in all cases, for women as well as for men. Most striking of all is the fact that among men aged twenty to twenty-four the proportion classified as married in 1970 was 99 per cent higher than the index for 1900. The percentage for those aged fifteen to nineteen increased almost threefold, but the numbers involved were relatively small. Next most pronounced were increases of 47 per cent in the proportion of males aged twenty-five to twenty-nine and 30 per cent in that of females aged twenty to twenty-four who were classified as married. But the percentages registered on the basis of the 1970 census were substantially above those evidenced by the 1900 enumeration in all cases. In all ages taken together, the proportions of those married increased by 24 per cent for the males and 11 per cent for the females.

In large part this change is due to the fact that both men and women are marrying at ages considerably younger than was the case at the opening of the century. As a result, during the seventy years under consideration, the proportions of the single among females of specified ages fell as follows: ages fifteen to nineteen, from 88.7 per cent to 88.1 per cent; ages twenty to twenty-four, from 51.6 per cent to 36.3 per cent; ages twenty-five to twenty-nine, from 27.5 per cent to 12.2 per cent; and ages thirty to thirty-four, from 16.6 per cent to 7.4 per cent. Likewise, the comparable proportions of the single male population decreased as follows: ages fifteen to nineteen, from 98.8 per cent to 95.9 per cent; ages twenty to twenty-four, from 77.6 per cent to 55.5 per cent; ages twenty-five to twenty-nine, from 45.8 per cent to 19.6 per cent; and ages thirty to thirty-four, from 27.6 per cent to 10.7 per cent.

To a considerable extent, however, the increasing proportions of the married in the population have resulted from the reduction that has taken place in the death rate, which in turn has substantially lowered the percentages of widows and widowers. Thus, between 1900 and 1970 the percentages of widowers in the male part of the population decreased as follows: ages thirty to thirty-four, from 2.0 per cent to 0.3 per cent; ages thirty-five to forty-four, from 3.6 per cent to 0.7 per cent; ages forty-five to fifty-four, from 6.8 per cent to 1.7 per cent; and ages fifty-five to sixty-four, from 11.9 per cent to 4.1 per cent. Similarly, during the same seventy-year period the proportions of widows among the females fell off as follows: ages thirty to thirty-four, from 4.6 per cent to 1.5 per cent; ages thirty-five to forty-four, from 8.6 per cent to 3.0 per cent; ages forty-five to fifty-four, from 17.6 per cent to 7.9 per cent; and ages fifty-five to sixty-four, from 32.3 per cent to 20.2 per cent.

Were it not for the increasing proportions of the divorced in the population, the percentages of the married would have mounted even more rapidly. It would be easy, though, to attach too much importance to this factor. The following facts are useful in helping to keep the proper perspective. Among males the maximum proportion of the divorced in any age category rose from 0.6 per cent among those forty-five to sixty-four in 1900 to 3.9 per cent among men aged fifty to fifty-four and those aged fifty-five to fifty-nine in 1970. Among females, the corresponding maximum rose from 0.7 per cent among women aged thirty to thirty-four in 1900 to 5.6 per cent among those aged forty to forty-four in 1970. The fact is, of course, that the great majority of those who divorce eventually remarries.

Between 1960 and 1970, however, some of those long-term trends were altered. In particular, the proportions of married women decreased as follows: ages fifteen to nineteen, from 15.7 per cent to 11.3 per cent; ages twenty to twenty-four, 69.5 per cent to 60.5 per cent; ages twenty-five to twenty nine, 86.2 per cent to 82.5 per cent; ages thirty to thirty-four, 88.7 per cent to 86.1 per cent; and ages thirty-five to forty-four, 87.1 per cent to 85.9 per cent. In all other age groups the percentages married increased during the decade. The net result was a decrease in the proportion of married women of all ages from 66.0 per cent in 1960 to 61.2 per cent in 1970. These changes can be attributed in some measure to increases in the proportions who were widowed and divorced, but they are chiefly the result of increased proportions remaining single. Thus, between the two census years in question, the proportions of single women increased as follows: ages fifteen to nineteen, 83.9 per cent to 88.1 per cent; ages twenty to twenty-four, 28.4 per cent to 36.3 per cent; ages twenty-five to twenty-nine, 10.5 per cent to 12.2 per cent; and ages thirty to thirty-four, 6.9 per cent to 7.4 per cent. In the ages thirty-five to forty-four, the proportion decreased from 6.1 per cent to 5.7 per cent. The overall result was a rise from 19.0 per cent of the women of all ages classified as single in 1960 to 22.6 per cent in 1970. The decrease in the proportion of married women and the increase in that of single women might be explained by a declining sex ratio were it not for the fact that the proportion of married men also dropped in the age groups from twenty through forty-four, while the percentages of single men rose in some of the same age categories, especially that from twenty to twenty-four. The proportion of married men of all ages fell from 69.5 in 1960 to 65.7 in 1970; that of single men rose from 25.0 per cent to 28.6 per cent. These facts can only be explained by a lesser propensity of young adults of both sexes, but especially females, to contract marriage, which in turn is influenced by wars, economic conditions, the demands of higher education, changing sex roles, and other fundamental sociocultural matters that are beyond the scope of this volume.

NOTES

1. See T. Lynn Smith, *Brazil: People and Institutions* (4th ed.), (Baton Rouge: Louisiana State University Press, 1972), pp. 462 - 465.

2. This is in accord with an earlier generalization to the effect that of all the people in the world, "Latin Americans are in a class by themselves when it comes to shying away from legal matrimonial ties." T. Lynn Smith, *Population Analysis* (New York: McGraw-Hill Book Company, 1948), p. 137. See also, Smith, *Brazil, op. cit.*, pp. 468 - 469.

3. For the 1940 materials, see Smith, *Population Analysis, op. cit.*, pp. 140 - 143.

4. For additional comparisons of the marital conditions of whites and Negroes, see T. Lynn Smith and Homer L. Hitt, *The People of Louisiana* (Baton Rouge: Louisiana State University Press, 1952), pp. 78 - 81; and Paul E. Zopf, Jr., *North Carolina: A Demographic Profile* (Chapel Hill: University of North Carolina Population Center, 1967), pp. 159 - 164.

SUGGESTED SUPPLEMENTARY READINGS

BERESFORD, JOHN, and ALICE M. RIVLIN. "Characteristics of 'Other' Families." *Demography*, Vol 1, No. 1 (1964), pp. 242 - 246.

BOGUE, DONALD J. *The Population of the United States*, Chap. 10. Glencoe, Ill.: The Free Press, 1959.

BOGUE, DONALD J. *Principles of Demography*, Chaps. 11, 12, and 17. New York: John Wiley & Sons, Inc., 1969.

BURCH, THOMAS K. "The Size and Structure of Families: A Comparative Analysis of Census Data" *American Sociological Review*, Vol. 32, No. 3 (June, 1967), pp. 347 - 363.

CARTER, HUGH, and PAUL C. GLICK. *Marriage and Divorce: A Social and Economic Study*. Cambridge: Harvard University Press, 1970.

CARTER, HUGH, and PAUL C. GLICK. "Trends and Current Patterns of Marital Status Among Nonwhite Persons." *Demography*, Vol. 3, No. 1 (1966), pp. 276 - 288.

COX, PETER R. *Demography*, 4th ed., pp. 87 - 97. London: Cambridge University Press, 1970.

LESLIE, GERALD R. *The Family in Social Context*, 2nd ed. New York: Oxford University Press, 1973.

RELE, J. R. "Trends and Differentials in the American Age at Marriage," in *Population and Society*, edited by Charles B. Nam, pp. 394 - 404. Boston: Houghton Mifflin Company, 1968.

SHRYOCK, HENRY S., JACOB S. SIEGEL, and associates. *The Methods and Materials of Demography*, Vol. 1, Chap. 10; Vol. 2, Chap. 19. Washington: Government Printing Office, 1971.

SMITH, T. LYNN. *Brazil: People and Institutions*, 4th ed., pp. 462 - 472. Baton Rouge: Louisiana State University Press, 1972.

SMITH, T. LYNN. "A Demographic Study of Widows." *Proceedings of the International Population Conference*, Vol. 2. London: UNESCO, 1963, pp. 311 - 315.

TAEUBER, CONRAD, and IRENE B. TAEUBER. *The People of the United States in the 20th Century* (A 1960 Census Monograph), Chaps. VI and VII. Washington: Government Printing Office, 1971.

U.S. BUREAU OF THE CENSUS. *U.S. Census of Population: 1970. Subject Reports. Marital Status*. Washington: Government Printing Office, 1973.

9
OCCUPATIONAL STATUS

The occupational status of the population deserves careful study for several reasons. First, all indicators of employment and unemployment must be based on the data on occupations. Second, occupational status is a major component in the establishment of general social and economic position or status. And, third, the classification of employed workers by occupation and industry offers a sound basis for significant comparisons of the social and economic functions of cities, states, and other political entities.

Abundant materials on the occupations of the population and the industries in which the workers are engaged are collected regularly in connection with the censuses of population taken throughout the world. These data constitute very substantial portions of the demographic reports which are issued by most countries, including the United States; and their practical application in securing knowledge about such matters as employment and unemployment, the supply and distribution of various types of manpower, and so forth, is readily apparent to all. Nevertheless, it is fair to say that their analysis is still among the least developed parts of the entire field of population study. In many ways the voluminous reports issued census after census, along with substantial compilations of information gathered annually or as the result of special surveys, represent practically unexplored social and economic jungles. As yet neither the frame of reference nor the methodology that has been developed is adequate for the purpose of gaining from this multitude of facts the knowledge which is so badly needed. The study of occupations, which promises so much for the understanding of basic similarities and differences between two or more societies or the various parts of any given society, is still in its swaddling clothes.

TERMINOLOGY AND CLASSIFICATIONS

Since 1930, and especially since the organization of the United Nations, much headway has been made in the development and refinement of meaningful termi-

239

nology to be employed in the analysis of occupational statistics, and familiarity with some of the results of these accomplishments is essential for all students of population.

The Labor Force or the Economically Active Population

Especially important are the distinctions, developed largely since 1930, designed to exclude from the tabulations and classifications of occupational statistics all persons who are neither actively engaged in economically productive activities nor seeking such employment. "Labor Force" is the term used by the United States Bureau of the Census to designate the large category of persons for which an occupational classification is of primary importance, and the meaning of this term corresponds closely with the "Economically Active Population" as used in the *Demographic Yearbook* and other publications of the United Nations.

It is not easy to design a set of criteria that are entirely adequate for distinguishing those in the labor force or in the economically active population from those who should be excluded from the category. This is illustrated by the procedures used in the 1970 census of the United States. In this fundamental compilation, three big groups of persons made up the labor force; namely, the employed, the unemployed, and members of the armed forces. The third of these included all persons on active duty with the United States Army, Air Force, Navy, Marine Corps, and Coast Guard, but the definition of the other two groups was considerably more difficult.

The *employed* class included all civilians aged sixteen and over who were either "at work," that is who during the week preceding the visit of the census enumerator "did any work at all as paid employees or in their own business or profession, or on their own farm, or who worked 15 hours or more as unpaid workers on a family farm or in a family business," and also those "with a job but not at work."[1] The latter was intended to include as employed persons and as members of the labor force those who had jobs or businesses from which they were absent temporarily "due to illness, bad weather, industrial dispute, vacation, or other personal reasons."[2]

The *unemployed* subcategory included the civilians of sixteen years of age and over who were not at work but who were looking for work, either within the "reference week" or the preceding four weeks as well as those who were available to accept a job. The unemployed group also included those who were waiting to be recalled to jobs from which they had been laid off.[3]

Persons classified as "not in the labor force" included all civilians of sixteen years and over who qualified for neither the employed nor the unemployed designations. It included also those doing "incidental" work on family farms or in family businesses. The category consisted primarily of "students, housewives, retired workers, seasonal workers enumerated in an 'off' season who were not looking for work, inmates of institutions, disabled persons, and persons doing only incidental unpaid family work."[4]

In the compilations of data for various nations presented in several issues of the *Demographic Yearbook,* the technicians of the United Nations sought to define the working or "economically active population" as including "all persons of either sex who furnish the supply of labour for the production of goods and services during the time reference chosen for the investigation." The endeavor was made to include the following:

1. Civilian employers, employees, own-account workers, unpaid family workers, and members of a producers' co-operative

2. Armed forces

3. Employed and unemployed persons, including those seeking work for the first time

4. Persons engaged in part-time economic activities

5. Domestic servants.[5]

The "not economically active" group, on the other hand, includes housewives, students, inmates of institutions, retired persons, children below the working ages, persons past the working ages, and so forth.

A glance at some of the materials presented in the fundamental compilations of the United Nations makes apparent some of the difficulties involved in the attempt to get comparable data on the economically active populations of various nations and serves to emphasize the necessity of much caution on the part of those making international comparisons of the assembled data. In the 1959 - 60 census of Nigeria, for example, 95.8 per cent of all persons aged fourteen years and over were classified as "economically active," with the ratio reaching 99.0 for those aged fourteen to nineteen and 99.8 for those thirty to thirty-nine, inclusive. Even among persons of seventy and over the figure was 47.4 per cent. On the other hand, in Australia (1961), only 57.4 per cent of the persons aged fifteen and over were placed in the economically active category, and the index was at its maximum in the twenty to twenty-four age group (73.7 per cent). Thereafter it continued to decrease, with increasing age of population, until it was a mere 9.2 per cent among those seventy years or more in age.

Still a different practice is evidenced in the data for Peru, in which 39.4 per cent of those six years of age and over at the time of the 1961 census were placed in the economically active group. This index was only 3.4 per cent for the age group six to fourteen, and then rose sharply to 41.2 for those fifteen to nineteen. Thereafter the figure rose to 60.1 among those aged thirty to thirty-four, after which it fell, with increasing age, to 30.9 per cent among persons of seventy and above.

All three of these practices are considerably different from that used in the statistical compilations of such countries as the United States, Japan, and Israel. In the United States, for example, on the basis of the 1970 census, only 55.5 per cent of the population aged fourteen and over figured in the economically active class. At the ages fourteen and fifteen the index was only 10.2 per cent. The percentage rose to a maximum of 72.0 per cent in the age group thirty-five to forty-four and then fell off to 16.2 per cent of those sixty-five and over.

Occupation and Industry

The classification of the experienced members of the labor force or the economically active population according to the major industries in which they are engaged and the major occupation groups or categories of workers is another fundamental procedure used in the preparation of modern census materials. The 1970 census of the United States made use of 226 categories of industries organized into the following thirteen major groups: (1) agriculture, forestry, and fisheries; (2) mining; (3) construction; (4) manufacturing (subdivided as to durable and nondurable goods); (5) transportation, communications, and other public utilities; (6) wholesale and retail trade; (7) finance, insurance, and real estate; (8) business and repair services; (9) personal services; (10) entertainment and recreation services; (11) professional and related services; (12) public administration; and (13) industry not reported. One who contemplates the use of any of these materials would do well to spend considerable time studying the specific components of each of these categories.[6]

Those in charge of assembling data on the economically active population for the publications of the United Nations use the set of nine major divisions from the International Standard Industrial Classification of All Economic Activities. These divisions are as follows: (1) agriculture, forestry, hunting, and fishing; (2) mining and quarrying; (3) manufacturing; (4) construction; (5) electricity, gas, water and sanitary services; (6) commerce; (7) transport, storage and communication; (8) services; and (9) activities not adequately described.[7]

The system used by the United States Bureau of the Census for the classification of occupations employs thirteen major groups which in turn are made up of 441 items. The major occupation groups are as follows: (1) professional, technical, and kindred workers; (2) managers and administrators, except farm; (3) sales workers; (4) clerical and kindred workers; (5) craftsmen, foremen, and kindred workers; (6) operatives, except transport; (7) transport equipment operatives; (8) laborers, except farm; (9) farmers and farm managers; (10) farm laborers and farm foremen; (11) service workers, except private household; (12) private household workers; and (13) occupation not reported.[8] In 1970, for the first time, the Census Bureau also designated four occupation divisions. They are as follows: (1) white collar, which includes the first four major occupation groups in the list presented above; (2) blue collar, which embraces occupation groups five through eight; (3) farm workers, which is made up of farmers, farm managers, farm laborers, and farm foremen; and (4) service workers, which consists of all persons so designated, including those in private households.[9]

As in the case of the classification of industries, the system used by the United States Bureau of the Census to designate occupations is slightly more detailed than that employed in the *Demographic Yearbook* and other publications of the United Nations. The classification used by this international agency is as follows: (1) professional, technical, and related workers; (2) administrative, executive, and managerial workers; (3) clerical workers; (4) sales workers; (5) farmers, fishermen, hunters, loggers, and related workers; (6) miners, quarrymen, and related workers; (7) workers in transport and communication occupations; (8) craftsmen, production process workers, and laborers not elsewhere classified; (9) service, sport, and recreation workers; (10) workers not classifiable by occupation; and (11) members of the armed forces.[10]

Class of Worker or Status in the Profession

The modern census also attempts to classify the members of the active labor force according to what the U.S. Bureau of the Census designates as "class of worker" and the United Nations calls "status" in English and *selon la situation dans la profession* in French. Probably none of these is a very adequate expression of the basic idea involved, for, as is apparent from the categories employed, the basic objective seems to be to separate those who are employers from the employees with some further subdivision of each of these groups. The United States census reports distinguish four categories: (1) private wage and salary workers; (2) government workers (subdivided as to federal, state, and local); (3) self-employed workers (subdivided as to "own business not incorporated" and "own business incorporated"); and (4) unpaid family workers.[11] The United Nations classifies the workers according to "status" as follows: (1) employer; (2) own-account workers; (3) employee; (4) family worker; (5) member of producers' co-operatives; and (6) persons not classifiable by status.[12]

SOME INTERNATIONAL COMPARISONS

Were it possible to determine accurately for various countries the extent to which the efforts of those who work are expended in the major lines of endeavor such as agriculture, manufacturing, trade and commerce, transportation, and personal services, some of the most enlightening comparative studies of various societies would be feasible. Casual observation, for example, would make it appear that some societies expend high proportions of the available manpower merely in adding to the ostentation with which the members of a small elite class are

244

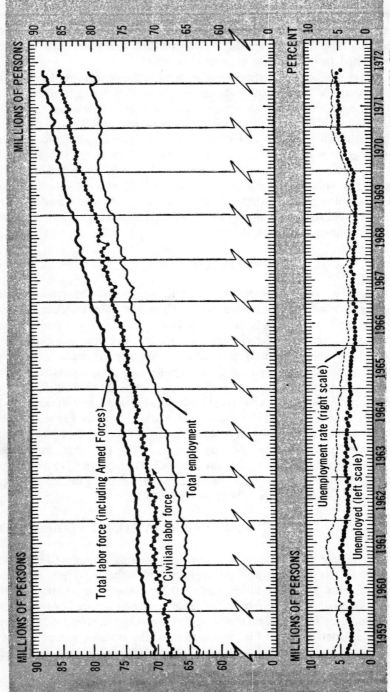

Figure 41. Trends in employment and unemployment in the United States, January, 1959, to September, 1972. Illustration from the Bureau of the Census.

privileged to live, whereas in others the number of domestic servants and other retainers has been reduced almost to the vanishing point. Again, in some societies the amount of human labor lavished on agriculture seems almost beyond belief to those from parts of the world in which each farmer combines large amounts of power and equipment with his own efforts in order to carry on various farm enterprises. Unfortunately, however, it is likely to be many years before the occupational data for various countries are sufficiently precise and comparable to justify their use in any except the most general studies of the situation in various nations.[13]

This conclusion seems adequately supported by the data assembled in Table 20 which show the proportions of the male labor force of selected countries classified as engaged in agriculture, manufacturing, commerce, and the services, respectively. Probably the extent to which the economically active population is occupied in agriculture is reflected fairly accurately, and therefore of considerable use for comparative purposes. Certainly, the fact that over half of the Latin American countries, along with such Asian countries as India, Iran, Malaysia, Pakistan, the Philippines, Syria, Thailand, and Turkey, have considerably more than one half of their economically active male workers employed in agriculture seems in accord with general impressions and information obtained in other ways. It is more difficult, though, to account for the extent to which the proportions of those reported as occupied in manufacturing or in commerce vary from country to country; and the "services" category, which indicates that less than 1 per cent of Yugoslavia's male labor force is so engaged, in comparison with 7 per cent of Hungary's or 24 per cent of Israel's, probably is entirely useless for comparative purposes.

In spite of the fact that inadequate data make significant international comparisons difficult or impossible, the materials for any given country are highly important for the study of the situation and trends within its borders. For obvious reasons, the discussion in the following pages of the various uses to which they may be put is illustrated with data for the United States.

EMPLOYMENT AND UNEMPLOYMENT

In modern society the number of jobs that are filled at any given time, the ratio of this to the number of persons in the labor force, and the indexes of employment and unemployment are vitally important as gauges of social and economic well-being. Obviously, fairly reliable and current information on the workers in all industries and in all occupations must be at hand for such purposes; and this information must come from well-done censuses taken periodically, supplemented by frequent surveys during the intercensal periods. Figure 41, showing trends in the United States in employment and unemployment from January, 1959, to September, 1972, illustrates two of the more important ways in which such ma-

TABLE 20

Proportions of the male economically active populations of selected countries
who are engaged in agriculture, manufacturing, commerce, and the services

Country	Year	Per cent Agri-culture	Manu-facturing	Commerce	Services
Africa					
Egypt	1960	58	9	8	6
Ghana	1960	60	8	6	7
South Africa	1960	35	13	8	12
Zaire (African population)	1955-57	72	6	3	6
America, North					
Canada	1961	15	25	16	19
Costa Rica	1963	57	10	10	8
El Salvador	1961	71	10	4	6
Honduras	1961	76	6	4	5
Jamaica	1960	52	12	7	10
Mexico	1960	59	14	8	8
Nicaragua	1963	71	10	5	6
Panama	1960	57	7	8	10
Puerto Rico	1960	30	14	16	11
Trinidad and Tobago	1960	22	15	12	16
United States	1970	5	28	18	16
America, South					
Argentina	1960	23	25	12	12
Bolivia	1950	68	8	4	2
Guyana	1960	37	16	9	10
Chile	1960	34	18	10	13
Ecuador	1962	64	12	6	8
Peru	1961	55	12	8	10
Uruguay	1963	18	21	13	27
Venezuela	1961	38	11	14	16
Asia					
India	1961	65	11	5	. . . .
Iran	1956	58	10	6	9
Iraq	1957	49	9	5	14
Israel (Jewish population)	1961	12	27	12	24
Japan	1960	26	24	17	14
Korea, Republic of	1960	60	7	8	13
Malaysia, East					
Sabah	1960	77	4	5	6
Sarawak	1960	74	6	7	7
Pakistan	1951	76	6	5	6
Philippines	1960	69	6	4	7
Singapore	1957	7	14	28	30
Syrian Arab Republic	1960	53	12	9	12
Taiwan	1956	49	11	7	14
Thailand	1960	78	4	5	6
Turkey	1960	61	10	5	8

TABLE 20 (Cont'd)

Proportions of the male economically active populations of selected countries
who are engaged in agriculture, manufacturing, commerce, and the services

Country	Year	Per cent Agriculture	Per cent Manufacturing	Commerce	Services
Europe					
Austria	1961	18	....	....	11
Denmark	1960	23	31	13	11
Finland	1960	38	22	9	7
France	1962	20	28	11	14
Germany, Federal Republic	1961	10	41	10	9
Greece	1961	48	14	9	12
Hungary	1960	37	24	5	7
Ireland	1961	41	15	13	11
Italy	1961	27	....	....	....
Netherlands	1960	13	32	14	17
Norway	1960	24	27	10	11
Portugal	1960	48	19	8	8
Romania	1956	59	....	4	7
Spain	1950	53	16	7	9
Sweden	1960	18	38	10	10
Switzerland	1960	15	41	11	11
Yugoslavia	1961	51	19	3	a
Oceania					
Australia	1961	13	28	17	14
New Zealand	1961	18	25	16	14
Western Samoa	1961	77	....	5	9

Source: Compiled and computed from data in United Nations, *Demographic Yearbook, 1964* (New York: United Naitons, 1965), pp. 240-291, Table 9; and U.S. Bureau of the Census, *U.S. Census of Population: 1970, General Social and Economic Characteristics,* Final Report PC(1)-C1, *United States Summary* (1972), p. 376, Table 82.
[a] Less than 1 per cent.

terials may be arranged. For some purposes, of course, the relative numbers showing percentages of the employed or the unemployed among all those in the labor force are even more significant than the absolute figures.

CLASS OF WORKER

The manner in which the occupational data for the United States are classified and tabulated makes it possible to determine the numbers and proportions of those in the civilian labor force who earn wages or salaries by working for private employers, who work for government at one level or another, who are self-employed, and who are unpaid family workers. When such materials are further subdivided according to sex and rural or urban residence, several highly important facts and relationships stand out. (See Table 21.) As late as 1970, it should

TABLE 21

The employed civilian labor force of the United States according to class of worker, by residence and sex, 1970

Residence and sex	Total		Class of worker							
			Private wage and salary workers		Government workers		Self-employed workers		Unpaid family workers	
	Number	Per cent	Number	Per cent	Number	Per cent	Number	Per cent	Number	Per cent
Total	76,553,599	100	57,917,538	75.7	12,320,637	16.1	5,911,204	7.7	404,220	0.5
Male	47,623,754	100	35,969,135	75.5	6,685,791	14.0	4,849,994	10.2	118,834	0.2
Female	28,929,845	100	21,948,403	75.9	5,634,846	19.5	1,061,210	3.7	285,386	1.0
Urban	57,873,851	100	44,722,863	77.3	9,571,209	16.5	3,370,740	5.8	209,039	0.4
Male	35,167,824	100	27,289,363	77.6	5,191,039	14.8	2,645,631	7.5	41,791	0.1
Female	22,706,027	100	17,433,500	76.8	4,380,170	19.3	725,109	3.2	167,248	0.7
Rural-nonfarm	14,835,655	100	11,191,609	75.4	2,300,466	15.5	1,250,808	8.4	92,772	0.6
Male	9,692,152	100	7,386,898	76.2	1,272,831	13.1	1,008,511	10.4	23,912	0.2
Female	5,143,503	100	3,804,711	74.0	1,027,635	20.0	242,297	4.7	68,860	1.3
Rural-farm	3,844,093	100	2,003,066	52.1	448,962	11.7	1,289,656	33.5	102,409	2.7
Male	2,763,778	100	1,292,874	46.8	221,921	8.0	1,195,852	43.3	53,131	1.9
Female	1,080,315	100	710,192	65.7	227,041	21.0	93,804	8.7	49,278	4.6

Source: Compiled and computed from data in U.S. Bureau of the Census, *U.S. Census of Population: 1970, General Social and Economic Characteristics*, Final Report PC(1)-C1, *United States Summary* (1972), pp. 396-397, Table 93.

be stressed, over 75 per cent of the civilian labor force were employed by private companies or individuals and about 16 per cent by government of all types. The self-employed, even including unpaid members of families, constituted only about one-twelfth of the total. Men are less likely than women to work for private employers or the government and more likely to be self-employed. Self-employment, long the rule in the rural-farm areas, fell to second place after 1960. In 1970, it accounted for 43 per cent of all the employed rural-farm males, but private wage and salary work was responsible for 47 per cent. The incidence of self-employment is still much higher than it is in the urban and rural-nonfarm populations because the family-sized farm system of agriculture retains its strength in many parts of the nation. For this reason, unpaid family labor is still important in the rural-farm areas. But due to the fact that the proportion of all workers engaged in agriculture grows smaller with each decade, both self-employed and unpaid family workers continue to become relatively less important among the four classes of the nation's workers.

MAJOR OCCUPATION GROUPS

The classification of occupations in the United States into major occupation groups also provides highly significant information pertaining to the manner in which the nation's workers gain their livelihoods. See Table 22, in which the materials have been assembled to show the absolute and relative importance of each of the twelve major categories in providing employment for the male labor force. To enhance the value of this information, the data are further classified according to residence. Even such a simple procedure brings out several highly significant facts and relationships. Thus, the two categories which include the craftsmen and the operatives are composed mostly of skilled workers, and the two together account for almost 35 per cent of the employed male workers in the nation. Domestic workers are conspicuous by their absence; and unskilled laborers, those who work on farms and all the others combined, make up just over 8 per cent of the males who were gainfully employed in 1970, a proportion substantially smaller than that of professional, technical, and kindred workers, and than that of managers and administrators exclusive of farmers. Only about 4.5 per cent of the nation's male labor force were employed in agriculture at the time of our latest enumeration, and even with numerous boys of less than twenty-one included, almost two-thirds of these were farm operators.

These data should also assist in making less tenable the position of many social scientists who are accustomed to using the data on residence as though they pertained to occupations. A specific error frequently encountered in social and economic literature is the practice of taking the ratio between the product produced on farms and dividing it by the number in the rural-farm population in order to determine the per capita production. However, it is evident from Table

TABLE 22

Occupations of employed males 16 years of age and over, by residence, 1970

Major occupation group	Total		Urban		Rural-nonfarm		Rural-farm	
	Number	Per cent of total	Number	Per cent of group	Number	Per cent of group	Number	Per cent of group
Total employed	47,623,754	100.0	35,167,824	73.8	9,692,152	20.4	2,763,778	5.8
Professional, technical, and kindred workers	6,798,887	14.3	5,679,109	83.5	1,008,564	14.8	111,214	1.6
Managers and administrators, except farm	5,315,768	11.2	4,207,338	79.1	974,097	18.3	134,333	2.5
Sales workers	3,302,324	6.9	2,758,325	83.5	476,302	14.4	67,697	2.0
Clerical and kindred workers	3,640,636	7.6	3,066,842	84.2	496,501	13.6	77,293	2.1
Craftsmen, foremen, and kindred workers	10,086,863	21.2	7,239,532	71.8	2,464,166	24.4	383,165	3.8
Operatives, except transport	6,481,836	13.6	4,534,435	70.0	1,664,023	25.7	283,378	4.4
Transport equipment operatives	2,825,883	5.9	2,009,765	71.1	687,368	24.3	128,750	4.6
Laborers, except farm	3,143,438	6.6	2,224,339	70.8	781,903	24.9	137,196	4.4
Farmers and farm managers	1,354,860	2.8	91,886	6.8	177,340	13.1	1,085,634	80.1
Farm laborers and farm foremen	799,442	1.7	184,538	23.1	351,469	44.0	263,435	33.0
Service workers, except private household	3,835,631	8.1	3,141,987	81.9	603,245	15.7	90,399	2.4
Private household workers	38,186	0.1	29,728	77.9	7,174	18.8	1,284	3.4

Source: Compiled and computed from data in U.S. Bureau of the Census, *U.S. Census of Population: 1970, General Social and Economic Characteristics,* Final Report PC(1)-C1, *United States Summary* (1972), pp. 392-393, Table 91.

22 that about 20 per cent of the nation's male farm operators and two-thirds of its male farm laborers did not live on farms, whereas all the other major occupational categories, including craftsmen, operatives, managers and administrators of businesses other than farms, and even professional men were found in considerable numbers in the rural-farm population.

MAJOR INDUSTRY GROUPS

The materials from the 1970 census make it evident that manufacturing is the most important source of employment for the nation's labor force, since 25.9 per cent of all employed workers were classified as engaged in manufacturing, although it is not as significant as it has been in some earlier decades. Wholesale and retail trade, accounting for 20.0 per cent of the jobs, was second, and professional and related services with 17.6 per cent, third. Then came transportation, communications, and other public utilities, 6.7 per cent; construction, 6.0 per cent; public administration, 5.5 per cent; finance, insurance, and real estate, 5.0 per cent; personal services, 4.6 per cent; agriculture, forestry, and fisheries, 3.7 per cent; business and repair services, 3.1 per cent; entertainment and recreation services, 0.8 per cent; and mining, 0.8 per cent.

Since a person's work is such a powerful determinant of what he is or what he becomes, it is interesting and important to note how the relative importance of several of the major industry groups varies from one state to another. For this purpose, the three major categories of manufacturing, wholesale and retail trade, and agriculture, which together in 1970 furnished employment for 50 per cent of the nation's workers, were selected. Data for them are assembled in Table 23. These materials fully support the widely held belief that the northeastern sections of the country are the manufacturing areas *par excellence*. It is interesting to note, however, that Delaware, North Carolina, South Carolina, Georgia, Tennessee, Alabama, and Arkansas also are states in which the proportions of the employed workers engaged in manufacturing exceeded the national average. At one end of the scale, North Dakota had less than 5 per cent of its workers employed in manufacturing, while at the other end more than 36 per cent of South Carolina's workers were so engaged. New Hampshire, Rhode Island, Ohio, Indiana, Michigan, and North Carolina are other states in which at least 35 per cent of the workers were employed in manufacturing; and South Dakota, Montana, Wyoming, New Mexico, Nevada, and Alaska are additional ones in which less than one worker in ten was in the manufacturing industry.

The most noticeable feature of the data about wholesale and retail trade is the slight extent to which the proportion engaged in it varies from state to state. Thus, the range is only from the low of 16.7 per cent in South Carolina to the high of 23.5 per cent in Florida. In this respect, the former is most closely rivaled by North Carolina and the latter by North Dakota.

TABLE 23

Relative importance of three major industry groups in providing work for all
employed persons in the United States, by divisions and states, 1970

Division and state	Agriculture, forestry, and fisheries	Manufacturing	Wholesale and retail trade
United States	3.7	25.9	20.0
New England	1.5	31.5	19.5
Maine	4.1	31.6	19.5
New Hampshire	1.9	35.5	18.5
Vermont	6.1	23.9	18.1
Massachusetts	0.9	29.2	20.2
Rhode Island	0.9	35.1	19.0
Connecticut	1.1	34.8	18.6
Middle Atlantic	1.4	28.8	19.3
New York	1.3	24.2	19.5
New Jersey	0.9	32.0	19.1
Pennsylvania	1.8	34.1	18.9
East North Central	2.8	33.7	19.8
Ohio	2.1	35.6	19.3
Indiana	3.4	35.9	19.1
Illinois	2.7	30.3	20.3
Michigan	1.8	35.9	19.5
Wisconsin	6.5	31.0	19.9
West North Central	9.6	19.6	21.7
Minnesota	7.6	21.1	22.0
Iowa	13.1	20.0	21.5
Missouri	5.1	24.4	21.5
North Dakota	21.3	4.7	23.1
South Dakota	22.2	7.4	21.6
Nebraska	13.7	13.7	22.3
Kansas	8.8	17.4	21.8
South Atlantic	3.8	24.1	19.3
Delaware	2.6	29.7	19.1
Maryland	1.9	19.5	19.1
District of Columbia	0.5	4.9	14.3
Virginia	3.3	22.4	18.0
West Virginia	2.1	23.2	19.1

TABLE 23 (Cont'd)

Relative importance of three major industry groups in providing work for all
employed persons in the United States, by divisions and states, 1970

Per cent employed in

Division and state	Agriculture, forestry, and fisheries	Manufacturing	Wholesale and retail trade
North Carolina	5.2	35.5	17.5
South Carolina	4.2	36.2	16.7
Georgia	4.3	27.2	19.6
Florida	4.6	14.1	23.5
East South Central	5.3	28.1	18.7
Kentucky	6.8	25.6	18.7
Tennessee	4.3	30.6	18.8
Alabama	3.9	28.6	19.0
Mississippi	7.5	25.9	17.9
West South Central	5.0	18.4	21.7
Arkansas	8.4	26. 1	19.2
Louisiana	4.1	15.9	21.2
Oklahoma	5.3	15.8	21.7
Texas	4.7	18.5	22.2
Mountain	5.9	12.6	21.7
Montana	13.4	9.7	22.3
Idaho	13.0	14.7	22.7
Wyoming	10.0	6.4	20.3
Colorado	4.6	14.6	22.3
New Mexico	4.8	6.8	21.0
Arizona	4.0	15.6	21.9
Utah	3.8	14.5	21.6
Nevada	2.4	5.2	19.1
Pacific	3.5	21.1	21.2
Washington	4.4	21.6	21.5
Oregon	5.5	21.4	22.1
California	3.1	21.6	20.9
Alaska	2.0	7.1	18.9
Hawaii	4.6	10.9	21.4

Source: Compiled and computed from data in U.S. Bureau of the Census, *U.S. Census of Population; 1970, General Social and Economic Characteristics,* Final Report PC(1)-C1, *United States Summary* (1972), pp. 526-528, Table 171.

The variations in the extent to which the jobs in the various states are directly in agriculture are of the same order as those in manufacturing. In this case, however, those states with higher proportions are somewhat less regionalized, since relatively high percentages are found in the Dakotas and some of their neighbors, and also in Mississippi and Arkansas. Nevertheless, the highest incidences of employment in agriculture tend to be in the states of the West North Central region and those of the northern portion of the Mountain division. The South is no longer the stronghold for those who make their livings from farming that it once was, although the percentages engaged in agriculture were above the national average in twelve of the sixteen states that constitute the "census South." In nine states, namely, New Hampshire, Massachusetts, Rhode Island, Connecticut, New York, New Jersey, Pennsylvania, Michigan, and Maryland, in 1970, less than 2 per cent of the gainfully employed were engaged in agricultural pursuits.

Functions of Cities

The census data on major industry groups have proved particularly useful to those geographers and sociologists who have been concerned with the study of the functions of cities.[14] It is easy for one to determine, for example, the extent to which the gainfully employed in a given city are engaged in manufacturing, trade and commerce, professional services, and each of the other major categories of industry groups; and this information, in turn, forms a sound basis for inferences about the functions in which each city specializes. An analysis of the pertinent materials from the 1970 census does much to bring out the roles played in the social and economic affairs of the United States by all its major cities.

Manufacturing is, of course, the principal activity on which is based the existence of most cities of the United States in their present form. As a matter of fact, in 1970, over 30 per cent of the male workers in sixty-seven of the nation's 153 cities of 100,000 or more inhabitants were employed in manufacturing activities, and the proportion rose as high as 64.1 per cent in Gary, Indiana, and 61.0 per cent in Flint, Michigan. There are, of course, cities in which manufacturing is practically nonexistent, and of these, Albuquerque, Alexandria, Las Vegas, and Washington, D.C., are the most striking examples. In none of them, in 1970, were as many as 9 per cent of the workers engaged in manufacturing. The extremes in the extent to which each of the other major groups of industries supplies the jobs from which the livelihoods of the families living in the various cities are derived are similar. A comprehensive analysis of all this is far beyond the scope of this chapter, but even so a glance at lists showing the cities which specialize to the greatest extent in each of the major industry categories is highly informative. In order to facilitate this, the index numbers used in the discussion below were computed using as bases of 100 the percentages of the nation's male urban workers engaged in each of nine major industries. The proportions are as follows: manufacturing, 29.9 per cent; wholesale and retail trade, 20.4 per cent; professional and related services, 11.5 per cent; transportation, communications, and other public utilities, 9.0 per cent; construction, 8.2 per cent; public administration, 6.8 per cent; finance, insurance, and real estate, 4.8 per cent; business and repair services, 3.9 per cent; and personal services, 2.3 per cent.

Gary, Indiana, as mentioned above, is the city with the highest proportion of its male workers engaged in manufacturing. The figure of 64.1 per cent for this city is 2.14 times as large as the corresponding one for the urban population of the United States as a whole, so that Gary may be said to have 214 per cent of its pro rata share of the nation's male workers employed in manufacturing. In 1970, it was most closely rivaled in this respect by the following: Flint, with an index of 204 per cent; Warren, 191; Hammond, 189; Canton, 178; Rockford, 173; Youngstown, 171; and Akron, 167.

Lubbock, Texas, was the city which, in 1970, had the highest proportion of its male workers engaged in wholesale and retail trade, and the 28.2 per cent so occupied was equivalent to an index of 138 per cent of its pro rata share of the nation's urban males who were employed in such activities. Charlotte, Amarillo, Fresno, Spokane, St. Petersburg, and Tampa, with indexes of 137, 136, 136, 136, and 133, respectively, were next highest in the list.

Cambridge, Massachusetts, in 1970, had 40.1 per cent of its male workers employed in professional and related services. This was the equivalent of 349 per cent of its pro rata share of such workers in the urban portions of the United States. It was most closely followed by Berkeley, Madison, Austin, Pasadena, New Haven, and Raleigh, with indexes of 343, 269, 198, 197, 190, and 180, respectively.

In 1970, Kansas City, Kansas, was the city specializing to the greatest extent in transportation, communications, and other public utilities. This category accounted for the employment of 19.0 per cent of its male workers, a proportion equal to 211 per cent of its pro rata share of those in the urban parts of the nation who were so engaged. Immediately below in the list came Hialeah (201), Jersey City (184), Amarillo (176), Topeka (176), New Orleans (163), and Savannah (158).

Hollywood, Florida, with 17.5 per cent (or 213 per cent of its pro rata share) of its male workers engaged in construction activities headed the list in this category. It was followed most closely by Fort Lauderdale, Honolulu, Baton Rouge, Santa Ana, Hartford, and Corpus Christi, with indexes of 204, 174, 160, 159, 154, and 151, respectively.

Public administration, which includes the civilian workers in national defense, is at its maximum in Alexandria, Virginia, which even surpassed the nation's capital in this respect. In that "bedroom suburb," 28.6 per cent of the male workers were employed in public administration in 1970, a proportion equivalent to 421 per cent of its pro rata share of such workers in the urban population of the nation.

The District of Columbia ranked second (374), followed by Huntsville (347), Sacramento (324), San Antonio (279), Norfolk (271), and Hampton (260). All but Sacramento, a state capital, are important centers of defense and related activities.

The fact that New York ranked first, in 1970, with respect to the relative importance of finance, insurance, and real estate in providing employment for its male workers is not surprising. The actual percentage is 9.7, which is equivalent to an index of 202 per cent of its pro rata share of the nation's urban males who were so employed. Fort Lauderdale, with its lively real estate market, ranked second (an index of 190), followed by San Francisco (186), Glendale (163), Des Moines (160), and St. Petersburg (150).

Employment in the business and repair activities category was at its maximum in Albuquerque, New Mexico, where, in 1970, 12.6 per cent of the male workers were so engaged. This was the equivalent of 323 per cent of that city's pro rata share of the nation's urban workers in this category. The other cities highest in the list were Las Vegas, Los Angeles, Stamford, Fort Lauderdale, and Minneapolis, which had indexes of 256, 167, 156, 151, and 149, respectively.

Personal services, increasingly rare as a source of jobs, accounted for the employment of 21.9 per cent of all male workers in Las Vegas in 1970, a proportion equal to an index of 952 per cent of its pro rata share of the urban men in this industry category. Miami (374), Hollywood, Florida (257), St. Petersburg (235), Fort Lauderdale (226), Honolulu (204), and San Francisco (200) were the other cities ranking highest in this list.

The remaining three categories of agriculture (including forestry and fisheries), entertainment and recreation services, and mining accounted for 1.4 per cent, 1.0 per cent, and 0.8 per cent, respectively, of the nation's male urban work force. The first and last of these are largely nonurban activities, but some cities contained relatively high proportions of workers in one or more of the three categories. Agriculture, forestry, and fisheries accounted for 5.5 per cent of the male work force in Stockton and for 4.7 per cent in Fresno, for indexes of 393 and 336, respectively. Entertainment and recreation services provided jobs for 6.8 per cent of the male workers in Las Vegas (index 680) and for 3.2 per cent in Los Angeles (300). Finally, mining activities provided the largest proportion of jobs in Tucson (7.7 per cent or an index of 962) and Tulsa (6.0 per cent or an index of 750).

By considering simultaneously the data on the extent to which the various cities have specialized in the several categories, it is possible to classify them into a few distinct types. Manufacturing, wholesale and retail trade, professional services, and transportation and communications are, of course, the functions to keep principally in mind for this purpose, since they are the ones in which the large majority of the nation's urban workers is engaged. Even in the state capitals and in the educational, recreational, cultural, and religious centers, they are economic activities which furnish employment to the bulk of the workers. After considerable experimentation with the data from the 1940, 1950, 1960, and 1970 censuses, the figure of 17.0 per cent was taken as the basic criterion and each city was studied to determine which of the specified categories of industries were supplying employment to that proportion or more of the gainfully employed males in its population. Then the 153 cities of 100,000 or more inhabitants at the time of the 1970 census were classified into the following seven categories or types:

1. *Manufacturing cities*. This group includes only those cities in which none of the general categories except manufacturing provided employment for as much as 17 per cent of the male workers. Most of them are, of course, almost purely industrial cities, and they proved to be fourteen in number: Akron, Canton, Cleveland, Dayton, Dearborn, Detroit, Erie, Flint, Gary, Hammond, Newport News, Trenton, Warren, and Youngstown.

2. *Manufacturing and trading centers*. Cities which are highly specialized in the two functions of manufacturing and trade include the large majority of all the nation's principal population centers. They in turn may be divided into two subgroups, namely, those in which manufacturing provides the jobs for more of the male workers than trade and commerce, and those in which the reverse is true. Of the ninety-six cities in the group as a whole, seventy-six were found to belong in the first of these subgroups, and twenty in the second. The cities in which manufacturing dominates are Allentown, Anaheim, Baltimore, Baton Rouge, Beaumont, Birmingham, Bridgeport, Buffalo, Camden (New Jersey), Cedar Rapids, Chattanooga, Chicago, Cincinnati, Columbus (Georgia), Columbus (Ohio), Elizabeth, Evansville, Fort Wayne, Fort Worth, Fremont, Garden Grove, Glendale, Grand Rapids, Greensboro, Hartford, Houston, Huntington Beach, Independence, Indianapolis, Jersey City, Kansas City (Missouri), Lansing, Livonia, Long Beach, Los Angeles, Louisville, Macon, Memphis, Milwaukee, Minneapolis, Mobile, Nashville, New Bedford, Newark, Oakland, Parma, Paterson, Peoria, Philadelphia, Pittsburgh, Portsmouth (Virginia), Providence, Richmond, Rochester, Rockford, St. Louis, St. Paul, San Diego, San Jose, Santa Ana, Savannah, Scranton, Seattle, South Bend, Springfield (Massachusetts), Stamford, Syracuse, Tacoma, Toledo, Torrance, Tulsa, Waterbury, Wichita, Winston-Salem, Worcester, and Yonkers. Those in which trade and commerce predominate are Atlanta, Charlotte, Dallas, Denver, Des Moines, Duluth, Jackson (Mississippi), Knoxville, Little Rock, Miami, New York, Oklahoma City, Omaha, Phoenix, Portland (Oregon), Shreveport, Springfield (Missouri), Stockton, Tampa, and Topeka.

3. *Trade Centers*. There were, in 1970, seventeen cities in which wholesale and retail trade was the only one of the large industry categories to provide employment to as many as 17 per cent of the male workers. They are Albuquerque, Amarillo, Colorado Springs, Corpus Christi, El Paso, Fort Lauderdale, Fresno,

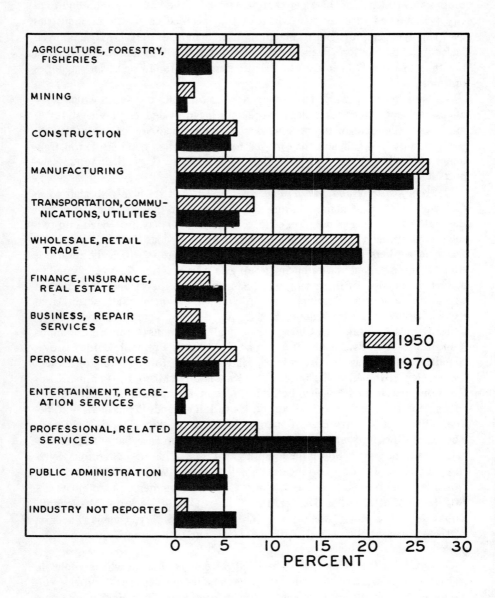

Figure 42. Changes in the proportions of employed persons who fell into thirteen industry groups in the United States, 1950 and 1970.

Honolulu, Jacksonville, Lubbock, Montgomery, New Orleans, St. Petersburg, San Bernardino, San Francisco, Spokane, and Virginia Beach.

4. *Trade and administrative centers.* In 1970, in three cities at least 17 per cent of the employed males worked in each of the categories of trade and public administration. These centers are Norfolk, Sacramento, and San Antonio.

5. *Trade and professional centers.* For an additional eight of the nation's large cities, the 1970 census data show that 17 per cent or more of the city's male workers were employed in the categories of trade and professional services. These centers are Albany (New York), Austin, Columbia (South Carolina), Lincoln, Madison, Raleigh, Salt Lake City, and Tucson.

6. *Manufacturing, trade, and professional centers.* In 1970, these three categories each contained at least 17 per cent of the male work force in five cities. They are Boston, Lexington (Kentucky), New Haven, Pasadena, and Riverside.

7. *Others.* Finally, ten cities had, on the basis of the 1970 data, principal functions in combinations that differed from any of the six types given above. In Hialeah and Kansas City, Kansas, manufacturing, trade, and transportation each accounted for the employment of 17 per cent or more of the male workers. The remaining eight cities and the industries, each of which accounted for 17 per cent or more of the male workers, are: Alexandria (public administration); Berkeley (professional services); Cambridge (manufacturing and professional services); the District of Columbia (professional services and public administration); Hampton (manufacturing and public administration); Hollywood, Florida (construction and trade); Huntsville (manufacturing, trade, and public administration); and Las Vegas (trade and personal services).

Trends in Industry Groups

The more important occupational fluctuations in the United States are reflected in changes in the relative importance of the various major industry groups. (See Figure 42.) For the most part, the variations which occurred between 1950 and 1970 are continuations of long-term trends. Most obvious among these, of course, is the rapid and highly significant decline in the number of workers engaged in agriculture (including forestry and fisheries) from over 7 million in 1950 to 2.7 million in 1970.[15] This represents a reduction from 12.5 per cent of the employed labor force in 1950 to only 3.5 per cent in 1970. Other industry groups in which both absolute and relative decreases took place are mining and personal services, especially those that involve work in private households. In the fields of construction, manufacturing, transportation, communications, and other public utilities, and entertainment and recreation services, the numbers of workers increased, but they became smaller proportions of the total work force because their growth rates were smaller than that of the latter. In the case of manufacturing, however, the proportion engaged in producing durable goods rose during the two decades, while the percentage of those producing nondurable goods fell. The percentage of workers involved in various kinds of trade remained about the same, although the number increased substantially. In all of the other industry groups, increases occurred both in the numbers of workers and their relative importance in the nation's work force. The greatest proportional gain by far was registered in the professions and related services. These workers increased from 4.7 million or 8.3 per cent of the total in 1950 to 12.8 million or 16.5 per cent of the total in 1970. Significant expansion also took place in finance, insurance, and real estate, public administration, and business and repair services, in that order. It is particularly interesting to note that in all of the industries taken together, the number of male workers increased about 19 per cent but that of female workers grew 86 per cent. Thus, agriculture continues to wane rapidly in relative importance as an employer of Americans, manufacturing to decline slowly in this respect, and commerce, finance, service industries, government, and especially the professions, to develop rapidly in the proportions of the work force which they employ.

1. In the 1940, 1950, and 1960 censuses, the data on the labor force were reported for persons aged fourteen and over. In 1970, relatively few materials included those aged fourteen and fifteen.

2. U.S. Bureau of the Census, *U.S. Census of Population: 1970, General Social and Economic Characteristics,* Final Report PC(1)-C1, *United States Summary* (1972), p. App-16.

3. *Ibid.*

4. *Ibid.*

5. United Nations, *Demographic Yearbook, 1970* (New York: United Nations, 1971), pp. 33 - 34.

6. For details of the classification see U.S. Bureau of the Census, *op. cit.*, pp. App-22 - App-23; and *U.S. Census of Population: 1970, Classified Index of Occupations and Industries* (Washington: Government Printing Office, 1971).

7. *Demographic Yearbook, 1964,* p. 28, and Table 9.

8. *General Social and Economic Characteristics, op. cit.,* pp. App-19 - App-22.

9. *Ibid.,* pp. App-21 - App.-22.

10. *Demographic Yearbook, 1964, op. cit.,* pp. 29 - 30, and Table 10.

11. *General Social and Economic Characteristics, op. cit.,* pp. App-23 - App-24.

12. *Demographic Yearbook, 1964, op. cit.,* pp. 30 - 31, and Table 11.

13. It should be noted that at this writing, the 1964 issue of the *Demographic Yearbook* is the most recent one in which either occupation or industry is reported, although summary information on the economically active population also was presented in the 1970 volume.

14. For a discussion of this subject and selected materials relating to it, see T. Lynn Smith and C. A. McMahan, *The Sociology of Urban Life* (New York: The Dryden Press, Inc., 1951), Chapter 3; T. Lynn Smith, *Current Social Trends and Problems in Latin America,* Latin American Monographs, No. 1 (Gainesville: University of Florida Press, 1957), pp. 5 - 7; and Paul E. Zopf, Jr., *North Carolina: A Demographic Profile* (Chapel Hill: University of North Carolina Population Center, 1967), pp. 253 - 261.

15. For a detailed study of this matter, see T. Lynn Smith, "Farm Labour Trends in the United States, 1910 - 1969," *International Labour Review,* 102, 2 (August, 1970), pp. 149 - 169.

SUGGESTED SUPPLEMENTARY READINGS

BLAU, PETER, and OTIS DUDLEY DUNCAN. *The American Occupational Structure.* New York: John Wiley & Sons, Inc., 1967.

BOGUE, DONALD J. *The Population of the United States,* Chaps. 16 - 19. Glencoe, Ill.: The Free Press, 1959.

BOGUE, DONALD J. *Principles of Demography,* Chaps. 9, 10, 13 and 14. New York: John Wiley & Sons, Inc., 1969.

COOK, ROBERT C., and TADD FISHER. "The U.S. Labor Force: 1950 - 1960: 'Islands of Obsolete Capacity and Unwanted Skills'," in *Population and Society,* edited by Charles B. Nam, pp. 604 - 625. Boston: Houghton Mifflin Company, 1968.

DUNCAN, OTIS DUDLEY, DAVID L. FEATHERMAN, and BEVERLY DUNCAN. *Socioeconomic Background and Achievement.* New York: Seminar Press, 1972.

HALL, RICHARD H. *Occupations and the Social Structure,* Part II. Englewood Cliffs: Prentice-Hall, Inc., 1969.

HATHAWAY, DALE E., J. ALLAN BEEGLE, and W. KEITH BRYANT. *People of Rural America* (A 1960 Census Monograph), Chaps. VII and VIII. Washington: Government Printing Office, 1968.

SHRYOCK, HENRY S., JACOB S. SIEGEL, and associates. *The Methods and Materials of Demography,* Vol. 1, Chap. 12. Washington: Government Printing Office, 1971.

SMITH, T. LYNN. *Brazil: People and Institutions,* 4th ed., pp. 88 - 96. Baton Rouge: Louisiana State University Press, 1972.

SMITH, T. LYNN. "Farm Labour Trends in the United States, 1910 - 1969." *International Labour Review,* Vol. 102, No. 2 (August, 1970), pp. 149 - 169.

SMITH, T. LYNN. "The Functions of American Cities," in *The Sociology of Urban Life,* edited by T. Lynn Smith and C. A. McMahan, pp. 97 - 103. New York: The Dryden Press, 1951.

SMITH, T. LYNN. *Studies of Latin American Societies,* Selection 22, New York: Doubleday & Co., Inc., 1970.

SWEET, JAMES A. *Women in the Labor Force.* New York: Seminar Press, 1973.

TAEUBER, CONRAD, and IRENE B. TAEUBER. *The People of the United States in the 20th Century* (A 1960 Census Monograph), pp. 175 - 188 and 205 - 231. Washington: Government Printing Office, 1971.

THOMLINSON, RALPH. *Population Dynamics,* pp. 472 - 484. New York: Random House, Inc., 1965.

UNITED NATIONS. *Demographic Yearbook, 1964,* pp. 26 - 34. New York: United Nations, 1965.

U.S. BUREAU OF THE CENSUS. *U.S. Census of Population: 1970. Subject Reports. Employment Status and Work Experience.* Washington: Government Printing Office, 1973.

U.S. BUREAU OF THE CENSUS. *U.S. Census of Population: 1970. Subject Reports. Industrial Characteristics.* Washington: Government Printing Office, 1973.

U.S. BUREAU OF THE CENSUS. *U.S. Census of Population: 1970. Subject Reports. Occupational Characteristics.* Washington: Government Printing Office, 1973.

WOLFBEIN, SEYMOUR. *Work in American Society.* Glenview, Ill.: Scott, Foresman and Company, 1971.

EDUCATIONAL STATUS

Among all the criteria employed to describe or characterize the quality of a population, educational status probably is second only to health. Indeed, the two seem to be very closely associated, so that a people that ranks high on the health scale also makes a good showing with respect to educational accomplishments, and one that is low on the health scale is also low on the educational one. For this reason those who describe the attributes of populations in various parts of the world almost inevitably couple such adjectives as the following: illiterate and unhealthy, uneducated and disease-ridden, uninformed and short-lived, and healthy and well-educated. But whereas it usually is impossible to secure any comprehensive, reliable, and current data about the health scores of a given population and most of the conclusions on this subject must be based upon inferences from study of causes of death and mortality rates, information relating to educational status usually figures among the earliest substantial compilations of demographic data made for a given nation, state, or city.

Throughout the world during the second half of the twentieth century, it is almost taken for granted that the average person must have the ability to communicate orally, to read well, to write legibly, and to make and check a variety of arithmetical computations. This is true of persons in all walks of life, for those who live in the rural districts as well as those who inhabit the towns and cities. As a matter of fact, in the space age the amount of schooling received by the oncoming generation is a direct reflection of the extent of effort that the parents, the community, the state, and the nation are putting forth for the well-being of the society, and the number of years of formal schooling attained by the adult population is one of the best indicators of its quality.

DATA AND INDEXES

Many modern censuses attempt to secure data that will enable the educational status of the population to be determined and that will permit comparisons of the educational attainments of the various segments into which the general population might be subdivided. Until quite recently it was deemed sufficient merely to ascertain whether or not those enumerated were able to read and write, so that judgments and comparisons could be made on the proportions of illiterates (or literates) in the total. An early refinement in many countries was to eliminate from consideration those children too young to have acquired the skills involved in reading and writing and to give the information only for persons who had passed a given age, such as six years (as in Mexico), ten years (as in the United States), or fourteen years (as in Argentina). Prior to 1940, these data on the numbers and proportions of illiterates and literates were the only comprehensive materials on the educational status of the population that were assembled in the United States and in the other nations of the world. By 1930, however, the percentage of those in the United States and many other parts of the Western world who were unable to read and write had been reduced to such an extent that this index had lost most of the value it once had both for diagnostic and comparative purposes.

In the 1940 census schedule employed in the United States (and in those developed at approximately the same time in several other parts of the world), a query was included as to the number of years of formal schooling that had been completed. The data so obtained were assembled in cross-tabulation with those pertaining to age, sex, residence, race, and other characteristics. With these materials it is possible for the demographer to compute a number of simple but highly significant indexes, such as the percentage of those above a given age who lack formal schooling (a close approximation to the percentage of illiteracy), the median years of schooling completed, the percentage of high school graduates in the population, and the percentage of those above a given age who have completed four years of work in a college or university.

SOME INTERNATIONAL COMPARISONS

Even in the last quarter of the twentieth century relatively few accurate generalizations may be made relative to the educational status of the population in many important parts of the world; and it is even more difficult if not impossible to rank the populations of the respective nations with respect to the educational level they have attained. It is true that the first issue of the *Demographic Yearbook* of the United Nations attempted to summarize the important data on this subject from around the world and that this endeavor has been continued with commendable vigor in the preparation of subsequent compilations.

But even if the fairly current information gathered by these coordinated efforts is supplemented by other data that are available, the gaps in our knowledge are still the most striking characteristics of such a summary as that persented in Table 24. It is also true that much headway has been made since the close of the Second World War, but even so much remains to be done before a comprehensive view of the world situation with respect to illiteracy or any other measure of the educational level of the population will be available to students of population.[1] Most discouraging of all is the fact that a great world organization has been unable to elicit data on the educational status of the population from most of the countries of Western Europe and from Australia and New Zealand, sections of the world in which undoubtedly the educational accomplishments of the population are fairly high.

Fragmentary though the data are, they still reveal the tremendous differences in educational status that prevail among populations in various parts of the earth. At one end of the scale are countries such as Canada, the United States, Japan, Czechoslovakia, Switzerland, and the Soviet Union in which all but a very small percentage of the adult population have acquired the skills involved in reading, writing, and elementary arithmetic. Were information available, many other European countries, along with Australia and New Zealand, also would be found in this group, since data for much earlier years showed the following proportions of illiteracy among those ten years of age and over: Belgium, 3.1 per cent in 1947: Finland, 0.9 per cent in 1930. France, 3.3 per cent in 1946; and Sweden, 0.1 per cent in 1930. Hungary, Poland, Argentina, and Uruguay are other countries in which the benefits of an elementary education have been extended to the masses of the population. All of these are in the greatest contrast with many other sections of the earth (virtually all of Africa along with India, Iran, Iraq, Pakistan, Malaysia, and Nepal) in which only the privileged few have ever studied in a schoolroom.

Between these two extremes falls the large majority of the countries for which materials are available. Among these, percentages of less than 30 in such parts of the earth as Costa Rica, Jamaica, Mexico, Panama, Puerto Rico, Chile, Colombia, Paraguay, Ceylon, Hong Kong, Israel, the Philippines, Taiwan, Bulgaria, Greece, Italy, Spain, and Yugoslavia are indicative of the fact that illiteracy today generally is recognized as one of the major social problems confronting the respective societies and that strenuous efforts are being made to develop systems of universal education;[2] whereas indexes of more than 50 per cent in most of the African nations, El Salvador, Guatemala, Honduras, Nicaragua, Indonesia, Jordan, the Syrian Arab Republic, and Turkey underscore the tremendous obstacles that these countries will have to overcome before the masses of their populations weigh very heavily in the scales of international affairs.

TABLE 24

Variations in the proportions of illiteracy among persons aged 15
years and over in countries of 1 million or more inhabitants
for which data are available, by sex

Country	Year	Per cent illiterate Total	Per cent illiterate Male	Per cent illiterate Female
Africa				
Algeria	1966	81.2	70.1	92.0
Egypt	1960	73.7	59.5	87.6
Ghana	1960	79.5[a]	70.0[a]	89.3[a]
Liberia	1962	91.1	86.1	95.8
Libyan Arab Republic	1964	78.3	62.5	95.8
Malawi (African pbpulation)	1966	77.9	66.2	87.7
Morocco	1960	88.8	80.2	97.2
Senegal (African population)	1960-61	94.4	89.6	98.6
Sierra Leone	1963	92.8[a]	80.2[a]	95.8[a]
South Africa (Bantu population)	1960	59.7	59.3	60.2
Southern Rhodesia (African population)	1962	95.3	94.4	96.3
Tunisia	1966	67.8[b]	53.6[b]	82.4[b]
Uganda (African population)	1959	74.9	63.2	86.1
United Republic of Tanzania				
Tanganyika	1967	72.1	57.6	85.2
Zanzibar	1967	64.3	47.1	81.5
Zambia	1969	52.6	38.8	65.4
America, North				
Canada	1961	1.5[a]	1.5[a]	1.4[a]
Costa Rica	1963	15.7	15.3	16.0
Dominican Republic	1960	35.5	33.3	37.6
El Salvador	1961	51.0	46.1	55.5
Guatemala	1964	62.0	55.7	68.4
Honduras	1961	55.0	51.3	58.5
Jamaica	1960	18.1	21.4	15.2
Mexico	1970	25.9	21.9	29.7
Nicaragua	1963	50.2	49.9	50.4
Panama	1960	26.7	25.8	27.6
Puerto Rico	1970	14.4[a,c]	12.3[a,c]	16.4[a,c]
United States	1970	1.4[a,d]	1.4[a,d]	1.4[a,d]
America, South				
Argentina	1960	8.6	7.5	9.7
Brazil	1970	33.0	29.9	36.1
Chile	1970	11.7	10.8	12.5
Colombia	1964	27.1	25.2	28.9
Ecuador	1962	32.7	27.9	37.3
Paraguay	1962	25.5	19.0	31.3
Peru	1961	38.9	25.6	51.6
Uruguay	1963	9.4	9.7	9.2
Venezuela	1961	36.7	32.0	41.6

TABLE 24 (Cont'd)
Variations in the proportions of illiteracy among persons aged 15 years and over tin countries of 1 million or more inhabitants for which data are available, by sex

Country	Year	Per cent illiterate Total	Male	Female
Asia				
Ceylon	1963	24.7	14.6	36.1
Hong Kong	1961	28.6	9.8	48.1
India	1961	72.2	58.6	86.8
Indonesia	1961	61.0	47.2	73.9
Iran	1966	77.2	67.2	87.8
Iraq	1965	73.7	63.0	84.5
Israel	1961	15.8[d]	9.5[d]	22.3[d]
Japan	1970	0.7[a]	0.4[a]	1.1[a]
Jordan	1961	67.6	49.9	84.8
Korea, Republic	1960	43.6[a]	31.8[a]	55.1[a]
Malaysia				
East				
Sabah	1960	76.5	65.6	88.5
Sarawak	1960	78.5	69.1	87.9
West	1957	53.0	34.1	73.5
Nepal	1961	91.2	83.3	98.5
Pakistan	1961	81.2	71.7	92.6
Philippines	1970	16.6[b]	15.4[b]	17.8[b]
Syrian Arab Republic	1960	69.2	51.2	87.3
Taiwan	1966	27.6	15.2	42.0
Thailand	1960	32.3	20.7	43.9
Turkey	1965	54.0	35.5	72.6
Europe				
Bulgaria	1965	9.8	4.8	14.7
Czechoslovakia	1961	0.7[a]	0.6[a]	0.8[a]
Greece	1961	19.6	8.3	30.0
Hungary	1963	2.6	2.1	3.1
Italy	1961	9.3[d]	7.3[d]	11.2[d]
Poland	1960	4.7[d]	2.9[d]	6.2[d]
Portugal	1960	37.2	30.0	43.4
Spain	1960	14.4	9.2	19.1
Switzerland	1960	0.2[a]	0.2[a]	0.2[a]
Yugoslavia	1961	19.7[b]	9.9[b]	28.8[b]
U.S.S.R.	1959	1.5[e]	0.7[e]	2.2[e]

Source: Compiled and computed from data in United Nations, *Demographic Yearbook, 1963,* pp. 338-339, Table 12; pp. 370-376, Table 13; pp. 378-427, Table 14; *1964,* pp. 704-706, Table 34; pp. 708-737, Table 35; *1970,* pp. 166-407, Table 6; pp. 583-594, Table 11; *1971,* pp. 160-328, Table 7; pp. 516-536, Table 18; pp. 538-577, Table 19; U.S. Bureau of the Census, *U.S. Census of Population: 1970, General Social and Economic Characteristics,* Final Report PC(1)-C53. *Puerto Rico* (1972), pp. 197-198, Table 45; *and Detailed Characteristics,* Final Report PC(1)-D1, *United States Summary* (1973), pp. 627-633, Table 99.

[a] Less than one year of schooling.

[b] 10 and over.

[c] 25 and over.

[d] 14 and over.

[e] 9 to 49.

DIFFERENTIALS IN EDUCATIONAL STATUS

Even within a given nation or state there are highly significant differences in the educational status of the various segments or categories into which the population may be divided. Few societies give males and females equal amounts of formal education, the rural population almost never receives as much instruction as the urban population, racial or ethnic identification may be a powerful determinant in establishing whether or not a child may be privileged to attend school, occupation frequently is closely related to educational opportunities, and so forth. Fortunately, the data for the United States are adequate for the study of most of these associations, and frequently they may be supplemented with information for other parts of the world in which one or more of these relationships is of particular significance. Consider first the materials in Table 25, which has been prepared in a manner that will enable one to determine the differences between the sexes, the residential groupings, and the white and Negro populations without running the risk of attributing to one of these factors any differences that may be merely a reflection of one of the others.

Sex Differentials

In the United States, there long was a significant and persistent tendency for girls to acquire more formal education than boys. This differential was evident from the materials gathered in the 1940, 1950, and 1960 censuses which indicated that among native whites and Negroes alike in each one of the three residential categories, the median years of schooling completed by those who were aged twenty-five years or more was lower for men than for women. Furthermore, in every one of the states and in the District of Columbia a similar differential was observed. By 1970 this differential had completely disappeared from the nation's population taken as a whole. It was virtually absent from the white urban population and was minimal though still present in the Negro urban population. It persists, however, in both of the rural residential categories for whites and Negroes alike, although it is most in evidence for both races in the rural-farm population. In twenty-five of the states the educational differential favoring women persisted in 1970, but in twenty-two of these women had median years of schooling that were only 0.5 year or less above the average for men. In North Dakota, females had an average of 1.4 years more schooling than men and in Kentucky and South Dakota the differences were 0.8 year and 0.7, respectively. In six states (Texas, New Mexico, Arizona, Utah, California, and Alaska), the median number of years of schooling completed was higher for men than for women, but in no case by more than 0.2 year. In the remaining nineteen states and the District of Columbia, in 1970, the educational statuses of the sexes were the same. As in the case of a number of other demographic characteristics, this

TABLE 25

Median years of schooling of the population aged 25 years and over in the United States, by sex, residence, and race, 1970

Sex and race	Total	Residence		
		Urban	Rural-nonfarm	Rural-farm
Total population	12.1	12.2	11.2	10.7
Male	12.1	12.2	10.9	9.9
Female	12.1	12.1	11.5	11.5
White population	12.1	12.2	11.6	11.0
Male	12.1	12.3	11.3	10.2
Female	12.1	12.2	11.8	11.8
Negro population	9.8	10.2	7.7	7.2
Male	9.4	10.0	7.1	6.2
Female	10.0	10.4	8.1	7.9

Source: Compiled from data in U.S. Bureau of the Census, *U.S. Census of Population: 1970, General Social and Economic Characteristics,* Final Report PC(1)-C1, *United States Summary* (1972), p. 368, Table 75.

pattern of convergence of the levels of education of the sexes is indicative of the process of homogenization of American society.

Since woman's role in passing on the cultural heritage from one generation to another is so much more important than man's, especially in highly urbanized societies in which fathers are separated from their children for all of the working day, the sociologist might suggest that women should be as well if not better educated than men. But the tendency either for girls to acquire more formal training than boys or for the sexes to be similar in educational status is a great rarity in the world, restricted largely to such countries as Canada, Uruguay, and the United States. Elsewhere the general rule is for the efforts of the parents to be concentrated to a much greater extent upon the education of their male off-spring than their daughters. Representative differentials, as computed from materials readily at hand in the 1963, 1964, 1970, and 1971 issues of the *Demographic Yearbook* and assembled in Table 24, make this obvious.

Several comments about these data seem to be in order. First, in general, the lower the educational status of a population the greater the extent by which the index for the male part of the population exceeds that for the female portion, sometimes being more than double. Second, in every country except Canada, Jamaica, the United States, Uruguay, and Switzerland the educational status of males is higher than that of females. Third, countries such as those just mentioned, along with Costa Rica, Argentina, Chile, Japan, the Philippines, Czechoslovakia, and Hungary, in which such remarkable progress in raising the educational status of their populations has been achieved during the last quarter of a century, are the ones in which the sex differentials are the smallest. Fourth, the African and Asian countries and most of those in Eastern Europe are the ones in which the educational status of women compares most unfavorably with that of men.

If the index used in making the comparisons between the sexes indicates the extent to which the higher and professional levels of training are achieved (such as the proportions of college and university graduates in the population), it is evident that in the United States higher percentages of men than of women receive such instruction. Thus, in 1970, among the population aged twenty-five and over in the United States 10.7 per cent had completed four years or more of college or university work, but whereas this index was 13.5 per cent for the men it was only 8.1 per cent for the women; and in 1960 the comparable figures were 7.7 per cent, 9.7 per cent, and 5.8 per cent, for the total, male, and female populations, respectively. There are, however, some departures from this general difference between the sexes in the various residential categories. For the white population, higher percentages of males than females are college graduates in the urban and rural-nonfarm groups, whereas the reverse is true in the rural-farm category. The net result is that 14.4 per cent of the nation's white men and 8.4 per cent of its white women completed four years or more of college. For the

Negro population, however, higher proportions of women than men are college graduates in all three of the residential groupings and, therefore, in the total Negro population as well, where the figure for men was 4.2 per cent and that for women was 4.6 per cent. The differences between the sexes are greatest for whites in the urban category, where 16.9 per cent of the men and 9.4 per cent of the women are college graduates and for Negroes in the rural-farm group, where 1.5 per cent of the men and 3.0 per cent of the women have attained this level of schooling. For the nation's total population, though, it is evident that girls are more likely than boys to complete the twelve years of pre-college schooling, but that at the higher levels this situation is reversed and that men are more likely than women to complete professional and other university courses of study. Nevertheless, the fact that in 1970, 11,717,226 (10.7 per cent of those aged twenty-five and over, or whose schooling might be thought of as completed) had secured at least four years of college and university training is indicative of an exceptionally high general level of educational achievement among the population of the nation.

Rural-Urban Differentials

The relationship between residence and educational status is definite and substantial: the urban population ranks considerably above the rural-nonfarm population, and persons in the rural-nonfarm category in turn make a far better showing than those classified as rural-farm. This is evident if such an index as the median years of schooling is employed in the comparisons, and it stands out even more clearly when gauges such as the percentage completing four years of high school or four years of college or university training are relied upon. Note in Table 25 that among the total, white, and Negro segments and in each of these groups further subdivided by sex, the median is highest for the urban category, intermediate for the rural-nonfarm, and lowest for the rural-farm portion of the nation's inhabitants, except among white females, who had identical indexes in both the rural-farm and rural-nonfarm categories. If the percentage of the population completing four years of high school is used in making the comparisons, these differences between the educational status of the various residential groups are even more striking. Thus, in 1970, 52.3 per cent of the population of the United States aged twenty-five and over had completed the four years required for graduation from high school. Among the urban population, however, the proportion was 55.2 per cent, compared with 44.9 per cent for the rural-nonfarm and 42.3 per cent for the rural-farm population. On the basis of the percentage completing at least four years of college or university training, the index is highest (12.1 per cent) for the urban, intermediate (7.2 per cent) for the rural-nonfarm, and lowest (4.6 per cent) for the rural-farm categories, respectively.

There can be little doubt but that similar rural-urban differentials prevail in other parts of the world. Indeed, the strong presumption is that in most countries the differences between the educational levels achieved by the residents of towns and cities and those of the rural districts are even more pronounced than they are in the United States. The materials assembled to date by the United Nations and other international agencies do not permit a thoroughgoing study of this matter, but the 1971 issue of the *Demographic Yearbook* does contain some data that underscore the rural and urban differentials in educational status for seven widely different countries. In three of them, the percentages of persons aged fifteen and over who were classified as illiterate were as follows: Bulgaria (1965), 5.2 per cent of the urban and 13.8 per cent of the rural; Chile (1970), 7.4 per cent of the urban and 26.7 per cent of the rural; and Ecuador (1962), 11.9 per cent of the urban and 44.5 per cent of the rural. In two countries, the proportions of those aged ten and over who were unable to read and write were the following: the Philippines (1970), 7.2 per cent of the urban and 21.3 per cent of the rural; Puerto Rico (1970), 7.6 per cent of the urban and 15.5 per cent of the rural. Finally, in Japan (1970), of those aged fifteen and over, 0.5 per cent of the urban population and 1.3 per cent of the rural had not completed the first grade; in Tunisia (1966), the comparable proportions were 20.6 per cent and 30.7 per cent, respectively. The examples are few, but the situation is obvious: rural people on the average receive substantially less formal education than do the urban and in those parts of the world in which overall levels of education are extremely low, the differentials by residence are certain to be even greater than those discussed above.

Racial Differentials

The information in Table 25 indicates that the median number of years of schooling attained by the Negro population of the United States is substantially lower than that secured by the white segment. This is true in the general population and in each of the fifty states except Maine, New Hampshire, Vermont, North Dakota, South Dakota, and Montana, none of which had more than 1,100 Negroes aged twenty-five and over. (See Table 26.) It also is the case at the national level and in forty-six of the states when the data for each race are further subdivided according to residence and sex, although the discrepancies in most cases were not as great in 1970 as they had been in 1960. Furthermore, the racial differentials are even more pronounced if the comparisons are based upon such indexes as the proportions of high school or college graduates in the population. Thus, in 1970, the proportion of the persons aged twenty-five and over who had completed four years of high school was only 31.4 per cent for the Negro population, whereas it was 54.5 per cent for the white; and the proportion completing four years or more of college or university work was only 4.4 per cent for the former in comparison with 11.3 per cent for the latter.

TABLE 26

State-to-state variations in the median years of schooling completed by the population aged 25 years and over, by race and residence, 1970

Region and state	Total	All groups White	All groups Negro	Urban White	Urban Negro	Rural-nonfarm White	Rural-nonfarm Negro	Rural-farm White	Rural-farm Negro
United States	12.1	12.1	9.8	12.2	10.2	11.6	7.7	11.0	7.2
New England	12.2	12.2	11.2						
Maine	12.1	12.1	12.3	12.2	12.4	12.1	11.3	12.1	....
New Hampshire	12.2	12.2	12.5	12.2	12.4	12.3	....	12.3	....
Vermont	12.2	12.2	12.2	12.3	....	12.2	....	12.0	....
Massachusetts	12.2	12.3	11.6	12.2	11.6	12.4	12.0	12.2	12.4
Rhode Island	11.5	11.6	10.8	11.5	10.8	12.1	11.2	11.8	....
Connecticut	12.2	12.2	10.8	12.1	10.7	12.5	12.1	12.2	....
Middle Atlantic	12.1	12.1	10.7						
New York	12.1	12.1	10.8	12.1	10.8	12.2	10.0	12.0	9.3
New Jersey	12.1	12.1	10.5	12.1	10.6	12.2	8.9	11.7	9.2
Pennsylvania	12.0	12.0	10.4	12.1	10.4	11.8	9.9	10.9	9.7
East North Central	12.1	12.1	10.6						
Ohio	12.1	12.1	10.6	12.2	10.6	12.0	9.9	12.0	10.2
Indiana	12.1	12.1	10.5	12.1	10.5	12.1	10.0	12.1	10.2
Illinois	12.1	12.1	10.7	12.2	10.7	11.8	9.0	11.8	8.3
Michigan	12.1	12.1	10.6	12.2	10.6	12.0	9.5	11.6	9.9
Wisconsin	12.1	12.1	10.4	12.2	10.4	11.9	10.0	10.5	....
West North Central	12.2	12.2	10.4						
Minnesota	12.2	12.2	12.0	12.4	12.0	11.7	11.4	10.1	....
Iowa	12.2	12.2	10.9	12.3	10.9	12.1	11.3	12.2	....
Missouri	11.8	12.0	10.0	12.1	10.2	10.5	7.9	10.5	7.5
North Dakota	12.0	12.0	12.5	12.4	12.5	10.2	....	10.2	....
South Dakota	12.1	12.1	12.3	12.4	12.4	11.2	....	11.8	....
Nebraska	12.2	12.3	11.2	12.4	11.2	12.0	....	12.1	....
Kansas	12.3	12.3	10.9	12.4	10.9	12.1	10.4	12.2	10.8
South Atlantic	11.4	12.0	8.8						
Delaware	12.1	12.2	9.9	12.3	10.3	12.0	8.9	10.7	8.1
Maryland	12.1	12.2	9.9	12.3	10.2	11.9	8.7	10.7	8.2
District of Columbia	12.2	13.2	11.3	13.2	11.3	....	....	....	....
Virginia	11.7	12.1	8.6	12.4	9.4	10.3	7.6	9.4	7.1
West Virginia	10.6	10.6	9.5	12.1	10.3	9.4	8.8	8.9	8.2
North Carolina	10.6	11.1	8.5	12.1	9.3	10.5	8.0	9.6	7.5
South Carolina	10.5	11.4	7.6	12.1	8.4	10.6	7.1	10.3	6.8
Georgia	10.8	11.5	7.9	12.2	8.7	10.2	6.7	9.9	6.5
Florida	12.1	12.2	8.8	12.3	9.0	11.8	7.6	11.1	7.5
East South Central	10.5	11.2	8.2						
Kentucky	9.9	10.0	9.3	12.0	9.7	8.8	8.5	8.7	8.0
Tennessee	10.6	11.1	8.7	12.1	9.0	9.3	8.1	8.8	7.3

TABLE 26 (Cont'd)

State-to-state variations in the median years of schooling completed by
the population aged 25 years and over, by race and residence, 1970

Region and state	Total	All groups White	All groups Negro	Urban White	Urban Negro	Rural-nonfarm White	Rural-nonfarm Negro	Rural-farm White	Rural-farm Negro
Alabama	10.8	11.6	8.1	12.2	8.8	10.1	6.8	10.0	6.7
Mississippi	10.7	12.1	7.5	12.4	8.3	11.1	7.0	11.0	6.6
West South Central	11.5	11.9	8.9						
Arkansas	10.5	11.1	7.9	12.2	8.4	9.8	7.1	9.3	6.9
Louisiana	10.8	12.0	7.9	12.2	8.5	10.5	6.6	9.9	5.9
Oklahoma	12.1	12.1	10.2	12.3	10.7	10.5	8.3	11.1	8.5
Texas	11.6	11.9	9.7	12.1	10.1	10.6	8.1	10.4	8.1
Mountain	12.3	12.4	11.2						
Montana	12.3	12.3	12.3	12.4	12.3	12.1	....	12.2	....
Idaho	12.3	12.3	12.1	12.4	12.1	12.1	....	12.2	....
Wyoming	12.4	12.4	11.1	12.5	11.2	12.2	....	12.3	....
Colorado	12.4	12.4	12.2	12.5	12.1	12.3	12.4	12.2	....
New Mexico	12.2	12.2	10.9	12.4	11.0	11.1	9.1	11.1	....
Arizona	12.3	12.3	9.7	12.3	9.8	12.2	8.6	12.0	....
Utah	12.5	12.5	11.5	12.5	11.3	12.3	....	12.3	....
Nevada	12.4	12.4	10.7	12.5	10.7	12.3	12.0	12.3	....
Pacific	12.3	12.4	12.0						
Washington	12.4	12.4	11.8	12.4	11.9	12.2	11.0	12.2	....
Oregon	12.3	12.3	11.1	12.4	11.1	12.1	12.2	12.1	....
California	12.4	12.4	11.9	12.4	12.0	12.2	10.2	12.1	9.6
Alaska	12.4	12.6	12.3	12.6	12.3	12.6	12.5	12.5	....
Hawaii	12.3	12.7	12.6	12.7	12.5	12.3	12.7	12.4	....

Source: Compiled from data in U.S. Bureau of the Census, *U.S. Census of Population:
1970, General Social and Economic Characteristics,* Final Report PC(1)-C1, *United States
Summary* (1972), p. 368, Table 75; p. 493, Table 156; p. 494, Table 157; Final Reports
PC(1)-C2-C52, reports for states (1971 and 1972), Table 51.

.... Fewer than 200 persons aged 25 and over.

Such racial differentials in educational status are decidedly more extreme in the other countries for which comparative data are available. For example, in Brazil, where the numbers of Negroes and mulattoes closely approximate those in the United States, the materials gathered in the 1950 census may be analyzed in ways that make the differentials under consideration stand forth clearly. When this is done, it is evident that Negroes and persons of mixed ancestry compare much less favorably in educational status with their white fellows than is true in the United States. Thus, among the population ten years of age and over the proportion of those unable to read and write, which was only 34.2 per cent for the white population (and only 17.4 per cent for the yellow or Japanese population), rose to 68.9 per cent among the mixed (*pardo* or brown category) and to 73.3 per cent among the sizable portion of the population that was classified as black. Likewise, if one studies the relevant materials, it is found that of a total number of 36,537,990 people aged ten years and over, only 158,070 (0.4 per cent) possessed degrees from institutions of higher learning. But this level of educational attainment had been achieved by 152,934 (or 0.7 per cent) of the whites, 3,568 (0.4 per cent) of the *pardos,* 924 (0.4 per cent) of the Japanese, and only 448 (0.01 per cent) of the blacks or Negroes.

Similar differences with respect to educational status exist between the white and Indian portions of the densely populated Andean sections of South America, a fact apparent to all who visit these portions of America. They are somewhat difficult to demonstrate statistically, however, since the racial or color classifications either are missing entirely from the census data or the racial materials are not cross-tabulated with those on educational status. For Bolivia, however, it is possible to secure the data which enable one to determine that 69.6 per cent of the population aged twenty and over was classified as illiterate, and that this index was 84.1 per cent for the adult Indian population and only 44.8 for the remainder of the inhabitants of the country.[3] Since those classified as Indian or "indigenous" constituted 63 per cent of the total, these figures make it readily apparent that the educational status of the white and mestizo part of the population is vastly superior to that of the Indian.

Since caste and class systems rooted in conquest and slavery prevail in most other parts of the world in which there are any considerable numbers of substantially different racial or ethnic stocks included in a given population, it is likely that the data as they become available will reveal differentials in educational status comparable to those demonstrated for the United States, Brazil, and Bolivia. In all cases it probably will be found that the groups once occupying a servile or semi-servile status have far to go before achieving a degree of schooling remotely approximating that of those who once were the masters, irrespective of whether the latter achieved their positions of dominance through conquest, economic exploitation, or by other means.

Regional and State-to-State Variations

In any given country, the educational status of the population differs substantially from one part of its territory to another. In a considerable measure, of course, such regional or state variations are merely a reflection of the fact that the rural and urban portions of the population and the racial or ethnic groups of which it is composed are distributed quite unequally among the various sections of the nation under consideration. Even after such rural-urban and racial or color differentials are taken into account, however, frequently there remain substantial differentials which must be attributed to regional differences or still other factors. This is apparent to anyone who will study the data for the various states of the United States which are given in Table 26.

Generally speaking, there is a tendency for the median years of schooling attained by the adult population to vary directly with the relative importance of the urban and the white components in its make-up. This is to say that the more urban the state and the smaller the proportion of Negroes or other nonwhite elements among its inhabitants, the higher the index of educational status. Therefore, it is not surprising that in their total populations, the median years of schooling is lowest for six southern states (Kentucky, Arkansas, South Carolina, North Carolina, Tennessee, and West Virginia) which contain either high proportions of Negroes or rural people or both. But neither the degree of urbanization nor the racial composition of the population explains completely why the scores are highest in Utah, Alaska, California, Colorado, Nevada, Washington, and Wyoming. Consequently, it is important to study the materials in Table 26 which show for each of the residential groups, further subdivided by race, the median years of schooling completed by the respective populations of the states and the District of Columbia.

If attention is centered upon the largest segment of the nation's population, that portion of the white population that also is urban, some very interesting results are apparent. Among this part of the population (63.5 per cent of the total), the District of Columbia is the subdivision of the nation having the highest index in 1970 (a median of 13.2 years of schooling), followed by Hawaii (12.7 years), Alaska (12.6 years), and Colorado, Nevada, Utah, and Wyoming (each with a score of 12.5 years). Rhode Island was the state in which the educational status of the urban white population was lowest (a median of 11.5 years), whereas the medians in all of the other states were 12.0 years or higher. Furthermore, by 1970 the nation's urban white population had acquired sufficient formal schooling so that no state except those mentioned above had an index that was higher than 12.4 years or lower than 12.0 years. Even the gap between the District of Columbia at the top of the scale and Rhode Island at the bottom was only 1.7 years. As compared with whites in the rural-nonfarm and rural-farm segments and with the Negro population in all of the residential categories, this is an extremely narrow range.

The data given in Table 26, since they are tabulated separately for the racial and residential groupings, make possible a wide variety of other significant state and regional comparisons of the educational status of the population. Among the rural population, both farm and nonfarm, and among whites as well as Negroes, the southern states without exception rank far down in the list. In New England, the Pacific states, the Mountain states except New Mexico, and in New York, Ohio, Indiana, Iowa, Nebraska, and Kansas, persons residing on farms have secured almost as much schooling as their fellows who live in the cities, and in New Hampshire, Rhode Island, and Connecticut the indexes for the rural-farm whites actually slightly exceed those for the urban whites. In the Middle Atlantic states collectively, the indexes for the white urban population are above those of the rural-farm group by approximately 0.6 year. In the East North Central division, the differences are about 0.5 year; in the West North Central division, they are roughly 1.0 year. But throughout the South the unfavorable situation of the farm population stands out. The relatively high educational status of its white urban population accompanied by the low educational status of its farm population, white and Negro, is one of the most striking features of the region. The differential between the amount of schooling achieved by the urban and rural-farm segments of the white population reaches its maximum (3.3 years) in Kentucky and Tennessee, followed by West Virginia (3.2 years), Virginia (3.0 years), Arkansas (2.9 years), and North Carolina (2.5 years), but it is 1.2 years or more in all of the southern states. It is important to note that differentials of 1.2 years or more also prevail in Pennsylvania, Wisconsin, Minnesota, Missouri, and North Dakota. As a result of these circumstances, the state-to-state variations in educational achievement among the rural populations are substantially greater than they are among the urban populations. In 1970, the range in the level of schooling attained by rural-farm whites extended from the high of 12.5 years in Alaska to the low of 8.7 years in Kentucky, a difference of 3.8 years. For the rural-nonfarm whites the extremes were the high of 12.6 years in Alaska and the low of 8.8 years in Kentucky, also a difference of 3.8 years.

Among all residential categories, the very low educational status of the Negro population in the various southern states is the most conspicuous regional difference exhibited by the data in Table 26. In 1970, the median years of schooling completed by Negroes in the entire South was about 8.6 years, compared with an average for the nation's total Negro population of 9.8 years. In some of the states outside of the South that contain appreciable numbers of rural Negroes, nearly all of them rural-nonfarm, the levels of schooling attained by persons in the rural and urban areas are roughly similar, but in the southern states without exception, urban Negroes receive more formal education than those in the rural-nonfarm population and substantially more than those in the rural-farm group. In the urban population, the range for Negroes in median years of schooling completed was from the highs of 12.7 years in Hawaii and 12.6 years in Alaska to the lows of 8.3 years in Mississippi and 8.4 years in Arkansas and South Carolina. In the rural-nonfarm segment, the range was from 12.7 years in Hawaii and 12.5 years in Alaska to 6.6 years in Louisiana and 6.7 years in Georgia. Finally, in the rural-farm population where Negroes have fared most badly, the highest indexes were 12.4 years in Massachusetts and 10.8 years in Kansas, the lowest were 5.9 years in Louisiana and 6.6 years in Mississippi. In no southern state, in 1970, had the average rural-farm Negro completed the ninth grade.

TRENDS

Any evaluation of trends in educational status in the United States becomes a study of at least some improvement in all of the race, sex, and residence categories, although these several groups vary considerably in their rates of improvement. (See Table 27.) In almost every case the result of the changes was a tendency toward greater similarity in the educational statuses of the various components of the national population. In 1960, as measured by the median years of schooling completed, males had received somewhat less formal education than females, nonwhites (mostly Negroes) had received substantially less than whites, rural people had received much less than urban inhabitants, and the rural-farm group had received less than the rural-nonfarm group. During the decade the index rose more rapidly for men than for women, for nonwhites than for whites, for rural people than for urbanites, and for persons in the rural-farm category than for those in the rural-nonfarm group. This homogenizing process also can be demonstrated by using as an index the percentages of those who had completed specified years of schooling. Thus, the proportions of persons aged twenty-five and over who had completed less than one year of schooling fell more rapidly for men than for women, for nonwhites than for whites, for rural people than for urban inhabitants, and for the rural-farm segment than for the rural-nonfarm group. Similarly, the percentages of high school graduates increased more rapidly in the categories that were at the greatest disadvantage in 1960 than they did in those for which the levels of education had been more favorable. Finally, the proportions of college graduates also changed in such a way that the homogenizing tendency persisted. That is, the percentages of persons who had attained this level of schooling increased more rapidly among nonwhites than among whites, among rural inhabitants than among the urban, and among rural-farm people than among rural-nonfarm inhabitants. They increased more rapidly for women than for men, but in 1960 women were at the disadvantage in this respect, so that the change also was in the direction of greater similarity in levels of education.

TABLE 27

Selected indicators of changes in educational status in the United
States, by sex, residence, and color, 1960 and 1970

Sex, residence, and color	No schooling		Per cent with Four years or more of high school		Four years or more of college		Median years completed	
	1960	1970	1960	1970	1960	1970	1960	1970
Total	2.3	1.6	41.1	52.3	7.7	10.7	10.6	12.1
Male	2.4	1.6	39.5	51.9	9.7	13.5	10.3	12.1
Female	2.2	1.6	42.6	52.8	5.8	8.1	10.9	12.1
Urban	2.2	1.6	44.3	55.2	8.9	12.1	11.1	12.2
Male	2.2	1.5	43.4	55.6	11.5	15.7	11.0	12.2
Female	2.2	1.7	44.9	54.9	6.5	9.0	11.2	12.1
Rural-nonfarm	2.6	1.8	34.4	44.9	5.3	7.2	9.5	11.2
Male	3.0	2.1	31.9	43.2	6.4	8.6	9.0	10.9
Female	2.2	1.6	36.9	46.5	4.2	5.8	10.0	11.5
Rural-farm	2.3	1.3	29.5	42.3	2.8	4.6	8.8	10.7
Male	2.7	1.6	24.9	37.8	2.6	4.5	8.6	9.9
Female	1.8	1.1	34.5	46.8	3.2	4.8	9.2	11.5
White	1.9	1.4	43.2	54.5	8.1	11.3	10.9	12.1
Male	2.0	1.4	41.6	54.0	10.3	14.4	10.7	12.1
Female	2.2	1.4	44.7	55.0	6.0	8.4	11.2	12.1
Urban	2.0	1.4	46.4	57.6	9.4	12.9	11.5	12.2
Male	1.9	1.3	45.7	58.0	12.3	16.9	11.3	12.3
Female	2.0	1.5	47.0	57.2	6.8	9.4	11.6	12.2
Rural-nonfarm	1.9	1.4	36.5	47.1	5.6	7.5	9.9	11.6
Male	2.2	1.6	34.0	45.3	6.9	9.1	9.4	11.3
Female	1.6	1.3	39.2	48.7	4.4	6.1	10.3	11.8
Rural-farm	1.5	1.0	31.6	43.9	3.0	4.8	8.9	11.0
Male	1.9	1.2	26.5	39.3	2.7	4.6	8.7	10.2
Female	1.2	0.8	36.9	48.6	3.3	4.9	9.7	11.8
Nonwhite	5.6	3.5	21.7	33.8	3.5	5.6	8.2	10.0
Male	6.8	4.1	20.0	32.9	3.5	5.8	7.9	9.7
Female	4.6	3.1	23.2	34.6	3.6	5.4	8.5	10.2
Urban	4.2	2.8	25.3	37.3	4.1	6.2	8.7	10.5
Male	5.0	3.2	23.7	36.7	4.2	6.6	8.5	10.3
Female	3.5	2.5	26.6	37.9	4.0	5.9	8.9	10.6
Rural-nonfarm	10.1	6.9	11.6	18.3	2.1	2.9	6.4	7.9
Male	11.9	8.1	10.5	17.0	1.8	2.5	5.8	7.3
Female	8.4	5.8	12.7	19.4	2.4	3.2	6.9	8.2
Rural-farm	10.0	6.9	7.1	15.1	1.1	2.3	5.7	7.4
Male	12.5	8.4	5.4	12.6	0.7	1.7	4.8	6.5
Female	7.6	5.5	8.8	17.4	1.6	2.9	6.5	8.0

Source: Compiled and computed from data in U.S. Bureau of the Census, *U.S. Census of Population: 1960,* Vol. I, *Characteristics of the Population,* Part 1 (1964), pp. 207-209, Table 76; *U.S. Census of Population: 1970, General Social and Economic Characteristics,* Final Report PC(1)-C1, *United States Summary* (1972), p. 368, Table 75.

Perhaps the most noteworthy of these various patterns of convergence in educational status that occurred between 1960 and 1970 is the one that took place for the two major color groups. During the decade the median years of schooling completed rose 11 per cent for whites but 22 per cent for nonwhites. Furthermore, changes in this index that brought the nonwhite group closer to the white in levels of education took place in all of the residence and sex categories. These relatively rapid rates of growth in the educational status of the nonwhite population are also reflected in the fact that the percentages of persons who had not completed even one year of schooling decreased more rapidly for nonwhites than for whites, whereas the percentages of those who ranked relatively high on the educational scale rose more rapidly for the former than for the latter. Most spectacular of all was the rise in the proportion of high school graduates. This increase amounted to 56 per cent for nonwhites as compared with 26 per cent for whites. Also highly significant was the 60 per cent increase in the proportion of nonwhite college graduates as compared with the 40 per cent increase in the proportion of whites who had attained this level. This reduction in the differences between whites and nonwhites in educational status is probably one of the most powerful social forces now at work in the United States to produce a long-term, genuine integration of the races.

1. For a summary discussion of the situation prevailing prior to the appearance of the first issue of the *Demographic Yearbook* in 1948, see T. Lynn Smith, *Population Analysis* (New York: McGraw-Hill Book Company, 1948), pp. 154 - 156.

2. Cf. T. Lynn Smith, *Current Social Trends and Problems in Latin America* (Gainesville: University of Florida Press, 1957), pp. 13 - 14 and 24 - 25; and T. Lynn Smith, *Brazil: People and Institutions* (4th ed.) (Baton Rouge: Louisiana State University Press, 1972), pp. 484 - 491 and 712 - 717.

3. The tabulations on which these computations are based are given in Asthenio Averanga Mollineado, *Aspectos Generales de la Población Boliviana* (La Paz: Editorial Argote, 1956), p. 101; and Mario Arce Vargas, *Monografía Estadística Indígena de Bolivia* (La Paz: Editorial Fenix, 1954), p. 41.

SUGGESTED SUPPLEMENTARY READINGS

BOGUE, DONALD J. *The Population of the United States,* Chap. 13. Glencoe, Ill.: The Free Press, 1959.

BOGUE, DONALD J. *Principles of Demography,* pp. 181 - 204. New York: John Wiley & Sons, Inc., 1969.

FOLGER, JOHN K., and CHARLES B. NAM. *Education of the American Population* (A 1960 Census Monograph). Washington: Government Printing Office, 1967.

HATHAWAY, DALE E., J. ALLAN BEEGLE, and W. KEITH BRYANT. *People of Rural America* (A 1960 Census Monograph), Chap VI. Washington: Government Printing Office, 1968.

JONES, GAVIN W. "Effect of Population Change on the Attainment of Educational Goals in the Developing Countries," in *Rapid Population Growth,* edited by a Study Committee of the National Academy of Sciences, Vol. II, Chap. IX. Baltimore: Johns Hopkins Press, 1971.

KIMBALL, SOLON T. "Education and the New South," in *The South in Continuity and Change,* edited by John C. McKinney and Edgar T. Thompson. Durham: Duke University Press, 1965.

SHRYOCK, HENRY S., JACOB S. SIEGEL, and associates. *The Methods and Materials of Demography,* Vol. 1, Chap. 11. Washington: Government Printing Office, 1971.

SIMPSON, GEORGE E., and J. MILTON YINGER. *Racial and Cultural Minorities,* 3rd ed., Chaps. 19 and 20. New York: Harper & Row, 1965.

SMITH, T. LYNN. *Brazil: People and Institutions,* 4th ed., Chap. XIX. Baton Rouge: Louisiana State University Press, 1972.

SMITH, T. LYNN, and LOUISE KEMP. *The Educational Status of Louisiana's Farm Population,* Louisiana Agricultural Experiment Station Bulletin No. 424. Baton Rouge: Louisiana State University, 1947.

SMITH, T. LYNN, and PAUL E. ZOPF, JR. *Principles of Inductive Rural Sociology,* Chap. 13. Philadelphia: F. A. Davis Company, 1970.

TAEUBER, CONRAD, and IRENE B. TAEUBER. *The People of the United States in the 20th Century* (A 1960 Census Monograph), pp. 188 - 205. Washington: Government Printing Office, 1971.

TAYLOR, LEE. *Urban-Rural Problems,* Chaps. 2 and 3. Belmont, Calif.: Dickenson Publishing Company, Inc., 1968.

THOMLINSON, RALPH. *Population Dynamics,* pp. 464 - 472. New York: Random House, Inc., 1965.

UNITED NATIONS. *Demographic Yearbook, 1971,* pp. 32 - 35. New York: United Nations, 1972.

UNESCO. *Manual of Educational Statistics.* Paris: UNESCO, 1961.

UNESCO. *World Illiteracy at Mid-Century.* Paris: UNESCO, 1957.

U.S. BUREAU OF THE CENSUS. *U. S. Census of Population: 1970. Subject Reports. Educational Attainment.* Washington: Government Printing Office, 1973.

PART FOUR

The Vital Processes

MEASURING THE RATE OF REPRODUCTION

The rate at which the population is reproducing is the central feature of population study. Reproduction itself quite properly is designated as one of the two *vital processes,* mortality being the other. Since in most populations throughout human history, births have substantially exceeded deaths in number, usually the rate of reproduction is considerably more important than the mortality rate in determining the number of inhabitants, their distribution, and the rate at which the population is changing. Only in rare cases is it rivaled in importance by the only other primary factor, namely migration, which may be involved in the changing number and distribution of the population.

A variety of terms may be used to denote the reproduction of the human species; and the student of population should be well acquainted with several of them. Those encountered most frequently are: birth rate, fertility, fecundity, and natality. Most demographers are now agreed that the term *fecundity* should be relied upon to designate the biological potential and the word *fertility* to specify the actual reproduction of the population. *Natality* as yet has received no specific connotations and is employed as synonymous with the reproduction of the population. The expression *birth rate* is used in popular terminology to refer to reproduction in general, although technically it refers to one specific way of measuring or gauging the fertility of the population.

INDEXES FOR MEASURING FERTILITY

Students of population long have been interested in objective methods for determining the level of reproduction in a given population at a stated time and for comparing the fertility of two or more populations. So far, two indexes, the birth rate and the fertility ratio, are in most general use, although several others sometimes are applicable and valuable for specific purposes.

Birth Rate

The measure known as the birth rate is by far the most commonly used index of the rate of reproduction. In its crudest and simplest form, the birth rate is merely the ratio of the number of births during a stated interval of time (one year) to the total number of persons in the population. Since the population is larger than the number of births, the decimal fraction resulting from this arithmetical operation generally is multiplied by a constant so that the index may be expressed as a simple number of two digits. Thus the birth rate for the United States in 1970 may be determined as follows:

$$\frac{\text{Number of births during 1970}}{\text{Population April 1, 1970}} \times 1{,}000 = \frac{3{,}718{,}000}{203{,}210{,}158} \times 1{,}000 = 18.3$$

Obviously, this index would be slightly more accurate if the population as of July 1 were used instead of that given by the census enumeration for April 1. Such a refinement is not particularly difficult, and the necessary estimate of population is not likely to be greatly in error, since the number of births registered during 1970 exceeded the number of deaths recorded that year by 1,797,000, and it is known that the net immigration during the three-month period could not have been great. Consider in this connection that the population of the United States as of July 1, 1970, as estimated by the U.S. Bureau of the Census, was 203,810,000 or very nearly that which would be secured by adding to the April 1 count of 203,210,158 one-fourth of the natural increase for the year (one-fourth of 1,797,000 or 449,250). Such a refinement would reduce the birth rate in question less than one-tenth of a point. However, there is little use in making such a correction in the denominator, unless one also is prepared to evaluate and correct for even more significant errors in the numerator. Tests of the completeness of birth registration in the United States indicate that in 1970 only about 99.2 per cent of the births were registered. If this is the case, then the actual number of births for the year was about 3,747,744, instead of the 3,718,000 used in the above calculation; and if this number and the estimated population for July 1 are used in the computations, the birth rate for 1970 is raised to 18.4. In most cases, however, so little is known about the extent of error in the reported number of births and in the estimated size of the population that such corrections are impossible; and even were this not the case, there is little point to such refinements of the crude birth rate.

Whoever uses vital statistics should realize that the unrefined or crude birth rate is a most unreliable gauge of human fertility. Variations in the age and sex composition of populations are large, and these influence so greatly the magnitude of the crude birth rate that little valid comparison of the fertility of different groups may be made until these variations have been corrected for or allowances have been made for their effects. For example, in Chapters 6 and 7 it was shown that the rural population of the United States contains high proportions of males and of children between five and fifteen years of age, whereas the urban population has high proportions of females and of those in the productive years of life. Obviously, a population which includes high percentages of males and of those who are physically immature should not be expected to produce as many babies per thousand population as one in which women in the childbearing ages constitute a disproportionately large share of the total. On the frontier, in the Yukon or the Amazon, where males constitute the bulk of the population, the crude birth rate is certain to be low even though each woman bears her maximum number of children. Thus, until proper allowances are made for the age and sex composition, it is impossible to make valid assertions concerning the rate of reproduction of a given population or to compare the fertility of one group with that of another.

In *Population Analysis*,[1] data for the white population of the United States in 1940 are used to demonstrate the process of correcting or standardizing the birth rate for the rural and urban portions of our country. For purposes of illustrating the technique this material may be summarized as follows. The total population of the United States in 1940 was taken as the standard or base to which the urban white and rural white segments of the population were to be equated. Next the birth rate of each specific age group in the population was determined, namely, the birth rates for the age groups fifteen to nineteen, twenty to twenty-four, twenty-five to twenty-nine, and so forth. Then in the urban population and in the rural population each of these age-specific birth rates was allowed the same weight or importance that it had in the base or standard population. This enabled a calculation to be made to show, on the basis of the observed age-specific rates, how many births would have occurred in the rural and urban populations of the given sizes providing each had had an age and sex composition corresponding exactly to that of the total population of the nation. The birth rates derived from these data, known as the *standardized birth rates* are the ones that would have prevailed among the rural and urban white populations of the nation, given the actual fertility of each group, had each of them had exactly the same age and sex composition. The arithmetic involved in the determination of such standardized birth rates is shown in Table 28.

The age distributions of the urban females and rural females (columns two and three) and the numbers of births classified according to the ages of the mothers (columns four and five), make the calculation of the age-specific birth rates for women (columns six and seven) very simple. The number of women in the standard population, and the proportion those of each stated age make up of the total population is shown in columns eight and nine. Applying the percentages in column nine to the total urban and the total rural populations produces the figures

TABLE 28

Illustration of the procedures involved in the standardization of the birth rates for the urban and rural white populations of the United States, 1940

Age (1)	Number of females of stated ages		Number of births to women of stated ages		Age-specific birth rates		Women in the standard[1] population		Number of women there would be if standard[1] age-sex distribution prevailed		Number of births there would be if standard[1] age-sex distribution prevailed	
	Urban (2)	Rural (3)	Urban (4)	Rural (5)	Urban (6)	Rural (7)	Number (8)	% of the total population (9)	Urban (10)	Rural (11)	Urban (12)	Rural (13)
Under 10	4,477,944	4,634,711	....	....	....	....	10,452,515	7.94	5,397,042	3,989,219	....	....
10-14	2,629,977	2,463,711	421	706	0.2	0.3	5,793,606	4.40	2,990,804	2,210,650	598	663
15-19	3,028,611	2,419,516	108,134	121,476	35.7	50.2	6,153,370	4.67	3,174,331	2,346,304	113,324	117,784
20-24	3,246,296	1,980,211	358,700	288,108	110.5	145.5	5,895,443	4.48	3,045,182	2,250,844	336,493	327,498
25-29	3,158,974	1,853,283	348,560	237,310	110.3	128.0	5,645,976	4.29	2,916,034	2,155,384	321,639	275,889
30-34	2,927,168	1,705,994	210,925	153,101	72.1	89.7	5,172,076	3.93	2,671,332	1,974,512	192,603	117,114
35-39	2,699,471	1,562,821	91,889	86,651	34.0	55.4	4,799,718	3.65	2,481,008	1,833,835	84,354	101,594
40-44	2,520,514	1,420,379	23,899	30,104	9.5	21.2	4,368,708	3.32	2,256,698	1,668,036	21,439	35,362
45-49	2,341,743	1,348,400	1,673	2,923	0.7	2.2	4,045,956	3.07	2,086,766	1,542,431	1,461	3,393
50-54	2,028,243	1,200,347	54	68	0.0	0.1	3,504,096	2.66	1,808,077	1,336,438	....	134
55 and over	5,609,181	3,509,033	....	....	....	....	9,776,219	7.42	5,043,583	3,727,960	....	....
Total	34,668,122	24,098,200	1,144,255	920,447	....	....	65,607,683	49.83	33,870,857	25,035,613	1,071,911	979,431

Source: Sixteenth Census of the United States, 1940, Population, Second Series, Characteristics of the Population, United States Summary Table 7, pp. 16-20; and *Vital Statistics of the United States,* Supplement, 1939-1940, Part III, Tables IV and V, pp. 28 and 40.

[1] The age and sex distribution of the total population of the United States as of 1940. The total white population numbered 118,214,873, the urban white group was 67,972,821, and the rural white segment was 50,242,052.

(columns ten and eleven) showing the number of women of each stated age there would be in each of these populations if it had the same age and sex distribution as the standard. Then from the age-specific birth rates (columns six and seven) it is easy to determine how many children would have been borne by each age group of women (columns twelve and thirteen) if the age and sex distribution had corresponded to the standard. These hypothetical totals of births are then used in the usual way along with the total urban and rural populations in the computation of the birth rates.

The objective of these computations and the effect of the adjustments so made is to correct for, to "iron out," or to eliminate the differences in the birth rates that are due solely to the variations in the age-sex distributions of the populations under study. The necessity of making such refinements before using the birth rate as the index upon which to base comparisons of fertility in rural and urban areas, or between any populations that have substantially different age and sex distributions, is emphasized by the results of the procedures illustrated in Table 28. Thus, in 1940, the reported crude birth rate of the white urban population was 16.8 compared with one of 18.3 for the white rural population. Correcting in the manner described for the differences in the age and sex distributions of the two populations lowers the urban rate to 15.8 and raises the rural rate to 19.5. Because, in 1940, the data on births in the United States were faulty, with more frequent failure to record the babies born in rural than in urban areas, even these standardized birth rates were not truly indicative of the rural-urban differentials in the fertility of the population. Nor would such be the case if 1970 materials were used in the computations. Indeed, before one engages in the lengthy arithmetical calculations involved in the standardization of birth rates, he should be as certain as possible that the data he is using are sufficiently accurate to justify such time-consuming endeavors. For most purposes this still is not the case for the United States and probably is even less so for most other parts of the world. In this, as in so many other portions of demography, and in the social sciences in general, improved observation, more reliable recording of the facts, and more useful classifications of the data, rather than the elaboration of highly refined mathematical procedures, seem to be the ways in which our knowledge of the field will be most greatly advanced.

The use of the birth rate as a measure of fertility has several distinct advantages, but it also has a few serious shortcomings. Among its advantages are the following: (1) it is simple to calculate and easy to understand; (2) where a registration system has been established, it can be secured annually; and (3) it is the index with which most people are familiar, and the only one with which many persons, including the scholars in many fields, are acquainted.

Among the most serious disadvantages of the birth rate as a gauge of human fertility are the following: (1) the crude birth rate when used by those with relatively little experience in population study is likely to be highly misleading, while the computation of standardized rates is involved and laborious; (2) rarely are birth rate statistics reasonably complete, so that most of the data presented and interpretations offered relating to levels, differentials, and trends in birth rates are vitiated by the faulty nature of the basic facts; and (3) births usually are not reported for small areas, so that at the community level only rarely can the birth rate be used to measure the rapidity with which the population is reproducing.

The Fertility Ratio

The second index in somewhat general use for gauging the fertility of the population is known as the *fertility ratio*. It differs from the birth rate, or any other measure based upon a count of the births, in that the data needed for its computation are not secured through the registration system. Instead, all materials needed for calculating this important index are secured by a census of the population, or even by the type of enumeration that is generally made in connection with most community surveys. This makes it especially useful for gauging the fertility of population in many parts of the world in which systems for registering births either are entirely lacking or are very faulty, as well as for determining the rate of reproduction in hundreds of small communities which wish to take stock of their human resources.

The fertility ratio is computed by taking the ratio between the number of young children and the number of women in the childbearing ages and multiplying this ratio by a constant to transform the result into a simple and easily manipulated number. Naturally, the specific age groupings used in the tabulation of census materials may produce variations in the age limits employed by various people for different countries, but insofar as it is feasible the present writers prefer to use children under five and women aged fifteen to forty-four. Those in charge of preparing the *Demographic Yearbook* of the United Nations, on the other hand, use children under five and women aged fifteen to forty-nine; and in many of the studies made between 1930 and 1940, when this index was gaining acceptance among population students, women aged twenty to forty-four figured in the computations. It has become conventional to use 1,000 as the constant in the formula for the fertility ratio, but this results in a figure containing three or even four digits, of which no more than the first two can be considered mathematically sound. Therefore, the present writers break with general practice and employ 100 rather than 1,000 in the computation of the index. To illustrate, the computation of the fertility ratio for Japan in 1970 is as follows:

$$\frac{\text{Number of children under five}}{\text{Number of women 15 to 44}} \times 100 = \frac{8,789,900}{26,156,000} \times 100 = 33.6$$

For most purposes this index is sufficiently refined. By its use in the comparison of fertility levels, differentials, and trends, any sex differences in the composition of the population are automatically eliminated, as are the effects of varying proportions of those too young to bear children and those who have passed the childbearing ages.

As compared with the birth rate, the fertility ratio has some rather obvious merits or advantages, and it also suffers from several disadvantages. Of primary importance is the fact that data secured by the registration of births, materials that often are highly defective, are not essential for its computation. Because it automatically is rather highly standardized for the age and sex composition of the population, it is far less likely than the birth rate to lead the nonspecialist astray. It also is easily calculated from the materials gathered in the census or even from those secured in the ordinary community survey. On the other hand, the usefulness of the fertility ratio may be impaired if there are significant differences between the populations being compared in the proportions of women in the younger one-half of the childbearing span, a matter which it is difficult or impossible to standardize. Likewise, even for large areas such as states or nations, it may not be computed annually, but only for the five-year period immediately preceding a census. In the United States, this means that the use of this index is limited mostly to such periods as April 1, 1965 through March 31, 1970, April 1, 1955 through March 31, 1960, and so forth. Since several years are required to prepare the details of a given census for publication, this signifies, in turn, that the fertility ratios for the period 1965 - 1970 will be the most recent ones available until about 1982, when the age-sex distributions from the twentieth census should be generally available. For many purposes, such a lag is a serious disadvantage. Finally, the fertility ratio may not be used to measure the rate of reproduction of any group, such as the foreign-born, in which mothers come in one category and their native-born children in another. Such is the present state of birth statistics throughout the world, however, that the fertility ratio is much to be preferred over the birth rate for studies of levels and differentials in fertility; and so defective are birth statistics for past years that if one would avoid deceiving himself and others with respect to historical and present trends in the rate of reproduction, he is almost forced to use the fertility ratio rather than the birth rate as the base for his comparisons.

Number of Children Ever Born

A third index, which has come into greater use in the United States since the publication of the results of the 1950, 1960, and 1970 censuses, is the number of children ever born per 1,000 women in specific age groups. The essential data necessary to prepare this ratio were acquired by census enumerators in response to the question asked about women who were ever married, "How many babies has she ever had, not counting stillbirths?" The materials for 1970 have been summarized and published for the nation with subdivisions by age, race, and residence,[2] and for each of the states with the same cross-classifications.[3] The latter volumes also contain some data for counties. This index has been computed by some users of the basic data for women aged fifteen to sixty-five and over, but for purposes of ascertaining differentials in fertility according to race, residence, and other characteristics, the ages fifteen to forty-four are the most used. The following illustrates the computation of the index for the United States in 1970 using the ages fifteen to forty-four:

$$\frac{\text{Number of children ever born}}{\substack{\text{Number of women aged 15-44} \\ \text{ever married}}} \times 1{,}000 = \frac{68{,}600{,}580}{29{,}067{,}204} \times 1{,}000 = 2{,}360$$

The number of children ever born per 1,000 women has the advantage of measuring actual childbearing performance by ages of married women. As indicated above, the fertility ratio or number of children under five years of age per 100 women aged fifteen to forty-four suffers as an index of differential fertility when women appear in abnormally large or small proportions in any of the five-year age groups that make up the total range. For example, one finds that such a tendency is especially pronounced when he attempts to compare fertility ratios for the urban, rural-nonfarm, and rural-farm populations of the United States. In this case, the migration from the farms to the cities of women in the ages eighteen to twenty-nine moves large numbers of women in the peak childbearing years from the former residence category to the latter, and when the fertility ratio is used it appears that the populations of the cities have higher rates of reproduction than those of the farming areas. This apparent differential is exaggerated further by the fact that the groups aged fifteen to nineteen and forty to forty-four, both of which have relatively low rates of reproduction simply because of age, are heavily represented on the farms and are comparatively scarce in the cities. As a result of these various distortions in the age profiles, the fertility ratio for the urban population appears abnormally high and that for the farm group excessively low. Therefore, when these conditions prevail, because it reflects actual childbearing, the ratio between the number of children ever born and the number of women ever married, controlled by age, constitutes a more refined measure of differential fertility.

This index also has some disadvantages. In the first place, the reported ratios refer only to children who have survived and do not account for differences between groups in infant mortality. Second, the essential data are based upon the necessity for women to recall the number of children they ever have borne, a fact which probably results in the reporting of too small a number. The magnitude of this deficiency may be reduced to a degree, however, by confining most analyses of the data thus acquired to the age group fifteen to forty-four. Third, the number of children ever born relates to no specific time period and does not reflect current fertility in the same way as do birth rates restricted to twelve-month registration periods. Fourth, the use of the ages fifteen to forty-four in connection with the index under consideration means that incomplete fertility is being examined, although this is no particular handicap for most purposes. Fifth, the index does not account for children born to women who report themselves as unmarried. Finally, this index of cumulative fertility is available only for the United States;[4] and the fertility ratio remains the most adequate index of levels of reproduction in the majority of the world's countries.

Other Indexes of the Rate of Reproduction

Demographers use a variety of other measures in their studies of human reproduction, of which it will suffice to mention two here, namely, the *gross reproduction rate* and the *net reproduction rate*.[5] Since the number of births, registered or estimated, enters into the computation of all of these, the cautions already indicated in connection with the defects in birth statistics should be kept in mind when using any of these.

The gross reproduction rate is an arithmetical fiction designed to determine how many female babies would be borne in the course of their lifetimes by 1,000 females all born at the same time, providing both of the following assumptions were true: (1) all of the 1,000 female babies lived through the childbearing period; and (2) all of them produced female children as they passed from age group to age group at the specific rates determined by an analysis of the birth statistics at the date on which they were born.

The net reproduction rate is the number of female children that would be borne in the course of their lifetimes by 1,000 women assumed to have been born at the same time, providing the age-specific death rates and birth rates prevailing at the time of their births were to continue until all of them had passed through the childbearing period. As described by the demographers of the United Nations, net reproduction rates are defined as:

> the average number of live daughters that would be born during their reproductive lifetime to a hypothetical female birth cohort which would be subjected not only to the current age-specific fertility schedule but also to the current mortality rates. It indicates the rate at which the number of births would eventually grow per generation if the fertility and mortality rates, on which the calculation is based, should remain in operation indefinitely.[6]

DATA ON THE FERTILITY OF THE POPULATION

Casual observation of standard sources is likely to make it appear that a plethora of material is readily available to anyone interested in studying the fertility of the population in various parts of the world. Data compiled from the registers of births occupy an important place in the *Statistical Yearbook* published each year by many countries. Reports on the numbers of births and computation of the birth rates for most of the independent countries, and for many colonies and possessions as well, figure prominently in the numerous issues of the *Statistical Yearbook* of the League of Nations, and they have been reproduced for the years 1905 to 1930 in the 1951 edition of the *Demographic Yearbook* of the United Nations. Other editions of the latter contain the materials from 1930 almost to date, and those for the years 1954, 1959, 1965, and 1969 have natality statistics as their special topics. In addition, various issues of the *Statistical Bulletin* supply the latest official data very shortly after they are received from the member governments as does the *Population and Vital Statistics Report,* issued four times a year. Various other statistical compendia contain substantial compilations of birth statistics for specific parts of the world; particular mention should be made of the *Summary of Biostatistics* for each of the Latin American countries prepared and published by the U. S. Bureau of the Census in cooperation with the Office of the Coordinator of Inter-American Affairs. These important volumes, which appeared during the early 1940's, contain substantial tabular and graphic materials on births and birth rates going back to 1900 in most cases. These are only a few of the sources, but a casual examination of them is sure to give the impression that all of the materials needed for thoroughgoing study of the birth rate in most parts of the earth are readily at hand.

Closer scrutiny of the data, however, is likely to dispel much of one's initial enthusiasm, and many students when attempting to use much of the data for comprehensive analysis or detailed comparisons are likely to become exasperated. For country after country, one is likely to find it difficult to establish any internal consistency among the data presented, although if he examines further the demographic publications of the United Nations, he will see that a slight beginning has been made in the evaluation of birth statistics throughout the world. Elementary details on the extent to which the data are presented on the year-of-occurrence rather than the year-of-registration basis, whether or not stillbirths are included in the totals, and the way in which multiple births are counted are given for the various countries. In addition, those responsible for the United Nations' demographic publications queried the national agency in each country responsible for the collection and tabulation of the birth statistics on the completeness of coverage and reliability of the data. On the basis of these reports, the nations, territories, and possessions were classified into three large quality categories: (1) "Data stated to be relatively complete, i.e., representing at least 90 per cent coverage of the events occurring each year"; (2) "Data stated to be unreliable, that is, less than 90 per cent coverage"; and (3) "Data concerning which no specific information is available."[7] For the most part the nations falling in the third category do not figure in the tabulations of birth statistics presented in the various issues of the *Demographic Yearbook.*

In order to simplify the examination of these materials, attention was restricted to those countries, territories, or possessions in which 25,000 or more births were reported for some year subsequent to 1950. Prior to the issuance of the 1969 edition of the *Demographic Yearbook*, those in charge of the demographic work of the United Nations had succeeded in securing from 100 of these countries and other areas materials deemed worthy of publication. Of these areas, fifty-six were classified as reporting that their birth statistics were complete or virtually complete, thirty-nine fell into the second category, and for five no comprehensive data were available. Important and populous mainland China does not figure in the list, nor do a number of other independent countries such as India, Haiti, Ethiopia, and North Viet-Nam.

All of the European countries were placed in the first group, of which they constitute the large majority, although data on any tests of completeness of the coverage in birth registration are given only for Poland. Other countries and territories classified as having complete or virtually complete coverage in birth registration are as follows: Algeria (excluding the Algerian or Moslem population, which fell into the second category), Mauritius, South Africa (excluding the Bantu population, which fell into the second category), Tunisia, Canada, Costa Rica, El Salvador, Guatemala, Jamaica, Mexico, Panama, Puerto Rico, Trinidad and Tobago, the United States, Argentina, Chile, Guyana (excluding the Amerindian population, which fell into the second category), Ceylon, Hong Kong, Israel, Japan, Jordan, West Malaysia, the Ryukyu Islands, Singapore, Taiwan, Australia (excluding full-blooded aborigines prior to 1967), New Zealand, and the Soviet Union. Information concerning tests of the completeness of birth registration is given only for Algeria, Ceylon, Jordan, and Chile. Furthermore, fifteen of the entities in the category with complete or virtually complete birth statistics are those in which the data are known to be by year of registration rather than by year of occurrence. They are as follows: Tunisia, Jamaica, Mexico, Guyana, Ceylon, Hong Kong, Israel (prior to 1963), Jordan, Taiwan, Denmark, Ireland, Northern Ireland, Scotland, Australia, and New Zealand.

The thirty-eight countries and territories in the second group, those in which the coverage of birth registration is far from complete, are as follows: Angola, Egypt, Ghana, Guinea (African population), Ivory Coast (African population), the Libyan Arab Republic, Madagascar, Malawi (excluding the European population, which fell into the first category), Mali, Morocco (excluding the non-Moroccan population, which fell into the first category), Rwanda, Senegal, Togo (African population), Upper Volta (African population), Zaire, Cuba, the Dominican Republic, Honduras, Nicaragua, Bolivia, Colombia, Ecuador, Paraguay, Peru, Uruguay, Venezuela, Burma, Indonesia, Iran, Iraq, Republic of Korea, Lebanon, Sabah and Sarawak in East Malaysia, the Philippines, the Syrian Arab Republic, Thailand, and the Republic of Viet-Nam. Tests of completeness of registration in this group are available only for Egypt, Madagascar, Honduras, Peru, the Republic of Korea, and Sarawak.

From the materials that have just been given, two things should be apparent to every student of population: (1) only the barest beginning has been made in the evaluation of the official birth statistics for most parts of the world; and (2) one should exercise a reasonable amount of skepticism before he accepts at face value the data and conclusions so liberally spread throughout the writings of sociologists, economists, geographers, and others who use population data relating to the magnitudes and trends in the birth rate in various parts of the world. Before concluding the discussion, however, it is necessary to indicate that the faulty nature of the birth statistics is not responsible for all of the large and puzzling discrepancies one finds in data for the same area and period published in two or more of the official sources or in various editions of the *Demographic Yearbook*. Sometimes the census data that are necessary for computing the birth rates also are seriously in error.

Fertility Data for the United States

The United States lagged badly, in comparison with many European countries, in the collection of basic data on the fertility of the population. The gathering and organization of birth statistics was one of the functions of government that long was left strictly to the states. Some of them, and some municipalities as well, developed fairly adequate systems for registering births, but such was not the case throughout large parts of the nation. When the Bureau of the Census was established by the Permanent Census Act, approved on March 6, 1902, the collection of birth statistics was one of the functions specifically assigned to the new agency. It was not until 1915, however, that the organization was established to begin this work, and then it was a cooperative venture between the Bureau and the states. Prior to this time federal attempts to gather and disseminate data on the fertility of the population had been limited to the highly unsatisfactory technique of trying to determine the number of births from the answers to questions that were included on the schedules used in the decennial census. The birth registration area that was established in 1915 included only ten states (Connecticut, Maine, Massachusetts, Michigan, Minnesota, New Hampshire, New York, Pennsylvania, Rhode Island, and Vermont) and the District of Columbia. Together these embraced about 30 per cent of the nation's population. Gradually other states were added, beginning with Maryland in 1916, until, with the admission of Texas to the birth registration area in 1933, birth data became available for the entire United States and each of its major subdivisions. As a result, one using the birth statistics for the period 1915 to 1932, inclusive, must be prepared to deal with two separate and distinct series: (1) the data for the original birth registration area and (2) the data for the expanding birth registration area. From 1933 on, of course, the data for the United States are those for the nation as a whole. Even so, studies made about 1930[8] showed the data to be seriously incomplete

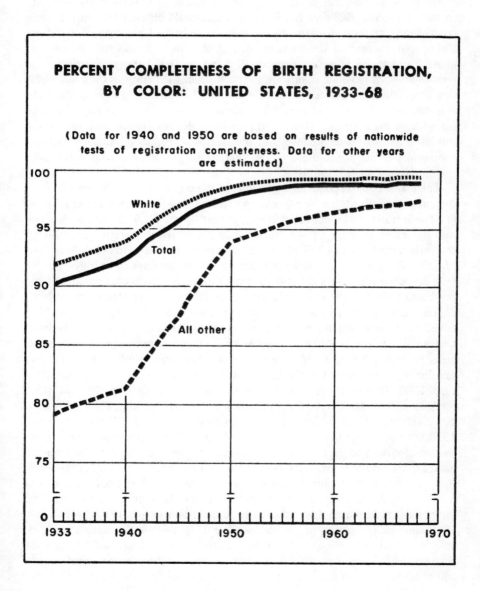

Figure 43. The completeness of birth registration in the United States, by color, 1933 to 1968. Illustration from the National Center for Health Statistics.

and two more decades were to elapse before fairly complete and reliable materials on births would be available for use by students in the United States.

By 1968 the coverage of birth registration had become sufficiently complete so that for many purposes the birth statistics could be used for fairly reliable comparisons of fertility. Even then, however, only 99.1 per cent of the births throughout the nation were registered, and the coverage was still quite inadequate for births to nonwhite parents (97.5 per cent) and those occurring in the remote sections in which significant proportions of the deliveries took place outside hospitals (88.2 per cent). (See Figure 43.) This makes the use of the birth rate difficult in racial and rural-urban comparisons of fertility, even for large areas such as regions or states; and it practically destroys the possibility of using this measure for fair comparisons of the rate of reproduction at the county or community levels, which are the ones that are of greatest significance for most theoretical and applied purposes.

The major bodies of data on the fertility of the population of the United States currently available for use by population students may be summarized as follows: (1) The birth statistics collected annually, first by the U. S. Bureau of the Census, and most recently by the National Center for Health Statistics. Although this series goes back to 1915, all of the states in the nation were not included until 1933, and even as late as 1968 tests showed the coverage to be only 99.1 per cent complete. It is very difficult to match exactly various components of the population, such as the residential and racial or color categories, with the birth data so as to get birth rates for such important groupings. These difficulties, added to those arising from the incompleteness of the coverage in birth registration, make the computation of reliable birth rates for counties and other small areas extremely difficult and time consuming if not impossible. (2) The age and sex distributions secured in the various decennial censuses of the United States since 1800. These materials may be used to compute the fairly well standardized measure of the rate of reproduction known as the fertility ratio. They are of fundamental importance for the study of fertility trends and differentials. From 1930 on, the availability of rather detailed age and sex distributions for the various residential and race or color categories for units as small as the counties makes these data of primary importance to all those interested in levels, differentials, and trends in fertility in specific parts of the United States. (3) Data from inquiries on the number of children ever born and the number of own children under five in the household conducted in connection with the 1910, 1940, 1950, 1960, and 1970 censuses of population. The 1910 and 1940 materials are available in a special report of the 1940 census,[9] those for 1950 in a special report of that census,[10] those for 1960 in a subject report of the census of that year,[11] and those for 1970 in a subject report of that enumeration, cited above.

NOTES

1. T. Lynn Smith (New York: McGraw Hill Book Company, 1948), pp. 194 - 196.

2. U.S. Bureau of the Census, U.S. Census of Population: 1970, General *Social and Economic Characteristics,* Final Report PC(1)-C1, *United States Summary* (Washington: Government Printing Office, 1972), pp. 369 - 370, Table 76; pp. 495 - 496, Table 158; and *Subject Reports, Women by Number of Children Ever Born* (Washington: Government Printing Office, 1973).

3. *General Social and Economic Characteristics, op. cit.,* Final Report PC(1)-C2-C52, reports for states (Washington: Government Printing Office, 1971 and 1972), Tables 45, 52, 63, 74, and 84.

4. For an examination of the index and its advantages and disadvantages see Donald J. Bogue, *Principles of Demography* (New York: John Wiley & Sons, Inc., 1969), pp. 690 - 691. For extensive use of the index, see Dale E. Hathaway, J. Allan Beegle, and W. Keith Bryant, *People of Rural America* (A 1960 Census Monograph, Washington: Government Printing Office, 1968), chapter IV.

5. For details on the nature and limitations of both rates, see United Nations, *Demographic Yearbook, 1969* (New York: United Nations, 1970), pp. 38 - 39; and for use of the indexes, see United Nations, *Population Bulletin of the United Nations,* No. 7-1963 (New York: United Nations, 1965), pp. 1 - 9.

6. *Demographic Yearbook, 1969, op. cit.,* p. 38.

7. *Ibid.,* p. 11.

8. See P. K. Whelpton, "The Completeness of Birth Registration in the United States," *Journal of the American Statistical Association, XXIX,* 186 (1934), pp. 125 - 136; and T. Lynn Smith, "Rural-Urban Differences in the Completeness of Birth Registration," *Social Forces* XIV, 3 (1936), pp. 368 - 372.

9. U.S. Bureau of the Census, *Sixteenth Census of the United States: 1940, Special Reports,* "Differential Fertility, 1940 and 1910" (Washington: Government Printing Office, 1947).

10. U.S. Bureau of the Census, *U.S. Census of Population: 1950,* Vol. IV, *Special Reports, Fertility* (Washington: Government Printing Office, 1955), Part 5, chapter C.

11. U.S. Bureau of the Census, *U.S. Census of Population: 1960, Subject Reports, Women by Number of Children Ever Born* (Washington: Government Printing Office, 1964).

BOGUE, DONALD J. *The Population of the United States,* Chap. 10. Glencoe, Ill.: The Free Press, 1959.

BOGUE, DONALD J. *Principles of Demography,* pp. 656 - 663. New York: John Wiley & Sons, Inc., 1969.

CAMPBELL, ARTHUR A., and others. *Natality Statistics Analysis* (National Center for Health Statistics, Series 21, No. 11). Washington: Government Printing Office, 1967.

CHO, LEE JAY. "Estimated Refined Measures of Fertility for all Major Countries of the World." *Demography,* Vol. 1, No. 1 (1964), pp. 359 - 374.

GRABILL, WILSON H., and LEE JAY CHO. "Methodology for the Measurement of Current Fertility from Population Data on Young Children." *Demography,* Vol. 2, No. 1 (1965), pp. 50 - 73.

GROVE, ROBERT D., and ALICE M. HETZEL. *Vital Statistics Rates in the United States, 1940 - 1960* (Public Health Service Publication No. 1677). Washington: Government Printing Office, 1968.

INTERNATIONAL SOCIOLOGICAL ASSOCIATION and UNESCO. "The Sociology of Human Fertility: A Trend Report and Bibliography." *Current Sociology,* Vols. 10 - 11 (1961 - 1962), pp. 35 - 121.

KEYFITZ, NATHAN, and WILHELM FLIEGER. *World Population: An Analysis of Vital Rates.* Chicago: University of Chicago Press, 1968.

SHRYOCK, HENRY S., JACOB S. SIEGEL, and associates. *The Methods and Materials of Demography,* Vol. 2, Chaps. 16 and 17. Washington: Government Printing Office, 1971.

SMITH, T. LYNN. *Population Analysis,* Chaps. 13 and 14. New York: McGraw-Hill Book Company, 1948.

SMITH, T. LYNN. "The Reproduction Rate in Latin America: Levels, Differentials, and Trends." *Population Studies,* Vol. XII, No. 1 (March, 1958), pp. 3 - 17.

THOMLINSON, RALPH. *Population Dynamics,* pp. 33 - 36 and 159 - 163. New York: Random House, Inc., 1965.

THOMPSON, WARREN S. *Ratio of Children to Women: 1920* (Census Monograph XI). Washington: Government Printing Office, 1931.

UNITED NATIONS. *Demographic Yearbook, 1969,* pp. 26 - 38. New York: United Nations, 1970.

U. S. BUREAU OF THE CENSUS. *U.S. Census of Population: 1970. Subject Reports. Women by Number of Children Ever Born.* Washington: Government Printing Office, 1973.

WHELPTON, PASCAL K. *Cohort Fertility: Native White Women in the United States,* Chaps. 1 - 3. Princeton: Princeton University Press, 1954.

WILLCOX, WALTER F. *Introduction to the Vital Statistics of the United States, 1900 - 1930,* pp. 55 - 81. Washington: Government Printing Office, 1933.

WILLCOX, WALTER F. *Studies in American Demography,* Chap. 17. Ithaca: Cornell University Press, 1940.

ZITTER, MEYER, and HENRY S. SHRYOCK, JR. "Accuracy of Methods of Preparing Postcensal Population Estimates for States and Local Areas." *Demography,* Vol. 1, No. 1 (1964), pp. 227 - 241.

The rate of reproduction varies greatly in time and space. Within the course of history the birth rate of a given people fluctuates widely; and at any one time there are likely to be vast differences between the birth rates of the various residential, racial, ethnic, religious, and socio-economic groups of which a population is composed. Thus, in colonial times, women in North America bore about as many children as physiology permitted, whereas in the 1930's the fertility of the population was so low that the question as to whether or not the women of the United States were bearing enough children to offset the then very low mortality rates was a matter of considerable concern. Nowadays, as will be indicated below, in most countries the birth rate of those who live in rural areas is much higher than that of city people, Negroes have higher rates of reproduction than whites, and certain ethnic and religious groups have greater fertility than others.

Differences in the fertility of various peoples, races, classes, residential groups, and so on are of tremendous social, economic, and political significance. To be specific, it is very likely that changes between 1870 and 1914 in the relative importance and strength of France and Germany as world powers were due in large measure to the higher birth rate and consequent more rapid growth of population in the latter. During the years under consideration, millions of Germans emigrated to other parts of the world, while relatively few Frenchmen sought new homes in other lands. Nevertheless, the population of Germany rose from slightly less than 36 million in 1870 to around 60 million in 1914, whereas that of France increased merely from 38 million to 40 million during the interval. Generations of future historians will be required to evaluate adequately the results of the momentous shift in relative importance and power that accompanied

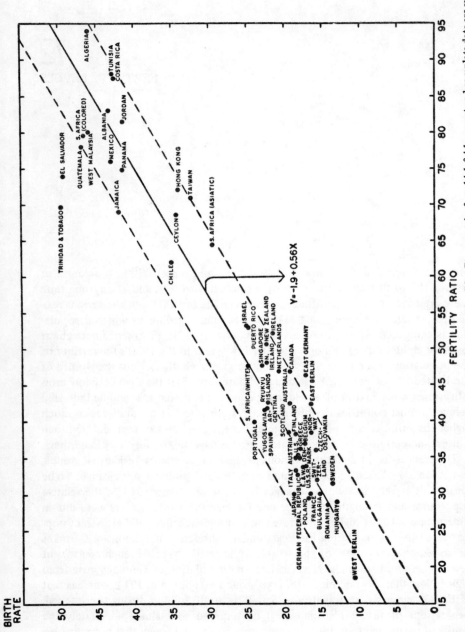

Figure 44. Correlation between the fertility ratio and the crude birth rate based on fifty-five countries for which fairly recent and complete data are available.

these changes. Largely responsible for this world-shaking change, however, were the differences reflected in the following birth rates of these two great powers: 1866 - 1870, France 26 and Germany 38; 1905 - 1909, France 20 and Germany 32; and 1911 - 1913, France 18 and Germany 27. The significance of these differences was not lost on such despots as Hitler and Mussolini, who later sought determinedly to increase the might of Germany and Italy by measures designed to increase the birth rates in these countries. Similarly, the extreme fluctuations in the official population policies of the Communist regime in mainland China in the 1950's and 1960's reflect wide internal differences of opinion as to whether a large population with a relatively high rate of increase constitutes a powerful political and military asset or a serious economic liability.[1]

RATES OF REPRODUCTION THROUGHOUT THE WORLD

A seemingly elementary task for students of population is the determination of the level of the rate of reproduction throughout the various parts of the world. One who attempts to get fairly complete and reliable birth statistics for the different nations and their possessions, however, discovers that this elementary task is by no means an easy one. Nor is the difficulty entirely overcome if one resorts instead to the data needed for the computation of fertility ratios. The present state of world affairs in this respect will become evident to anyone who examines Table 29 with care and attention. It contains the most recent crude birth rates and fertility ratios for all countries and for all territories of 1 million or more inhabitants for which data are available. In addition, it gives the present writers' estimates of the actual birth rates for those countries in which the birth data are admittedly or obviously incomplete. These estimates, in turn, were made in the following manner.

According to the materials supplied in the more recent issues of the *Demographic Yearbook* of the United Nations, fifty-five of the countries in which fairly recent censuses have been taken also figure as those in which birth registration is complete or fairly complete. Therefore, for these fifty-five areas one is able to determine the correlation between the two measures of the rate of reproduction, the fertility ratio and the birth rate. (See Figure 44.) When this is done, the value of the Pearsonian coefficient of correlation (r) is found to be +0.947, indicating that about 89.7 per cent of the variation in the magnitude of the crude birth rate is accounted for by differences in the size of the fertility ratio. As is readily observed in Figure 44, the straight line is an adequate description of the relationship between the two variables; and when such a line is fitted by the method of least squares, the resulting equation is $Y = -1.9 + 0.56 X$, with X designating the fertility ratio and Y the crude birth rate. This indicates that on the average an increase of 1.0 point in the fertility ratio is accompanied by an increase of 0.56 in the birth rate. This formula, in turn, can be applied to determine the most reasonable values for the birth rates in those countries or territories listed in Table 29 for which adequate birth statistics are lacking but for which fairly recent age and sex distributions of the population are available.

In interpreting the ratio between the birth rate and the fertility ratio in any given country, there are, of course, a number of factors that may make for a relatively high score in the one in comparison with that registered for the other. Thus, if infant and child mortality rates are high, the birth rate tends to be relatively large in comparison with the fertility ratio. In such cases, an estimate of the birth rate from the regression equation given above is likely to be somewhat too low. This may help explain in part the positions in Figure 44 of the points representing Trinidad and Tobago and El Salvador, as well as the fact that for a number of the African, South American, and Asian countries listed in Table 29, the estimated birth rates are somewhat lower than the reported rates. On the other hand, if considerable numbers of young women give birth to their first children in one place or country and soon thereafter migrate to another, the birth rate will be inflated in the former and the fertility ratio in the latter. Irrespective of the reasons for the situation of any given country, however, the closeness of the correlation between the fertility ratio and the birth rate makes it possible to estimate the latter with a considerable degree of accuracy providing the former is known. Since most persons, including the majority of those working in the field of population study, are accustomed to thinking of fertility levels in terms of the birth rate, and since relatively accurate age and sex distributions are available for many more areas than are reliable birth statistics, it has been deemed advisable to make the estimates of the crude birth rates given in Table 29. In particular, the discrepancies between the reported rates and the estimated rates of most of the Asian nations should make this need abundantly clear.

Before proceeding with a brief discussion of fertility levels throughout the world, it is well to consider briefly the manner in which fertility and the two other factors that affect populations (mortality and migration) bear upon changes in the number and distribution of the inhabitants. At most times and places, the number of births is the major factor, with deaths in second position and migrations in third. Births also may be regarded as the primary moving force in population changes, since obviously men and women must be born before they can move about or die. Therefore, the significance of any level of reproduction rests largely upon its relationship to the mortality rate, and, generally to a lesser degree, upon the extent to which the population is increased or decreased by migration to or from the area under consideration. If, for example, the death rate is above 30, as it probably has been at most times among the various peoples who have inhabited the earth, a birth rate of 40 or above is required to produce an increase of population of 1 per cent per annum; whereas, if the death rate is

TABLE 29

Fertility ratios and crude birth rates for countries and territories
with 1 million or more inhabitants for which data are available

Country or territory	Year	Number of children under 5 per 100 women 15-49	Crude birth rate (reported)	Crude birth rate (estimated)
Africa				
Algeria	1966	94.0	46.2	*
Angola	1960	70.2	20.3	39
Burundi	1965	95.2	46.1	53
Central African Republic (African population)	1959-60	55.7	48.0	31
Chad (African population)	1963-64	64.3	45.0	36
Dahomey (African population)	1961	83.7	54.0	47
Egypt	1960	70.2	43.0	39
Ghana	1960	83.1	49.5	47
Kenya	1969	90.1	47.8	50
Liberia	1962	60.0	44.0	34
Libyan Arab Republic	1964	85.7	25.1	48
Madagascar	1966	43.7	35.3	24
Mali	1960-61	75.7	55.0	42
Morocco	1960	84.5	47.0	47
Niger (African population)	1959-60	76.2	52.0	43
Senegal	1960-61	75.0	43.3	42
South Africa				
(Asiatic population)	1960	64.4	29.7	*
(Colored population)	1960	79.5	46.7	*
(White population)	1960	47.7	24.9	*
Southern Rhodesia (African population)	1969	75.0	48.4	42
Togo	1961	89.4	55.0	50
Tunisia	1966	88.0	42.8	*
Uganda	1969	89.2	43.2	50
Upper Volta	1960-61	69.7	53.0	39
Zambia	1969	79.3	49.8	44
America, North				
Canada	1966	46.8	19.3	*
Costa Rica	1963	87.5	42.7	*
Cuba	1953	50.3	25.0[a]	28
Dominican Republic	1960	76.9	36.3	43
El Salvador	1961	73.9	49.4	*
Guatemala	1964	78.1	47.0	*
Honduras	1961	85.7	42.9	48
Jamaica	1960	69.3	42.0	*
Mexico	1970	76.2	43.4	*
Nicaragua	1963	82.4	45.3	46
Panama	1960	74.8	41.5	*

TABLE 29 (Cont'd)

Fertility ratios and crude birth rates for countries and territories
with 1 million or more inhabitants for which data are available

Country or territory	Year	Number of children under 5 per 100 women 15-49	Crude birth rate (reported)	Crude birth rate (estimated)
Puerto Rico	1970	53.1	24.8	*
Trinidad and Tobago	1960	69.6	49.8	*
United States	1970	35.2	18.3	*
America, South				
Argentina	1960	41.7	22.5	*
Bolivia	1950	62.9	42.0	35
Brazil	1960	66.7	42.0	37
Chile	1960	61.9	35.0	*
Colombia	1964	77.9	42.5	44
Ecuador	1962	75.2	48.5	42
Paraguay	1962	76.6	43.5	43
Peru	1961	73.5	43.0	41
Uruguay	1963	40.5	24.5	23
Venezuela	1961	83.9	47.0	47
Asia				
Burma	1957	61.1	36.0	34
Ceylon	1963	68.6	34.4	*
Hong Kong	1961	72.2	34.2	*
India	1961	65.9	41.7	37
Indonesia	1961	71.4	27.7	40
Iran	1966	85.1	42.0	48
Iraq	1965	99.4	15.2	56
Israel	1961	53.2	25.1	*
Japan	1970	30.0	18.8	*
Jordan	1961	81.5	41.6	*
Khmer Republic	1962	65.0	50.0	36
Korea, Republic of	1966	67.3	17.1	38
Malaysia				
East				
Sabah	1960	78.8	35.3	44
Sarawak	1960	75.5	25.1	42
West	1957	80.0	46.1	*
Nepal	1961	57.0	41.1	32
Pakistan	1961	83.2	55.0[b]	47
Philippines	1960	72.9	29.6	41
Ryukyu Islands	1970	42.6	22.3	*
Singapore	1970	47.7	23.0	*
Syrian Arab Republic	1960	95.6	32.4	54
Taiwan	1966	70.9	32.4	*

TABLE 29 (Cont'd)
Fertility ratios and crude birth rates for countries and territories
with 1 million or more inhabitants for which data are available

Country or territory	Year	Number of children under 5 per 100 women 15-49	Crude birth rate (reported)	Crude birth rate (estimated)
Thailand	1960	69.7	34.7	39
Turkey	1965	67.3	43.0c	38
Viet-Nam, North	1960	66.5	35.0	37
Europe				
Albania	1960	83.0	43.4	*
Austria	1961	34.8	18.6	*
Belgium	1961	36.8	17.3	*
Bulgaria	1965	30.0	15.3	*
Czechoslovakia	1961	35.9	15.8	*
Denmark	1965	35.0	18.0	*
Finland	1960	38.2	18.5	*
France	1968	29.8	16.7	*
Germany				
Democratic Republic	1964	46.3	17.2	*
Federal Republic	1961	32.7	18.3	*
East Berlin	1964	42.3	16.6	*
West Berlin	1961	18.6	10.6	*
Greece	1961	36.2	17.9	*
Hungary	1963	27.9	13.1	*
Ireland	1966	52.1	21.6	*
Italy	1961	33.1	18.6	*
Netherlands	1960	46.9	20.8	*
Norway	1970	38.4	16.6	*
Poland	1970	29.4	16.8	*
Portugal	1960	39.8	24.2	*
Romania	1966	28.4	14.3	*
Spain	1960	38.2	21.8	*
Sweden	1970	31.3	13.7	*
Switzerland	1970	31.9	15.8	*
United Kingdom				
England and Wales	1961	33.6	17.6	*
Northern Ireland	1966	47.9	22.5	*
Scotland	1961	38.5	19.5	*
Yugoslavia	1961	41.5	22.7	*
Oceania				
Australia	1966	42.3	19.3	*
New Zealand	1966	50.6	22.5	*
U.S.S.R.	1970	33.7	17.4	*

Source: Compiled and computed from data in various issues of the *Demographic Yearbook.*
*Estimate not given for countries in which birth data are considered by the United
Nations as complete or virtually complete.
aData are for 1952.
bData are for 1962.
cData are for 1966.

only 10, a level attained by many contemporary peoples, and one that is coming to prevail over additional large sections of the earth, a birth rate of 35 is sufficient, assuming no migration, to make the population mount at 2.5 per cent per annum. During the latter part of the twentieth century there has been much alarm in some circles of a "population explosion" or a "population bomb," because of the recent rapidly mounting number of people on the earth. This has developed largely because of the high death rates which prevailed until recently in large and densely populated sections of the world have been cut sharply, whereas there has as yet been little or no corresponding fall in the birth rates. Therefore, the birth rates of 35 or above presently prevailing in many parts of the world are making for tremendous change, and this is giving rise to considerable alarm at home and abroad. A few decades ago such levels of reproduction were offset by high mortality rates and occasioned little thought in the countries involved or elsewhere.

With these facts in mind, it is well to observe with some care the data given in Table 29. Possibly it will facilitate comparisons if birth rates of various levels are designated as follows: 40 or above, *very high*; 30 to 39, *high*; 20 to 29, *medium*; and less than 20, *low*. On this basis, the Latin American area, generally speaking, has the greatest extent of very high rates of reproduction, although some parts of Africa (Algeria, Burundi, Dahomey, Ghana, Kenya, the Libyan Arab Republic, Mali, Morocco, Niger, Senegal, the "colored" population of South Africa, Southern Rhodesia, Togo, Tunisia, Uganda, and Zambia), Indonesia, Iran, Iraq, Jordan, the Khmer Republic, Malaysia, Pakistan, the Philippines, the Syrian Arab Republic, and Albania also are characterized by very high birth rates. Among all of the Latin American countries, only Argentina, Bolivia, Brazil, Chile, Cuba, and Uruguay, along with Puerto Rico, do not belong in the category with the highest birth rates. One of the immediate effects of these very high reproduction levels may be mentioned. Because the birth rates have remained high throughout much of Latin America, while drastic reductions in the death rate were being accomplished, the proportion of Latin Americans in the world population has moved up from about 2.7 per cent in 1900 to approximately 7.8 per cent in 1970. One should also note that the parts of Latin America with the very highest rates of reproduction constitute a significant portion of what frequently are designated as the "underdeveloped" parts of the world.

Likewise, other underdeveloped areas are the ones in which, for the most part, high birth rates prevail. In most of Africa, in addition to the countries mentioned above, and in the sections of Asia for which information is available, the birth rates range between 30 and 39. Israel, Japan, the Ryukyu Islands, and Singapore are notable exceptions.

Birth rates designated here as medium currently prevail in about one-fifth of the countries of Europe, Cuba, Puerto Rico, Argentina, Uruguay, Israel, the Ryukyu Islands, Singapore, and New Zealand, and among the non-African populations of a few African states. Low birth rates, on the other hand, are limited to Canada, the United States, Japan, Australia, the Soviet Union, and the large majority of European countries, with those in West Berlin, Hungary, Sweden, and Romania commanding particular attention. Mortality rates in much of Europe are so low, of course, that even these low birth rates make for a considerable increase in population, except in those countries in which they are offset to some extent by emigration.

In concluding this section on the rate of reproduction throughout the world, it is well to fill as much as possible the most obvious gap in the data presented in Table 29, namely, the lack of data for China. Fortunately, France's leading demographer, Alfred Sauvy, has presented the results of two comprehensive attempts to determine the rate of reproduction in the world's most populous nation. One of these, based on materials secured in 1953 from 30 million persons, indicated a birth rate of 30; the other, a study of sixteen districts with a total population of over 1.8 million made in the years 1951 - 1954, indicated a birth rate of 42.[2] In addition, Leo Orleans, Senior Research Analyst at the Library of Congress, suggests that the birth rate in mainland China is between 40 and 45.[3]

FERTILITY LEVELS IN THE UNITED STATES

Throughout the twentieth century the rate of reproduction in the United States has proved to be highly variable, in time, in space, and from group to group. Since 1900, the sharp reversals in the trend of the birth rate have scarcely been equalled in any other major nation; the state and regional differences in fertility hardly can be matched in other parts of the world; and the rural-urban and other differentials have been of a magnitude that should command attention by every student of population. All of this makes the study of fertility levels, differentials, and trends in the United States particularly significant, but there are other reasons as well why a comprehensive study of these matters in this country is of unusual importance for the demographer.

First, census taking and registration procedures are now at a level of perfection that is surpassed in few parts of the world. This means that fairly accurate and reliable data may be used for various comparisons, with less need for various makeshifts and improvisations than is the case if one is studying rates of reproduction in many other parts of the world. Second, the extensive and highly diverse territory of the nation is divided into fifty states and the District of Columbia, for each of which every effort is made to collect, tabulate, and publish exactly comparable data, information that is as comprehensive in all essential respects as is that for the country as a whole. This applies alike to the materials obtained through the registration of births and those secured in the decennial census. Much of the detail is also made available separately for the thousands of counties into which the states are subdivided and for other thousands of cities, towns, and villages found throughout the nation. Indeed, large portions of the information may be had for the minor civil divisions of which the counties are composed and for small segments of the various cities. Third, despite the nation's political solidarity, it is composed of highly diverse elements (ethnic, racial, cultural, religious, agricultural, industrial, educational, and so forth), all of which are distributed very unequally throughout the various states, although not to the extent that prevailed in earlier times. Thus, a summary of existing knowledge relative to fertility levels, differentials, and trends in the United States is especially important to the student of population; and the materials available for study offer unusual opportunities for gaining additional understanding of the reproduction rate and the factors responsible for its variations.

As indicated above, since about 1957 the level of fertility in the United States has dropped off rather sharply. As measured by the birth rate it has gone from 24.1 in 1950, to 23.7 in 1960, to 18.3 in 1970, and to 15.6 in 1972. The last figure is lower than that for any other year in the entire period during which birth registrations have been kept in the United States and is one of the lowest in the world. As gauged by the ratio between children under five years of age and women aged fifteen to forty-four years, the level of fertility rose from 47.9 in 1950 to 56.3 in 1960 and dropped to 40.4 in 1970, although it should be remembered that the fertility ratio for any year reflects the birth patterns for the preceding five-year period.

The rate of reproduction for the United States represents, of course, a net product which comes from including the widely divergent birth rates or fertility ratios prevailing in the various subdivisions of the nation. The actual rate in each of these, in turn, is influenced by the extent to which its people are rural or urban, white or nonwhite, native-born or foreign-born, of one religious persuasion or another, or composed of other ethnic, social, or economic groupings which affect in one way or another the reproductive behavior of mankind. Therefore, it is highly important to observe how fertility levels vary throughout the United States.

Tables 30 and 31 have been prepared to enable the reader to examine carefully the extent to which the rate of reproduction varies from one part of the United States to another. The first of these presents fertility ratios computed by the present writers from the materials gathered in the 1970 census (that is, fertility data for the period April 1965 to 1970) and crude birth rates for the years 1969 - 1971. Since one of the most obvious reasons for variations in the rate of reproduction is the degree to which the populations of the various states are rural or urban, information is also included showing the percentage of the total population of each state in 1970 that was classified as rural. Birth rates centered on the year 1970 are given, rather than those for a later period, for the

TABLE 30

The fifty states and the District of Columbia ranked according
to the fertility levels of their populations and proportions of the population classified as rural

State	Fertility ratio, 1970[a]		Birth rate, 1969-1971		Rural population, 1970	
	Index	Rank[b]	Index	Rank	% of total	Rank
United States	40.4	....	17.7	....	26.5	....
Alaska	48.9	1	23.9	3	51.2	8
Utah	48.7	2	25.1	2	19.4	42
Mississippi	46.8	3	21.1	5	55.5	4
Idaho	44.7	4	18.9	14	45.7	13
New Mexico	44.3	5	21.6	4	30.0	29
New Hampshire	43.8	6	17.1	35	43.5	14
Vermont	43.6	7	17.7	25	67.8	1
Maine	43.2	8	17.6	29	49.1	10
Wisconsin	43.1	9	17.0	38	34.1	23
Michigan	43.0	10	18.6	19	26.1	34
North Dakota	43.0	11	18.2	23	55.7	3
Arizona	43.0	12	20.7	6	20.5	39
Minnesota	42.8	13	17.4	31	33.6	26
South Dakota	42.4	14	17.2	34	55.4	5
South Carolina	42.2	15	19.5	11	52.4	7
Georgia	42.1	16	20.3	8	39.7	18
Iowa	42.0	17	16.9	39	42.8	15
Indiana	41.8	18	18.3	20	35.1	22
Texas	41.8	19	20.0	10	20.2	40
Wyoming	41.7	20	18.3	22	39.6	19
Arkansas	41.7	21	17.6	26	50.0	9
Alabama	41.5	22	18.8	15	41.6	16
Hawaii	41.5	23	20.5	7	17.0	44
Nevada	41.4	24	19.0	12	19.1	43
Montana	41.2	25	17.3	32	46.4	12
Ohio	41.0	26	18.0	24	24.7	35
Kentucky	41.0	27	18.3	21	47.6	11
Delaware	41.0	28	18.6	18	27.9	32
Rhode Island	40.8	29	16.8	43	13.0	48
Illinois	40.7	30	17.6	28	17.0	45

TABLE 30 (Cont'd)

The fifty states and the District of Columbia ranked according
to the fertility levels of their populations and proportions of the population classified as rural

State	Fertility ratio, 1970[a]		Birth rate, 1969-1971		Rural population, 1970	
	Index	Rank[b]	Index	Rank	% of total	Rank
Nebraska	40.6	31	17.2	33	38.4	20
Connecticut	40.5	32	15.8	47	22.7	37
Maryland	40.4	33	15.3	51	23.4	36
Massachusetts	40.3	34	16.9	40	15.4	46
New Jersey	40.0	35	15.8	48	11.1	49
Washington	39.5	36	16.8	44	27.4	33
North Carolina	39.4	37	18.7	17	55.0	6
Missouri	39.3	38	17.5	30	29.9	30
West Virginia	39.0	39	17.0	37	61.0	2
Pennsylvania	38.8	40	15.8	49	28.5	31
New York	38.8	41	16.7	45	14.4	47
Kansas	38.8	42	15.5	50	33.9	24
Virginia	38.7	43	17.1	36	36.9	21
Tennessee	38.7	44	19.0	13	41.2	17
Colorado	38.4	45	18.8	16	21.3	38
California	38.3	46	17.6	27	9.1	50
Florida	38.0	47	16.8	41	19.5	41
Oregon	37.9	48	16.7	46	32.9	27
Oklahoma	37.8	49	16.8	42	32.0	28
Louisiana	36.1	50	20.0	9	33.9	25
District of Columbia	32.9	51	33.6	1	....	....

Source: Birth rates are from National Center for Health Statistics. *Monthly Vital Statistics Report,* Vol. 19, No. 13, *Annual Summary for the United States, 1970 (1971), p. 13,* Table 1; Vol. 20, No. 13, *Annual Summary for the United States, 1971* (1972), p. 12, Table 1. Fertility ratios were computed from data in U.S. Bureau of the Census, *U.S. Census of Population: 1970, General Population Characteristics,* Final Report PC(1)-B1, *United States Summary* (1972), pp. 297-309, Table 62. Percentages of rural people compiled from *ibid., General Social and Economic Characteristics,* Final Report PC(1)-C1, *United States·Summary* (1972), pp. 470-471, Table 142.

[a]Number of children under 5 per 100 women 15-44.

[b]Rank figured to two decimal places when states are tied.

TABLE 31

Number of children ever born per 1,000 women aged 15-44 who
were ever married, for states, by race, 1970

State	Rank[a]	Number of children ever born per 1,000 women aged 15-44 who were ever married			
		Total	White	Negro	Other races
United States	....	2,360	2,285	2,976	2,436
South Dakota	1	2,774	2,726	2,592	3,797
North Dakota	2	2,756	2,731	2,519	3,892
Mississippi	3	2,727	2,196	4,073	2,551
Utah	4	2,692	2,685	3,054	3,005
New Mexico	5	2,664	2,581	3,016	3,724
Louisiana	6	2,655	2,383	3,442	2.687
Wisconsin	7	2,642	2,622	3,157	2,922
Idaho	8	2,617	2,614	2,633	2,847
Montana	9	2,607	2,570	1,770	3,528
Minnesota	10	2,601	2,595	2,758	3,051
Vermont	11	2,560	2,563	....	....
Maine	12	2,558	2,557	2,321	2,854
Iowa	13	2,540	2,536	2,941	2,359
Michigan	14	2,512	2,476	2,800	2,836
Nebraska	15	2,508	2,491	3,047	2,646
Wyoming	16	2,490	2,478	3,291	2,817
Arizona	17	2,480	2,390	3,229	3,658
South Carolina	18	2,460	2,105	3,572	2,357
West Virginia	19	2,443	2,418	3,514	1,289
Arkansas	20	2,434	2,196	4,031	2,152
New Hampshire	21	2,429	2,429	2,859	1,791
Massachusetts	22	2,409	2,399	2,735	2,064
Indiana	23	2,404	2,365	2,967	2,243
Alabama	24	2,396	2,118	3,496	2,065
Ohio	25	2,393	2,358	2,764	2,042
Alaska	26	2,379	2,114	2,135	4,039
Kentucky	27	2,377	2,336	3,062	2,158
Texas	28	2,377	2,302	2,963	2,213
Illinois	29	2,367	2,298	2,819	1,947
Pennsylvania	30	2,366	2,327	2,785	1,852

TABLE 31 (Cont'd)
Number of children ever born per 1,000 women aged 15-44 who
were ever married, for states, by race, 1970

State	Rank[a]	Number of children ever born per 1,000 women aged 15-44 who were ever married			
		Total	White	Negro	Other races
Hawaii	31	2,346	2,061	1,849	2,571
Missouri	32	2,344	2,269	3.045	2,053
Oregon	33	2,341	2,334	2,945	2,404
Rhode Island	34	2,337	2,320	2,977	2,234
Kansas	35	2,337	2,304	3,022	2,469
Washington	36	2,323	2,311	2,680	2,513
Georgia	37	2,311	2,067	3,212	1,921
Delaware	38	2,307	2,196	3,087	2,075
Colorado	39	2,302	2,292	2,631	2,333
Connecticut	40	2,285	2,251	2,766	2,031
Florida	41	2,272	2,104	3,215	2,042
New Jersey	42	2,264	2,203	2,736	1,987
Maryland	43	2,263	2,144	2,863	2,006
New York	44	2,258	2,227	2,466	2,061
North Carolina	45	2,247	2,018	3,278	2,935
Oklahoma	46	2,242	2,161	3,255	2,758
Tennessee	47	2,230	2,086	3,213	1,893
District of Columbia	48	2,223	1,273	2,462	1,596
California	49	2,217	2,186	2,636	2,165
Virginia	50	2,196	2,040	3,067	2,002
Nevada	51	2,191	2,134	3,056	2,448

Source: Compiled and computed from data in U.S. Bureau of the Census, *U.S. Census of Population: 1970, General Social and Economic Characteristics,* Final Report PC(1)-C1, *United States Summary* (1972), pp. 369-370, Table 76; Final Report PC(1)-C2-C52, reports for states (1971 and 1972), Table 52.

.... Data not shown where number of women aged 15-44 who were ever married is less than 200.

[a]Rank figured to one decimal place when states are tied.

reason that 1970 is the most recent year for which accurate data are available, or will be available prior to about 1981, on the number of inhabitants in each of the states. This is because even for the nation as a whole computations of birth rates for the years subsequent to 1970 are subject to considerable error, solely because estimates of the population must be used in their calculation; and those for the various states are likely, for the same reason, to be seriously wrong. The averages for the three years 1969 - 1971 are used instead of the rates for 1970 in order to reduce the effects of random variations that may be present in the indexes for a given year. In comparing the standing of a given state on the basis of the two indexes used in Table 30, it should be remembered that the fertility ratios are fairly well standardized for age and sex differences in the respective populations, whereas the crude birth rates are not. As a result, a highly urbanized unit, such as Delaware, Hawaii, or the District of Columbia (to whose cities large numbers of young women have been attracted) ranks much higher in the list when the birth rate is employed as a basis for the rating than it does when the fertility ratio is used in making the comparisons. In fact, this situation is so pronounced in the District of Columbia that, in 1970, it ranked first on the basis of the birth rate but last on the basis of the fertility ratio. On the other hand, the most rural state, Vermont, from which large numbers of young women have migrated to towns and cities in other parts of the nation, ranks much higher when the fertility ratio is used than it does if the birth rate is employed. Still other states such as Arizona and California, which received such large contingents of migrants from other states, including thousands of women in the child-bearing ages during the decade 1960 to 1970, rank much higher on the basis of the birth rate than they do according to the fertility ratio.

Table 31 presents the number of children ever born per 1,000 women aged fifteen to forty-four who were ever married for the total, white, and nonwhite populations of the various states, ranked according to the magnitude of their respective indexes. If one centers his attention upon the state-to-state variations, it will be noted that three states, Mississippi, Utah, and New Mexico, appear among the five leaders in levels of reproduction irrespective of the index used as a basis for the rankings. When variations in the age and sex composition of the various populations are accounted for by means of the number of children ever born per 1,000 women aged fifteen to forty-four who were ever married, the ten states whose rates of reproduction are highest in the nation are South Dakota, North Dakota, Mississippi, Utah, New Mexico, Louisiana, Wisconsin, Idaho, Montana, and Minnesota. Utah, Mississippi, Idaho, New Mexico, and Wisconsin also are among the leading ten states when the fertility ratio is used as an index, although it is somewhat less satisfactory as a measure of actual reproduction than is the number of children ever born. Furthermore, of the states with the lowest levels of fertility, five (Virginia, California, Tennessee, Oklahoma, and Florida) appear when the fertility ratio is used in making the comparisons, but only Oklahoma and Florida are on the list of ten states with the lowest levels of fertility according to all three of the indexes used in this chapter. The District of Columbia, whose fertility ratio is lower than that for any of the fifty states and whose number of children ever born per 1,000 women ever married is lower than those for forty-seven of them, has a birth rate that ranks first in the nation. Two factors probably account for most of this difference. First, thousands of young women have flocked to the national capital, so that women of childbearing age constitute an excessively large percentage of the residents of the District. Even though comparatively small proportions of them marry and give birth to children while they are in Washington, enough of them do to make the ratio of births to population fairly large. However, when this abnormal age-sex distribution is adjusted for either through the use of the fertility ratio or the number of children ever born, the resulting index is very low. Second, there is a possibility that the attempt to allocate the births actually taking place in the hospitals of the nation's capital to the states in which the mothers reside, a complicated problem at best, is not entirely successful. In any case, it should be obvious that the reported levels of fertility in the various states vary tremendously according to the index used and that the most dependable indexes are those that make it possible to control for variations in the age and sex composition of the population.

It is also apparent from the data in Tables 30 and 31 that the sections of the country with the lowest rates of reproduction generally are highly urban and that there is a tendency for the rate to increase as the degree of urbanization decreases, although this relationship was more pronounced in 1960 than it was in 1970. However, neither New Mexico nor Utah, for which all of the indexes are among the highest, is to be classed as among the more rural states of the Union. This suggests that other factors are largely responsible for the high birth rates in those states, and one immediately thinks of the Spanish-American heritage of the former and the influence of the Mormon religion in the latter as probably responsible for their high rates of reproduction. Somewhat comparable to the Spanish-Americans, in that it is an ethnic group that has held tenaciously to its distinctive social and cultural patterns, is the French-speaking population of southern Louisiana. Therefore, it is interesting to note that Louisiana also ranks far higher in the number of children ever born and the birth rate than would be predicted solely on the basis of the degree to which its population resides in urban areas. Likewise, the large Mormon populations of Idaho and Arizona may account in part for the relatively high rates of reproduction in those states.

The varying importance of Negroes, whose birth rate generally is higher than that of whites, also may be a factor in accounting for the relative rankings of the various states, although the proportions of the black population that are rural and urban greatly influence its level of reproduction. In this connection it may be noted that Mississippi, which ranks fifth from the top among the states on the basis of the birth rate and third on the basis of the fertility ratio and the number of children ever born, is only thirty-fourth in rank with respect to the number of children ever born among the white population but first with respect to that index among its Negro population. Similarly, the other states with very high proportions of Negroes in their populations (South Carolina, Louisiana, Georgia, and Alabama) rank considerably higher on the various scales of fertility for the total population than they do on the basis of those for the white population separately. But it is hardly profitable to pursue such analysis further, since a study of differential fertility is the better way to determine the nature and significance of such variations.

1. For a discussion of this matter, see Leo A. Orleans, "The Population of Communist China," in *Population: The Vital Revolution,* edited by Ronald W. Freedman (New York: Doubleday & Co., Inc., 1964), pp. 234 - 236. See also Pi-Chao Chen, "China's Birth Control Action Programme," *Population Studies,* XXIV, 2 (July, 1970), pp. 141 - 158.

2. Alfred Sauvy, "La Population de la Chine," *Population,* 12 année, no. 4 (1957), 697 - 698.

3. Orleans, *op. cit.,* p. 232.

BOGUE, DONALD J. *Principles of Demography*, pp. 663 - 689. New York: John Wiley & Sons, Inc., 1969.

COX, PETER R. *Demography*, 4th ed., pp. 97 - 118. London: Cambridge University Press, 1970.

FREEDMAN, RONALD. "Norms for Family Size in Underdeveloped Areas," in *Readings on Population,* edited by David M. Heer, Chap. 10. Englewood Cliffs: Prentice-Hall, Inc., 1968.

GENDELL, MURRAY. "Fertility and Development in Brazil." *Demography*, Vol. 4, No. 1 (1967), pp. 143 - 157.

GRABILL, WILSON H., CLYDE V. KISER, and PASCAL K. WHELPTON. *The Fertility of American Women*, Chaps. 1 - 3. New York: John Wiley & Sons, Inc., 1958.

HEER, DAVID M. "Fertility Differences Between Indian and Spanish-Speaking Parts of Andean Countries." *Population Studies*, Vol. 18, No. 2 (July, 1964), pp. 71 - 84.

LORIMER, FRANK, and others. *Culture and Human Fertility*, pp. 22 - 57. Paris: UNESCO, 1954.

PETERSEN, WILLIAM. *Population*, 2nd ed., Chap. 18. New York: The Macmillan Company, 1969.

RYDER, NORMAN B., and CHARLES F. WESTOFF. *Reproduction in the United States, 1965.* Princeton: Princeton University Press, 1971.

SHRYOCK, HENRY S., JACOB S. SIEGEL, and associates. *The Methods and Materials of Demography*, Vol. 2, Chap. 18. Washington: Government Printing Office, 1971.

SMITH, T. LYNN. *Brazil: People and Institutions,* 4th ed., Chap VI. Baton Rouge: Louisiana State University Press, 1972.

SMITH, T. LYNN. *Latin American Population Studies*, Chap. 3. Gainesville: University of Florida Press, 1960.

SMITH, T. LYNN. *Studies of Latin American Societies*, Selection 6. New York: Doubleday & Co., Inc., 1970.

TAEUBER, CONRAD, and IRENE B. TAEUBER. *The People of the United States in the 20th Century* (A 1960 Census Monograph), Chap. VIII. Washington: Government Printing Office, 1971.

THOMLINSON, RALPH. *Demographic Problems,* Chaps. 3 and 4. Belmont, Calif.: Dickenson Publishing Company, Inc., 1967.

UNITED NATIONS. *Human Fertility and National Development.* New York: United Nations, 1971.

WESTOFF, CHARLES F. "The Fertility of the American Population," in *Population: The Vital Revolution,* edited by Ronald Freedman, Chap. 8. New York: Doubleday & Co., Inc. (Anchor Books), 1964.

WHELPTON, PASCAL K., and ARTHUR A. CAMPBELL. "Fertility Tables for Birth Cohorts of American Women, Part I." National Office of Vital Statistics. *Vital Statistics – Special Reports,* Vol. 51, No. 1 (January, 1960).

WHELPTON, PASCAL K., ARTHUR A. CAMPBELL, and JOHN E. PATTERSON. *Fertility and Family Planning in the United States.* Princeton: Princeton University Press, 1966.

13

DIFFERENTIAL FERTILITY

There is much interest in and importance attached to the facts with respect to the differences in the rate of reproduction of white and Negro, rural and urban segments of a population. Even greater significance may be attached by some to any differentials, much more difficult to establish, that may be found between the fertility of those who belong to the lower social and economic classes and those who are in the middle and upper classes of their respective societies. Likewise, there is considerable interest in knowing what differences if any exist between the birth rates of different religious groups, occupational groups, and those who live in various regions of a country. There is good reason for having an interest in and attaching importance to any differential fertility of these types.

Within a given nation differences in the birth rate, and especially in the net reproduction rate, of various ethnic, color, residential, and other categories can quickly bring about fundamental changes in the biological make-up of its population. The following illustration should serve to demonstrate the rapidity with which such a change can occur. In 1940, when regional differentials in the fertility of the white population were greater than they are at present, Illinois had a white population of 7,504,202 persons, a figure only slightly below that for the four East South Central states (Kentucky, Tennessee, Alabama, and Mississippi) which annually send such large contingents of migrants to Chicago and other parts of the state. Suppose for illustrative purposes that the total were exactly 15 million persons, of whom one-half were in Illinois and the other half in the East South Central states. Net reproduction rates for the white population in 1940 were as follows: Illinois, 82; and the East South Central states, 121. Differences in the mortality rates, if any, were very slight, so that the differentials were almost entirely due to the higher birth rate in the four southern states. If there were no changes in the age-specific birth rates and death rates, such a generation of Illinoisans would leave only 6,150,000 descendants, who in turn would produce 5,043,000 offspring, who in their turn would give rise to a generation of

327

TABLE 32

Residential and racial differentials in fertility in the United States, by age of mother, 1970

Number of children ever born per 1,000 women ever married

Age	White				Negro			
	Total	Urban	Rural-nonfarm	Rural-farm	Total	Urban	Rural-nonfarm	Rural-farm
15 and over	2,455	2,324	2,771	3,142	3,011	2,780	4,088	4,808
15–44	2,285	2,197	2,463	2,973	2,976	2,820	3,842	4,535
15–19	579	568	610	622	1,026	1,018	1,069	1,010
20–24	1,006	943	1,191	1,270	1,631	1,577	1,953	1,959
25–29	1,922	1,834	2,136	2,325	2,541	2,438	3,194	3,585
30–34	2,734	2,645	2,919	3,187	3,395	3,236	4,381	4,902
35–39	3,086	2,994	3,275	3,584	3,839	3,618	5,068	5,835
40–44	3,012	2,913	3,240	3,579	3,795	3,522	5,207	6,029
45–49	2,791	2,671	3,101	3,393	3,394	3,079	4,925	5,762
50–54	2,553	2,405	2,938	3,186	3,030	2,698	4,509	5,152
55–59	2,378	2,206	2,833	3,016	2,834	2,500	4,164	4,859
60–64	2,352	2,152	2,890	3,017	2,731	2,421	3,904	4,472
65 and over	2,743	2,544	3,342	3,483	3,093	2,779	4,134	4,750

Source: Compiled and computed from data in U.S. Bureau of the Census, *U.S. Census of Population: 1970, Detailed Characteristics,* Final Report PC(1)-D1, *United States Summary* (1973), pp. 671–674, Table 212.

4,135,260 persons. In the East South Central states, the numbers in the corresponding generations would be 9,075,000, 10,980,750, and 13,286,708, respectively. Since the duration of a generation in the United States is only slightly more than twenty-five years, these calculations indicate that the net reproduction rates employed would increase the total size of the generation from 15 million assumed for the first to 17,421,968 for the fourth. However, assuming no intermixture after 1940 only 23.7 per cent of the latter would be the descendants of the 7.5 million Illinoisans (50 per cent of the total) and 76.3 per cent would be the descendants of the 7.5 million white southerners. This demonstrates fairly well the rapidity with which differential birth rates such as those presently prevailing in the United States and many other parts of the world may change the basic ethnic components of a given population. Similar differences, if continued over several generations, could result in greatly varying numbers of descendants of persons presently in the lower, middle, and upper classes of a given society; in the proportions of whites and Negroes in countries such as the United States, Brazil, and Cuba; and in the numbers contributed to future national populations by those presently living on the farms and in the cities of various countries.

RURAL-URBAN DIFFERENTIALS

Its magnitude, the extent to which it persists from decade to decade, and its general social significance all make the rural-urban differential in fertility of prime importance. Whenever one takes a bird's-eye view of the rates of reproduction in a given country, as is possible for the United States by observation of Tables 32 and 33, it is at once evident that the more urban an area the lower the fertility of the population and the more rural an area the higher the rate of reproduction. In our own country, the highest birth rates prevail in the southern Appalachians, in others of the most rural portions of the southern region, and in the remote sections of the Rocky Mountains. On the other hand, the rate of reproduction is very low in all the great cities, which even seem to exert a depressing effect upon the birth rates of the population in the rural districts surrounding them.

In order to determine whether or not there are significant rural and urban, racial, and state or regional differentials in fertility, it is necessary to have the data subsorted as they are in Tables 32 and 33. Otherwise when the various racial groups are so unequally represented .in the different residential categories and each of these in the several regions, as is the case in the United States, one is likely to conclude that a given differential exists when in reality it is merely a reflection of another. In other words, one who goes to the trouble to compare the rates of reproduction in the Northeast and the South wants to demonstrate something more than that the latter is more rural or that it contains a higher proportion of Negroes than the former. These facts are already well known and easily demonstrated.

TABLE 33

Residential and racial differentials in fertility in the United
States, by states, 1970

State	White Urban	White Rural-nonfarm	White Rural-farm	Negro Urban	Negro Rural-nonfarm	Negro Rural-farm
New England						
Maine	2,454	2,630	3,009	2,450	....	....
New Hampshire	2,381	2,467	2,788	2,881	....	....
Vermont	2,482	2,537	3,257	....	....	....
Massachusetts	2,370	2,532	2,650	2,731	2,900	....
Rhode Island	2,301	2,442	2,537	3,251	....	....
Connecticut	2,199	2,403	2,417	2,772	2,594	....
Middle Atlantic						
New York	2,147	2,852	2,962	2,462	2,577	2,856
New Jersey	2,183	2,328	2,527	2,712	3,294	3,229
Pennsylvania	2,255	2,432	2,803	2,778	3,080	3,224
East North Central						
Ohio	2,263	2,555	2,930	2,759	3,004	3,443
Indiana	2,271	2,442	2,813	2,971	2,530	....
Illinois	2,240	2,470	2,756	2,810	4,071	4,016
Michigan	2,379	2,657	3,028	2,786	3,545	....
Wisconsin	2,445	2,767	3,468	3,166	....	....
West North Central						
Minnesota	2,390	2,810	3,514	2,750	....	....
Iowa	2,349	2,576	3,124	2,951	....	....
Missouri	2,157	2,428	2,743	2,990	4,571	5,075
North Dakota	2,377	2,819	3,383	2,457	....	....
South Dakota	2,426	2,757	3,304	....	....	....
Nebraska	2,326	2,588	3,044	3,048	....	....
Kansas	2,162	2,485	2,915	3,018	3,179	....
South Atlantic						
Delaware	2,185	2,169	2,618	2,947	3,456	....
Maryland	2,075	2,331	2,627	2,766	3,450	3,938
District of Columbia	1,273	....	....	2,462	....	....
Virginia	1,932	2,210	2,445	2,809	3,496	3,719
West Virginia	2,112	2,592	2,762	3,202	3,733	....
North Carolina	1,922	2,058	2,304	2,888	3,616	4,032
South Carolina	2,021	2,160	2,446	3,193	3,806	4,298
Georgia	1,962	2,188	2,429	2,909	3,890	4,439
Florida	2,050	2,295	2,418	3,101	3,884	3,897

TABLE 33 (Cont'd)

Residential and racial differentials in fertility in the United
States, by states, 1970

State	White Urban	White Rural-nonfarm	White Rural-farm	Negro Urban	Negro Rural-nonfarm	Negro Rural-farm
East South Central						
Kentucky	2,137	2,500	2,695	2,947	3,615	3,665
Tennessee	1,961	2,199	2,436	3,078	3,827	4,237
Alabama	2,005	2,258	2,381	3,202	4,023	4,532
Mississippi	2,046	2,305	2,502	3,505	4,441	5,046
West South Central						
Arkansas	1,989	2,358	2,617	3,649	4,565	4,831
Louisiana	2,255	2,595	2,861	3,187	4,025	4,751
Oklahoma	2,030	2,437	2,617	3,166	3,992	3,654
Texas	2,237	2,568	2,715	2,848	3,893	3,765
Mountain						
Montana	2,450	2,622	3,007	....	....	....
Idaho	2,406	2,734	3,272	....	....	....
Wyoming	2,371	2,595	2,824	3,265	....	....
Colorado	2,213	2,526	2,803	2,627	....	....
New Mexico	2,467	2,924	3,014	3,037	....	....
Arizona	2,339	2,622	2,902	3,222	3,291	....
Utah	2,585	3,084	3,730	3,167	....	....
Nevada	2,087	2,324	2,586	3,071	....	....
Pacific						
Washington	2,204	2,544	2,909	2,684	2,481	....
Oregon	2,177	2,618	2,846	2,925	....	....
California	2,149	2,538	2,712	2,626	3,304	....
Alaska	1,984	2,288	2,642	2,044	2,646	....
Hawaii	1,994	2,465	3,000	1,887	....	....

Source: Compiled and computed from data in U.S. Bureau of the Census, *U.S. Census of Population: 1970, General Social and Economic Characteristics,* Final Report PC(1)-C2-C52, reports for states (1971 and 1972), Table 52.

. . . . Data not shown where number of women aged 15-44 ever married is less than 200.

The data in Tables 32 and 33 are based upon the number of children ever born per 1,000 women ever married rather than upon the fertility ratio (number of children under five per 100 women aged fifteen to forty-four), which is the most satisfactory index for making comparisons in most countries of the world. As indicated in Chapter 11, the use of the number of children ever born avoids the distortions introduced into the fertility ratio by extreme variations in five-year age groups within the overall range of fifteen to forty-four, found when the residential and racial groups are compared. This is especially important when one is considering these various groups in the populations of individual states.

When the appropriate comparisons are made of the data in Table 32 (Chapter 13), it is observed that the fertility of the urban population is substantially lower than that of either the rural-nonfarm or the rural-farm populations in the United States as a whole, and that this is the case for each one of the age groups represented. Furthermore this differential prevails not only for the population as a whole, but also for both the white and Negro populations taken separately. In every case the levels for the rural-farm population also are above those for the rural-nonfarm group, except among Negroes aged fifteen to nineteen.

If one makes even more refined comparisons using the data for states given in Table 33, the strong and consistent tendency of the rural population to multiply more rapidly than the urban is even more convincingly demonstrated. Among the white population in every one of the states but Delaware for 1970, the level of fertility of the urban population is substantially lower than those of the rural-nonfarm and the rural-farm categories; and except in Connecticut, New Jersey, Oklahoma, Texas, and Washington, in most of which the numbers of rural persons involved are small, the same is true among the Negro population. The tendency of the birth rate of the rural population of the United States to exceed that of the urban has been known, of course, for some time,[1] as has something about the factors responsible for the differential. Nevertheless, it is important to see the degree to which it persists throughout the length and breadth of the country, even after the upsurge in the urban birth rate between 1935 and 1957, the remarkable decline after that time, and the elimination of so much of the difference between the rural and urban ways of life that has accompanied the perfection of modern means of communication and transportation.

Such rural-urban differentials in fertility are by no means limited to the United States. Indeed, that the birth rates of rural people have greatly exceeded those of city residents in various European countries and in other parts of the world for which even partially reliable data have been available long has been known.[2] More recently it has become possible to compare the fertility of rural and urban populations in most of the Latin American countries. (See Table 34.) This is especially significant because the Latin American countries taken together occupy a very substantial part of the earth's surface; the world division they constitute is the one in which current rates of population increase are the highest;[3] these nations make up a highly important part of the so-called "underdeveloped" areas of the world; and the various improvisations necessary in order to make the comparisons illustrate the types of difficulties encountered by those who undertake to study the populations of the areas containing the vast majority of the earth's people.

Even on the basis of these highly imperfect materials, it is readily evident that throughout Latin America the fertility ratio of the rural population is much higher than that of the urban population.

Study of the data in Table 34 also leads one to the following conclusion: the lower the general rate of reproduction in a country, the greater the rural-urban differential in fertility. Therefore, since the factors presently in operation lead

TABLE 34

Rural-urban differences in the fertility ratios of the Latin American countries[a]
Number of children under 5 per 100 women aged 15-44

Country	Year	Total population	Urban population	Rural population
Costa Rica	1963	94.8	73.8	112.4
Cuba	1953	55.3	41.5	79.2
Dominican Republic	1960	90.0	68.1	102.7
El Salvador	1961	80.3	66.0	90.8
Guatemala	1964	84.1	71.0	91.8
Haiti	1970[b]	64.9	....	....
Honduras	1961	92.5	73.0	99.5
Mexico	1960	78.7	73.4	84.7
Nicaragua	1963	88.9	77.3	98.2
Panama	1960	81.7	60.9	100.7
Argentina	1960	47.1	....	....
Bolivia	1950	68.5	....	....
Brazil	1960	72.4	47.1	78.6
Chile	1960	68.3	60.2	91.7
Colombia	1964	84.3	72.0	101.0
Ecuador	1962	81.9	73.9	86.8
Paraguay	1962	84.5	63.6	98.3
Peru	1961	79.7	70.2	89.3
Uruguay	1963	44.2	41.7	58.1
Venezuela	1961	91.4	82.0	115.1

Source: Compiled and computed from data in various editions of United Nations, Demographic Yearbook.
[a]Barbados, Jamaica, Trinidad and Tobago, and Guyana are not included.
[b]United Nations estimate.

one to expect the continued urbanization and industrialization of the Latin American countries, the prevailing rural-urban differential in the birth rate is likely to be maintained for some decades to come. It may even become more pronounced in most parts of Mexico, Central America, the island republics, and South America. Eventually, of course, the point should be reached at which this tendency will produce a falling birth rate throughout the length and breadth of the area, for as the urban population becomes a more significant proportion of the total population, many national birth rates are certain to fall, perhaps sharply.

A special set of tabulations prepared as a part of the 1970 census of the United States which gives the characteristics of the inhabitants according to the size of the places in which they lived, enables one to explore two other significant aspects of the relationship between urbanization and the rate of reproduction. These are (1) the ways in which fertility varies as one passes from the greatest metropolitan cities, to cities of fewer inhabitants, to towns and villages, to the open country; and (2) the differentials between the rates of reproduction of people living in the central cities of the urbanized areas and those living in the densely populated districts immediately adjacent to such incorporated cities. To facilitate such comparisons, Table 35 was prepared. Observation of the data it contains makes it readily apparent that, among both the white and the Negro segments of the population, the number of children ever born per 1,000 women aged thirty-five to forty-four increases steadily as the size of community decreases. In fact, by comparing the two extremes it is noted that the index for the rural-farm districts is one-fifth again as large as that for the central cities of urbanized areas. Furthermore, among the Negro population the index for the rural-farm group is two-thirds again as large as the one for those living in central cities. For the total population the index is slightly higher for persons residing in the central cities than it is for those living in the urban fringes. This, however, is due to the particular distribution of women and children in the two racial groups and when each is considered separately, it is found that whites and Negroes living in the central cities both have lower fertility levels than those residing in the urban fringes. This, of course, is in line with the general belief that many young couples, especially the white, establish residences in the suburbs to have a more advantageous environment in which to rear their families. Moreover, for both races, fertility levels are lower in cities of 1 million or more inhabitants than they are in centers of 250,000 to 999,999, just as they are lower in the latter than they are in cities of fewer than 250,000 persons.

Before leaving the subject of rural-urban differentials in fertility, it is well to return to the matter of the variations within the open country districts themselves, and especially the manner in which the fertility of the population changes as the distance from centers of manufacturing, trade, and transportation increases. The farther the distance from such large urban centers, the higher the birth rate seems apparent from Figure 45. In each of the regions of the nation, levels of

TABLE 35

Number of children ever born per 1,000 women aged 35–44 ever married,
by size of place and race, 1970

| Size of place | Number of children ever born per 1,000 women aged 35–44 ever married | | |
	Total population	White population	Negro population
Urbanized areas			
Total	2,991	2,916	3,478
Central cities	3,019	2,890	3,463
Urban fringe	2,964	2,937	3,557
Other urban			
10,000 or more	3,145	3,051	4,106
2,500–9,999	3,215	3,131	4,402
Rural			
Nonfarm	3,381	3,242	5,140
Farm	3,671	3,574	5,939

Source: Compiled and computed from data in U.S. Bureau of the Census, *U.S. Census of Population: 1970, General Social and Economic Characteristics,* Final Report PC(1)-C1, *United States Summary* (1972), p. 406, Table 100; p. 426, Table 119; *Detailed Characteristics,* Final Report PC(1)-D1, *United States Summary* (1973), pp. 675–676, Table 213.

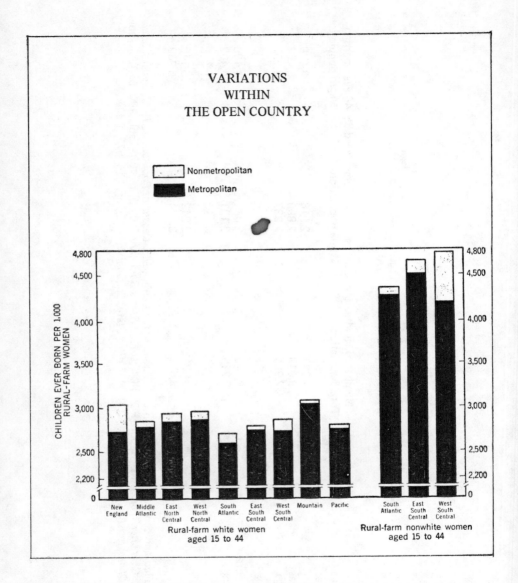

Figure 45. Number of children ever born per 1,000 rural-farm white women (and nonwhite women in the South) aged 15 - 44 ever married, by metropolitan and nonmetropolitan residence, for regions of the United States, 1960. Reproduced from Dale E. Hathaway, J. Allan Beegle, and W. Keith Bryant. *People of Rural America.* A 1960 Census Monograph, Washington: Government Printing Office, 1968.

fertility are lower for farm people who reside in or near the most highly urbanized metropolitan portions of the country than they are for those who live in the less urbanized nonmetropolitan sections; and this is true no matter which racial groups are involved.[4] The amount of detail shown for 1960 in Figure 45 is not available for 1970, but materials for the nation as a whole demonstrate that the situation persists. That is, in 1970 the number of children ever born per 1,000 rural-farm women aged fifteen to forty-four who were ever married was only 2,789 in the metropolitan parts of the nation but was 2,955 in the nonmetropolitan sections. The rural-nonfarm population is similarly influenced by the proximity of large cities, inasmuch as the index for this residential group was 2,486 for the metropolitan segment and 2,575 for the nonmetropolitan contingent.

 ## RACIAL DIFFERENTIALS

There is a widespread belief that the Negro and other nonwhite elements of the population are multiplying much more rapidly than the white population in the United States and other parts of the Western Hemisphere. Coupled with this is the belief that the populations of the parts of the world inhabited chiefly by various nonwhite races are growing more rapidly than those of Europe, the white populations of the American continents, and the descendants of Europeans in other parts of the world such as Australia, New Zealand, and South Africa. Indeed thousands, if not millions of well-educated persons in the United States have a haunting fear that very shortly the white population of this country will be completely drowned, at home and abroad, in the surging masses of Negro and other nonwhite peoples. Even if such a phobia is absent, the differences, if any, between the rates of reproduction of whites, Negroes, and other races, in the United States, of whites, Negroes, and Indians in the Latin American countries, and so on are of considerable interest. This may be illustrated by a short quotation of a generalization by Frank Tannenbaum, noted historian and long-time student of the Negro in the Americas. After pointing out that the Negro has physical occupancy or possession of a large part of the two American continents, aptly described as the area within a huge half circle extending from Washington, D. C., to Rio de Janeiro, Brazil, this authority succinctly states:

> And the density as well as the extent of this empire is increasing because Negro fertility is relatively high in comparison to the white. The only place where this biological expansion is being challenged is in Trinidad by the East Indians.[5]

Thus, it is important for the student of population to establish what differentials, if any, exist between the rates of reproduction of the various racial groups in such countries as the United States, Brazil, Cuba, and South Africa, in which the population is composed of large groups of persons of highly diverse racial stocks.

In the United States, as was shown in Table 9, the proportion of Negroes in the population fell steadily from the time of the first census in 1790 until 1930. Throughout most of our history, although the birth rate of the Negro population may have been above that of the white, the results of the differential were more than offset by the higher mortality rate of the Negroes, or by the immigration of whites, or a combination of these two factors. Reliable birth rates are, of course, not available for any part of this historical period, but fertility ratios for whites and Negroes separately may be computed from the materials gathered in each census from 1890 to date. These (the number of children under five per 100 women fifteen to forty-four) are as follows, the index for the white population given first in each case: 1890, 52 and 62; 1910, 48 and 52; 1920, 47 and 44; 1930, 39 and 43; 1940, 32 and 37; 1950, 47 and 51; 1960, 55 and 69; and 1970, 39 and 49. Thus, it appears that for the most part, from 1885 on, the Negro population actually had a slightly higher birth rate than the white population. Between 1915 and 1920, however, this seemingly was not the case. But prior to 1935 the effective fertility of the Negro population was not sufficient to offset the other two factors (mortality and immigration) related to population change, and the proportion of Negroes in the population declined.

By 1930 it was possible to make fairly satisfactory comparisons of the rates of reproduction of whites and Negroes in the various residential categories. Then, and until 1950, it was apparent that the fertility of the Negro population equaled or exceeded that of the white population only because the former lived in rural-farm areas in considerably greater proportions than the latter.[6] With this in mind, the data in Tables 32, 33, and 35 should be analyzed to determine what, if any, differentials prevailed in 1970 in the rates of reproduction of whites and Negroes in the United States. Among the total population, as is evident from Table 32, the fertility level of the Negroes is somewhat above that for the whites. (See also Figure 46.) Moreover, in the four major regions of the nation similar differentials exist between the races although they are not great except in the South. Thus, in 1970, the regional differences in the number of children ever born per 1,000 women aged fifteen to forty-four ever married were as follows among whites and Negroes, respectively: Northeast, 2,286 and 2,608; North Central, 2,413 and 2,853; South, 2,173 and 3,242; and West, 2,270 and 2,663. This regional situation immediately suggests that outside the South Negroes live in urban centers in much greater proportions than whites; and in the South higher percentages of Negroes than of whites also are classed as urban, but the difference is not great. In any event, the residential factor must be controlled before fair comparisons may be made. When this is done, as the information given in Tables 32 and 35 makes possible, it is seen that the difference between the rates of reproduction of the white and Negro residents of the central cities of urbanized areas is about 20 per cent. However, turning attention from the inhabitants of the urbanized areas to those residing in nonurban places, the fertility differentials between

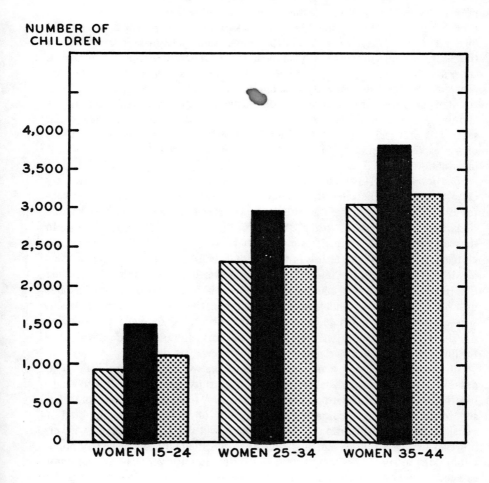

Figure 46. Number of children ever born per 1,000 women ever married, the United States, by age and race, 1970.

the races are seen to become greater; and this divergence grows in the rural-non-farm population and reaches its zenith in the rural-farm group. In the last category the number of children ever born to Negro mothers aged thirty-five to forty-four is 66 per cent greater than that born to white mothers in the same age range. But it is highly significant that the ratio for rural-farm Negroes also is 71 per cent greater than that for Negroes living in urbanized areas, suggesting strongly that any important racial differences in fertility probably arise from the fact that comparatively high proportions of Negroes who now reside in cities have left the poverty levels of agriculture in the recent past and retain many of the sociocultural features which originated in that background, one of which is relatively high rates of fertility. These conditions are especially important, of course, in the South, which contains nearly all of the Negro farm population and in which, generally speaking, those Negroes who still reside in rural areas tend to be concentrated in the most poverty-stricken and agricultural portions of the open country. Because many Negroes are still residents of the most rural region of the country and probably because they tend to live in the poorest and most rural sectors of that region, their rate of reproduction is considerably higher than that of whites. Such a conclusion receives further support from a study of the detailed information for the fifty states given in Table 33.

The levels of fertility among the races other than Negro and white are very close to those of the latter. (See Figure 46.) An examination of Table 31 (Chapter 12) indicates, however, that this is the net result of wide state-to-state variations that are influenced strongly by the particular racial identities of those in the category of other races. In general, where the group is made up almost exclusively of rural Indians, as it is in the Dakotas, North Carolina, Oklahoma, New Mexico, and Arizona, the number of children ever born per 1,000 women aged fifteen to forty-four ever married tends to be relatively high, although in states in which the Indian population is largely urban the indexes are much lower. Where Chinese and Japanese, who are almost entirely urban, make up a substantial share of the category, as they do in New York, Illinois, and California, the fertility levels for other races are comparatively low.

In Latin America and many other parts of the world, it is more difficult to determine what, if any, racial differentials in fertility prevail than it is to establish the rural-urban differentials presented above. A few countries, it is true, classify births according to color or race, and many of them include some kind of racial or ethnic classification of the population in the censuses. Almost never, however, is it possible to match the births so classified with the necessary population data in order to compute reliable birth rates for various racial or color categories; and even if one could, there still would be many questions of completeness or lack of it in the registration of the births. Even more disheartening to the population student is the fact that the age and sex distributions of the various racial groups, data needed for the computation of the fertility ratios, generally are lacking. One who attempts to determine the extent of racial differentials in fertility throughout Latin America and most other parts of the world must be prepared to make even more improvisations than those generally called for in population analyses made in the United States and the European countries.

Some significant comparisons, though, are possible. For example, a number of students of population have for some time been convinced that differential fertility was producing a rapid "bleaching" or whitening of the Brazilian population. The most complete census available to them to study this matter, however, and the latest one in which the data are presented for various color categories in such a way to make the comparison of fertility differentials possible is that for 1950. Yet the subject is so important that these materials must be relied upon. Since almost 6 million persons were classified as black or Negro by Brazil's 1950 census, since the number of mulattoes must be fully as large if not larger, and since the total population of Brazil was about 52 million at the time, the racial differentials in fertility in that large country have much to do with determining the nature of and direction of the changes in the racial composition of the population of the Americas. Fortunately, the improved classifications used in the 1950 Brazilian census make it easy to compute the indexes needed for comparisons of the rates of reproduction of Brazil's white, black, yellow, and mixed-blood populations. (See Table 36.)

A study of these materials makes it readily apparent that whites are multiplying more rapidly than Negroes and by a considerable margin. Throughout Brazil the fertility ratios for the Negro population are consistently lower than those for the white population. The ratios for the mixed category are inflated, of course, by any racial mixing in which either the whites or the Negroes are involved, but despite this fact, the indexes for the white population compare very favorably with those for the mixed group. The difficulties the Negro woman has in securing a mate, and the relative freedom of access which the upper class (white or whitish) man has to the (colored) women in the lower social classes probably are two of the more important factors explaining the differentials observed.[7]

A few data for some of the other countries also are available. Thus, for Cuba, in 1953, the fertility ratios for the four racial or color categories are as follows: white, 52.4; Negro, 57.2; yellow, 57.8; and mixed, 68.8. For Costa Rica, in which the numbers and proportions of Negroes are very small, the fertility ratios for 1950 are 74.3 for whites and mestizos combined and 54.6 for Negroes; and in Panama, a veritable "melting pot," the fertility ratios for the various racial or color groupings used in the 1940 census are as follows: whites, 40.5; Negroes, 34.2; mestizo (largely mulatto), 68.9; and others, 55.2. All told these fragments of data do not fully support the hypothesis, based on Brazilian materials, that the white elements in the Latin American population are reproducing more rapidly than the nonwhite ones, but neither do they fortify the belief so widely held that exactly the opposite is true.[8]

TABLE 36

Number of children under five per 100 women aged 15-49 for each Brazilian state
and territory, by color, 1950

Region and state or territory	Total	White	Negro	Yellow	Pardo (mixed)
Brazil	65.3	65.3	55.6	79.6	69.2
North					
Guaporé†	73.0	70.7	51.9	....	76.9
Acre†	90.0	90.1	58.7	....	92.1
Amazonas	73.7	74.5	50.5	119.1	74.4
Rio Branco†	83.6	82.1	62.0	....	86.0
Pará	67.2	67.0	47.2	91.5	69.0
Amapa†	73.5	77.9	43.2	....	75.7
Northeast					
Maranhão	64.9	69.4	52.2	....	65.7
Piauí	75.6	78.5	60.5	....	77.6
Ceará	77.0	78.2	68.3	....	80.9
Rio Grande do Norte	73.1	74.5	61.1	....	73.9
Paraiba	70.0	72.3	60.0	....	69.1
Pernambuco	65.2	67.3	52.0	....	66.0
Alagôas	68.6	71.3	51.0	....	69.2
Fernando de Noronha†	65.2	....	....	....	....
East					
Sergipe	69.2	75.0	55.6	....	66.7
Bahia	65.4	66.9	54.1	....	68.9
Minas Gerais	67.5	69.7	56.2	82.1	69.3
Espírito Santo	74.5	76.5	63.0	....	75.7
Rio de Janeiro	66.9	65.5	65.4	78.6	71.2
Distrito Federal	36.8	36.2	34.0	56.7	41.3
South					
São Paulo	57.4	56.6	55.4	78.3	65.7
Paraná	72.9	73.4	64.5	89.4	70.1
Santa Catarina	80.5	81.2	71.5	....	73.0
Rio Grande do Sul	66.0	66.6	57.9	52.3	64.0
West Central					
Mato Grosso	76.7	77.9	63.9	81.5	78.4
Goiás	72.0	76.7	53.0	94.1	69.5

Source: Computations based on data from the *VI Recenseamento Geral do Brasil.*
†Territory.
.... Rates not given for a category in which there were less than 100 women aged fifteen to forty-nine.

REGIONAL DIFFERENTIALS

When the data are assembled in the forms used in Table 33 and Figure 45, the nature of the regional differences in the United States is rather readily apparent. There are great variations, but most of them seem due to the fact that the north-eastern states are highly urban and industrial whereas the South, the West North Central division, and the Rocky Mountain states are more rural. The heavy representation of Negroes in some of the more rural sections of the South also seems to be a factor in making the birth rate for the area in general somewhat higher than that for the nation, although the comparatively low rates of whites in the region have offset this to a substantial degree. In urban areas, and especially those of the North and the West, the increasingly large Negro populations still multiply more rapidly than their white fellows but not nearly to the extent that prevails where rural influences are strong. As indicated in Chapter 12 and as seen in Table 33, two western states, Utah and New Mexico, and one in the South, Mississippi, consistently have extremely high levels of fertility no matter which index is used to measure the rate of reproduction. When the data are subsorted for residence and race, the indexes for the urban, the rural-nonfarm, and the rural-farm white populations of Utah are the highest in the nation. New Mexico's white population ranks third in the nation with respect to the fertility levels of its urban group, second with respect to those if its rural-nonfarm segment, but eleventh with respect to the rural-farm contingent. These facts hardly should be interpreted, however, as indicating that the rate of reproduction tends to be unusually high in the region as such; rather they suggest that above and beyond the rural-urban differentials, factors associated with the Spanish-American and the Mormon social and cultural heritages make for high birth rates in the communities in which these groups reside. Census data are not available to measure the fertility of religious groups,[9] but those that permit some gauging of the birth rates of the Spanish-American population are. These materials indicate that in New Mexico, in 1970, the number of children ever born per 1,000 women aged fifteen to forty-four ever married in the population of "Spanish language or Spanish surname" was 38 per cent higher than that of the other residents of the state. The high position of Mississippi in the ranking of states by fertility levels is due to its large number or rural Negroes, for that state's Negro population, in 1970, ranked first in levels of fertility, but its white population ranked only thirty-seventh. Similar wide differentials by race prevail throughout much of the South, with the result that the fertility levels for the region's Negroes are higher than those in any of the other major regions, whereas the rates of reproduction of whites are lower than those in any other region.

The most satisfactory generalization with respect to regional differences may be formulated as follows: every refinement introduced into the analysis of the rate of reproduction in the United States tends to emphasize the importance of rural-urban, educational, and socioeconomic differentials and to minimize the importance of racial and regional differences in fertility. When the residential, educational, and socioeconomic differentials have been fully isolated, including effects of a rural background that may persist for a time after migrants from the farms enter cities, there is little if anything left to attribute to race and region.

EDUCATIONAL DIFFERENTIALS

In most countries there is a considerable tendency for fertility levels to be higher for people at the lower levels of educational attainment than for those who rank closer to the top in the amount of formal schooling received. In fact, as indicated above, a considerable part of the fertility differential between whites and non-whites may be explained by differences in levels of education,[10] and, of course, by variations in residence. In order to examine the relationship between variations in fertility and the levels of education attained by women, Table 37 was prepared, taking the characteristics of age, color, and residence into account in making the comparisons. The level of educational attainment of women rather than that of their husbands was used because the former appears to have significantly greater influence upon levels of reproduction than the latter.[11] The materials are for 1960, because those for 1970 do not provide the highly important separation between rural-farm and rural-nonfarm residence. The data for the latter year that are presented in Table 38, however, bear out the same general observations about the relationships between fertility levels and educational status. Both tables show that fertility levels decrease dramatically as the number of years of schooling completed increases. In fact, the rates of reproduction among women who have had no schooling along with those who have completed fewer than five years of formal schooling, the group sometimes classified as "functional illiterates," generally are at least twice as high as those for women who have completed four years of college. Moreover, this relationship obtains in all of the residence groups and in both the white and the nonwhite populations. It also appears in all four of the age categories shown in Table 37, although it is most pronounced for women aged fifty and over; that is, for those whose childbearing is essentially completed.

As mentioned previously, when educational attainment is considered, a substantial part of the fertility differential between whites and nonwhites also is accounted for. In fact, in the ages past thirty-five, if the years of schooling completed and residence both are held constant, nonwhite women frequently are found to have somewhat lower rates of reproduction than white women, particularly at the various levels of high school and college training. This has considerable significance, for it suggests that as the gap in educational attainment which now exists between whites and nonwhites in the United States is reduced and finally eliminated, differential fertility by race also is certain to become substantially less pronounced.[12]

TABLE 37

Number of children ever born per 1,000 women ever married, by educational attainment, according to selected age groups, color, and residence, 1960

Years of schooling completed, by age groups	Number of children ever born per 1,000 women ever married							
	White				Nonwhite			
	Urbanized areas	Other urban	Rural-nonfarm	Rural-farm	Urbanized areas	Other urban	Rural-nonfarm	Rural-farm
Ages 20-24								
None	2,167	....	2,085	....	....	....	2,974	....
Elementary								
1-4 years	1,895	2,100	2,307	2,650	2,153	2,786	2,633	3,060
5-7 years	1,859	2,008	2,088	2,022	2,398	2,546	2,721	3,046
8 years	1,792	1,961	1,982	1,931	2,380	2,534	2,480	2,757
High school								
1-3 years	1,683	1,790	1,913	1,962	2,189	2,360	2,409	2,416
4 years	1,126	1,221	1,305	1,428	1,489	1,632	1,626	1,806
College								
1-3 years	841	887	1,008	1,156	1,137	1,384	1,168	....
4 years	508	544	674	682	718	741	....	....
5 or more	426	520	579	....	....	....	....	....
Ages 30-34								
None	3,601	4,544	4,419	....	2,719	4,047	4,962	....
Elementary								
1-4 years	3,244	3,891	3,979	4,252	3,039	4,023	4,806	5,299
5-7 years	2,861	3,071	3,375	3,481	3,297	3,899	4,728	5,470
8 years	2,553	2,811	3,082	3,423	3,078	3,597	4,324	5,534
High school								
1-3 years	2,531	2,681	2,916	3,159	2,994	3,607	4,002	4,895
4 years	2,326	2,448	2,560	2,940	2,418	2,923	3,213	3,548
College								
1-3 years	2,308	2,488	2,502	2,875	2,257	2,525	2,934	....
4 years	2,213	2,319	2,264	2,360	1,666	1,625	1,828	....
5 or more	1,735	1,934	1,903	2,301	1,461	1,171	....	....
Ages 40-44								
None	3,567	5,258	4,815	5,671	2,725	3,267	4,630	5,578
Elementary								
1-4 years	3,219	3,973	4,307	4,737	2,487	3,462	4,677	5,986
5-7 years	2,650	3,142	3,601	3,919	2,593	3,439	4,801	6,177
8 years	2,370	2,742	3,214	3,520	2,439	3,703	4,250	5,466

TABLE 37 (Cont'd)

Number of children ever born per 1,000 women ever married, by educational
attainment, according to selected age groups, color, and residence, 1960

Years of schooling completed, by age groups	Number of children ever born per 1,000 women ever married							
	White				Nonwhite			
	Urban-ized areas	Other urban	Rural-nonfarm	Rural-farm	Urban-ized areas	Other urban	Rural-nonfarm	Rural-farm
High school								
1-3 years	2,341	2,576	2,891	3,167	2,482	3,293	4,014	5,304
4 years	2,132	2,270	2,483	2,937	2,080	2,598	3,164	3,738
College								
1-3 years	2,146	2,323	2,442	2,925	1,971	2,255	3,058	....
4 years	2,244	2,296	2,286	2,583	1,789	1,537	1,576	....
5 or more	1,933	1,999	2,114	1,892	1,261	1,164	....	....
Ages 50 and over								
None	4,015	5,140	5,302	5,349	3,383	3,778	4,546	4,856
Elementary								
1-4 years	3,521	4,320	4,858	4,997	2,833	3,474	4,414	5,008
5-7 years	2,857	3,522	3,989	4,206	2,639	3,484	4,390	5,417
8 years	2,454	3,014	3,379	3,610	2,516	2,948	4,122	4,967
High school								
1-3 years	2,076	2,525	2,860	3,190	2,290	3,197	3,863	4,774
4 years	1,793	2,035	2,237	2,718	2,115	2,521	2,845	3,973
College								
1-3 years	1,702	1,916	2,054	2,518	1,799	2,102	2,354	2,802
4 years	1,617	1,721	1,743	2,030	1,425	1,217	1,980	1,997
5 or more	1,324	1,408	1,451	1,579	1,191	1,223	1,414	....

Source: Compiled from U.S. Bureau of the Census, *U. S. Census of Population: 1960,
Subject Reports, Women by Number of Children Ever Born* (1964), pp. 100-108, Table 25.
.... Data not shown where number of women is less than 1,000.

Differences in fertility by educational status, however, explain only a part of
the variation which exists on the basis of residence. Thus, the data in Table 37
demonstrate that even when age, race, and the years of schooling completed can
be taken into account by subsorting, the rural-urban differential discussed earlier
continues to exist. At virtually every level of education and among members of
both color groups, rates of reproduction are lower in urban centers than they are
in rural-nonfarm areas and they are lower in the latter places than they are on
the farms. To be sure, residential differences tend to be greatest for those in the
lowest ranks of educational status and are likely to diminish greatly as the highest levels are reached, but in most cases they persist in some magnitude through-

TABLE 38

Number of children ever born per 1,000 women ever married, by
educational attainment, according to selected age
groups and race, 1970

Years of schooling completed, by age groups	Number of children ever born per 1,000 women ever married			
	Total	White	Negro	Other races
Ages 20-29				
Elementary				
Less than 8 years	2,475	2,380	2,931	2,105
8 years	2,429	2,319	3,083	2,501
High school				
1-3 years	2,204	2,107	2,706	2,170
4 years	1,470	1,440	1,762	1,569
College				
1-3 years	1,071	1,053	1,311	1,050
4 years or more	754	743	951	786
Ages 30-39				
Elementary				
Less than 8 years	3,847	3,626	4,636	3,766
8 years	3,529	3,378	4,366	3,451
High school				
1-3 years	3,395	3,249	4,065	3,533
4 years	2,840	2,820	3,091	2,707
College				
1-3 years	2,667	2,676	2,628	2,321
4 years or more	2,247	2,279	1,936	1,934
Ages 40-49				
Elementary				
Less than 8 years	3,862	3,689	4,302	4,429
8 years	3,297	3,193	3,946	3,736
High school				
1-3 years	3,087	2,965	3,782	3,709
4 years	2,759	2,742	3,027	2,796
College				
1-3 years	2,751	2,750	2,792	2,625
4 years or more	2,574	2,610	2,072	2,461

Source: Compiled and computed from data in U.S. Bureau of the Census, *U.S. Census of Population 1970, Subject Reports, Women by Number of Children Ever Born* (1973), pp. 146-149, Table 35; pp. 150-153, Table 36; pp. 154-157, Table 37.

out the entire range of educational achievement. In the case of residential differentials in fertility, however, the degree of difference between the urban, rural-nonfarm, and rural-farm groups, both white and nonwhite, tends to be greater in the older age groups than in the younger.

CLASS DIFFERENTIALS

The determination of differentials in the fertility of the various social classes in a society is extremely difficult, and until very recently there had been little comprehensive study of the subject. This was particularly true in the United States. But since the birth rates began to move downward in the late 1950's, a number of students of population have attempted to analyze the relationship between various criteria of socioeconomic status and rates of reproduction. A major criterion, education, has already been discussed. These studies have established comparatively easily and clearly that there are important associations between class and fertility, but the precise nature of the associations, the causes involved, the isolation of socioeconomic variables related to decreases in fertility and those connected with increases and the ways in which specific aspects of class standing have affected the fertility rates of various segments of the population have proved to be considerably more difficult matters with which to contend.

Historically, two viewpoints concerning the relationship of class levels to the birth rate have prevailed. The first, apparently derived deductively from the principles formulated by Thomas R. Malthus at the close of the eighteenth century, holds that increases in socioeconomic status promote higher fertility; and the second, usually associated with those who have employed the "Demographic Transition" as a conceptual device, implies that improvements in status tend to inhibit fertility.[13] However, the relationship seems to be considerably more complicated than either position would have it. The direct and early effect of economic improvement in a society often may be the stimulation of fertility to higher levels, but such factors as a rise in the overall level of education and reductions in infant mortality, which ordinarily are parts of the entire set of changes designated as socioeconomic development, seem to have a depressing effect on rates of reproduction.[14] Moreover, when these are joined by the awareness on the part of individual couples that their economic standing may be enhanced if family size is limited, increases in status often are allied with decreases in rates of reproduction. Therefore, the relationship between socioeconomic status and fertility levels may vary widely from one country to another, from one group to another or from one period of time to another within the same society, and so on.

Deborah Freedman has carried out one of several studies of the relationship between economic factors and fertility in the United States, the results of which may be summarized briefly.[15] During the period of urban growth and industrial development, higher economic status typically was associated with lower levels of fertility, a fact demonstrated several decades ago by Thompson in his highly competent study of differential fertility in Butler County, Ohio.[16] But recently this differential has decreased and for some groups has even been reversed, essentially for two reasons: (1) knowledge of birth control methods and the incentive to use them as one way of translating rising standards of living (aspirations) into reality no longer are confined to the middle and upper classes; and (2) as the American economy has lost its agricultural character, children have lost their economic utility,[17] which is consistent with the observation made earlier in this chapter that one of the most persistent differentials in fertility levels in the United States is residential.

Turning attention to the association between fertility and the income of husbands, Freedman concludes that a crucial factor in determining the nature of this association is not merely the actual level of income but the manner in which couples *perceive* this level in relation to that of others who follow similar occupations. That is, when income is felt to be comparatively low or normal for the particular job, fertility rates tend to be rather low; when it is perceived as more than adequate for a given occupational niche, birth rates are significantly higher. It appears, however, that middle- and upper-class families are more sensitively attuned to this factor than lower-class families; those at the lowest income levels (under $3,000) are still the least likely to plan family size and are the ones whose rates of reproduction are the highest. In general, fertility rates tend to decrease as income increases until some level is reached at which the persons involved feel that they have the financial ability to care for somewhat larger families. Under these conditions, children may be looked upon as desirable "consumer items." The data in Tables 39 and 40, prepared by the present writers, for 1960 and 1970, respectively, support this set of conclusions, although the relationship is more clear-cut for urban groups than for rural. Furthermore, it is especially noteworthy that in 1970 the slightly higher fertility rates for whites that were found in the income range between $10,000 and $14,999 than in the bracket just below did not occur in the Negro group or among the members of other races. Finally, Freedman suggests that as a larger proportion of the American population comes to perceive their respective incomes as described above, it is likely that fertility differentials by economic status will continue to diminish within each of the residential groups and that the principal distinctions between members of the various classes will be in the pattern of child-spacing rather than in the total number of children born per couple by the end of the childbearing period.[18] This tendency is only one of a large number of other sociocultural changes which are bringing about the greater homogenization of American society.[19]

Data on levels of fertility by occupational status show that in general the people with the higher (more desired, better paid, and more difficult to enter)

TABLE 39

Number of children ever born per 1,000 white mothers in the age groups 35-39
and 40-44, by income of husband in 1959 and residence, the United States, 1960

Income of husband	Number of children ever born per 1,000 mothers			
	Urbanized areas	Other urban	Rural-nonfarm	Rural-farm
Ages 35-39				
All levels	2,773	2,917	3,205	3,501
None	2,793	2,976	3,839	3,733
$1-1,999 or less	3,075	3,451	3,909	3,599
$2,000-2,999	3,018	3,253	3,576	3,522
$3,000-3,999	2,829	3,001	3,272	3,470
$4,000-4,999	2,760	2,864	3,134	3,486
$5,000-6,999	2,724	2,824	3,063	3,451
$7,000-9,999	2,754	2,822	2,975	3,379
$10,000-14,999	2,772	2,874	2,960	3,314
$15,000 and over	2,854	3,078	3,120	3,525
Ages 40-44				
All levels	2,677	2,871	3,243	3,592
None	2,920	3,272	3,836	3,698
$1-1,999 or less	3,011	3,474	4,028	3,682
$2,000-2,999	2,971	3,300	3,575	3,550
$3,000-3,999	2,801	2,964	3,351	3,598
$4,000-4,999	2,672	2,841	3,206	3,636
$5,000-6,999	2,631	2,759	3,066	3,568
$7,000-9,999	2,627	2,732	2,871	3,409
$10,000-14,999	2,638	2,714	2,823	3,444
$15,000 and over	2,672	2,842	2,914	3,367

Source: Compiled from U.S. Bureau of the Census, *U.S. Census of Population: 1960, Subject Reports, Women by Number of Children Ever Born* (1964), pp. 181-186, Table 37.
[18]*Ibid.*, p. 421. See also Ronald Freedman and Lolagene Coombs, "Child-spacing and Family Economic Position," *American Sociological Review*, 31, 5 (October, 1966), pp. 634-639.

occupations or professions have lower rates of reproduction than those lower in the occupational scale, and they also show a marked decrease in the fertility of rural people as one passes up the agricultural ladder from the farm laborers at the bottom to the farm owners at the top. In an early study, Clyde V. Kiser, working with data from the National Health Survey, which was attempted in 1935 and 1936, demonstrated a close relationship between occupation or social class and the rate of reproduction. Specifically, he computed standardized birth rates for women aged fifteen to forty-four, married to native white men, and living in Oakland, Newark, Grand Rapids, St. Paul, and Fall River at the time of

TABLE 40

Number of children ever born per 1,000 women aged 35–44 ever married, by income of husband in 1969 and race, 1970

| Income of husband[a] | Total | Number of children ever born per 1,000 women aged 35–44 ever married | | Other races |
		White	Negro	
All levels	3,145	3,080	3,874	3,183
Less than $2,000	3,589	3,318	4,534	4,127
$2,000 to $2,999	3,785	3,473	4,787	4,135
$3,000 to $3,999	3,739	3,463	4,538	4,007
$4,000 to $4,999	3,491	3,306	4,175	3,695
$5,000 to $6,999	3,213	3,118	3,781	3,336
$7,000 to $9,999	3,057	3,025	3,440	2,999
$10,000 to $14,999	3,038	3,035	3,248	2,832
$15,000 and over	3,020	3,024	2,914	2,774

Source: Compiled and computed from data in U.S. Bureau of the Census, *U.S. Census of Population: 1970, Detailed Characteristics,* Final Report PC(1)-D1, *United States Summary* (1973), pp. 675–676, Table 213.

[a] Includes only husbands present.

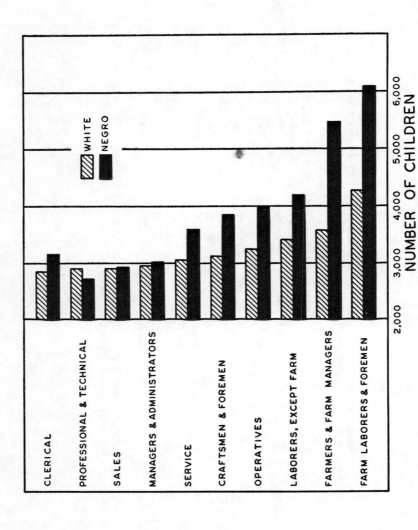

Figure 47. Number of children ever born per 1,000 women aged 35 - 44 ever married, by occupation of husband and race, 1970.

the survey. In these cities the number of live births per 1,000 women varied according to the occupational category of the head of the family as follows: professional, 101; proprietors, 85; clerks-salesmen, 96; skilled workers, 101; semiskilled workers not in manufacturing, 110; semiskilled workers in manufacturing, 122; and unskilled workers, 137.[20] A similar conclusion is drawn from more recent data on rates of reproduction by occupation of husbands, but there now are a few important departures from the general inverse relationship between fertility and job status. In particular, the lowest birth rates among whites appear for those who occupy clerical jobs, white-collar occupations that generally confer status in the lower part of the middle class. (See Figure 47.) Sales workers and professional and technical personnel are virtually tied for the second lowest level of fertility among the whites. The sales workers, too, generally occupy the lower portion of the middle class although the professional workers usually rank far above them in the middle stratum. On the other hand, those who are managers and administrators of businesses other than farms, most of whom attain status in the upper portion of the middle class, have somewhat higher rates of reproduction. In the case of the clerical and sales workers, very low fertility probably reflects the fact that the couples involved construe their occupational statuses and incomes as inadequate relative to their aspirations and are strongly impelled to plan families sufficiently small to minimize the demands on their limited financial resources. Added to this is the fact that relatively high proportions of wives in such couples also work outside the home and may be less available for childbearing than those who do not. In the case of the managers and administrators of nonfarm businesses who in 1969 had higher average levels of income than any other occupational group, the somewhat higher rates of reproduction probably reflect the fact that above a certain level additional improvements in socioeconomic status, as measured by occupation and income, may serve to stimulate increases in the number of children desired and born, provided the income and job status are perceived as relatively high. However, as one looks further at the ranking in Figure 47, he finds that the farmers and the laborers of various kinds have the highest fertility. This is the case for both whites and Negroes, except that in these occupational categories the racial differentials are far greater than they are in the four occupations with the lowest rates of reproduction. The racial difference is the greatest for farmers and farm managers, which testifies to the fact that the group of "farmers" involves great diversity in class standing. The typical Negro farmer, confined almost exclusively to the South, usually is a tenant or an operator of some other modest type which places him close to the bottom of the social scale; whereas the white farmer is much more likely to be one who owns and operates a family-sized farm and who belongs in the middle class.[21]

A few lines from Donald J. Bogue summarize the fertility differentials according to occupation:

White husbands who hold unusually high status positions tend to have above-average fertility. White husbands who hold unusually low status positions tend also to have above-average fertility. Lowest fertility is exhibited among those who do clerical work. Among Negroes, there is a rather consistent inverse relationship between occupational status and fertility.[22]

It is important to keep in mind that most of the studies that show fertility to be higher at the lower-class level than in the middle and upper strata have been made in the most highly urbanized and industrialized areas of the Western world. It does not follow necessarily that the same is true in those areas in which agricultural and pastoral ways of life dominate and in which hoary patriarchal patterns of family organization continue to function. As a matter of fact, and with much reason, Sorokin and Zimmerman, in explaining why vertical social mobility is so much greater in urban society than in rural, listed as one of the principal reasons differences in the differential fertility of the upper and lower classes in the two residential groups. On the basis of a considerable amount of evidence, they concluded that among city populations "the differential fertility of the upper and lower classes is far greater than in rural populations."[23]

Although quantitative data of the kind they would like to have are lacking, the present writers have become thoroughly convinced, through some thirty-five years of personal observation and study by the senior author, that in Brazil, Colombia, and most other Latin American countries the fertility of the upper classes is fully as great as that of the lower social and economic strata. In fact, they have come to believe that the very high rates of reproduction of the upper classes in Latin America have had much to do with shaping and maintaining some of the more distinctive psycho-social traits of the population in these parts of the world.[24] Similarly, a comprehensive study made in Poland shows rather definitely that the size of the farm family is positively correlated with the size of the farm and this factor is then used to help explain the rapidity with which inheritance is decreasing the size of agricultural holdings.[25]

OTHER DIFFERENTIALS

Undoubtedly, there are many other differentials in fertility between various groups of mankind, such as those between ethnic groups and religious groups that were mentioned above. Unfortunately, very few studies have been made, with residential and other variables sufficiently controlled, that would enable one to judge the nature and magnitude of such differences. Unfortunately, too, the complete lack of comprehensive data on the religious affiliations of the population of the United States makes practically impossible what otherwise would be the fairly easy task of disentangling possible differences in the rates of reproduction of the various religious elements in the population from those more properly attributed to rural-urban, racial, or other influences. A few data collected by the Bureau of the Census in 1957 as part of the *Current Population Survey* support the general impression that Jews have the lowest birth rates of any of the major religious groups, Protestants next lowest, and Roman Catholics the highest. Thus, the number of children ever born per 1,000 women aged fifteen to forty-four ever married, by religious affiliation, was as follows: Jewish, 1,749; Protestant, 2,220; and Roman Catholic, 2,284. Among the major Protestant groups, the numbers of children were as follows: Presbyterian, 2,001; Lutheran, 2,013; Methodist, 2,155; Baptist, 2,359; and other Protestant, 2,237.[26] These data are undifferentiated by race, residence, or any other characteristic except the general age range of the women involved. Therefore, they provide only the most fragmentary evidence of birth rate differentials by religious affiliation. Nevertheless, the impression which they give seems to be supported by the few studies of this matter done with sufficient care and skill to be significant.

The study of fertility in Indianapolis, conducted among 41,498 native-white married couples, indicated that when economic status, as measured by the amount of rent paid per month or its equivalent, was held constant, the couples in which both the man and the wife were Roman Catholics definitely produced more children than those in which both were Protestants, and those in which one of the mates was Catholic and the other Protestant had the lowest birth rates of all.[27] Likewise, a detailed study of the rate of reproduction in Louisiana showed very clearly that "the residents of the French, Catholic portion of Louisiana are characterized by much higher rates of reproduction than those of the Anglo-Saxon, Protestant portion. This is true for both racial groups in all of the residential classifications."[28] An investigation by Ronald Freedman and others, employing careful controls for several social and economic variables (occupation of husband, education of wife, income of husband, duration of marriage, metropolitan character of residence, and farm background), reiterated the fact that Jews have the lowest rates of reproduction and Roman Catholics the highest, with Protestants falling in an intermediate position.[29] However, the study also showed that differences in socioeconomic status account for most of the fertility differentials between Protestants and Jews but for little if any of the variation between Catholics and members of the other two groups.[30] Furthermore, Protestants and Jews were found to express very similar attitudes toward the use of birth control methods, whereas Catholics either expressed disapproval or qualified their approval in a relatively high proportion of cases. Yet, as significant as are the fertility differentials between Catholics on the one hand and Jews and Protestants on the other, the fact remains that Catholics, along with members of the other two religions, tend to favor families which are moderate in size (two to four children) over those which are much larger.[31] Therefore, the fertility variations between the three groups generally occur within these rather narrow limits, and while the latter may change, it is unlikely that they would do so very drastically or very differently among members of the three religious groups.

Finally, the data for the various states presented above underscore the conclusion of Hastings, Reynolds, and Canning that the birth rate of the Mormons is substantially higher than those of the Catholics and other major religious groups in the United States.[32] The point to stress, however, is the extent to which we lack adequate census data on the differences between the birth rates of the principal religious segments of the population.

NOTES

1. See the data and literature cited in T. Lynn Smith, *Population Analysis* (New York: McGraw-Hill Book Company, 1948), pp. 209 - 211; and T. Lynn Smith and Paul E. Zopf, Jr., *Principles of Inductive Rural Sociology* (Philadelphia: F. A. Davis Company, 1970), pp. 61 - 65.

2. The most comprehensive summaries of the facts and indications of the relevant literature on the subject are contained in P. A. Sorokin and Carle C. Zimmerman, *Principles of Rural-Urban Sociology* (New York: Henry Holt and Company, 1929), pp. 205 - 220; and P. A. Sorokin, Carle C. Zimmerman, and Charles J. Galpin, *A Systematic Source Book in Rural Sociology* (Minneapolis: University of Minnesota Press, 1932), III, 135 - 225.

3. See T. Lynn Smith, "The Reproduction Rate in Latin America: Levels, Differentials and Trends," *Population Studies*, XII, 2 (July, 1958), pp. 4 - 17; and *Latin American Population Studies* (Gainesville: University of Florida Press, 1960), pp. 42 - 45.

4. See the discussion of this matter in Dale E. Hathaway, J. Allan Beegle, and W. Keith Bryant, *People of Rural America* (A 1960 Census Monograph, Washington: Government Printing Office, 1968), pp. 86 - 95. Cf. J. Allan Beegle, "Social Structure and Changing Fertility of the Farm Population," *Rural Sociology*, 31, 4 (December, 1966), pp. 415 - 427.

5. "Discussion." In *Caribbean Studies: A Symposium*, edited by Vera Rubin (Jamaica, B.W.I.: Institute of Social and Economic Research, 1957), p. 62.

6. See Smith, *Population Analysis, op. cit.*, pp. 212 - 216; and Paul E. Zopf, Jr., *North Carolina: A Demographic Profile* (Chapel Hill: University of North Carolina Population Center, 1967), pp. 279 - 281 and 291 - 293.

7. See T. Lynn Smith, *Brazil: People and Institutions* (4th ed.), (Baton Rouge: Louisiana State University Press, 1972), pp. 101 - 106; John Van Dyke Saunders, *Differential Fertility in Brazil* (Gainesville: University of Florida Press, 1958), pp. 58 - 62; and Giorgio Mortara, "The Brazilian Birth Rate: Its Economic and Social Factors," in *Culture and Human Fertility*, by Frank Lorimer, and others (Paris: UNESCO, 1954), p. 497, *passim.*

8. See Smith, *Latin American Population Studies, op. cit.*, pp. 48 - 51.

9. For a discussion of Mormon birth norms, see Donald W. Hastings, Charles H. Reynolds, and Ray R. Canning, "Mormonism and Birth Planning: The Discrepancy between Church Authorities' Teachings and Lay Attitudes," *Population Studies*, 26, 1 (March, 1972), pp. 19 - 28.

10. See Donald J. Bogue, *Principles of Demography* (New York: John Wiley & Sons, Inc., 1969), pp. 693 - 696; and Robert M. Dinkel, "Education and Fertility in the United States," in *Population and Society,* edited by Charles B. Nam (Boston: Houghton Mifflin Company, 1968), pp. 517 - 519.

11. Dinkel, *op. cit.,* pp. 518 - 519.

12. See Bogue, *op. cit.,* p. 696.

13. For a statement of these two views and an effort to reconcile them, see David M. Heer, "Economic Development and Fertility," *Demography,* 3, 2 (1966), pp. 423 - 444.

14. *Ibid.,* pp. 439 - 440.

15. Deborah Freedman, "The Relation of Economic Status to Fertility," *American Economic Review,* LIII, 3 (June, 1963), pp. 414 - 426.

16. Warren S. Thompson, *Average Number of Children per Woman in Butler County, Ohio, 1930 − A Study in Differential Fertility* (Washington: U. S. Bureau of the Census, 1941), p. 9.

17. Freedman, *op. cit.,* p. 415.

18. *Ibid.,* p. 421. See also Ronald Freedman and Lolagene Coombs, "Child-spacing and Family Economic Position." *American Sociological Review,* 31, 5 (October, 1966), pp. 634 - 639.

19. On this point, see T. Lynn Smith, "The Homogenization of Society in the United States," *Memoire du XIX Congress International de Sociologie,* II (Mexico, 1960), pp. 245 - 275.

20. Clyde V. Kiser, "Variations in Birth Rates According to Occupational Status," *Milbank Memorial Fund Quarterly,* 16 (1938), p. 46.

21. See Smith and Zopf, *op. cit.,* chapter 11.

22. Bogue, *op. cit.,* p. 720. See also C. Shannon Stokes, "Family Structure and Socio-economic Differentials in Fertility," *Population Studies,* 27, 2 (July, 1973), pp. 295 - 304.

23. Sorokin and Zimmerman, *op cit.,* p. 43. Cf. Pitirim A. Sorokin, *Social Mobility* (New York: Harper and Brothers, 1927), *passim.*

24. See T. Lynn Smith, "Values Held by People in Latin America which Affect Technical Cooperation," *Rural Sociology,* 21, 1 (March, 1956), pp. 72 - 74.

25. W. Stys, "The Influence of Economic Conditions on the Fertility of Peasant Women," *Population Studies,* XI, 2 (July, 1957), pp. 136 - 148.

26. U. S. Bureau of the Census, *Statistical Abstract of the United States: 1963* (Washington: Government Printing Office, 1963), p. 57, Table 58.

27. Pascal K. Whelpton and Clyde V. Kiser, "Social and Psychological Factors Affecting Fertility; I. Differential Fertility Among 41,498 Native-White Couples in Indianapolis," *Milbank Memorial Fund Quarterly,* 21 (1946), p. 238.

28. J. Allan Beegle and T. Lynn Smith, *Differential Fertility in Louisiana,* Louisiana AES Bulletin No. 403 (Baton Rouge: Louisiana State University, 1946), p. 27.

29. Ronald Freedman, Pascal K. Whelpton, and John W. Smit, "Socio-Economic Factors in Religious Differentials in Fertility," *American Sociological Review*, 26, 4 (August, 1961), pp. 608 - 614. Cf. Ronald Freedman, Pascal K. Whelpton, and Arthur A. Campbell, *Family Planning, Sterility, and Population Growth* (New York: McGraw-Hill Book Company, Inc., 1959).

30. Freedman, Whelpton, and Smit, *op. cit.,* p. 610.

31. *Ibid.,* p. 614.

32. Hastings, Reynolds, and Canning, *op. cit.,* p. 28.

BEEGLE, J. ALLAN. "Social Structure and Changing Fertility of the Farm Population." *Rural Sociology*, Vol. 31, No. 4 (December, 1966), pp. 415 - 427.

BOGUE, DONALD J. *Principles of Demography*, pp. 690 - 751. New York: John Wiley & Sons, Inc., 1969.

DINKEL, ROBERT M. "Education and Fertility in the United States," in *Population and Society*, edited by Charles B. Nam, pp. 517 - 520. Boston: Houghton Mifflin Company, 1968.

DRIVER, EDWIN D. *Differential Fertility in Central India.* Princeton: Princeton University Press, 1963.

DUNCAN, OTIS DUDLEY. "Farm Background and Differential Fertility." *Demography*, Vol. 2, No. 1 (1965), pp. 240 - 249.

FREEDMAN, DEBORAH. "The Relation of Economic Status to Fertility." *American Economic Review*, Vol. LIII, No. 3 (June, 1963), pp. 414 - 426.

FREEDMAN, RONALD, PASCAL K. WHELPTON, and JOHN W. SMIT. "Socioeconomic Factors in Religious Differentials in Fertility." *American Sociological Review*, Vol. 26, No. 4 (August, 1961), pp. 608 - 614.

GRABILL, WILSON H., CLYDE V. KISER, and PASCAL K. WHELPTON. *The Fertility of American Women*, Chaps. 4 - 7. New York: John Wiley & Sons, Inc., 1958.

HATHAWAY, DALE E., J. ALLAN BEEGLE, and W. KEITH BRYANT. *People of Rural America* (A 1960 Census Monograph), Chaps. IV, V, and VI. Washington: Government Printing Office, 1968.

KISER, CLYDE V. "Social, Economic and Religious Factors in the Differential Fertility of Low Income Countries." *Proceedings of the World Population Conference, 1965*, Vol. II (1967), pp. 219 - 222.

KISER, CLYDE V., and PASCAL K. WHELPTON. "Social and Psychological Factors Affecting Fertility." *Milbank Memorial Fund Quarterly*, Vol. 36, No. 3 (July, 1958), pp. 282 - 319.

PETERSEN, WILLIAM. *Population*, 2nd ed., Chap. 9. New York: The Macmillan Company, 1969.

SAUNDERS, JOHN V. D. *Differential Fertility in Brazil.* Gainesville: University of Florida Press, 1958.

SMITH, T. LYNN. "The Reproduction Rate in Latin America: Levels, Differentials and Trends." *Population Studies*, Vol. XII, No. 2 (July, 1958), pp. 4 - 17.

SMITH, T. LYNN, and HOMER L. HITT. *The People of Louisiana*, pp. 142 - 161. Baton Rouge: Louisiana State University Press, 1952.

SPENGLER, JOSEPH J. "Values and Fertility Analysis." *Demography*, Vol. 3, No. 1 (1966), pp. 109 - 130.

TAEUBER, CONRAD, and IRENE B. TAEUBER. *The People of the United States in the 20th Century* (A 1960 Census Monograph), Chap. IX. Washington: Government Printing Office, 1971.

TAEUBER, IRENE B. "Demographic Transitions and Population Problems in the United States." *Annals of the American Academy of Political and Social Sciences*, Vol. 369 (January, 1967), pp. 131 - 140.

THOMPSON, WARREN S., and DAVID T. LEWIS. *Population Problems*, 5th ed., Chaps. 10 and 11. New York: McGraw-Hill Book Company, 1965.

$$14$$

FERTILITY TRENDS

Four specific fertility trends weigh heavily in the thinking of most contemporary students of population. The first is the rapid and sustained fall in the birth rate that took place in many Western countries during the century which started about 1830 and ended during the great world economic depression. The second is really not a trend at all, but rather the absence of one. This is the tendency observed in recent decades throughout much of the world, and especially in the more densely populated parts of it, for the birth rate to remain at a high level, at the same time that the death rate was falling sharply. The third is the fairly substantial increase that took place in the birth rate of the United States and Canada during the period 1935 to 1957. The fourth is the substantial decline of the birth rate in the United States in the late 1950's, all of the 1960's, and well into the 1970's. As demographic knowledge increases, other equally significant trends in the birth rate may be observed and described, but for the present a discussion of these four will suffice.

THE LONG-CONTINUED FALL IN THE BIRTH RATE
IN SELECTED COUNTRIES

Throughout most of the nineteenth century and the first three decades of the twentieth century, the falling birth rate throughout large parts of Western civilization was among the most important social and economic determinants in world affairs. France frequently is credited with being the original center from which the phenomenon of the falling birth rate spread to other countries. This may or may not actually be the case. There can be no doubt, however, that France was the first to develop a set of birth statistics that was sufficiently

accurate for analysis to reveal what was going on in this important part of
Europe during the opening half of the nineteenth century. (See Figure 48.)
Either the data for other European countries were not sufficiently accurate or
the fall in the birth rate began later in them, for, with the exception of Sweden,
the curves for the other countries included in this chart did not start to fall
until after 1870. In interpreting these materials, one should make liberal allowance for improvements in the registration of births. This means that probably

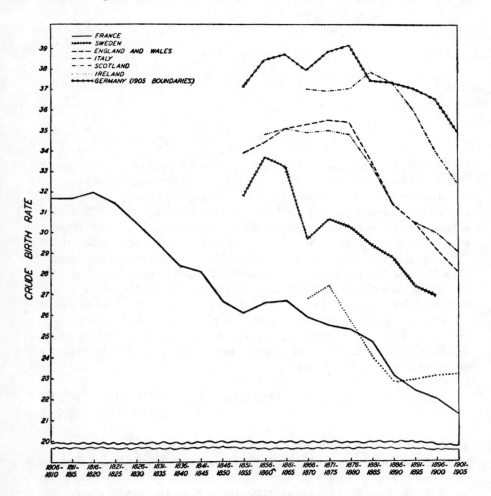

FIGURE 48. The trend of the crude birth rate in selected European countries
during the nineteenth century. Based on data in *Statistique Internationale du
Mouvement de la Population.* Paris: Imprimerie Nationale, 1907.

the declines in the various countries actually began earlier and were more rapid than would appear from this chart. Although they are extremely fragmentary, these materials do indicate that the decline in the birth rate got well underway in many of the Western countries before the end of the nineteenth century.

For the present century the data are, of course, much more abundant and far more reliable. Nevertheless, the materials for the years prior to 1945, and especially those for the period 1900 to 1930, leave a great deal to be desired. From the information presented in Figure 49, however, one may gain a fair idea of the trends in the birth rate in selected important countries, for which the statistics are most reliable, between 1900 and 1940. It is important to note that the first one-third of the twentieth century was characterized by a precipitous decline in the rate of reproduction in all of the larger European countries, in the United States, and in Japan; and also that this particular trend ended and the birth rate began to rise in most of the countries between 1930 and 1940. The

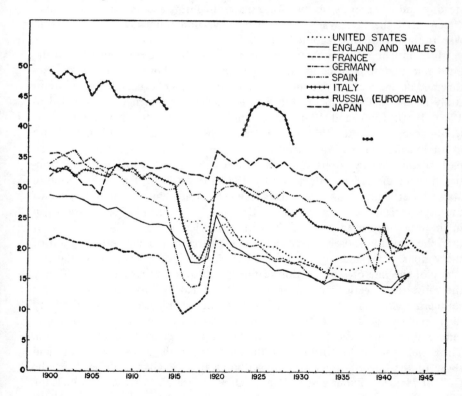

FIGURE 49. Variations in the reported crude birth rates of selected countries during the first part of the twentieth century.

effects of the First World War and the Spanish Civil War upon the birth rate are so clearly revealed by Figure 49, however, that it should be studied in that connection as well.

Since comprehensive birth statistics for the United States go back only to 1915, our own country is not included in Figure 48; and it also is represented for only a part of the period included in Figure 49. By means of the fertility ratio, however, it is possible to demonstrate that the rate of reproduction in the United States fell rapidly throughout the entire nineteenth century (see Figure 50); and from the curve showing the birth rate adjusted for underregistration of births (Figure 51) one may obtain a fairly accurate idea of the extent of the decrease in the fertility of the population between 1909 and 1936. The materials on fertility ratios presented in Figure 50 and the birth data charted in Figure 51 indicate that the birth rate in the United States during the opening decade of the nineteenth century probably was above 50, from which it fell steadily and persistently, except for a sharp dip during and an abrupt rise immediately after the Civil War[1] and a slighter gyration following the First World War, to the low of 18.4 recorded for 1933 and also for 1936.

Much insight into the factors responsible for the long-continued fall in the birth rate that took place in the United States throughout the nineteenth century and during the first one-third of the twentieth may be gained from a careful study of the materials mapped in Figure 52. The analysis may be extended to 1940, 1950, 1960, and 1970 by examining those presented in Table 41. It would seem that in the first few decades of the existence of the United States as an independent nation, fertility was rather uniformly high, throughout all parts of the country. Apparently, though, it was somewhat higher on the frontier than in the older settlements. By 1840 the fertility of the population in Massachusetts and Connecticut had declined considerably and that in some of the other original states perceptibly. Obviously, the declining birth rate began in the most urbanized parts of the nation, and just as obviously the spread of this phenomenon closely paralleled the industrialization and urbanization of the various states and regions. Successively in the decades after 1840, the tendency of the rate of reproduction to fall spread over the nation. By 1930 only the most rural sections of the nation (in the Rocky Mountain area, in the southern region, and in the Dakotas) retained any semblance of their earlier very high fertility ratios. By 1940 the few areas in which the rate of reproduction remained at a high level stood out like the scattered peaks on an old peneplain. These were the rural settlements of the Mormons in the Rocky Mountains and those of the Spanish-Americans spread along the Rio Grande Valley from the Gulf of Mexico to southern Colorado. Other scattered localities in which the birth rate had not fallen to any great extent by 1940 were found in Montana, the Dakotas, and northern Michigan. More important, because of the much larger populations involved, are the high fertility ratios that still prevailed in the

TABLE 41

Number of children under five per 100 women aged 15-44, for states,
by color, 1940 to 1970

State	Number of children under 5 per 100 women 15-44							
	White				Nonwhite			
	1940	1950	1960	1970	1940	1950	1960	1970
United States	32.4	46.7	54.6	39.2	37.7	52.1	69.2	48.2
New England								
Maine	37.6	51.5	58.9	43.1	57.9	66.2	81.4	53.6
New Hampshire	32.2	48.0	57.1	43.8	....	....	79.9	49.9
Vermont	38.9	53.1	59.6	43.6	....	....	....	46.0
Massachusetts	26.8	42.5	53.8	39.9	29.9	44.5	63.6	49.0
Rhode Island	26.1	42.3	52.4	40.4	40.1	52.4	77.1	50.4
Connecticut	25.4	41.8	53.3	39.6	30.1	44.1	67.1	52.1
Middle Atlantic								
New York	24.4	39.6	49.2	38.1	20.3	33.5	50.3	42.8
New Jersey	23.9	40.5	50.5	38.7	28.5	40.4	60.4	48.6
Pennsylvania	30.0	42.0	50.8	38.2	28.5	41.4	59.3	44.6
East North Central								
Ohio	30.7	47.5	56.9	40.6	28.3	42.5	66.2	44.5
Indiana	33.9	48.8	57.2	41.3	27.6	44.0	72.3	48.2
Illinois	28.0	42.8	54.4	39.5	25.1	39.8	68.9	47.2
Michigan	34.7	49.0	60.5	42.1	28.0	43.8	66.8	49.4
Wisconsin	35.1	50.6	62.2	42.5	47.3	55.9	84.0	56.3
West North Central								
Minnesota	35.1	52.6	64.4	42.4	54.7	65.6	79.4	58.1
Iowa	36.1	51.4	59.6	41.8	35.3	52.0	69.6	53.2
Missouri	31.3	44.5	54.5	38.2	27.5	41.7	73.0	47.9
North Dakota	42.6	58.5	67.7	42.1	78.6	89.1	105.5	71.1
South Dakota	39.1	56.6	66.2	40.6	70.5	75.5	85.3	74.7
Nebraska	34.5	50.0	60.3	40.2	32.6	51.9	81.1	51.5
Kansas	33.6	49.3	58.4	38.1	29.6	47.4	74.6	50.2
South Atlantic								
Delaware	29.8	44.6	57.4	39.1	31.9	47.2	73.4	52.0
Maryland	29.8	46.2	53.7	39.0	34.0	48.9	67.4	46.2
District of Columbia	19.3	30.4	29.7	15.4	24.9	36.8	57.7	39.0
Virginia	21.1	48.4	51.6	37.0	40.7	53.1	68.0	46.4
West Virginia	44.2	53.3	51.9	38.8	35.4	51.0	65.7	43.6
North Carolina	40.6	49.1	48.9	36.7	45.8	61.4	72.3	48.6
South Carolina	39.7	50.3	50.8	37.8	51.1	67.8	77.1	52.8
Georgia	38.4	49.8	51.7	38.9	41.8	58.3	72.4	51.1
Florida	32.0	44.5	51.2	35.1	30.2	48.1	74.7	51.7

TABLE 41 (Cont'd)

Number of children under five per 100 women aged 15–44, for states,
by color, 1940 to 1970

| | Number of children under 5 per 100 women 15-44 | | | | | | | |
| | White | | | | Nonwhite | | | |
State	1940	1950	1960	1970	1940	1950	1960	1970
East South Central								
Kentucky	44.9	55.1	56.7	40.5	29.8	45.1	70.1	47.2
Tennessee	40.1	49.5	49.5	36.7	32.1	50.1	72.9	48.9
Alabama	41.8	50.4	51.5	38.0	43.7	60.8	75.9	51.9
Mississippi	41.1	50.3	52.6	38.4	47.2	70.0	89.1	62.3
West North Central								
Arkansas	43.0	52.9	50.6	38.1	41.2	64.7	87.9	59.0
Louisiana	36.7	50.2	57.8	41.5	41.8	62.5	78.3	54.8
Oklahoma	39.1	48.1	51.4	36.2	40.1	58.9	76.9	51.0
Texas	36.1	50.7	57.9	40.5	33.7	50.2	71.1	50.2
Mountain								
Montana	38.2	54.8	64.0	40.1	72.2	88.3	99.1	63.7
Idaho	44.4	57.9	64.0	44.4	50.9	72.5	84.0	56.8
Wyoming	39.1	54.6	61.9	41.3	66.1	68.0	90.7	53.9
Colorado	37.2	50.5	58.5	38.1	30.3	46.5	68.3	45.3
New Mexico	50.5	61.3	67.9	42.4	69.1	72.1	86.6	61.0
Arizona	42.5	52.2	59.9	41.1	65.1	72.3	93.4	61.1
Utah	45.9	61.4	70.2	48.6	52.5	62.5	78.1	51.6
Nevada	35.8	46.0	53.1	40.0	54.9	56.4	79.4	56.1
Pacific								
Washington	30.5	51.2	56.2	39.1	36.8	60.1	74.3	46.2
Oregon	30.2	49.5	54.1	37.7	36.5	53.7	71.7	43.6
California	27.4	45.5	53.5	37.7	28.9	46.4	63.6	43.1
Alaska	32.8	52.6	70.4	45.2	77.5	84.5	97.3	63.9
Hawaii	30.7	48.7	61.2	42.9	50.4	59.4	59.9	40.5

Source: Compiled and computed from data in U.S. Bureau of the Census, *U.S. Census of Population: 1970, General Population Characteristics,* Final Report PC(1)-B1, *United States Summary* (1972), pp. 276-277, Talbe 53; Final Report PC(1)-B2-B52, reports for states (1971 and 1972), Table 21.

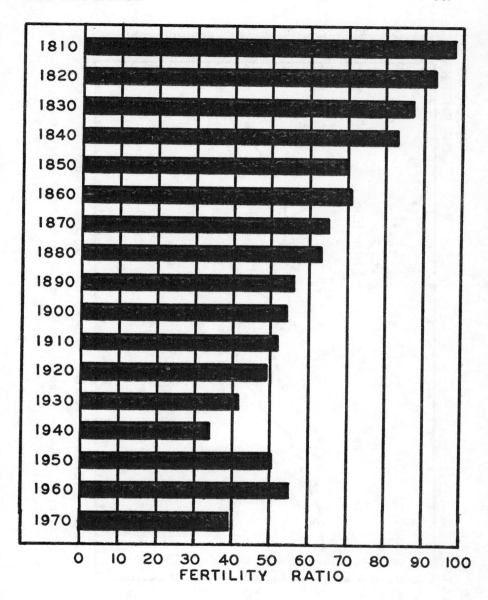

Figure 50. Trends in the number of children under five per 100 women aged 16 - 44 in the United States, 1810 to 1970.

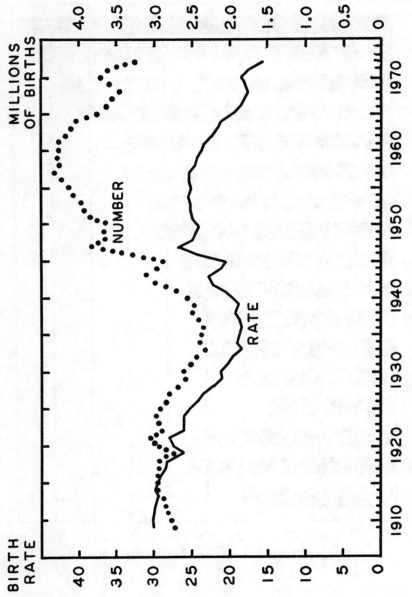

Figure 51. Variations in the crude birth rate and the number of births in the United States, 1909 to 1972. Includes the adjustments for states not in the birth-registration area prior to 1933 and for underegistration until 1959.

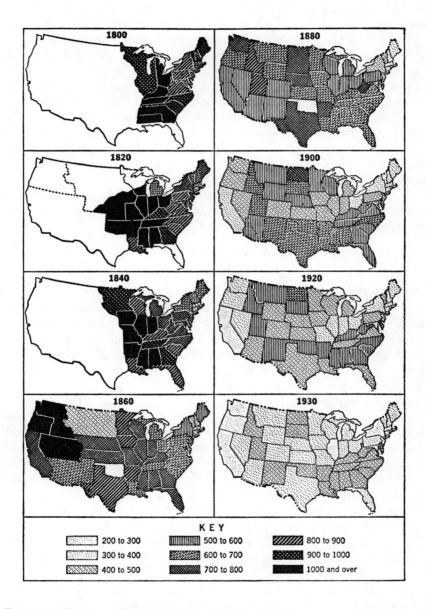

Figure 52. Number of children under five per 1,000 women aged 15 - 49 in the United States, 1800 to 1930. After O. E. Baker. "The Effect of Recent Public Policies on the Future Population Prospect." *Rural Sociology,* 2, 2 (June, 1937), p. 124.

Southern Appalachians, portions of the Ozarks, the hills of southeastern Oklahoma, in some areas along the South Atlantic Coast, and among the French-
speaking people of south Louisiana. The only factor common to all the sections
with high fertility ratios in 1940 is their geographical and cultural isolation. It
therefore is evident that the falling birth rate in the United States was first a
function of the developing urban and industrial way of life, that as these aspects
of our civilization gained in size and momentum they exerted a depressing effect
upon the rate of reproduction throughout the nation, and that by 1940 only in
areas most removed from such urban influences had the fertility ratio maintained its previously high level. Following 1936, however, as will be indicated
below, the tendency for increasing urbanization and decreasing fertility of the
population to accompany one another came to an end, at least temporarily. The
former proceeded at a pace rarely equalled in the United States or any other part
of the world, and the latter ceased its downward course and moved sharply upward. Furthermore, the increase in the birth rate was more rapid in the urban
areas than it was in the rural.

THE PERSISTENCE OF HIGH BIRTH RATES
IN UNDERDEVELOPED COUNTRIES

Since the close of World War II, population control by means of family planning has become a major concern of scientists in many fields, political and religious leaders, and whole societies. In fact, most population experts have devoted
large segments of their time to various aspects of this topic, and agencies such as
the Population Reference Bureau and the Population Council have concentrated
almost exclusively on this matter. The literature on the subject is voluminous
and ranges from the neo-Malthusian position at one extreme which forecasts
"standing room only" and even cannibalism, to the Marxist stance at the other
which acknowledges no problem of overpopulation but only one of under-
employment. In the view of the present writers, the matter requires both a
serious concern evoked by the present size of many populations and their rapid
growth rates, and a rational perspective generated by the fact that these rates
cannot be extrapolated indefinitely into the future with any degree of accuracy.

As a recent milestone in the worldwide concern over rapid population growth,
the heads of thirty nations, including Australia, Colombia, India, Japan, Pakistan,
the United Arab Republic, the United Kingdom, and the United States, prepared
a statement on the matter for presentation at the United Nations in December,
1967. It expresses the situation clearly and in a reasoned manner, as follows:

> The peace of the world is of paramount importance to the community of nations,
> and our governments are devoting their best efforts to improving the prospects for
> peace in this and succeeding generations. But another great problem threatens the
> world—a problem less visible but no less immediate. That is the problem of unplanned
> population growth.

It took mankind all of recorded time until the middle of the last century to achieve a population of one billion. Yet it took less than a hundred years to add the second billion, and only thirty years to add the third. At today's rate of increase, there will be four billion people by 1975 and nearly seven billion by the year 2000. This unprecedented increase presents us with a situation unique in human affairs and a problem that grows more urgent with each passing day.

The numbers themselves are striking, but their implications are of far greater significance. Too rapid population growth seriously hampers efforts to raise living standards, to further education, to improve health and sanitation, to provide better housing and transportation, to forward cultural and recreational opportunities—and even in some countries to assure sufficient food. In short, the human aspiration, common to men everywhere, to live a better life is being frustrated and jeopardized.

As heads of governments actively concerned with the population problem, we share these convictions:

We believe that the population problem must be recognized as a principal element in long-range national planning if governments are to achieve their economic goals and fulfill the aspirations of their people.

We believe that the great majority of parents desire to have the knowledge and the means to plan their families; that the opportunity to decide the number and spacing of children is a basic human right.

We believe that lasting and meaningful peace will depend to a considerable measure upon how the challenge of population growth is met.

We believe that the objective of family planning is the enrichment of human life, not its restriction; that family planning, by assuring greater opportunity to each person, frees man to attain his individual dignity and reach his full potential.

Recognizing that family planning is in the vital interest of both the nation and the family, we, the undersigned, earnestly hope that leaders around the world will share our views and join with us in this great challenge for the well being and happiness of people everywhere.[2]

In comparison with most other analysis in these pages, any reasoning about the trend in the birth rate in most of the underdeveloped areas of the world must rest upon fragmentary and highly unreliable data. Probably the soundest procedure of all is to note in Table 29 the high rates of reproduction that currently prevail in most parts of Asia for which data are available, in Africa, and in the Latin American countries; and then to reason that these levels are still so high that no substantial reductions could have taken place during the preceding twenty-five years.

For two extensive parts of the so-called underdeveloped portion of the world, however, enough data have been assembled and enough critical study of the rates of reproduction has been done to permit a direct approach to the matter under consideration. One of these is that dealt with by Kingsley Davis in his fundamental demographic analysis of the "teeming millions" of India and Pakistan.[3] Unlike most of those who have used the data on fertility for various parts of the world, Davis was not content to pass along official statistics at their face value. Instead he attempted to determine as nearly as possible the actual rate of reproduction in the subcontinent once called India and now divided into the large and densely populated independent nations of India, Pakistan, and Bangladesh. In this work, he had as precedent the substantial work of Mr. G. F. Hardy, an actuary who was employed by the Indian Census to make life tables for the period 1891 - 1911. Hardy had made estimates of the birth rates of the various provinces for the decades 1881 - 1891, 1891 - 1901, and 1901 - 1911, and these estimates were all very much above the reported birth rates for the last of these decades. Hardy's computations gave no basis whatsoever for concluding that the birth rate in India was declining, but rather indicated that it continued at a level of about 50 throughout the thirty years studied.[4] Davis himself calculated the numbers of births during each decade from data on the numbers of children under ten reported at each census and the appropriate values from the life tables. For the four decades 1901 to 1941 his estimates of the actual birth rates, followed in each case by the officially reported rate, are as follows: 1901 - 1911, 48 and 37; 1911 - 1921, 49 and 37; 1921 - 1931, 46 and 33; and 1931 - 1941, 45 and 34. As a result of his studies Davis concluded that since 1921 the crude birth rate in India had fallen slightly; but he summarized the general situation as one of continued high fertility, "somewhat lowered mortality, and a growing rate of natural increase which is adding huge increments to India's population."[5]

Another comprehensive study of the levels and trends of fertility in the so-called underdeveloped areas is Smith's work on the rate of reproduction in Latin America. Working first with Brazilian data, he attempted to go beyond the published rates and to determine the extent to which the official statistics reflected the birth rates actually prevailing. By analyzing materials on baptisms by the Roman Catholic church and other fragments of data, he concluded that in 1940 the birth rate in Brazil at the time of the Second World War was about 40, and not 12, as reported in the official publications, and that in 1970 it was also about 40.[6] In the meantime, efforts were extended to include the other Latin American countries, beginning with El Salvador, where he found that the birth rate must be about 45.[7] In 1953, he published the preliminary results of his attempts to determine the levels of the rate of reproduction throughout Latin America.[8] More recently the present writers have determined the changes in the fertility ratios in the various countries which have taken two or more censuses, thus making possible a study of the changes taking place in the rate of reproduction.[9] These data are presented in Table 42.

A study of these materials, along with those for some of the other countries for which data on current levels are available (see Table 34) makes it evident that the rate of reproduction remains high throughout most of Latin America. In the 1960's, in most of the countries, the birth rate was still at levels comparable to those prevailing in the United States and Canada at the beginning of the nineteenth century. Only in Argentina and Cuba are there rather definite indications that the fertility of the population is decreasing. In and of themselves the indexes for most of the countries are high enough to indicate that little or no decrease could have taken place during recent decades. Furthermore, for fifteen of the seventeen countries for which successive censuses make possible a determination of trends, the fertility ratio for the most recent year is higher than the one at the time of the preceding census. One should hardly assert on the basis of this evidence that the birth rate is rising in these countries (improvement in census procedures is probably the more likely cause of the observed changes), but it does lend strong support to the proposition that it is not falling significantly. Furthermore, there is little reason for supposing that the present high levels will not continue in most parts of Latin America for a time. In the meantime, as indicated in Chapter 17, since 1900 the death rate in most of these countries has been reduced substantially. Therefore, it is not surprising that currently the Latin American area is the major division of the earth's surface in which the growth of population is most rapid. (Between 1900 and 1970, according to the computations of the present writers, the proportion of the world's population made up of the inhabitants of the independent Latin American republics rose from 2.7 per cent to 7.8 per cent.)

Although the results, in terms of population increase, of the continued high level of fertility combined with sharply reduced mortality in India and Pakistan, on the one hand, and the Latin American countries, on the other, are similar, the implications of such changes in these two important parts of the world are considerably different. India and Pakistan are already among the most densely populated parts of the earth's surface. They are areas in which the man-land ratio already is at or beyond the point at which mankind's present knowledge of resources and command over the ways of utilizing them permit a satisfactory level of production per person. In sharp contrast, throughout Latin America there are still immense areas devoid of inhabitants, sections capable of furnishing an abundant livelihood to many additional persons provided large-scale organized human effort is devoted to the wise use of these important sections of the earth's surface. All that this means in practical terms, however, is that the Latin Americans simply have a bit more time than India and Pakistan and other densely settled areas in which to devise effective ways of fertility limitation and a better distribution of the population before they, too, are beset by the consequences of excessively large numbers of people.

Serious efforts to decrease fertility actually are taking place in some of the underdeveloped areas. Moreover, the sharp reductions in the birth rate in Japan since 1949 and the decreases which have come about in Eastern and Southern Europe indicate the speed with which such changes can occur despite traditional value systems and other sociocultural factors which once were believed to be nearly insurmountable obstacles to effective family planning. Furthermore, as the mere existence of the statement on population by the world leaders implies, many societies now have begun to make the extremely difficult change from a world view shaped by high death rates and the problems associated with exces-

TABLE 42

Number of children under five per 100 women aged 15-44 in the Latin American countries at various census dates

Country	Date	Fertility ratio
Costa Rica	1892	68.3
	1927	68.8
	1950	73.9
	1963	94.8
Cuba	1931	62.2
	1943	57.4
	1953	55.3
Dominican Republic	1935	78.2
	1950	79.8
	1960	90.0
El Salvador	1930	66.8
	1950	67.4
	1961	80.3
Guatemala	1940	72.2
	1950	75.2
	1964	84.1
Haiti	1950	49.7
	1967	64.7
	1970	64.9[a]
Honduras	1935	56.6
	1945	71.2
	1950	72.7
	1961	92.5
Mexico	1930	62.1
	1940	63.0
	1950	68.4
	1960	78.7
Nicaragua	1940	71.9
	1950	70.2
	1963	88.9
Panama	1940	64.4
	1950	75.4
	1960	81.7
Argentina	1914	67.2
	1947	46.8
	1960	47.1
Bolivia	1950	68.5
Brazil	1920	66.8[b]
	1940	68.9
	1950	70.5
	1960	72.4

TABLE 42 (Cont'd)

Number of children under five per 100 women aged 15-44 in the Latin American countries at various census dates

Country	Date	Fertility ratio
Chile	1940	52.3
	1952	56.7
	1960	68.3
Colombia	1938	67.6
	1964	84.3
Ecuador	1950	76.5
	1962	81.9
Paraguay	1950	75.2
	1962	84.5
Peru	1940	71.5
	1961	79.7
Uruguay	1963	44.2
Venezuela	1936	58.3
	1941	64.1
	1950	76.7
	1961	91.4

Source: Computed from data given in the censuses of the respective countries and in various editions of the *Demographic Yearbook.*

[a]United Nations estimate.

[b]54.5 per cent women aged forty to forty-nine considered as being forty to forty-four.

sively small populations to one which takes account of the relatively new problems generated by low death rates, rapid growth rates, and extremely large base populations. Subsequent changes in attitudes, motivations, and values, necessary before birth-control programs can be promulgated successfully, already are well along in some sections of the earth. Their success seems not to be especially dependent upon prior socioeconomic development, the extension of education to all the masses, nor the replacement of one generation by another. Rather, wide distribution of information about birth-control methods and rapid development of the motivations that result in family planning appear to be conditions that can and do occur without the establishment of an elaborate set of prerequisite conditions.[10] Even in Latin America, the region which has become the most spectacular example of rapid population growth, significant changes already are underway.

> There is some evidence to indicate that many residents of the rapidly growing cities are beginning to practice birth control on a fairly large scale. This appears to be the case especially on the part of the numerous descendants of the upper classes who find it extremely difficult to maintain even an appearance of upper-class status; and it also seems evident on the part of those who are genuine members of the middle class. In view of this it is likely that by about 1980 a sharp reduction of the birth rate, comparable to that which took place in the United States between 1900 and 1935, will get underway throughout Latin America. As a matter of fact the fall in the birth rate in Latin America may be even more precipitous and dramatic than that which brought about such tremendous social and economic changes in the United States. Meanwhile, though, the tidal wave of population growth in Latin America is likely to continue rising until it crests, probably about 1970, at a rate of about 3.5 per cent per year. Thereafter the influence of further successes in the control of mortality probably will be more than offset by the quickening pace of a falling birth rate.[11]

THE RISE IN THE BIRTH RATE IN THE UNITED STATES AND CANADA, 1935 - 1957

The upward movement of the rate of reproduction in the United States and Canada which took place between 1935 and 1948 and the maintenance until 1957 of the 1948 level is one of the most significant demographic happenings on record. In many ways it also is one of the most puzzling. Considerably more study will be needed to identify and evaluate fully the various factors responsible for the revolutionary change in the reproductive pattern of the populations of the two countries. The actual changes in the birth rate of the United States since 1935 are clearly portrayed in Figure 51. In 1936, it will be noted, the birth rate once more equalled the all-time low recorded in 1933. Then a recovery commenced, haltingly at first, but soon becoming more rapid. As was to be expected, the all-out mobilization for the Second World War and the dispatching of millions of men overseas halted the upswing and produced the dip, for the years 1944 and 1945, typical of a country in the midst of a serious struggle. With the end of the war and demobilization, the birth rate shot up to a peak in 1947, after which it dropped slightly and stabilized at a level of about twenty-five births per thousand population. In 1955, the rate was the same as it had been in 1925.

The changes in the birth rate in Canada, over the comparable period, were rather closely similar, although the general level at which they occurred was somewhat higher. (See Figure 53.) The rise in Canada after 1935, however, was somewhat less abrupt, and the dip occasioned by the war was somewhat less pronounced, than the comparable changes in the United States. These probably reflect the fact that Canada's all-out war effort was spread over a longer period than was that of her neighbor.

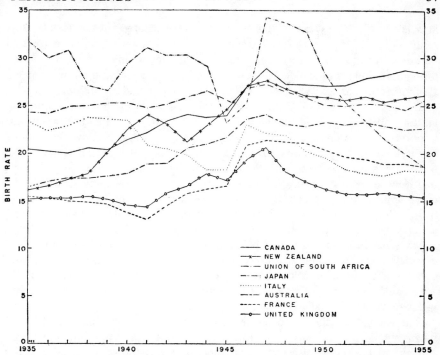

FIGURE 53. Trends in the crude birth rates in Canada and other selected countries, 1935 to 1955.

In order to facilitate comparison of trends between 1935 and 1955 in the United States and Canada with those of other selected countries, the curves for the United Kingdom, the white population of South Africa, France, Italy, Australia, New Zealand, and Japan also are shown in Figure 53. This list embraces most of the larger nations of the so-called Western world for which the birth statistics are believed to be fairly complete and for which changes in territory and boundaries do not almost preclude the possibility of fairly accurate comparisons. It also includes Japan, the only large Asiatic power for which the records cover enough years and are sufficiently complete to justify their use.

Observation of this figure makes it evident that New Zealand is the nation in which the trends in the birth rate, following 1935, most closely paralleled those in the United States and Canada. France and Australia, however, are countries in which the birth rate stabilized following the close of the war at a considerably higher level than that prevailing before the outbreak of the conflict. In the United Kindgom, on the other hand, the entire upswing in the birth rate, from the low level at which it stood in 1935, took place during the war years and the ones immediately following. Then the index dropped back down and stabilized at a level only barely above that which prevailed throughout the 1930's. As a result, after 1945 the United Kingdom replaced France as the large Western nation with the lowest rate of reproduction. The lack of any major trends in the birth rate is the most striking feature of the line representing the white population of South Africa. Throughout the entire period under consideration, one marked by recovery from deep economic depression, world military conflict on an unparalleled scale, and the tensions of the postwar years, the birth rate in this important part of Africa fluctuated only slightly above and below the level of twenty-five births per thousand population. In Italy, the general trend in the birth rate was downward, with the extent of the dip during the war years, the relatively low postwar peak, and the comparatively low level at which the curve appears to have stabilized being other significant features. By 1955 the birth rate in Italy was only slightly higher than that in the United Kingdom and actually was lower than that in France. Finally, the trend of the birth rate in Japan since 1935 should command particular interest. Three of its features are especially striking, namely, the pronounced dip during the war, the rapid up-surge following the cessation of hostilities, and the precipitous drop since 1949. Who could have believed, as late as 1950, that only five years later, the birth rate in Japan would have fallen to the same level as that in France!

The general conclusion to be derived from these comparisons is that by no means should these trends in the birth rate in the United States and Canada be thought of as representative of those going on during the same period in other parts of the Western world, or in other countries, such as Japan, on which Western standards have had such a tremendous impact. Somewhat similar trends did take place in New Zealand, and there are some resemblances of the changes in France and Australia to those in the United States. In general, though, the trends in the birth rate in other parts of the world have been quite different from those which took place in the United States and Canada.

Among the various racial and residential groups within the United States, there also existed between 1935 and 1955 trends in the fertility levels which were similar to those just described for the population of the nation as a whole. (See Figure 54 and Table 41.) As measured by the fertility ratio, rates of reproduction rose substantially from the beginning to the end of this period for all of the groups except the rural-farm white population. The increases were especially precipitous for nonwhites in all three of the residential categories, with that for the urban group rising especially sharply from extreme lows which existed not only in 1935 - 1940, but in 1905 - 1910, and in all of the intervening years.

As indicated above, the factors responsible for the changes in the birth rate in the United States between 1935 and 1957 have not been fully identified and evaluated. It is clear, however, that there was a change in the pattern of fertility within the typical family. Indeed, for almost ten years after 1950 the number of mothers giving birth to a second child, the number bearing a third child, and

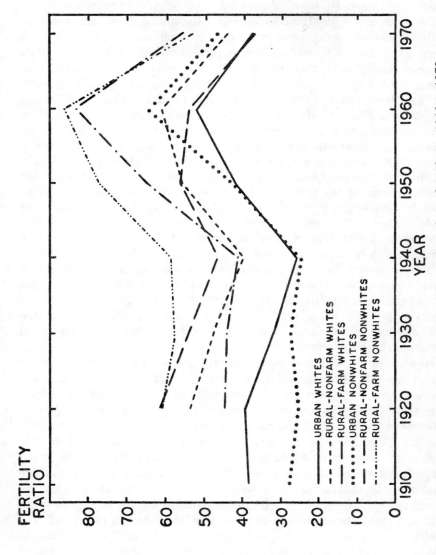

Figure 54. Trends in fertility ratios in the United States, by color and residence, 1910 to 1970.

the number having a fourth child, out of each 1,000 white women of child-bearing ages, was significantly above what it had been in 1940 (see Figure 55) and was about double what it was at the lowest point during the 1930's. As is evident from this chart, the number of first births per 1,000 women aged fifteen to forty-four rose in 1947 to a level almost two-thirds again as high as that for 1940. Similar increases occurred in the rates for each successive child, with the exception of the eighth, until peaks were reached for the second child in 1952, the third child in 1957, the fourth in 1960, and the fifth, sixth and seventh children in 1961. This period from 1947 to 1961, therefore, is the one during which the "baby boom" reached its crest and after which it began to wane significantly. The curves in Figure 55 also indicate that the "baby boom" resulted essentially from large increases in the numbers of second, third, and fourth children rather than from any substantial growth in the proportion of couples producing five or more children. They also indicate that many couples concluded their childbearing after the third baby had been born.[12] Furthermore, the times at which the curves representing the births of different orders began to move upward were 1934 for first births, 1936 for second births, 1940 for third births, and 1943 for fourth births. This suggests that the same generation of women was responsible for the reversal of earlier trends in all four cases, just as a study of trends in the age-specific birth rates of women in the United States over the period 1920 to 1945 indicated that "the particular women who entered the childbearing period just after the close of the first world war are more responsible than the others for the low point to which fertility fell."[13] If this is the case, then cyclical variations in the attitudes and general behavior patterns of successive generations of young women may be the key to an understanding of the fundamental changes in the rate of reproduction.

Irrespective of the factors responsible for the upswing in the birth rate in the United States during the period under consideration, the fact of the increase is among the most significant demographic phenomena of the twentieth century. It meant, to begin with, that the population of the United States could pass the 170 million mark in 1957 and could continue until 1965 to increase by more than 2.5 million per year. In contrast, had the birth rate continued at its 1936 level, population increase would hardly have exceeded 1 million per year, and it probably would have been 1958 before the United States contained 150 million inhabitants. In addition to this, a wide variety of other important social, economic, and military facts should be attributed rather directly to the rise in the birth rate that began in the mid-1930's and ended in the late 1950's and early 1960's. The following are a few of these: (1) the overcrowding of the schools that became so acute immediately after the Second World War; (2) the housing shortage and the housing boom which have figured so largely in national affairs since 1946; (3) the mushrooming of suburban areas since 1950; (4) the shortage of facilities for higher education which became acute in the late 1950's; (5) an

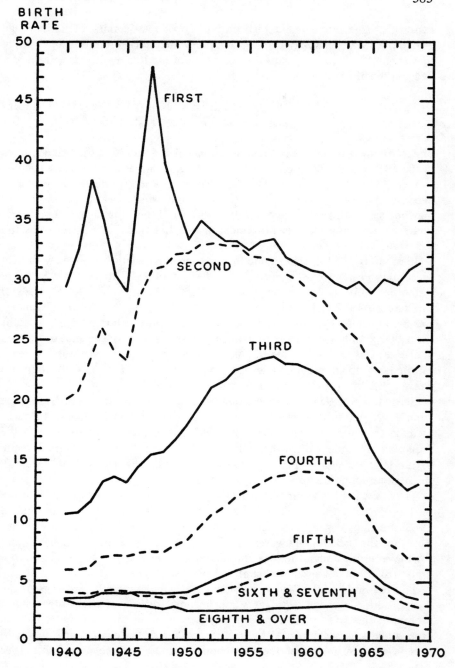

Figure 55. Number of births per 1,000 white women aged 15 - 44, by birth order, the United States, 1940 to 1969.

extremely large number and high proportion of men coming of military age during the 1960's; and (6) a large generation which started into the childbearing ages about 1968; although this may or may not result in another significant upswing in the birth rates.

DECLINE OF THE BIRTH RATE IN THE UNITED STATES IN THE 1960's AND 1970's

The sharp decrease in rates of reproduction which occurred in the United States in tfie 1960's and 1970's is a trend fully as significant as those discussed above. In fact, if it continues, as seems likely, the birth rate and the death rate well may become equal about 1975 or shortly thereafter, which means that the nation may be faced with a declining population with all of the advantages and problems that such a situation entails. Movement in this direction is demonstrated by the following facts.

First, after 1957, the birth rate for the general population dropped with each succeeding year up to the present. By the end of 1972 it was only 15.6 live births per 1,000 population as contrasted with 25.3 in 1957. (See Figure 51.) The rate for 1972 was the lowest in the nation's history. Moreover, this change was accompanied by only a very slight decline in the death rate from 9.6 deaths per 1,000 population in 1957 to 9.4 in 1972, so that the convergence of the two vital rates was exclusively the product of declining fertility. Nor was the death rate moving downward in advance of the birth rate so that an early complete convergence of the two is entirely possible.

Second, since 1957, the annual number of births also has declined, dropping from 4,308,000 in that year to 3,256,000 in 1972, although there was a slight increase each year between 1958 and 1961. It is especially important that the reduction in numbers of births took place despite the fact that by 1972, many of the large number of babies born during the postwar fertility boom were in the peak reproductive ages.

Third, by 1961, the birth rates had begun to decline significantly in all of the birth-order categories from the first birth through the seventh birth, and in 1963 the rates began to decrease in that representing eight and more births. Rates for the first child, however, have dropped at a slower pace than have those for the second through the seventh children and have shown the greatest instability, rising and falling somewhat after 1963. (See Figure 55.)

Fourth, both whites and nonwhites have exhibited similar patterns of decrease, both in general birth rates and in those for various birth-order groups. Moreover, this took place for both major races in all three of the residential groups and was accompanied by a tendency for the rates of reproduction of these various segments of the total population to become more alike. (See Figure 54.)

Fifth, since the late 1950's, significant decreases in rates of reproduction have appeared, irrespective of the indexes used to measure them. For example, for the white population, not only did the crude birth rates decline from 24.0 in 1957 to 15.5 in 1970, but the fertility rate (number of births per 1,000 women aged fifteen to forty-four) fell from 117.7 in 1957 to 82.4 in 1969; the net reproduction rate declined from 1,765 in 1957 to 1,116 in 1968; and the age-sex adjusted birth rate dropped from 30.9 in 1957 to 20.3 in 1968. In addition, for the white population the fertility ratio fell from 54.6 in 1960 to 39.2 in 1970. (See Figure 50 and Table 41.) Finally, the number of children ever born per 1,000 women aged fifteen to forty-four ever married seemed to go against the trend, for it increased slightly from 2,253 in the former year to 2,285 in the latter. This situation existed, however, only for women aged thirty-five to forty-four whose fertility is largely a product of the birth norms and other factors influencing reproduction that prevailed in the period of high birth rates after World War II. The indexes dropped during the decade under consideration for the two younger age groups of women as follows: aged fifteen to twenty-four, from 1,236 to 933; aged twenty-five to thirty-four, from 2,379 to 2,306. Their fertility, of course, is more influenced by contemporary birth norms and other sociocultural features than is that of the older women whose reproduction is largely complete. For the nonwhite population, the various indexes also consistently show reductions in fertility. The crude birth rate dropped from 35.3 in 1957 to 25.2 in 1970; the fertility rate fell from 163.0 in 1957 to 114.8 in 1969; the net reproduction rate decreased from 2,206 in 1957 to 1,495 in 1968; and the age-sex adjusted birth rate dropped from 41.2 in 1957 to 27.5 in 1968. The fertility ratio among the nonwhite population fell from 69.2 in 1960 to 48.2 in 1970; the number of children ever born per 1,000 women aged fifteen to forty-four ever married followed the same pattern that appeared in the white population. That is, the overall index for the nonwhites rose from 2,788 in 1960 to 2,912 in 1970 and that for women aged thirty-five to forty-four increased from 3,067 to 3,739 during the decade, whereas the index for women aged fifteen to twenty-four fell from 1,820 to 1,468 and that for women aged twenty-five to thirty-four declined from 2,963 to 2,875. When the results of the fertility reductions of the 1970's appear in the data of the 1980 census of population, this index for both races will be seen to have declined substantially, provided, of course, that no actual increases in fertility occur in the interim.

Finally, between 1957 and 1972, substantial decreases in the crude birth rate were registered in all of the major regions of the United States and in each of the fifty states. In the District of Columbia, however, the rate increased from 26.8 in 1957 to 28.8 in 1972 because of the large increase in the proportion of Negroes in its population and the concomitant decrease in that of whites. But for whites and nonwhites separately, the birth rates in the nation's capital also fell significantly during the decade.

Among other things, the rise between 1960 and 1970 in the number of children ever born per 1,000 women aged thirty-five to forty-four, accompanied by the decreases in the two younger age groups, demonstrates how recent is the trend of declining birth rates in the United States. The question as to whether it will continue to take the shape which it assumed between 1957 and 1973, subside and level off, or even be reversed, remains unanswered. To be sure, a relatively large group of young adults is just now coming into the peak childbearing ages and their fertility levels could generate a new upsurge in the overall levels of reproduction. For example, the number of women aged fifteen to forty-four increased about 2 per cent between 1971 and 1972 and the Bureau of the Census projects another 6 per cent increase by 1975.[14] In the ages twenty to twenty-nine, when births are most likely to occur, the increase between 1971 and 1972 was about 3 per cent and the projection to 1975 is for an additional 10 per cent growth. Obviously, if the age-specific birth rates do not change or even if they decline slightly, the number of births will increase, although much of this could be negated by a continuation of the decline in the age-specific reproduction rates. Moreover, the marriage rate, which declined from a high of 16.4 marriages per 1,000 population in 1946 to a low of 8.4 in 1958, had risen modestly but steadily to 10.9 by the end of 1972. These and other conditions may help to generate new increases in fertility levels in the United States. Yet Bogue suggests that "the generation that is just now starting to bear children is having the first child at a slower rate than did the preceding generation and is having a second and third child at an even slower pace," and he also holds that "by 1965 it appeared that the 'baby boom' was definitely over."[15] But not only must further examination of the matter await the appearance of additional data for all of the 1970's; some highly sophisticated analyses of economic conditions, birth norms, philosophies of childrearing, attitudes toward marriage, and other factors which underlie patterns of fertility also need to be carried out in connection with this recent trend before it can be understood fully. Nevertheless, the trend of declining birth rates in the 1960's and the 1970's ranks as one of the most spectacular demographic changes occurring in the United States.

NOTES

1. On this point see T. Lynn Smith, "The Demographic Basis of Old Age Assistance in the South," *Social Forces,* 17, 3 (March, 1939), pp. 356 - 361.

2. "Statement on Population by World Leaders," in *World Leaders Declaration on Population* (New York: Population Council, Inc., 1967), pp. 13 - 15.

3. *The Population of India and Pakistan* (Princeton, N. J.: Princeton University Press, 1951).

4. See the materials in *ibid.*, p. 68, which follows Gyan Chand, *India's Teeming Millions* (London: Allen & Unwin, 1939), pp. 97 - 98.

5. *Ibid.*, p. 69.

6. T. Lynn Smith, *Brazil: People and Institutions* (4th ed.), (Baton Rouge: Louisiana State University Press, 1972), pp. 99 - 100 and p. 635. Giorgio Mortara, with age and sex data from the 1940 Brazilian census at hand, concluded that the true rate was somewhere between 39.5 and 47.8, with 42.3 being a reasonable estimate of its magnitude. See his *Estimativas da Taxa de Natalidade paro o Brasil, as Unidades da Federãçao e as Principais Capitais,* Estudos de Estatística Teórica e Aplicada, Estatística Demográfica, No. 4 (Rio de Janeiro: Instituto Brasileiro de Geografia e Estatística, 1949).

7. T. Lynn Smith, "Notes on Population and Rural Social Organization in El Salvador," *Rural Sociology,* 10, 4 (December, 1945), pp. 366 - 367.

8. T. Lynn Smith, "The Reproduction Rate in Latin America," *Eugenical News Quarterly,* XXXVIII, 3 (1953), pp. 64 - 70.

9. See also T. Lynn Smith, *Latin American Population Studies* (Gainesville: University of Florida Press, 1960), pp. 51 - 52.

10. For several of these and related observations, see Donald J. Bogue, *Principles of Demography* (New York: John Wiley & Sons, Inc., 1969), pp. 741 - 742.

11. T. Lynn Smith, "The Population of Latin America," in *Population: The Vital Revolution,* edited by Ronald Freedman (New York: Doubleday and Company, Inc., 1964), p. 182.

12. On these points, see Bogue, *op cit.,* pp. 685 - 686.

13. T. Lynn Smith, *Population Analysis* (New York: McGraw-Hill Book Company, 1948), p. 228.

14. Reported in U. S. Department of Health, Education, and Welfare, "Births, Marriages, Divorces, and Deaths for 1972," *Monthly Vital Statistics Report,* 21, 12 (March 1, 1973), p. 1.

15. Bogue, *op. cit.,* p. 732.

SUGGESTED SUPPLEMENTARY READINGS

BERELSON, BERNARD. "Beyond Family Planning." *Studies in Family Planning,* No. 38 (1969), pp. 1 - 16.

BLAKE, JUDITH. "Ideal Family Size Among White Americans: A Quarter of a Century's Evidence." *Demography,* Vol. 3, No. 1 (1966), pp. 154 - 173.

BOGUE, DONALD J. *Principles of Demography,* Chap. 20. New York: John Wiley & Sons, Inc., 1969.

BOGUE, DONALD J., ed. *Progress and Problems of Fertility Control around the World. Demography,* Vol. 5, No. 2 (1968).

CHANDRASEKARAN, C. "Fertility Trends in India." *Proceedings of the World Population Conference, 1954,* Vol. I. New York: United Nations, 1955.

DAVIS, KINGSLEY. *The Population of India and Pakistan,* Part III. Princeton: Princeton University Press, 1951.

DAVIS, KINGSLEY. "Population Policy: Will Current Programs Succeed?" *Science,* Vol. 158 (November 10, 1967), pp. 730 - 739.

FARLEY, REYNOLDS. "Recent Changes in Negro Fertility." *Demography,* Vol. 3, No. 1 (1966), pp. 188 - 203.

FORD, THOMAS R., and GORDON F. DeJONG. "The Decline of Fertility in the Southern Appalachian Mountain Region." *Social Forces,* Vol. 42, No. 1 (October, 1963), pp. 89 - 96.

FREEDMAN, RONALD, PASCAL K. WHELPTON, and ARTHUR R. CAMPBELL. *Family Planning, Sterility, and Population Growth.* New York: McGraw-Hill Book Company, 1959.

GRABILL, WILSON H., and MARIA DAVIDSON. "Recent Trends in Childspacing." *Demography,* Vol 5, No. 1 (1968), pp. 212 - 225.

KISER, CLYDE V., WILSON H. GRABILL, and ARTHUR A. CAMPBELL. *Trends and Variations in Fertility in the United States.* Cambridge: Harvard University Press, 1968.

STOLNITZ, GEORGE J. "The Demographic Transition: From High to Low Birth Rates and Low Death Rates," in *Population: The Vital Revolution,* edited by Ronald Freedman, Chap. 2. New York: Doubleday & Co., Inc. (Anchor Books), 1964.

TAEUBER, IRENE B. *The Population of Japan,* Chaps. XII and XIII. Princeton: Princeton University Press, 1958.

THOMLINSON, RALPH. *Demographic Problems,* Chaps. 5 and 6. Belmont, Calif.: Dickenson Publishing Company, Inc., 1967.

UNITED NATIONS. *Demographic Yearbook, 1969,* Chap. I. New York: United Nations, 1970.

WESTOFF, CHARLES F., and NORMAN D. RYDER. "Contraceptive Practices in the United States," in *Family Planning Today,* edited by Alan Rubin, Chap. 1. Philadelphia: F. A. Davis Company, 1969.

WRONG, DENNIS H. *Population and Society,* 3rd ed., Chap. 4. New York: Random House, Inc., 1967.

Mortality is the second of the vital processes and also the second of the three primary factors affecting the number and distribution of the population to receive attention in this volume. Ordinarily it is considerably less important than the other vital process (fertility) as a primary factor in population change, although now and.then throughout human history years of plague and famine have contributed striking exceptions to this rule. Ordinarily, too, it is far more important than the third of the primary factors (migration) in producing changes in the size and distribution of any large population, although frequently an exodus of people or an influx of those from elsewhere may be the principal factor in the gain or loss of inhabitants of a given village, town, city, or county over a short period of time. In times of great upheaval, migration may even lead among the factors in producing increases or decreases of population at national or regional levels; and sustained mass movements of population, such as those taking place in the United States since 1940, may make migration more important than mortality or even fertility in accounting for the increase of population in some states such as Arizona, Florida, and California. For the most part, though, mortality is the second most important factor in population change. For this reason the student of population must be well acquainted with the ways and means of measuring the mortality of a population.

It would be a mistake, however, to assume that the significance of the study of mortality is limited to the role this factor plays in population change. Longevity as such is one of the important criteria of the quality of a population. Moreover, from analysis of the data on mortality comes the most useful information on such matters of universal interest as the control of tuberculosis and other transmissible diseases; the progress if any in the fight against cancer, diseases of the heart, cirrhosis of the liver, and other causes of death that result from the deterioration of the body's vital organs; the "score" with respect to fatalities from automobile accidents, suicides, homicides, and other violent causes of death;

and the situation with respect to the hazards of infancy. Indeed, because comprehensive data on morbidity are almost entirely lacking in most nations, mortality data have come to be the most commonly accepted means of measuring the health of a population; and society is almost entirely dependent upon indexes of mortality and longevity for accurate information concerning the effectiveness and efficiency of medical and sanitary sciences in the improvement of the welfare of mankind. In fact, one of the specific mortality indexes, the infant mortality rate, long was regarded as "the most sensitive index of social welfare and of sanitary improvements which we possess."[1] This is still the case in most parts of the world, although efforts to ascertain the state of health, such as the National Health Survey taken periodically in the United States, are beginning to provide some of the basic data necessary for the investigation of this fundamental topic in an increasing number of countries. Finally, mention should be made of the fact that the mortality indexes, arranged in the form of life tables, constitute the scientific basis for one of the largest and most important financial institutions of modern times, namely, the life insurance business.

MORTALITY DATA

In nearly every modern nation, the keeping of mortality records has come to be an essential function of government. The value these data have in the control and prevention of transmissible diseases alone more than justifies the organization and expense necessary to secure them. Fortunately, the problems inherent in the registration of deaths are considerably less difficult than those involved in the registration of births, so that the coverage of the former usually is far more complete than that of the latter. But even so, to secure the registration of every death in a county, state, or nation, along with a record of the essential characteristics of the deceased (age, sex, race or color, rural or urban residence, marital condition, occupation, and so on) and an accurate diagnosis of the cause of death, is no simple matter. In this connection it is important to have in mind that the information from the registers of vital statistics must be matched with those secured in the census enumeration before indexes can be computed for the various segments of the population. Back of every valid statement on how mortality varies with age, or the differences in the death rates of males and females, whites and Negroes, farmers and industrial workers, or city people and country people, is a painstaking effort on the part of thousands of efficient public servants.

In every country the evolution of the registers of vital statistics is a long and involved story. The experience of the United States, however, serves to illustrate many of the problems that had to be faced and overcome. Prior to 1900 the responsibility for registration of vital statistics rested upon the states. A few of them maintained fairly adequate organizations for recording deaths, but in the majority of them little or no reliance could be placed upon the completeness and accuracy of the data. During the last half of the nineteenth century repeated efforts were made to secure comprehensive and reliable mortality statistics for the nation by means of queries included in the decennial censuses of population. The numerous bulky volumes of mortality statistics published in connection with every census from that of 1850 to that of 1900 supplied little or no trustworthy information on the subject. This was recognized by the ingenious J. D. B. DeBow, who stated in connection with the statistics resulting from the first attempt that the data "can be said to have little value," and then elucidated as follows:

> Upon the subject of the Deaths no one can be deceived by the figures of the Census, since any attempt to reason from them would demonstrate a degree of vitality and healthfulness in the United States unparalleled in the annals of mankind. . . . The truth is, but a part of the deaths have been recorded.[2]

It also was well known to Dr. J. S. Billings, who worked with the compilations made in connection with the censuses of 1870 and 1880. Some of his most telling comments are as follows:

> The fact that it is impossible, in any large community, to collect complete and reliable data with regard to births and deaths by means of any inquiry made only at the end of the year for which the data are desired, is well known to all who are practically familiar with the subject of vital statistics; and the experience of the United States census furnishes no exception to this rule. The results of each of the four censuses in which an attempt has been made to ascertain the number of persons who died in the United States during the preceding year, have shown that the enumerators did not obtain and record more than 60 to 70 per cent of the actual number of deaths.[3]

In spite of these evaluations by those in charge of the work, attempts to secure mortality data in connection with census enumerations continued in 1890 and 1900.

When the Bureau of the Census was established on a permanent basis, by action of Congress in 1902, the collection of vital statistics for the nation was one of the functions specifically assigned to it. The organization the Bureau established for the registration of deaths rested entirely upon voluntary cooperation between the states and the federal government, and it remains so today. Willcox has given an excellent summary of the major features of the cooperative venture:

> 1. It recommends a State law and is not satisfied with a municipal ordinance.
>
> 2. The model law prohibits disposing of a corpse by burial, cremation, transportation, or otherwise until a burial or transportation permit has been secured.
>
> 3. To secure this permit a certificate of death properly made out on the standard form and including a statistical description of the deceased and a professional statement of the cause of death must be filed with the office issuing the permit.
>
> 4. The duty of preparing this certificate of death rests upon the undertaker, aided by a relative or friend of the deceased and by the attending physician, the coroner or other qualified person.

5. A standard nomenclature and classification of the causes of death, excluding vague and unsatisfactory ones like fever or old age, has been prepared and periodically revised.

6. Physicians, registrars, and other officers having to do with registration, are given detailed instructions about the nomenclature.

7. The local registrar is the only person authorized to issue a burial or transit permit and he only in exchange for a certificate of death.

8. The local registrar files with the State registrar each month the certificates of death which he has received.

9. The State registrar examines them and corresponds with the local registrars who are dilatory or send in defective returns.

10. At this point the Federal Government intervenes, for the first time, by purchasing copies of the certificates of death filed in a state or city office, but only if it is convinced that the returns are complete enough to have statistical value.

11. From these copies the Bureau of the Census prepares uniform tables for the registration states and their main divisions.[4]

The first report on national mortality statistics issued under provisions of the 1902 law appeared in 1906 and contained data for the years 1900 to 1904, inclusive. The statistics presented were those for the states of Connecticut, Indiana, Maine, Massachusetts, Michigan, New Hampshire, New Jersey, New York, Rhode Island, and Vermont, along with the District of Columbia. These have since been known as the Original Registration States. Materials for 153 cities scattered throughout the remaining states also were given in the initial report. Following 1904, additional states gradually adopted the required standards and were admitted to the registration area until with the admission of Texas in 1933 the coverage included the entire continental United States. Because of the manner in which registration of vital statistics evolved, one who uses historical series relating to mortality in the United States must be prepared to deal with some tabulations for the "original registration area" and with others pertaining to the "expanding registration area."

A large share of the space devoted to mortality statistics in the official reports of most countries is given over to presentation of data concerning the causes of death. This is as it should be, for one must go further than a study of the gross rates if he would learn many of the most significant facts and relationships in the field of mortality.

The causes of death, of course, lack precise scientific definition and standardization. Indeed, they may not always be recorded as accurately as the knowledge possessed would make possible. For example, it frequently is said that attending physicians refrain from reporting syphilis as the cause of death of prominent and well-to-do members of a community, even though it is evident to them that it was the principal factor in the complex involved. They may not hesitate to do so, however, in comparable cases involving less-esteemed residents in the locality. Nevertheless, much progress has been made in securing comparability in the reported causes of death throughout the world, due in large part to the use and per-fection of the *International List of Causes of Death.*

This list had its inception in 1853, when the First Statistical Congress (con-vened at Brussels) appointed Dr. William Farr and Dr. Marc d'Espine to develop a system of classifying deaths that would be suitable for international use. After working for two years, these men submitted to the Congress two separate lists, and the one finally adopted by it in 1855 was a compromise. It received little acceptance by the various nations involved. Nevertheless, it served as a basis for more work, and in 1893 a greatly revised system prepared by Dr. Jacques Bertil-lion, was presented to and immediately adopted by the Congress. Several countries began at once to use it in their official compilations, and from 1900, when the mortality statistics for the United States began, to the present time, it has been employed in this country. Since 1893, the list has been revised several times, so that the latest revision, that of 1965, is known as the *Eighth Revision.*

The Eighth Revision, use of which is specified for member nations by the World Health Organization, was employed for the first time in the United States for the classification of the 1968 data. However, it is not entirely comparable with the previous revision, used in the United States between 1958 and 1967. Further-more, many of the countries of the world employed the causes of death as given in the Seventh Revision when they last reported their data on this subject to the United Nations, so that at the international level, too, complete comparability over time is not possible.[5] Most of the changes involve the transfer of specific causes from one large class to another with the result that comparability in the major categories is more difficult to achieve than is that in the more detailed specific causes. The Eighth Revision is used by the present writers in making the analyses of causes of death, but in tracing trends they have attempted to achieve as uniform a classification as possible by relying on specific causes rather than merely the major groups of causes. The Eighth Revision consists of sixteen large categories of diseases and morbid conditions and one large category of accidents, poisonings, and violence.[6] A total of 671 specific categories of disease or morbid conditions make up the former and 182 classes of causes are used with the latter. The detailed list is prescribed for classification purposes, but condensed and ab-breviated lists are provided for use in tabulating and publishing the materials.

INDEXES OF MORTALITY

Four principal measures are employed in the study of mortality. The *death rate* is one of these, and the rather special indexes called the *infant mortality rate* and the *maternal mortality rate* are others. The fourth, and in many ways the most important, is the set of *arithmetic averages* included in the life table, or the values commonly known as the *expectation of life.*

The Death Rate

The computation of the death rate is very similar to that of the birth rate. That for the total population of the United States in 1970 may be secured as follows:

$$\frac{\text{Number of deaths during 1970}}{\text{Population (April 1, 1970)}} \times 1,000 = \frac{1,921,000}{203,210,158} \times 1,000 = 9.5$$

Strictly speaking, the population as of July 1 should be used rather than that of the census date, but such corrections are hardly worthwhile in the computation of crude death rates. Likewise, there would be little point in using the average number of deaths per year for the years 1969, 1970, and 1971, rather than that for 1970 alone, in connection with the crude measure, whereas such a procedure is highly recommended if the death rate is to be adjusted or refined in any way. It should be added that death rates reported for years other than those in which censuses are taken must be calculated using estimates rather than enumerations of the total population. For instance, in 1972, the registered number of deaths for the year (1,962,000), divided by the population estimated as of July 1 (208,232,000), multiplied by 1,000, results in a death rate of 9.4.

Those who use either the data or the conclusions on mortality should realize that for most purposes the crude death rate is a highly unsatisfactory index, because the mortality rates of males and females are so different and especially because mortality is so closely related to age. (See the second column in Table 43.) Observe that the death rate is high for the very young, extremely low for those between one and fifty, and very high for those aged sixty-five and over. Therefore, since the age distribution differs so greatly from one population to another, from time to time in the same population, and between the various residential and racial groups in a given population, the crude death rate is a very unsatisfactory measure to use for comparative purposes.

If one is to make any pretense of accuracy, the specific rates for particular age and sex groups must be employed. The arithmetical procedures for calculating these are exactly the same as those for determining the rate for the general population, except that the data used pertain to a specific age and sex segment of the population. For example, one could compute the death rate for males of twenty-six years of age, or for females aged thirty-one. If these age-specific death rates are then combined so that the one for each age and sex segment is given the same weight that it would have in a normal or standard population, the results are compressed into what is called the *standardized death rate*. The procedures used in doing this are closely comparable to those employed in the standardization of the birth rate (see Chapter 11). Usually, however, there is little point to such computations, because, for most purposes, the construction of a *life table* is the procedure generally employed for adjusting the mortality rates of various

TABLE 43

Abridged life table for the total population of the United States, 1969 to 1971

(1) Age interval — Period of life between two exact ages stated x to x + n	(2) Mortality rate — Number dying per 1,000 alive at beginning of age interval $n q_x$	(3) Of 100,000 born alive — Number living at beginning of age interval l_x	(4) Number dying during age interval $n d_x$	(5) Stationary population — In the age interval $n L_x$	(6) Stationary population — In this and all subsequent age intervals T_x	(7) Average remaining lifetime — Average number of years of life remaining at beginning of age interval e_x
0-1	19.27	100,000	1,927	98,555	7,100,737	71.0
1-5	3.13	98,073	307	391,680	7,002,182	71.4
5-10	2.03	97,766	198	488,335	6,610,502	67.6
10-15	2.00	97,568	195	487,352	6,122,167	62.7
15-20	5.37	97,373	523	485,557	5,634,815	57.9
20-25	7.10	96,850	688	482,530	5,149,258	53.2
25-30	6.80	96,162	654	479,175	4,666,728	48.5
30-35	8.10	95,508	774	475,605	4,187,553	43.8
35-40	11.70	94,734	1,108	470,900	3,711,948	39.2
40-45	17.73	93,626	1,660	463,980	3,241,048	34.6
45-50	27.37	91,966	2,517	453,538	2,777,068	30.2
50-55	41.93	89,449	3,751	437,865	2,323,530	26.0
55-60	63.17	85,698	5,414	414,955	1,885,665	22.0
60-65	95.43	80,284	7,662	382,265	1,470,710	18.3
65-70	137.70	72,622	10,000	338,110	1,088,445	15.0
70-75	202.57	62,622	12,685	281,400	750,335	12.0
75-80	284.23	49,937	14,194	214,200	468,935	9.4
80-85	393.97	35,743	14,082	143,510	254,735	7.1
85-over	1,000.00	21,661	21,661	111,225	111,225	5.1

Source: Compiled and computed from data in National Center for Health Statistics, *Vital Statistics of the United States, 1969,* Vol. II, Section 5, *Life Tables* (1971), p. 8, Table 5-2; *Monthly Vital Statistics Report,* Vol. 19, No. 13, *Annual Summary for the United States, 1970* (1971), p. 15, Table 3; Vol. 20, No. 13, *1971* (1972), p. 14, Table 3.

populations for differences in their age and sex distributions. It should not be forgotten, of course, that the actual number of deaths occurring and the crude death rate are the materials that must be used in computing population changes or determining the amount and rate of natural increase.

The Arithmetic Averages Commonly Called Expectation of Life

A life table is made up of the results of a series of arithmetical computations designed to show the average number of years that would be lived by a number of persons born at the same time, called an age cohort, or for those of any given age who are alive at the same time if the age-specific death rates prevailing during the year for which the table is constructed were to remain unchanged until all of the persons involved had died. Table 43 for the total population of the United States, 1969 - 1971, is an example of an abridged life table. The figures in this table most commonly used are the arithmetical averages shown in the last column. The first of these values, 71.0, is the average amount of time that would be lived by 100,000 persons born at the same time in the United States were the age-specific death rates in this country to remain at the levels which prevailed during the years 1969 to 1971 until they died. Providing these mortality levels were to remain unchanged until all in the age cohort had died, this is the same average that would be obtained were a group of Methuselahs to amuse themselves by observing the length of life of people in the United States. Suppose that such a group of "demographers" were to start stop watches at the birth of 100,000 babies born during 1970 to measure and record accurately the amount of time each lived. When the last of these babies had passed away, if they added the figures to secure the total amount of time lived by the group as a whole, and then divided by 100,000, the resulting arithmetic average should be 71.0 years. This particular average refers to the time measured from the moment of birth. Similarly, the second figure in the last column, 71.4, is the average measured from the beginning of the second year of life; the third figure, 67.6, that secured if the beginning of the sixth year of life is taken as the point of departure; and so on. When other knowledge is lacking, the best guess with respect to the value of any one item in a frequency distribution is the arithmetic average of all the items in the distribution; hence, the average length of life of the group measured from birth commonly is called the *expectation of life* at birth. Likewise, it is customary to speak of expectation of life at age ten, age forty, age sixty-five, and so on. In each case the expression denotes what the average duration of life would be for persons of the stated age who are alive at the beginning of the year for which the table is constructed if the age-specific death rates shown in the table were to remain unchanged until all the persons involved had died. Any specific characteristics possessed by a particular person in the group, which makes him likely to die earlier or live longer than the others, makes it less likely that the average is a fair approximation of the number of years he personally may expect to live.

The precise methods used by actuaries in the construction of life tables are too involved to be of general interest or significance. They suffer from many of the defects that arise when highly refined mathematical techniques are applied to observations or measurements which themselves are grossly lacking in precision. Nevertheless, the general outlines of life-table construction are fairly simple. To begin with, one must have a distribution of the population by single years of age for a complete life table or by five-year age ranges for the abridged version and also a distribution of deaths (for the year corresponding to the census of population, or preferably the three-year period centered on the census year) by age. With these in hand the computation of the death rate for each age group is a simple matter, and these in turn can readily be transformed into the conventional life table. One of the principal technical difficulties is the determination of the population of less than one year of age and another is the calculation of the average age at death of those who die before attaining the age of one year. In other words, the lack of precision in enumerating children of less than one year of age, the deficiencies of birth registration, and the rapid flow of vital events during the first year of life introduce some technical difficulties into the determination of the population and the specific death rate of those under one year of age. Another obstacle is the obvious errors in the reporting of age, and this is true both with respect to the living and those who die. Therefore, in the construction of life tables the calculated age-specific death rates are subjected to a rather elaborate mathematical smoothing process in order to remove the fluctuations that are due merely to random events or pure chance. As Raymond Pearl once wrote, a highly esoteric cult has grown up around this particular phase of life-table construction.[7]

Notwithstanding the difficulties inherent in determining the death rate of persons of less than one year of age and the correction of the other age-specific death rates, understanding the life table is not difficult.[8] The steps involved in computation and the values derived may be noted through a careful examination of Table 43. Column 1 gives the age classification by five-year ranges; column 2 contains the age-specific mortality rates; column 3 shows the number alive at the beginning of each age interval, starting with the hypothetical number of 100,000; column 4 indicates how many persons would die within given age intervals, calculated by applying the age-specific death rates shown in column 2 to the respective numbers of persons alive at the beginning of the intervals shown in column 3; column 5 indicates the total number of years lived by the survivors in each age interval; column 6 rearranges in cumulative form the data from column 5, with the cumulating process starting from the bottom of the table; and column 7 presents the series of computations showing the averages that are secured when the figures in column 6 are divided by the figures in the corresponding rows as given in column 3. This last operation is, of course, the actual computation of the arithmetic averages, and in each case the number of persons alive at the beginning of each age period is divided into the total number of years of life remaining to the group as a whole.

The materials indicate that during the period 1969 to 1971, 1,927 out of each 100,000 babies born in the United States had died before attaining the age of one. (This, of course, corresponds closely to an infant mortality rate of 19.3.) Accordingly, of the theoretical population of 100,000 born at the same time, only 98,073 would be alive to start the second year of life. If these died at the rate of 3.13 per 1,000 (column 2), 307 of them would pass away in the course of the four years, leaving 97,766 children alive to commence the sixth year of life. In this way, by applying the age-specific death rates to each succeeding number of survivors until all are accounted for, all of the values in column 4 may be determined.

The calculation of the values entered in column 5 presents some difficulties, and it will help to recall that the entries in this column represent the total number of years lived by those in the particular age intervals. The 98,555 entered for the age group zero to one represents 98,073 years contributed by the contingent who were still alive at the beginning of the second year of life, plus 482 years credited to the account by the 1,927 babies who died in the course of the first year of life. Thus, by the procedures employed, it has been estimated that 0.25 year was the average length of life of those who died before reaching the age of one. The procedures for the other age groups are slightly different because of the use of age intervals rather than single years of age. For most ages, the value to be entered in column 5 may be determined by multiplying the number of survivors at the end of the age interval by the number of years in the interval (usually five), by ascertaining the number who died during the interval and multiplying half of that number by the years in the interval, and by adding the two products thus obtained. For example, the 482,530 entry in column 5 corresponding to the age group twenty to twenty-five represents a total of 480,810 years lived during the five-year period by the 96,162 persons who survived to the end of the age interval plus 1,720 years lived by the 688 persons who died during the interval.

Next, begin at the bottom of the table and observe that of the original 100,000, given the age-specific death rates prevailing from 1969 to 1971, 21,661 persons would celebrate their eighty-fifth birthdays. All told, these 21,661 persons would have a total of 111,225 years still to live, the data for each interval being given in column 5. By cumulating from the bottom to the top in column 6 the values that are entered in column 5, one secures the total number of years still to be lived by the persons in any given age group. Accordingly, at age zero or birth, the entire group of 100,000 persons has a total of 7,100,737 years ahead of them, or an average of 71.0 years per person. After the risks of infancy have been passed, however, the 7,002,182 remaining years of lifetime divided by the 98,073 persons who were alive at the beginning of the second year of life produces an average of 71.4 years. Similarly, the average remaining lifetime for each of the other age groups may be computed and entered in column 7.

Infant Mortality and Maternal Mortality Rates

For simple gauging of the general welfare of the populations of most countries, the infant mortality rate has few serious rivals. As has been repeatedly indicated by those best informed on the subject, people who lack either the knowledge or the desire to care properly for their own helpless offspring are unlikely to have the knowledge or the will to care for themselves.

The infant mortality rate is computed by dividing the number of infant deaths taking place during the course of one year by the number of live births registered during the year and then multiplying by a constant to secure an index of two digits. Thus, for the United States in 1972, the infant mortality rate may be computed as follows:

$$\frac{\text{Number of infants (children under one)}}{\text{Number of live births, 1972}} \times 1{,}000 = \frac{60{,}200}{3{,}256{,}000} \times 1{,}000 = 18.5$$

It is important to note that the infant mortality rate is not the age-specific death rate of children of less than one year of age, although the values of the two are approximately equal. Note that the year used in this illustration is 1972 and that any other year might just as well have been chosen. The death rate of children under one, though, can be computed with accuracy only for years in which a census is taken, such as 1960 or 1970 in the United States. Even then, between three and four years elapse before the age tabulations can be completed and the data made available. The fact that the information on both infant deaths and live births is secured annually adds much to the usefulness of the infant mortality rate.

The maternal mortality rate also has many uses in gauging the well-being of various populations. Its computation may be illustrated with the following materials for the United States in 1972:

$$\frac{\substack{\text{Number of women dying from causes}\\ \text{arising from deliveries and complications}\\ \text{of pregnancy, childbirth, and the}\\ \text{puerperium, 1972}}}{\text{Number of live births, 1972}} \times 10{,}000 = \frac{780}{3{,}256{,}000} \times 10{,}000 = 2.4$$

As with the infant mortality rate, the usefulness of the maternal mortality rate is greatly enhanced by the fact that it may be secured annually.

NOTES

1. George C. Whipple, *Vital Statistics* (New York: John Wiley & Sons, Inc., 1923), p. 393.

2. *The Seventh Census of the United States, 1850* (Washington: Robert Armstrong, Public Printer, 1853), pp. xxxix - xl.

3. *Report on the Mortality and Vital Statistics of the United States*, Part I Washington: Government Printing Office, 1885), p. xi.

4. Walter F. Willcox, *Introduction to the Vital Statistics of the United States, 1900 to 1930* (Washington: Government Printing Office, 1933), p. 14. Cf. Robert D. Grove and Alice M. Hetzel, *Vital Statistics Rates in the United States: 1940 - 1960*, Public Health Service Publication No. 1677 (Washington: Government Printing Office, 1968), pp. 3 - 9.

5. See the United Nations, *Demographic Yearbook, 1971* (New York: United Nations, 1972), pp. 45 - 47.

6. These seventeen categories are as follows: infective and parasitic diseases; neoplasms; endocrine, nutritional, and metabolic diseases; diseases of the blood and blood-forming organs; mental disorders; diseases of the nervous system and sense organs; diseases of the circulatory system; diseases of the respiratory system; diseases of the digestive system; diseases of the genito-urinary system; complications of pregnancy, childbirth, and the puerperium; diseases of the skin and subcutaneous tissue; diseases of the musculo-skeletal system and connective tissue; congenital anomalies; certain causes of mortality in early infancy; symptoms and ill-defined conditions; and accidents, poisonings, and violence.

7. *Introduction to Medical Biometry and Statistics* (Philadelphia: W. B. Saunders Company, 1923), p. 196.

8. The interested student will find practical and relatively nontechnical discussions of this matter, with data to assist in the construction of a life table, in Grove and Hetzel, *op. cit.*, pp. 31 - 34 and p. 306, Table 48. See also Donald J. Bogue, *Principles of Demography* (New York: John Wiley & Sons, Inc., 1969), pp. 551 - 559.

ANDERSON, ODIN W., and MONROE LERNER. "Measuring Health Levels in the United States, 1900 - 1968," in *Population and Society*, edited by Charles B. Nam, pp. 170 - 177. Boston: Houghton Mifflin Company, 1968.

BOGUE, DONALD J. *Principles of Demography*, pp. 548 - 560. New York: John Wiley & Sons, Inc., 1969.

COX, PETER R. *Demography*, 4th ed., Chaps. 8 and 11. London: Cambridge University Press, 1970.

DUBLIN, LOUIS I., and ALFRED J. LOTKA. *Length of Life: A Study of the Life Table*, Rev. ed., Chaps. 1 and 2. New York: The Ronald Press Company, 1949.

GROVE, ROBERT D., and ALICE M. HETZEL. *Vital Statistics Rates in the United States, 1940 - 1960*, Chaps. II and III (Public Health Service Publication No. 1677). Washington: Government Printing Office, 1968.

METROPOLITAN LIFE INSURANCE COMPANY. "Increase in Survivorship Since 1840." *Statistical Bulletin*, Vol. 45 (1965), pp. 1 - 3.

MORIYAMA, IWAO M. "The Eighth Revision of the International Classification of Diseases." *American Journal of Public Health*, Vol. 56, No. 8 (1966), pp. 1277 - 1280.

PETERSEN, WILLIAM. *Population*, 2nd ed., Chap. 10. New York: The Macmillan Company, 1969.

SHRYOCK, HENRY S., JACOB S. SIEGEL, and associates. *The Methods and Materials of Demography*, Vol. 2, Chaps. 14 and 15. Washington: Government Printing Office, 1971.

SMITH, T. LYNN. *Brazil: People and Institutions*, 4th ed., Chap. VII. Baton Rouge: Louisiana State University Press, 1972.

SMITH, T. LYNN. *Population Analysis*, Chap. 15. New York: McGraw-Hill Book Company, 1948.

STOLNITZ, GEORGE J. *Life Tables from Limited Data: A Demographic Approach*. Princeton: Office of Population Research, 1956.

THOMLINSON, RALPH. *Population Dynamics*, Chap. 6. New York: Random House, Inc., 1965.

UNITED NATIONS. *Demographic Yearbook, 1961*, Chap. I. New York: United Nations, 1962.

UNITED NATIONS. *Demographic Yearbook, 1967*, pp. 26 - 42. New York: United Nations, 1968.

UNITED NATIONS. *Principles for a Vital Statistics System; Recommendations for the Improvement and Standardization of Vital Statistics*. New York: United Nations, 1953.

U.S. NATIONAL CENTER FOR HEALTH STATISTICS. *An Index of Health: Mathematical Models* (Public Health Service Publication No. 1000). Washington: Government Printing Office, 1965.

WILLCOX, WALTER F. *Introduction to the Vital Statistics of the United States, 1900 to 1930*, pp. 13 - 54. Washington: Government Printing Office, 1933.

WINKLER, WILHELM. "Relations Between Crude and Life Table Death Rates." *Journal of the Royal Statistical Society*, Vol. 127, No. 4 (1964), pp. 534 - 543.

WORLD HEALTH ORGANIZATION. *Measurement of Levels of Health* (WHO Technical Report Series No. 137). Geneva: World Health Organization, 1957.

16

MORTALITY LEVELS,
DIFFERENTIALS, AND CAUSES

The mortality rate differs from the fertility rate in at least three fundamental ways. First, in modern times at least and in most large nations the level of mortality is much lower than the level of fertility—deaths are considerably fewer than births. In the United States, for example, even when the birth rate was very low in 1972 there were about 3,256,000 births in this country and 1,962,000 deaths, so that the natural increase of population was about 1,294,000 persons. When the rate of reproduction was at the postwar peak, in 1947, there were about 3,820,000 births and only 1,450,000 deaths, with natural increase alone producing an increase of 2,370,000 in the population. Because the rate of reproduction generally is above the mortality rate, populations usually tend to increase—the fact that has given Malthusian principles their tremendous appeal. Second, the fluctuations in the death rate usually are far less pronounced, seemingly less capricious, than those in the birth rate. Again using the United States as an example, only in 1918, the year of the great influenza epidemic, were the number of deaths and the death rate in a given year strikingly above or below those for the preceding or the succeeding year. This means that ordinarily the number of deaths in a given population for the years immediately ahead may be predicted with a far greater degree of reliability than can the number of births. This, in turn, has much importance to those who need reliable bases for estimating populations for the years that have elapsed since a census or to those who need quick, simple, and fairly reliable ways of testing the accuracy of the estimates that others may make. For example, by the procedure illustrated in Chapter 21, the official in Arizona or Alabama who needs to know the population of his state for a year such as 1973, well after the last census was taken and eight or nine years before the results of the next one will be available, may use the death rates for earlier years and the number of deaths registered in 1973 as bases for making a simple and reliable estimate. Third, and closely related to the preceding difference, changes in the death rate generally take place more evenly and

gradually than those in the birth rate. That is, the curve representing the pro-
longed trend in the former moves up or down more slowly and steadily than
does that depicting the long-time changes in the latter. In turn, the gradual manner in which the trend in the death rate usually proceeds adds greatly to the value that may be derived from knowledge about the mortality of a population for
purposes of estimating current changes in its number and distribution.

SOME INTERNATIONAL COMPARISONS

Some of the most significant and reliable information on the levels of mortality
throughout the world has been selected for presentation in Tables 44 and 45.
The first of these gives, for all countries or territories with 1 million or more inhabitants for which the data are available, the recent information on the crude
death rate and the infant mortality rate. As much as possible, the crude death
rates are given for the latest census year to minimize any variations that might
be due merely to overestimates or underestimates of the population. However,
with some exceptions, the estimates prepared by the United Nations for Africa,
Latin America, and Asia for the period 1965 - 1970 generally are more dependable than the recorded rates, even for census years. Therefore, they have been
used in Table 44. Table 45 presents, for all countries for which life tables have
been constructed in fairly recent years, the expectation of life at selected ages as
shown in the latest available compilations. The ages are zero (or birth), twenty,
forty-five, and sixty-five. Wherever possible the information is given separately
for males and females.

Mortality Level

A lengthy treatise would be required to explain fully the nature of and reasons
for all the differences these various indexes reveal. Most striking is the great contrast between the relatively low death rates, the low infant mortality rates, and
the high expectation of life at birth in most of Europe, Puerto Rico, the United
States, Canada, Hong Kong, Israel, Japan, Australia, New Zealand, and the Soviet Union, and the high death rates, high infant mortality rates, and low life expectancy in West Cameroon, Nigeria, Togo, Zaire, Haiti, India, and the Khmer
Republic. Whereas, at birth children in the first group of countries have an average of about seventy years of life ahead of them, in the latter the corresponding
figure is only forty. A few countries of Southern and Eastern Europe, most portions of Latin America, and the other Asiatic nations for which data are available
rank substantially below the first group mentioned above.

Nonwhites (mostly Negroes) in the United States make a poor showing in
comparison with their white countrymen, but even so they have an expectation
of life at birth that compares favorably with that in most of Latin American

TABLE 44
Crude death rates and infant mortality rates for countries and
territories of 1 million or more inhabitants for
which data are available

Country	Crude death rate		Infant mortality rate	
	Year	Rate	Year	Rate
Africa				
Algeria	1965-70	16.9[a]	1960	113.0
Angola	1965-70	30.2[a]	1965-70	20.8
Burundi	1965-70	25.2[a]	1965-70	150.0[a]
Cameroon, West	1965-70	22.8[a]	1962	76.0[a]
Central African Republic (African population)	1965-70	25.1[a]	1959-60	190.0[a]
Chad (African population)	1965-70	25.0[a]	1963-64	160.0[a]
Dahomey (African population)	1965-70	25.5[a]	1967	109.6[a]
Egypt	1966	15.8	1966	127.1
Ghana	1965-70	17.8[a]	1960	156.0[a]
Guinea (African population)	1965-70	25.1[a]	1955	216.0[a]
Ivory Coast	1965-70	22.7[a]	1957-58	164.0
Kenya	1965-70	17.5[a]	1965-70	55.0
Liberia	1971	20.9[a]	1971	159.2
Libyan Arab Republic	1965-70	15.8[a]	....	....
Madagascar	1966	25.0[a]	1966	102.0[a]
Malawi	1965-70	25.0[a]	1953	148.3
Mali	1965-70	26.6[a]	1960-61	120.0[a]
Mauritania	1965-70	22.7[a]	1964-65	187.0[a]
Morocco	1965-70	16.5[a]	1962	149.0[a]
Mozambique	1965-70	22.9[a]	1969	92.5
Niger	1965-70	23.3[a]	1960-61	200.0[a]
Nigeria	1965-70	24.9[a]	....	....
Rwanda	1965-70	23.3[a]	1970	132.8[b]
Senegal	1965-70	22.8[a]	1960-61	92.9[a]
Sierra Leone	1965-70	22.7[a]	1968	136.3
South Africa	1965-70	16.6[a]	....	....
Southern Rhodesia	1965-70	14.4[a]	1954	122.2[a]
Sudan	1965-70	18.4[a]	1956	93.6[a]
Togo	1965-70	25.5[a]	1961	127.0[a]
Tunisia	1967-70	16.0[a]	1969	77.7
Uganda	1965-70	17.6[a]	1959	160.0[a]
Upper Volta	1965-70	29.1[a]	1965-70	182.0[a]
Zaire	1965-70	22.7[a]	1955-58	104.0[a]
Zambia	1965-70	20.7[a]	1950	259.0[a]
America, North				
Canada	1971	7.3	1971	17.6
Costa Rica	1971	5.9	1971	56.5
Cuba	1965-70	7.5[a]	1971	35.5
Dominican Republic	1965-70	14.7[a]	1970	50.1
El Salvador	1971	8.1	1971	52.5
Guatemala	1971	14.1	1971	83.1

TABLE 44 (Cont'd)

Crude death rates and infant mortality rates for countries and
territories of 1 million or more inhabitants for
which data are available

Country	Crude death rate		Infant mortality rate	
	Year	Rate	Year	Rate
Haiti	1965-70	19.7[a]	....	....
Honduras	1965-70	17.1[a]	1971	39.5
Jamaica	1970	7.1	1970	32.3
Mexico	1970	9.2	1970	67.4
Nicaragua	1965-70	16.5[a]	1971	45.0
Panama	1965-70	8.8[a]	1971	37.6
Puerto Rico	1970	6.6	1970	28.6
United States	1970	9.4	1970	19.8
America, South				
Argentina	1968	9.5	1967	58.3
Bolivia	1965-70	19.1[a]	1966	77.3
Brazil	1965-70	9.4[a]	1940-50	170.0[a]
Chile	1970	9.4	1970	78.8
Colombia	1965-70	10.6[a]	1968	70.4
Ecuador	1965-70	11.4[a]	1970	76.6
Paraguay	1965-70	10.8[a]	1970	35.6
Peru	1965-70	11.1[a]	1967	72.5
Uruguay	1971	9.8	1971	40.4
Venezuela	1965-70	7.8[a]	1970	48.7
Asia				
Afghanistan	1965-70	26.5[a]	....	....
Burma	1965-70	17.4[a]	....	....
Ceylon	1971	7.6	1968	50.3
China	1965-70	15.3[a]	....	....
Hong Kong	1971	5.0	1971	17.7
India	1965-70	16.7[a]	1951-61	139.0
Indonesia	1965-70	19.4[a]	1962	74.7
Iran	1965-70	16.6[a]	....	....
Iraq	1965-70	15.5[a]	1970	19.7
Israel	1971	7.0	1971	20.4
Japan	1970	6.9	1970	13.1
Jordan	1965-70	16.0[a]	1971	36.3
Khmer Republic	1965-70	15.6[a]	1959	127.0[a]
Korea,				
Democratic Peoples Republic	1965-70	11.2[a]	....	....
Republic of	1965-70	11.0[a]	....	....
Malaysia	1965-70	10.8[a]	1970	39.4
Nepal	1965-70	22.9[a]	....	....
Pakistan	1965-70	18.4[a]	1962-65	142.0
Philippines	1965-70	12.0[a]	1971	62.0
Singapore	1970	5.2	1970	20.5
Syrian Arab Republic	1965-70	15.3[a]	1971	23.5

TABLE 44 (Cont'd)

Crude death rates and infant mortality rates for countries and
territories of 1 million or more inhabitants for
which data are available

Country	Crude death rate		Infant mortality rate	
	Year	Rate	Year	Rate
Thailand	1965-70	10.4[a]	1970	25.5
Turkey	1967	14.6[a]	1967	153.0[b]
Viet-Nam, Democratic				
Republic	1965-70	16.1[a]	1965	36.7[a]
Europe				
Albania	1960	10.4	1960	83.0
Austria	1970	13.4	1971	25.9
Belgium	1970	12.3	1970	20.5
Bulgaria	1965	8.2	1965	30.8
Czechoslovakia	1970	11.4	1970	22.1
Denmark	1970	9.8	1970	14.2
Finland	1970	9.5	1970	12.5
France	1968	11.1	1968	20.4
Germany, Federal Republic	1970	11.6	1970	23.5
Democratic Republic	1972	13.7	1972	17.7
East Berlin	1970	16.2	1970	19.6
West Berlin	1970	19.0	1970	25.8
Greece	1971	8.3	1971	27.0
Hungary	1970	11.7	1970	35.9
Ireland	1971	10.6	1970	19.6
Italy	1971	9.6	1971	28.3
Netherlands	1960	7.7	1960	17.9
Norway	1970	9.8	1970	12.7
Poland	1970	8.2	1970	33.2
Portugal	1970	9.7	1970	58.0
Romania	1966	8.2	1966	46.6
Spain	1970	8.6	1970	27.9
Sweden	1970	9.9	1971	11.1
Switzerland	1970	9.1	1970	15.1
United Kingdom				
England and Wales	1971	11.6	1971	17.6
Northern Ireland	1971	10.6	1971	23.0
Scotland	1971	11.8	1971	19.9
Yugoslavia	1971	8.7	1971	48.8
Oceania				
Australia	1970	9.1	1971	17.3
New Zealand	1970	8.8	1971	16.5
U.S.S.R.	1970	8.2	1970	24.4

Source: Compiled from data in United Nations, *Demographic Yearbook*, various issues;
and *Population and Vital Statistics Report*, Vol. XXIII, No. 4; Vol. XXIV, No. 2; Vol.
XXV, No. 2.

[a]Estimate-prepared by the United Nations.
[b]Estimate prepared by the country.

TABLE 45

Expectation of life at selected ages for countries and territories
of 1 million or more inhabitants for which life tables
are available, by sex

Country	Year	Sex	Age 0	20	45	65
Africa						
Cameroon, West (African population)	1964-65	Male	34	35	18	9
		Female	37	35	17	10
Egypt	1960	Male	52	48	26	12
		Female	54	53	31	14
Ghana (African population)	1960	Male	48	36	20	9
Nigeria	1965-66	Male	44	39	21	10
		Female	43	38	21	11
South Africa						
(Asiatic population)	1965-70	Male	58	44	22	10
		Female	60	46	24	10
(Colored population)	1959-61	Male	50	43	23	12
		Female	54	47	27	13
(White population)	1959-61	Male	65	48	26	12
		Female	72	54	31	15
Southern Rhodesia (European population)	1961-63	Male	67	49	26	12
		Female	74	56	33	16
Togo	1961	Male	32	30	17	7
		Female	38	38	21	10
Zaire (African population)	1950-52	Male	38	34	18	9
		Female	40	36	20	10
America, North						
Canada	1965-67	Male	69	52	29	14
		Female	75	57	34	17
Costa Rica	1962-64	Male	62	51	29	14
		Female	65	53	30	15
Dominican Republic	1959-61	Male	57	49	27	11
		Female	59	50	28	11
El Salvador	1960-61	Male	57	48	28	14
		Female	60	51	30	16
Guatemala	1963-65	Male	48	43	25	12
		Female	50	45	25	12
Haiti	1950		33	34	22	14
Jamaica	1959-61	Male	63	49	27	13
		Female	67	53	30	15
Mexico	1965-70	Male	61	....	....	....
		Female	64	....	....	....
Panama	1960-61	Male	58	49	28	13
		Female	72	56	34	17
United States						
(White population)	1967-68	Male	68	50	27	13
		Female	75	57	33	16

TABLE 45 (Cont'd)

Expectation of life at selected ages for countries and territories
of 1 million or more inhabitants for which life talbes
are available, by sex

Country	Year	Sex	Age 0	20	45	65
(nonwhite population)	1967-68	Male	60	44	24	12
		Female	68	51	29	15
America, South						
Argentina	1959-61	Male	63	49	27	13
		Female	69	55	32	16
Bolivia	1949-51	Male	50	47	. . . .	. . . .
		Female	50	47	. . . .	. . . .
Brazil	1965-70		61	. . . .	. . . .	. . . .
Chile	1960-61	Male	54	45	25	12
		Female	60	50	29	14
Colombia	1950-52	Male	44	40	21	9
		Female	46	41	23	10
Ecuador	1961-63	Male	51	46	26	12
		Female	54	48	28	13
Peru	1960-65	Male	53	45	25	12
		Female	55	47	27	13
Uruguay	1963-64	Male	66	50	27	13
		Female	72	55	32	16
Venezuela	1961		66	52	30	16
Asia						
Ceylon	1962	Male	62	49	27	11
		Female	61	48	27	10
China	1965-70		50	. . . .	. . . .	. . . .
Hong Kong	1968	Male	67	50	27	13
		Female	73	57	33	17
India	1951-60	Male	42	37	19	10
		Female	41	36	20	11
Israel	1970	Male	70	52	29	14
		Female	73	55	31	15
Japan	1968	Male	69	51	28	13
		Female	74	56	32	15
Jordan	1959-63	Male	53	44	25	12
		Female	52	46	27	13
Khmer Republic	1958-59	Male	44	39	21	9
		Female	43	38	22	11
Korea, Republic of	1966	Male	60	46	25	11
		Female	64	51	29	13
Malaysia, West	1969	Male	64	49	27	13
		Female	67	52	29	14
Pakistan	1962	Male	54	48	27	12
		Female	49	43	24	13

TABLE 45 (Cont'd)

Expectation of life at selected ages for countries and territories
of 1 million or more inhabitants for which life talbes
are available, by sex

Country	Year	Sex	Age 0	20	45	65
Taiwan	1965	Male	66	49	27	12
		Female	70	53	30	14
Europe						
Albania	1965-66	Male	65	53	30	15
		Female	67	56	33	16
Austria	1970	Male	66	49	27	12
		Female	74	56	32	15
Belgium	1959-63	Male	68	50	27	12
		Female	74	56	32	15
Bulgaria	1965-67	Male	69	52	29	13
		Female	73	56	32	15
Czechoslovakia	1966	Male	67	50	27	12
		Female	74	56	32	15
Denmark	1968-69	Male	71	53	29	14
		Female	76	57	33	16
Finland	1961-65	Male	65	48	25	11
		Female	73	54	31	14
France	1969	Male	68	50	27	13
		Female	75	57	33	16
Germany, Federal Republic	1966-68	Male	68	50	27	12
		Female	74	56	32	15
Democratic Republic[a]	1967-68	Male	69	52	29	13
		Female	74	56	33	16
West Berlin	1960-62	Male	66	49	27	13
		Female	72	55	30	14
Greece	1960-62	Male	67	53	29	13
		Female	71	56	32	15
Hungary	1964	Male	67	51	28	13
		Female	72	55	31	14
Ireland	1960-62	Male	68	51	28	13
		Female	72	54	31	14
Italy	1964-67	Male	68	52	28	13
		Female	73	56	33	16
Netherlands	1970	Male	71	53	29	14
		Female	76	58	34	16
Norway	1961-65	Male	71	53	30	14
		Female	76	58	34	16
Poland	1965-66	Male	67	51	28	13
		Female	73	56	32	15
Portugal	1970	Male	65	51	29	13
		Female	71	56	33	15
Romania	1964-67	Male	66	51	28	13
		Female	71	55	31	14

TABLE 45 (Cont'd)

Expectation of life at selected ages for countries and territories
of 1 million or more inhabitants for which life talbes
are available, by sex

Country	Year	Sex	Age 0	20	45	65
Spain	1960	Male	67	51	28	13
		Female	72	55	32	15
Sweden	1967	Male	72	53	30	14
		Female	77	58	34	16
Switzerland	1958-63	Male	69	51	28	13
		Female	74	56	32	15
United Kingdom						
England and Wales	1968-70	Male	69	51	27	12
		Female	75	57	33	16
Northern Ireland	1968-70	Male	68	50	27	12
		Female	73	55	32	15
Scotland	1968-70	Male	67	49	26	11
		Female	73	55	31	15
Yugoslavia	1967-68	Male	64	50	27	12
		Female	69	54	31	14
Oceania						
Australia	1960-62	Male	68	50	27	12
		Female	74	56	32	16
New Zealand	1960-62	Male	68	51	28	13
		Female	74	56	32	15
U.S.S.R.	1968-69	Male	65	....	....	....
		Female	74	....	....	....

Source: Compiled from data in United Nations, *Demographic Yearbook, 1971* (New York:
United Nations, 1972), pp. 746-765, Table 34.
[a]Includes East Berlin.

countries and in the parts of Asia, other than Japan, Israel, and Hong Kong, for which it has been possible to prepare life tables. Similarly, in South Africa the expectation of life of the colored population and that of the Asiatic population are substantially lower than that of the white population.

As age increases, the differentials are greatly decreased. Thus, at birth the extreme range, among the countries represented in Table 45, is from seventy-seven for females in Sweden to thirty-two for males in Togo, whereas at age twenty the greatest disparity is between the index of fifty-eight years for females in Norway and the one of thirty for males in Togo. At age forty-five the differences are even more sharply reduced, with the upper extreme being the average of thirty-four years of future lifetime left to women in Canada, Puerto Rico, the Netherlands, Norway, and Sweden, and the lower that of seventeen years for females in West Cameroon and males in Togo. At age sixty-five the highest of the calculations (seventeen) is for women in Canada, Puerto Rico, and Hong Kong; the lowest (seven), for males in Togo. This means that much of the difference noted throughout the world in life expectation at birth is due to the varying levels of infant and child mortality.

Additional light is shed on this observation by comparing, in various countries, the age at which the expectation of life is reduced to an average equal to that at birth. (Since the very slight contributions made to the total years lived by the group by infants dying during the first year of life must be included in calculating the average, the expectation of life at age one always is higher than that at birth; and if high child mortality rates prevail, the same may be the case at various ages beyond one.) Such comparisons are permitted, to a considerable extent, by the values from the life tables for various countries which have been assembled in the 1971 edition of the *Demographic Yearbook* of the United Nations. A careful scrutiny of these materials indicates that in nine of the countries on the list the expectation of life is approximately equal at the time of the first birthday or the beginning of the second year of life to that at birth. These, of course, are the countries in which deaths during the first twelve months of life have been reduced to the lowest levels and the average length of life has been expanded to the greatest extent by the saving of infant and child lives. They are as follows: Japan, Denmark, Finland, France, the Netherlands, Norway, Sweden, England and Wales, and Australia. These nine countries are most closely rivaled in this respect by the following in which at approximately the second birthday or the start of the third year of life the amount of future lifetime is again equal to that at birth: South Africa (white population), Southern Rhodesia (European population), Canada, the United States, Israel, Taiwan, Austria, Belgium, Czechoslovakia, East and West Germany, East and West Berlin, Ireland, Italy, Switzerland, Scotland, and New Zealand. Next comes a group of nations in which and child mortality rates have been reduced to the extent that expectation of life at birth and at the third birthday are approximately equal. The countries in this category are: Hong Kong, West Malaysia, Bulgaria, Hungary, Poland, Romania, and Spain. In three countries (Puerto Rico, Uruguay, and Northern Ireland), the expectation of life is about equal to that at the fourth birthday; in five (Venezeula, the Republic of Korea, Greece, Portugal, and Yugoslavia) the average remaining lifetime at birth is about the same as that at the fifth birthday.

At the other extreme are Haiti, in which only at age twenty-four is life expectation again approximately equal to what it was at birth; Nigeria, in which the corresponding age is twenty-three; West Cameroon and Bolivia, in which it is twenty; Togo, in which it is about nineteen; Ghana (African population) and Egypt, where it is seventeen; and Zaire (African population), where the average future lifetime at birth and at age fifteen are approximately the same. Finally, the approximate age at which expectation of life is equal to that at birth in various other countries may be summarized as follows: age six, South Africa (Asiatic population), Jamaica, and Ceylon; age seven, Argentina; age eight, Costa Rica and Albania; age ten, El Salvador, Panama, Chile, and Peru; age eleven, the Dominican Republic; age twelve, South Africa (colored population) and Jordan; age thirteen, Pakistan; and age fourteen, Guatemala, Colombia, Ecuador, India, and the Khmer Republic.

In passing, it should be pointed out that these data offer little support for the thesis, which has enjoyed such wide popularity, that high infant and child mortality rates eliminate the weaklings, leaving only the strong and virile. Such a thesis would be supported if the countries in which expectation of life at birth is high were the ones in which expectation of life at age sixty-five is low, and if those in which the average calculated from birth is low were those in which the index for persons aged sixty-five is high. Such is definitely not the case. Generally speaking, the nations with high expectation of life at birth maintain their superiority at all ages throughout the life span.

The almost universal tendency for females of all ages to enjoy a longer expectation of life than males also deserves comment. When the expectation of life at birth is used as the index, the exceptions to this rule among the countries listed in Table 45 are Nigeria, Ceylon, India, Jordan, the Khmer Republic, and Pakistan. Females are at the disadvantage at some other ages in these same countries, although in a few other places at some ages the values for men and women are equal. In no case, however, is the expectation of life shorter for women than for men in the highly industrialized countries and, in fact, the differentials between the sexes generally are greater in those places than they are in the underdeveloped areas. In the latter, women are still subject to a relatively high degree of risk from the various causes of maternal mortality.

Causes of Death

The tabulations prepared for the *Demographic Yearbook* of the United Nations now make it possible to explore, with comparative ease, the extent to which the various causes of death are assigned by those who prepare the death certificates in different parts of the world. Although one may be certain that uniformity in procedures is still far from being attained, for certain broad purposes this information probably is sufficiently reliable to make worthwhile comparisons possible. In general, one may be quite sure that the extent to which the deaths are attributed to "symptoms and ill-defined conditions" and "all other diseases" (categories B45 and B46 in the abbreviated list of the Eighth Revision of the International List of Causes of Death) is somewhat indicative of the need for substantial improvement in recording and reporting mortality statistics. Thus, one might conclude that the rates given for various important causes of death, such as heart ailments or cancer, are more trustworthy for Denmark, in which only 1.4 per cent of the deaths are classified as due to symptoms and ill-defined conditions and 10.4 per cent to the residual set of all other causes, than they are for France, in which the corresponding percentages are 10.2 and 12.3, respectively. Even so, the death rate in France from symptoms in 1970 of 107 per 100,000 population is exceeded by those in El Salvador (360), Guatemala (271), Ecuador (233), Venezuela (157), Panama (134), and Mexico (133); and the residual class of all other diseases is assigned frequently enough to account for rates of 355 per 100,000 population in the German Democratic Republic, 148 in Poland, 146 in El Salvador and Hungary, 144 in Austria, 136 in Belgium, and 131 in Ecuador. In view of this, great care is needed in comparing the absolute and relative importance of the different causes of death in the various nations.

Where modern methods of preventive medicine and sanitation, based on the germ theory of disease, have been applied on a large scale, the deteriorative ailments (heart disease, cancer, cerebrovascular disease or "stroke," and so on) stand at the top of the list of the causes of death; where such applications of modern science have not been adequately made, organism-transmitted diseases continue to rank high in the list of killers. For this reason, even with all the limitations of the data indicated in the preceding paragraph, it is interesting to identify the three most important causes of death reported for various nations throughout the world. Unfortunately, many of the most populous countries have not supplied the necessary information or have not yet done so according to the Eighth Revision of the list of causes, but even so the compilations presented in Table 46 deserve careful study. (The residual category of all other diseases was omitted from consideration in making this tabulation.)

Two patterns are evident in these materials. Where much has been done to control the ravages of preventable diseases (as is especially true in almost all of Europe, the United States and Canada, Uruguay, Israel, Australia, and New Zealand), heart disease, cancer, and cerebrovascular disease are the leading causes of death; and collectively the three account for the large majority of all fatalities. In many other countries, symptoms and ill-defined conditions, enteritis and related maladies, and one other of the transmissible ailments make up the three most impor-

TABLE 46
Three leading causes of death

Country	Year	Cause	Rate*
Africa			
South Africa			
(Asiatic population)	1969	1. Ischaemic heart disease (B28)	101
		2. Cerebrovascular disease (B30)	79
		3. Pneumonia (B32)	76
(Colored population)	1969	1. Enteritis, etc. (B4)	322
		2. Pneumonia (B32)	179
		3. Cerebrovascular disease (B30)	93
(White population)	1969	1. Ischaemic heart disease (B28)	212
		2. Malignant neoplasms (B19)	135
		3. Cerebrovascular disease (B30)	100
Southern Rhodesia			
(European population)	1970	1. Ischaemic heart disease (B28)	148
		2. Malignant neoplasms (B19)	123
		3. Cerebrovascular disease (B30)	75
America, North			
Barbados	1970	1. Cerebrovascular disease (B30)	123
		2. Malignant neoplasms (B19)	100
		3. Other forms of heart disease (B29)	85
Canada	1969	1. Ischaemic heart disease (B28)	230
		2. Malignant neoplasms (B19)	141
		3. Cerebrovascular disease (B30)	74
Costa Rica	1969	1. Enteritis, etc. (B4)	83
		2. Malignant neoplasms (B19)	68
		3. Pneumonia (B32)	46
El Salvador	1969	1. Symptoms, ill-defined conditions (B45)	360
		2. Enteritis, etc. (B4)	93
		3. Bronchitis, emphysema, asthma (B33)	31
Guatemala	1969	1. Enteritis, etc. (B4)	392
		2. Symptoms, ill-defined conditions (B45)	271
		3. Influenza (B31)	159
Jamaica	1969	1. Cerebrovascular disease (B30)	107[a]
		2. Malignant neoplasms (B19)	84[a]
		3. Pneumonia (B32)	48[a]
Mexico	1970	1. Pneumonia (B32)	147
		2. Enteritis, etc. (B4)	141
		3. Symptoms, ill-defined conditions (B45)	133
Panama	1970	1. Symptoms, ill-defined conditions (B45)	133
		2. Ischaemic heart disease (B28)	63
		3. Pneumonia (B32)	50
United States	1970	1. Ischaemic heart disease (B28)	325
		2. Malignant neoplasms (B19)	162
		3. Cerebrovascular disease (B30)	102

TABLE 46 (Cont'd)
Three leading causes of death

Country	Year	Cause	Rate*
America, South			
Chile	1968	1. Pneumonia (B32)	133
		2. Malignant neoplasms (B19)	101
		3. Ischaemic heart disease (B28)	55
Ecuador	1969	1 Symptoms, ill-defined conditions (B45)	233
		2. Bronchitis, emphysema, asthma (B33)	92
		3. Enteritis, etc. (B4)	80
Paraguay	1969	1. Symptoms, ill-defined conditions (B45)	102
		2. Enteritis, etc. (B4)	46
		3. Malignant neoplasms (B19)	33
Uruguay	1970	1. Malignant neoplasms (B19)	190
		2. Ischaemic heart disease (B28)	149
		3. Cerebrovascular disease (B30)	114
Venezuela	1969	1. Symptoms, ill-defined conditions (B45)	157
		2. Malignant neoplasms (B19)	54
		3. Enteritis, etc. (B4)	51
Asia			
Hong Kong	1970	1. Malignant neoplasms (B19)	100
		2. Pneumonia (B32)	50
		3. Symptoms, ill-defined conditions (B45)	50
Israel	1970	1. Ischaemic heart disease (B28)	184
		2. Malignant neoplasms (B19)	116
		3. Cerebrovascular disease (B30)	88
Japan	1970	1. Cerebrovascular disease (B30)	175
		2. Malignant heoplasms (B19)	116
		3. Symptoms, ill-defined condition (B45)	51
Singapore	1970	1. Malignant neoplasms (B19)	77
		2. Symptoms, ill-defined conditions (B45)	61
		3. Cerebrovascular disease (B30)	50
Europe			
Austria	1970	1. Malignant neoplasms (B19)	262
		2. Ischaemic heart disease (B28)	232
		3. Cerebrovascular disease (B30)	199
Belgium	1969	1. Malignant neoplasms (B19)	240
		2. Ischaemic heart disease (B28)	181
		3. Cerebrovascular disease (B30)	170
Bulgaria	1970	1. Cerebrovascular disease (B30)	187
		2. Ischaemic heart disease (B28)	178
		3. Malignant neoplasms (B19)	133
Czechoslovakia	1968	1. Ischaemic heart disease (B28)	230
		2. Malignant neoplasms (B19)	215
		3. Cerebrovascular disease (B30)	143

TABLE 46 (Cont'd)
Three leading causes of death

Country	Year	Cause	Rate*
Denmark	1969	1. Ischaemic heart disease (B28)	294
		2. Malignant neoplasms (B19)	221
		3. Cerebrovascular disease (B30)	102
Finland	1969	1. Ischaemic heart disease (B28)	247
		2. Malignant neoplasms (B19)	166
		3. Cerebrovascular disease (B30)	137
France	1970	1. Malignant neoplasms (B19)	206
		2. Cerebrovascular disease (B30)	146
		3. Other forms of heart disease (B29)	111
Germany			
Federal Republic	1969	1. Malignant neoplasms (B19)	243
		2. Cerebrovascular disease (B30)	186
		3. Ischaemic heart disease (B28)	177
Democratic Republic[b]	1969	1. Malignant neoplasms (B19)	220
		2. Ischaemic heart disease (B28)	151
		3. Other forms of heart disease (B29)	123
Greece	1970	1. Malignant neoplasms (B19)	131
		2. Cerebrovascular disease (B30)	117
		3. Symptoms, ill-defined conditions (B45)	101
Hungary	1970	1. Ischaemic heart disease (B28)	228
		2. Malignant neoplasms (B19)	216
		3. Cerebrovascular disease (B30)	170
Ireland	1970	1. Ischaemic heart disease (B28)	264
		2. Malignant neoplasms (B19)	188
		3. Cerebrovascular disease (B30)	156
Italy	1968	1. Malignant neoplasms (B19)	174
		2. Cerebrovascular disease (B30)	136
		3. Ischaemic heart disease (B28)	129
Netherlands	1970	1. Malignant neoplasms (B19)	195
		2. Ischaemic heart disease (B28)	182
		3. Cerebrovascular disease (B30)	97
Norway	1969	1. Ischaemic heart disease (B28)	264
		2. Malignant neoplasms (B19)	188
		3. Cerebrovascular disease (B30)	159
Poland	1970	1. Malignant neoplasms (B19)	138
		2. Other forms of heart disease (B29)	92
		3. Symptoms, ill-defined conditions (B45)	83
Romania	1970	1. Other forms of heart disease (B29)	179
		2. Cerebrovascular disease (B30)	131
		3. Malignant neoplasms (B19)	120

TABLE 46 (Cont'd)
Three leading causes of death

Country	Year	Cause	Rate*
Spain	1968	1. Malignant neoplasms (B19)	131
		2. Cerebrovascular disease (B30)	109
		3. Other forms of heart disease (B29)	95
Sweden	1969	1. Ischaemic heart disease (B28)	314
		2. Malignant neoplasms (B19)	203
		3. Cerebrovascular disease (B30)	109
Switzerland	1969	1. Malignant neoplasms (B19)	194
		2. Other forms of heart disease (B29)	130
		3. Ischaemic heart disease (B28)	104
United Kingdom			
England and Wales	1970	1. Ischaemic heart disease (B28)	284
		2. Malignant neoplasms (B19)	236
		3. Cerebrovascular disease (B30)	162
Northern Ireland	1970	1. Ischaemic heart disease (B28)	295
		2. Malignant neoplasms (B19)	184
		3. Cerebrovascular disease (B30)	161
Scotland	1970	1. Ischaemic heart disease (B28)	337
		2. Malignant neoplasms (B19)	242
		3. Cerebrovascular disease (B30)	191
Oceania			
Australia	1970	1. Ischaemic heart disease (B28)	272
		2. Malignant neoplasms (B19)	145
		3. Cerebrovascular disease (B30)	126
New Zealand	1970	1. Ischaemic heart disease (B28)	242
		2. Malignant neoplasms (B19)	160
		3. Cerebrovascular disease (B30)	114

Source: Compiled from data in United Nations, *Demographic Yearbook, 1971* (New York: United Nations, 1972), pp. 728-744, Table 33, Part B.
*Rates are per 100,000 population.
[a]Estimate.
[b]Includes East Berlin.
Abbreviations:
Enteritis, etc. (B4) = Enteritis and other diarrheal diseases.
Malignant neoplasms (B19) = Malignant neoplasms, including neoplasms of lymphatic and haematopoietic tissue.

tant categories. This is underscored by the importance of various causes of death in several developing countries as classified according to the Seventh Revision of the list. The country, the year of reporting, and the three leading causes in descending order of importance are as follows:[1] Angola (1969), gastritis, senility, and pneumonia; Egypt (1969), gastritis, senility, and bronchitis; Nicaragua (1965), senility, gastritis, and residual diseases of early infancy; Bolivia (1966), senility, pneumonia, and residual diseases of early infancy; Colombia (1967), gastritis, senility, and pneumonia; Peru (1964), senility, pneumonia, and residual diseases of early infancy; Ceylon (1968), senility, residual diseases of early infancy, and gastritis; India (1963), senility, pneumonia, and residual diseases of early infancy; and the Philippines (1969), senility, pneumonia, and tuberculosis of the respiratory system. Nevertheless, the fact that malaria, infective and parasitic diseases, tuberculosis, and various deficiency ailments now figure among the top three causes of death in so few countries reflects the high degree to which the control of these maladies throughout the world has become an international concern. Nowadays the presence of yellow fever in a Latin American port, a violent scourge of malaria in some part of Africa, or an outbreak of cholera in Egypt is considered and dealt with as a menace to peoples in many lands.

Infant Mortality

The deaths of children of less than one year of age constitute such a large proportion of all deaths that infant mortality deserves special analysis. As indicated above, the rates for all the principal portions of the globe for which data are available are presented in Table 44. A fair approximation of the situation around the world at the opening of the last three decades of the twentieth century may be secured through a study of these materials.

The fact that by 1971 the infant mortality rate in Sweden had been reduced to 11 is a remarkable achievement, as are the other rates of less than 20 achieved in Canada, the United States, Hong Kong, Denmark, Finland, the German Democratic Republic, East Berlin, Ireland, the Netherlands, Norway, Switzerland, England and Wales, Scotland, Australia, and New Zealand. Only slightly less impressive are rates that are between 20 and 30 in Puerto Rico, Israel, Singapore, Thailand, Austria, Belgium, Czechoslovakia, France, the Federal Republic of Germany, West Berlin, Greece, Italy, Spain, Northern Ireland, and the Soviet Union.[2] It seems reasonable to expect, therefore, that within a few more decades, a rate approaching the minimum possible may be registered by one or more of these countries. At the other end of the scale are parts of the world in which very high proportions of all the children born fail to live through the first year of life. The population of Zambia, in which the reported rate would indicate that more than one child in every four dies before attaining the age of one year, is in a class by itself; but rates of 120 or above also are listed for Burundi, the Central African

Republic (African population), Chad (African population), Egypt, Ghana, Guinea (African population), Ivory Coast, Liberia, Malawi, Mali, Mauritania, Morocco, Niger, Rwanda, Sierra Leone, Southern Rhodesia, Togo, Uganda, Upper Volta, Brazil, India, the Khmer Republic, Pakistan, and Turkey. In addition, in descending order according to the rates, Algeria, Dahomey (African population), Zaire, Madagascar, Sudan, Senegal, and Mozambique all have rates of 90 or more. It should be indicated that any tendency for birth registration to be incomplete is likely to result in an artificial inflation of the infant mortality rate, and that the high indexes for some of the countries may be due in part to this factor. In Colombia, for example, it is highly probable that the reported infant mortality rate is inflated by 10 to 20 per cent merely because the number of births used in the calculation of the rate is too small. This same factor is certainly present in the relatively old data for Brazil as well.

The white population of the United States has a much lower infant mortality rate than the nonwhite population, the indexes in 1972 being 16 and 29, respectively. However, the rate for nonwhites (mostly Negroes) is relatively close to those in such countries as Puerto Rico, Bulgaria, Greece, Italy, and Spain; and it is substantially lower than the ones for Albania, Hungary, Portugal, Romania, and Yugoslavia.

These data indicate that in many of the most populous parts of the earth infant mortality rates are still very high. However, the deaths of young infants are among those most easily prevented through the proper application of modern scientific knowledge in the fields of preventive medicine, the care and feeding of children, care of mothers during childbirth, sanitation, and so on. During the last part of the twentieth century, this knowledge is being widely diffused, and it is being applied to safeguard the lives of the very young. If this trend continues, as appears to be certain, during the decades immediately ahead the world may very well see an upsurge of population that will dwarf the increases that have taken place since 1950 provided, of course, that no decline of similar magnitude takes place in the birth rate.

MORTALITY IN THE UNITED STATES

A study of mortality in the United States does much to bring out the factors responsible for variations in the death rates and in the expectation of life generally, even though our data and procedures must be greatly improved before accurate measurements and comparisons of the levels of mortality in the various states and regions will be possible. The basic difficulty is the extremely high mobility of our population, which often results in deaths being charged to states to which the persons involved had been sent for their health and not to the sections of the country in which they had contracted their fatal illnesses. Any measures that show the risks of life in the United States to be relatively great in the states of Arizona and New Mexico, and least in the Plains States, obviously leave a great deal to be desired. Likewise, it probably is absolutely impossible, with the data available, to secure a reliable answer to a question of what effect, if any, retirement to an area such as southern California, Arizona, the Gulf Coast, or peninsular Florida may have upon the longevity of the persons making such a move. We are unable to charge properly the deaths occurring in our population to the areas to which the debits should be given. Nevertheless, the data we do have enable the demographer to explore many important aspects of mortality.

Age and the Death Rate

The close relationship between age and the death rate has already been referred to in connection with Table 45. Even in the United States, with its very low infant mortality rate, the hazards of life are great during infancy. This is especially true during the first hours and days of the baby's life, but the death rate then declines precipitously during the first year of life, rapidly for another two or three years, and slowly but gradually until the age of twelve. During late childhood and early adolescence the chances of loss of life during a given year are near their minimum, but by the time the person reaches fifteen the age-specific mortality rate has begun to rise perceptibly. Henceforth the trend is ever upward, although not until age fifty-five or thereabouts has been attained is the increase greatly accelerated. Eventually, after the mark of "threescore years and ten" has been passed, the rates soar. At age seventy there is one chance out of five that a given person will pass away before attaining his seventy-fifth birthday, at age eighty there are almost two chances in five that he will die before reaching his eighty-fifth birthday.

Sex and the Mortality Rate

That females have a longer expectation of life than males has already been indicated in connection with analysis of the materials in Table 45. All of the data for the United States are in absolute accord. For the years 1969 - 1971, for example, the life tables indicate that at every age from birth to eighty-five and over, and for the nonwhite population as well as the white, the age-specific death rate for males was higher than the one for females, although the differential by sex was greater for the whites than for the nonwhites. Moreover, irrespective of the manner in which the data are presented, it can be asserted with a reasonable degree of certainty that among whites and Negroes (regardless of whether they live in cities or in the open country), and in all sections of the country, the death rates of males are higher than those for females of comparable ages; and life expectancy of the former is less than that of the latter. For this reason, the mortality data should always be subdivided by sex before any other comparisons are attempted, although for most purposes this is not necessary in the use of the infant mortality rate.

Race or Color and the Mortality Rate

As indicated above, from the standpoint of longevity the white population enjoys a distinct advantage over the nonwhite (mostly Negro) population. This was true in 1901, the year for which our first life tables were constructed, when the life expectation at birth of Negro males was only 34.1 years compared with 50.2 years for white males and when the corresponding averages for Negro and white females were 35.0 and 51.1 years, respectively. The same pattern prevailed at every subsequent date at which the census of population supplied the age distributions essential for making the computations, including 1970, when the expectation of life at birth among males was 68.1 years for whites and 60.5 years for nonwhites and when the corresponding indexes among females were 75.4 and 68.9, respectively. However, it will be noted that the differential between whites and Negroes was greatly reduced in the course of the seventy years covered by our inventories of the length of life of the population. Thus, in 1901, the materials given above indicate that the life expectation at birth of white males was 47 per cent above that of Negro males, and that the average for the white females was 46 per cent higher than the index for nonwhite females. By 1970, though, the increase in life expectancy had been so much more rapid among Negroes than among whites that the corresponding differences for males and females had been reduced to 13 per cent and 9 per cent, respectively.

Residence and the Mortality Rate

It now is very difficult to prepare life tables and other indexes of mortality in a manner that will permit valid comparisons of mortality in rural and urban areas, and this apparently is becoming more difficult with the passing of each decade. The mushrooming of the suburbs, the development of rural residential areas for those who work in the city, the growing tendency for farm owners and farm laborers to reside in towns and cities, the greater use of hospitals, and the rapidly increasing territorial mobility of the population all serve to complicate the work. Probably it already is almost impossible to match population counts and mortality records in a way that will make it possible to compute reliable age-specific death rates for rural residents and those who live in urban districts. In 1900 and 1910, the task was not so involved, and the first official life tables prepared in the Bureau of the Census included separate computations for the rural and urban populations.[3] These were supplemented with fairly comparable compilations prepared for 1930 by the *Metropolitan Life Insurance Company*.[4] In 1943, the

United States Bureau of the Census published abridged life tables for the year 1939 for the rural and urban, white and nonwhite portions of the population.[5] These were the first using data in which deaths were recorded by place of residence of the deceased rather than by place of occurrence. In the early 1960's, the National Public Health Service published for each state, separately by color and rural and urban residence, the number of all deaths, that of infants under one year of age, and that of babies under 28 days.[6] These materials were subdivided for the nation as a whole according to size of place although never into categories which distinguished the rural-nonfarm and the rural-farm populations. The data made it possible to gain a few impressions of the variations in mortality rates by residence. Even so, these materials were not subsorted by sex, nor were the data on general mortality adjusted for age in the various residence categories. Beginning with 1964, however, the rural and urban distinctions were abandoned. Since then some data on general mortality and infant deaths have been compiled for urban places with 100,000 or more inhabitants but the materials for places with 2,500 to 9,999 inhabitants (classified as urban by the Bureau of the Census) are included with the "balance of area," which is a conglomeration of small-urban, rural-nonfarm, and rural-farm populations.[7] Moreover, the publication of these materials is generally delayed by at least three years after the date to which they apply. These data, subdivided by color, give only a few impressions of rural and urban differentials in mortality levels for the nation and the various states, although they are now reported separately for infants under one year of age and do at least allow that particular accounting for age. They provide no insights into the variations in expectation of life among urban and rural inhabitants. As a result of these severe limitations, the analysis of mortality differentials by residence is based upon the materials for 1960. (See Tables 48 and 49.) The fact remains that any comparisons of rural and urban mortality in which the necessary control is exercised over the factors of age, sex, and color or race must rest upon the results of special endeavors by a few students working with the data for selected states.

From the data given in Table 47, it is evident that among the white population in 1901, 1910, and 1930, rural persons, both male and female, enjoyed a considerably longer expectation of life at birth, and also at age fifty, than did people living in the cities of the United States. A similar conclusion can be derived from the results of later efforts to determine the nature and extent of rural-urban differences in mortality.[8] Among both males and females, the expectation of life has been greater in rural than in urban areas. However, a study of infant mortality rates, employed to account for the factor of age, indicates that in 1960 the rates of the rural population were not uniformly lower than those of people residing in urban centers of all sizes and that the relationship between levels of mortality and residence is quite different for whites and nonwhites. (See Tables 48 and 49.) Among whites the mortality rates of those under one year of age are higher in the urban than in the rural population; but among nonwhites the reverse is true. This difference also exists in the majority of states. That is, the death rates of white infants are lower in the urban than in the rural populations of only fifteen states, whereas those of nonwhite infants are lower in the urban than in the rural populations of thirty-eight of them. The tendency for rural whites to have lower infant mortality rates than urban whites and for urban nonwhites to have lower rates than rural nonwhites appears even when the

TABLE 47

Changes in the expectation of life of the white population of the original registration area, 1901, 1910, and 1930, by residence and sex

Age and class	Expectation of life		
	1901	1910	1930
At birth:			
Urban males	43.97	47.32	56.73
Urban females	47.90	51.39	61.05
Rural males	54.03	55.06	62.09
Rural females	55.41	57.35	65.09
At age twenty:			
Urban males	39.13	40.51	44.20
Urban females	41.86	43.51	47.35
Rural males	45.97	45.92	48.32
Rural females	46.09	46.86	50.37
At age fifty:			
Urban males	18.56	18.59	19.78
Urban females	20.28	20.53	22.40
Rural males	22.78	22.43	23.39
Rural females	23.54	23.27	24.77
At age seventy:			
Urban males	8.20	8.14	8.50
Urban females	8.97	8.99	9.70
Rural males	9.56	9.36	9.88
Rural females	10.10	9.76	10.43

Source: James W. Glover, *United States Life Tables, 1890, 1901, 1910, and 1901 - 1910* (Washington: Government Printing Office, 1921); and the *Statistical Bulletin* of the Metropolitan Life Insurance Company, Vol. 16 (July, 1935). Urban in 1901 refers to cities of 8,000 or more inhabitants and in 1910 and 1930 to those with 10,000 or more residents.

TABLE 48

Number of deaths of children under one year of age per 1,000 live births, by color and residence, for states, 1960

State	White		Nonwhite	
	Urban	Rural	Urban	Rural
United States	23.2	22.4	40.9	48.5
Alabama	23.8	26.1	43.9	46.1
Alaska	34.4	24.0	44.6	75.2
Arizona	25.7	28.7	51.4	64.7
Arkansas	22.2	22.7	38.8	38.7
California	22.2	23.1	29.3	31.6
Colorado	26.9	26.8	37.7	90.4
Connecticut	19.4	21.0	36.6	43.0
Delaware	20.9	16.8	47.6	53.7
District of Columbia	29.4	....	39.6	....
Florida	25.9	21.7	45.9	46.5
Georgia	26.8	22.6	45.7	51.0
Hawaii	20.9	21.8	21.2	27.3
Idaho	22.8	22.7	35.7	31.6
Illinois	22.2	22.0	39.5	42.6
Indiana	24.0	20.5	37.9	31.0
Iowa	24.3	18.5	33.9	60.0
Kansas	23.1	18.4	33.1	36.8
Kentucky	25.9	26.0	45.6	54.7
Louisiana	24.3	20.5	44.3	50.6
Maine	27.2	24.8	7.2	17.4
Maryland	25.2	20.5	41.4	52.5
Massachusetts	21.2	21.1	33.5	43.7
Michigan	21.2	23.5	40.5	38.5
Minnesota	22.3	20.4	24.8	18.3
Mississippi	27.1	26.2	53.3	54.7
Missouri	22.5	19.7	44.6	52.9
Montana	23.6	24.9	36.8	33.9
Nebraska	21.8	20.6	31.9	53.6
Nevada	30.5	27.3	31.8	39.7
New Hampshire	24.2	23.1	....	71.4
New Jersey	21.7	23.0	41.8	41.4
New Mexico	29.6	33.5	44.9	56.3
New York	22.0	20.5	41.7	41.5
North Carolina	23.1	21.7	50.6	53.5
North Dakota	24.5	23.8	18.9	48.3
Ohio	23.0	21.0	39.5	38.6
Oklahoma	22.8	22.3	44.5	39.6

TABLE 48 (Cont'd)

Number of deaths of children under one year of age per 1,000 live births, by color and residence, for states, 1960

State	White Urban	White Rural	Nonwhite Urban	Nonwhite Rural
Oregon	24.2	22.0	29.3	28.8
Pennsylvania	23.6	21.0	40.9	35.9
Rhode Island	22.5	22.1	44.2	45.5
South Carolina	24.3	23.8	44.7	50.0
South Dakota	26.8	21.9	63.3	79.7
Tennessee	24.3	26.0	41.6	47.8
Texas	26.0	27.2	43.1	46.4
Utah	17.9	20.4	53.8	54.1
Vermont	26.5	22.7	....	....
Virginia	24.7	24.6	43.2	47.8
Washington	24.8	20.1	25.4	61.2
West Virginia	21.5	27.0	44.7	32.1
Wisconsin	21.9	20.2	35.2	35.7
Wyoming	31.1	22.0	37.3	58.4

Source: Compiled from National Center for Health Statistics, *Vital Statistics of the United States: 1960,* Vol. II, *Mortality,* Part B,Section 9 (1963), pp. 60-77, Table 2.

TABLE 49

Infant mortality rates in the United States, by size of place and color, 1960

Size of place	Total population	White population	Nonwhite population
All urban	26.3	23.3	40.9
Places of 1,000,000 or more	27.7	22.9	39.7
Places of 500,000 to 1,000,000	29.0	24.8	38.5
Places of 250,000 to 500,000	28.1	24.8	38.4
Places of 100,000 to 250,000	26.8	23.5	40.7
Places of 50,000 to 100,000	24.4	22.6	37.7
Places of 25,000 to 50,000	23.9	21.8	44.3
Places of 10,000 to 25,000	24.5	22.3	47.7
Places of 2,500 to 10,000	26.6	24.3	48.8
All rural	25.7	22.4	48.5

Source: Compiled from National Center for Health Statistics, *Vital Statistics of the United States: 1960,* Vol. II, *Mortality,* Part B, Section 9 (1963), pp. 60-77, Table 2.

"urban" and "balance of area" designations described above are employed. At the national level in 1968, the white population living in places of 10,000 or more had an infant mortality rate of 19.7, while those living in smaller places and in the open country had one of 18.7. Urban nonwhites, however, had a rate of 33.3 compared with one of 37.2 for those in the nonurban category. In the urban centers of various sizes given in Table 49, the infant mortality rates for whites are lower in the rural areas than in the cities of all sizes except those with 10,000 to 25,000 people and those with 25,000 to 50,000 inhabitants. The rates for nonwhites are higher in the rural districts than in the cities of all sizes with the single exception of those containing 2,500 to 10,000 inhabitants.

Marital Status and the Mortality Rate

That married people have lower mortality rates, or longer expectation of life, than the single, the widowed, and the divorced is rather generally known. If anyone were inclined to question this generalization, an examination of the data for the period 1959 - 1961, the latest comprehensive materials available for the United States, should remove any reasonable doubt. For these years among males and females alike, and for the nonwhite population as well as the white, at every age the death rate of those who were married was substantially below that of those who had remained single, those who were widowed, and those who were classified as divorced.[9] The second lowest position is consistently held by single persons, and highest of all are the death rates of those whose marriages have been terminated by divorces and who have not remarried.

The exact reasons for these differences are not fully known. Probably a tendency to avoid marriage on the part of those afflicted with various disabilities is part of the answer, but this could hardly explain why the single have lower mortality rates than the widowed and the divorced. A better adjustment to life on the part of the married person certainly is involved. This seems to be indicated especially by the fact that the death rates of married persons are particularly low for such causes of death as syphilis, homicide, and suicide.

Regional Differences

The available data suggest that mortality rates do not differ greatly from one region to another if the comparisons are made separately for whites and non-whites, using the infant mortality rate to control for age. (See Table 50.) For the white population in 1968, the range was from a rate of 18.5 in the West North Central and Pacific divisions to one of 20.9 in the East South Central division. For nonwhites the differences were greater, ranging from a low of 22.9 in the Pacific division to a high of 40.5 in the East South Central section. In large part, however, the low level of infant mortality in the Pacific states is due to the inclu-

TABLE 50

Infant mortality rates for geographic divisions of the United States, by color, 1968

Division	Total population	White population	Nonwhite population
United States	21.8	19.2	34.5
New England	19.9	19.2	31.8
Middle Atlantic	21.2	18.6	35.0
East North Central	21.6	19.4	35.4
West North Central	19.5	18.5	31.8
South Atlantic	24.3	19.6	36.2
East South Central	26.2	20.9	40.5
West South Central	22.7	19.4	35.0
Mountain	21.2	19.7	36.1
Pacific	19.1	18.5	22.9

Source: Compiled from data in National Center for Health Statistics, *Vital Statistics of the United States, 1968,* Vol. II, *Mortality,* Part A, Section 2 (1972), p. 6, Table 6.

sion of Hawaii in that division, the nonwhite population of which does not suffer from the same degree of disadvantage in health and nutrition borne by a substantial segment of the nonwhite (largely Negro) population of the mainland. Therefore, the mortality rate of the nonwhite group in the Pacific division is substantially below that of nonwhites in any other region, just as nonwhites in Hawaii average more future years of life than do nonwhites in any other state and have lower infant mortality rates than do those in all other states except Maine and North Dakota. When the Pacific division is eliminated from consideration, the lowest infant mortality rate for nonwhites is that of 31.8 in the New England and West North Central divisions, and while this means that the regional differences are greater for nonwhites than for whites, they too are relatively minor. All in all, it appears that regional variations in longevity and levels of mortality are not very significant and that the available data do not permit a very comprehensive study of them in any case.

Other Differences

Two other differentials in levels of mortality that deserve brief mention are those that accompany variations in educational attainment and in family income. A study by the National Center for Health Statistics, using infant mortality rates from the National Natality Survey of 1964 - 1966, enables some general observations to be made on both of these matters.[10] Infant mortality rates tend to decline substantially as the number of years of schooling attained by mothers increases until the level representing the completion of high school is reached. At higher levels of educational attainment, however, no additional important reductions in infant mortality seem to take place. The same pattern prevails when the educational attainment of the father rather than that of the mother is used as a basis for comparison. In the case of family income, a similar tendency appeared in the study. That is, in the range below $3,000 of annual family income, infant mortality rates were the highest and they decreased progressively and significantly through the $3,000 to $4,999 range and the $5,000 to $6,999 range. Beyond that point, however, no appreciable reductions took place as average family income increased. These findings suggest that the longevity and the survival potential of those who are the poorest and the least well-educated in the United States are seriously limited, but that the sanitation techniques, the medical technology, the knowledge of nutrition, and so on, which save infant lives and extend the expectation of life, have rather uniform results in this respect for those who are members of the middle and upper classes. Once again, this appears to be a reflection of the pervasive process of homogenization of American society.

Causes of Death

Since 1965, the number of deaths in the United States has averaged about 1.9 million per year. In 1972, the total registered was 1,962,000; in 1971, 1,921,000; in 1970, also 1,921,000; in 1969, 1,916,000. These figures correspond to crude death rates of 9.4, 9.3, 9.4, and 9.5, respectively, for the years indicated. An examination of the causes assigned to these deaths is another essential aspect of the study of mortality. The most significant of abundant recent materials on the subject are presented in Table 51, which shows the rates per 100,000 population for the twenty-five leading causes of death in 1969. In this compilation, motor vehicle accidents are considered a separate category and are not combined with other accidents, a practice also followed by the National Center for Health Statistics. The causes are classified according to the Eighth Revision of the international list and the category "diseases of the heart" is somewhat more inclusive than is the class "ischaemic heart disease" used in Table 46.

In the last part of the twentieth century, diseases of the heart are the cause of almost two-fifths of all deaths occurring in the United States, and the death rate from this specific set of ailments is more than double that for any other cause of death. Malignant neoplasms (cancer), including neoplasms of the lymphatic and hematopoietic tissues, rank in second place, followed by cerebrovascular diseases ("strokes"), influenza and pneumonia, and accidents other than those in which motor vehicles are involved, in the order named. Motor vehicle accidents, certain causes in early infancy, diabetes mellitus, arteriosclerosis, and the class including bronchitis, emphysema, and asthma, in the order named, round out the list of the ten most important killers.

There is a pronounced difference between the rates at which males and females are decimated by the various important causes of death. In general, the rates for males are very much higher than those for females, and this is true of most of the degenerative ailments (such as heart disease and cancer), the transmissible diseases (such as tuberculosis, influenza, and syphilis), and the causes in which external factors are involved (such as suicide, homicide, and accidents). Even the death rates from diseases of early infancy and congenital anomalies are substantially higher for males than for females, and in the residual category of all other causes, a similar situation is seen. For a few of the twenty-five categories given in Table 51, however, the rates for women are higher than those for men. Among whites, these are cerebrovascular diseases, diabetes mellitus, arteriosclerosis, infections of the kidney, hernia and intestinal obstructions, benign and unspecified neoplasms, and cholelithiasis and related maladies. Among nonwhites the causes of death for which women have higher rates than men are cerebrovascular diseases, diabetes mellitus, benign and unspecified neoplasms, and cholelithiasis and related maladies.

TABLE 51
Death rates in the United States for the 25 leading causes of
death, by color and sex, 1969

Cause of death	Total population	White Male	White Female	Nonwhite Male	Nonwhite Female
All causes	951.9	1,092.7	815.1	1,132.8	798.7
Diseases of heart	366.1	443.9	315.4	316.1	246.7
Malignant neoplasms	160.0	181.6	146.3	159.1	112.4
Cerebrovascular diseases	102.6	94.4	109.5	105.2	106.9
Influenza and pneumonia	33.9	36.4	28.9	53.2	33.8
Accidents (other than motor vehicle)	30.0	38.7	19.0	58.7	22.8
Motor vehicle accidents	27.6	40.0	15.1	47.0	14.5
Certain causes in early infancy	21.4	22.2	14.5	51.5	36.3
Diabetes mellitus	19.1	15.7	21.0	17.3	29.5
Arteriosclerosis	16.4	15.2	19.3	9.7	9.6
Bronchitis, emphysema, and asthma	15.4	26.7	6.5	13.2	4.7
Cirrhosis of the liver	14.8	19.1	9.5	23.9	14.4
Sypmtoms and ill-defined conditions	13.0	12.4	7.4	41.8	29.0
Other diseases of arteries, arterioles, and capillaries	12.4	16.5	9.7	9.3	7.6
Suicide	11.1	17.2	6.8	8.1	2.8
Congenital anomalies	8.4	9.0	7.3	11.6	9.6
Homicide	7.7	6.0	2.0	58.1	11.7
Nephritis and nephrosis	4.7	4.5	3.6	10.3	8.6
Peptic ulcer	4.6	6.5	3.1	4.9	2.1
Infections of kidney	4.3	3.8	4.4	5.7	6.3
Hypertension	4.2	3.8	3.5	8.8	7.4
Hernia and intestinal obstructions	3.7	3.4	4.0	4.3	3.2
Tuberculosis	2.8	3.3	1.2	9.5	4.1
Benign and unspecified neoplasms	2.3	2.2	2.3	2.2	3.1
Cholelithiasis, cholecystitis, cholangitis	2.1	2.0	2.5	0.7	1.4
Other infective and parasitic diseases	2.0	2.0	1.8	3.4	3.3
All other causes	61.3	66.2	50.5	99.2	66.9

Source: Compiled from data in National Center for Health Statistics, "Final Mortality Statistics, 1969," *Monthly Vital Statistics Report,* Vol. 21, No. 4 (July 25, 1972), pp. 8-9, Table 5.

The principal causes of death for the white population also differ substantially from those for the nonwhite (largely Negro) population of the United States. Among the former the rates of fatalities attributed to eight causes definitely are much higher than they are among the latter. These are diseases of the heart; cancer; arteriosclerosis; bronchitis, emphysema, and asthma; other diseases of the arteries, arterioles, and capillaries; suicide; peptic ulcer; and cholelithiasis and related diseases. In sharp contrast, the death rates from the following seventeen causes are substantially higher for nonwhites than for whites: cerebrovascular diseases (males only); influenza and pneumonia; accidents not involving motor vehicles; vehicular accidents (males only); certain causes in early infancy; diabetes mellitus; cirrhosis of the liver; symptoms and ill-defined conditions; congenital anomalies; homicide; nephritis and nephrosis; infections of the kidney; hypertension; hernia and intestinal obstructions (males only); all forms of tuberculosis; benign and unspecified neoplasms (females only); and other infective and parasitic diseases. The only items in the list of twenty-five for which there appear to be no significant differences between the death rates of the white and nonwhite segments of the population are motor vehicle accidents involving the deaths of women and benign and unspecified neoplasms among men.

There are such broad differences between the races in rates of death by suicide and homicide that the two deserve special comment. In 1969, the rate of death by suicide among white men was more than twice as high as that among nonwhite men and the rate for white women was two and one-half times as high as that for nonwhite women. On the other hand, the death rate from homicide for nonwhite males was nearly ten times as high as that for the whites and homicide was, in fact, the fifth leading cause of death among the former but only the seventeenth among the latter. The rate of death from homicide for nonwhite females was almost six times as high as that for white females. An elaborate explanation of these wide variations is beyond the scope of this volume, but it does seem that the low suicide rate among Negroes comes at least in part from the persistence of fundamentalist religious beliefs, mostly Baptist, and the impact that they have had on behavior. The extremely high homicide rates among Negroes seem to be a product of the plantation system, which was sustained first by slavery and later by the sharecropping arrangement. In both cases, an important part of the system was the reliance upon physical, rather than psychosocial, means of social control. The cotton planters, through their overseers, drivers, gang bosses, and other representatives, inflicted corporal punishment as the means of controlling their workers; and direct action was resorted to by the slaves and sharecroppers in their dealings with one another.[11] The habitual order-and-obey social relationships characteristic of the plantation system, the physical means of control relied upon to exercise social control, and the direct action involved in settling disputes among the workers and their families themselves, provided little training of those born and reared in the system in the psychosocial means of social control which govern most of the actions of middle-class people. Indeed, our hypothesis posits the proposition that the descendants of slaves and sharecroppers have not yet internalized psychosocial controls to the degree required to reduce the homicide rate to the level that exists in the white population. It should be added, of course, that the exercise of violence prevails largely in the lower class and is directed mostly against other Negroes. One might speculate that when the gap between the races in suicide and homicide rates begins to close, genuine integration will probably be underway, but an examination of the trends in the causes of death indicates that this is happening only very slowly. For example, in 1950, the death rate from suicide was 2.8 times higher for whites than for nonwhites but, in 1969, it was 2.2 times higher for the former than for the latter. The degree of convergence between the races for males and females separately was about the same. In 1950, the death rate by homicide was 10.8 times higher for nonwhites than for whites and, in 1969, it was 8.5 times higher for the former than for the latter. The convergence of the rates was about the same for the sexes taken separately. Thus, there has been some reduction of the racial differentials in the death rates by suicide and homicide in these twenty-nine years, but it is not sufficient to demonstrate any great amount of integration of the races.

The relative importance of the causes of death varies significantly by age, of course, with many of them being highly specific to persons in the several age groups. These variations among the causes by age may be summarized as follows:

(1) Under one year of age, congenital anomalies, immaturity, respiratory ailments, birth injuries, and ill-defined causes, especially malnutrition, exact a comparatively heavy toll.

(2) In the ages one through fourteen, deaths from any cause are relatively few, with accidents accounting for about half of all fatalities among male children and about one-third of those among females. Respiratory ailments and the lingering effects of congenital anomalies also are important, as are various types of malignancies, over half of which are leukemia and aleukemia. Ill-defined causes remain among the most important ones, with nonwhite boys and girls being especially susceptible to the variety of illnesses included in this category.

(3) During the ages fifteen through thirty-four, the death rate begins its gradual rise for members of both races and sexes. Accidents continue to be the major cause of death, but heart disease and cancer become increasingly important. Suicide and homicide take on greater significance for persons in this age range.

(4) In the age range from thirty-five to fifty-four, the degenerative diseases have become the major maladies causing death, with heart disease in first place and cancer in second. Accidents continue to kill a significant number of persons, as do suicide and homicide. Strokes and related ailments and cirrhosis of the liver also figure prominently in the list of causes of death for members of this age group.

(5)   Among those aged fifty-five through seventy-four, the death rate continues to accelerate, taking an especially heavy toll of men of both races. The deteriorative or degenerative diseases are by far the major causes; and among them heart disease, cancer, cerebrovascular diseases, diabetes mellitus, and cirrhosis of the liver are the most important. Accidents and suicides continue to be important causes and influenza and pneumonia and other respiratory ailments also exact increasingly heavy tolls among this aging group. Ill-defined causes and symptoms also appear now as significant causes.

(6)   In the group seventy-five and over, heart disease kills almost three times as many persons as any other cause. Cerebrovascular diseases are in second place and cancer is in third, while influenza and pneumonia, arteriosclerosis, accidents, and diabetes mellitus round out the list.[12]

1. The abbreviations for specific causes of death along with the code designation in the abbreviated Seventh Revision are as follows:
   Gastritis (B36) = gastritis, duodenitis, enteritis, and colitis, except diarrhea of the newborn;
   Residual diseases of early infancy (B44) = other diseases peculiar to early infancy, and immaturity unqualified;
   Senility (B45) = senility without mention of psychosis, ill-defined and unknown causes.

2. The relatively low rates reported for Angola, Iraq, and the Syrian Arab Republic are almost certainly substantially inaccurate.

3. See James W. Glover, *United States Life Tables, 1890, 1901, 1910, and 1901 - 1910* (Washington: Government Printing Office, 1921).

4. Published in the company's *Statistical Bulletin,* 16 (July, 1935).

5. Republished in "United States Abridged Life Tables, 1939: Urban and Rural, by Regions, Color, and Sex," *Vital Statistics - Special Reports,* 23, No. 15 (1947), 297 - 316.

6. *Vital Statistics of the United States: 1960,* Vol. II, *Mortality,* Part B, Section 9 (Washington: Government Printing Office, 1963), pp. 60 - 77, Table 2.

7. See National Center for Health Statistics, *Vital Statistics of the United States, 1968,* Vol. II, *Mortality* (Washington: Government Printing Office, 1972), Part A, Section 6, p. 7.

8. See the summary of these attempts in C. A. McMahan, "Rural-Urban Differentials in Longevity, in *The Sociology of Urban Life,* edited by T. Lynn Smith and C. A. McMahan (New York: The Dryden Press, 1951), pp. 281 - 289. See also T. Lynn Smith and Paul E. Zopf, Jr., *Principles of Inductive Rural Sociology* (Philadelphia: F. A. Davis Company, 1970), pp. 65 - 69.

9. See Grove and Hetzel, *op. cit. in Chap. 15, r. 4,* pp. 334 - 336, Table 57; and National Center for Health Statistics, "Mortality from Selected Causes by Marital Status: United States, 1959 - 1961," *Vital and Health Statistics,* Series 20, No. 8 (1970).

10. "Infant Mortality Rates: Socioeconomic Factors," *Vital and Health Statistics,* Series 22, No. 14 (1972).

11. See T. Lynn Smith, *The Sociology of Rural Life* (3rd ed.) (New York: Harper and Brothers, 1953), pp. 307 - 311.

12. For a study of death rates by age from specific causes, see National Center for Health Statistics, "The Change in Mortality Trend in the United States," *Vital and Health Statistics,* Series 3, No. 1 (1964), pp. 11 - 37.

BOGUE, DONALD J. *The Population of the United States,* Chap. 9. Glencoe, Ill.: The Free Press, 1959.

FREEDMAN, RONALD, and others. "Social Correlates of Fetal Mortality." *Milbank Memorial Fund Quarterly,* Vol. 44, No. 3 (1966), pp. 327 - 344.

GLASS, DAVID V. "Some Indicators of Differences Between Urban and Rural Mortality in England and Wales and Scotland." *Population Studies,* Vol. 17, No. 3 (March, 1964), pp. 263 - 267.

HAMILTON, C. HORACE. "Ecological and Social Factors in Mortality Variation." *Eugenics Quarterly,* Vol. 2, No. 4 (1955), pp. 212 - 223.

ISKRANT, A. P., and P. V. JOLIET. *Accidents and Homicide.* Vital and Health Statistics Monographs, American Public Health Association. London: Oxford University Press, 1968.

JACOBSON, PAUL H. "Mortality of Native and Foreign Born Population in the United States." *Proceedings of the International Union for the Scientific Study of Population, 1961,* Vol. I (1963).

MADIGAN, FRANCIS C. "Are Sex Mortality Differences Biologically Caused?" In *Population and Society,* edited by Charles B. Nam, pp. 152 - 164. Boston: Houghton Mifflin Company, 1968.

METROPOLITAN LIFE INSURANCE COMPANY. "Mortality and Social Class." *Statistical Bulletin,* Vol. 40 (October, 1959), pp. 9 - 10.

PETERSEN, WILLIAM. *Population,* 2nd ed., Chap. 10. New York: The Macmillan Company, 1969.

PRESTON, SAMUEL H., NATHAN KEYFITZ, and ROBERT SCHOEN. *Causes of Death: Life Tables for National Populations.* New York: Seminar Press, 1972.

SPIEGELMAN, MORTIMER. "Longevity and Mortality in the American Population," in *Population: The Vital Revolution,* edited by Ronald Freedman, Chap. 7. New York: Doubleday & Co., Inc. (Anchor Books), 1964.

STOCKWELL, EDWARD G. "Socioeconomic Status and Mortality in the United States," in *Population and Society,* edited by Charles B. Nam, pp. 164 - 177. Boston: Houghton Mifflin Company, 1968.

TAEUBER, CONRAD, and IRENE B. TAEUBER. *The People of the United States in the 20th Century* (A 1960 Census Monograph), pp. 511 - 579. Washington: Government Printing Office, 1971.

THOMLINSON, RALPH. *Demographic Problems,* Chap. 7. Belmont, Calif.: Dickenson Publishing Company, Inc., 1967.

UNITED NATIONS. "The Situation and Trends of Mortality in the World." *Population Bulletin,* No. 6 (1963).

WRONG, DENNIS H. *Population and Society,* 3rd ed., Chap. 3. New York: Random House, Inc., 1967.

ZELNIK, MELVIN. "Age Patterns of Mortality of American Negroes: 1900 - 02 to 1959 - 61." *Journal of the American Statistical Association,* Vol. 64, No. 326 (June, 1969), pp. 433 - 451.

The falling death rate in most of the world which has characterized the twentieth century is one of the most significant items in history. This striking evidence of mankind's growing control over the forces responsible for disease and death became apparent in Sweden, the Netherlands, and Denmark shortly after 1850. Before the end of the nineteenth century the mortality data for England and Wales, Scotland, France, Germany, and Italy made it clear that expectation of life definitely was on the increase in all of these countries. Furthermore, the evidence shows that by 1900 the curves showing the average duration of life in all these portions of Europe were moving upward at an increasing rate.[1] Probably the results of improvements in education and preventive medicine were having similar results in other portions of the Western world, but the statistical data needed to establish this satisfactorily are lacking.

After 1900, spectacular increases in the expectation of life took place throughout most of Europe, in Australia and New Zealand, and in the United States and Canada; and in all of these the upward trend in the average duration of life has continued unabated well into the second half of the twentieth century. In addition, since 1925 the educational, health, sanitary, and medical measures which had worked such wonders in conserving lives in these portions of the Western world were extended to or copied by peoples elsewhere in the world. The full impact of these efforts, as reflected in plummeting mortality rates, or increasing life expectation, has been felt for the most part only in the years since the outbreak of the Second World War. Since midcentury the trends have been particularly rapid.

As must be stressed again and again, the data available for the study of mortality trends throughout the world are far from satisfactory. This will be evident to anyone who attempts to add substantially, with comparable materials, to the facts presented in Table 52. Even so, the information in this compilation substantiates the statements made above. In addition, one may see from these data that during the twentieth century in such countries as South Africa (white population), Canada, the United States, Israel, Denmark, all parts of Germany, Norway, Sweden, Scotland, Australia, and New Zealand the life expectation of the male population has increased annually by under .30 of a year, and that the gain among the female population has been somewhat greater. The rates of increase have been slightly more pronounced in South Africa (colored population), Southern Rhodesia (European population), Guatemala, Argentina, Burma, India, Japan, Thailand, Belgium, Finland, France, Ireland, Italy, the Netherlands, Romania, Switzerland, England and Wales, and Northern Ireland. Finally, the most spectacular increases have taken place in many of those countries which have been styled as "underdeveloped" but which have begun to make rapid strides in the control of various causes of death, particularly those which often strike as epidemics. The rates of increase in expectation of life at birth amounting to at least .66 of a year annually in nations such as Egypt, Barbados, El Salvador, Ceylon, the Republic of Korea, West Malaysia, the Philippines, the Ryukyu Islands, and Albania are due principally to this factor. Furthermore, the rapid gains in these places have taken place largely since the end of the Second World War and in most of them the starting point was extremely low, even as late as the middle of the twentieth century. For example, between 1937 and 1960, Egypt registered an average annual gain in expectation of life at birth of .69 of a year for males and .54 of a year for females, but the starting points in 1937 were 35.6 years and 41.5 years, respectively. In India, the average annual increases between 1906 and 1955 of .39 of a year for males and .35 of a year for females represent improvements over the extremely low expectation of life in 1906 of 22.6 years and 23.3 years, respectively. Nevertheless, the improvements during the forty-nine year period resulted in an average expectation of life in 1955 of only 41.9 years for males and 40.6 years for females. On the other hand, many of the countries which registered the smallest average annual gains during the time ranges indicated in Table 52 already had a relatively high expectation of life early in the twentieth century due to prior successful grappling with the various causes of death. New Zealand is a case in point. Between 1904 and 1962 the average annual rates of increase in expectation of life at birth were only .18 of a year for males and .23 of a year for females, but the starting points in 1904 were 58.1 years and 60.6 years, respectively. The situation is similar in a substantial number of the world's highly developed nations, particularly those in Western Europe, North America, and Oceania.

TABLE 52

The increase in expectation of life at birth in selected countries
during the twentieth century

Country	Period	Males		Females	
		Increase (in years)	Average per year	Increase (in years)	Average per year
Africa					
Egypt	1937-60	16.0	.69	12.3	.54
South Africa					
(Asiatic population)	1946-60	7.0	.50	9.8	.70
(Colored population)	1936-60	9.4	.39	13.4	.56
(White population)	1921-60	9.1	.23	12.5	.32
Southern Rhodesia					
(European population)	1936-62	8.4	.32	11.4	.44
America, North					
Barbados	1946-60	13.6	.97	14.5	1.04
Canada	1931-66	8.8	.25	13.1	.37
Costa Rica	1950-63	7.2	.56	7.8	.60
El Salvador	1950-60	6.6	.66	8.0	.80
Guatemala	1950-64	4.5	.32	6.2	.44
Jamaica	1911-60	23.6	.48	25.2	.51
Mexico	1922-67	29.3	.65	30.3	.67
Puerto Rico	1902-60	37.3	.64	40.9	.70
Trinidad and Tobago	1901-60	25.4	.43	27.6	.47
United States	1901-70	19.2	.28	23.9	.35
America, South					
Argentina	1914-67	18.9	.36	22.7	.43
Chile	1930-60	14.0	.47	18.9	.63
Guyana	1911-60	29.1	.59	30.6	.62
Asia					
Burma	1926-54	10.2	.36	12.8	.46
Ceylon	1921-62	29.2	.71	30.7	.75
Hong Kong	1961-68	3.1	.44	2.8	.40
India	1906-55	19.3	.39	17.2	.35
Israel	1950-70	3.3	.17	3.5	.18
Japan	1901-68	25.1	.37	29.4	.44
Korea, Republic of	1957-66	8.6	.96	10.3	1.14
Malaysia, West	1957-69	8.0	.67	8.5	.71
Philippines	1902-47	37.3	.83	39.4	.88
Ryukyu Islands	1928-60	22.1	.69	24.2	.76
Thailand	1947-60	4.9	.38	6.8	.52
Europe					
Albania	1956-66	7.7	.77	8.4	.84
Austria	1903-70	27.2	.41	32.5	.49
Belgium	1930-61	11.7	.38	13.7	.44
Bulgaria	1900-66	28.8	.44	32.3	.49

TABLE 52 (Cont'd)

The increase in expectation of life at birth in selected countries
during the twentieth century

Country	Period	Males		Females	
		Increase (in years)	Average per year	Increase (in years)	Average per year
Czechoslovakia	1900-66	28.4	.43	31.9	.48
Denmark	1904-69	17.8	.27	19.4	.30
Finland	1905-63	20.1	.35	24.5	.42
France	1901-69	22.3	.33	26.6	.39
Germany					
Democratic Republic	1953-68	4.1	.27	5.3	.35
Federal Republic	1950-67	3.0	.18	5.1	.30
West Berlin	1950-61	2.3	.21	3.5	.32
Greece	1920-61	24.6	.60	24.2	.59
Hungary	1900-68	29.5	.43	34.0	.50
Ireland	1901-61	18.8	.31	22.3	.37
Italy	1906-66	23.6	.39	28.5	.48
Netherlands	1904-70	19.7	.30	23.1	.35
Norway	1905-63	16.2	.28	18.3	.32
Poland	1932-66	18.7	.55	21.4	.63
Portugal	1941-70	16.7	.58	18.2	.63
Romania	1956-68	4.0	.33	4.8	.40
Spain	1900-60	33.5	.56	36.2	.60
Sweden	1906-67	17.3	.28	19.6	.32
Switzerland	1905-60	19.5	.35	22.0	.40
United Kingdom					
England and Wales	1906-69	20.1	.32	22.5	.36
Northern Ireland	1901-69	20.8	.31	26.8	.39
Scotland	1921-69	13.8	.29	16.7	.35
Yugoslavia	1933-68	14.2	.41	14.7	.42
Oceania					
Australia	1906-62	12.7	.23	15.3	.27
New Zealand[a]	1904-62	10.4	.18	13.2	.23
U.S.S.R.	1961-69	4.0	.50	7.0	.89

Source: Compiled and computed from data in United Nations, *Demographic Yearbook,*
1967 (New York: United Nations, 1968), pp. 704-741, Table 29; *1971* (1972), pp. 746-
765, Table 34.
[a]Prior to 1950, includes European population only.

For two reasons the present writers believe that increases in expectation of life throughout the world as a whole are likely to be fully as spectacular in the decades just ahead as they have been up to the present. First, during the most recent intercensal period in some parts of the Western world there was only a slight tendency for the rate of change to be less than it was in the decades immediately before. Second, in much of Africa, Latin America, and Asia, the death rates from many of the transmissible diseases still are very high, and it seems reasonable to suppose that shortly these causes of death will be brought under control to a degree comparable with that achieved in many other parts of the world. Consider in this connection the mortality rates per 100,000 population for a few selected causes of death as reported for years since 1962 by recent issues of the *Demographic Yearbook* of the United Nations: *tuberculosis,* 78 in Brazil, 74 in Burma, 72 in the Philippines, 61 in India, 59 for the colored population of South Africa, 50 in Sabah, 45 in Turkey, 36 in Hong Kong, and 33 in Chile, Peru, and Taiwan; *typhoid fever,* 36 in Burma, 7 in the Dominican Republic and Nicaragua, 6 in Mexico, and 5 in Egypt; *malaria,* 115 in Nigeria, 41 in Sabah, 33 in Burma, 28 in Nicaragua, and 21 in the Dominican Republic; and *pneumonia,* 312 in Burma, 246 in India and Nigeria, 195 in Turkey, 179 for the colored population of South Africa, 147 in Mexico, 133 in Chile, and 122 in Guatemala. In addition, the numbers of deaths per 100,000 live-born infants attributable to *infections of the newborn* (as given in the Seventh Revision of the international list of causes) were 1,584 in Guatemala, 1,299 in Chile, 877 in Colombia, 833 in Mexico, 741 in Burma, 728 in Bolivia, 721 in the Dominican Republic, and 710 in Brazil. Were data available for China and many other populous parts of the world, it is likely that even greater opportunities for saving lives through the applications of modern sanitary, health, and medical measures would be revealed. Much of this work certainly will be done in the next few decades. The resulting decreases in mortality probably will keep the rates of natural increase so high that fear of world overpopulation will continue for some time to come.

TRENDS IN THE UNITED STATES

The general nature of mortality trends in the United States during the first seventy years of the twentieth century, the only period for which comprehensive information is available, may be observed easily from the data presented in Figure 56. The fact that the materials have been classified according to color, further subdivided by sex, and adjusted for changes in the age composition adds greatly to the reliability of any comparisons based upon them.

The most striking features of these historical series are: (1) the rather consistent manner in which the death rate fell over the period under consideration until about 1955, and (2) the way in which the rate tended to level off after

TABLE 53

Trends in the expectation of life among the white population
of the United States, 1900-1902 to 1967-1969, by sex

Average future lifetime

| | At birth | | Age 20 | | Age 45 | | Age 70 | |
Period	Males	Females	Males	Females	Males	Females	Males	Females
1900-02	48	51	42	44	24	26	9	10
1919-21	56	59	46	47	26	27	10	10
1929-31	59	63	46	49	25	27	9	10
1939-41	63	67	48	51	26	29	9	11
1949-51	66	72	50	55	27	31	10	12
1959-61	68	74	50	56	27	33	10	12
1967-69	68	75	50	57	27	33	10	13

Source: Compiled from data in Elbertie Foudray and Thomas N.E. Greville, "United
States Life Tables 1930-1939 (Preliminary) for White and Nonwhite by Sex," *Vital Statistics—Special Reports,* 23, No. 13 (1947), p. 265; Robert D. Grove and Alice M. Hetzel,
Vital Statistics Rates in the United States, 1940-1960, Public Health Service Publication
No. 1677 (1968), p. 308, Table 50; National Center for Health Statistics, *Vital Statistics
of the United States, 1968,* Vol. II, *Mortality,* Part A, Section 5 (1972), p. 11, Table 5;
and *Vital Statistics of the United States, 1969,* Vol. II, *Mortality,* Part A, Section 5
(1973), p. 11, Table 5.

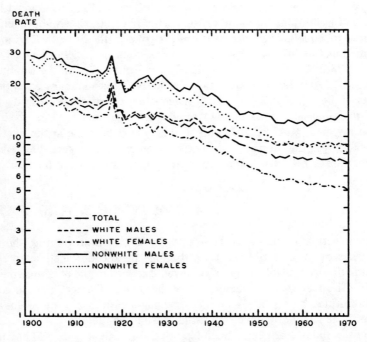

Figure 56. Trends in the age-adjusted death rate in the United States, by color
and sex, 1900 to 1970.

1955, although it was subject to a slight decrease after 1968. The major exception to the decrease in the earlier years is the pronounced peak corresponding to 1918, the year of the great influenza epidemic. The various other fluctuations prior to 1930 should be discounted liberally, due to the fact that data are for the expanding death registration area. The gradual addition of data for the southern states and the Negro population, with their somewhat different mortality patterns, to the national series may very well be responsible for many of the gyrations. The 1937 peak probably is truly indicative of a slightly higher mortality rate for the year, although the reasons for such an increase are not readily apparent. The striking feature of the chart is the sharp and consistent fall in the death rate from 1937 until 1955, when the rate of decrease dropped sharply. In the latter year, the death rate for nonwhite males even began to rise slightly, beginning a pattern which continued at least to 1968. The fact that Negro males in increasing numbers moved to different parts of the country and had to adjust to climate and society amid quite different surroundings probably is largely responsible for this exception. After 1968, however, the rates for all groups represented in Figure 56 again moved downward somewhat.

By consulting Figure 57 one may see at a glance the trends among ten important age groups into which the total population may be divided. From the materials presented in this illustration one should note especially that, in 1970, the mortality rate of children aged one to four had been reduced to a level that was only 4 per cent as high as that prevailing in 1900, and that the one for children aged five to fourteen was only 10 per cent as high as it was at the beginning of the century. Similarly for the other age groupings represented on the chart, the 1970 death rates as percentages of those for 1900 are as follows: under one, 13 per cent; fifteen to twenty-four, 22 per cent; twenty-five to thirty-four, 19 per cent; thirty-five to forty-four, 30 per cent; forty-five to fifty-four, 48 per cent; fifty-five to sixty-four, 61 per cent; sixty-five to seventy-four, 65 per cent; and seventy-five to eighty-four, 63 per cent.

Trends in mortality in the United States also may be gauged by the increase in life expectation that has taken place in this country since 1900 - 1902, the years for which our first life tables were constructed. Some of the most reliable and pertinent of the data, those for the white population subdivided according to sex, are presented in Table 53.

These materials give ample evidence of the phenomenal increase in the average length of life that took place during the first sixty-eight years of the twentieth century. For white males the expectation of life at birth increased from 48.2 years in 1900 - 1902 to 67.7 in 1967 - 1969, a gain of 19.5 years or 40.5 per cent; and the increase for females was even greater, from 51.1 to 75.0, a change of 23.9 years or 46.8 per cent. Much of the increase was due to the saving of lives of infants and young children, but it is easy to overstress this point. It should be observed in Table 53 that among both males and females

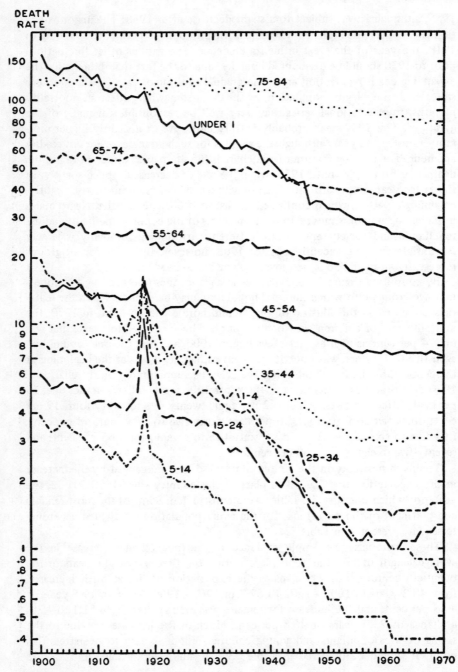

Figure 57. Trends in the death rates of principal age groups in the United States, 1900 to 1970.

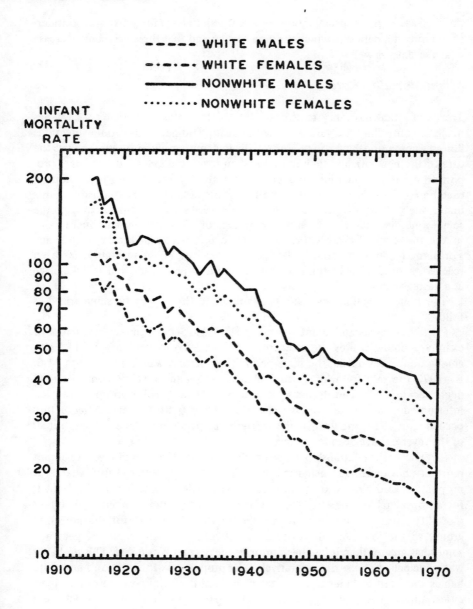

Figure 58. Trends in the infant mortality rate in the United States, by color and sex, 1915 to 1969.

the increase in life expectancy at age twenty and at age forty-five was considerable during the period to which the data pertain and that there was some increase
at age seventy as well.

Infant Mortality Rates

Trends in infant mortality rates generally reflect the progress that a society has
made in controlling the various causes of death. Ordinarily, as various infectious
illnesses come under adequate control, as epidemics grow more rare, and as the
care of the newborn and their mothers is improved and extended to a larger proportion of the population, the infant mortality rate decreases precipitously.
(See Figure 58.) This means that the index, or the number of deaths of infants
under one year of age per 1,000 live births, is very sensitive to differences in the
socioeconomic well-being of various segments of a population; and fluctuations
in the index usually are closely attuned to differences in the level of living.
Furthermore, after a certain relatively low level of infant mortality has been
reached, additional reductions tend to diminish in magnitude and to take place
at a decreasing rate.

The trends in infant mortality in the United States may be summarized as
follows:

(1) The decrease in infant mortality since 1915 has been spectacular. For
example, among whites the rate dropped from 98.6 in 1915 to 18.4 in 1969;
among nonwhites during the same period the decrease was from 181.2 to 31.6.
By 1972 the rate for whites had declined to 16.3 and that for nonwhites had
decreased to 29.0. The declines for members of both color groups have been
interrupted and reversed briefly at various times, with the major fluctuation
occurring in 1918, the year of the influenza epidemic mentioned above, but all
of the reverses have been temporary.

(2) The basic relationship between the two racial groups in levels of infant
mortality has remained unchanged throughout the twentieth century. That is, at
no point have the rates for nonwhites dropped below those for whites. In fact,
for a considerable time after World War II there was some tendency for infant
mortality rates to decline more rapidly for the white than for the nonwhite
group, so that by 1966 the divergence between the races in this respect was
somewhat greater than it had been prior to the Second World War. This probably
was principally because a comparatively large proportion of the nation's nonwhite
babies was born to parents who lived in the least healthful portions of its largest
cities, although it certainly also involved in part the improvements which were
made in the registration of the deaths of nonwhite infants. After 1966, however,
the infant mortality rate for nonwhites fell faster than did that for whites and by
1972 the rates had converged somewhat. It appears that nonwhites, having the
greatest initial disadvantage to overcome, finally are obtaining a somewhat more

equitable share of the technology that saves infant lives than they have had during most of their tenure in the United States.

(3) For every year in the 1915 - 1969 period and within each color category the mortality rate of male infants has been significantly higher than that of female infants. The reasons for this persistent differential are still largely speculative although it seems clear that the various factors of the cultural environment which help to bring about the higher death rates of males than females in the older ages operate only in a minor way, if at all, to produce the difference in the first year of life.

(4) Between 1950 and 1966 the rates of decrease in infant mortality became smaller than they had been, but after 1966 they grew greater. For example, between 1915 and 1950 the mortality rate for white infants declined by an average of 2.1 per cent per year, but between 1950 and 1966 the average annual decrease was only 1.4 per cent. Between 1966 and 1972, however, the average annual rate of reduction in infant mortality rose to 3.5 per cent. Even though the mortality rates for white infants may be approaching some lower limit, beyond which no major reductions are likely, it is obvious that somewhat more modest decreases are still possible. Much of the improvement after 1966 came about as a result of substantially better control of influenza and pneumonia, asphyxia, birth injuries and the problems associated with immaturity, and somewhat better control of various gastrointestinal diseases of the newborn. The rates of death from congenital anomalies remained almost unchanged. For nonwhites similar fluctuations took place in the rate of decline of infant mortality. Between 1915 and 1950, the average annual rate of decrease was 2.2 per cent, but between 1950 and 1966 it was only 0.8 per cent. As a result, nonwhites seemed to reach a plateau on which the substantial potential for reducing their infant mortality rates close to those of whites went unrealized for almost two decades. Between 1966 and 1972, however, the situation changed significantly, for the infant mortality rate of nonwhites dropped by an annual average of 4.2 per cent, which was well above the rate of decrease for the white population. It is true, of course, that the rates continue to be high compared with those for whites, largely because some of the most advanced medical technology and health and sanitary measures, especially those relating to prenatal and immediate postnatal care of mothers and infants, have not yet been extended to the Negro population as effectively as they have to the white population. Nevertheless, it seems clear that the nonwhite population is no longer bound to the virtually changeless infant mortality rates of the 1950's and the early 1960's and that their general well-being, at least as measured by this index, is on the increase.

Causes of Death

The primary factors underlying the trends in mortality are the various causes of death to which the fatalities are attributed. In studying these matters, however, it must be recognized that the changes or trends observed in the magnitude of the various specific causes are due to two sets of influences: (1) the antecedents making for an actual increase or decrease in the risks of life from any particular disease, ailment, or external cause; and (2) the changing age distribution of the population. Thus, in a period such as that between 1900 and 1940 the decreasing proportion of children in the population of the United States should have caused the total number of deaths from children's diseases to fall, even though such dangers had not been substantially reduced; and the aging of the population, such as has occurred in the United States since 1900, should increase the mortality from heart disease, cancer, cirrhosis of the liver, and other degenerative ailments even though a given person's risks from them had remained unchanged.

To facilitate the study of the trends in mortality from specific causes in the United States since 1900, Table 54 has been prepared. In this table, the death rates for each of thirty-three categories of causes are given for the years 1900, 1920, 1940, 1960, and 1970. In studying these materials, it is well to keep in mind that the data for the years after 1925 probably are considerably better than those for the first quarter of the century.

The most striking of the changes or trends shown by these materials is the tremendous reduction in mortality from tuberculosis. In the United States, in 1900, respiratory tuberculosis alone was responsible for the death of 175 persons per 100,000 population, whereas in 1970 the corresponding index was only two. Success in the control of this scourge was particularly rapid following 1940.

The control of acute infectious diseases also proceeded rapidly, with deaths from many once deadly microorganisms being almost eliminated. The reduction in deaths attributed to influenza and pneumonia (from 202 per 100,000 population in 1900 to 31 in 1970) closely rivals the control of fatalities from tuberculosis. Typhoid fever, scarlet fever, whooping cough, diphtheria, dysentery, malaria, and measles, all responsible for sizable numbers of deaths in 1900, had been reduced to statistically negligible proportions by 1970. Even syphilis, which as late as 1920 was assigned as the cause of 16.5 deaths per 100,000 population, accounted for only 0.2 per 100,000 in 1970.

However, these accomplishments of preventive medicine and other safeguards to health were accompanied by substantial increases in the numbers and proportions of deaths attributed to heart disease, malignant neoplasms, diabetes mellitus, and other ailments associated with aging. Indeed, by 1970 heart disease alone was responsible for almost two-fifths of the deaths in the United States. In all of these increases, better reporting of the causes of death and the substantial reduction in the numbers relegated to residual and poorly defined categories probably are of some significance. Of much greater significance, surely, is the effect of the changing age distribution, but the fact that various revisions of the international list of causes of death figured in the tabulations makes it impracticable if not impossible to control this factor adequately.

TABLE 54

Specific death rates for selected causes in the death registration
states, 1900, 1920, 1940, 1960, and 1970

	Number of deaths per 100,000 population				
Cause of death	1900	1920	1940	1960	1970
Pneumonia and influenza	202.2	207.3	70.3	37.3	30.5
Tuberculosis of the respiratory system	174.5	99.8	42.2	5.6	2.1
Diarrhea, enteritis, and ulceration of the intestines	142.7	53.7	10.3	5.2	1.1
Diseases of the heart	137.4	159.6	292.5	369.0	360.3
Intracranial lesions of vascular origin	106.9	93.0	90.9	108.0	101.7
Nephritis	88.6	88.8	81.5	7.6	3.9
Congenital malformations, etc.	74.6	84.4	49.2	12.2	8.1
Other accidents	72.3	60.7	47.4	31.0	28.0
Cancer and other malignant tumors	64.0	83.4	120.3	149.2	162.0
Senility	50.2	14.2	7.7	11.4	14.1
Bronchitis	45.2	13.2	3.0	2.5	3.2
Diphtheria	40.3	15.3	1.1	0.0	0.0
Typhoid and paratyphoid fever	31.3	7.6	1.1	0.0	0.0
Puerperal causes (females only)	26.9	38.6	13.5	0.9	0.9
Tuberculosis (other forms)	19.9	13.4	3.7	0.5	0.6
Measles	13.3	8.8	0.5	0.2	0.0
Cirrhosis of the liver	12.5	7.1	8.6	11.3	15.8
Whooping cough	12.2	12.5	2.2	0.1	0.0
Dysentery	12.0	4.0	1.9	0.2	0.0
Syphilis	12.0	16.5	14.4	1.6	0.2
Hernia and intestinal obstruction	11.9	10.5	9.0	5.1	3.6
Diabetes mellitus	11.0	16.1	26.6	16.7	18.5
Suicide	10.2	10.2	14.4	10.6	11.1
Scarlet fever	9.6	4.6	0.5	0.0	0.0
Appendicitis	8.8	13.2	9.9	1.0	0.7
Malaria	6.2	3.4	1.1	0.0	0.0
Alcoholism	5.3	1.0	1.9	1.2	2.3
Diseases of the prostate (males only)	3.3	8.2	13.3	2.5	2.1
Ulcer of stomach or duodenum	2.7	3.6	6.8	6.4	4.1
Homicide	1.2	6.8	6.2	4.7	7.6
Pellagra	0.0	2.5	1.6	0.0	0.0
Cerebrospinal meningitis	....	1.6	0.5	1.1	0.9
Motor vehichle accidents	....	10.3	26.2	21.3	26.2

Source: Compiled from data in Forrest E. Linder and Robert D. Grove, *Vital Statistics Rates in the United States, 1900-1940* (1943), pp. 258-273; Robert D. Grove and Alice M. Hetzel, *Vital Statistics Rates in the United States, 1940-1960* (1968), pp. 595-603; National Center for Health Statistics, *Vital Statistics of the United States, 1966,* Vol. II, *Mortality,* Part A, Section 1 (1968), pp. 53-86, Table 22; and "Annual Summary for the United States, 1970," *Monthly Vital Statistics Report,* Vol. 19, No. 13 (September 21, 1971), p. 18, Table 7.

A few words about the trends in mortality from suicide, homicide, and accidents are in order. The increase in homicide between 1900 and 1920 was due to the inclusion in the death registration area of southern states with their large Negro populations, among whom the incidence of this cause has been considerable.[2] Automobile accidents did not, of course, figure at all in 1900, whereas from 1925 on they have been prominent as a cause of death. The curve representing mortality from this cause began about 1910, rose steadily to a rate of slightly more than 25 per 100,000 population in 1931, fluctuated about that level until 1941, dropped sharply during the years of the Second World War, and has fluctuated between 21 and 27 from 1947 until the present. The one for other accidents, on the other hand, dropped rather consistently between 1900 and 1970, except for sharp upturns in 1936 and during the Second World War.

In summary, the causes of death associated with advancing age have increased in importance both among whites and nonwhites. On the other hand, those contagious diseases and other ailments which are attributable more or less directly to neglect, poverty, lack of medical facilities and attention, dietary deficiencies, and improper diagnosis have decreased in importance as killers of members of both races. Finally, violent deaths, except suicide, have remained a far more important cause of mortality in the nonwhite than in the white group.

NOTES

1. See T. Lynn Smith, *Population Analysis* (New York: McGraw-Hill Book Company, 1948), pp. 270 - 271.

2. Charts showing the trends in the homicide and suicide rates of whites and Negroes in the United States during the period 1920 to 1940 will be found in T. Lynn Smith and Homer L. Hitt, *The People of Louisiana* (Baton Rouge: Louisiana State University Press, 1952), pp. 196 - 197.

BOGUE, DONALD J. *Principles of Demography,* pp. 560 - 622. New York: John Wiley & Sons, Inc., 1969.

DAVIS, KINGSLEY. *The Population of India and Pakistan,* Part II. Princeton: Princeton University Press, 1951.

LERNER, MONROE, and ODIN W. ANDERSON. *Health Progress in the United States, 1900 - 1960.* Chicago: University of Chicago Press, 1963.

MORIYAMA, IWAO M. *The Change in Mortality Trends in the United States* (U.S. National Center for Health Statistics, Analytical Studies Series 3, No. 1). Washington: Government Printing Office, 1964.

SPIEGELMAN, MORTIMER. "Mortality Trends for Causes of Death in Countries of Low Mortality." *Demography,* Vol. 2, No. 1 (1965), pp. 115 - 125.

SPIEGELMAN, MORTIMER. *Significant Mortality and Morbidity Trends in the United States since 1900.* Philadelphia: American College of Life Underwriters, 1960.

STOLNITZ, GEORGE J. "A Century of International Mortality Trends." *Population Studies,* Vol. IX, No. 1 (1955), pp. 24 - 55, and Vol. X, No. 1 (1956), pp. 17 - 42.

STOLNITZ, GEORGE J. "A Century of International Mortality Trends." *Popu-*Africa." *Population Studies,* Vol. XIX, No. 2 (1965), pp. 117 - 138.

TAEUBER, CONRAD, and IRENE B. TAEUBER. *The People of the United States in the 20th Century* (A 1960 Census Monograph), pp. 495 - 511. Washington: Government Printing Office, 1971.

THOMLINSON, RALPH. *Population Dynamics,* Chap. 5. New York: Random House, Inc., 1965.

THOMPSON, WARREN S., and DAVID T. LEWIS. *Population Problems,* pp. 373 - 379. 5th ed. New York: McGraw-Hill Book Company, 1965.

UNITED NATIONS. *Demographic Yearbook, 1966,* Chap. I. New York: United Nations, 1967.

WORLD HEALTH ORGANIZATION. *Trends in the Study of Morbidity and Mortality* (Public Health Papers No. 27). Geneva: World Health Organization, 1965.

PART FIVE

Migration

18
EMIGRATION and IMMIGRATION

Migration is the last of the three factors affecting changes in the number and distribution of populations to be discussed in this volume. From a strictly demographic point of view it usually is considerably less important than births or deaths in effecting changes in the populations of nations or even of regions within a given nation. However, it frequently becomes the most important of the three primary factors involved in population changes within a given community, county, or state. Furthermore, the social and economic effects upon the societies involved due to the exodus of population from one area and the influx of migrants in another often greatly outweigh the influences exerted by variations in the birth rate or those in the death rate, though the results of the changes in the vital processes should by no means be depreciated. Finally, international migration is much more a subject of expressed public policy and legal regulation than are either the fertility or the mortality of the population. This is not to say that the modern state does not assume a heavy responsibility in the control of transmissible diseases and that it does not in many other ways implement the general belief that life is better than death. Neither is it to deny that some national and state governments may maintain clinics for the dissemination of knowledge and the distribution of apparatus related to birth control. Nor is it to maintain that modern governments lack the legal enactments which make it a crime to practice infanticide or to engage in other forms of homicide. But it is to state flatly that all such attempts at direct regulation of the factors of fertility and mortality are slight in comparison with the legal provisions and the administrative machinery established to deal with immigration and emigration.

THE SOCIAL SIGNIFICANCE OF MIGRATION

Consider briefly some of the significant social and economic aspects of the movement of people from one place to another. Migration affects directly the physical

459

constitutions and health of the populations involved. It has a powerful impact upon the structures and processes of the societies concerned, and it exerts tremendous influences upon the personalities of the migrants themselves. All of these are, of course, at a minimum in a nomadic society in which a wandering existence is the normal way of life; for then each group of nomads carries along with it all of the institutional accoutrements of its particular society. Consequently, little social disruption is brought about because of the movement of persons in physical space, and the influences of migration upon human personalities are reduced to the minimum. Nevertheless, the individuals involved must adjust to new or constantly varying physical surroundings. In addition, in nomadic societies man's devices for sheltering himself from the weather, along with all other portions of the protective shield of manmade environment or culture that the members of social groups place between themselves and the natural environment, are less highly developed and perfected than they are in more stable and sedentary groups. Hence, the social repercussions of migration are at a minimum in societies where people are always on the move.

A wandering existence also sets definite limits upon the social structures that may be developed and put into use. For example, nomadic groups must necessarily be small — the limitations of securing food for man and beast dictate this. In turn, the limitation of numbers precludes the high development of specialization by tasks and industries and of any elaborate division of labor. Therefore, among such groups the economy has to be a simple one, based as a rule upon mere collecting, hunting and fishing, or herding. The elaboration of great systems of communication and transportation is impossible among people who are always on the move; a nomadic society could never develop the telephone, the telegraph, the radio, television, the superhighway, the automobile, and the airplane; and attempts to overcome the effects of earth's gravitational pull must take the fictionalized form represented by magic carpets or winged steeds instead of the intricate missiles, launching pads, and space ships that are the concern of scientists and engineers during the last part of the twentieth century. Great and enduring institutions, universities, churches, and cathedrals, and many other familiar portions of the social structure of a great modern society are all made absolutely impossible by a wandering type of existence. It should hardly be necessary to say more to indicate that the role of migration is no small one, even in a nomadic society.

When a sedentary type of living is the normal situation for the bulk of the population, such migration as takes place is of even greater significance. Most important under these circumstances are the effects of migration upon societal processes and structures and human personalities. In a society where permanent settlements are the norm, the movement of persons from one location to another severs the most significant social ties and bonds. Emigration disrupts established social structures in the communities of origin, and immigration introduces new and oftentimes conflicting ethnic and cultural groups into the social groups at the place of settlement. Therefore, migration necessitates social and economic adjustments on the part of the communities in which the migrants originated, the ones to which they move, and personal and social adjustments on the part of the persons who move from one place to another. The community of origin, that which the newcomer enters, and the migrant himself are never again the same. If the number of persons involved in the exodus or the influx forms a very large proportion of the total population, the repercussions may be paralyzing in their effects.

The influences of migration upon the individual and his personality are tremendous. By moving from one place to another a person severs most of the ties and bonds that bound him to his old groups and gave him status in them. Through migration he sheds most of his social obligations, and, in turn, he is shorn of nearly all of the benefits and privileges of group association. For him position and status in the groups and classes of the new community do not come automatically, but he must find his place in them during a period of trial and testing. The migrant's status in a new community may be vastly different from what it was in the old, and the greater the role of inheritance (or caste) in establishing the person's position within the society involved, the more important this discrepancy is likely to be. Cut adrift from all his primary and interest groups, separated from his class identification, the individual must gain a place for himself in the new groups and establish the social level at which he is to operate in the new community. Since he is forced to abandon the role of "native" and assume that of "stranger," the process of becoming accepted and established in the new locality may be neither pleasant nor rapid.

Whenever migration involves a shift between radically different societies or cultures, and especially if a change of language is necessitated, a complete adjustment may be impossible for the migrant and even for his children. At best assimilation is a slow, difficult, and painful process. Thousands of immigrants to countries such as Argentina, Australia, Brazil, Canada, New Zealand, the United States, and Venezuela have never succeeded in becoming fully attuned to the new society. As long as they live, they bear some of the social markings of the foreigner and are unable to adapt themselves fully to the changed social surroundings. Many of them continue to live for the most part in the Old World. Frequently, the effect upon the second generation is disastrous, the immigrants themselves remaining enmeshed in patterns and tensions of the old country, and the children going to all extremes in their endeavors to break away, throw off all identification with the heritage of their fathers, and to achieve full acceptance into the new. In portions of the world in which immigrants are less numerous, all of these effects upon the migrant himself and his offspring probably are even more pronounced.

DEFINITION AND TYPES

The verb *migrate* is given three shades of meaning in the *New Merriam-Webster Dictionary*: (1) to move from one place to another, especially to move from one country, region, or place of abode or sojourn to another, with a view to residence; (2) to pass periodically from one region or climate to another; and (3) to transfer. In accordance with these definitions, the term *migration* seems generally to be employed to refer to all movements in physical space — with the assumption more or less implicit that a change of residence or domicile is involved. Obviously, the dictionary definitions and current usages are adjusted to a society in which settled living is the normal situation and in which nomadism is absent or largely lacking. In a society in which residential instability seems to be increasing, it is likely that more shades of meaning need to be developed. In sociology, where the practice of using migration and mobility (or even social mobility) as interchangeable terms is almost universal, this seems particularly essential. Additional attention is given to this point in the following chapter.

For demographic purposes it is useful to divide the subject of migration into two large parts, the first of which involves the changes of residence from one country to another and the second of which covers all kinds of migratory movements that take place within the boundaries of a given nation. The first of these is designated as *emigration,* from the standpoint of the nation from which the movement occurs, and *immigration* from the point of view of the receiving country. All of the intranational migrations conventionally are grouped together under the designation of *internal* migration. Emigration and immigration are discussed in the remaining pages of this chapter, and internal migration is the subject of the two that follow.

SOURCES OF DATA

Data on emigration and immigration leave a great deal to be desired. Despite the widespread interest in and concern about the subject, within the entire realm of population study the paucity of reliable information about international migrations of populations is matched only by the lack of comprehensive materials relating to internal migration. This presents a curious paradox in a world which has succeeded in overcoming so many intricate problems connected with the definition, counting, and measurement of so many elusive phenomena.

The fact that the mass movement of population from one country to another was a highly important feature of world affairs during the first half of the twentieth century and well into the second half is so obvious that it hardly calls for comment. Merely to mention that approximately one out of every forty persons in the United States on January 1, 1915, had been living in his native European country on the corresponding date in 1913 is sufficient to demonstrate this point, but even an abbreviated list of recent mass dislocations of population through migration would have to include comparable movements of persons from other parts of the world to Argentina, Brazil, Canada, and Australia, to mention only four other large takers of immigrants. Even more significant to many in other parts of the world would be the uprooting of many millions of Europeans during the First World War; the flight from a Hitlerized Central Europe in the 1930's; the displacement of millions that resulted from the marching of armies, the shifts in factories, and the remaking of the maps of Europe and Asia during and immediately after the Second World War; the partition of India and Pakistan, the struggles between them, and the resulting mass migrations and transfers of population; the establishment and growth of the new nation of Israel; the flight of population from East Germany to West Germany; the Hungarian uprising and its aftermath; the expulsion of the Dutch from the East Indies; the movement of European colonials from Africa and parts of Asia as one territory after another has established its independence; the migration of large numbers from mainland China to Taiwan and Hong Kong; and the flight of Koreans, Vietnamese, and Cambodians from one part to another of their respective war-torn territories. Regardless of whether migration of these types are produced principally by developments in the homelands which lead to the flight of large numbers of persons from their native countries or whether attractions in other nations are responsible for the movements, these gigantic streams of human migration are of vital concern nationally and internationally.

Some countries, such as Argentina, Brazil, and Venezuela, now receive fewer immigrants than they once did. But for the most part and despite some temporary reductions around 1960, the various streams continue and the problems and policies of immigration still are of basic concern to all branches of the modern state, executive, legislative, and judicial; to capital and labor alike; to church as well as state; to those whose principal professional interest is social welfare as well as those engaged in manufacturing, transportation, agriculture, commerce, and banking; and to all those who devote time to the intellectual activities connected with the social sciences, and particularly to sociologists and economists. Since national policies eventually must rest upon public opinion in the countries involved, the debates on immigration problems and policies which seem to be on the "regular agenda" of contemporary parliaments have widespread repercussions in local communities of which the nations are composed, and much of the stimulus for these debates comes from these same small localities.

In spite of this, in·most parts of the world the first steps still are to be taken toward the collection of comprehensive, reliable, informative, and comparable data on emigration and immigration. It hardly is an accident that those responsible for the preparation of the *Demographic Yearbook* of the United Nations selected "natality" as the special topic to be stressed in five of the first twenty-three issues of this indispensable compendium and have still to single out emigration and immigration for special consideration in one of the annual volumes. Indeed in the 1953, 1955, 1956, 1958, 1960, 1961, 1963, 1964, 1965, 1967, 1969, and 1971 editions of the *Yearbook*, statistics on this highly important portion of demography do not figure at all. The 1948, 1949 - 50, 1951, 1952, 1954, 1957, 1959, 1962, 1966, 1968, and 1970 compilations do give such fragmentary materials as could be secured with respect to the following aspects: continental and intercontinental migration (1948 issue only), major categories of departures and arrivals, emigrants by country of intended permanent residence, emigrants by age and sex, immigrants by age and sex, and immigrants by country of last residence. In addition, the 1952 volume includes data on refugees settled by the International Refugee Organization and on refugees repatriated by this organization for the years 1947 - 1951.

The 1970 edition of the *Yearbook* not only contains the most recent set of materials, but also includes an enlightening discussion of the problems inherent in the collection and collation of data on immigration and emigration, pertinent extracts from the recommendations adopted by the Population and Statistical Commissions of the Economic and Social Council, and some indications as to why the tabulations presented fail to meet the standards proposed in the recommendations. The student of population would do well to attend carefully to what is said in this volume concerning the difficulties inherent in definitions and nomenclatures pertaining to the international movements of persons. The proposals set forth by this international agency are a far cry from those that sufficed in the days in which it could almost be assumed that data about persons debarking as third-class or steerage passengers from transoceanic vessels could be considered statistics on immigration.

Two basic categories of compilations are included in these recommendations and in the tabulations resulting from them as contained in the 1970 issue of the *Yearbook:* (1) statistics on arrivals from other countries and (2) statistics on departures to other countries. The first of these should consist of six subgroups, namely, *long-term immigrants*, or nonresidents, nationals and aliens, intending to remain for a period exceeding one year; *short-term immigrants*, or nonresidents intending to exercise for a period of one year or less an occupation remunerated from within the country; *visitors*, or nonresidents intending to remain in the country for less than one year and to engage in no occupation for renumeration; *transit visitors; cruise-ship visitors;* and *residents*, nationals and aliens, returning after a short-term sojourn abroad. The second category also should be subdivided into six subgroups: *long-term emigrants*, that is residents, both nationals and aliens, intending to remain abroad for a period exceeding one year; *short-term immigrants departing; visitors* departing on completion of visit; *transit visitors; cruise-ship visitors;* and *residents*, nationals and aliens, intending to go abroad for one year or less. Obviously, it would be laborious, involved, and expensive to secure materials of this type even if well-trained international agents were stationed at all places of entry to take charge of all the bookkeeping involved. When this must be done volunatarily by all of the governments individually, working through such personnel as they station on their frontiers, and complicated by the frequently quite different sets of categories provided the visas required by each, the prospects of obtaining satisfactory information do not appear very bright. Adding to the complications is the large illegal movement across international boundaries, of which the influx of "wetbacks" from Mexico to the United States is merely one of the more publicized examples. For years to come those working with international migration statistics probably will have to do the best they can to piece together fragments of information drawn from a variety of sources and highly lacking in comparability.

The best evidence that this is the case is gained from an examination of the materials on the international movements of population assembled in the 1970 volume of the *Demographic Yearbook,* which at the time of this writing is the latest one to give any data on emigration and immigration. The four tabulations attempted were concerned with the major categories of arrivals, 1963 - 1969, the major categories of departures, 1963 - 1969; long-term immigrants by age and sex, 1962 - 1969; and long-term emigrants by age and sex, 1962 - 1969. Unfortunately, information concerning the immigrant's last country of permanent residence and the emigrant's country of intended residence do not appear in the 1966, 1968, or 1970 issues of the *Yearbook* and one must go to those for 1959 and some earlier years in order to find these valuable data. Nevertheless, an examination of the most general of the recent materials, the classification of departures into permanent emigrants and other subcategories and of arrivals into permanent immigrants and other subcategories, suffices for present purposes. The only countries for which data are presented showing the number of long-term immigrants arriving for all of the years from 1962 to 1969 are as follows: Canada, Mexico, Panama, the United States, Argentina, Colombia, Israel, Austria, Iceland, the Netherlands, Sweden, Australia, and New Zealand. Several others provide data for some of the years designated and still others give information on long-term and short-term immigrants combined. Many of these data present problems in analysis, largely because they are not comparable. For example, prior to 1964, the materials for the United Kingdom pertained only to movements of nationals of Commonwealth countries arriving by ship from places outside Europe and the Mediterranean area. Beginning in 1964 the data were based on estimates from a sample survey of passenger traffic at airports and seaports, but even they excluded movement to and from Ireland and along the Scandinavian sea routes. The data for the United States are for aliens admitted for the first time for one year or more and former alien residents returning after a sojourn abroad for a year or more; those for Italy apply only to Italian nationals returning by sea or air from non-European countries, and so on. Obviously, much remains to be done before comprehensive, accurate, and comparable statistics on emigration and immigration will be available even for the countries which are sending out the most emigrants and those which are receiving the most immigrants.

INTERNATIONAL MIGRATIONS AND THEIR MAGNITUDE

Great historical importance is attached to overseas movements of Europeans during the second half of the nineteenth century and the first quarter of the twentieth, especially to countries such as the United States, Canada, Argentina, Brazil, Australia, and New Zealand whose national destinies were so strongly influenced by the millions of immigrants they received.[1] More important for most contemporary demographic matters, however, are the tremendous shifts of populations from their native hearths to other lands brought about by the scrambling of national boundaries and the uprooting of millions of families produced by the two world wars. This can best be considered by examining the international movements of population in the interval between the First and the Second World Wars and those that have taken place since the close of the latter. The tremendous dislocations of populations during the wars themselves hardly should be treated under the heading of emigration and immigration.

The Inter-War Period

In an earlier work,[2] all of the fairly reliable, available information on world immigration movements for the period between the two world wars was assembled and analyzed. Naturally, the data were sadly inadequate. The most serious shortcomings were the lack of anything at all comprehensive and reliable for mainland China, Soviet Russia, a large part of Africa, and some parts of Central and South America. However, for most of the European countries, the then Union of South Africa, India, New Zealand, Australia, and much of North and South America the materials for the decade immediately preceding the outbreak of the Second World War are fairly complete and reasonably accurate. The most trustworthy information is that for the years 1926 to 1936, inclusive, and the materials for this period are the ones that figure in the following discussion.[3]

Exclusive of Turkey and Russia, there was an annual migration of about 1 million persons from the various European countries during the period 1926 to 1930. The great economic depression brought about a sharp decline in the number of persons leaving one European country for another or for an overseas destination, and the number fell to slightly over 600,000 in 1931 and then to approximately 380,000 in 1936.

At the beginning of the period, in 1926 and 1927, some 700,000 persons annually were immigrating to these same European countries, either by leaving one of them for another or by returning to Europe from overseas. The economic depression greatly accelerated these movements, and the number of immigrants to European countries rose to above 1 million in 1930. Then the figure gradually declined until by 1936 it was only 400,000.

The result attained by balancing European emigration and immigration during this period indicates a slight loss of people by the continent prior to 1930, an almost exact balance in 1930, an annual excess of immigrants over emigrants in 1931 and in 1932, and a return to a near balance by 1936.

Considerable significance is attached to the situation in the various countries. Italy was the source of far more emigrants (1.5 million) than any other country during the eleven-year period under consideration. Poland (1.25 million) ranks second, followed by Great Britain and Northern Ireland, France, the Netherlands, Spain, Germany, and Portugal, in the order named. On the receiving end, France outranked all other European countries, with more than 1.14 million immigrants. Italy and Germany also were heavy takers, each receiving more than 1 million immigrants during the period. In third place is Great Britain and Northern Ireland, and fourth is Poland, followed in descending order by Switzerland, Spain, Belgium, and Portugal.

Most significant is the net amount of movement in these exchanges of population. Of these European countries in which immigration exceeded emigration, Germany led the list with a net gain of 638,736 for the period 1926 to 1936, followed by Switzerland (515,741), France (446,831), and Belgium (108,912). The country losing most heavily was Poland, with a net loss of 511,622 persons, followed by Italy (506,246), Czechoslovakia (266,046), Yugoslavia (131,096), Great Britain and Northern Ireland (100,934), Ireland (94,914), Bulgaria (94,621), Romania (84,230), and Greece (77,059).

Unfortunately, the data for most of the Asiatic countries are so inadequate that no significant conclusions may be established. The Philippines, Japan, India, and Palestine, however, are exceptions. In the Philippines, emigration and immigration both were heavy in the years 1926 to 1936, resulting in a net gain of 34,326 persons. In that period, for every two persons leaving Japan one returned and the net loss of population was 95,799. Palestine sustained a net gain of 50,672 persons by losing large numbers of Arabs and gaining many Jews. The flow from India was very large, but the reverse movement was slightly larger, so that a population gain of 90,000 is to be credited to migration.

For Africa, only the materials for the then Union of South Africa merit attention. This was an important area of absorption but one of small losses during the period 1926 to 1936, so that the net gain by migration was 931,244 persons.

Latin America long has been one of the principal takers of international migrants, although large numbers of persons also leave the various countries. Fortunately, relatively good information is available for Argentina, Brazil, Chile, Mexico, Uruguay, and Venezuela, countries which contain the bulk of the Latin American population. Between 1926 and 1936, the rates of emigration and immigration fluctuated considerably. Prior to 1930 the countries collectively incurred net gains of 150,000 to 200,000 persons a year, but by 1936, the number had fallen to only 3,000. The net gain for the entire period was the greatest in Argentina (423,000), followed by Mexico (374,000), Brazil (308,000), and Uruguay (104,000). For the six countries taken together the net gain was 1,232,000.

Detailed information for the United States is presented later in this chapter, but for comparative purposes the following information is given for the period 1926 to 1936: total immigration, 1,606,000; total emigration, 876,000; net gain from migration, 730,000.

Finally, in Oceania, Australia received a net immigration of more than 100,000 and New Zealand a net gain of about 24,000 persons during the eleven-year period under consideration.

All in all, emigration and immigration were much less important during the period between the two world wars than they were in the first fourteen years of the twentieth century. In part, and especially during the 1920's, this was due to the restrictions on immigration instituted by the various countries. Later on, however, it was because of the great worldwide economic depression.

The Period Following the End of the Second World War

After the Second World War, immigration increased substantially over that which took place between the two world conflicts. Some countries became more important recipients of migrants than they had been and others became less significant in this respect. Moreover, some of the nations that accepted large numbers of immigrants in the late 1940's and the 1950's virtually closed their doors in the 1960's or became less attractive to the migrants, whereas others welcomed increasing numbers of the migrants into their territories. Argentina and Brazil are examples of nations in which immigration decreased greatly, Australia and the United Kingdom of those in which it increased markedly. In order to present the principal facts on the matter for the period from 1946 through 1969, inclusive, Table 55 has been prepared. It shows the ten countries that received the largest contingents of immigrants after the Second World War, but because the time periods in some cases are for years other than 1946 - 1969, the ranking in descending order is according to the average annual amount of immigration rather than gross immigration.

In the years from 1946 through 1969, immigration to these ten countries totaled over 22.7 million persons. When adjustments are made for the fact that for a few countries not all of the years of the entire period are represented, this is an average annual immigration to the ten countries of about 973,000 persons. In the last several years, however, immigration to three of the ten countries under consideration has slowed considerably while that to seven has accelerated, with the result that the rate of immigration to the ten countries combined has been somewhat greater since 1960 than it was previously. During the period from 1946

TABLE 55

Immigration to the ten countries receiving the largest
numbers of international migrants, 1946 to 1969

Country	Period	Immigration Total	Annual average
United States	1946-69	6,362,237	265,093
Canada	1946-69	3,263,124	135,964
Australia	1946-69	3,248,591	135,358
United Kingdom	1946-69	2,471,500	102,979
France	1946-68	2,232,509	97,066
Israel	1946-69	1,376,933	57,372
Belgium	1948-69	1,157,738	52,624
Brazil	1946-63	798,000	44,333
Netherlands	1951-69	831,833	43,781
Argentina	1946-69	926,761	38,615

Source: Compiled and computed from data in various editions of United Nations, *Demographic Yearbook* and from those supplied by the International Labor Office to the world conference on "The Cultural Integration of Immigrants," held in Havana, Cuba, 1956.

TABLE 56

Emigration from the ten countries contributing the largest
numbers of international migrants, 1960 to 1969

Country	Period	Emigration Total	Annual average
Germany, Federal Republic	1960-69	4,351,492	435,149
United Kingdom	1960-69	2,119,478	211,948
West Berlin	1960-69	868,288	86,829
Greece	1960-68	693,959	77,107
Australia	1960-69	742,136	74,214
Portugal	1960-68	576,797	64,089
Mexico	1961-69	508,057	56,451
Italy	1960-69	552,314	55,231
Spain[a]	1960-69	489,771	48,978
Netherlands	1960-69	430,355	43,036

Source: Compiled and computed from data in various editions of United Nations, *Demographic Yearbook*.
[a]Prior to 1966, includes intercontinental movement only.

through 1959, the average annual number of immigrants was about 883,000, but from 1960 through 1969 it was approximately 1,088,000.

Between 1946 and 1969, the United States received about 28 per cent of the total number of immigrants admitted to the ten leading countries or almost twice as many as Canada, which was in second place, and Australia, which was third. Together these three countries absorbed nearly 57 per cent of the total. They are among the seven in which the rate of immigration was slower between 1946 and 1959 than it was from 1960 through 1969. These seven countries, with their average annual numbers of immigrants admitted during the two parts of the postwar period, respectively, are as follows: the United States, 224,892 and 321,375; Canada, 135,650 and 136,403; Australia, 107,107 and 174,909; the United Kingdom, 63,334 and 158,482; France, 88,426 and 110,504 (from 1960 through 1968); Belgium, 46,753 (from 1948 through 1959) and 59,670; and the Netherlands, 34,112 (from 1951 through 1959) and 52,482. The three countries in which the average annual numbers of immigrants were smaller in the second part of the postwar period than in the first segment are Israel, 73,336 between 1946 and 1959 and 35,023 from 1960 through 1969; Brazil, 47,519 and 33,183 (from 1960 through 1963); and Argentina, 62,183 and 5,619.

The origins of the immigrants entering each of the ten leading countries is another basic aspect of the topic. At this writing, however, the most recent materials available for all of the nations that identify the origins of the immigrants who went to each country are those for 1958. Obviously, these data provide no information for the second part of the postwar period. Yet there are some studies that provide more recent data on the matter for specific countries and these, together with the earlier materials, make it possible to identify the chief contributors of immigrants in recent years to the countries listed in Table 55. In the decade or so just after the Second World War, the United States received its largest contingents from Germany, Canada, the United Kingdom, and Poland, but in the years from 1960 through 1969, the greatest number came from Mexico, followed by those from Canada, Cuba, the United Kingdom, and Germany, in the order named. Canada, in the period from 1946 to 1967, accepted its largest numbers from the United Kingdom, Italy, the United States, and Germany. The group that migrated to Australia during the postwar years came chiefly from the United Kingdom and Ireland, Italy, various Eastern European countries, the Netherlands and several of its former colonies, and Germany. The immigrants received in the United Kingdom have come largely from Ireland, Poland, which sent nearly 100,000 of the members of its armed forces just after the war, Germany, Italy, the Eastern European countries, and recently the West Indies, India, and Pakistan. It should be added, however, that the United Kingdom is also a heavy contributor of emigrants to various other countries. France admitted the great bulk of its immigrants from Italy, followed by those from Spain and Germany, with a sizable contingent also arriving from Algeria. Those who went to

Israel are, of course, largely Jews from the European countries, mainly Romania, Poland, Bulgaria, and Hungary, although many also came from North Africa and from Iraq, Yemen, Turkey, Iran, and other parts of Asia. The great bulk of this migration took place from 1948 through 1952, after which the influx was comparatively small. Immigrants to Belgium after the Second World War came principally from Italy, France, the Netherlands, Germany, and Spain. Brazil received its largest postwar numbers from Portugal, Italy, and Spain, although immigrants from any source were relatively few after 1960. The persons who migrated to the Netherlands arrived mostly from Indonesia, with smaller contingents from Surinam, Morocco, Australia, Germany, Belgium, Italy, and Spain. Finally, those who entered Argentina came largely from Italy, Germany, Poland, and Portugal although, like Brazil, Argentina has received relatively few immigrants since 1960.

The counterpart of immigration is, of course, emigration and the available data make it possible to identify the countries contributing the largest numbers of migrants to the international flow between 1960 and 1969. Table 56 gives the major countries of emigration during this period, ranked in descending order according to the average annual amount of emigration in order to adjust for the somewhat variable time periods involved for a few of the countries.

In the years between 1960 and 1969, inclusive, emigration from these countries totaled over 11.3 million persons. When the adjustments are made for the slightly variable time ranges, this amounts to an average annual movement from the ten nations of about 1.15 million persons. The Federal Republic of Germany alone accounted for 38 per cent of the movement and West Berlin was responsible for an additional 8 per cent. The United Kingdom was in second place and together these three political entities sent out almost two-thirds of the total between 1960 and 1969. But even within the decade, emigration continued to increase up to 1969 in some countries but to diminish in several others. In West Berlin, Australia, Mexico, and Spain, the peak emigration occurred in 1969, which suggests that the magnitude of movement from these countries is continuing to increase. In the other countries, however, the peaks were reached in 1965, 1966, or 1967, after which the numbers decreased substantially. This condition may, of course, be temporary, but despite the moderate increase in movement in the second part of the postwar period over that which occurred in the first segment, it does underscore Bogue's observation that "almost everywhere in the world, since 1960 international migration is a comparatively insignificant component in population growth or change in population composition."[4] Clearly, it pales in significance beside natural increase and the changes in population characteristics that are produced by fluctuations in the two vital processes.

Other countries that sent out more than 15,000 emigrants annually during the period under consideration are Belgium, Denmark, Poland, New Zealand, and Sweden, in the order named. Some of them, along with several of those given in Table 56, are among the countries to which immigration also is relatively great, so that international migration tends to involve large-scale exchanges of persons among a fairly small number of nations. Also included in the list of nations sending out comparatively large numbers of emigrants are several that are among neither the most highly developed nor the least developed in the world. In fact, the latter are completely absent from the group losing the most emigrants despite the fact that one might expect large numbers of persons to be fleeing the low levels of living that prevail in them in search of more attractive places. In part, the absence of such countries from the list is a consequence of the nonexistence of data for many of them and the poor quality of the materials that are to be had for others. This problem precludes any thorough analysis of the movements of people from such countries as China, India, Pakistan, and Viet-Nam, as well as those from more developed ones such as Cuba and East Germany, all of which are known to have lost comparatively large numbers of emigrants in the 1960's. But three other things also seem to be involved. First, most of the countries of heavy immigration, including the United States, are no longer interested in receiving the least fortunate from the underdeveloped areas and have promulgated policies to exclude them. Second, it should be noted that voluntary emigration is a hopeful action in the sense that most of those making such a move expect to improve their lives in some way. In the underdeveloped areas in which the level of living is so low as to produce dejection and fatalistic acceptance on a large scale, there may be little impetus to migrate. In fact, given a resigned philosophy of life, migration may be an irrational act. On the other hand, where the level of living is tolerable but below that desired by many of the inhabitants, a powerful motivation may arise to transform the restless aspirations into reality. Emigration is one of the possible actions under these conditions and persons in such straits often are strongly impelled to leave their homelands for more attractive places. Third, some countries attempt to prevent emigration for various political reasons and while such policies do not necessarily succeed entirely, they may at least be effective in reducing the flow of emigrants to relatively small proportions. Present-day Cuba and East Germany are examples of this situation.[5]

IMMIGRATION TO THE UNITED STATES

To those who live in the Americas, immigration is a subject of more than usual interest, for to new nations in general and to those of the Western Hemisphere in particular, immigration has been a basic factor in their histories. Except for the Indians, who are of minor importance numerically in the larger American nations such as Argentina, Brazil, Canada, and the United States, the inhabitants of the New World are either themselves immigrants or the descendants of persons who migrated from one of the other continents. Even in countries such as Bolivia, Chile, Colombia, Cuba, Peru, Venezuela, and those of Central America, the upper classes generally are composed of persons of European ancestry. The growth of population in the United States during the nineteenth century and the first quarter of the twentieth would have been much slower had there been no immigration; the ethnic composition of our people would have been quite different had we never permitted millions of immigrants to come to our shores; and the national origins and backgrounds of our inhabitants would still be changing radically had the Immigration Act of 1924 never been put into effect. Thus, immigration has been so significant in the life history of our nation that it is well to consider briefly the highlights in the history of the phenomenon.

History of Immigration to the United States

The history of immigration to the United States falls rather logically into five distinct periods. The first of these embraces the years from the establishment of the first settlements to the emergence of the national state in 1783; the second, the period of free immigration, ended about 1830; the third, extending until 1882, was the period of state regulation; the fourth, beginning with the passage of the first national immigration act in 1882 and lasting until 1917, was a period of federal regulation with individual selection; and the fifth, the present stage of restricted immigration, began in 1917 when both the House and the Senate passed by two-thirds majority, over the veto of President Woodrow Wilson, the law whose purpose Wilson stated clearly was "restriction and not selection." Let us consider briefly each of these five eras in the history of immigration in the United States.

Those who came from overseas to the northern portions of the Western Hemisphere during the colonial period were in a situation vastly different from that encountered by later arrivals. They came to an unclaimed wilderness and not to an established nation with fixed boundaries, laws, well-grounded customs, and a definite status in the family of nations. Unfortunately, though, there are few reliable data concerning the number and origin of persons coming to the United States before the Revolutionary War. During this period the natural increase of population doubtless was very rapid; but on the other hand, there were large influxes of population through such important migrations as that of the Scotch-Irish during the early part of the eighteenth century. It is estimated that 20,000 of these Ulstermen left Ireland for America between 1700 and 1730, and it is known that 6,000 of them debarked in Philadelphia in the year 1729 alone. In fact, it has been calculated that by 1750 they and their children comprised one-fourth of the total population of Pennsylvania.[6] Natural increase and immigration combined to produce a population of approximately 4 million at the time of the first census in 1790.

The era which began with the adoption of the federal constitution and ended about 1830 was one of free immigration. Rarely in the history of any nation has the freedom of ingress been so complete. During these years of infancy of the new

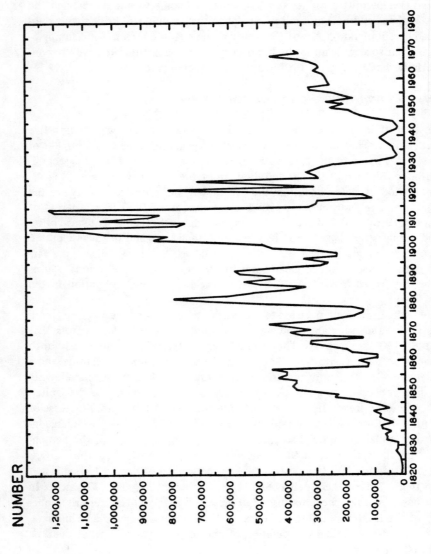

Figure 59. Immigration to the United States, 1820 to 1970. Data for 1820 - 1867 are for "alien passengers arriving," those for 1868 - 1891 and 1895 - 1897 are for "immigrants arriving," those for 1892 - 1894 and for 1898 to the present are for "immigrants admitted." When not for twelve months, coverage is as follows: 1834, fifteen months; 1843, nine months; 1850, fifteen months; and 1868, six months.

nation the immigrants arriving were similar in kind and heritage to those who had preceded them. For decades there was little or no thought given to the advisability of limiting in any way the number or types of persons permitted to land. By 1830, however, enough agitation had arisen over asserted drawbacks to the system of free immigration that this year is selected as the closing one for this period in the immigration history of the nation. We lack precise information of the numbers of persons coming to our shores during these formative years. Official estimates place the number of persons admitted during the years 1783 to 1820 at 250,000, a figure thought by some to be too low.[7] From 1820 on data are available. (See Figure 59.) Even then, no distinction was made between visitors and those who came with the avowed intention of remaining. In any case the numbers were small and the arrival each year of a few thousand newcomers aroused little interest or concern on the part of the earlier arrivals. It was not until 1825 that the number of debarkations reached 10,000 per year. Thereafter, immigration increased rapidly; and as the incoming tide swelled in volume, there arose a belief that the newcomers were partially responsible for some of the nation's pressing social and economic problems.

The regulation of immigration and emigration was not one of the functions attributed to the federal government when the constitution was adopted in 1787. Consequently, when widespread belief arose that absolutely unrestricted and unregulated immigration was undesirable, agitation arose for control at the state level. Among all the factors leading to attempts by various states to control immigration none was more important than the tendency for paupers and criminals to immigrate either of their own accord or by means of subsidies supplied by those who wished to be rid of them. As early as 1830 *Nile's Register* contained a bitter protest because the British ship *Anacreon* put off in Norfolk 168 passengers, of whom more than three-fourths were said to be transported paupers. By 1838 the immigration of such indigents, large numbers of whom were duped into migrating by means of a subsidy[8] paid by the overseers in the home parishes in England, was of such moment that it was the subject of a voluminous report prepared by the then Secretary of State John Forsyth.[9] In addition, competition from the immigrant workers with low standards of living, opposition to the Roman Catholic religion of the Irish who had begun swarming to the United States, and asserted clannishness on the part of the Irish and Germans were effective in helping generate opposition to continued unrestricted immigration. They crystalized in a nativist political movement which made considerable headway in this country in the years immediately before the ones in which the conflict over slavery entered its final stages. The economic depression of 1857, followed closely by the Civil War, pushed immigration problems temporarily into the background. In fact, the low number of immigrants during 1862 was never again equalled until the depth of the great world economic depression in 1932. As soon as the war ended, however, the struggle over immigration policy was resumed, and in this the opposition to the Irish, widely publicized by the Molly Maguire disturbances in the coal mining districts of Pennsylvania and the alarm on the West Coast over the coming of the Chinese, were major issues. The agitation eventually was responsible for the passage in 1882 of federal legislation excluding the Chinese and other provisions designed to keep paupers, criminals, and those suffering from various diseases from gaining admission to the United States. By these acts the federal government definitively took control of matters pertaining to immigration and emigration, thus ushering in the fourth period in the history of migration to and from the United States.

The first epoch in the federal control of immigration was based on the principle of individual selection. It began in a year (1882) in which the arrival of 788,992 immigrants, the highest to that time, was recorded. But while the federal government was designing and placing into effect its immigration policy, the tide of newcomers was destined to move to much higher levels. In 1884, Congress corrected a discrimination in favor of those arriving overland at our borders in comparison with those coming by sea; and in 1885, it was made

> . . .unlawful for any person, company, partnership, or corporation, in any manner whatsoever, to prepay the transportation, or in any way to assist or encourage the importation or migration of any alien or aliens, any foreigner or foreigners, into the United States, its Territories, or the District of Columbia, under contract or agreement, parol or special, express or implied, made previously to the importation or migration of such alien or aliens, foreigner or foreigners, to perform labor or service of any kind in the United States, its Territories, or the District of Columbia.[10]

Thereafter, with debate over immigration policy annually on its regular agenda, Congress continued year after year to develop in piecemeal fashion legislation regulating immigration. Additions in 1887 and 1888 were minor, those during the last decade of the nineteenth century somewhat more substantial, and those in 1903 of considerable importance. In 1903, the exclusion of the mentally ill, beggars, anarchists, prostitutes, and procurers was decreed. Thereafter, year after year Congress filled gaps in the legislation and responded to tremendous pressures from its constituents in the states for laws restricting immigration. Specifically there was a widespread popular demand that immigration from southern and eastern Europe should be stopped.

The particular device proposed to achieve this goal was the literacy test. Thirty-two times between 1882 and 1917, an act establishing such a test was passed either in the House or in the Senate. Four times it was passed by both houses of Congress, only to be vetoed—in 1897 by Cleveland, in 1913 by Taft, and in 1915 and 1917 by Wilson. Finally, on February 5, 1917, over Wilson's second veto, the House and the Senate passed a bill providing for the exclusion of "all aliens over sixteen years of age, physically capable of reading, who cannot read the English language, or some other language or dialect, including Hebrew or Yiddish," but providing some exceptions for near relatives of citizens and for refugees from religious persecution. The final passage of this bill was a triumph for the forces advocating restriction of immigration, and it marked the end of the period of individual selection and the beginning of the fifth epoch, that of immigration restriction.

The literacy test soon proved ineffective, for after the end of the First World War, a heavy tide of immigration once more got underway. Thereupon the proponents of restriction quickly set about to secure the passage of legislation that effectively would reduce the numbers of immigrants to the United States and would limit those who did come largely to persons from the countries of northern and western Europe. The quota system, under which immigration has been controlled from shortly after the end of the First World War until the present, was put into effect temporarily by a 1921 act and more definitively by one passed in 1924. The National Origins Plan provided for by the latter was designed to apportion a total of about 150,000 immigrants annually among the various countries in about the same proportions as natives of those nations were represented in the population of the United States in 1920. This was reworked to some extent by the Immigration and Nationality Act of 1952 under which quotas were established that prevailed until 1965. Roughly, the formula employed allowed to each country an annual quota of immigrants equal to one-sixth of 1 per cent of the number of persons born in that country who were residing in the United States in 1920. There were no quotas restricting immigration of persons born in Canada, Mexico, Cuba, Haiti, the Dominican Republic, the Canal Zone, or in one of the independent countries of Central and South America; nor were there any for the spouses and children of such persons who accompanied or followed to join them in this country. At various times the quotas set forth in the law have been modified to permit the entry of relatively large contingents of refugees from Hungary, Cuba, and some other countries whose political conditions precipitated sudden emigrations. In 1965, the 1952 Act was amended in such a way that beginning on July 1, 1968, the total annual quota of immigrants was increased to 290,000. This was apportioned in such a way that only 120,000 immigrants could come each year from the countries of the Western Hemisphere, which previously had not had quota restrictions imposed upon them and the remaining 170,000 could come from all other countries taken together. Under the 1965 amendment, the national quotas were eliminated in favor of a first-come, first-served system, although a limit of 20,000 is not to be exceeded by the contingent from any one nation.[11] Furthermore, "selection is made on the basis of preferences favoring family reunification and persons with skills and talents needed here."[12] The amendment eliminates much of the obsession with racial and national origins in determining the eligibility of potential immigrants for entry into the United States, but it does not alter significantly the total number who may be admitted.[13] Its basic element is restriction and it seems likely to remain so.

The Number of Immigrants

As indicated above, the data on immigration to the United States leave a great deal to be desired. Prior to 1820 no comprehensive records were kept, and from then until 1868 the statistics pertained only to aliens arriving from overseas. In 1868, the attempt to assemble data on immigrants as such began. In 1908, those entering the United States were classified as immigrant or nonimmigrant, and that practice has been continued until the present. With the year 1908 also begins the series of data pertaining to departures, with the materials recorded also divided into those for emigrants and nonemigrants, at least through 1956. In 1957 and later years, the categories of emigrant aliens departed and nonemigrant aliens departed were combined into one. In that year also, those leaving the United States for Canada were excluded from the category of aliens departing.

Charted in Figure 59 are the materials for the years 1820 to 1970. This covers the entire period in which the migration of people to the United States was an important factor in our demographic processes. Observation of these materials enables one to identify the peaks and depressions in the movement of persons from abroad, with those recorded in 1855, 1874, 1908, 1914, and 1921 deserving special attention. From 1908 on, the period for which the materials are most reliable, the detailed figures also are presented in Table 57. This table also supplies the recorded information about departures from this country along with the balance secured by subtracting the number of departures from the number of arrivals. It is important to note from this table that at no time between 1924 and 1957 did the number of arrivals registered exceed by 300,000 a year the number of departures recorded. In 1957, the migration balance rose above one-half million, but the exclusion from the data in that and subsequent years of persons departing from the United States for Canada probably was responsible for most of the apparent increase. A more realistic picture of immigration into the United States in the period 1957 to 1970, inclusive, is provided by the data in the "immigrant" column of Table 57 or that for immigrant aliens admitted. This number has changed relatively little in the 1960's, generally fluctuating between one-quarter and one-half million annually. Furthermore, these numbers are so small as proportions of the total population that the major importance of immigration in recent decades involves the social, economic, and political, rather than the strictly demographic aspects of the subject.

Before closing this section, it is important to indicate that these records are by no means a complete accounting of the migration of persons to the continental United States. Three additional movements of persons into the nation must be noted. The first of these is the heavy influx of Puerto Ricans into New York City and other heavily populated areas of the country. Technically, this is not immigration at all, nor is the amount of such migration known. However, the 1970 census accounted for a total of 764,960 persons born in Puerto Rico who

TABLE 57

Immigration and emigration, United States, 1908 to 1970

	Aliens admitted		Aliens departed		
Year	Immigrant	Non-immigrant	Emigrant	Non-emigrant	Migration balance†
1908	782,870	141,825	395,073	319,755	209,867
1909	751,786	192,449	225,802	174,590	543,843
1910	1,041,570	156,467	202,436	177,982	817,619
1911	878,587	151,713	295,666	222,549	512,085
1912	838,172	178,983	333,262	282,030	401,863
1913	1,197,892	229,335	308,190	303,734	815,303
1914	1,218,480	184,601	303,338	330,467	769,276
1915	326,700	107,544	204,074	180,100	50,070
1916	298,826	67,922	129,765	111,042	125,941
1917	295,403	67,474	66,277	80,102	216,498
1918	110,618	101,235	94,585	98,683	18,585
1919	141,132	95,889	123,522	92,709	20,790
1920	430,001	191,575	288,315	139,747	193,514
1921	805,228	172,935	247,718	178,313	552,132
1922	309,556	122,949	198,712	146,672	87,121
1923	522,919	150,487	81,450	119,136	472,820
1924	706,896	172,406	76,789	139,956	662,557
1925	294,314	164,121	92,728	132,762	232,945
1926	304,488	191,618	76,992	150,763	268,351
1927	335,175	202,826	73,366	180,142	284,493
1928	307,255	193,376	77,457	196,899	226,275
1929	279,678	199,649	69,203	183,295	226,829
1930	241,700	204,514	50,661	221,764	173,789
1931	97,139	183,540	61,882	229,034	−10,237
1932	35,576	139,295	103,295	184,362	−112,786
1933	23,068	127,660	80,081	163,721	−93,074
1934	29,470	134,434	39,771	137,401	−13,268
1935	34,956	144,765	38,834	150,216	−9,329
1936	36,329	154,570	35,817	157,467	−2,385
1937	50,244	181,640	26,736	197,486	7,302
1938	67,895	184,802	25,210	197,404	30,083
1939	82,998	185,333	26,651	174,758	66,922
1940	70,756	138,032	21,461	144,703	42,624
1941	51,776	100,008	17,115	71,362	63,307
1942	28,781	82,457	7,363	67,189	36,686
1943	23,725	81,117	5,107	53,615	46,120
1944	28,551	113,641	5,669	78,740	57,783
1945	38,119	164,247	7,442	85,920	109,004

TABLE 57

Immigration and emigration, United States, 1908 to 1970

Year	Aliens admitted		Aliens departed		Migration balance†
	Immigrant	Non-immigrant	Emigrant	Non emigrant	
1946	107,721	203,469	18,143	186,210	106,837
1947	147,292	366,305	22,501	300,921	190,175
1948	170,570	476,006	20,875	427,343	198,358
1949	188,317	447,272	24,586	405,503	205,500
1950	249,187	426,837	27,598	429,091	219,335
1951	205,717	465,106	26,174	446,727	197,922
1952	265,520	516,082	21,880	487,617	272,105
1953	170,434	485,714	24,256	520,246	111,646
1954	208,177	566,613	30,665	568,496	175,629
1955	237,790	620,946	31,245	634,555	192,936
1956	321,625	686,259	22,824	692,376	292,684
1957	326,867	758,858	574,608[a]		511,117
1958	253,265	847,764	710,428		390,601
1959	260,686	1,024,945	885,913		399,718
1960	265,398	1,140,736	1,004,377		401,757
1961	271,344	1,220,315	1,093,937		397,722
1962	283,763	1,331,383	1,158,960		456,186
1963	306,260	1,507,091	1,266,843		546,508
1964	292,248	1,744,808	1,431,000		606,056
1965	296,697	2,075,967	1,735,000		637,664
1966	323,040	2,341,923	1,920,000		744,963
1967	361,972	2,608,193	2,144,000		826,165
1968	454,448	3,200,336	2,473,742		1,181,042
1969	358,579	3,645,328	2,807,618		1,196,289
1970	373,326	4,431,880	3,246,481		1,558,725

Source: Compiled from National Office of Vital Statistics, *Vital Statistics—Special Reports,* No. 9 (1940), p. 456; U.S. Bureau of the Census, *Continuation to 1952 of Historical Statistics of the United States, 1789-1945* (1954), p. 6; and *Statistical Abstract of the United States,* various editions, 1957-1972.

†Balance of total aliens admitted and total aliens departed.

[a]Figures for emigrant and nonemigrant aliens departed combined after 1956.

were enumerated in the continental United States, of whom 485,139 were in New York City. This compares with totals for 1960 of 615,384 and for 1950 of 429,710. The proportion of the total living in New York City in 1970, however, was 63.4 per cent as compared with 69.8 per cent in 1960 and 82.9 per cent in 1950, which indicates a gradual dissemination of persons of Puerto Rican birth throughout the nation.[14]

Second is the flow of migrants without benefit of passport or visa across the border between the United States and Mexico. This reached enormous proportions in the 1950's, with over a half-million either leaving the United States voluntarily or being deported in 1950 alone. Since then, cooperative efforts between Mexico and the United States designed to control this current of migration and to safeguard the conditions of work for the laborers who were given permission to enter (largely for seasonal work in agriculture) helped to reduce somewhat the numbers of such illegal entrants to the United States. Furthermore, after January 1, 1965, Mexican agricultural laborers brought into the United States have been allowed to enter legally only under the provisions of the general Immigration and Nationality Act rather than under a special law which prevailed previously. This, too, has brought about some reduction in the number who either arrive or remain illegally. Nevertheless, despite these various efforts, Bridges, in his careful study of the population of our southern neighbor, evaluates the movement of Mexicans into the United States in recent years as follows:

> While an average of about 45,000 each year have been admitted legally during the 1960's, probably at least five times this number find entrance to the country through illegal channels, and some years a total of over 300,000 Mexican nationals have been expelled.[15]

Obviously, the latter figure does not include the unknown number that goes undetected. In any case, the border between the two countries is still a great sieve and the flow of illegal entrants continues to be so large that in many of the western states, their employment is taken as a matter of course. The migrants are also subject to the wide range of abuse and exploitation that can be imposed upon any group of illegal entrants who dare not appeal to the police, the courts, or the other legal institutions of the country in which they are residing for fear of being discovered and expelled.

Third is the movement of persons into the United States under the Cuban Refugee Program. Originally, Cuban refugees were designated as "parolees" without recognized immigrant status and often without sufficient promise of permanence or official recognition to obtain jobs. As a result of their dilemma, legislation that became effective in 1966 was passed to enable Cubans who came to the United States after January 1, 1959, and who had been in the country for two years or longer to have their status adjusted to that of permanent residents. However, the numerical limitation on Western Hemisphere natives that went into effect on July 1, 1968, also applies to Cubans, with the result that they now must compete with other Western Hemisphere natives for the 120,000 visa numbers allocated annually. Under these various concessions and restrictions, between 1961 and 1970, 402,497 Cubans were registered as having passed through the Cuban Refugee Center in Miami. Moreover, the 1970 census enumerated a total of 444,356 persons who had been born in Cuba, 105,148 of whom had become naturalized citizens. Of the total, 48 per cent were residing in Florida at the time of the latest census, 16 per cent were in New York, 13 per cent in New Jersey, and 9 per cent in California.

IMMIGRATION POLICY

The immigration policies of a given country rarely are the result of careful, cool, deliberate, and systematic analysis of the problems and alternatives involved, nor are the specific provisions put into effect those that would prove most advantageous to it socially and economically. Rather, the immigration policies of most nations grow out of rough and tumble struggle between political forces in which special interests of all kinds fight for the measures that will best serve their own ends. Some employers, for example, may use all means at their disposal to promote the adoption of immigration policies that seem to promise a more abundant supply of labor at lower wages than they otherwise would be obliged to pay. Labor organizations, on the other hand, are likely to oppose strongly proposals designed to have this effect. However, many labor leaders and members of the unions may fiercely champion measures that would permit the entry of greater numbers of people from the countries in which they or their parents originated or of the religious faith which they profess. Doctors, lawyers, dentists, and members of the other professions may personally advocate liberal immigration policies, at the very same time that their professional associations are effective in securing the adoption of provisions that make it extremely difficult, or even impossible, for highly trained immigrants to practice those particular professions. In general, immigrants are welcome, provided they offer no threat of competition in the fields in which given persons or groups are occupied.

Along with these clashes of economic interests, many considerations of a cultural or religious nature are involved. If the prospective immigrants are of a different religious faith than the majority of those in the country in question, their coming in any great numbers is likely to be viewed with alarm by the older settlers. In many countries, the adoption of laws relating to the operation and control of cemeteries has proved especially effective in preventing the immigration of persons whose religious faith differs from that of the majority of those already in the country. Likewise, if the suspicion arises that the newcomers will seek to preserve their language and other cultural forms, in preference to those of the country to which they are immigrating, bitterness and opposition are almost certain to arise. As a result of all of this the immigration policies arrived at through the democratic process may be far different than those that might be designed by a commission of impartial, competent, and well-informed statesmen who had only the welfare of the nation as a whole under consideration. This is probably the reason so many countries seek as immigrants primarily those in the category of agricultural laborers (the least skilled, least informed, and least organized portion of society), although any nation should shun, as it would the plague, any immigrants who would be satisfied permanently with the status of agricultural laborers.

For these reasons a given nation may have at any particular time rather unsatisfactory answers to such problems as the following: How many immigrants shall be admitted annually? From which countries shall they come, and in what numbers and proportions? In the selection of the immigrants, which occupations and professions are to receive preference? Is there to be any restriction with respect to the localities in which the immigrants may settle and with respect to the proportions those of a given origin may constitute of the population of a given community? What restrictions, if any, shall govern the eligibility of individuals for admission from the standpoint of health, record of convictions for offenses against the law, and previous affiliations with various ideological groups? What preference, if any, shall be given those closely related to citizens of the receiving country, such as wives or husbands, children, parents, cousins, and so forth? What sponsorship, if any, shall be required for each immigrant on the part of those already citizens of the country?

Whether or not would-be emigrants shall have freedom of egress from their respective homelands is another item of population policy that seems to be calling for more attention than it has received in the past. In recent decades, perhaps the best-known abridgements of the right of egress have been imposed on the citizens of Cuba and the German Democratic Republic and on Jews in the Soviet Union, but restrictions of various kinds exist elsewhere as well. Even where stringent restrictions are not imposed, the official attitude toward intended emigrants often is that they are practically guilty of sedition because of their desire to leave for other countries. Undoubtedly, for a long while and in many places, those who have seized control of the governments in one way or another have sought to prevent their enemies, who often had been their oppressors, from fleeing to other parts of the world. For those in the Western Hemisphere, however, the case of Cuba, where hundreds of thousands already have fled their native land, considerable numbers of others have perished in the attempt to do so, and other hundreds of thousands are searching for ways and means to flee, brings this matter into focus as never before. Indeed, it seems to be a problem calling not only for attention in the United States, which has received large numbers of the Cuban refugees, but for hemispheric and even general international consideration as well. To this end, the Organization of American States and the United Nations might well enunciate some of the principles involved and establish some guidelines for various types of emigration.

1. Probably the nearest to a definitive compilation of the statistical data on emigration and immigration for this period that has been made is found in Walter F. Willcox, *International Migrations* (New York: National Bureau of Economic Research, Inc., 1920), 2 vols.

2. T. Lynn Smith, *Population Analysis* (New York: McGraw-Hill Book Company, 1948).

3. For the detailed figures for each country see *ibid.*, pp. 302 - 304.

4. Donald J. Bogue, *Principles of Demography* (New York: John Wiley and Sons, Inc., 1969), p. 801.

5. For an excellent discussion of the topic treated in this section, see Gunther O. Beijer, "Modern Patterns of International Migration," in *Migration,* edited by J. A. Jackson (London: Cambridge University Press, 1969), pp. 11 - 59.

6. See Constance Lindsay Skinner, *Pioneers of the Old Southwest* (New Haven: Yale University Press, 1921), pp. 1 - 6; and John R. Commons, *Races and Immigrants in America* (New York: The Macmillan Company, 1907), pp. 31 - 32.

7. See Henry Pratt Fairchild, *Immigration: A World Movement and Its American Significance* (rev. ed.) (New York: The Macmillan Company, 1928), p. 57.

8. See on this point, Marcus Lee Hansen, *The Atlantic Migration, 1607 - 1860* (Cambridge: Harvard University Press, 1940), p. 281.

9. Fairchild, *op. cit.*, p. 70.

10. From Act of February 26, 1885, Section 1, quoted in *ibid.*, p. 113.

11. For a discussion and evaluation of the 1965 amendment, see Ralph Thomlinson, *Demographic Problems* (Belmont, Calif.: Dickenson Publishing Company, Inc., 1967), pp. 82 - 84.

12. U.S. Bureau of the Census, *Statistical Abstract of the United States, 1972* (Washington: Government Printing Office, 1972), p. 90.

13. Thomlinson, *op. cit.*, p. 83.

14. See U.S. Bureau of the Census, *U.S. Census of Population: 1970, Subject Reports* PC(2)-1C, *Persons of Spanish Origin* (Washington: Government Printing Office, 1973), pp. 32 - 45, Table 4.

15. Julian C. Bridges, *The Population of Mexico: Its Composition and Changes,* Ph.D. dissertation, University of Florida (1973), pp. 265 - 266.

BEIJER, GUNTHER. "Modern Patterns of International Migratory Movements," in *Migration,* edited by J. A. Jackson, Chap. 2. London: Cambridge University Press, 1969.

BOGUE, DONALD J. *The Population of the United States,* Chap. 14. Glencoe, Ill.: The Free Press, 1959.

BOGUE, DONALD J. *Principles of Demography,* pp. 800 - 823. New York: John Wiley & Sons, Inc., 1969.

BORRIE, W. D., and others. "The Cultural Integration of Immigrants: A Survey Based upon the Papers and Proceedings of the UNESCO Conference Held in Havana, April, 1956." *Population and Culture Series,* No. 4. Paris: UNESCO, 1959.

COX, PETER R. *Demography,* 4th ed., Chap. 9. London: Cambridge University Press, 1970.

DAVIS, KINGSLEY. *The Population of India and Pakistan,* Chaps. 12 and 13. Princeton: Princeton University Press, 1951.

HANDLIN, OSCAR, ed. *Immigration as a Factor in American History.* Englewood Cliffs: Prentice-Hall, Inc., 1959.

HERNÁNDEZ ALVAREZ, JOSÉ. "A Demographic Profile of the Mexican Immigration to the United States, 1910 - 1950." *Journal of Inter-American Studies,* Vol. 8, No. 3 (July, 1966), pp. 471 - 476.

LEE, EVERETT. "A Theory of Migration," in *Migration,* edited by J. A. Jackson, Chap. 10. London: Cambridge University Press, 1969.

PETERSEN, WILLIAM. *Population,* 2nd ed., Chap. 5. New York: The Macmillan Company, 1969.

RUBIN, ERNEST. "The Demography of Immigration to the United States." *Annals of the American Academy of Political and Social Science,* Vol. 367 (September, 1966), pp. 15 - 22.

SHRYOCK, HENRY S., JACOB S. SIEGEL, and associates. *The Methods and Materials of Demography,* Vol. 2, Chap. 20. Washington: Government Printing Office, 1971.

SMITH, T. LYNN. *Brazil: People and Institutions,* 4th ed., Chap. VIII. Baton Rouge: Louisiana State University Press, 1972.

SMITH, T. LYNN. "Migration from One Latin American Country to Another," in *International Population Conference,* edited by Louis Henry and Wilhelm Winkler, pp. 695 - 702. Vienna: Selbstverlag, 1959.

TAEUBER, ALMA F., and KARL E. TAEUBER. "Recent Immigration and Studies of Ethnic Assimilation." *Demography*, Vol. 4, No. 2 (1967), pp. 798 - 808.

TAEUBER, CONRAD. "American Immigration and Population Growth," *International Migration Review*, Vol. VI, No. 1 (Spring, 1972), pp. 7 - 17.

TAEUBER, CONRAD, and IRENE B. TAEUBER. *The People of the United States in the 20th Century* (A 1960 Census Monograph), Chap. III. Washington: Government Printing Office, 1971.

THOMAS, BRINLEY. *Migration and Economic Growth*, 2nd ed. New York: Cambridge University Press, 1972.

THOMLINSON, RALPH. *Demographic Problems*, Chap. 8. Belmont, Calif.: Dickenson Publishing Company, 1967.

UNITED NATIONS. *Demographic Yearbook, 1970*, pp. 20 - 21. New York: United Nations, 1971.

UNITED NATIONS. *International Migration Statistics. Organization and Operation; Recommended Standards; Sampling*. New York: United Nations, 1953.

WHEELER, THOMAS C., ed. *The Immigrant Experience*. Baltimore: Pelican Books, 1971.

INTERNAL MIGRATION

The preceding chapter should have made it clear that the student of population must be prepared to deal with immigration and emigration as factors in the changing number of inhabitants in a given country. In all that has to do with the changing number and distribution of population within a given nation, however, it is even more important that he have professional proficiency in handling data on various kinds of internal migration. This is because the role of internal migration in the increase or decrease of population in a given region, state, district, county, city, town, or minor civil division frequently is much greater than that of natural increase, whereas only in a few countries, for brief periods and under exceptional circumstances, does immigration or emigration become the principal factor in population change. In addition, poor as they are, the data on international migrations usually are better than those pertaining to the rural-urban exchange of population, state-to-state movements of persons, or any of the other varieties of internal migration. Because the poorer the data the greater is the skill needed to make reasonable approximations, the student who works with population materials should leave nothing undone in order to become as conversant as possible with the theory and method that have been developed in the study of internal migrations. Finally, it should be recognized that the flow of population from areas in which the natural increase of population is rapid to those in which it is slow, such as the immense movement in the years since 1920 of persons from south of the Mason-Dixon line to sections north of it, may be the principal factor in keeping a radical redistribution of population among the regions from taking place. In brief, in all that has to do with the number, distribution, redistribution, and growth of population within a country the demographer who is thoroughly conversant with the subject of internal migration will be substantially more competent than the one who is not.

TYPES OF INTERNAL MIGRATION

The varieties of internal migration are numerous, but a great deal of work remains to be done before they all may be classified into a number of clearly defined, mutually exclusive categories or types. The mere mention of some of the principal kinds of internal movements of population makes this abundantly evident.

During the nineteenth century the mass movement of people from the country to the city got underway on a large scale throughout much of Europe and North America. In the course of the twentieth century this exodus from rural areas to urban districts has become rampant in all parts of the world. Indeed, even in the so-called underdeveloped sections of the earth, such as the independent Latin American countries, many of them with huge, unoccupied areas still awaiting the fructifying effects of man's efforts, a rush of people to the cities took on great proportions before the outbreak of the Second World War, and since the close of that epic struggle it continues at an accelerated pace.

Indeed, since 1950 the migration of people from the country to the city well may be considered as the most important current demographic fact in that immense section of the earth's surface.[1] As a matter of fact, throughout the entire world the phenomenal growth of cities which has taken place in the course of the last century was possible only because of the flow of population from the rural to the urban districts. The continuous migration of population from farm to city is one of the primary characteristics of Western civilization, and this feature presently is one of those being copied most widely by societies in other parts of the world. Certainly it is the most extensive and significant of all the varieties of internal migration.

In many parts of the earth the pushing forward of the frontier still looms large in national affairs. The gradual process that in the United States edged settlement forward from the Atlantic to the Pacific in the course of two centuries, mostly in the nineteenth, has its parallels elsewhere. The westward and northwestward trend of settlement in Canada, the push to the north in Australia, the "march to the west" in Brazil, the advancement of settlement down the slopes of the eastern Cordillera and out into the heavily forested Montaña in Peru, a comparable edging down to and out on the plains at the base of the Andes in Colombia, the surge of population from the high sierras down into the coastal plain in Ecuador, and the crowding of Argentine settlers northward into the Chaco are only a few of the important cases of contemporary expansions of the frontier. If the facts were known, undoubtedly remarkable extensions of settlement would be discovered within the boundaries of the Soviet Union.

Nor is the mass movement of people from a region, whether propelled by un-bearable circumstances in their old locations or attracted by brighter prospects in a new home, to be relegated merely to the realm of history. The depopulation of the Great Plains area of the United States, so greatly dramatized by the "dust bowl" epic of the 1930's, did not end with the coming of the rains but continued through 1950 and thereafter. The abandonment of southern plantations by hundreds of thousands of Negroes who were lured to the West Coast by jobs in war plants during the early years of the Second World War has been followed by sustained heavy migrations of Negroes from the South in the decades that have followed. Such phenomena are paralleled in Brazil by the periodic flights from the terrific droughts that every ten or fifteen years make life practically impossible in a vast area in the northeastern portion of the country and by the long trek south to the cities of Rio de Janeiro and São Paulo by hundreds of thousands of northeasterners ever since the first road passable by trucks was put through from these cities to Fortaleza, on the northern coast, in 1951. Undoubtedly, these interregional movements of population in the two largest nations of the Western Hemisphere could be matched with many others in various parts of the earth, and especially by interregional migrations of population in China, India, and the Soviet Union. Finally, in the United States at least, in recent decades and as the social status and financial circumstances of the aged have changed, there has developed a tremendous movement from one region to another of those in or near the retirement ages.

Nomadism is still to be reckoned with, even in countries such as the United States. At a time when civilization already is well within the space age, there are still in this country hundreds of thousands of persons who lead a wandering existence "following the crops." These people are constantly on the move from one place to another in order to participate as laborers in the harvest of fruits, vegetables, and other crops. Furthermore, the high degree of specialization achieved in some industries, such as the building of bridges and other construction activities, serves to make seminomads out of large numbers of highly skilled workers. For example, the men who handle the steelwork on a new bridge over the Mississippi River at New Orleans may find after a stay in the Crescent City of from two to three years that their company's next contract is in New England or on the Pacific Coast. Likewise, specialization and division of labor have reached the point that the technicians who instruct workers in Dallas in the use of a new machine during the first half of a year may be engaged in similar activities in Ohio in the fall.

Finally, in the agricultural districts of most countries there is always much shifting of people from one farm to another. In the United States, this is particularly important in the areas in which the farms are large and in which agricultural laborers are numerous, but it also is prevalent where any considerable proportions of the farm operators are tenants or renters.

In the United States and in the Latin American countries, the fragmentary nature of the data determines to a large extent the categories into which internal migrations may be classified. Furthermore, there is little in the literature that would lead one to suspect that the situation is substantially different in any other part of the world. Such sources as we do have make it possible for the student to advance our understanding of the subject somewhat by dividing these migrations into the rural-to-urban, urban-to-rural, state-to-state or region-to-region, and farm-to-farm varieties. Not all of these categories are mutually exclusive, but in this case pragmatic considerations must weigh heavily. It may be that a student with considerable ingenuity, abundant time, and much perseverance could with the existing data learn enough about migration from city to city to enable us to add this category to those listed above.

DATA AND INDEXES

As is mentioned repeatedly in this volume, every competent student of population always has uppermost in his mind the fact that there are only three primary factors influencing the changing number and distribution of the population, migration being one of them and births and deaths the other two. But whereas for many nations and even for the various subdivisions of some of them, it is possible to determine rather well the fertility and mortality of the population, the data on migration for most of the countries are probably the most deficient in amount and quality of those relating to any major aspect of population study. This is especially true of internal migration, which does not appear even as an incidental topic in any of the issues of the *Demographic Yearbook*. Several studies for individual countries and regions, of course, have been carried out, but even they together do not permit many international comparisons to be made. Therefore, the present writers have attempted only a few such comparisons in the discussion of this matter and have addressed it only in a general way, finding it necessary instead to direct their attention largely to the situation in the United States. When it does become possible for the subject to be dealt with for a large number of the world's countries, the following topics should be analyzed: (1) the amount of migration to and from each of the states (departments, provinces, and so forth), counties or comparable subdivisions, and cities of which a given nation is composed; (2) the nature of the selective processes at work in the rural-urban exchanges of population and in other types of internal migration; (3) the absolute and relative importance of the movement of operators and laborers from farm to farm within the various areas in a nation, and the extent to which this is associated with vertical social mobility and other social, demographic, and economic phenomena which may be regarded either as causes or effects of the shifting of families from one farm to another; and (4) the migration of agricultural laborers, the number of persons involved and how it fluctuates, the principal routes followed and the seasonal ebb and flow of movement over each, and the social and economic effects of their migratory mode of existence, with respect both to the migrants themselves (especially the children involved) and the neighborhoods and communities through which they pass.

Even in the United States, where volumes of data are gathered that treat various aspects of internal migration, a substantial part of what is known about the matter is inference based on materials derived from successive counts of the inhabitants and a knowledge of fertility and mortality levels. Furthermore, it was not until 1940 that the United States Census included a question on migration in the population schedule, and the results obtained were hardly such as would enable one to answer most of the elementary questions about the subject. Other somewhat different attempts in later censuses yielded results that are a little better but which still fail to meet many needs. Specifically, in 1940, persons in a sample of the population were queried about where they were residing on April 1, 1935; in 1950, those in another sample were questioned concerning their residences on April 1, 1949; and in 1960, those who made up a 25 per cent sample were asked about their residences on April 1, 1955. In 1970, persons in a 15 per cent sample of the population were asked where they were born, which yielded data on the state and country of birth. They also were asked where they were living on April 1, 1965, which produced information on the numbers of persons who resided in the same or a different house five years prior to the census date, and in the same or a different county, state, or nation. These data resulted in summary tables published in *General Social and Economic Characteristics* for the states and the nation and in several *Subject Reports,* which are as follows: *State of Birth, Mobility for States and the Nation, Mobility for Metropolitan Areas, Lifetime and Recent Migration,* and *Migration Between State Economic Areas.* In addition, for each state and county the Census Bureau has published estimates of net migration between 1960 and 1970.[2] These data were produced, however, by subtracting natural increase from total population change over the decade, called the "residual method," which means that they are subject to a variety of possible errors, including those that occur in the registration of births and deaths. The same is true of the estimates made of net migration to the central cities and the outlying portions of standard metropolitan statistical areas that occurred during the 1960 - 1970 decade, arrived at by the same method.[3]

Clearly, much could be learned about internal migration in the United States if the materials from the last four censuses were adequately analyzed. However, because of their nature and the span covered, these materials cannot be employed, in combination with those on births and deaths and successive census counts of the inhabitants, for the purpose of drawing up a population balance sheet for a given state or county covering any or all of the complete decades from 1940 to 1970. Nor is one even safe in assuming accuracy in the figures purporting to show the net flow of population between farms and urban and other nonfarm areas in the nation as a whole during the various periods represented in the four censuses. This is because residence in the earlier year of the time range employed in each case is merely the person's report on where he was living five years earlier for the 1940, 1960, and 1970 materials, and one year earlier for the 1950 census data, whereas residence at the census date was determined by the enumerator's own application of specified criteria. An analysis of the results of the various queries makes it appear beyond doubt that (especially in 1940) many persons who actually had moved from farms and other portions of the fringes surrounding various urban centers to homes within the corporate limits of others were counted merely as moving from one urban center to another. The information gathered in these four attempts, which does seem to be fairly reliable, shows the amount of movement from one state to another during the stated periods and the absolute and relative importance of migrants (that is, of persons who had moved from one county or quasi-county to another) in the populations of the various states and some other subdivisions. Indeed, the data secured in the 1970 census were tabulated to show the numbers of persons who had moved from one house to another in the twelve months prior to April 1, 1970, and these materials were published not merely for the various regions, divisions, and states but also for each of 510 "state economic areas" into which the nation has been divided for certain statistical purposes, for each standard metropolitan statistical area, and for each urban place that had a population of 50,000 or more.

Also of importance in any effort to understand internal migration in the United States is the first of a series of reports that deal with rural-to-urban migration produced jointly by the University of Georgia and the Office of Economic Opportunity.[4] This volume presents data on several aspects of the total migration and that of the poor specifically from farm to cities, including their places of origin and destination, levels of education, health status, marital status, fertility, occupation and industry, and so on. Yet the data are estimates based on materials collected in the Survey of Economic Opportunity taken in 1967, which means that the matters reported do not coincide with any census year or complete intercensal period. Even though the migration data collected in this survey were intended to be cumulative in effect rather than to relate to any limited span of time and are useful in that respect, the fact that they are not entirely comparable with any of the materials on migration that appear in various publications of the U.S. Bureau of the Census is a substantial disadvantage. Nevertheless, this report is a significant step in the direction of better comprehension of the rural-to-urban flow of people in the United States. One of its major contributions is that it contains information on each move actually made by each person interviewed and not merely data on where he was living at two different times.

The materials just described amount to a formidable amount of information which is just beginning to receive some of the study that it deserves. Perhaps the failure of demographers to make better use of this voluminous and expensive information is because it is difficult or impossible to make it serve a useful purpose in connection with the demographic problems with which almost perforce they must occupy their time. It would appear that the best way of improving the migration data would be to make the question on the census schedule pertain to residence at the time of the preceding census for those who had passed their tenth birthdays and to place of birth of those under ten years of age and to ask the question of each person enumerated, similar to the procedure with respect to age, sex, occupation, and so forth. This would enable tables to be prepared for each state, county, and quasi-county showing the number of persons who had migrated to it in the interim between the two censuses. With such data at hand, along with the census counts and the materials from the registries of births and deaths, population students in all sections of the country would be able to check fully the reliability of the information and, if the data were all correct, to determine the absolute and relative influence of each of the factors in population change. They also would be in position to estimate, with much greater accuracy than is now possible, the populations of states, cities, and counties (a service for which there is a tremendous demand in every state) in postcensus years. Of course, in many cases it probably would be found that formulas such as the following would fail to check out:

Population in 1960 plus Natural Increase,
April 1, 1960, to March 31, 1970, plus or
minus Net Migration, 1960 - 1970 = population in 1970.

If so, it would be obvious that something was wrong: one or more of the two census counts, the count of the number of births, the count of the number of deaths, the amount of net migration, or two or more of these items. Nevertheless, this type of accounting has become imperative in the present stage of population studies, and only the migration data are needed to make it feasible. If such procedures reveal shortcomings in the materials presently available, they will also point the way to the necessary corrections or improvements in registration systems or enumeration techniques. As to cost, it is entirely possible that such materials could be supplied in substantially less space than was devoted to the publication of migration data in the reports of the last four censuses.

In addition to the migration data, as such, certain other information secured in the decennial census in the United States, and likewise in the censuses of many other countries, is of great utility in the study of internal migration. Most important of these are the materials showing state-of-birth of the inhabitants in cross-tabulation with state-of-residence. For the United States such information has been secured and published in connection with every census from 1850 to 1970, inclusive.

One of our most useful bodies of data relative to internal migration in the United States is the series of annual estimates of the movement of population away from and to the farms of the nation. These data are assembled and published by the U.S. Department of Agriculture; the former Bureau of Agricultural Economics had the responsibility for the materials assembled for the years 1920 to 1949 and the Agricultural Marketing Service and the Economic Research Service for the estimates for subsequent years. These data are secured along with and in the same manner as the facts upon which the crop estimates are prepared. This is to say that they come from thousands of farmers throughout the country who voluntarily fill in questionnaires for their own farms and those of their neighbors. The materials from these sources are carefully assembled, analyzed, and weighted to eliminate as many sources of error as possible. Even so users are warned not to attach any great significance to variations from one year to the next because of the effects of sampling errors upon the calculations for any given year.

Much can also be learned about the geographical distribution and intensity of the movement from one farm to another through an analysis of the materials assembled each five years by the U. S. Census of Agriculture relative to the length of time farm operators have occupied the farms upon which they are located. The reports of most recent censuses of agriculture contain elaborate materials on this subject, but, unfortunately, students of population have made relatively little use of them.

As yet few indexes have been developed that are of any particular value in the study of internal migration. No doubt this is largely due to the defective nature of the data and the fact that the attention of investigators has had to be devoted to ways of approximating or estimating the extent to which migration has been a factor in various demographic changes. Worthy of emphasis in this connection, however, is the method of estimating migration by comparing the number of persons in a certain age group at a given census, decreased by the expected mortality over an intercensal period for the specific age groups involved, with the same contingent at the next census. In the United States, for example, the number of persons aged forty to forty-four in 1960, decreased by the expected mortality of persons in these and progressively older ages over a ten-year span, may be compared with the number of persons aged fifty to fifty-four in 1970, with the difference being attributed to migration. This technique has been used by a number of students to add substantially to our knowledge of the currents of internal migration in the United States, their volume, and the directions in which they flow. Some of these demographers have used the life tables as the basis for computing the expected mortality, whereas others have maintained that the proportion by which a given contingent of the national population decreases during the course of the ten-year period in which it moves up the age ladder (as, for example, it ceases to be the group aged forty to forty-four in 1960 and becomes that aged fifty to fifty-four in 1970) is a better indicator of the importance of the mortality factor in the various parts of the nation. The former sets of computations are sometimes designated as *life table survival ratios,* and the latter as *census survival ratios.* At present it seems rather well agreed that the second of these procedures is the more practicable and reliable, and it is likely to be relied upon rather heavily until such time as the necessary improvements are made in the collection of migration data.[5]

Also deserving of consideration is the device of comparing the age configuration of segments of a population with that of the whole, and inferring that migration is the factor responsible for persistent concentrations or deficiencies such as the exceedingly high proportions of people in the productive ages in the urban population or the low percentage of persons in the productive ages in the rural-farm population. This, of course, entered into the discussions in Chapter 6.[6]

The simple expedient of taking the population of a county (or other administrative unit) at a given census, adjusting the number by the natural increase (births minus deaths) for the ensuing decade, comparing the result with the population enumerated at the next census, and attributing the difference to migration eventually may become highly useful in the study of internal migration. This will only be the case, though, if birth registration is improved to the point that the number of births reported for a given county in the course of a decade is a fair approximation of the number actually born to mothers whose residences are located in that county. This definitely was not the case in the 1930's when this index was used in all seriousness as the principal basis for one of the most ambitious studies of internal migration ever made in the United States.[7]

RURAL-URBAN MIGRATION IN OTHER COUNTRIES

The present migration of population from rural areas to urban districts throughout the world is on a scale unparalleled at any other period of human history. However, in Western civilization the constant flow of people from the country to the city has been going on for hundreds of years, and it is likely that the large-scale movement of persons from farms to cities also has been underway in other parts of the earth for centuries. As early as 1662, as indicated in Chapter 2, John Graunt, "Citizen of London," concluded that there was constant and heavy migration of people from the surrounding districts to that metropolis. As a result of his study of death certificates, and in a manner that would warm the hearts of modern investors in real estate, he observed "that, let the *Mortality* be what it will, the City repairs its loss of Inhabitants within two years, which Observation lessens the Objection made against the value of houses in *London,* as if they were liable to great prejudice through the loss of Inhabitants by the *Plague.* "[8] This ingenious pioneer gave details to show that in London there were many more burials than christenings, and then employed the same sort of reasoning that contemporary demographers are forced to rely upon in their studies of internal migration. Thus, from the facts on fertility, mortality, and observed changes in the number of inhabitants, the founder of population study and statistics generalized that: "from this single Observation it will follow, That *London* hath decreased in its People, the contrary whereof we see by its daily increase of Buildings upon new Foundations, and by the turning of great Palacious Houses into small Tenements. It is therefore certain, that *London* is supplied with People from out of the *Countrey*, whereby not onely to repair the overplus difference of *Burials* above-mentioned, but likewise to increase its *Inhabitants* according to the said increase of housing."[9]

The data on fertility and mortality for the United States and other parts of the Western world also seem to demonstrate that, until very recently, cities would have dwindled away, as would have London in the sixteenth century, had the numbers of their inhabitants not been replenished constantly by migration from the rural districts. All through the nineteenth century and well into the twentieth it seems that the cities of Europe and the United States were sorts of colonies which had to be partially repopulated every year by the rural portions of these societies; and it is entirely possible that this situation still prevails in many parts of the world.

There are, of course, no comprehensive materials on the amount of movement from rural districts to urban centers in most parts of the world. Nor are we likely to have such information in the near future. By comparing the rates of natural increase in rural and urban areas and the growth of population in country and city, one establishes a firm basis for the conclusion that there is a heavy movement of people from the farms and villages to the urban districts. This proposition also gains substantial support from an analysis of materials assembled by the censuses of many countries showing state or province of birth in cross-tabulation with place of residence, especially where such information is classified separately for some of the principal cities, or in countries such as the United States, Brazil, Mexico, and Venezuela, in which the limits of the nation's capital city are roughly comparable to those of the federal district in which it is located. For example, the senior author has made such an analysis of the information for the Latin American countries; Kingsley Davis has reached similar conclusions by studying the materials for India and Pakistan;[10] Minoru Tachi has demonstrated in similar ways the importance of the migration from the rural districts to the four largest metropolitan areas in Japan,[11] J. Clyde Mitchell has evaluated urban growth in Southern Rhodesia by this means,[12] and so on.[13]

The factors responsible for the mass movement on a world-wide scale of population from the agricultural districts into towns and cities also deserve comment, even though the task of identifying these and determining their relative importance is still largely to be done. In the United States, it is generally assumed, and probably correctly, that economic attractions in the cities have been responsible for most of the rural-urban migration taking place in this country. In sharp contrast, Kingsley Davis[14] describes the economic situation in Indian villages that would lead "anyone acquainted with the mass flight of farmers from the blighted areas in the United States" to expect a general exodus of population from the villages. This does not occur, however, because the glitter of city life, the faster pace, the greater opportunities, and the broader social horizons seem to mean little to the villager. The peasant goes to the city merely to work, is not accompanied by his wife and family, and desires to remain only as long as it is necessary. "To the peasant the city is simply a bit of hell which fortunately is not eternal."[15] This analysis not only emphasizes the strictly economic nature of the factors responsible for the movement of people, mostly males, from villages to urban centers in India, but also serves to emphasize the importance of social and cultural factors in drawing persons from the country to the city in the United States.

Mass migrations of people from rural districts throughout the world, but especially in the so-called "underdeveloped" countries, are intertwined with a vast network of factors, forces, and media. The broad social and cultural changes that have generated the massive movements and that have been instrumental in the development of the urban centers that receive the migrants are: (1) the development and extension of modern means of communication and transportation, both those that link one country with another and those that unite the various parts of a given country; (2) the first steps in the development of what may eventually become a system of universal education in large numbers of the countries; (3) greatly increased contacts between the less-developed societies and those in various parts of the Western world, especially those in which relatively strong middle-class standards and values and a high degree of industrialization have combined to produce exceptionally high levels and standards of living; (4) great social ferment among the masses, especially among the descendants of those who for centuries were so docile and tractable in the hands of the aristocratic elements that dominated their societies but who now are increasingly motivated by rising expectations to bring about change; (5) the enactment in some countries of large bodies of social legislation relating to hours of work, minimum wages, security of tenure, paid vacations, severance pay, and so forth, all of which have been much more effective in urban districts than in rural, thus helping to broaden the differentials in working conditions in the two; (6) the growing conviction of political and other leaders that industrialization offers the most promising solutions for a host of the acute and chronic problems with which their countries must deal; (7) the onslaught in some countries, such as Viet-Nam, of extended periods of serious internal strife which has caused hundreds of thousands of rural people to seek safety in towns and cities; and (8) some fundamental changes in the nature and functions of cities, leading to the expansion of employment opportunities. In turn the following seem to be important in a long list of immediate influences or media which cause specific persons to transfer their residences from rural areas to urban districts: (1) word-of-mouth reports and letters describing the advantages of life in the city by some earlier migrants which are taken or sent back to their friends and relatives in the rural communities; (2) the location of almost all secondary schools and institutions of higher learning in towns and cities, which induces many a large landowner to move his family to one of them so that the children may continue their education; (3) the recruitment by many upper-class families of rural people for jobs as urban house servants and grounds keepers; (4) hiring in the rural districts of workers for construction and other projects in which foreign and national companies are engaged; (5) the temptation among young women in the rural districts to accept at face value the attractions of urban living described by young men who pass through or return to the countryside; and (6) descriptions of the virtues of urban living presented to rural people by a wide variety of persons, including transportation workers who pass through the rural districts, schoolteachers who have been reared and trained in cities but whose jobs take them into the countryside, friends and relatives of rural folk who return from the city periodically to visit with their comrades and kinsmen, and many others who form a human link between the city and the outlying rural areas. It is obvious from this enumeration of the media helping to precipitate rural-to-urban migration that a great deal of the motivation to move is supplied through various kinds of personal interaction between the city dwellers or visitors, who know the city well, and the rural people, to whom it is merely an illusion. There is, perhaps, no better illustration of the importance of word of mouth and personal influence in bringing about the wide and rapid transplantation of an idea or practice.[16]

RURAL-URBAN MIGRATION IN THE UNITED STATES: THE MASS TRANSFER OF POVERTY[17]

From 1933 on the migration of persons from the farms has been a mass transfer of the rural poor and of their sociocultural syndrome of poverty to the cities and towns of the United States. As of April 1, 1930, about 45 per cent of the nation's 125 million inhabitants were classified as rural and 37 per cent resided outside of places having as many as 1,000 inhabitants. There were only thirty-seven cities with 250,000 or more inhabitants and almost no suburbs. Moreover, so serious was the economic depression and so desperate the plight of millions that, in 1931 and 1932, three-quarters of a million more people returned to farms than left them, thus adding to a large reserve of potential rural-to-urban migrants. After 1932, however, many millions of rural people did migrate to the cities and the magnitude and characteristics of the flow are of major concern to one who would understand internal migration in the United States.

The Societal Threshold of the Exodus

The great movement of the rural poor into the cities and towns of the nation after 1932 was prompted by a variety of circumstances and societal features. Three of the, however, stand out as fundamental and necessary conditions that helped to get the movement underway on an unprecedented scale and to sustain it for about forty years.

First, by 1932 the awareness that the nation's frontier days had passed had become general although relatively little good land was available for homesteading after 1900. As a result, by 1930 most people were aware that they could not solve their various economic problems by migrating to essentially unsettled areas and establishing farms. Many looked instead to other alternatives to remaining in poverty in the older agricultural areas, and migration to the cities and towns became the most important of these alternatives.

Second, several traditional sources of people to build and maintain the cities were shut off prior to 1930, which created the opportunity for the rural poor to fill the vacuum thus produced. The two principal traditional sources of new urban migrants were (1) European immigration, which was almost entirely shut off by transportation problems and dangers during the First World War and by extremely restrictive legislation in the 1920's; and (2) the flow of young people from the middle-class family-sized farms of the northeastern and midwestern sections of the country. Representatives of this group of middle-class farmers had gone in such large numbers to the industrializing cities of their own regions in the 1920's that by 1930 not only were the rural areas depleted of their youth, the products of a large natural increase, but of older farmers and their wives and young children as well. As these two sources of new urban inhabitants atrophied and the demands for industrial workers increased, prompted by the exigencies of the First World War, large numbers of Negroes were recruited in southern cities and rural districts to help fill the jobs in northern factories. This great migration continued after the war and by 1930 it was affecting significantly the racial composition of most of the large northern cities. In addition, considerable numbers of unskilled Mexican-Americans were recruited in the Southwest to perform menial agricultural tasks in parts of the Midwest where crops such as sugar beets and potatoes were grown. This practice eventually funneled many of these people into Minneapolis, St. Paul, Chicago, Detroit, and other large cities and opened the way for a continuing flow of substantial numbers of them, a considerable proportion of whom ended up on the welfare rolls of those cities. During and after the Second World War the rural Mexican-Americans flocked into Los Angeles, Phoenix, Albuquerque, and Denver, and to all of the smaller cities of the Southwest.

Third, and most important, was the reversal of the flow of energy between farm and city. More specifically, the internal combustion engine in its various applications became the principal cause and also the major means of reversing the flow of energy between the farms and the cities, although the railroads also played an important part in the process. In turn, the reversal produced the great exodus of sharecroppers, wage hands, and subsistence farmers that took place after 1930. In 1910, the farms themselves produced the horses and the mules that powered the farm implements, the vehicles that transported people and products in the farming areas and from the farms to the shipping points, and those that carried freight and people about in the towns and cities themselves. Moreover, the feed that sustained the animals in these places was produced on the farms. All of this meant that in 1910, the farms were nearly the exclusive source of energy for the farms and for locomotion and transportation within the cities. By 1920, however, automobiles and trucks powered by industrially produced sources of energy (gasoline, oil, and electricity) had become the major components of the intraurban system of transportation and motorized tractors were being widely employed in farm work throughout the Midwest and some other sections of the country.

By 1930, horses and mules were of little significance in the transportation systems of the towns and cities and had even become relatively unimportant on the farms. Electric streetcars had become common, but it was the internal combustion engine that propelled most of the vehicles used in intraurban transportation and locomotion. It also drove the industrially produced machines and vehicles that were used to carry on the work on the farms and to transport people, supplies, and products between the farms and the trade and service centers. It propelled the heavy equipment used to construct and maintain the network of highways and farm-to-market roads, thereby displacing thousands of animal-powered scrapers owned by farmers and used previously in these projects. Furthermore, farm-produced hay and grain as the sources of energy were supplanted by urban-produced gasoline, oil, and electricity as the sources of energy. The speed with which all of this occurred is indicated by the following facts: in 1910, the number of horses classified by the census of that year as "not on farms" was 3,182,789, but by 1920 the number had dwindled to 1,705,611, and by the time of the 1930 census so few horses were being used in cities and towns that no data about them appeared in the reports of that enumeration. On the other hand, in 1920, tractors were in use on only 229,332 of the nation's farms, but in 1930 the number had risen to 851,457. All of this is to say that by 1930 farm-produced energy was virtually gone from the cities and had declined greatly on the farms as well, so that by the time this process was essentially complete, the one-way flow of energy from farm to city had been replaced by a one-way flow of energy from urban industries to the farm. This created a situation in which the efficient application of the new sources of energy on the farms made it possible for a much smaller farm population to produce the necessary food and fiber for a much larger national population and great amounts for export as well. In turn, this mechanization and increased productivity in agriculture helped to convert many farm people into a surplus commodity in the rural areas and to make them highly available to migrate to the cities. Those who were at the bottom of the socioeconomic scale were the most expendable and they moved in droves into the nation's urban centers immediately after 1930. Finally, the reversal of the flow of energy destroyed the self-sufficient nature of farming, greatly fostered specialization in crop and live-stock enterprises, and forced many rural people who had known only their immediate communities into a much wider range of contacts. This process, too, helped to induce migration to the cities and towns, which were becoming more and more attractive to large numbers of the farm people.

Public Relief and Welfare Become the "Employer of Last Resort"

The tremendous role played by the reversal of the flow of energy and the other factors just mentioned, which helped to force people out of agriculture, was complemented by features of the cities that attracted them. One of these major attractive elements of the complex migratory process came into play just as the reversal of the flow of energy was being completed in many of the agricultural areas of the United States. It is the fact that after 1932, and especially under Franklin Roosevelt's "New Deal," public relief and welfare became the "employer of last resort." Prior to this, general or subsistence farming on a small scale and various types of farm labor together constituted the "marginal industry" in the national economy, providing a means of survival for those who were crowded out of other industries, including the more rewarding kinds of agriculture. After 1932, the public welfare and relief rolls rapidly took over the part long played by these rural types of endeavor. Moreover, the various welfare and related efforts were conducted almost exclusively in the towns and cities, where they became a powerful magnet to attract millions of small farmers, tenants, and sharecroppers and other laborers, especially from the South, to the towns and cities of the United States. There seem to be three basic parts of this feature in rural depopulation and the flight to the cities.

First, the federal government reluctantly moved into the field of public relief and welfare, initially under the provisions of the Relief and Construction Act of 1932. This legislation provided for the distribution of funds to state and local agencies for public works and various programs to relieve economic distress. It first began to make the welfare and relief programs of the states into the marginal industry; and after the inauguration of Franklin Roosevelt, it was supplemented by other legislation that became the basis for the highly institutionalized activities of the federal government as the employer of last resort that have prevailed since 1933. And, of course, ready access to these various benefits and programs was to be had only in the county seats, that is, the towns and cities.

Second, these relief and welfare efforts had an almost immediate impact upon the semi-servile white and Negro sharecroppers of the densely populated agricultural parts of the South, the region where more than half of the rural-farm population lived. The various funds allocated to the states of the region were first put to use in their major cities and soon afterward they also were disbursed to the county seats in the more rural areas. After the cotton was picked in the fall of 1932, public assistance programs drew great numbers of farm tenants, sharecroppers, and wage laborers into these population centers. Many planters themselves had the families of workers on their places put on the relief rolls during the slack winter months. In the spring, when the laborers were again needed to prepare the land for cotton, efforts were made to purge them from the welfare rolls of the towns and to force them back to the plantations, but these pressures were never fully successful. As a result, the 1935 Census of Agriculture showed a decrease of over 60,000 sharecroppers in the South between 1930 and 1935, even though the number of farms had increased substantially during the period. The migration of this group to the towns and cities picked up so greatly in volume that when the agricultural censuses of 1964 and 1969 were taken, data about them were no longer tabulated separately. They are now virtually nonexistent in American agriculture.

Third, the initiation, in 1932, of public assistance as the employer of last resort did not have the immediate effect upon the traditional role of small general farming and subsistence agriculture that it had upon the sharecroppers and other farm laborers. In fact, as the economic depression deepened, most youths on the small subsistence farms could find no urban jobs and they practically all remained in the rural areas; many others who had previously left the farms for the cities returned to their farm homes. All of this swelled the rural population and produced temporarily a sharp increase in the number of small subsistence farms. For example, in the United States between 1930 and 1935, there was a net increase of 336,162 farms of less than twenty acres and an increase of 523,702 farms of all sizes. This is the only period between 1920 and 1970 in which there was such growth. Thus, those depression years were the "final fling" of the nation's traditional employer of last resort. Subsequently, the public relief and welfare rolls, which apparently can operate effectively only in the towns and cities, were in ascendancy, drawing wage hands, tenants, sharecroppers, subsistence operators, and others away from the farms. As a result, by 1970 the mass transfer of poverty from the farms to the towns and cities of the United States was about complete, primarily because so few farm laborers and small general farmers were left in the rural areas. This is supported by the fact that between 1970 and 1972, the average annual net migration from the farms was a mere 87,000 persons, which was fewer than at any time in our history except for 1930 - 1932 and 1945.

The Extent of the Rural-to-Urban Migration

The volume of the great exodus just described is not easy to ascertain, despite the existence of many official statistics on various aspects of the matter. Nevertheless, it is important to determine the total migration and the net movement of persons from the farms over the entire span 1933 to 1970. Estimates prepared annually by the Agricultural Marketing Service and later by the Economic Research Service of the United States Department of Agriculture are available for the period from 1910 through 1969. Those from 1920 to 1969, inclusive, appear in Table 58. It should be noted that the data for each year after 1953 apply to the period from April 1 of the stated year to April 1 of the following year, so that the data for 1969, for example, apply to the year that ends with April 1, 1970, the date of the latest census. Furthermore, the data for the years 1940 through 1953 do not include movement between farms and the armed services. These materials indicate that from 1933 to April 1, 1970, about 54 million persons left farms in the United States. Offsetting this to some degree is a total of more than 25 million persons who moved to farms during the same period. On this basis, therefore, the recorded net loss involved about 29 million individuals. But even these figures on the losses by migration are probably somewhat too small and it is more likely that the total migration from farms involved more than 55 million persons and that the net loss was at least 30 million. During the period under consideration, the natural increase of the farm population was about 10.4 million, but as a result of the losses by migration of the natural increase and much of the "seed stock" as well, the number of people living on farms declined from 32,393,000 in 1933 to 9,712,000 on April 1, 1970.[18] This was a fall of 70.0 per cent and it reduced the farm population from about 25.8 per cent of the total in 1933 to a mere 4.8 per cent in 1970.[19]

Two other sets of materials serve as indicators of the volume of the exodus from farming that took place after 1932. The first is the change in the number of farms, which is the same as the change in the number of farm operators. The amount of land in farms actually rose slightly from 1,027 million acres in 1930 to 1,060 million in 1970, but the number of farms dropped from 6,602,000 in the former year to 2,726,000 in the latter.[20] Therefore, the number of farms decreased by almost 59 per cent during the period under discussion.

The second indicator of the great exodus is the decrease in the number of workers employed on farms. This number was at its all-time high (13,632,000) in 1916, dropped slowly and somewhat erratically to 12,816,000 in 1932, almost held its own until 1935 (12,733,000), and then began the long, uninterrupted downward trend that reduced the total to a monthly average of only 4,373,000 in 1972. For the period 1932 to 1972, this amounts to a reduction of 65.9 per cent.[21] In 1930, there was an average of about 2.0 workers per farm and this ratio remained practically unchanged until 1964, when it was 1.9. In

TABLE 58

Annual estimates of the number of persons moving to and from farms in the
United States, 1920 to April 1, 1970

Year	Number moving (thousands)		Net movement from farms (thousands)
	From farms	To farms	
1920	896	560	336
1921	1,323	759	564
1922	2,252	1,115	1,137
1923	2,162	1,355	807
1924	2,068	1,581	487
1925	2,038	1,336	702
1926	2,334	1,427	907
1927	2,162	1,705	457
1928	2,120	1,698	422
1929	2,081	1,604	477
1930	2,046	1,985	61
1931	1,762	1,918	†156
1932	1,219	1,826	†607
1933	1,433	970	463
1934	1,310	783	527
1935	1,624	825	799
1936	1,553	719	834
1937	1,533	872	661
1938	1,368	823	545
1939	1,522	819	703
1940	1,254	696	558
1941	2,035	822	1,213
1942	2,940	824	2,116
1943	2,053	995	1,058
1944	1,180	816	364
1945	1,530	1,691	†161
1946	1,458	1,062	396
1947	2,633	900	1,733
1948	1,463	1,112	351
1949	2,262	931	1,331
1950	1,660	564	1,096
1951	693	598	95
1952	2,309	425	1,884
1953	1,686	561	1,125
1954	635	544	91
1955	753	497	256
1956	2,695	459	2,236
1957	1,051	475	576
1958	988	440	548
1959	1,498	356	1,142
1960	1,309	309	1,000
1961	933	287	646
1962	1,391	305	1,086
1963	842	309	533
1964	998	295	703

TABLE 58 (Cont'd)

Annual estimates of the number of persons moving to and from farms in the
United States, 1920 to April 1, 1970

Year	Number moving (thousands)		Net movement from farms (thousands)
	From farms	To farms	
1965	1,127	269	858
1966	1,092	299	793
1967	732	251	481
1968	481	283	198
1969	746	104	642

Source: Compiled from data in Agricultural Marketing Service, *Farm Population, Migration to and from Farms, 1920-54,* AMS 10 (1954); Agricultural Marketing Service, *Farm Population Estimates for 1950-59,* AMS 80 (1959); Economic Research Service, *Farm Population Estimates for 1910-62,* ERS 130 (1963); Economic Research Service, *Farm Population Estimates,* annual issues, 1963-1970.

The data for the years 1940 to 1953, inclusive, exclude movements to and from the armed forces. The materials for 1954 on pertain to the periods between April 1 of the year stated and April 1 of the following year.

†Net movement to farms.

506

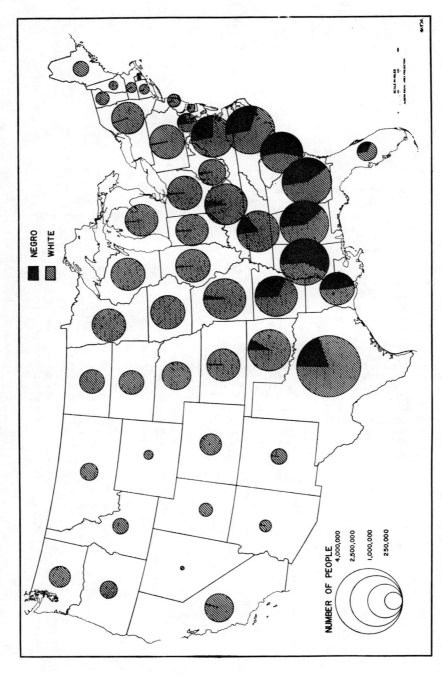

Figure 60. Estimated numbers of migrants from the farms of each state to cities and towns between 1930 and 1970, by race.

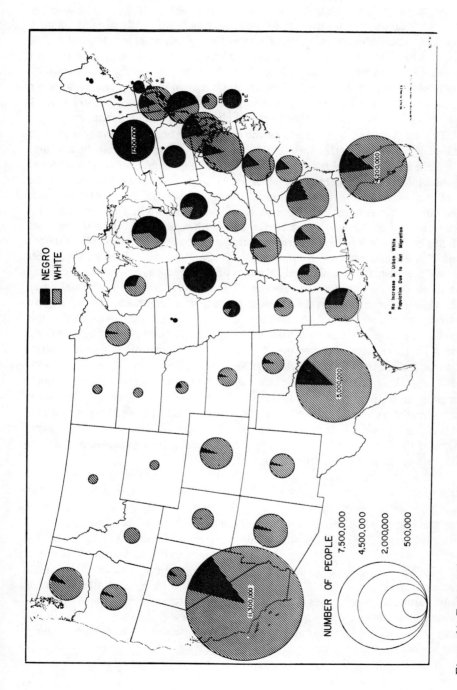

Figure 61. Estimated increases in the urban populations of states as a result of migration from farms between 1930 and 1970, by race.

1970, however, it was only 1.6. This trend offers scant support for the idea that American agriculture is changing into a system in which hosts of laborers on a few large establishments are producing the food, feed, and fiber for our highly industrialized society. It is true that the average size of farms has increased, from about 156 acres in 1930 to 389 acres in 1970, largely by the elimination of many small, marginal enterprises. But if size is measured in terms of workers per farm, since 1964 the decrease in size has been dramatic. Moreover, in 1972, 74 per cent of the workers on farms were still classified as "family labor."[22]

The numbers and proportions of the farm population who have migrated to villages, towns, and cities vary greatly, of course, from one state to another. Urban areas exhibit no more uniform gains by net migration than rural areas show uniform losses. Between 1930 and 1970, however, our estimates indicate that the movement has been especially heavy from the farms of Louisiana, Oklahoma, the eastern two-thirds of Texas, the southern half of Arkansas, the western third of Mississippi, the central and southeastern two-thirds of Alabama, all of Georgia except the northern quarter, the central portion of South Carolina, and the eastern parts of Kentucky, North Carolina, and Virginia. Figure 60 shows the estimated numbers of migrants of each major race who left the farms of these and the other states between 1930 and 1970 for the towns and cities throughout the nation. In 1930, most farming areas in the South were quite densely populated, so that the numbers of persons who have participated in the exodus are large. As expected, relatively large proportions of the migrants from most of these states are Negroes.[23] Heavy rates of migration from the rural-farm areas also have occurred in large sections of New Mexico, Arizona, Colorado, and Montana, but in these cases the numbers involved generally were much smaller. All of the states of the North Central region also have lost comparatively large numbers of farm people by migration, but not to the extent that has prevailed throughout the South. Finally, New England, New Jersey and Delaware, parts of the Southwest, and most of the Pacific states have sustained a relatively low rate of migration from the farms.

The migration of farm people from throughout the nation to the towns and cities has been especially heavy in California, Texas, Florida, and New York as well as in a number of other states along the eastern seaboard and in the nation's capital. Figure 61 shows the estimated numbers of farm people who swelled the urban ranks of these and the other states between 1930 and 1970. Of particular interest is the selectivity by race that is represented in this movement. The urban populations of New York, Illinois, Pennsylvania, and the District of Columbia sustained large increases in their Negro populations because of the migration from farms, but they experienced no important increases in their white populations by this means. This was also true in Maine, New Hampshire, and Massachusetts, although the numbers involved are small. Furthermore, Negroes accounted for at least half of the urban increase by migration from farms in New Jersey,

Ohio, Missouri, and Michigan. Many of the states of the South experienced comparatively large gains in their urban populations by the migration of white farm people. Particularly heavy growth by this means occurred in Texas, Florida, Virginia, and Georgia. In most of the southern states the migration of farm Negroes to the cities also has been substantial, although this cannot compare in magnitude with their exodus from the region to urban centers elsewhere in the nation. Finally, Washington, Colorado, Arizona, Oregon, Wisconsin, New Mexico, Utah, Nevada, and Kansas also experienced substantial urban growth, mostly of whites, by the influx of migrants from the farms.

Relatively few data are available for the study of the 25 million who migrated to farms from nonfarm areas after 1932, although it can be shown that increasing proportions of those who live on tracts of land classified as farms earn their incomes from sources other than agriculture. In 1940, of the male labor force resident on farms, 56.1 per cent were employed as farmers and farm managers and 15.9 per cent as farm laborers and foremen. By 1970 the comparable proportions were down to 39.3 and 9.5, respectively. Clearly, many of those who have moved to farms in recent decades are men and women who choose the open country primarily for residential reasons rather than for business purposes. As a result, much of the nonfarm-to-farm migration was not a movement of persons into agriculture or even into a strictly rural way of life. Moreover, the increasing extent to which the homes of farmers and those of persons primarily engaged in other occupational pursuits are intermingled in rural neighborhoods is indicative of the rapid progress of homogenization of society in the United States.

Social Characteristics of the Migrants

The social characteristics of those taking part in the great exodus of about 55 million persons from the farms of the United States since 1932 probably will never be known with any degree of certainty. Surely the migrants were about as diverse as the extremely heterogeneous population of the nation itself. The mass migration included such varied ethnic and racial components as a vast segment of the Negro population, and the children and grandchildren of the immigrants from many lands who contributed so greatly to the development of farming in this country. It also involved most of the small farmers who inhabited Louisiana and the Southwest when these portions of the national territory were secured from France and Mexico, respectively. Likewise, it embraced many millions of the descendants of the "Old Americans" of Scotch-Irish, German, and other origins who long carried on a subsistence type of agriculture in the comparatively unproductive mountainous and hilly sections of the nation, and especially in the Southern Appalachians, the Ozarks, and the upland portions of the South generally. Four major tenure categories of those who left the farms for the cities in the period 1933 through 1969, however, are of particular interest. These are as follows: (1) farm wage hands and members of their families who were estimated at about 5,250,000 persons or 17.5 per cent of the net migration of more than 30 million; (2) sharecroppers and share "tenants" on southern plantations and farms and the members of their households who numbered roughly 8,250,000 persons and who made up 27.5 per cent of the net migration; (3) the operators of small general or subsistence farms and the members of their households, approximately 11,000,000 persons or 36.7 per cent; and (4) the operators of fairly large and considerably commercialized farms and the members of their families, around 5,500,000 individuals or 18.3 per cent.

A few comments about the persons in these categories are in order. The estimates given above indicate that about 45 per cent of the net migration from farms during the period 1933 - 1969, inclusive, was made up of wage workers, sharecroppers, and share "tenants," which is to say that about 13.5 million of the net movement of 30 million from the farms to the cities were unequivocally of lower-class socioeconomic status. Even this is a conservative figure, for some of the operators of small general and subsistence farms would fall into the lower class as well, although the bulk of them probably belongs in the lower part of the middle class. It should be emphasized, though, that about 28 per cent of those in the lower-class group consisted of southern sharecroppers and share "tenants" and their families, both black and white. In a very literal sense this means that the southern cotton plantation, with its semi-servile labor system, has been one of the great rural tap roots of our urban poverty and much of the crime, violence, and despair that accompany it. Our society has only begun to pay the price for this institutionalization by a few entrepreneurs of a highly specialized type of agriculture featuring large units and highly regimented gangs of "cheap" laborers.

The 11 million operators of small general and subsistence farms and their families account for the great bulk of the decrease in the number of farms. If this category is considered to consist of the operators of farms of less than 100 acres, and the 1 million places attributed to southern sharecroppers and share "tenants" are eliminated, about 67 per cent of the decrease that occurred in the number of farms from 1930 to 1970 was in establishments of less than 100 acres and only 33 per cent in larger places. Most of the 11 million persons who left the smaller farms were in the bottom stratum of the middle class and most of the 5.5 million who left the larger ones were above that level. It is these high proportions of wage workers, sharecroppers and share "tenants," and of small general and subsistence farm operators that constitute the basis for the contention that rural-to-urban migration in the United States from 1933 to 1970 has amounted to a mass transfer of poverty from the farms to the cities of the nation.

Some Additional Factors Producing the Exodus

Early in this section the reversal of the flow of energy between farm and city and the growth of public relief and welfare as the employer of last resort were emphasized as major factors generating rural-to-urban migration in the United States. Several others, however, also were involved in this complex process and deserve mention.

First, the extensive social differentiation, division of labor, and specialization, along with the transfer of many functions and services from the country to the city, that accompanied the rise of mechanized and motorized ways of production, helped to prompt the exodus. By 1930 many of the tasks and functions for which the self-sufficient farm family had been responsible were transferred to the cities, leaving those on the farms to become increasingly specialized themselves. As a result, lines of contact between the farm family and a variety of urban establishments and services became more numerous and the city became more familiar and more necessary to the farm family. For example, as late as 1930 only one birth in three in the United States took place in a hospital. At that time the overwhelming proportion of all children borne by farmers' wives took place in the farm homes. By 1970 practically all deliveries, including those of farm women, took place in hospitals, which also is to say in towns and cities. In turn, these features made the urban centers more accessible and attractive to farm youth, and they migrated in large numbers.

Second, in some types of farming, such as the production of poultry and citrus, vertical integration of production and marketing has become an important feature. It involves the shift of many of the managerial activities once performed by the farm operator to various specialists who live in and work out of towns and cities. It is often combined with corporation farming. In turn, vertical integration helps to open contacts between rural people and the cities, it places many farm functions in the hands of those who live and work in the · urban centers, it decreases the self-sufficiency of the farm, and in general it promotes migration to the cities.

Third, much of the exodus from the farms since 1933 must be attributed to the severely reduced role of cotton production in American agriculture, and in lesser degree to the dwindling production of wool. Involved in the former are the various "cotton control" programs that decreased production, the burgeoning of cotton production abroad, the loss of foreign markets for domestic cotton, and especially the boom in various kinds of synthetic fibers. These factors, along with the rapid progress of mechanization in cotton production since 1935, all helped to convert much of the labor in the cotton-growing areas into a "surplus" and to promote the mass movement of people from the farms of these once densely populated agricultural districts of the South.

Fourth, a great deal of the depopulation of the open-country districts of the Great Plains since 1930 is due to the rise of "suitcase farming." Particularly in wheat production, this consists of an arrangement whereby the owner or renter of a sizable tract of semi-arid land maintains his residence in a town or city and goes out to his land only briefly at planting time and again at the harvest to perform the necessary functions in a completely mechanized fashion. In many cases he may even have these tasks done on a custom basis. Obviously, all of this reduces substantially the number of those who live on farms. Similar results occur in areas devoted to the production of fruits and vegetables in such states as California and Florida, where high proportions of farm operators and farm laborers alike reside in towns and cities.

Fifth, and most important, is the mechanization of agriculture by which internal combustion engines and electric motors supply the energy that heretofore had been provided by humans of all ages and by draft animals. These revolutionary changes made it possible for the average farm worker, who produced enough to meet the needs of 9.8 persons in 1930, to supply enough for 45.3 people in 1969. They also enabled a reduction in the agricultural labor force from an average of 12,816,000 per month in 1932 to a mere 4,373,000 in 1972, while facilitating vastly increased production. Mechanization, coupled with national agricultural policies that tend to favor the large producers of single crops, has not only reduced the need for laborers but has played a major role in forcing the small general and subsistence farmer from the land. It has helped to make both groups part of the net movement to towns and cities of over 30 million since 1932.

In analyzing the relationship between the mechanization of agriculture and the huge exodus from the farms since 1932, it is essential to keep in mind that the amount of land in the farms of the United States changed very little between 1932 and 1970, that the average farm more than doubled in size during this period, that the average number of workers per farm actually fell, and that there was a tremendous increase in agricultural production during the period involved. Moreover, it is important to recall the points made above relative to the reversal of the flow of energy between farm and city and that this was part and parcel of the long-continued transfer of economic and social functions from the rural to the urban parts of the country. As a result, by 1970 the farms were dependent upon urban industries, not only to build the tractors and associated implements, the motor trucks and automobiles on which they rely for transportation, the electric and gasoline motors required in the modern milking parlors, feed lots, drying sheds, and so on, but also for the gasoline, oil, and electricity that are required to supply the power for all these machines. The mechanical devices needed for the great transformation already had reached a considerable degree of perfection by 1930. From then on the change consisted largely of the substitution of mechanical and motor power for manpower in the various processes involved in agricultural production, processing, and transportation. And as "mechanical hands" made human hands superfluous, the city's attractions, including its burgeoning public welfare rolls, exerted more and more drawing power.

Underlying the complex socioeconomic process of mechanization of agriculture is the set of sociocultural values that helped to give rise to it and to rationalize it. In this connection it is important to emphasize that the complicated machines and implements that save labor on the farms were developed by or in response to the needs of middle-class operators of fairly large family-sized farms in the midwestern United States. Their basic attiture toward labor was to use it as efficiently and as productively as possible and they sought large, strong, and light machines and implements to enable them to do so. The labor, after all, was their own and that of the members of their families. This is in stark contrast with the attitude that pervailed in the South, where large cotton, sugarcane, and rice plantations-dominated the rural scene. There labor was used lavishly, essentially because it was plentiful and cheap and was performed by someone other than the farm operator and the members of his family. This situation provided little incentive to devise labor-saving techniques and devices, either for the benefit of the slaves or the sharecroppers who followed them. The laborers themselves, of course, were in no position to undertake such efforts. Indeed, departures from the prescribed activities, even though they might represent a substantial improvement in efficiency, would evoke not a reward, but at least a reprimand and more frequently the lash. Therefore, a high degree of mechanized efficiency was achieved in the regions of substantial family-sized farms long before even its rudiments were accepted in the plantation areas. Nevertheless, even though a high degree of mechanization existed in some places much earlier than in others, it became a universal feature of American agriculture between 1930 and the present, with the result that large numbers of those who had been the laborers and their families not only were released from agriculture to migrate to the cities, but were virtually forced to do so by the planters, the managers employed by corporations, and other large-scale operators who no longer needed them. They were joined by the operators whose farms were too small and too poor to make mechanization feasible. Now the problems of both groups are the problems of the cities.

NOTES

1. For a discussion of various types of internal migration in Latin America, especially the rural-urban, see the collection of papers published as "Internal Migration in Latin America," *International Migration Review*, 6, 2 (Summer, 1972), the entire issue. Cf. T. Lynn Smith, "Rural-Urban Migration in Brazil," *Sociologia Internationalis*, 10, 2 (1972), pp. 243 - 249.

2. U.S. Bureau of the Census, "Components of Population Change by County: 1960 to 1970," *Current Population Reports*, Series P-25, No. 461 (June, 1971).

3. U.S. Bureau of the Census, *General Demographic Trends for Metropolitan Areas, 1960 to 1970*, Final Report PHC (2)-1, *United States Summary* (Washington: Government Printing Office, 1971).

4. Gladys K. Bowles, A. Lloyd Bacon, and P. Neal Ritchey, *Poverty Dimensions of Rural-To-Urban Migration: A Statistical Report* (Washington: Government Printing Office, 1973).

5. For descriptions of the methodology and examples of the types of analyses in which it has been employed, see Vera J. Banks and Calvin L. Beale, *Farm Population Estimates, 1910 - 70* (Washington: Rural Development Service, 1973); Vera J. Banks, Calvin L. Beale, and Gladys K. Bowles, *Farm Population Estimates, 1910 - 60* (Washington: Economic Research Service, 1963); Donald J. Bogue, *Principles of Demography* (New York: John Wiley and Sons, Inc., 1969), p. 759; C. Horace Hamilton and F. M. Henderson. "Use of Survival Rate Method in Measuring Net Migration," *Journal of the American Statistical Association*, 39, 226 (1944), pp. 197 - 206; Everett S. Lee, "Migration Estimates," in *Population Redistribution and Economic Growth, United States, 1870 - 1950, I, Methodological Considerations and Reference Tables*, edited by Everett S. Lee, Ann Ratner Miller, Carol P. Brainerd, and Richard A. Easterlin (Philadelphia: The American Philosophical Society, 1957), pp. 15 - 55; Homer L. Hitt, "America's Aged at Mid-Century," in *Living in the Later Years*, edited by T. Lynn Smith (Gainesville: University of Florida Press, 1952), pp. 20 - 27; T. Lynn Smith, "The Migration of the Aged," in *Problems of America's Aging Population*, edited by T. Lynn Smith (Gainesville: University of Florida Press, 1951), pp. 15 - 28; and T. Lynn Smith, "The Migration of the Aged," in New York State Joint Legislative Committee on Problems of the Aging, *Growing With the Years* (Albany: Legislative Document No. 32, 1954), pp. 69 - 80.

6. Other examples are to be found in T. Lynn Smith and Paul E. Zopf, Jr., *Principles of Inductive Rural Sociology* (Philadelphia: F. A. Davis Co., 1970), p. 97; C. A. McMahan, *The People of Atlanta* (Athens: University of Georgia Press, 1950), pp. 180, 190 - 191; and Homer L. Hitt, "Migration and Southern Cities," in *The Sociology of Urban Life,* edited by T. Lynn Smith and C. A. McMahan (New York: The Dryden Press, 1951), pp. 332 - 334.

7. See Carter Goodrich, and others, *Migration and Economic Opportunity* (Philadelphia: University of Pennsylvania Press, 1936), pp. 685 - 686, plate VIII-A, and *passim.*

8. The most convenient edition of Graunt's work is that edited by Walter F. Willcox, *Natural and Political Observations Made upon the Bills of Mortality by John Graunt* (Baltimore: The Johns Hopkins Press, 1939). See p. 50.

9. *Ibid.,* p. 52.

10. *The Population of India and Pakistan* (Princeton: Princeton University Press, 1951), pp. 114 - 115 and 134 - 137.

11. "Regional Income Disparity and Internal Migration of Population in Japan," *Economic Development and Cultural Change,* 12, 1 (January, 1964), pp. 186 - 204.

12. "Structural Plurality, Urbanization and Labour Circulation in Southern Rhodesia," in *Migration,* edited by J. A. Jackson (London: Cambridge University Press, 1969), pp. 156 - 180.

13. A brief summary of the situation in each of fourteen countries appears in Bogue, *op. cit.,* pp. 771 - 776.

14. *Op. cit.,* p. 135.

15. *Ibid.,* p. 136.

16. For a more detailed discussion of factors, forces, and media at work in rural-to-urban migration, see Smith and Zopf, *op. cit.,* pp. 79 - 84.

17. The materials and discussion in this section are adapted from T. Lynn Smith, *Studies of the Great Rural Tap Roots of Urban Poverty in the United States* (New York: Carlton Press, 1974), chapter II. See also T. Lynn Smith, "Some Major Rural Social Trends in the United States of America," *International Social Science Journal,* XXI, 2 (1969), pp. 272 - 285.

516

18. For the data on these changes and the components involved, see Rural Development Service, *Farm Population Estimates, 1910 - 70*, U.S. Department of Agriculture Statistical Bulletin 523 (1973), pp. 14 - 15, Table 1; pp. 32 - 46, Table 6. The estimates of the farm population made periodically by this and other agencies of the U.S. Department of Agriculture in cooperation with the U.S. Bureau of the Census are somewhat larger and probably more accurate than the enumerations made of the farm population in the decennial census. This was especially true in 1970, when the farm and nonfarm components of the rural population as enumerated in the census were seriously in error. See U.S. Bureau of the Census, *U.S. Census of Population: 1970, General Social and Economic Characteristics*, Final Report PC(1)-C1, *United States Summary* (Washington: Government Printing Office, 1972), p. 359.

19. Rural Development Service, *op. cit.*, pp. 14 - 15, Table 1.

20. Economic Research Service, *Farm Real Estate Historical Series Data: 1850 - 1970*, ERS 520 (1973), p. 1, Table 1.

21. Crop Reporting Board, *Farm Labor* (monthly mimeographed release), especially January, 1959, and October, 1973.

22. For a discussion of changes in farm labor in the United States, see T. Lynn Smith, "Farm Labour Trends in the United States, 1910 - 1969," *International Labour Review*, 102, 2 (August, 1970), pp. 149 - 169.

23. These estimates are from as yet unpublished studies by T. Lynn Smith. For related materials, however, see T. Lynn Smith, "The Redistribution of the Negro Population of the United States, 1910 - 1960," *Journal of Negro History*, LI, 3 (July, 1966), pp. 155 - 173; and C. Horace Hamilton, "The Negro Leaves the South, *Demography*, I, 1 (1964), pp. 273 - 295.

ABRAMSON, JANE A. *Rural to Urban Adjustment* (ARDA Research Report No. RE-4). Ottawa: Department of Forestry and Rural Development, 1968.

BAALI, FUAD. "Social Factors in Iraqi Rural-Urban Migration." *American Journal of Economics and Sociology,* Vol. 25, No. 4 (October, 1966), pp. 359 - 364.

BANKS, VERA J., and CALVIN L. BEALE. *Farm Population Estimates, 1910 - 70.* Washington: Rural Development Service, 1973.

BEALE, CALVIN L. "Rural Depopulation in the United States: Some Demographic Consequences of Agricultural Adjustments." *Demography,* Vol. 1, No. 1 (1964), pp. 264 - 272.

BOGUE, DONALD J. *Principles of Demography,* pp. 756 - 800. New York: John Wiley & Sons, Inc., 1969.

BRODY, EUGENE B. *Behavior in New Environments: Adaptation of Migrant Populations,* Part II. Beverly Hills: Sage Publications, Inc., 1973.

BROWN, JAMES S., and GEORGE A. HILLERY, JR. "The Great Migration, 1940 - 1960," in *The Southern Appalachian Region,* edited by Thomas R. Ford, Chap. 4. Lexington: University of Kentucky Press, 1962.

DAVIS, KINGSLEY. *The Population of India and Pakistan,* Chaps. 14 and 15. Princeton: Princeton University Press, 1951.

HAMILTON, C. HORACE. "The Vital Statistics Method of Estimating Net Migration by Age Cohorts." *Demography,* Vol. 4, No. 2 (1967), pp. 464 - 478.

HERRICK, BRUCE H. *Urban Migration and Economic Migration in Chile.* Cambridge: The M.I.T. Press, 1965.

HITT, HOMER L. "Peopling the City: Migration," in *The Urban South,* edited by Rupert B. Vance and Nicholas J. Demerath, Chap. 4. Chapel Hill: University of North Carolina Press, 1954.

PETERSEN, WILLIAM. *Population,* 2nd ed., Chap. 7. New York: The Macmillan Company, 1969.

PRICE, DANIEL O. "Rural to Urban Migration of Mexican Americans, Negroes and Anglos." *Internal Migration Review,* Vol. V, No. 3 (Fall, 1971), pp. 281 - 291.

SCHWARZWELLER, HARRY K., and JAMES S. BROWN. "Social Class Origins, Rural-Urban Migration, and Economic Life Chances: A Case Study." *Rural Sociology,* Vol. 32, No. 1 (March, 1967), pp. 5 - 19.

SHRYOCK, HENRY S., JR. *Population Mobility Within the United States,* Chaps. 1 - 10. Chicago: Community and Family Study Center, University of Chicago, 1964.

SHRYOCK, HENRY S., JACOB S. SIEGEL, and associates. *The Methods and Materials of Demography*, Vol. 2, Chap 21. Washington: Government Printing Office, 1971.

SMITH, T. LYNN. "The Redistribution of the Negro Population of the United States, 1910 - 1960." *Journal of Negro History*, Vol. LI, No. 3 (July, 1966), pp. 155 - 173.

SMITH, T. LYNN. *Studies of the Great Rural Tap Roots of Urban Poverty in the United States*. New York: Carlton Press, 1974.

SMITH, T. LYNN. *Studies of Latin American Societies*, Selection 7. New York: Doubleday & Co., Inc., 1970.

SMITH, T. LYNN, and PAUL E. ZOPF, JR. *Principles of Inductive Rural Sociology*, Chap. 4. Philadelphia: F. A. Davis Company, 1970.

TAEUBER, CONRAD, and IRENE B. TAEUBER. *The People of the United States in the 20th Century* (A 1960 Census Monograph), Chaps. XII - XIV. Washington: Government Printing Office, 1971.

TAEUBER, KARL E. "The Residential Redistribution of Farm-Born Cohorts." *Rural Sociology*, Vol. 32, No. 1 (March, 1967), pp.20 - 36.

THOMLINSON, RALPH. *Population Dynamics*, Chap. 11. New York: Random House, Inc., 1965.

UNITED NATIONS. *Methods of Measuring Internal Migration.* New York: United Nations, 1970.

U.S. BUREAU OF THE CENSUS. *U.S. Census of Population: 1970. Subject Reports. Lifetime and Recent Migration.* Washington: Government Printing Office, 1973.

U.S. BUREAU OF THE CENSUS. *U.S. Census of Population: 1970. Subject Reports. Mobility for States and the Nation.* Washington: Government Printing Office, 1973.

ZOPF, PAUL E., JR. *North Carolina: A Demographic Profile*, Chap. XII. Chapel Hill: University of North Carolina Population Center, 1967.

INTERNAL MIGRATION

(Continued)

Much can be learned about the net result of the interchange of population among the various states of the United States by an analysis of the state-of-birth data in the reports of the various censuses from 1850 to the present. The same is true through study of comparable materials assembled in recent censuses in other countries, such as those for India which were analyzed by Davis,[1] those for Mexico which have been studied by Whetten and Burnight,[2] and those for Brazil which have been utilized by Giorgio Mortara and other Brazilian scholars, as well as by T. Lynn Smith.[3] Of course, these data give us no information other than the state of birth and the state of residence on the movement of persons from one state to another. The thousands of persons born in Illinois who spent most of their lives in Iowa and then moved to California as they neared the retirement ages are shown only as moving from Illinois to California; Iowa does not figure one way or the other in the tabulations. Likewise, in Brazil the thousands of persons born and reared in the northeastern portion of that great country who made the long migration into the Amazon Basin during the Second World War in the attempt to rejuvenate rubber production in the area in which it originated and then later found their way to the south are shown merely as born in Ceará or one of the other northeastern states and residing in the Federal District, the state of São Paulo, or one of the other states.

STATE-TO-STATE MIGRATION

The data on the interstate exchanges of population assembled in the 1970 census of population in the United States may be used to determine the extent to which each state has sent out and received migrants. In this case the tendency for a state to be a heavy gainer or loser of people by migration is reflected in the percentages of the native population born in a state other than the one in which they were residing on April 1, 1970. (See Figure 62.)[4] Most striking in this con-

520

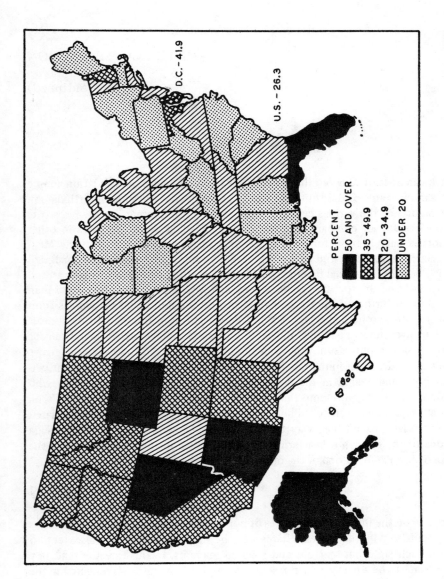

Figure 62. Percentage of the population born in a state other than the state of residence, 1970.

nection is the fact that 65 per cent of those who make their homes in Nevada and 61 per cent of those who reside in Alaska were born in other states. In addition, over half of those residing in Arizona, Florida, and Wyoming, in 1970, had come from other states. At the opposite extreme, with less than 15 per cent of the population able to claim other states as birthplaces, are Pennsylvania, New York, Mississippi, and Kentucky. The latter two states long have been heavy contributors of migrants to other parts of the nation but the former two have become so more recently. These four along with several other states of the South, the great majority of those in the North Central region, and some in the Mountain division sent out substantially larger numbers of migrants in the 1960's than they received. It should be remembered, though, that the reliability of conclusions based upon the data for such a seemingly straightforward matter as state of birth, gathered from a sample of the population in connection with the 1970 census, may be open to serious question. This probably will occur to many of the readers of these pages as they study the nature and implications of the statements in the following paragraphs, summarizing some of the materials on interstate migration assembled in the 1970 enumeration.

As a basis for such study and reflection, Table 59 was prepared. It shows the net migration to or from each of the states and the District of Columbia during the ten years prior to April 1, 1970. Figures are given separately for the total, the white, and the nonwhite populations. These data indicate first of all that among the nine major divisions of the nation four — New England, the South Atlantic, the Mountain, and the Pacific — experienced net gains of 300,000 or more persons by migration during the decade. In addition, the Middle Atlantic division received almost 9,000 more persons than it lost by migration. The remaining four divisions incurred net losses, with the South Central division losing most heavily, followed in descending order by the West North Central, the East North Central, and the West South Central. The largest proportional gains by net migration took place in the Pacific division (12.0 per cent of the population enumerated in 1960) and the South Atlantic division (5.1 per cent); the greatest losses occurred in the East South Central division (5.8 per cent); and the West North Central (3.9 per cent). All of these exchanges produced net gains by migration in the West (2,849,527 persons or 10.2 per cent), the South (589,804 persons or 1.1 per cent), and the Northeast (318,855 persons or 0.7 per cent). They produced a net loss in the North Central region of 757,015 persons or 1.5 per cent of the population in 1960.

Among the fifty states and the District of Columbia, twenty-four gained more migrants than they lost. However, the gains in only twelve of them accounted for 95 per cent of the total increase by migration experienced by the four states. This clearly testifies to the fact that migration continues to concentrate rather than to disperse the American population although it also helps to distribute some of its components more evenly throughout the nation. Heading

TABLE 59

Net interstate migration in the United States, by color, 1960-1970

State	Total population		White population		Nonwhite population	
	Number	Per cent[a]	Number	Per cent[a]	Number	Per cent[a]
New England						
Maine	+310,077	+3.0	+206,365	+2.0	+103,714	+39.8
New Hampshire	−70,940	−7.3	−69,478	−7.2	−1,462	−24.5
Vermont	+68,881	+11.3	+67,638	+11.2	+1,243	+48.0
Massachusetts	+14,526	+3.7	+13,736	+3.5	+790	+100.1
Rhode Island	+74,232	+1.4	+23,052	+0.5	+51,180	+40.8
Connecticut	+9,551	+1.1	+5,422	+0.6	+4,129	+28.6
	+213,827	+8.4	+165,993	+6.8	+47,834	+42.9
Middle Atlantic	+8,778	b	−724,521	−2.3	+733,299	+25.4
New York	−101,205	−0.6	−637,503	−4.2	+536,298	+35.9
New Jersey	+488,152	+8.0	+335,711	+6.1	+152,441	+28.9
Pennsylvania	−378,169	−3.3	−422,729	−4.0	+44,560	+5.1
East North Central	−153,057	−0.4	−613,381	−1.8	+460,324	+15.5
Ohio	−125,581	−1.3	−191,401	−2.1	+65,820	+8.3
Indiana	−15,878	−0.3	−57,956	−1.3	+42,078	+15.4
Illinois	−42,988	−0.4	−212,580	−2.4	+169,592	+15.8
Michigan	+27,236	+0.3	−122,445	−1.7	+149,681	+20.3
Wisconsin	+4,154	+0.1	−28,999	−0.8	+33,153	+35.7
West North Central	−603,958	−3.9	−654,829	−4.4	+50,871	+7.9
Minnesota	−25,495	−0.7	−38,911	−1.2	+13,416	+31.7
Iowa	−183,592	−6.7	−189,468	−6.9	+5,876	+20.4
Missouri	+868	b	−25,218	−0.6	+26,086	+6.6
North Dakota	−94,497	−14.9	−94,450	−15.2	−47	−0.4
South Dakota	−95,067	−14.0	−91,667	−14.0	−3,400	−12.4
Nebraska	−73,209	−5.2	−76,452	−5.6	+3,243	+8.9
Kansas	−132,966	−6.1	−138,663	−6.7	+5,697	+5.7

South Atlantic	+1,332,358	+5.1	+1,806,752	+9.0	-474,394	-8.0
Delaware	+38,075	+8.5	+32,309	+8.4	+5,766	+9.3
Maryland	+384,672	+12.4	+289,921	+11.3	+94,751	+18.0
District of Columbia	-99,975	-13.1	-137,067	-39.7	+37,092	+8.9
Virginia	+140,958	+3.6	+205,717	+6.5	-64,759	-7.9
West Virginia	-264,874	-14.2	-247,281	-14.0	-17,593	-19.5
North Carolina	-94,399	-2.1	+80,998	+2.4	-175,397	-15.2
South Carolina	-149,414	-6.3	+44,028	+2.8	-193,442	-23.3
Georgia	+51,007	+1.3	+198,369	+7.0	-147,362	-13.1
Florida	+1,326,308	+26.8	+1,339,758	+33.0	-13,450	-1.5
East South Central	-698,934	-5.8	-152,934	-1.6	-546,000	-20.1
Kentucky	-153,329	-5.0	-157,704	-5.6	+4,375	+2.0
Tennessee	-45,139	-1.3	+531	b	-45,670	-7.7
Alabama	-233,072	-7.1	-5,351	-0.2	-227,721	-23.2
Mississippi	-267,394	-12.3	+9,590	+0.8	-276,984	-30.1
West South Central	-43,620	-0.3	+152,897	+1.1	-196,517	-6.9
Arkansas	-70,869	-4.0	+38,055	+2.7	-108,924	-27.9
Louisiana	-132,117	-4.1	+25,856	+1.2	-157,973	-15.1
Oklahoma	+13,349	+0.6	-3,858	-0.2	+17,207	+7.8
Texas	+146,017	+1.5	+92,844	+1.1	+53,173	+4.4
Mountain	+305,215	+4.5	+300,392	+4.6	+4,823	+1.5
Montana	-58,153	-8.6	-56,544	-8.7	-1,609	-6.7
Idaho	-42,029	-6.3	-43,507	-6.6	+1,478	+15.1
Wyoming	-39,349	-11.9	-39,392	-12.2	+43	+0.6

TABLE 59 (Cont'd)

Net interstate migration in the United States, by color, 1960-1970

State	Total population		White population		Nonwhite population	
	Number	Per cent[a]	Number	Per cent[a]	Number	Per cent[a]
Colorado	+215,491	+12.3	+187,374	+11.0	+28,117	+52.8
New Mexico	−129,691	−13.6	−120,167	−13.7	−9,524	−12.7
Arizona	+226,171	+17.4	+247,984	+21.2	−21,813	−16.4
Utah	−10,958	−1.2	−11,000	−1.2	+42	+1.1
Nevada	+143,733	+50.4	+135,644	+51.5	+8,089	+37.0
Pacific	+2,544,312	+12.0	+1,974,384	+10.2	+569,928	+30.3
Washington	+249,023	+8.7	+220,217	+8.0	+28,806	+28.4
Oregon	+158,655	+9.0	+145,411	+8.4	+13,244	+36.1
California	+2,113,079	+13.4	+1,528,384	+10.6	+584,695	+46.3
Alaska	+14,285	+6.3	+22,066	+12.6	−7,781	−15.1
Hawaii	+9,270	+1.5	+58,306	+28.8	−49,036	−11.4

Source: Compiled and computed from data in U.S. Bureau of the Census, "Components of Population Change by County: 1960 to 1970," *Current Population Reports,* Series P-25, No. 461 (June, 1971), pp. 5-74.
[a]Expressed as a percentage of the population in 1960.
[b]Less than 0.1 per cent.

the list with well over 2 million is California, followed by Florida with over 1.3 million. New Jersey, with 488,152 persons, is a poor third. Maryland and Washington are fourth and fifth, respectively, followed by Arizona, Colorado, and Connecticut, in the order named. Others that incurred net gains of 100,000 or more during the decade are Oregon, Texas, Nevada, and Virginia.

If attention is directed to the heavy losers of population through net migration, as evidenced by the data in Table 59, there appears little reason to question Pennsylvania's right to first place or Mississippi's claim to second. West Virginia, Alabama, Iowa, Kentucky, South Carolina, Kansas, Louisiana, New Mexico, Ohio, and New York, in the order named, round out the list of those which lost at least 100,000 more people than they gained by exchanges with other states. Significant, too, is the net loss from the nation's capital of just under 100,000 persons, many of whom moved to suburban areas in neighboring Virginia and Maryland.

If the white population is considered separately, the six states showing the largest increases for the ten-year period due to net migration are the same and rank in nearly the same order given above for the total population. That is, California and Florida are in first and second places, respectively, followed by New Jersey, Maryland, Arizona, and Washington. On the other hand, New York, Pennsylvania, West Virginia, Illinois, Ohio, and Iowa, in the order named, were the ones losing most heavily by net migration to other parts of the nation. In the case of the District of Columbia, the net loss of whites was over 137,000, placing the nation's capital ninth in the amount of net loss by migration of members of that race. Quite different, however, is the list of heavy gainers and losers of population during the ten-year period produced by net migration of the nonwhite population. Among the states on the receiving end of such a movement, California outranked all the others, followed by New York, Illinois, New Jersey, Michigan, and Maryland, in the order named. Among those sending more nonwhite migrants to other parts of the nation than they received from them, Mississippi led the list, followed by Alabama, South Carolina, North Carolina, Louisiana, and Georgia.

An examination of the materials in Table 59 indicates the great extent to which the patterns of net migration between 1960 and 1970 produced a redistribution throughout the nation of whites and nonwhites. Most striking is the fact that among the sixteen states and the District of Columbia that make up the South for census purposes, only six experienced net gains of nonwhites, but twelve incurred net gains of whites. The result of all of this was a net loss in the region of more than 1.2 million nonwhites, but a net gain of 1.8 million whites. On a proportional basis, net migration increased the white part of the population of the South by 4.2 per cent, but decreased the nonwhite segment by 10.6 per cent. On the other hand, of the twelve states that make up the North Central region, ten received more nonwhites than they lost by interstate migration, but all twelve lost more whites than they acquired by this means. The result was a net loss from the region of almost 1.3 million whites, who were 2.6 per cent of the white population in 1960, but a net gain of over 0.5 million nonwhites who swelled that part of the region's population by 14.1 per cent. The situation is somewhat different in the Northeast. In that region, six of its nine states gained whites by net migration and eight gained nonwhites. The end product of all of this, however, was a net loss of whites amounting to over 0.5 million (1.2 per cent) and a net gain of nonwhites of more than 0.8 million (26.6 per cent). Finally, in the thirteen states that make up the West, eight had net gains of whites by migration between 1960 and 1970 and seven had net gains of nonwhites. The West is the only one of the four major regions that had net gains of members of both major races. They amounted to 2.3 million whites (8.8 per cent) and 0.6 million nonwhites (26.0 per cent).

The materials on these various exchanges by race make it clear that the flow of Negroes into areas that were almost completely inhabited by whites at the turn of the century continued at a very substantial rate in the 1960's, while the losses from their traditional homeland – the South – continued unabated. At the same time large numbers of whites have been moving to the South, to the Pacific Coast, into some of the Mountain states, and to New England. As a consequence of these migrations by members of the two races, no major region of the nation possesses the great predominence of one race or the other that existed seventy years ago. It is clear that this part of the process of homogenization of American society is going on briskly, although it may be producing relatively little genuine integration of the races. Moreover, even though the nonwhite population is becoming more evenly distributed throughout the nation, it should be remembered that the great bulk of this redistribution is to urban centers.

One particularly interesting aspect of state-to-state migration is the movement from one section of the nation to another of persons in or near the retirement ages. Data on the number of persons aged 65 and over who migrated to and from each state between 1965 and 1970 were collected as part of the 1970 census of population. From these materials it is a simple matter to compute the net gains or losses by migration of the elderly sustained by each state and to calculate the net change as a percentage of the total population aged 65 and over enumerated in each state in 1970. The results of such computations are shown in Table 60. Comparison of these materials with those for earlier periods indicates that the currents of migration of elderly persons have remained about the same since 1940 except that the volume has increased. It is obvious, however, that relatively few states are important recipients of this net movement. There were 159,338 more persons aged 65 and over in Florida in 1970 than there would have been had there been no migration during the five years ending that year; and for California the corresponding number is 29,713. As may be seen from Table 60, Arizona, Texas, Oregon, and Maryland are the other states attracting the largest numbers

TABLE 60

Net gains and losses of persons aged 65 and over in 1970 by
interstate migration between 1965 and 1970

State	Number migrating		Net gain or loss	
	In	Out	Number	Per cent[a]
New England	37,472	51,112	−13,640	−1.1
Maine	4,075	4,179	−104	−0.1
New Hampshire	5,449	4,069	+1,380	+1.8
Vermont	2,516	2,352	+164	+0.3
Massachusetts	11,933	23,202	−11,269	−1.8
Rhode Island	2,667	3,736	−1,069	−1.0
Connecticut	10,832	13,574	−2,742	−0.9
Middle Atlantic	80,337	188,146	−107,809	−2.7
New York	23,894	111,476	−87,582	−4.5
New Jersey	32,395	35,629	−3,234	−0.5
Pennsylvania	24,048	41,041	−16,993	−1.3
East North Central	89,571	178,174	−88,603	−2.3
Ohio	23,437	39,262	−15,825	−1.6
Indiana	13,968	20,931	−6,963	−1.4
Illinois	22,965	63,749	−40,784	−3.7
Michigan	16,805	39,996	−23,191	−3.1
Wisconsin	12,396	14,236	−1.840	−0.4
West North Central	53,527	72,223	−18,696	−1.0
Minnesota	9,061	15,885	−6,824	−1.7
Iowa	8,225	11,461	−3,236	−0.9
Missouri	17,778	19,312	−1,534	−0.3
North Dakota	2,047	4,000	−1,953	−2.9
South Dakota	2,279	3,586	−1,307	−1.6
Nebraska	5,160	6,968	−1,808	−1.0
Kansas	8,977	11,011	−2,034	−0.8
South Atlantic	269,104	112,574	+156,530	+5.3
Delaware	2,615	2,177	+438	+1.0
Maryland	18,451	13,234	+5,217	+1.7
District of Columbia	2,962	14,110	−11,148	−15.7
Virginia	15,914	14,483	+1,431	+0.4
West Virginia	4,178	8,501	−3,323	−1.7
North Carolina	10,884	8,616	+2,268	+0.5
South Carolina	6,282	4,875	+1,407	+0.7
Georgia	10,721	9,819	+902	+0.2
Florida	196,097	36,759	+159,338	+16.1

TABLE 60 (Cont'd)

Net gains and losses of persons aged 65 and over in 1970 by
interstate migration between 1965 and 1970

State	Number migrating		Net gain or loss	
	In	Out	Number	Per cent[a]
East South Central	33,953	34,742	−789	−0.1
Kentucky	8,212	10,113	−1,901	−0.6
Tennessee	12,017	10,140	+1,187	+0.5
Alabama	7,943	7,520	+423	+0.1
Mississippi	5,781	6,969	−1,188	−0.5
West South Central	57,008	42,303	+14,705	+0.8
Arkansas	11,703	8,629	+3,074	+1.3
Louisiana	6,315	5,943	+372	+0.1
Oklahoma	11,566	9,056	+2,510	+0.8
Texas	27,424	18,675	+8,749	+0.9
Mountain	66,717	43,777	+22,940	+3.3
Montana	2,833	4,024	−1,191	−1.7
Idaho	3,772	3,583	+189	+0.3
Wyoming	1,630	2,274	−644	−2.1
Colorado	11,459	9,350	+2,109	+1.1
New Mexico	6,455	5,273	+1,182	+1.7
Arizona	32,492	12,468	+20.024	+12.4
Utah	3,238	3,427	−189	−0.2
Nevada	4,838	3,378	+1,460	+4.7
Pacific	114,774	79,412	+35,362	+1.5
Washington	14,773	13,073	+1,700	+0.5
Oregon	14,644	9,298	+5,346	+2.4
California	82,852	53,139	+29,713	+1.6
Alaska	562	1,992	−1,430	−20.8
Hawaii	1,943	1,910	+33	+0.1

Source: Compiled and computed from data in U.S. Bureau of the Census, *U.S. Census of Population: 1970, General Population Characteristics,* Final Report PC(1)-B1, *United States Summary* (1972), pp. 297-309, Table 62; *Subject Reports, Mobility for States and the Nation,* Final Report PC(2)-2B (1973), pp. 355-422, Table 59.

[a]Percentage of those aged 65 and over in 1970.

of those in or near the retirement ages. Together these six states received 91 per cent of the net gain through interstate migration of those aged 65 and over. On a relative basis, also, in Florida migrants make up the highest proportions of the elderly population, followed by Arizona, Nevada, and Oregon, in the order given. Also readily determined from the data presented in this table are the absolute and relative losses for the twenty-six states and the District of Columbia from which elderly persons were migrating to the states on the Pacific Coast, Arizona, the Gulf States, and peninsular Florida. Chief among them is New York, which had a net loss of 87,582 elderly people, followed by Illinois, Michigan, Pennsylvania, Ohio, Massachusetts, and the District of Columbia, in that order. All of these exchanges produced net losses by migration of the elderly in the Northeast (121,449 persons or 2.3 per cent of the 1970 population aged 65 and over) and the North Central region (107,299 persons or 1.9 per cent). They generated net gains in the South (170,446 persons or 2.8 per cent) and in the West (58,302 persons or 1.9 per cent). In the case of the South, 93.4 per cent of the total increase was accounted for by that in Florida.

It would be easy to attach too much importance to the migration of the elderly in producing population change, however, when in fact they are less than half as likely as persons of all ages to be involved in interstate migration. For example, about 802,000 persons aged 65 and over migrated from state to state between 1965 and 1970, representing 4.0 per cent of the population in this age group enumerated in 1970. During the same period, however, about 17 million persons of all ages moved from one state to another and they made up 9.1 per cent of the nation's total population aged five and over. Furthermore, even though persons aged 65 and over were 9.9 per cent of the total population, they were only 4.7 per cent of the total number of interstate migrants. Finally, interstate migration is an exceptionally rare phenomenon among elderly Negroes. In 1970, Negroes made up 7.9 per cent of all persons aged 65 and over, but they accounted for only 4.0 per cent of the persons in this age group who moved from one state to another between 1965 and 1970. During these five years, 4.0 per cent of the nation's elderly whites but only 1.9 per cent of its aged Negroes were interstate migrants.[5]

Before closing this section on interstate migration of all types, it is well to point out the relative importance of the movement during the period from 1850 to 1970. The data on the state of birth of the native population indicate that Americans have been highly mobile during the entire period under consideration and that interstate migration was about as significant a factor in American life over a century ago as it is now. For example, in 1850, 24 per cent of the native or nonimmigrant population (excluding Indians and slaves) had been born in other states or territories than the ones in which they were residing; in 1970, the figure was 26 per cent. Furthermore, in no census year during the period from 1850 to 1970 did the proportion rise above 26 per cent or fall below 21 per cent.

Even the reports of the 1940 census which reflect many demographic consequences of the hardships experienced during the economic depression, one of which was a temporarily reduced rate of interstate migration, showed that 22.4 per cent of the native inhabitants had moved to a state other than that in which they were born. During the time between 1850 and 1970 the directions of migration have changed somewhat, some states which were the origins and some which were the destinations of migrants have declined in importance and others have increased, and the characteristics of the migrants have been altered as frontiersmen and settlers gave way to urbanites and suburbanites and as Negroes joined what had been a movement composed almost exclusively of whites. Nevertheless, no matter how much these various aspects of interstate migration have changed, the overall movement has continued at about the same rate for well over a century.

FARM-TO-FARM MIGRATION

The movement of the farm population, especially in some sections of the country, is a third important variety of internal migration. A considerable amount of reliable data on the subject for the United States is available in the reports of the agricultural censuses that were taken each five years through 1964. However, in the latest census of agriculture, that for 1969, the materials that would make it possible to study the basic aspects of farm-to-farm migration were not collected. In fact, that census deals almost exclusively with various aspects of agricultural production, costs, and income and contains very little information on the agricultural population. Therefore, the discussion of differential migration by tenure status that follows is based upon the information for 1964. The significant data on the shifting about from one farm or plantation to another are those secured from the tabulations of answers to the question on the 1964 farm schedule which asks for the "year when you began to operate *this* farm." The answers were tabulated to show for each tenure category the numbers of farm families who had been occupying their farms for less than two years, less than five years, five to nine years, and ten years or more.

For the United States as a whole, the average period of farm occupancy in 1964 was about fifteen years, or, the average year of occupancy for all farm operators was 1949. Full owners had been on their farms for an average of seventeen years, part owners for sixteen years, and tenants for only eight years. Furthermore, the varying proportions of these tenure categories and other factors caused the index to differ greatly from one part of the nation to another. Within each of the major tenure categories, however, variations from state to state are relatively minor, essentially because tenure class and the socioeconomic features which it involves are principal elements in determining different rates of migration of the farm population. The data in Table 61, based on the percentages of farm operators in various tenure statuses who were reported in the 1964 census of agriculture as having lived on their farms for ten years or more, indicate that only about 31 per cent of the full owners and part owners had moved from one farm to another between 1954 and 1964, whereas 55 per cent of the managers and 62 per cent of the tenants had made such moves. By groups of states, full and part owners in the Mountain and Pacific divisions had operated their farms for somewhat shorter periods on the average than those in the other divisions of the United States. With the single exception of Alaska, whose population has grown largely as a result of recent migration, in every state well over half of those with ownership of some kind had been on the same farm for at least ten years. Alaska excluded, the proportions reached highs for full owners of 81 per cent in North Dakota and 77 per cent in North Carolina and Nebraska and lows of 53 per cent in Arizona, 54 per cent in Nevada, and 56 per cent in Oregon. Among part owners the highs were 79 per cent in North Dakota and Kansas and 76 per cent in New Jersey and Nebraska; the lows were 59 per cent in Kentucky, 60 per cent in Nevada, and 61 per cent in Tennessee. Among the tenants, clearly a much less permanent group, in no state were as many as half living on the same farms in 1954 and 1964. In addition to Alaska, especially striking are the extremely small proportions in Nevada (17 per cent), Kentucky (23 per cent), and Arizona (24 per cent). Tenancy seems to involve the least amount of migration and the highest level of stability in those states where the family-sized farm rather than the plantation, the huge "factory" farm, or some other type of the large landed estate dominates agriculture.[6] For example, in 1964, 49 per cent of all tenants in Illinois and Kansas had occupied their farms for at least ten years. In general, then, the nature of the rights that agriculturists have to the land is highly significant in producing particular rates of movement from one farm to another. Stable rights, which permit the exercise of suitable management techniques and encourage a high level of investment in land, buildings, equipment, and so on, are associated with a comparatively low rate of movement from farm to farm. Conversely, the lack of rights to the soil or even those tenuous rights associated with low-status tenancy are reflected in much greater mobility. Under these conditions, farm-to-farm movement produces little improvement for agricultural families.

One of the phases of farm-to-farm migration in which society as a whole must be most concerned is that involving migratory agricultural laborers. Prior to the Second World War, persons who "followed the crops," farm laborers for whom being always on the move was a way of life, numbered between 200,000 and 350,000 according to the estimates of Paul S. Taylor[7] or an even million as estimated by the President's Commission on Migratory Labor.[8] The discrepancies among the various figures underscore how little was known about this unfortunate segment of the population. The number fell to about 600,000 during the war years and then increased once more to over 1 million,[9] at least for a time. In 1970, the Economic Research Service of the U.S. Department of Agriculture

TABLE 61

Percentages of farm operators in various tenure classes who had lived on their present farms for ten or more years, by states, 1964

State	Full owners	Part owners	Managers	Tenants
United States	69.2	69.8	44.7	37.7
New England				
Maine	70.2	70.8	42.3	26.9
New Hampshire	68.4	68.0	47.6	42.0
Vermont	67.5	67.1	43.8	28.6
Massachusetts	73.6	71.7	54.8	34.8
Rhode Island	73.3	74.9	72.7	40.0
Connecticut	72.8	73.3	58.8	35.2
Middle Atlantic				
New York	69.3	70.7	49.3	33.2
New Jersey	73.4	75.5	50.7	36.7
Pennsylvania	70.6	69.3	52.0	33.6
East North Central				
Ohio	67.6	70.2	45.6	44.3
Indiana	67.6	70.0	51.8	43.1
Illinois	69.8	72.9	48.8	49.5
Michigan	70.3	69.4	49.0	37.3
Wisconsin	69.9	68.9	39.8	33.0
West North Central				
Minnesota	72.3	70.1	42.6	36.6
Iowa	72.3	70.8	40.7	41.6
Missouri	65.5	67.8	41.1	34.9
North Dakota	80.8	78.8	53.3	39.0
South Dakota	76.3	73.4	39.6	37.2
Nebraska	76.5	75.9	48.1	43.2
Kansas	72.0	78.8	51.7	49.4
South Atlantic				
Delaware	73.3	73.0	72.4	41.9
Maryland	69.9	68.1	44.0	38.1
Virginia	74.0	71.0	51.7	33.9
West Virginia	72.3	68.5	41.7	32.5
North Carolina	77.2	68.4	47.2	32.0
South Carolina	75.2	70.2	48.4	36.7
Georgia	72.0	68.7	41.3	35.2
Florida	61.0	64.1	46.2	25.2
East South Central				
Kentucky	68.7	58.6	44.3	22.9
Tennessee	69.1	60.5	39.1	27.1
Alabama	71.4	65.6	51.9	39.5
Mississippi	74.1	65.2	44.4	35.7
West South Central				
Arkansas	64.6	63.5	38.1	34.0

TABLE 61 (Cont'd)

Percentages of farm operators in various tenure classes who had lived on their present farms for ten or more years, by states, 1964

State	Full owners	Part owners	Managers	Tenants
Louisiana	74.9	68.6	48.7	41.5
Oklahoma	62.7	71.9	38.7	39.1
Texas	67.8	69.8	44.5	39.8
Mountain				
Montana	65.4	74.6	33.9	35.9
Idaho	62.4	68.4	35.1	28.0
Wyoming	65.0	70.4	49.6	28.4
Colorado	61.1	72.2	40.7	35.9
New Mexico	66.0	70.6	43.5	27.0
Arizona	53.4	61.5	36.6	24.1
Utah	73.1	75.2	39.1	28.1
Nevada	53.7	59.7	32.7	16.8
Pacific				
Washington	58.4	64.8	41.4	34.5
Oregon	55.8	65.1	41.0	24.9
California	57.4	67.0	45.5	28.7
Alaska	37.3	38.5	50.0	16.7
Hawaii	57.3	61.6	36.8	46.2

Source: Compiled and computed from data in U.S. Bureau of the Census, 1964 *Census of Agriculture,* Vol. II, Chapter 5, *Characteristics of Farm Operators and Persons Living on Farms* (1967), pp. 542-551, Table 15.

estimated domestic migratory workers at about 196,000,[10] and in 1972, that agency placed their number at about 184,000 or 6.5 per cent of the total number of farm workers hired for wages in the United States.[11] About 38 per cent were classified as heads of households and the remainder as other members of their households, but even so the total estimate probably omits a relatively large number of the members of families headed by migratory laborers. In 1972, 90 per cent of the group were white as compared with 85 per cent of all farm workers hired for wages, which means that Negroes are underrepresented in the migratory group. Puerto Ricans and Mexican-Americans, on the other hand, are substantially overrepresented. Of the total, 34 per cent were identified as having come from the South and another 38 per cent as being from the West, although their nomadic existence makes it difficult to identify them with any relatively permanent place of residence. About 46 per cent also did some work for wages off the farms, which is not surprising considering that their average annual earnings in agriculture were only $1,391 and the median number of days worked in agriculture during the year was only 65. In any case, the disadvantages of the group as a whole make their rapidly diminishing numbers no surprise and certainly no misfortune, although many have simply abandoned the migratory rural life for the public assistance to be found in the cities.

Each of the crops with which the migratory laborers are involved tends to generate a particular stream of migration. The major ones that have existed in the twentieth century and their present importance are as follows: (1) The wheat belt migration, which, from 1900 until the 1920's, saw the movement of large numbers of workers to Texas in June, and from there northward to the Dakotas and even Canada. Some workers followed the entire route, others from local areas participated in harvests in their own regions. At present, the mechanization of wheat production has made this flow largely historical. (2) The cotton belt migration, which is confined principally to its western portion, especially the states of Arizona, California, New Mexico, and western Texas, largely because sharecropping persisted so long and stubbornly in the "Deep South" that no other system requiring the lavish use of labor became widespread before the 1950's. (3) The movement in areas where small fruits and vegetables are grown. Such crops as strawberries, grapes, beans, tomatoes, and others require careful handpicking and have generated a great deal of migration northward from the Gulf of Mexico to Lake Michigan, with stops in Florida, Louisiana, central Arkansas, Kentucky, Illinois, Michigan, and New York. Many of these people also participate in the harvest of tree fruits and vegetables along the way, and some eventually fan out toward the Northwest and the fruit-growing sections of Washington and Oregon. Another group moves northward each summer along the eastern seaboard, harvesting most of the same crops. (4) The movement of sugar workers. Including those who harvest both beets and cane, this group is highly localized; workers harvesting cane in Louisiana are drawn from the immediate vicinity, laborers cultivating and harvesting sugar beets in the Mountain States and the Middle West are recruited in their general areas, and so on. "Following the crop" is hardly possible in sugar production. (5) The migration to and within California following fruit and truck crops. Much of the nation's migratory labor population now is confined to California and the other states of the Pacific Coast because of the nature of farming in that area. The Imperial Valley of California is perhaps the single most important area insofar as the recruitment of migratory agricultural laborers is concerned.

Of all the migrations of rural people, the shifting of migratory laborers from one seasonal crop to another is fraught with the most serious social consequences. Earnings are low and sporadic, exploitation is frequent, expenditures for transportation are high, and there is little possibility of accumulating any reserve to tide the workers and their families over periods of unemployment or adversity. Housing of such workers is mostly a makeshift affair, with little or no care given to sanitation, despite a few modest improvements since 1968. Attachment to or participation in the activities of social institutions such as churches and schools is almost out of the question for the migrant laborer or the members of his family. Even the whites are not accepted by the communities in which they work temporarily, and workers of other races and of foreign birth find still greater discrimination. A system of agriculture based on migratory labor breeds the most demoralizing social results that can be contemplated. However, the Economic Research Service reports on the effort to improve these conditions as follows:

> Legislation now in effect on either a national or State basis deals mainly with migratory farmworkers. Certain States regulate labor camps, conditions of travel, day care for children, working hours of children under 16, farm-labor contractors and crew leaders, and other working arrangements of migratory farm laborers. Federal legislation requires crew leaders to register with the Employment Service and regulates their activities. The Economic Opportunity Act has special provisions for programs to improve housing, sanitation, and day care for migratory children. The Migrant Health Act provides for special programs to improve the health conditions and medical facilities available to migratory workers and their family members.
>
> The Economic Opportunity Act was given about $20 million in 1965 for special programs for migratory and other seasonal workers. By June 30, 1965, 50 projects from 26 States for these special programs had been approved. Grants totaled more than $14 million, with about 28 per cent for projects in California. Most of the projects included educational programs for children in migrant-worker families; supervised day care for children is often provided. New approaches are now being tried to meet housing and sanitation needs.[12]

In addition to various governmental efforts, those of some labor organizations to unionize the migrant laborers have produced some modest improvements in levels of living. Most notable was the campaign conducted in 1968 by the United Farm Workers Organizing Committee to organize the grape pickers in California. The effort produced some awareness of the plight of the laborers and resulted in a union contract between the migrants and the growers, but it also speeded the process of mechanized harvesting so as to reduce the reliance on hand labor.[13]

Finally, it should be noted that certain changes in the nature of American agriculture have increased the tendency for farm laborers to mill around locally. In particular, the rapid conversion of cotton growing in the South from a system involving sharecroppers to one employing wage hands on large-scale units has made many of the workers even more mobile than they had been prior to 1960. In turn, the seasonality of employment is associated with changes in residence; many workers move to nonfarm residences in the off-season and back to the farms when the work demands are great. Many of them, however, do not move to and from the same farms or nonfarm homes and they frequently change employers during a single year or even a single growing season. These short-distance, temporary moves imply, of course, that the wage hand is even less likely than was the sharecropper to find any great level of stability in his relationship with the land or with a local community. For example, on April 1, 1972, about 76 per cent of all self-employed people in agriculture were living on farms but about 67 per cent of the wage workers in agriculture lived in nonfarm residences.[14]

THE SELECTIVITY OF MIGRATION

How do those who migrate compare with those who do not? Do those who leave the country for the city differ in significant ways from those who remain in the communities in which they were born? What distinguishing characteristics, if any, are possessed by those who participate in the back-to-the-land movement? Those who move from one state to another? Those who follow the crops? In a word, does migration select persons with any particular set of bio-social attributes or qualities?

These questions are of considerable moment, even though there generally is much more speculation than fact in the answers presented. Consider, for example, the implications of rural-urban migration if it should be that there are any particular features or qualities, especially those having to do with innate or inherited characteristics, which distinguish the migrants from the ones who stay at home. That like tends to produce like is a biological generalization known to all. Therefore, if those who migrate are more intelligent than the other members of their families or if in any other way they tend to be the "cream of the population" or the "better lives," the substantial differences in the rates of natural increase in city and country are fraught with serious implications for the societies concerned. But in spite of the significance of the subject, it is still one of the portions of demography in which the glib phrase is most likely to take the place of the tested fact. To find in the early sociological literature statements similar to the following is easy:

> No doubt rural decline from this cause has occurred sporadically for thousands of years, but it assumes acute forms in the United States because the double pull of city and frontier, propagated by schools and newspapers, has worked on our old rural population like a cream separator. In New England there are rural counties which have been losing their best for three or four generations, leaving the coarse, dull, and hidebound. The number of loafers in some slackwater villages of the Middle States indicates that the natural pacemakers of the locality have gone elsewhere to create prosperity. In parts of southern Michigan, Illinois, Wisconsin, and even as far west as Missouri, there are communities which remind one of fished-out ponds populated chiefly by bull-heads and suckers.[15]

More difficult to find, however, are reports of studies in which various possibilities have been tested with substantial and reliable quantitative data.

Before considering the specific characteristics for which migration may or may not be selective, it is well to have in mind that the type of migration involved no doubt has much to do with the attributes of the migrants. One could hardly expect the migrants who fled the "dust bowl" during the 1930's to have the same characteristics as the ones who moved from California to Texas and Oklahoma in 1949, nor is it likely that those leaving the farms for the cities resemble in most respects those moving in the opposite direction. Again the characteristics of the migrants are almost certain to differ as the incentives to migration vary.

For example, the highly remunerative jobs that attracted hundreds of thousands of Negroes from the cotton belt to the Pacific Coast during the Second World War probably called forth persons with characteristics substantially different from those of persons who left the same area as a result of the tensions produced by the attempts to desegregate the schools of the various southern states.

Race

In countries such as the United States, Brazil, or the Soviet Union, in which sharply different racial and ethnic groups make up substantial portions of the population, the extent to which the various racial or ethnic elements participate in the various forms of migration is of considerable importance. In the United States, this long was true in the South, where most students of population accepted as axiomatic that an essential element in any demographic analysis was the subdivision of the data according to race. It attained national importance after the flood of Negro migration into northern cities during the First World War, the heavy migration of Negroes to the West Coast during the Second World War, and the sustained movement of Negroes from the South to other parts of the nation from 1946 on.

For decades following their political emancipation, the Negroes remained for the most part in the same districts where they had lived as slaves. But as education gradually emancipated their minds, and as information they trusted about alternatives came to them from venturesome relatives and friends who had migrated to the North, Negroes by the hundreds of thousands began abandoning the farms of the southern region. To demonstrate this one needs merely to show that the Negro population long was urbanizing more rapidly than the white. This is easily done. In 1910, only 27 per cent of the Negroes were classified as urban in comparison with 48 per cent of the white population. By 1940 the Negro population was 49 per cent urban, the white population 58 per cent; by 1950 the corresponding percentages had risen to 62 and 63 per cent; by 1960, 73 per cent of the Negroes and only 70 per cent of the whites fell into the urban category. By 1970 the proportions had risen to 72.4 per cent for the whites but to 81.3 per cent for the Negroes. As a result of all of this, the Negro farm population has become so depleted that the 1969 census of agriculture reported that only 87,393 Negro farm operators of all tenure classes remained in the United States and that a mere 17,548 of them were tenants. Finally, the great magnitude of the movement of Negroes from the rural South and their comparatively small rate of return to it during much of the present century are indicated by the fact that in 1970, only 8 per cent of all Negroes living in the South had been born outside of the region, whereas 32 per cent of those residing in the other three major regions had been born in the South. In the West, 41 per cent of the Negroes had been born in the South; in the North Central region, 32 per cent;

and in the Northeast, 28 per cent. Obviously, since 1910 the tremendous flow of population from the rural districts of the South to the urban centers in all parts of the country has been selective of Negroes.[16]

In view of the foregoing data, it is not surprising that Negroes have participated in interstate movements of population to a much greater extent, relatively, than have white people. Even as early as 1930, 25.3 per cent of the nation's Negroes were enumerated in a different state from the one in which they had been born, whereas for native whites the corresponding percentage was only 23.4. Exactly comparable data are not available for 1950, but at the time of that census 29.2 per cent of the nonwhite population (of which the overwhelming proportion is Negro) were living in a state other than the one in which they were born, in comparison with 25.1 per cent of the native white population. In 1960, 28.5 per cent of the nation's nonwhite group were living in a state other than the one of birth as contrasted with 27.1 per cent of the native white segment. In 1970, however, 26.6 per cent of the native whites but only 24.6 per cent of the Negroes were residing in a state other than that of birth. These data from the 1970 census indicate, therefore, that while the interstate migration of members of both races continues, the Negro group that migrated from the South in earlier years is now so large and so likely to remain in the cities and regions to which they moved, that for increasing proportions of their children the state of birth and the state of residence in 1970 were the same. In turn, this is gradually increasing the number of urban-born Negroes who have had no personal experience in the South or in the type of agriculture which was an integral part of the lives of their parents and grandparents, although its influences may persist for generations in the cities. Furthermore, it is to be expected that the migration of Negroes from the South to other parts of the nation cannot continue indefinitely at a peak rate. To be expected also are patterns of migration which eventually will vary even less between the two major races than they did in 1960 and 1970 and which will be largely a matter of movement between various cities and between the urban centers and the areas immediately surrounding them.

Age

At most times and in most places voluntary migration is largely a phenomenon of youth. The bulk of the persons who abandon the farming districts of a nation for its towns and cities, those who leave one country in order to become citizens of another, and those who transfer their residences from one state to another generally are less than twenty-five years of age. (See Figure 63.) This is true even for persons who migrate only from one county to another within their respective states of birth and for those who move only from one house to another within the same county. For example, between 1965 and 1970, the highest rates of interstate migration and of movement from county to county within a given state occurred for people aged twenty to twenty-four, resulting in median ages of the migrants in these two categories of twenty-three and twenty-four years, respectively. In fact, the mobility of the group aged twenty to twenty-four is so great that only 25 per cent of them was living in the same house in 1965 and 1970. Furthermore, the peak years for both males and females generally are those from twenty to twenty-four.[17] The migrants leave the communities in which they were born and reared for the city, a new homeland, or another state just at the time their contemporaries are marrying and establishing homes of their own. Of course, these statements need some qualification. Populations torn from their homes by war, those fleeing from oppression in their native lands, and those driven out by famine or pestilence include persons of all ages. Also, in all probability, a considerable share of the migrants from city to country is middle-aged or beyond, individuals born in the rural districts who have spent their most productive years in the city and who return to the rural villages to spend their remaining years.

That immigrants and migrants from farm to city are young, most of them in late adolescence or early adulthood, long was generally agreed upon by those who had given most study to the subject. Hart, Sorokin and Zimmerman, Thomas, McMahan, and others, who made exhaustive examinations of the available materials, all arrived at this conclusion. Hart found, for example, that three-fourths of the immigrants to the United States came to this country before attaining the age of thirty, and that more than one-fourth of them were less than twenty when they arrived. He also discovered that migrants from the farms to the cities were even younger than the immigrants, more than half of them being less than twenty.[18] The results of many studies summarized by Sorokin and Zimmerman,[19] Thomas,[20] and McMahan[21] are in agreement.

The age distribution of immigrants is changing somewhat, however. Taeuber found that in the population that immigrated into the United States between 1960 and 1970, the relative concentrations of young adults had declined below that of earlier decades and the percentages of children and of somewhat older adults had increased.[22] For example, of the immigrants who came to the United States between 1900 and 1910, 15 per cent were under fifteen years of age and 5 per cent were over forty-four; but between 1960 and 1970, 24 per cent were under fifteen and 14 per cent were over forty-four. Even so, 62 per cent of the immigrants who arrived between 1960 and 1970 were in the ages fifteen to forty-four as compared with only 41 per cent in those ages in the total population.[23] Thus, immigration is still largely a phenomenon of young adulthood, although not to the great extent that it was a few decades ago. In large part, the legislation that favors immigrants who have certain skills is responsible for this change in the age distribution, simply because the highly skilled occupations that are now most wanted are generally those of older adults. For example, in the group that arrived in the first decade of the twentieth century, 1 per cent was professional

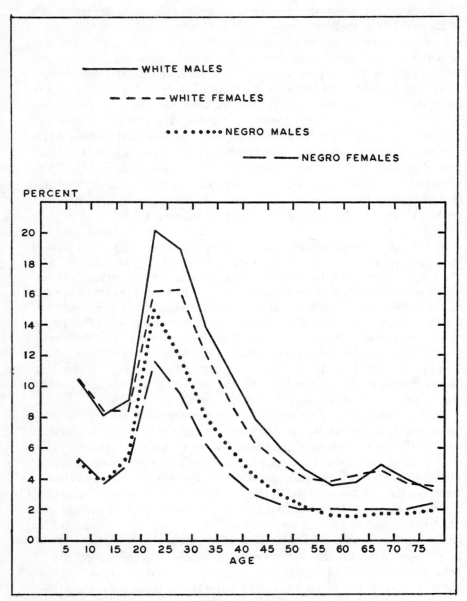

Figure 63. Percentages of persons in the United States who had migrated from one state to another between 1965 and 1970, by age, race, and sex in 1970.

and technical workers and 33 per cent were laborers; in the group that came in the 1960's, 10 per cent were in the professional category and only 4 per cent were laborers.[24] This change in occupational emphasis also means that large percentages of the immigrants are already married and have children, which helps to explain the increase in the proportion of children among the recent arrivals.

The age composition of persons involved in internal migration in the United States has changed relatively little in several decades. For example, for all types of migration, ranging from that between counties in the same state to that between noncontiguous states and for migrants of both sexes, the peak rates in the 1940's, the 1950's, and the 1960's all occurred in the ages from twenty to twenty-four. The only change in this pattern in the three decades has been for the peak rate of interstate migration of females to occur in the ages twenty-two to twenty-four in the late 1960's rather than in the ages twenty and twenty-one as it did in the early 1940's. For females who move only within a given county, however, which includes a great deal of rural-to-urban movement, the highest rate still occurs in the younger age span. The peak rates for males who move either long or short distances have continued to be in the ages twenty-two to twenty-four.

As indicated earlier, information now available indicates that those in the more advanced ages are participating to an increasing extent in the various types of internal migration within the United States. Table 60 indicates that state-to-state movements of persons aged sixty-five and over is by no means to be ignored and that increasingly large numbers and proportions of those nearing or in the retirement ages have left the sections of the country in which they lived and worked throughout their productive years to establish new homes in southern California, Arizona, all along the Gulf Coast, and in peninsular Florida. In addition, the elderly are more disposed than they once were to migrate from the farms of the nation to nearby small towns and villages and sometimes even large cities. Places of 1,000 to 2,500 receive an especially large percentage of those who can no longer operate their farms but who do not wish to leave the local community. In general, however, the rate of migration of the elderly is well below that of the population of most other ages.

Sex

Migration is also highly selective for sex, but again the nature of the selection depends largely upon the type of migration involved. If long distances are spanned, such as in immigration, the migration of Negroes from southern farms to cities in the North or on the Pacific Coast, or the movement from northeastern Brazil to São Paulo or Rio de Janeiro, males usually greatly outnumber females. On the other hand, if migration covers only a short distance, as with most of the movement from farms to towns and cities, females usually participate in the exodus in much greater numbers than males. These conclusions are in agreement with the

the detailed information presented in Chapters 6 and 7 on the differences between the sex composition of urban and rural populations and results of the
various studies which are summarized in the works of Sorokin and Zimmerman,
Thomas, McMahan, and others cited above.

The sex ratio (number of males per 100 females) is probably the most useful
index yet devised for studying the sex selectivity of migration. In evaluating the
import of this statement, the population student should remember that (1) the
sex ratio at birth can be determined accurately from registration statistics, (2)
age-specific death rates show that at nearly all times and in nearly all places the
death rates of females of all ages are lower than those of males, and (3) the data
frequently are available for color and nativity groups so that the influences of
immigration can be largely eliminated. Therefore, it is possible to determine
quickly in a general way and precisely by more painstaking methods the fact of
considerable sex selectivity in the various types of internal migration. For example, it is easily demonstrated that the migration of native whites from the rural to the urban districts of the United States includes many more women than
men. The sex ratio at birth among native whites in this country is approximately
105 and in any year that one wishes to examine between 1900 and the present,
at all ages the expectation of life for females can be found to be higher than that
for males. Yet, after the movement of tens of millions of persons from the farms
to the cities of the United States, the sex ratios among native whites in 1930
were 96 in the urban population and 112 in the rural-farm population. In 1940,
1950, 1960, and 1970, the comparable indexes were 95 and 112, 94 and 111,
94 and 108, and 94 and 106, respectively. The predominance of females among
the migrants from the farms to the cities is the only hypothesis that fits all these
facts. However, where societal arrangements are radically different from those in
the United States, such as in India, rural-urban migration seems to result in the
transfer from farm to city of much higher proportions of males than females.[25]

In addition to the low sex ratios prevailing in nations that have lost heavily by
emigration and the high sex ratios among the foreign-born populations of such
countries as Argentina, Australia, Brazil, Canada, and the United States, there is
much other evidence that long-distance migration usually is highly selective of
males, short-distance movement of females. One of the more convenient bodies
of such information is that relating to various types of movement in the United
States between 1965 and 1970. The general pattern is for the proportion of males
to rise and that of females to decline progressively as the distance covered increases. The short-distance moves from one house to another within the same
county during these five years involved only 92 males for each 100 females, but
the migration from one county to another within the same state produced a
somewhat higher index of 96. Interstate migration generally involves larger numbers of males than females, but in this case too the distances involved are crucial in shaping the sex composition. Thus, the sex ratio for the population migrat-

ing from one state to a contiguous state was 99, but the index for the group migrating between noncontiguous states was 111. The movement from one major region to another also involves larger numbers of males than females, producing a sex ratio of 111 for the total inter-regional migration. The greatest preponderance of males appears in the migration to the West from the Northeast and from the South, in the movement to the South from the three other regions, and in that to the North Central region from the Northeast. Finally, the population which migrated the longest distance — from abroad — had the very high sex ratio of 120. These facts are strictly in accord with the principle that males greatly predominate among those who migrate long distances.

An interesting exception to this rule, however, is encountered in the study of migration to the city of Rio de Janeiro from other parts of Brazil. For some time, there has been a very heavy influx of migrants from nearby states, among whom females greatly outnumbered males, and another one from the northeastern states, thousands of miles away, in which males were much more numerous than females. As a matter of fact, in the extremely heavy movement of people to the former national capital from the state of Paraíba the newcomers included almost three times as many males as females. All of this was strictly in line with expectations. But in the migrations from the most distant parts of Brazil, such as those from the territory of Acre, and the states of Amazonas, Pará, Mato Grosso, and Maranhão, the sex ratios were very low, with the actual indexes ranging from 55 males per 100 females for Amazonas to a comparable figure of 75 for Maranhão. These are even lower than the sex ratios among the migrants from the nearby states of Rio de Janeiro and Minas Gerais, which were 78 and 76, respectively. To explain this departure from the rule it is hypothesized that the employees of the federal government who are sent to the outermost parts of Brazil as civil servants consist largely of young, unmarried men. In their distant ports many of them marry local girls and start their families. When opportunity permits, they return to the nation's former capital with their brides. When state-of-birth and state-of-residence data alone are available for use in estimating internal migration, the men involved do not figure as migrants but their wives do.[26]

Education

Since 1960 a considerable amount of effort has been devoted to studies of the relationships between migration and educational status. Two principal areas of interest in many of these investigations are as follows: (1) the differences, if any, between poorly educated and well educated persons in rates, directions, and distances of migration; and (2) the effects, if any, which selectivity has upon the educational levels of the populations at the points of origin and destination of the migrants.

Insofar as the levels of education of the migrants themselves are concerned, the general tendency has been for the better educated to have higher rates of migration than the poorly educated, at least over comparatively long distances. For example, Folger and Nam found that "persons with higher levels of education are more migratory than persons with lower levels of education, and the difference in migration rates between poorly educated and well educated persons increases for longer distance moves."[27] The data for the migration that occurred in the United States between 1965 and 1970 support their conclusions. During this five-year period college-educated people made up about 11 per cent of the nation's population aged twenty-five and over, but they accounted for 25 per cent of the group which migrated between noncontiguous states. Much the same situation appeared in each of the age ranges within the span from twenty-five to sixty-five and over, and there was about as much tendency for this particular type of interstate migration to be selective of the best educated among the elderly as among the young adults. On the other hand, those who had completed eight or fewer years of schooling were 28 per cent of the population aged twenty-five and over but only 12 per cent of the group which migrated. Similar differences occurred in each of the specific age ranges. Furthermore, those who had completed four years of high school but did not enter college were overrepresented in the migration between noncontiguous states, whereas those who ranked lower in educational attainment were underrepresented. It appears that these same general patterns exist in the bulk of rural-to-urban migration, but the census data that are necessary to demonstrate this conclusively and directly are not yet available.[28]

The migration just described involves relatively long distances. When short distances are involved, as in moves from one house to another in the same county, if one provides the necessary cross-classifications for age, the situation is the reverse of that which prevails in long-distance migration, although the extent of the variation is not as great. That is, in short-distance movement the most poorly educated are somewhat overrepresented and the best educated are somewhat underrepresented. For example, among persons who moved from house to house in the same county between 1965 and 1970, 9.2 per cent of those aged twenty-five to twenty-nine had attained eight grades or less of schooling as compared with 8.9 per cent for the national population in those ages. For the group aged sixty-five and over, 59.6 per cent of those who moved and 57.4 per cent of the nation's total elderly population had completed eight grades or less. The same patterns exist in all other age groups from thirty to sixty-four. On the other hand, at every age among these short-distance movers, the proportion of college graduates was below the national averages in the comparable ages. For instance, among persons aged twenty-five to twenty-nine, 10.6 per cent of the intracounty movers but 16.1 per cent of the national population were college graduates. Similar variations of somewhat lesser magnitude exist in the other age groups, including that sixty-five and over, in which 4.6 per cent of the movers and 5.5 per cent of the national population had graduated from college. In general, then, long-distance migration tends to attract disproportionately large numbers of the well educated and comparatively small numbers of the poorly educated; short-distance movement seems to be somewhat deficient in members of the former group and to have somewhat more than its fair share of the latter. But even so, it is difficult to identify any universal pattern of selectivity by level of education.

Regarding possible changes in the educational status of populations at the points of origin and destination of migrants, the existing evidence suggests that significant changes in either place are the exception rather than the rule. Folger and Nam, summarizing the findings of several studies, conclude that "the effects of interregional migration on the educational attainment of the resident population are small."[29] Even when exceptions do appear, generally among relatively small populations which have lost or received comparatively large numbers of migrants, they tend to be small when compared with the rise that has occurred in the educational status of people throughout the country.[30] In part, the fact that many currents of migration are largely offset by countercurrents tends to reduce the differentials in educational status which would develop if some areas only received migrants and others only contributed them.

Occupation

Persons in some occupations are substantially more likely to migrate than those in others. In general, workers in the occupations that provide the highest status are much more heavily represented in long-distance migration in the United States than are those whose occupations place them lower in the status hierarchy. In this sense, the parallel between educational and occupational selectivity of migration is a close one. Table 62 has been prepared to show the patterns of occupational selectivity in the migration that took place in the United States between 1965 and 1970, but in order to reduce the variations that might be the result of differences in age and sex, the data are given separately for employed males and females aged twenty-five to forty-four, inclusive. Moreover, index numbers are employed to show the degree to which the workers in specified occupations are overrepresented or underrepresented in the various types of movement. The percentage of all employed workers of each sex aged twenty-five through forty-four who fell in each of the occupations is used as the base. For example, sales workers made up 6.7 per cent of the total male work force aged twenty-five through forty-four, but they were 9.0 per cent of the group who had migrated between contiguous states sometime during the 1965 - 1970 period. Therefore, the proportion of sales workers in the male work force is expressed as an index of 100 and the proportion of sales workers in the migration to contiguous states, being 134 per cent of the proportion in the entire group, is expressed as an index of

TABLE 62

Index numbers showing the extent to which employed persons aged 25-44
in eleven major occupational groups were represented in various
types of migration between 1965 and 1970, by sex

Occupational group	Same house (non-mover)	Moved, same county	Migrated, different county same state	Migrated to contiguous state	Migrated to noncontiguous state
Males					
Professional, technical, and kindred workers	76	85	138	165	187
Managers and administrators, except farm	97	91	121	139	124
Sales workers	91	100	119	134	119
Clerical and kindred workers	104	100	94	84	93
Craftsmen, foremen, and kindred workers	110	103	88	75	73
Operatives, except transport	104	113	77	70	67
Transport equipment operatives	106	116	84	69	56
Laborers, except farm	104	114	73	65	61
Farmers and farm managers	175	65	50	35	20
Farm laborers and foremen	104	102	103	79	58
Service workers	102	107	83	57	69
Females					
Professional, technical, and kindred workers	83	89	148	167	172
Managers and administrators, except farm	102	97	109	114	106
Sales workers	112	87	88	94	99
Clerical and kindred workers	103	101	100	96	95
Craftsmen, foremen, and kindred workers	108	104	83	73	67
Operatives, except transport	106	110	73	62	54
Transport operatives	125	87	83	59	56
Laborers, except farm	106	106	77	77	68
Farmers and farm managers	150	55	50	50	35
Farm laborers and foremen	119	89	77	62	62
Service workers	101	107	80	75	81

Source: Compiled and computed from data in U.S. Bureau of the Census, *U.S. Census of
Population: 1970, Subject Reports,* Final Report PC(2)-2B, *Mobility for States and the
Nation* (1973), pp. 26-37, Table 6.

134. The various mobility categories are the following: residence in the same house in 1965 and 1970, movement within the same county, migration to a different county in the same state, migration to a contiguous state, and migration to a noncontiguous state.

These data show that the interstate migration of men aged twenty-five through forty-four, whether to contiguous or noncontiguous states, is most heavily selective of professional, technical, and kindred workers, followed by managers and administrators, and sales workers. Men in all of the other occupations appear with less frequency in interstate migration than they do in the total male work force aged twenty-five through forty-four. In fact, except for farm laborers and foremen, all of these other groups are underrepresented even in the comparatively short distance involved in migrating from one county to another in the same state. The professional, managerial, and sales workers, of course, are also heavily overrepresented in that flow. On the other hand, comparatively small percentages of professional workers and managers are found in the movement from one house to another in the same county and they are less likely than all of the other occupational groups to have remained in the same house during the five-year period. Transport operatives are the most likely to be part of intracounty movement, followed by nonfarm laborers, other operatives, service workers, craftsmen and foremen, and farm laborers and farm foremen. As might be expected, farmers and farm managers are relatively scarce in any kind of migration, whether over short or long distances, and they are far more likely than any other occupational group to have remained in the same house during the period under consideration. All of these patterns of migration are about the same for the other age groups of male workers except, of course, that the rate of migration in any occupational group tends to diminish with increasing age.

The patterns of migration of female workers in the various occupations are not greatly different than those of the males. Women employed in professional and technical positions are heavily overrepresented in the migration between counties in the same state and in both types of interstate migration; managers and administrators are overrepresented in these three forms of migration, but to a lesser degree than the professional workers. Those in all other occupational groups are substantially underrepresented in interstate migration and except for clerical workers who are equitably represented, they are comparatively scarce in the movement between counties in the same state as well. On the other hand, movement from house to house within the same county involves a larger-than-average share of female operatives in fields other than transportation, service workers, nonfarm laborers, craftsmen and foremen, and clerical workers. Farmers and farm managers are the least likely to move at all, followed by transport operatives, farm laborers, sales workers, craftsmen and foremen, and other operatives. As is the case with men, the propensity of women to migrate relatively long distances decreases as the status of their various occupational categories decreases. As is also the case with men, the relationship between job status and short-distance migration is not clear-cut, although for both sexes there is a relatively large amount of shifting about within a specific county on the part of those whose jobs place them in an intermediate position on the scale of occupational status. Craftsmen and foremen and industrial operatives are especially likely to be involved in this type of movement. Yet there is also considerable intracounty movement on the part of male laborers and service workers of both sexes, all of whom tend to fall near the bottom of the status system associated with occupation.[31]

1. Kingsley Davis, *The Population of India and Pakistan* (Princeton, N. J.: Princeton University Press, 1951), pp. 108 - 109.

2. Nathan L. Whetten and Robert G. Burnight, "Internal Migration in Mexico," *Rural Sociology,* 21, 2 (1956), pp. 141 - 151.

3. T. Lynn Smith, *Brazil: People and Institutions* (4th ed.) (Baton Rouge: Louisiana State University Press, 1972), pp. 145 - 157. See also T. Lynn Smith, "Rural-Urban Migration In Brazil," *Sociologia Internationalis,* 10, 2 (1972), pp. 243 - 249.

4. For the data, see U. S. Bureau of the Census, *U.S. Census of Population: 1970, General Social and Economic Characteristics,* Final Report PC(1)-C1, *United States Summary* (Washington: Government Printing Office, 1973), p. 472, Table 143.

5. For more details on this subject, see T. Lynn Smith, "The Migration of the Aged," in *Growing with the Years,* A Report of the New York State Joint Legislative Committee on Problems of the Aging (Albany: Legislative Document No. 32, 1954), pp. 69 - 80; T. Lynn Smith and Douglas G. Marshall, *Our Aging Population: The United States and Wisconsin,* Wisconsin's Population Series No. 5 (Madison: University of Wisconsin, 1963), pp. 31 - 37; Homer L. Hitt, "The Role of Migration in Population Change Among the Aged," *American Sociological Review,* 19, 2 (April, 1954), pp. 194 - 200; and Jacob S. Siegel and William E. O'Leary, "Some Demographic Aspects of Aging in the United States," *Current Population Reports,* Series P-23, No. 43 (February, 1973), pp. 9 - 14.

6. Many excellent studies have been made of the excessive amount of shifting from farm to farm that goes on in the plantation districts of the southern part of the United States. Some of the best early work on this subject is that by Alfred H. Stone, "Plantation Experiment," *Quarterly Journal of Economics,* XIX (February, 1905), pp. 271 - 275. Later contributions in the long list that might be compiled are Rupert B. Vance, *Human Factors in Cotton Culture* (Chapel Hill: University of North Carolina Press, 1929), pp. 134 - 135, 151 - 154, *passim;* Charles S. Johnson, *Shadow of the Plantation* (Chicago: University of Chicago Press, 1934), pp. 25 - 27; B. O. Williams, "Mobility," in *Landlord and Tenant on the Cotton Plantation,* by T. J. Woofter, Jr., and associates. Research Monograph V (Washington: Works Progress Administration, 1936), chapter VIII; Max R. White, Douglas Ensminger, and Cecil Gregory, *Rich Land–Poor People,* Research Report 1 (Indianapolis: Farm Security Administration, 1938), p. 4, *passim;* Homer L. Hitt, *Recent Migration into and within the Upper Mississippi Delta of Louisiana,* Louisiana Agricultural Experiment Station Bulletin No. 364 (Baton Rouge: Louisiana Agricultural Experiment Station, 1943);

Paul E. Zopf, Jr., *North Carolina: A Demographic Profile* (Chapel Hill: University of North Carolina Population Center, 1967), pp. 384 - 389; and T. Lynn Smith and Paul E. Zopf, Jr., *Principles of Inductive Rural Sociology* (Philadelphia: F. A. Davis Co., 1970), pp. 92 - 94).

7. "Migratory Farm Labor in the United States," *Monthly Labor Review*, 44, 3 (1937), pp. 537 - 549.

8. *Migratory Labor in American Agriculture* (Washington: Government Printing Office, 1951), p. 1.

9. *Ibid.*

10. *The Hired Farm Working Force of 1970*, ERS 201 (Washington: Government Printing Office, 1971), p. 10.

11. *The Hired Farm Working Force of 1972*, ERS 239 (Washington: Government Printing Office, 1973), p. 1.

12. *Rural People in the American Economy* (Washington: Government Printing Office, 1966), pp. 50 - 51. See also Office of Economic Opportunity, *The Quiet Revolution* (Washington: Government Printing Office, 1967), pp. 52 - 55; and President's National Advisory Commission on Rural Poverty, *The People Left Behind* (Washington: Government Printing Office, 1967).

13. On this point, see Everett M. Rogers and Rabel J. Burdge, *Social Change In Rural Societies* (2nd ed.) (New York: Appleton-Century-Crofts, 1972), pp. 381 - 382.

14. U.S. Bureau of the Census and Economic Research Service, "Farm Population of the United States: 1972," *Current Population Reports*, P-27, No. 44 (June, 1973), p. 3, Table C; p. 9, Table 5.

15. Edward Alsworth Ross, *The Outlines of Sociology* (New York: Century Company, 1924), pp. 23 - 24. Reprinted by permission.

16. For a discussion of the matter, see Calvin L. Beale, "Rural-Urban Migration of Blacks: Past and Future," *American Journal of Agricultural Economics*, 53, 2 (May, 1971), pp. 302 - 307.

17. For the data, see U.S. Bureau of the Census, *U.S. Census of Population: 1970, Subject Reports,* Final Report PC(2)-2B, *Mobility for States and the Nation* (Washington: Government Printing Office, 1973), pp. 5 - 11, Table 2.

18. Hornell N. Hart, *Selective Migration,* University of Iowa Studies No. 53 (Iowa City: University of Iowa, 1921), p. 32, *passim.*

19. Pitirim A. Sorokin and Carle C. Zimmerman, *Principles of Rural-Urban Sociology* (New York; Henry Holt and Company, 1929), pp. 540 - 544.

20. Dorothy S. Thomas, *Research Memorandum on Migration Differentials* (New York: Social Science Research Council, 1938), pp. 11 - 54; and Dorothy S. Thomas, "Age and Economic Differentials in Interstate Migration," *Population Index,* 24, 4 (October, 1958), p. 324.

21. C. A. McMahan, "Selectivity of Rural-to-Urban Migration," in *The Sociology of Urban Life,* edited by T. Lynn Smith and C. A. McMahan (New York: The Dryden Press, 1951), pp. 334 - 340. See also Henry S. Shryock, Jr., *Population Mobility within the United States* (Chicago: Community and Family Study Center, University of Chicago, 1964), pp. 384 and 346 - 402; Zopf, *op. cit.,* pp. 369 - 373; and Smith and Zopf, p. 97.

22. Conrad Taeuber, "American Immigration and Population Growth," *International Migration Review,* 6, 17 (Spring, 1972), p. 8.

23. See Richard Irwin, "Changing Patterns of American Immigration," *International Migration Review,* 6, 17 (Spring, 1972), p. 22.

24. *Ibid.,* p. 23.

25. See Kingsley Davis, *op. cit.,* pp. 139 - 141.

26. See Smith, *Brazil, op. cit.,* pp. 145 - 150.

27. John K. Folger and Charles B. Nam, *Education of the American Population,* A 1960 Census Monograph (Washington: Government Printing Office, 1967), p. 210.

28. See, however, the following excellent studies on the subject: C. Horace Hamilton, "Educational Selectivity of Rural-Urban Migration: Preliminary Results of a North Carolina Study," *Proceedings of the Annual Milbank Memorial Fund Conference,* Part III (New York: Milbank Memorial Fund, 1958), pp. 110 - 122; C. Horace Hamilton, "Educational Selectivity of Migration from Farms to Urban and Other Nonfarm Communities," in *Mobility and Mental Health,* edited by Mildred B. Kantor (New York: Charles C. Thomas, 1965); Irene B. Taeuber and Conrad Taeuber, *People of the United States in the 20th Century,* A 1960 Census Monograph (Washington: Government Printing Office, 1971), pp. 932 - 938; and Thomas, *Research Memorandum, op. cit.,* p. 111 and *passim.*

29. Folger and Nam, *op. cit.,* p. 185.

30. *Ibid.,* p. 186.

31. The process of collecting the data on which the observations made about migration are based involves asking the respondent to recall his place of residence in 1965. This should be a simple and accurate procedure but any materials in which one element is based upon recall and another upon observations of a current situation made by the census taker are open to error.

FOLGER, JOHN K., and CHARLES B. NAM. *Education of the American Population* (A 1960 Census Monograph), pp. 178 - 186. Washington: Government Printing Office, 1967.

FRIEDLAND, WILLIAM H., and DOROTHY NELKIN. *Migrant Agricultural Workers in America's Northeast.* New York: Holt, Rinehart and Winston, 1971.

HAMILTON, C. HORACE. "Educational Selectivity of Migration from Farms to Urban and to Other Nonfarm Communities," in *Mobility and Mental Health,* edited by Mildred B. Kantor. New York: Charles C. Thomas, 1965.

HAMILTON, C. HORACE. "Educational Selectivity of Rural-Urban Migration: Preliminary Results of a North Carolina Study." *Proceedings of the Annual Milbank Memorial Fund Conference,* Part III, pp. 110 - 122. New York: Milbank Memorial Fund, 1958.

HITT, HOMER L. "Migration between the South and Other Regions, 1949 to 1950." *Social Forces,* Vol. 36, No. 1 (October, 1957), pp. 9 - 16.

LESLIE, GERALD R., and ARTHUR H. RICHARDSON. "Life-Cycle, Career Pattern, and the Decision to Move," in *Population and Society,* edited by Charles B. Nam, pp. 349 - 358. Boston: Houghton Mifflin Company, 1968.

McMAHAN, C. A. "Selectivity of Rural-to-Urban Migration," in *The Sociology of Urban Life,* edited by T. Lynn Smith and C. A. McMahan, pp. 334 - 340. New York: The Dryden Press, 1951.

PRESIDENT'S NATIONAL ADVISORY COMMISSION ON RURAL POVERTY. *The People Left Behind.* Washington: Government Printing Office, 1967.

RAMSEY, CHARLES E., and WALFRED A. ANDERSON. *Migration of the New York State Population* (Cornell AES Bulletin No. 929). Ithaca: Cornell University, 1958.

RAVENSTEIN, E. G. "The Laws of Migration." *Journal of the Royal Statistical Society,* Vol. 48, Part 2 (June, 1885), pp. 167 - 227.

SHRYOCK, HENRY S., JR. *Population Mobility Within the United States,* Chaps. 11 - 13. Chicago: Community and Family Study Center, University of Chicago, 1964.

SHRYOCK, HENRY S., JR. and CHARLES B. NAM. "Educational Selectivity of Interregional Migration." *Social Forces,* Vol. 43, No. 3 (March, 1965), pp. 299 - 310.

SMITH, T. LYNN. *Brazil: People and Institutions,* 4th ed., Chap. IX. Baton Rouge: Louisiana State University Press, 1972.

SMITH, T. LYNN. "The Migration of the Aged," in *Problems of America's Aging Population,* edited by T. Lynn Smith, pp. 15 - 28. Gainesville: University of Florida Press, 1951.

SOROKIN, PITIRIM A., and CARLE C. ZIMMERMAN. *Principles of Rural-Urban Sociology*, Chaps. XXIII - XXVI. New York: Henry Holt & Company, 1929.

TAEUBER, KARL E., LEONARD CHIAZZE, JR., and WILLIAM HAENSZEL. *Migration in the United States, An Analysis of Residence Histories.* Washington: Government Printing Office, 1968.

TARVER, JAMES D. "Interstate Migration Differentials." *American Sociological Review,* Vol. 27, No. 3 (June, 1963), pp. 448 - 451.

U.S. DEPARTMENT OF AGRICULTURE, ECONOMIC RESEARCH SERVICE. *Rural People in the American Economy,* pp. 49 - 53. Washington: Government Printing Office, 1966.

U.S. SENATE, COMMITTEE ON LABOR AND PUBLIC WELFARE, SUBCOMMITTEE ON MIGRATORY LABOR. "The Migratory Farm Labor Problem in the United States." *Report No. 934, 88th Congress,* Vol. X. Washington: Government Printing Office, 1964.

PART SIX

Growth of Population

THE GROWTH OF POPULATION

Growth of population[1] is the second most important subject in the entire realm of demography. From the standpoints of general interest, theoretical significance, and utility or application, matters having to do with the number and distribution of the inhabitants are the only ones that may be thought of as more important than those which constitute the subject of population growth. In this volume, the treatment of this subject has been postponed until the three primary factors that may be involved (fertility, mortality, and migration) in the changing number of the inhabitants have all been examined.

The study of the growth of population falls naturally into two parts: an analysis and description of changes that already have occurred and the attempt to project or forecast what the population of a given area or territory will be at stated dates in the future. In our present state of knowledge, no very high degree of dependability may be placed upon efforts made in connection with the second of these; and the longer the period for which the forecasts or projections are made, the greater will be the unreliability of the estimates. Even for short periods in the future, unless one can foretell with a high degree of accuracy the numbers of births that will take place in ensuing years, the projections or predictions quickly get out of line with reality. If, on the other hand, the experts making the projections merely supply the reader with various sets of computations based upon different assumptions with respect to the future course of births (or deaths and migrations as well), the results are of still more dubious value. Such a procedure merely transfers the responsibility for making the most reasonable inferences on the subject from the ones who have at their disposal all of the available facts and who supposedly have studied thoroughly all aspects of the problem to those who do not have access to many of the data and who may have given little or no previous attention to the problems involved. If those engaged professionally in such studies are unable to judge the respective probabilities of the various alternatives, what reason is there to suppose that the ordinary reader will be able to do so?

There likewise are two basic approaches used in studies of population growth. One of these attempts to take into account the absolute and relative importance of the three factors that may be involved and to base all conclusions upon a knowledge of births, deaths, and migrations. The other would explain and predict variations in the numbers of people on the earth or any of its respective parts in terms of the workings of some inexorable mathematical law. Most of the so-called mathematical "laws" of population growth appear to be merely excellent illustrations of jumping to a conclusion that something actually occurred in a given way simply because it might have happened in that manner, or of reasoning out a possible connection between two phenomena and then gradually coming to the stage of asserting that they are in fact related. Approaches of the latter kind are afforded no space in this volume.

WORLD POPULATION GROWTH

As was indicated in Chapter 3, even in the 1970's the total population of the earth is not known with any degree of precision. Nevertheless, current knowledge on the populations of various sections of the world is vastly superior to that available a hundred years ago. This means, however, that statements about the absolute and relative increases in world population, even those pertaining to happenings during the last century, or indeed changes during the twentieth century, are in considerable part mere conjecture. For earlier periods there is no likelihood that any fairly accurate knowledge ever will be attained.

If one wishes to consider world population trends during the eighteenth and nineteenth centuries (and there is little scientific basis for any earlier estimates), the materials assembled by the French *Ministère du travail et de la prévoyance social* probably are as satisfactory as any. This authority arrived at the figure of 750 million as the number of inhabitants of the earth in 1761 and of 1.15 billion as that in 1861. The estimated increase in the population of the various continents during this hundred-year period are as follows: Africa, from 80 to 100 million; America, from 20 to 70 million; Asia (including Oceania), from 520 to 700 million; and Europe from 130 to 280 million.[2]

In order to set forth the more significant facts on this subject as simply and concisely as possible, Figure 64 is presented. Plotting population (the dependent variable) on a logarithmic scale, as is done in this illustration, has two advantages: (1) it enables one to keep the diagram within reasonable dimensions; and (2) since any variable that is increasing at a constant rate results in a straight line when it is plotted on a semi-logarithmic basis, it permits one to tell at a glance from a diagram such as this whether the rate of increase is holding its own, falling off, or increasing. The comparison of trends in the various continents is particularly facilitated by the use of this device. The student is again warned, however, against placing any considerable degree of confidence in the data for the eighteenth and nineteenth centuries which were used in the preparation of this chart.

Only a few comments are called for in discussing the trends portrayed in Figure 64. The phenomenal growth of population on the North American continent is the most striking feature of demographic history in the course of the last 220 years. Since 1900 the South American continent also has commanded attention by the rapidity with which its inhabitants have been multi-

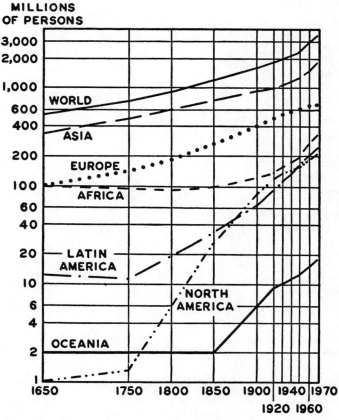

FIGURE 64. Population growth in the major world divisions, 1650 to 1970.

TABLE 63
Estimates of the annual growth of population in major world
regions, 1963 to 1971

Region	Population at mid-year 1971 (millions)	Annual growth 1963-1971	
		Millions	Rate
World	3,706	68.5	2.0
Africa	354	8.1	2.6
Western Africa	104	2.4	2.5
Eastern Africa	100	2.2	2.5
Northern Africa	89	2.2	3.0
Middle Africa	37	0.8	2.1
Southern Africa	23	0.5	2.3
America	522	10.1	2.1
Northern America	230	2.8	1.3
Latin America	291	7.3	2.9
Tropical South America	155	4.1	3.0
Middle America	70	2.1	3.4
Temperate South America	40	0.6	1.8
Caribbean	26	0.5	2.3
Asia	2,104	43.8	2.3
East Asia	946	15.5	1.8
Mainland region	779	13.0	1.8
Japan	105	1.1	1.1
Other	63	1.5	2.6
South Asia	1,158	28.3	2.8
Middle South Asia	783	18.9	2.7
South East Asia	295	7.4	2.8
South West Asia	79	2.0	2.9
Europe	466	3.6	0.8
Western Europe	150	1.2	0.8
Southern Europe	130	1.2	0.9
Eastern Europe	105	0.8	0.8
Northern Europe	81	0.4	0.6
Oceania	20	0.4	2.1
Australia and New Zealand	16	0.3	1.9
Melanesia	3	0.1	2.4
Polynesia and Micronesia	1	a	3.2
U.S.S.R.	245	2.5	1.1

Source: Compiled and computed from data in United Nations, Demographic Yearbook,
1971 (New York: United Nations, 1972), p. 111, Table 1.
aLess than 0.1 million.

plying, and, indeed, the twentieth century is one in which the rate of population growth in that continent is unmatched by that of any other major portion of the world. The populations of Asia and Europe continue to increase, thus adding each year many millions of additional people to the earth's total, even though the rate of increase in Europe is comparatively low. In Oceania, on the other hand, the rates are high, but the absolute numbers involved are not large. If the curve for Africa is starting to rise to parallel the trends on the other continents, as the data in Table 63 seem to indicate actually is happening, another very potent factor is being added to those currently producing a rapid upsurge in world population.

The most reliable information on world population trends in the last third of the twentieth century is contained in Table 63. Not until about 1976, when the bulk of the data from censuses taken becomes available, will it be possible for another somewhat reliable assessment of the situation to be made. The student of population should bear in mind that by 1971 the earth's inhabitants already numbered over 3.7 billions, that each succeeding year has added about 69 million persons to this total, and that at the end of the year there are approximately 1,020 persons alive for each thousand in existence at its beginning. Other interesting and significant details of current world population trends, on the absolute basis, are as follows: (1) well over one-half of the annual increase in world population is taking place in Asia, most of it in south Asia, whose "teeming millions" already have produced the greatest overcrowding the earth has ever seen; (2) all of Europe, the Soviet Union omitted, is adding each year to the world total only slightly more persons than are the United States and Canada together, and somewhat less than are the nations of South America; and (3) the annual increase of population in the United States and Canada is only slightly larger than that in the U.S.S.R.

The rate of population growth is most rapid in the various Latin American countries, or in Middle America and tropical South America in terms of great world regions, followed by South Asia, Africa, and Oceania. It is lowest in Northern Europe, where the index is less than one-third as high as that for the world as a whole, followed most closely by the rates for Western Europe, Eastern Europe, and Southern Europe. Interestingly enough, the index for the Soviet Union and that for the United States are the same, and both of them are little more than half that for the members of the human race collectively. Noteworthy also is the fact that the rate of growth in temperate South America is slightly over half that in Middle America and about three-fifths that in tropical South America.

THE GROWTH OF POPULATION IN SELECTED COUNTRIES

The practice of taking a census of population at regular intervals has been so limited, and the changes in national boundaries so frequent and extensive, that it is difficult to obtain successive accurate counts of population for various nations. These are essential to study the growth of population in the different important sections of the earth's surface. Therefore, any extensive and exact comparative analysis of the growth of population throughout the countries of the world is impossible. Nevertheless, for a considerable number of selected countries some data that are of value may be presented. (See Table 64.) In choosing the materials to be presented in this form, first consideration was given to making the coverage of nations or territories having a million or more inhabitants as complete as possible for a recent intercensal period. Therefore, a considerable number of countries is included, even though comparable materials for the early portion of the twentieth century are lacking. Wherever possible, however, the table contains the annual rate of increase for an intercensal period early in the present century as well as the most recent one near or after its middle.

It is interesting to note that on the basis of the census counts on which these rates are based (and it should be emphasized that all estimates have been excluded), Kuwait is the nation with the highest rate of population growth in the world.[3] Between 1965 and 1970 the number of inhabitants in that world-famous producer of petroleum increased at the rate of almost 12 per cent per annum. It was most closely rivaled in this respect by Nigeria, for which the rate established by the comparison of censuses of population taken in 1953 and 1963 was 5.7 per cent per year. Venezuela was in third position with a rate of 4.2; Costa Rica and El Salvador were tied for fourth place with an index of 4.1. Uganda, in which the rate of population growth was 3.9 per cent per year during the latest intercensal period, was in fifth position; the Libyan Arab Republic and Southern Rhodesia (Africans only), whose populations grew by 3.7 per cent between the two most recent censuses, were tied for sixth place; and Mexico and the Philippines (index 3.5) were matched for the seventh place. Growth rates of 3.4 per cent per year occured in Kenya, South Africa, Togo, Peru, Sabah, and Taiwan. Indexes of 3.3 were registered in Malawi and the Syrian Arab Republic. Twelve other countries have experienced recent increases in population that were 3.0 per cent or more per year. They are Colombia and Albania with 3.2 per cent; Tanganyika, Guatemala, Nicaragua, Iran, and Iraq with 3.1 per cent; and the Dominican Republic, Honduras, Panama, Ecuador, and Mongolia with 3.0 per cent.

There are two countries listed in Table 64 in which population decreased during the most recent intercensal period, although the falling off in the number of inhabitants was not large in either case. The population of Portugal declined by 221,125 persons between 1960 and 1970 and that of West Berlin decreased by 26,369 persons between 1956 and 1961. In addition, long-term population decreases were halted in two countries in the latest intercensal periods. In the Democratic Republic of Germany, the population declined by almost 1.3 million people between 1950 and 1964, largely as a result of migration to the Federal

TABLE 64

Rates of population growth in selected countries during intercensal periods early in and about the last third of
the twentieth century

Country	Intercensal period	Annual rate of growth	Intercensal period	Annual rate of growth
Africa				
Algeria	1901-1906	2.0	1960-1966	1.7
Angola	....	....	1960-1970	1.7
Egypt	1907-1917	1.3	1960-1966	2.5
Ghana	....	....	1960-1970	2.4
Kenya	....	....	1962-1969	3.4
Libyan Arab Republic	....	....	1954-1964	3.7
Malawi	....	....	1945-1966	3.3
Morocco	....	....	1960-1971	2.9
Mozambique	....	....	1960-1970	2.5
Nigeria	....	....	1953-1963	5.7
South Africa	1904-1911	2.1	1960-1970	3.4
Southern Rhodesia	....	....	1962-1969	3.7[a]
Togo	....	....	1960-1970	3.4
Tunisia	1911-1921	0.8	1956-1966	1.8
Uganda	....	....	1959-1969	3.9
United Republic of Tanzania				
Tanganyika	....	....	1957-1967	3.1
Zanzibar	....	....	1958-1967	1.8
Zambia	....	....	1963-1969	2.6[a]
America, North				
Canada	1901-1911	2.9	1966-1971	2.1
Costa Rica	1892-1927	1.9	1950-1963	4.1
Cuba	1907-1919	2.9	1953-1970	2.2
Dominican Republic	....	....	1960-1970	3.0
El Salvador	....	....	1961-1971	4.1
Guatemala	1893-1921	1.4	1950-1964	3.1
Honduras	1905-1910	2.1	1950-1961	3.0
Jamaica	1891-1911	1.3	1960-1970	1.5
Mexico	1900-1910	1.1	1960-1970	3.5
Nicaragua	1906-1920	1.7	1963-1971	3.1
Panama	1911-1920	3.2	1960-1970	3.0
Puerto Rico	1899-1910	1.5	1960-1970	1.4
Trinidad and Tobago	1901-1911	2.0	1960-1970	1.3
United States	1900-1910	2.0	1960-1970	1.3
America, South				
Argentina	1895-1914	3.7	1960-1970	1.5
Brazil	1890-1900	1.9	1960-1970	2.8
Chile	1907-1920	1.1	1960-1970	1.9
Colombia	1905-1912	2.2	1951-1964	3.2

TABLE 64 (Cont'd)

Rates of population growth in selected countries during intercensal periods early in and about the last third of
the twentieth century

Country	Intercensal period	Annual rate of growth	Intercensal period	Annual rate of growth
Ecuador	....	....	1950-1962	3.0
Guyana	1891-1911	0.6	1960-1970	2.5
Paraguay	....	....	1950-1962	2.6
Peru	1876-1940	1.3	1961-1972	3.4
Uruguay	1900-1908	1.5	1908-1963	1.8
Venezuela	1920-1926	3.4	1961-1971	4.2
Asia				
Ceylon	1901-1911	1.8	1953-1963	2.6
Cyprus	1901-1911	1.5	1956-1960	2.0
Hong Kong	1901-1911	1.6	1961-1971	2.6
India	1901-1911	0.6	1961-1971	2.6
Indonesia	....	....	1961-1971	2.3
Iran	....	....	1956-1966	3.1
Iraq	....	....	1957-1965	3.1
Israel	1922-1931	8.4	1961-1972	4.3
Japan	1920-1925	1.3	1965-1970	1.1
Jordan	....	....	1952-1961	2.7
Korea, Republic of	....	....	1966-1970	1.9
Kuwait	....	....	1965-1970	11.6
Malaysia				
East				
Sabah	1921-1931	0.5	1951-1960	3.4
Sarawak	....	....	1947-1960	2.5
West	1901-1911	3.5	1947-1957	2.5
Mongolia	....	....	1963-1969	3.0
Nepal	....	....	1961-1971	2.0
Pakistan	1901-1911	0.8	1951-1961	2.1
Philippines	1903-1918	1.9	1960-1970	3.5
Ryukyu Islands	1920-1925	−0.5	1960-1965	1.1
Singapore	1901-1911	3.3	1957-1970	2.8
Syrian Arab Republic	....	....	1960-1970	3.3
Taiwan	1920-1925	1.8	1956-1966	3.4
Thailand	1911-1919	1.4	1960-1970	2.7
Turkey	1927-1935	2.1	1965-1970	2.7
Europe				
Albania	1923-1930	3.2	1955-1960	3.2
Austria	1900-1910	1.0	1961-1971	0.6
Belgium	1900-1910	1.0	1961-1970	0.6
Bulgaria	1900-1905	1.5	1956-1965	0.9
Czechoslovakia	1900-1910	0.7	1961-1970	0.5

TABLE 64 (Cont'd)
Rates of population growth in selected countries during intercensal periods early in and about the last third of
the twentieth century

Country	Intercensal period	Annual rate of growth	Intercensal period	Annual rate of growth
Denmark	1901-1906	1.1	1965-1970	0.7
Finland	1900-1910	1.0	1960-1970	0.4
France	1901-1906	0.2	1962-1968	1.1
Germany	1900-1910	1.4	....	....
Democratic Republic	....	....	1964-1971	b
Federal Republic	....	....	1961-1970	1.2
East Berlin	....	....	1964-1971	0.2
West Berlin	....	....	1956-1961	−0.3
Greece	1920-1928	1.6	1961-1971	0.4
Hungary	1900-1910	1.1	1960-1970	0.4
Ireland	1901-1911	−0.3	1966-1971	0.3
Italy	1901-1911	0.9	1961-1971	0.6
Netherlands	1899-1909	1.4	1947-1960	1.4
Norway	1900-1910	0.6	1960-1970	0.8
Poland	1921-1931	1.7	1960-1970	0.9
Portugal	1900-1911	0.9	1960-1970	−0.2
Romania	1899-1912	1.4	1956-1966	0.9
Spain	1900-1910	0.8	1960-1970	1.1
Sweden	1900-1910	0.7	1965-1970	0.8
Switzerland	1900-1910	1.3	1960-1970	1.5
United Kingdom	1901-1911	1.0	1966-1971	0.6
England and Wales	1901-1911	1.0	1966-1971	0.6
Northern Ireland	1901-1911	0.1	1966-1971	0.6
Scotland	1901-1911	0.6	1966-1971	0.2
Yugoslavia	1921-1931	1.5	1961-1971	1.1
Oceania				
Australia	1901-1911	1.7	1966-1971	2.1
New Zealand	1901-1906	2.8	1966-1971	1.4
U.S.S.R.	1926-1939	1.2	1959-1970	1.3

Source: Compiled and computed from data in United Nations, Demographic Yearbook, 1955, pp. 128-150, Table 4; 1964, pp. 156-168, Table 6; 1970, pp. 408-431, Table 7; and Population and Vital Statistics Report, Series A. XXV, 3-4 (October, 1973), passim.

aAfrican population only.
bLess than 0.1 per cent.

Republic of Germany, but between 1964 and 1971, the former registered a very slight increase (26,369 persons). In Ireland, prior to 1961, the demographic situation was characterized by over a century of net losses of people by migration, resulting in substantial reductions in absolute numbers. Between 1961 and 1966, however, the population grew by over 65,000 and between 1966 and 1971 it increased by more than 94,000.

European countries also make up the entire list of the other seventeen nations whose rates of population growth at the time of the most recent census were less than 1 per cent per annum. Among the countries of Europe, Albania, France, the Federal Republic of Germany, the Netherlands, Spain, Switzerland, and Yugoslavia constitute the group in which the rate of population increase is 1 per cent per annum or higher, although with the exception of Albania, in none of them is the figure above 1.5 per cent. Outside of Europe, the only countries that had average annual rates of population increase in their latest intercensal periods that were less than 1.5 per cent are Japan and the Ryuku Islands, each with 1.1 per cent; Trinidad and Tobago, the United States, and the Soviet Union, each with 1.3 per cent; and Puerto Rico and New Zealand, each with 1.4 per cent.

Twenty-one of the twenty-five independent Latin American countries are among the nations for which data are given in Table 64. The discussion that follows, however, is limited to twenty and does not include the Bahamas, Barbados, Guyana, Jamaica, or Trinidad and Tobago because their sociocultural backgrounds and present features are not "Latin." Fourteen of the twenty that have Iberian or French backgrounds are in the group of forty-six countries in which the rate of population increase is 2.5 per cent per annum or higher. Cuba, Argentina, Chile, and Uruguay are the only ones of these Latin American countries in which the annual rate of increase is less than 2.5 per cent. Therefore, what is happening to the populations of Mexico and Central America, the republics that are located in the Caribbean, and South America is of mounting importance in world affairs. Some of the materials for them may be used to illustrate the need for more concerted efforts to get indexes that are comparable for the various parts of the earth. In this connection it is essential that the period of time involved in the comparisons be the same for each of the nations under study and that estimates as reliable as possible be used for the years and countries for which census data are lacking. The results of efforts to determine the absolute and relative increases of population in the twenty Latin American countries between 1960 and 1970 are given in Table 65, with materials for the United States and Puerto Rico included for comparative purposes.

One should note that even for this important part of the Western Hemisphere, an area in which much effort of representatives of all of the Latin American countries and the United States was expended in connection with the 1950 census of the Americas and with subsequent enumerations, it is necessary to use estimates for the majority of the countries, for although censuses were taken in

TABLE 65
Increase of population in the Latin American countries, 1960 to 1970

Country	Population 1960	Population 1970	Increase 1960-1970 Number	Increase 1960-1970 Per cent
North America	60,055,740	82,184,429	22,128,689	36.8
Costa Rica	1,171,000[a]	1,737,000[a]	566,000	48.3
Cuba	6,797,000[a]	8,553,395	1,756,395	25.8
Dominican Republic	3,047,070	4,006,405	959,335	31.5
El Salvador	2,450,000[a]	3,534,000[a]	1,084,000	44.2
Guatemala	3,765,000[a]	5,111,000[a]	1,346,000	35.8
Haiti	3,505,000[a]	4,867,000[a]	1,362,000	38.9
Honduras	1,845,000[a]	2,582,000[a]	737,000	39.9
Mexico	34,923,129	48,381,547	13,458,418	38.5
Nicaragua	1,477,000[a]	1,984,000[a]	507,000	34.3
Panama	1,075,541	1,428,082	352,541	32.8
South America	141,939,245	186,799,403	44,860,158	31.6
Argentina	20,008,945	23,362,204	3,353,259	16.8
Bolivia	3,462,000[a]	4,931,000[a]	1,469,000	42.4
Brazil	70,967,185	93,204,379	22,237,194	31.3
Chile	7,374,115	8,834,820	1,460,705	19.8
Colombia	14,132,000[a]	21,117,000[a]	6,985,000	49.4
Ecuador	4,317,000[a]	6,093,000[a]	1,776,000	41.1
Paraguay	1,768,000[a]	2,386,000[a]	618,000	35.0
Peru	10,020,000[a]	13,586,000[a]	3,566,000	35.6
Uruguay	2,540,000[a]	2,886,000[a]	346,000	13.6
Venezuela	7,350,000[a]	10,399,000[a]	3,049,000	41.5
Latin America	201,994,985	268,983,832	66,988,847	33.2
United States	179,323,175	203,210,158	23,886,983	13.3
Puerto Rico	2,349,544	2,712,033	362,489	15.4

Source: Compiled and computed from data in United Naitons, *Demographic Yearbook, 1970* (New York: United Nations, 1971), pp. 127-135, Table 4; pp. 408-431, Table 7.
[a]United Nations estimate.

1960 and 1970 in six of them, the times when the two most recent enumerations were made vary substantially in the remainder. Even so, no attempt was made to compensate for variations in census dates so that exactly the same period would be involved for all of the nations. For example, the 1970 census in Brazil was taken as of September 1, whereas that in Mexico was taken as of January 28. It is believed that the data are not sufficiently reliable to justify such refinements and that the use of the period from 1960 to 1970 provides sufficient accuracy for present purposes.

The population increase of 33.2 per cent during the decade in the twenty Latin American republics taken collectively, which represents the sum of these computations, corresponds to an annual rate of 3.2 per cent. This compares with rates of about 2.0 per cent for the world as a whole, 1.3 per cent in the Soviet Union, and 1.3 per cent in the United States.

When the twentieth century opened, there were only about 43 million inhabitants in all of Latin America. As well as can be determined, this was only about 2.7 per cent of the world total.[4] By 1970 the total had risen to approximately 269 million, or 7.8 per cent of the inhabitants of the earth. Subsequent to 1970 there have been about 8 million more Latin Americans alive at the end of a given year than there were at its beginning, and this number is likely to become somewhat greater as the years of the 1970 decade succeed one another. This is suggested by the fact that the rate of population growth in the region was greater in the 1960's than in the 1950's, when it was 31.2 per cent. Moreover, the rate was greater in the 1960's in thirteen of the twenty countries, the exceptions being Brazil, Chile, Cuba, Nicaragua, Panama, Uruguay, and Venezuela. Indeed, the increasing absolute and relative importance of Latin Americans among the members of the human race is one of the more important demographic trends underway as we move through the last quarter of the twentieth century.[5]

GROWTH OF POPULATION IN THE UNITED STATES

There were only 3,929,214 persons enumerated by the first census of the United States in 1790. For the next half century the increase was well over 30 per cent per decade, so that by 1850 the new nation with a total population of more than 23 million inhabitants (see Table 66) ranked among the more populous countries of the world. The rate of growth fell sharply during the second half of the nineteenth century, but it was rapid enough to bring the total population of the nation to almost 76 million by 1900. Thereafter, the annual rate of growth declined sharply until 1940, when the sixteenth census enumerated a total of 131,669,275 persons in the United States, and then rose abruptly to bring the total population of the nation up to 203,210,158 at the time of the nineteenth census in 1970. Since an increase of 30 per cent during a decade is only slightly less than an annual rate of 3 per cent, the data in Table 66 indicate that the

TABLE 66

The growth of population in the United States, 1790 to 1970

Year	Number of inhabitants	Increase over preceding census (per cent)
1790	3,929,214	....
1800	5,308,483	35.1
1810	7,239,881	36.4
1820	9,638,453	33.1
1830	12,866,020	33.5
1840	17,069,453	32.7
1850	23,191,876	35.9
1860	31,443,321	35.6
1870	38,558,371	22.6
1880	50,155,783	30.1
1890	62,947,714	25.5
1900	75,994,575	20.7
1910	91,972,266	21.0
1920	105,710,620	14.9
1930	122,775,046	16.1
1940	131,669,275	7.2
1950	150,697,361	14.5
1960	179,323,175	19.0
1970	203,210,158	13.3

Source: Compiled from data in U.S. Bureau of the Census, *U.S. Census of Population: 1970, Number of Inhabitants,* Final Report PC(1)-A1, *United States Summary* (1971), p. 42, Table 2; *General Social and Economic Characteristics,* Final Report PC(1)-C1, *United States Summary* (1973), p. 361, Table 68.

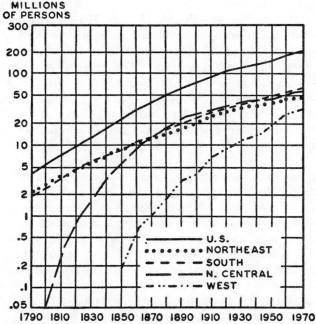

Figure 65. Growth of population in the United States, by regions, 1790 to 1970.

population of the United States was growing at a rate of more than 3 per cent per year at all times prior to the Civil War. Thereafter, it remained above 2 per cent per annum until 1910, after which it fell off sharply to an all-time low in the decade 1930 to 1940. From 1950 to 1960 the rate at which the population of this nation increased was closest to that prevailing between 1890 and 1900. Given the decreases in the birth rate in the United States since 1957, however, the percentage of growth between 1960 and 1970 was only seven-tenths as high as that of the preceding decade, producing an annual rate of 1.3 per cent.

From Figure 65 one may see at a glance how the population growth of the nation's four principal regions compares from the time the respective divisions first figured in the census of population until 1970. Particularly interesting is the closeness with which the curve representing the South corresponds to that for the Northeast, although after 1870 the former moved forward along a higher level than the latter, and after 1930 the differential widened considerably. The curve for the North Central states is striking because of the steepness with which it rose from 1800 to 1880—the period of settlement in this region—and the comparatively low rate of growth from 1890 to 1970. Most rapid of all has been the population growth in the West, and from the nature of past trends one might anticipate that the number of inhabitants in this region would equal those in each of the other three sections before the end of the twentieth century. Between 1960 and 1970, for example, the population of this region grew by 24.1 per cent as compared with 14.2 per cent in the South, 9.8 per cent in the Northeast, and 9.7 per cent in the North Central region. As may be seen in Figure 65, the net result of these rates of growth from 1790 to 1970 has been a much more equitable distribution of the nation's population among its four major regions.

The rates at which the various states of the nation have grown during recent decades also is of considerable interest to all students of population in the United States. To make this information available in simple, compact form, Table 67 and Figure 66 are presented. The first of these gives the rankings of the fifty states and the District of Columbia according to changes between 1960 and 1970 in absolute numbers of people and also according to relative changes in their populations during the decade. The diagram shows the percentage changes that took place during the decade in the populations of counties.

Many of the principal changes are continuations of those that have been going on for some time while others are relatively new. The decade 1930 to 1940 was characterized by rapid increases of the population in California and some other parts of the West, in Florida, and in and around the nation's capital; and by a substantial loss of population throughout the Great Plains. Much the same pattern of change prevailed between 1940 and 1950, except that the growth of population was much more rapid and also more widespread throughout the West and Southwest, in Florida, and in the District of Columbia and the neighboring states. Likewise, for that decade, there were substantial rates of increase of

TABLE 67

States ranked by absolute and relative changes in population,
1960 to 1970

State	Absolute change		Relative change	
	Number	Rank	Per cent	Rank
California	4,235,930	1	27.0	5
Florida	1,837,883	2	37.1	2
Texas	1,617,053	3	16.9	17
New York	1,454,663	4	8.7	33
New Jersey	1,101,382	5	18.2	14
Michigan	1,051,889	6	13.4	20
Illinois	1,032,818	7	10.2	27
Ohio	945,620	8	9.7	31
Maryland	821,710	9	26.5	6
Virginia	681,545	10	17.2	16
Georgia	646,459	11	16.4	18
Washington	555,955	12	19.5	12
Massachusetts	540,592	13	10.5	26
Indiana	531,171	14	11.4	25
North Carolina	525,904	15	11.5	23
Connecticut	496,475	16	19.6	11
Pennsylvania	474,543	17	4.2	41
Arizona	468,739	18	36.0	3
Wisconsin	465,954	19	11.8	21
Colorado	453,312	20	25.8	7
Minnesota	391,107	21	11.5	24
Louisiana	384,284	22	11.8	22
Missouri	356,688	23	8.3	34
Tennessee	356,598	24	10.0	29
Oregon	322,698	25	18.2	15
Oklahoma	230,945	26	9.9	30
South Carolina	207,922	27	8.7	32
Nevada	203,460	28	71.3	1
Kentucky	180,550	29	5.9	38
Alabama	177,425	30	5.4	39
Utah	168,646	31	18.9	13
Arkansas	137,023	32	7.7	35
Hawaii	135,789	33	21.5	10
New Hampshire	130,760	34	21.5	9
Delaware	101,812	35	22.8	8
Rhode Island	87,237	36	10.1	28
Alaska	74,215	37	32.8	4
Nebraska	72,163	38	5.1	40
Kansas	67,967	39	3.1	42
Iowa	66,839	40	2.4	44

TABLE 67 (Cont'd)

States ranked by absolute and relative changes in population,
1960 to 1970

State	Absolute change		Relative change	
	Number	Rank	Per cent	Rank
New Mexico	64,977	41	6.8	37
Vermont	54,449	42	14.0	19
Idaho	45,376	43	6.8	36
Mississippi	38,771	44	1.8	46
Maine	22,783	45	2.4	45
Montana	19,642	46	2.9	43
Wyoming	2,350	47	0.7	47
District of Columbia	−7,446	48	−1.0	48
North Dakota	−14,685	48	−2.3	50
South Dakota	−15,007	50	−2.2	49
West Virginia	−116,184	51	−6.2	51

Source: Compiled from data in U.S. Bureau of the Census, *U.S. Census of Population: 1970, Number of Inhabitants,* Final Report PC(1)-A1, *United States Summary* (1971), p. 50, Table 9.

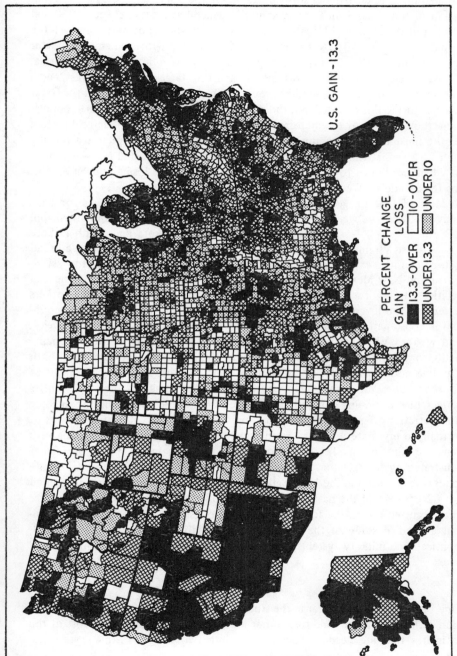

Figure 66. Percentage changes in the population of counties, 1960 to 1970.

population in Michigan and adjacent states. On the other hand, the loss of population in the Great Plains area was not as general as it was between 1930 and 1940, but Arkansas and Mississippi also figured in the list of states in which the population declined. The years between 1950 and 1960 witnessed an even greater acceleration of the already rapid population growth in Florida, California, Alaska, western Oregon and Washington, and the states of the Southwest, and a continuation of the more modest growth in the Northeast and around the Great Lakes. During this decade, too, the states of the Great Plains all gained population, though most of the increases were comparatively small and largely limited to the most urbanized counties. Furthermore, the nation's capital lost population for the first time, generally to the suburbs of Virginia and Maryland, both of which continued to show substantial gains. The states losing population during the decade are West Virginia, Arkansas, and Mississippi.

Most of the changes just described as occurring in the 1950's went on basically unaltered between 1960 and 1970, except that Arkansas and Mississippi left the list of states losing population and North Dakota and South Dakota joined West Virginia and the District of Columbia on it. Furthermore, a broad belt of counties extending from Montana and the Dakotas southward to western Texas and New Mexico and including Iowa and northern Missouri, experienced relatively heavy losses of population. The same was true of a number of others extending southward from Illinois along the Mississippi River and of many counties in those parts of "Appalachia" that lie in West Virginia, eastern Kentucky, and western Virginia. A fairly large number of counties in southern Alabama and Georgia and in the tidewater sections of Virginia, North Carolina, and South Carolina also lost heavily, as did some of those in northern Maine and most of those in upper Michigan. In general, the patterns of gains and losses by counties reflect the continuing depopulation of the most rural districts and the ongoing concentration of people in the urban areas. This is true within the borders of virtually every state and even in those which are losing people or gaining very few, the piling up in a few urban counties is still going on. The pattern is further illustrated by the fact that the ten states which experienced the largest absolute gains of population in the 1960's all are highly urbanized and together accounted for 62 per cent of the national increase. A full interpretation of all the changes that occurred during the four decades under consideration would, however, entail a detailed study of the impact of our rapidly changing economic, social, political, and military systems, and that is far beyond the scope of this volume.

POPULATION ESTIMATES

One cannot proceed very far in the study of any given population before population estimates of one kind or another must figure in the analyses. Most of the estimates that are needed, however, fall into two sharply distinct categories, *interpolation* and *extrapolation*. The first of these is comprised of the calculations designed to show the most reasonable population figures to use for years or other units or points in time which fall between two dates on which census counts of the number of inhabitants have been taken. Examples of such estimates are those for the United States as a whole, or any one of its parts, for such years as 1842, 1914, and 1968. Such information is in demand for a myriad of purposes, including the computation of birth rates, death rates, and many other indexes which the student of population himself must use. The second category is made up of estimates which seek to approximate reasonably what the population of a given area is or was at dates subsequent to the latest census counts, along with those which seek to forecast what it will be at specified times in the future. Since planning for the future in all fields—educations, industrial, military, community, and so on—is quite unrealistic unless the numbers of persons who will be involved are known, there always is a strong demand for population estimates of this second type, especially for those pertaining to the future. There is a growing tendency to designate attempts to forecast future populations as population *projections.*

The need for estimates of current populations is patent, and the student of population must accept the responsibility of making calcualtions that are as reasonable as possible. As is the case with respect to intercensal years, he himself must have such figures for use in his studies of fertility, mortality, and other demographic matters. The extent to which a demographer should engage in population forecasts, predictions, or projections, however, is a more debatable matter. As has been shown throughout this volume, the birth rate, the death rate, and migration (the three primary factors in population change) are influenced directly by a host of factors such as war, the business cycle, advancements in the medical and sanitary sciences, changes in the educational accomplishments of the population, and so on. Therefore, unless someone is prepared to supply them with knowledge of what is to be expected along these lines, that is, with respect to the independent variables responsible for changes in population (the dependent variable), the present writers are unwilling to spend very much time and effort in population forecasts or projections of any type. They are especially unwilling to engage very extensively in any such mental gymnastics which presuppose an ability to foretell the numbers of births that will occur in future years—and fertility usually is the major component in population change.

Interpolation

Two methods, the arithmetic and the geometric, are generally relied upon for purposes of interpolation, and there appears to be little need for additional ones unless the intercensal period is very long. The arithmetic method involves the assumption that the annual increment remains constant or that the population increases or decreases by a given amount during each of the years in the period between two censuses. Therefore, the procedures are very simple. One merely has to determine the total amount of change, divide this change into as many equal parts as there are years in the intercensal period, and attribute one of these parts to each of the years. (See Table 68.) Thus, if one wished to use this method to estimate how many inhabitants there were in the United States on April 1, 1962, he would proceed as follows: subtract 179,323,175, the population enumerated in 1960, from 203,210,158, that given by the 1970 count, to obtain 23,886,983, or the gain for the decade. Dividing this total increase by ten, the number of years in the intercensal period, gives 2,388,698 per year; and adding two such amounts, one for the year ending April 1, 1961 and another for that ending April 1, 1962, to the 1960 population gives 184,100,571 as the estimate needed. The weakness of this method is that it allows for an annual increase on the part of 179,323,175 persons alive at the beginning of the first year of the decade as great as that attributed to almost 201 million persons in the population at the beginning of the tenth year. The longer the intercensal period, the more serious this defect becomes. However, if the rate of increase of the population is falling off, as was true in the United States between 1960 and 1970, the arithmetic method generally is to be recommended.

The geometric method of interpolation rests upon the assumption that the rate of population growth is constant throughout the period involved. Unless the rate of growth is declining, it generally is to be preferred over the arithmetic method. If the annual rate of growth is constant, it can be determined from the formula: $\log (l + r) = \log P_1 - \log P_0/N$, in which P_1 equals the population at the end of the period, P_0 the population at the beginning of the period, N the number of years included, and r the annual rate of increase. Applying this formula to the data for the United States for the period 1960 to 1970 gives these results:

$$\log (l + r) = \frac{\log 203,210,158 - \log 179,323,175}{10}$$

$$= \frac{8.30794 - 8.25364}{10}$$

$$= 0.005430$$

$$l + r = 1.012543$$

$$r = 0.012543 \text{ or } 1.2543 \text{ per cent}$$

If the rate of population increase is low and if the intercensal period is short, it makes very little difference whether the arithmetic or the geometric method of interpolation is used. This is readily evident from the materials in Table 68 showing the calculations by each of these methods for the population of the United States for each year between 1960 and 1970. In this case the maximum difference is of the order of 411,456 for the year 1965, the midpoint in the intercensal period.

As indicated above, the annual increments are all equal (in the amount of 2,388,698 persons) when the arithmetic method is employed. The geometric method, on the other hand, gives an increase of only 2,249,251 for the first year of the decade, followed by steadily rising increments until the figure for the last of the ten years is 2,516,282. If the estimates so made are to be used in the computations of such indexes as the birth rate or the death rate, it is well for one to bear in mind that interpolation by the arithmetic method gives a slightly larger population than the geometric method for every one of the ten years in an intercensal period.

Extrapolation

If fairly adequate data on births, deaths, and migrations are available, the student would do well to make use of them in the preparation of any postcensal estimates of population that he may be called upon to make. If these essential data are lacking, however, the arithmetic and the geometric methods may be used as a basis for computing probable populations for a short period following any given census. It should be stressed, however, that such estimates should be used with the greatest of caution, and that they should not be relied upon if information on fertility, mortality, and migration are available for use in making the necessary computations. For illustrative purposes the estimates presented in Table 69 were prepared; along with them are given the estimates for the comparable years through 1973 prepared by the personnel of the U. S. Bureau of the Census and published by that responsible agency.

An examination of these materials makes it readily apparent how rapidly the results obtained by using the arithmetic method of extrapolation come to differ substantially from those secured by employing the geometric method. In the case of extrapolation, however, it should be noted that, if the population is increasing at all, the geometric procedure yields a higher estimate for every year than the arithmetic method. Even more important is the fact that, in the course of only a few years, either of these methods of extrapolation may give results radically different from those which will result if fairly accurate knowledge of the number of deaths, a less satisfactory inventory of the births, and a crude approximation of the amount of migration are used by skilled persons as a basis for preparing estimates of the population. If in a country such as the United States, even the geometric method of estimating the population for the years immediately following a census results in less than three years in a figure that is

TABLE 68

Estimates of the population of the United States for
each year, 1960 to 1970, according to the
arithmetic and geometric methods

Number of inhabitants on April 1

Year	Arithmetic method	Geometric method (Annual rate = 1.2543 per cent)
1960[a]	179,323,175	179,323,175
1961	181,711,873	181,572,426
1962	184,100,571	183,849,889
1963	186,489,270	186,155,918
1964	188,877,968	188,490,871
1965	191,266,666	190,855,210
1966	193,655,364	193,249,107
1967	196,044,063	195,673,031
1968	198,432,761	198,127,358
1969	200,821,459	200,612,470
1970[a]	203,210,158	203,210,158

[a]Census figure.

TABLE 69

Estimates of the population of the United States, 1970 to 1979,
according to the arithmetic and geometric methods, with
estimates prepared by the U.S. Bureau of the Census included for comparative purposes

Year	Arithmetic method	Geometric method (Annual rate = 1.2543 per cent)	Estimate by the U.S. Bureau of the Census[a]
1970	203,210,158[b]	203,210,158[b]	203,849,000
1971	205,598,856	205,759,023	206,072,000
1972	207,987,554	208,339,858	209,089,000
1973	210,376,252	210,953,064	209,717,000
1974	212,764,950	213,599,048	....
1975	215,153,648	216,278,220	....
1976	217,542,346	218,990,997	....
1977	219,931,044	221,737,800	....
1978	222,319,742	224,519,057	....
1979	224,708,440	227,335,199	....

[a]Data are from U.S. Bureau of the Census, "Estimates of the Population of the United States to September 1, 1973," *Current Population Reports,* Series P-25, No. 507 (October, 1973), p. 2.
[b]Census figure.

1.2 million more than the one based upon a knowledge of the primary factors involved, what degree of confidence may one place upon the results obtained for the various parts of the nation and for other parts of the world? Furthermore, as mentioned above, the arithmetic method is to be preferred to the geometric method when the rate of population increase is falling off as was the case in the United States throughout the 1960's and the early 1970's. Furthermore, if the birth rate continues to move downward and the death rate remains relatively steady, as certainly seems likely in the foreseeable future, within a few years estimates of the population that are based upon the assumption of any growth at all may become greatly inaccurate. All of this points to the need for great caution in placing very much reliance upon any estimates of population for post-censal years or any forecasts of what the number of inhabitants of a given area will be at some date in the future. The more removed the date from that of a fairly accurate census, the greater the amount of error in the figures involved. Since, as indicated above, the number of inhabitants of a given area is a dependent variable directly influenced by such independent variables as fluctuations in the business cycle, wars and internal disturbances, progress or the lack of it in the medical and sanitary sciences, and so on, it could not be otherwise. There seems to be little reason for believing that population forecasting or the making of population projections will ever become an exact science.

The Use of the Death Rate in Making Estimates of Population

For some purposes and in many situations a fairly reliable current estimate of the population in the years following a census may be based upon a knowledge of the death rate and the trends in it. This procedure is especially useful in making population estimates for such areas as states or large cities, or for evaluating the estimates that others make for such units. It is not very accurate if the population involved is a small one. One using this method assumes that the changes in the death rate are not capricious, that for any large population the annual fluctuations are small, and that the trend is fairly constant and gradual. Hence, if one makes the supposition that the change in the death rate is very slight, or that it is moving in a given direction to a stated degree, for any year in which the number of deaths in a city or state is known, the population is easily estimated from the formula for the death rate. One needs merely to solve for the one unknown, that is, the population, in the formula:

$$\text{Death rate} = \frac{\text{Number of deaths}}{\text{Population}} \times 1,000$$

As a check, comparable procedures based upon the formula for the birth rate may be used.

NOTES

1. Changes in the number of the inhabitants of a given area naturally may involve decreases as well as increases in population. For convenience, though, the present writers follow rather conventional procedures and use the expression "growth of population" to denote the entire subject.

2. *Statistique internationale du mouvement de la population,* II (Paris: Imprimerie Nationale, 1913), p. X.

3. Because of the special circumstances involved, Israel and Hong Kong are omitted from consideration in this connection.

4. T. Lynn Smith. *Population Analysis* (New York: McGraw-Hill Book Company, 1948), p. 372.

5. For a detailed analysis of these matters, see T. Lynn Smith, "The Growth of Population in Central and South America," in U.S. House of Representatives, Committee on the Judiciary, Subcommittee No. 1, *Study of Population and Immigration Problems,* Special Series No. 6 (1963), pp. 125 - 186.

SUGGESTED SUPPLEMENTARY READINGS

BOGUE, DONALD J. *Principles of Demography*, Chaps. 2, 3, 6, and 21. New York: John Wiley & Sons, Inc., 1969.

BROWN, HARRISON, and ALAN SWEEZY, eds. *Population: Perspective 1971*. San Francisco: Freeman, Cooper & Company, 1972.

COX, PETER R. *Demography*, 4th ed., Chaps. 22 and 23. London: Cambridge University Press, 1970.

COX, PETER R., and JOHN PEEL, eds. *Resources and Population*. London: Academic Press, 1973.

GRAUMAN, JOHN V. "Population Estimates and Projections," in *The Study of Population: An Inventory and Appraisal*, edited by Philip M. Hauser and Otis Dudley Duncan, Chap. 23. Chicago: University of Chicago Press, 1959.

HAUSER, PHILIP M. "The Population of the World: Recent Trends and Prospects," in *Population: The Vital Revolution*, edited by Ronald Freedman, Chap. 1. New York: Doubleday & Co., Inc. (Anchor Books), 1964.

KEYFITZ, NATHAN. "Population Trends in Newly Developing Countries," in *Population: The Vital Revolution*, edited by Ronald Freedman, Chap. 11. New York: Doubleday & Co., Inc. (Anchor Books), 1964.

NATIONAL ACADEMY OF SCIENCES. *Rapid Population Growth*. Vol. 1. Baltimore: Johns Hopkins Press, 1971.

PETERSEN, WILLIAM. *The Politics of Population*, Part 1. New York: Doubleday & Co., Inc., 1964.

PETERSEN, WILLIAM. *Population*, 2nd ed., Chap. 11. New York: The Macmillan Company, 1969.

SHRYOCK, HENRY S., JACOB S. SIEGEL, and associates. *The Methods and Materials of Demography*, Vol. 2, Chaps. 23 - 25. Washington: Government Printing Office, 1971.

SMITH, T. LYNN. *Brazil: People and Institutions*, 4th ed., pp. 44 - 50 and Chap. XXIV. Baton Rouge: Louisiana State University Press, 1972.

SMITH, T. LYNN. *Studies of Latin American Societies*, Selection 4. New York: Doubleday & Co., Inc., 1970.

SMITH, T. LYNN, and HOMER L. HITT. *The People of Louisiana*, Chap. XIV. Baton Rouge: Louisiana State University Press, 1952.

TAEUBER, CONRAD, and IRENE B. TAEUBER. *The People of the United States in the 20th Century*, Chaps. I, XI, and XVI. Washington: Government Printing Office, 1971.

582

THOMLINSON, RALPH. *Demographic Problems,* Chap. 2. Belmont, Calif.: Dickenson Publishing Company, Inc., 1967.

UNITED NATIONS. *Demographic Yearbook, 1970,* Chap. I. New York: United Nations, 1971.

UNITED NATIONS. *World Population: Challenge to Development.* New York: United Nations, 1966.

U.S. COMMISSION ON POPULATION GROWTH AND THE AMERICAN FUTURE. *Population Growth and the American Future.* Washington: Government Printing Office, 1972.

VANCE, RUPERT B. "The Growth of the American Population," in *Population: The Vital Revolution,* edited by Ronald Freedman, Chap. 10. New York: Doubleday & Co., Inc. (Anchor Books), 1964.

WESTOFF, CHARLES F., and ROBERT PARKE, JR., eds. *Demographic and Social Aspects of Population Growth.* Washington: U.S. Commission on Population Growth and the American Future, 1972.

CONCLUSION

It is neither necessary nor desirable to conclude a volume such as this with an elaborate summary of its contents. The usefulness of this book to the student of population would be enhanced little if any by a detailed restatement of the more significant facts, procedures, principles, and relationships already set forth. Indeed, these are all more easily understood and more fully appreciated in the specific contexts in which they have been given where they are closely supported by the data on which they are based. It is in order, however, to make a few general comments relating to the current situation and prospects of population study.

Since about 1930 at least three significant tendencies or trends have been underway in the field of population research and teaching in the United States and other parts of the world. Probably these have been more noticeable in the teaching than in the research aspects, due no doubt to the fact that a broadening of interests on the part of those doing research in the field of demography eventually resulted in modifications in the subject matter of courses. In any case, in contrast to the situation during the first quarter of the twentieth century, since about 1930 the following tendencies have been rather pronounced: (1) the emphasis on "population problems" has ceased to dominate the field, and concern with the normal or nonpathological aspects of the subject have become for the most part the chief concern of those teaching population courses and doing research in demography; (2) whereas as late as 1925 the major attention of most of those engaged in population study was with the numbers of people, during recent decades more and more attention has been given to the characteristics of the population and the factors involved in population change; and (3) closely related to the second tendency, there seems to have been a marked decrease in the once rather widespread tendency to apply supposed general mathematical laws of population growth and decline and an upsurge of endeavor to understand and account for population changes through a knowledge of the three primary factors involved, namely, fertility, mortality, and migration. In the preparation of this textbook, an effort has been made to keep all of the sections of this volume attuned to these three important current developments and trends.

It is hoped that the specific manner in which the various aspects of population study have been developed in this volume has made it apparent to the beginning student that the field already is a scientific discipline of creditable standing. The frame of reference, or the systematized arrangement of all the topics and concepts involved in the study of population, from those relating to the study of the number and distribution of the inhabitants to those connected with mortality, fertility, and migration, is a substantial one. Thousands of persons working during many centuries have contributed to building it, and throughout the entire world there is remarkable agreement in theory and practice with respect to its principal elements.

The facts that are ready for use by all those engaged in population study, and especially the quantitative data available to all because of the many censuses that have been taken and the lengthy and detailed records that have been kept of births, deaths, and migrations, are of an order of magnitude undreamed of in most other portions of social science. Each decade the ingenuity of the men and women concerned with population study brings these data, many of them assembled over a hundred years ago, to bear in testing ideas or hypotheses of immediate practical or theoretical concern. Furthermore, every year that passes enables those in charge of censuses and registers of vital statistics throughout the world to enrich substantially with new compilations of population data the invaluable store already in existence.

In addition to its well-established and systematized frame of reference and its rich store of facts, the field of population study includes a host of analytical devices and techniques that are of prime utility. Over the decades population students have devised and tested a host of such methods or techniques that are extremely useful in the organization, analysis, and interpretation of demographic facts, relationships, and trends. Many of these are statistical in nature, ranging from the simple, direct, and conclusive varieties of tabulation or subsorting, which the plentitude of data makes possible, to highly involved correlation procedures. Many of the devices are graphical. Indeed, it may be said with some degree of certainty that the manipulation of population data has been one of the principal sources of the improvements in graphical devices that have taken place during the last several decades. Many of the tables and charts used in this volume were, of course, designed by the authors themselves, but others were selected from a wide variety of sources. They deserve special study solely from the standpoint of the methods of analysis and presentation presently readily available to those working with demographic data.

The general field of population theory has not been overlooked in the preparation of the specific sections and chapters which make up this book. Generalizations about demographic matters that are based upon careful observations and are in agreement with all the known facts, tested hypotheses, and established relationships between two or more attributes or variables are rapidly accumulating. Such inductions are the warp and woof of scientific theory in any field of knowledge. In this volume almost every section has dealt with some aspect of population theory, and in all cases an endeavor has been made to have conclusions reached confronted with the relevant facts, previously established relationships, and verified hypotheses. Because they have survived such exacting and searching tests, they merit the careful consideration of those concerned with population theory in particular or social theory in general.

Population facts and principles also are the keys to an understanding of many existing social conditions and current social changes. Therefore, throughout this volume there are many suggestions of the manner in which a demographic factor, as an independent variable, is involved in many social and economic matters of public interest. The relation of population facts and relationships in the proper planning of health, welfare, business, educational, agricultural, industrial, and a host of other public policies is so obvious that further comment is unnecessary. However, the impression should not be left that interest in them is limited to those concerned with public problems. Private organizations, enterprises, and individuals, too, make much use of reliable population information when they are formulating plans for the future. Apparently this use will increase as the years go by and we increase substantially our knowledge about the number, distribution, characteristics, vital processes, migration, and growth of the population.

Finally, a word should be said about population policies, or the public and private measures designed to get and maintain the kind of population that is desired, from the standpoints of number, quality, and distribution. Only a little thought is necessary to determine that the formulation and execution of such policies hardly are, or can be, the sole or even the main responsibility of those engaged in the study of population as such. A state or national policy with respect to birth control, the limitation of immigration, measures designed to extend the expectation of life, or the encouragement or discouragement of migration between urban and rural areas — to mention only a few of the possible issues — involve knowledge and interests far beyond the special province of the demographer. Nevertheless, in all of these matters there is no substitute for the facts, and the student of population is the one most likely to possess the knowledge and skill needed to assemble many of the most pertinent facts concerning the topic. Therefore, it is not surprising that the general body of fact and theory that has been developed in the field of population study finds many of its most important applications in connection with population policies.

BOGUE, DONALD J., ed. *Applications of Demography: Composition and Distribution of the U.S. Population in 1975* (Scripps Foundation Studies in Population Distribution, No. 13). Oxford, Ohio: Scripps Foundation, 1957.

CARR-SAUNDERS, ALEXANDER M. *World Population: Past Growth and Present Trends.* Oxford: Clarendon Press, 1936.

COWGILL, DONALD O. "Transition Theory as General Population Theory," in *Social Demography*, edited by Thomas R. Ford and Gordon F. DeJong, pp. 627 - 633. Englewood Cliffs: Prentice-Hall, Inc., 1970.

COX, PETER R. *Demography*, 4th ed., Chap. 24. London: Cambridge University Press, 1970.

EASTERLIN, RICHARD A. "Long Swings in the United States Demographic and Economic Growth: Some Findings in Historical Patterns." *Demography*, Vol. 2 (1965), pp. 490 - 507.

FORD, THOMAS R., and GORDON F. DeJONG, eds. *Social Demography*, Chaps. 1 and 12. Englewood Cliffs: Prentice-Hall, Inc., 1970.

HATHAWAY, DALE E., J. ALLAN BEEGLE, and W. KEITH BRYANT. *People of Rural America* (A 1960 Census Monograph), Chap. 10. Washington: Government Printing Office, 1968.

HAUSER, PHILIP M., ed. *Population and World Politics.* Glencoe, Ill.: The Free Press, 1958.

KIRK, DUDLEY. "A New Demographic Transition?" in *Rapid Population Growth*, edited by a Study Committee of the National Academy of Sciences, Vol. II, Chap. II. Baltimore: Johns Hopkins Press, 1971.

LORIMER, FRANK. "Issues of Population Policy," in *The Population Dilemma*, edited by Philip M. Hauser, Chap. 8. Englewood Cliffs: Prentice-Hall, Inc., 1963.

MANGALAM, J. J., and HARRY K. SCHWARZWELLER. "Some Theoretical Guidelines Toward a Sociology of Migration." *International Migration Review*, Vol. IV, No. 2 (Spring, 1970), pp. 5 - 21.

TAEUBER, IRENE B. *The Population of Japan*, Chaps. XVI - XVIII. Princeton: Princeton University Press, 1959.

THOMLINSON, RALPH. *Demographic Problems*, Chap. 10. Belmont, Calif.: Dickenson Publishing Company, Inc., 1967.

UNITED NATIONS, POPULATION DIVISION. "History of Population Theories," in *Population and Society*, edited by Charles B. Nam, pp. 63 - 97. Boston: Houghton Mifflin Company, 1968.

587

WHITNEY, VINCENT H. "Some Interrelations of Population and Atomic Power," in *Population and Society,* edited by Charles B. Nam, pp. 640 - 647. Boston: Houghton Mifflin Company, 1968.

ZOPF, PAUL E., JR. *North Carolina: A Demographic Profile,* Chap. XIV. Chapel Hill: University of North Carolina Population Center, 1967.

CHAPTER 1: THE SCOPE AND METHOD OF POPULATION STUDY

1. Consult a recent issue of *Population Index* and make a list of the principal headings used in classifying population materials in this comprehensive annotated bibliography.
2. Outline the basic elements of the scientific method as it is applied in population study.
3. Study carefully the table of contents of this volume, and then indicate which of the subjects included must be studied largely through use of materials gathered in population censuses and which must be studied for the most part by use of data from various registration systems.
4. List five ways in which population materials may be applied in social and economic planning.
5. In what way is demography or the study of population related to the following disciplines: biology, economics, political economy, sociology, and geography?
6. Give in your own words a definition of demography.
7. Is it wise to place the study of the growth of population at the end of a volume such as this? Explain.
8. Why are fertility, mortality, and migration the only *primary* factors influencing the number of inhabitants and the distribution of the population?
9. Select a city, county or state and then examine the reports of the latest U. S. Census of Population and determine specifically the items of information that are available for it. Which ones should be present but are not?

CHAPTER 2: IMPORTANT LANDMARKS IN THE DEVELOPMENT OF POPULATION STUDY

1. Write a paper of 500 words criticizing or defending the proposition that the history of demography or population study should begin with the work of John Graunt.

2. Indicate why the census of the United States may be called a political accident and why the year 1790 should figure as one of the landmarks in the development of population study.

3. Consult J. D. B. DeBow's *Compendium of the Seventh Census,* and then write a 500-word exposition setting forth its importance for the study of population.

4. Consult *Studies in American Demography* by Willcox, *Population Analysis* by Smith, and the *Handbook of Vital Statistics Methods* by the Statistical Office of the United Nations, and then write a brief history of the development of mortality statistics in the United States.

5. Of what significance for the study of population was the publication of the first issue of the *Demographic Yearbook* in 1949?

6. What must be done before students of population will have available for their use the necessary statistics about internal migration?

7. Compile a short bibliography of the demographic works of one of the following authors: Donald J. Bogue, Gladys K. Bowles, A. M. Carr-Saunders, Ansley J. Coale, Kingsley Davis, Louis I. Dublin, Otis Dudley Duncan, Ronald Freedman, David Glass, Wilson H. Grabill, C. Horace Hamilton, Philip M. Hauser, Frank Lorimer, Charles B. Nam, Frank W. Notestein, William F. Ogburn, Alfred Sauvy, Henry S. Shryock, Joseph J. Spengler, Conrad Taeuber, Irene B. Taeuber, Warren S. Thompson, Rupert B. Vance, Charles F. Westoff, Pascal K. Whelpton, and Walter F. Willcox.

8. Revise the list of landmarks in the development of population study given in Chapter 2 of this volume, deleting those that are not entitled to a place in such a list and adding others that are.

9. Should the elements of genetics be included in a course on population? Explain.

CHAPTER 3: THE NUMBER AND GEOGRAPHIC DISTRIBUTION OF THE POPULATION

1. Indicate in your own words the meanings of the following concepts: census, density of population, center of population, *de jure,* minor civil division, census tract, township, incorporated center, enumeration, and population.

2. Why is the determination of the number and distribution of the inhabitants the most important single task in population study?

3. Why is the tabulation of census data by small and homogeneous sub-divisions of counties and municipalities, territorial units having boundaries that are easily identified and stable, of such tremendous significance in the study of the distribution of the population?

4. Discuss briefly the more important reasons why we do not know rather accurately how many people there are on earth at the present time.

5. Set forth briefly the more important facts about the present distribution of population in the United States.

6. Using the data from the most recent census publications and the techniques which you think most appropriate, construct a map showing the distribution of population in the country in which you reside.

7. How do the estimates of population in current use in a nation, state, or city at the beginning of a census year usually compare with the results of the population counts made by the census in the course of the year?

8. What is the present population of the state in which you live?

9. Indicate why it is inaccurate to assume that each inhabitant of the United States has one and only one usual place of residence.

10. What is the correlation between the size of the states of the United States in terms of area and size and the number of inhabitants? What implications if any, does this have for the mapping of demographic data for the nation?

CHAPTER 4: RURAL OR URBAN RESIDENCE

1. How do the definitions of urban and rural categories employed by the United States Census compare and contrast with those used in the following countries: England, Canada, Mexico, Cuba, Australia, Sweden, France, Brazil and India?

2. Indicate specifically how the "new" definitions of urban, rural-nonfarm, and rural-farm employed in the 1950, 1960, and 1970 censuses of the United States differ from those used in 1940 and 1930.

3. Is the practice of the U. S. Census in making the urban-rural classification of the population a primary one on most of its tabulations a sound procedure? Why or why not?

4. Suggests ways in which the residential classification used by the U. S. Census might be improved.

5. Why is it that definitions of urban and rural that are highly satisfactory for statistical purposes would be entirely inadequate for more theoretical sociological purposes, and vice versa?

6. How may one determine the degree of urbanization or rurality of various states, counties, or other civil divisions?

7. Which is the most urban state in the United States? Which the most rural? Explain.

8. In what ways, if at all, is one's personality affected by the fact that he resides in a highly urban, a strictly rural, or a suburban environment?

9. Who is the typical American: the resident of a large city? the one who lives on a farm in the open country? or the person whose home is in one of the "Middletowns" or "Littletowns" spread about throughout the nation? Explain.

CHAPTER 5: RACE, COLOR, ETHNIC STOCK AND NATIVITY

1. Consult the 1956, 1963, 1964, and 1971 issues of the *Demographic Yearbook* of the United Nations, and then write a 500-word paper on the present status of racial, color, and ethnic classifications of the populations in the censuses of five countries selected by the instructor.

2. What are the basic procedures of the U. S. Census in classifying the population according to color, race, and nativity?

3. Is the practice of the U. S. Census in making the color and racial classifications of the population a primary one in most of its tabulations a sound procedure? Why or why not?

4. Why is it that definitions of white and Negro that are highly satisfactory for statistical purposes would be entirely inadequate for more theoretical anthropological purposes, and vice versa?

5. How does the relative importance of the native white, the foreign-born white, and the Negro populations vary throughout the United States?

6. Describe recent changes in the distribution of the Negro population in the United States.

7. To what extent are the foreign-born portions of the population of the United States concentrated in the urban districts?

8. From the series of maps given in Chapter 5, indicate the sections of the United States in which the immigrants of each nationality have made their largest contributions to the nation's civilization and culture.

9. Compare and contrast the race and nativity make-up of the population of the United States in 1970 with that prevailing in 1850.

10. In which states is the Negro population still concentrated in the rural districts and in which is it concentrated in the cities?

CHAPTER 6: AGE COMPOSITION

1. What similarities would you expect to find between the age-sex pyramid for a predominantly rural state in the South such as Mississippi, and that of Italy? Why?

2. Give a critical appraisal of the method used in the text for the purpose of scoring populations with respect to the accuracy of age reporting.

3. Construct an age-sex pyramid for the population of a given country, city, or state, and then identify the factor or factors responsible for each "scar" or irregularity it exhibits.

4. Discuss in some detail the social and economic significance of the "aging" of the population in the United States that has taken place since 1900.

5. Construct a diagram (similar to Figures 31, 32, and 33) showing the extent to which the population of a given state contains more or less than its pro rata share of each age group from zero to four to seventy-five and over in the nation's population. What factors are chiefly responsible for the surpluses and deficits?

6. Why do cities located in the western portions of the United States have relatively high proportions of aged persons whereas most cities in the South have relatively low proportions?

7. Using the data in Table 10 construct a scatter diagram showing the relationship between educational status (the independent variable, or X, as measured by the percentage of illiteracy) and the index of correctness in age reporting (the dependent variable or Y).

CHAPTER 7: SEX COMPOSITION

1. How may one explain the high sex ratios that prevail in the populations of Liberia, Alaska, Cuba, India, and Kuwait and the low sex ratios in those of Austria, Germany, Portugal, Spain, and the United Kingdom?

2. Using the latest census data, determine the sex ratios for the white and Negro populations of the six largest cities in your state. Compare these findings with the sex ratios among the rural-farm population of six of the most rural counties in your state. What factors have produced these differences?

3. Why is the sex ratio of the Negro population so much lower than that of the native white population?

4. Other things remaining equal, what will be the affect upon the sex ratio of a population of (a) a fall in the birth rate, (b) an increase in the expectation of life, (c) a strong current of immigration, and (d) the arrival of large numbers of migrants from distant portions of the country itself?

5. How may one determine that the S-shape of the curve showing sex ratios by age is due to the understatement of women's ages rather than the overstatement of men's ages?

6. Why is the sex ratio high among children of less than ten years of age? Why is it low among those aged sixty-five and over?

7. Is the relatively high sex ratio in some of the western portions of the United States and the comparatively low sex ratio in the South likely to persist for several decades to come?

8. Identify the factors responsible for the fall in the sex ratio of the population of the United States from 106.0 in 1910 to 94.8 in 1970.

CHAPTER 8: MARITAL CONDITION

1. With data from the 1968 and 1971 issues of the *Demographic Yearbook* of the United Nations construct charts similar to Figure 37 showing the marital status of the population of four countries which are selected by the instructor.
2. The data make it evident that women are much more likely than men to remain single throughout life. Write a 500-word paper in which you (a) identify the factors responsible for this difference and (b) describe the principal social consequences of the differential.
3. Discuss the reasons for and the social significance of the fact that widowers are much more likely to remarry than widows.
4. Describe in your own way how the marital status of a population changes as age advances.
5. How does the marital status of the white population of the United States compare with that of the Negro population?
6. How does the geographic maldistribution of the sexes in the United States hinder marriage and affect mate selection?
7. As the expectation of life of a population increases, what changes take place in the proportions of widows and widowers in the country concerned?
8. In what ways does the marital status of the urban, the rural non-farm, and the rural-farm populations differ?
9. In 1970 the percentages of married persons among those fourteen years of age and over in the United States were as follows: urban males, 65.0; rural-farm males, 65.7; urban females, 59.4; and rural-farm females, 69.1. Does this mean that urban men are about as likely to marry as those living on farms but that urban women are much less likely to marry than their farm counterparts? Explain.
10. For census purposes exactly who should be included in and who excluded from the married category?

CHAPTER 9: OCCUPATIONAL STATUS

1. Of what importance is one's occupation in the determination of one's personality?
2. How does the category of the "economically active" population differ from one country to another?
3. Why is it that in the United States both the total number of persons employed and the index of unemployment generally rise during the month of June?

4. How may the occupational statistics be employed by urban sociologists in the study of city functions?
5. Describe the principal occupational trends in the United States since 1900.
6. How does the relative importance of each of the major industry groups in the city or country in which you reside compare with the national average?
7. Which portions of the United States are most dependent upon agricultural activities? Which upon manufacturing? And which upon trade and commerce?
8. Look up the concepts of "organic" and "mechanistic" social solidarity as developed by Emile Durkheim. How are these related to occupational specialization and industrial division of labor?
9. What is the usefulness and what are the limitations of employing the data on occupations to ascertain socioeconomic status?

CHAPTER 10: EDUCATIONAL STATUS

1. Under what circumstances is it preferable to use each of the following indexes of educational status: the percentage of illiterates in the population of ten years of age and over, the median years of schooling attained by the adult population, and the percentage of high school graduates among the adult population?
2. Sometimes a given state or county will rank fairly high if the percentage of high school graduates is used as the index of educational status and low if the median years of schooling is employed. Of what important social phenomenon is this indicative?
3. As a general rule, in most parts of the world, how does the educational status of women compare with that of men? Under what circumstances is the situation reversed?
4. Indicate how the educational status of the population varies throughout the world, and evaluate the position of the United States in this respect.
5. In which portions of the United States is the educational status of the population the highest? The lowest? Explain.
6. How does the educational status of Negroes in the United States compare with that of whites? With that of populations in other selected parts of the world?
7. Analyze the factors responsible for the very high educational status of the urban white population in the southern states.
8. Use the latest census data to compare the educational status of the population of Illinois with that of the population of Mississippi, making sure that you are not merely using a cumbersome method of showing that the former is much more urban and contains a far lower proportion of Negroes than the latter.

CHAPTER 11: MEASURING THE RATE OF REPRODUCTION

1. What conditions must be met before one is justified in using the birth rate as a measure of the fertility of a population?

2. What are the advantages and disadvantages of the fertility ratio as a measure of fertility?

3. Suppose you wish to compare the rate of reproduction of the population of the United States at intervals over the period 1850 to 1970. What index of fertility will you use? Explain.

4. Consult the appropriate pages in *Studies in American Demography* by Walter F. Willcox and *Population Analysis* by T. Lynn Smith, and then write a 500-word paper dealing with Dr. J. S. Billings' effort to measure the birth rate in the United States and to determine its trend.

5. Who was responsible for developing the fertility ratio as a measure of the rate of reproduction? Trace the development of its use.

6. Of what value is the net reproduction rate in the study of fertility?

7. Why should one not employ the fertility ratio for comparisons of the rates of reproduction of the native-born and foreign-born white populations? What changes in census tabulations would be necessary to obviate this difficulty?

8. Consult the volumes of *Vital Statistics* published by the National Center for Health Statistics and determine the categories of population for which birth statistics are available for the country in which you live; and consult the publications of the U. S. Bureau of the Census and determine the categories for which fertility ratios may be computed.

CHAPTER 12: FERTILITY LEVELS

1. How does the present rate of reproduction in the United States compare with that in such countries as Japan, France, Great Britain, India, Argentina, Brazil, and Mexico?

2. Compute the fertility ratios for representative urban and rural counties of the state in which you reside. How do these compare with the indexes for the urban and rural-farm populations of the United States as a whole?

3. From the data in Table 29 make a list of the countries in which you judge that the actual level of fertility is rather accurately depicted by the reported crude birth rates.

4. In which sections of the United States are the actual birth rates the highest? The lowest? Nearest the average for the nation as a whole?

5. Describe the manner in which, for whites, the number of children ever born per 1,000 women aged fifteen to forty-four who were ever married varies throughout the United States.

6. What factors probably account for the fact that Utah and New Mexico have exceptionall high rates of reproduction irrespective of the indexes used in making the comparisons?
7. Why is the fertility ratio of the population in the District of Columbia the lowest in the United States?
8. Since the birth rates of the populations in various parts of the world are no higher at present than they were in 1900, why is it that since 1950 so many people have been concerned about the "population bomb" or "population explosion"?
9. How does a serious war affect the birth rates of the populations in the nations taking part in it?

CHAPTER 13: DIFFERENTIAL FERTILITY

1. If one reasoned from Malthusian theory, what relationship between socioeconomic status and the birth rate would he postulate? How would this compare with the actual results of a study in a country such as the United States in which some measure of economic position (such as the rent or rent equivalent of the home) was correlated with an index of the number of children in the family?
2. As the proportion of Negroes in the population increases in the various parts of the United States, what happens to the birth rate or other index of the rate of reproduction?
3. Discuss the validity and implications of the following statement:
"Every refinement introduced into the analysis of the rate of reproduction in the United States tends to emphasize the importance of rural-urban, educational, and socioeconomic differentials and to minimize the importance of racial and regional differences in fertility."
4. Of what biological and social significance is the sharp rural-urban differential in fertility that has prevailed in the United States for many decades?
5. Compute fertility ratios for the white and Negro portions of the urban, rural-nonfarm, and rural-farm populations of your state. Basing your judgement upon these indexes, which differential is the greater, that between the races or that between the rural and urban segments of the population?
6. As the United States urbanized swiftly between 1850 and 1935, the birth rate of the population fell rapidly; and in 1930, 1940, 1950, 1960, and 1970 the birth rate decreased rapidly as one passed from the most highly urbanized and industrialized sections of the nation to the most remote of the agricultural areas. How, then, may one account for the fact that between 1930 and 1947, a period in which the urbanization of the nation was proceeding very rapidly, the birth rate ceased to fall and then rose abruptly?

1. Prepare a chart showing the trends in the rate of reproduction of population of your state over the period 1860 to 1970. How do the fluctuations that occurred in this state compare with those in the nation as a whole?

2. Is the birth rate in most parts of Latin America likely to fall much during the next decade? That in China? In Russia? In Japan? In Germany? Explain.

3. Outline some of the social effects of the rise in the birth rate in the United States that took place between 1935 and 1957.

4. To what extent may one predict the trend in the birth rate a decade ahead from a knowledge of the trends during the preceding twenty-five years?

5. Give as much detail as you can about the falling birth rate of the population of the United States during the period 1830 to 1930.

6. Following 1935, how did the trend in the rate of reproduction of the urban population of the United States compare with that of the rural-farm population?

7. Prepare a chart showing how the changes since 1930 in the fertility ratios of the Negro population compare with the changes in those of the white population.

8. Prepare an annotated bibliography of fifteen items on the subject of current trends in the rate of reproduction of the population of the United States.

9. Indicate some of the reasons why the birth rate in the United States fell steadily after about 1957 as well as some of the social and demographic implications of that decline.

CHAPTER 15: THE MEASUREMENT OF MORTALITY

1. What data must one have for the making of a life table, and precisely what steps are involved in constructing one?

2. What are the *pros* and the *cons* with respect to the use of the crude death rate as the index on which is based a comparative study of the mortality in different countries and among various segments of a nation's population such as the white and the Negro, the rural and the urban, and so forth?

3. How is the infant mortality rate computed? How does it differ from the death rate of children of less than one year of age? And why is this index so important as an indicator of the social and economic well-being of the people involved?

4. Of what value is the *International List of Diseases and Causes of Death?*

5. Why is the coverage secured in the registration of deaths usually more complete than that secured in the registration of births?
Is the expectation of life at birth in a given state an accurate indicator of healthfulness in that state? Explain.

6. If you were to undertake the construction of life tables for the population of your state, precisely which years out of the decade would you select for such purposes? Explain.

7. Note in any lifetable to which you have ready access that the expectation of life at age one is higher than at birth. How is this possible?

CHAPTER 16: MORTALITY LEVELS, DIFFERENTIALS, AND CAUSES

1. How does the death rate of females of all ages generally compare with that of males? In what places and under what circumstances is this situation sometimes reversed?

2. In what parts of the world are current mortality rates the highest? In which areas are they the lowest? And in which other countries is the expectation of life at birth most closely comparable with that of the population of the United States?

3. How does the expectation of life at birth of the Negro population of the United States compare with that of the white population? With that in various Latin American countries and the Mediterranean countries of Europe?

4. In countries such as the United States and Canada, how do the mortality rates of the rural populations compare with those of the urban populations?

5. In which states of the United States is the expectation of life at birth of the white population the highest? In which is it the lowest? What conclusion, if any, does this lead you to with respect to the validity of such a measure for the purpose of comparing health and morbidity in one state with that in another?

6. Assemble the available mortality data for the county in which you live. To what extent may you use this information to compare the mortality of the population in your county with that of the people in the state as a whole?

7. From the *Vital Statistics* published annually by the National Center for Health Statistics, determine the ten leading causes of death in the state in which you live. How do these compare with or differ from the list for the nation as a whole?

8. Determine the infant mortality rate for the county or city in which you live. How does this compare with that for the state as a whole? And what are the probable reasons for any differences observed?

1. The changes in the death rate in the United States since 1920 are best described as a "trend," those in the birth rate as "fluctuations." Explain why this is the case.

2. Between 1900 and 1970 the expectation of life at birth of the white population of the United States rose from about fifty years to approximately seventy-two years. Is there any possibility that a comparable increase will take place between 1970 and the year 2000? Explain.

3. Write a short paper (not over 1,000 words) on the social significance of falling death rates throughout the world during the period since 1925.

4. What relationship, if any, is there between the trends since 1900 in fatalities from diseases of the heart on the one hand and those from tuberculosis, typhoid fever, scarlet fever, and other transmissible diseases on the other?

5. In the long-continued increase in the expectation of life of the population of the United States, what has been the effect of (a) the decreasing infant mortality rate, (b) the prolongation of life for those seventy years of age or over, and (c) the urbanization of the nation?

6. To what extent is the current rapid increase in world population due to changes in the mortality rate and to what extent has it been produced by changes in the birth rate?

7. Reexamine the data in Table 46 and then make a list of the countries in which you expect substantial reductions in the death rate to take place prior to 1985.

8. How do the trends in the expectation of life of the white population compare with those of the nonwhite (Negro) population? If the same relative rates of change are maintained subsequent to 1970, about when should the expectation of life at birth for the two come to be equal?

CHAPTER 18: EMIGRATION AND IMMIGRATION

1. The 1970 issue of the *Demographic Yearbook* of the United Nations carried an estimate of 2,886,000 for the population of Uruguay in 1970 and the 1971 volume one of 2,921,000 in that year. The same sources published a birth rate for the country of 22.5 for the 1970–1971 period and a death rate of 9.5 for the same period. Using these data, estimate the amount of net immigration or emigration that would have had to occur during 1970 in order to make the figure of increase of population during the year a reasonable one.

2. Under what circumstances may a stream of immigration that is negligible from the standpoint of population increase have profound social and economic consequences for a country?

3. Make a list of the countries which have been the principal sources of emigrants in the years since 1900 and make another showing the countries which have been most important as receivers of immigrants.

4. Into what five periods may the history of immigration to the United States be divided?

5. Describe the manner in which the composition of the immigration stream to the United States changed, decade by decade, between 1850 and 1970.

6. What elements, groups, organizations, and so forth favor rather free immigration of Mexicans to the United States? Which ones are opposed? Why?

7. In what ways are a nation's immigration policies determined?

8. What has been the fate of the millions of "displaced persons" who were found in Central Europe at the close of the second World War?

9. In what ways was the Immigration Act of 1924 modified and changed by the McCarran-Walter Act? By the 1965 amendment?

10. How important is immigration as a factor in population change?

CHAPTER 19: INTERNAL MIGRATION

1. What are the principal varieties of internal migration? And from what sources may one secure pertinent information about each of them?

2. What difference, if any, is there between migration and social mobility? Is one justified in referring to migration as territorial social mobility? Explain.

3. Prepare an annotated bibliography of ten items on the subject of rural-urban migration.

4. Of what value for the study of internal migration are the U. S. Census tables showing state of birth cross-tabulated with state of residence?

5. What is the role of rural-to-urban migration in the maintenance and growth of towns and cities?

6. To what extent is the United States becoming a nation of nomads? Explain.

7. How do the "factors" and "media" related to rural-urban migrations in Latin American countries, as set forth in the text, compare with those presently of importance in the United States?

8. Why are the data on migration the most deficient of all those required in population study?

9. Suppose you require information on the movement of people to or from the county in which you live. Precisely what data would you be able to obtain from the various publications of the United States Census of Population?

10. How does the relative importance of farm-to-city migration vary from one part of the United States to another?

11. In what ways is one justified in referring to rural-urban migration in the United States after 1932 as "the mass transfer of poverty"? Why did it take place?

12. What is the significance of the reversal of the flow of energy in producing rural-to-urban migration in the United States? What are the prospects for the "energy crisis" producing a large-scale migration from the cities to the farms? Explain.

CHAPTER 20: INTERNAL MIGRATION (Continued)

1. How does the residential stability of the farm population in the state in which you reside compare and contrast with that of the farmers in other parts of the United States?

2. Describe the principal regional interchanges of population which took place from 1965 to 1970 (the period to which the 1970 census data apply).

3. Of what value to society in general is the movement of the farm population from one farm to another?

4. How does the resdiential stability of the farmers in the "cotton belt" compare with that of those in the "corn belt"?

5. In what ways is the migration from rural to urban areas selective?

6. What differences, if any, are there between the migrants who move long distances and those who move short distances?

7. Give some of the social characteristics of migratory farm laborers.

8. Are Negroes more migratory than white people? Explain.

9. Write a paper approximately 1,000 words in length outlining the principal migrations of the Negro population of the United States in the period 1915 to the present.

10. How may charts showing age and sex distributions of the population be used to make inferences with respect to recent migrations to or from the population under consideration?

CHAPTER 21: THE GROWTH OF POPULATION

1. About how many people will there be in the United States in 1980, and where will the center of population be at that time?

2. Why is it extremely difficult or impossible to trace the growth of population in most countries from the time the national state emerged until the present?

3. Should the growth of population be considered for analytical purposes as an independent variable or a dependent variable? Explain.

4. Using semilogarithmic paper prepare a chart on which you compare the growth of population since 1900 in the county in which you live, the state in which it is located, and the United States as a whole.

5.   Set forth what appear to you to be the social correlates of a rapid growth of population, and also those of a decreasing population.

6.   Prepare a chart on which you show the growth of population in your state from 1900 to the present, along with extrapolations, both arithmetic and geometric, until the year 1980.

7.   What is the present population of the state in which you reside?

8.   Note the percentage increase in the population of the United States during each intercensal period from 1790 - 1800 to the present time, and comment upon the principal causes of the variations which occurred from one decade to another.

9.   In recent decades what has been the absolute and relative importance of fertility, mortality, and migration (immigration or emigration) in accounting for changes in the numbers of inhabitants in the following countries: Canada, India, France, the United States, and Brazil?

CONCLUSION

1.   What is the general nature of population theory? And how does the method by which it is produced differ, if at all, from theory in the fields of zoology, astronomy, geology, philosophy, and psychology?

2.   What tested hypotheses derived from the empirical study of population materials may legitimately be designated as theories?

3.   What should be the role of population experts in the development of national population policies?

4.   Set forth what appear to you to be the most important ways in which population facts and principles may be applied in connection with social problems and social and economic policies and planning.

5.   What are the major features of the population policy of the United States? And what facts, fears, and forces have enabled each of these to prevail?

6.   Indicate at least six demographic principles or relationships that should be included in the subject matter taught in the introductory courses in sociology and economics.

7.   What are the principal population problems of the United States at the present time?

8.   How do the population problems of Japan compare with those of Brazil?

9.   Prepare a paper in which you identify and briefly describe the most important demographic factors that are both producing and resulting from the homogenization of society in the United States.

10.   From your studies in various areas of the social sciences, what seem to be the most important elements that should be accounted for in the formulation of demographic theory?

AUTHOR AND TITLE INDEX

SUBJECT INDEX